COMMUNICATION AND SOCIAL ORDER

HUGH DALZIEL DUNCAN

With a New Introduction by
Carol Wilder

Transaction Publishers
New Brunswick (U.S.A.) and Oxford (U.K.)

Second printing, 1989
New material this edition copyright © 1985 by Transaction Publishers,
New Brunswick, New Jersey 08903. Original edition copyright © 1962
by The Bedminster Press. Reprinted from the 1968 Oxford University
Press edition.

Library of Congress Catalog Number: 84-2495
ISBN: 0-87855-971-X (paper)
Printed in the United States of America

Library of Congress Cataloging in Publication Data

Duncan, Hugh Dalziel.
  Communication and social order.
  Reprint. Originally published: London; New York:
Oxford University Press, 1968.
    Bibliography: p.
    Includes index.
    1. Communication. 2. Social interaction. 3. Organization. I. Title.
HM258.D8 1984   302.2   84-2495
ISBN 0-87855-971-X (pbk.)

To Hal, my friend of many years,
whose help brought my books into life,
and to his beloved wife, Ruthie,
who now lives among us in memory and in music.

Introduction to the Transaction Edition
Carol Wilder

How is social experience organized? How is social order expressed? In what ways do human motives become known? Can symbolic interaction be studied as a social fact? How can we come to understand the relationship between art and society, and its further relation to varieties of social order and disorder? And, centrally, how can we think at all about societal events unless we use forms of thought of how humans *communicate* as they act together in society?

The answers, argues Hugh Duncan in this classic work, lie in exploring the belief that "human communication in society is an attempt to create symbols whose use is believed to uphold social order." Moreover, it is not in attention to the content of symbols that a theory of communication and social action is to be found, but rather in symbolic forms, relationships, interactions. What are these symbolic forms? How can they be identified? How do they work, how do they operate, to create and sustain social order?

Communication and Social Order is Duncan's pathfinding attempt to clear the way for a theory of symbols in society, a theory which treats communication not as an epiphenomenon to be reckoned with only in passing, but as an activity which lies at the very heart of social experience. Kenneth Boulding, reviewing the first publication of this work for *Scientific American*, finds Duncan's central idea to be that "the dynamics of society cannot be understood without an understanding of the process of communication, by which the great artist changes the taste of millions, the dramatist arouses images that deflect the course of history and the orator stirs men to glory or to madness."[1]

Such a notion may not strike us as remarkable in the 1980s, when communicational models (e.g. loosely, Mead, Bateson, Kelly, Blumer, Watzlawick, Geertz, Goffman, Burke, Sullivan) have indisputably taken their place—albeit second place—in the social and behavioral sciences. Recall, however, that Duncan was writing *Communication and Social Order* more than two decades ago, at a time close to the height of fashion for mechanistic, quantifiable social theorizing and research. Duncan begins his argument virtually at square one because he is specifically challenging the formidable foe of Parsonian functionalism, a theory which relegates language to the status of a "mechanism" for the transmission of culture, a mechanism sharing a role similar to that of money in Parsons's view.

Given the advantage we now have of hindsight over Duncan's full range of work, it becomes clear that *Communication and Social Order* serves in large measure as an extensive prologue to his systematic theoretical statement presented in *Symbols in Society,* written six years later. *Communication and Social Order* has all the hallmarks of a pioneering journey; here and there it falters or bewilders, here and there again we share a moment of inspired discovery. As such, this is not an easy book to travel through, not comfortable to travel with. Some of its byways turn out to be blind alleys and some of its treasure is hidden; Duncan leaves it to the reader to map the true course of his search for a theory of symbolic action which will unify our understanding of the creation and maintenance of social order.

Perhaps a brief look "ahead" to Duncan's system as articulated in *Symbols in Society* will reflect some light back upon the less orderly volume at hand. If *Communication and Social Order* can best be seen as an intellectual journey, *Symbols in Society* is surely Duncan's fullest account of the destination. This later work is structured around seventy-one propositions, twelve of which Duncan terms "axiomatic," with the remainder divided between "theoretical" and "methodological" propositions. It is the axiomatic propositions which are of most interest here, for these dozen statements taken together represent the credo Duncan courts without consummation in *Communication and Social Order.* Before turning to look directly at the present work, the axiomatic propositions of *Symbols in Society* merit repetition:

1. Society arises in, and continues to exist through, the communication of significant symbols.
2. Man creates the significant symbols he uses in communication.
3. Emotions, as well as thought and will, are learned in communication.
4. Symbols affect social motives by determining the forms in which the contents of relationships can be expressed.
5. From a sociological view motives must be understood as man's need for social relationships.
6. Symbols are directly observable data of meaning in social relationships.
7. Social order is expressed through hierarchies which differentiate men into ranks, classes, and status groups, and, at the same time, resolve differentiation through appeals to principles of order which transcend those upon which differentiation is based.

8. Hierarchy is expressed through the symbolization of superiority, inferiority, and equality, and of passage from one to the other.
9. Hierarchy functions through persuasion, which takes the form of courtship in social relationships.
10. The expression of hierarchy is best conceived through forms of drama which are both comic and tragic.
11. Social order is created and sustained in social dramas through intensive and frequent communal presentations of tragic and comic roles whose proper enactment is believed necessary to community survival.
12. Social order is always a resolution of acceptance, doubt, or rejection of the principles that are believed to guarantee such order.[2]

Note the key terms here: society, symbols, communication, motive, form, order, hierarchy, drama. Expressed discursively, society exists in and through the communication of symbolic forms, forms which determine the ways in which social motives can be expressed. Social order is inescapably hierarchical, and most suitably analyzed through a dramatistic representation. This is the case argued in the present volume.

Duncan is scrupulous in his payment of intellectual debts. Nearly all his final work, *Symbols and Social Theory*,[3] is devoted to this task, as is the first third of *Communication and Social Order*. Here Duncan summarizes the contributions to a theory of symbolic interaction made by Freud, Simmel, Malinowski, James, Dewey, Mead, and Burke. However labored the reader may find these excursions (Boulding writes that "it is as if the author were working a little too hard to establish his reference group"), Duncan's main points are worthy of mention here for the insight they provide into his subsequent formulations.

Sigmund Freud may seem a peculiar point of departure for the development of a theory of symbolic interaction, yet this is where Duncan begins. Freud's monadic, intrapsychic psychoanalytic theory is hardly helpful in understanding forms of relationships: Freud is the bête noire of contemporary family ("interactional") therapy. Family systems therapists and theorists (e.g. Gregory Bateson) most often present Freud and his interest in processes *within* people as a counterpoint to their concern with processes *between* people. Yet this distinction is not entirely lost on Duncan, who recognizes the limitations of Freud's emphasis on communication as cathexis and sees that "the basic problem for human scientists interested in social communication of how to explain emotion, not as motion but as communication, is not solved by Freud."

Duncan uses Freud, rather, because of the importance of symbols in his work. Freud may not be interactional, but he is surely symbolic. And while Freud may have "refused to study motivation in terms of symbols, he often illustrated what he had studied and conclusions he had reached, through illustrations drawn from symbolic works." Duncan draws a distinction between Freud's theorizing and his exemplifications: "It is not so much Freud's theory of repression, but his remarks on the expression of the repression, which are significant to those seeking to develop a theory of social action based on communication." Duncan is especially taken with Freud's treatment of jokes, dreams, and the unconscious elements in communication, pointing to the fact that many illustrations of condensations and displacement reveal the involvement of social as well as sexual elements. Duncan also externalizes Freud's dream censor to become the conscious audience of address. Duncan is taken with Freud's symbolic descriptions "as a *source* for the development of a specific sociological approach, but a source is only a beginning."

Were Duncan to have examined the work of Georg Simmel a decade after writing *Communication and Social Order,* he likely would have attended more closely to Simmel's theorizing about social conflict, a major concern of Simmel's which receives little notice here. Later, at least by 1970, Duncan could state clearly that "a model of rhetoric as used in a democratic society must be a conflict rhetoric."[4] Herein, however, Duncan invokes Simmel to exploit the potential of a focus on social *forms*. Simmel's search for a "pure form of sociation" led him to consider the varieties of human play, where form achieves autonomy from material causes and can thus be studied in its purest sense: In conversation we talk for the sake of talking, at parties we socialize for the sake of socializing, we flirt for the sake of flirting. It is no accident, suggests Duncan, that we place so much emphasis on "good form" in social relationships. Sociability is the "primary sociological category": It has no objective purpose, no content, and no extrinsic results. Tact, manners, discretion, and the like are forms which constitute primary data for the drama of social relationships. Play is to reality as art is to reality, for both activities can be represented as pure form. Content is important ("the subject of talk must be interesting and fascinating"), but in all cases is subordinated to form, in this instance meaning the rules which govern social discourse.

Yet in the end, Simmel falls short of developing a theory of symbolic interaction. Art and play are used by Simmel to illustrate rather than to constitute his social theory, a theory at its roots mechanical rather than symbolic. Simmel "reduces social process to a natural process." Just as Duncan found Freud's focus on symbols useful despite the limitations of psychoanalytic theory, he finds Simmel's attention to form of value even though it stops short of a full symbolic theory.

Malinowski comes closer to presenting a social theory of communication by making language an organizing principle of society. Language is a "mode of action," and no meaning can be ascertained apart from an understanding of the "context of situation." Utterance carries no intrinsic significance. Meaning is not contained *within* symbols; it is to be found in the *relationship* of symbols to social context. Purely social talk, where the talk itself becomes self-referentially the context, Malinowski calls "phatic communication." And beyond pragmatic language and social talk lies Malinowski's special interest, the language of magic. The magical act, with its distinctive form and context and rhetorical function, provides a rich source of data for the analysis of communication processes. In the end, however, Malinowski's strict attention to magical communication—an essentially authoritarian mode—limits the range of his contribution by neglecting the dialectical and rhetorical functions of language so central to democratic social organization. Also, in Duncan's view, Malinowski disregards art, form, and the relationship between language and social change, further restricting his contribution.

James, Dewey, and Mead turned social philosophy around by arguing that the way in which people express themselves about their experience *is* their experience. While there may well exist some form of experience behind the "veil of words," all we can observe—hence all that can constitute a science of society—is what people *say*. James viewed religion from this perspective: Religious experience exists in its expression, regardless of what sorts of "laws" may be said to be operating behind the scenes.

But what forms does this data of expression assume which best allow of symbolic analysis? Duncan decisively chooses art here, a form of expression "unique among the acts of men because it is both instrumental and consummatory." Duncan singles out John Dewey because of the centrality of art to his theory of social action. Art integrates consummatory and instrumental aspects of events, giving the meaning to experience which is essential to social communication. The artist, through creating "forms which make possible participating in community life," thus creates also social interaction. The study of art replaces the study of the supernatural in Dewey's scheme; perhaps art is the most refined form of observable human expression. Duncan faults Dewey for not providing a functional model of art in society, for telling *what* communication as art in society does but not *how* this is accomplished.

Far more functional is the work of George Herbert Mead, who addressed interaction between self and society as a primary concern. Interpersonal reality is a socially bestowed phenomenon. To become conscious of self one must learn to take the attitude of others, to stand as an object to oneself. The complicated games and role plays through which self is created and maintained can be represented by a dramatic model: "The basic *form* of communication as a social act, whatever its content, is histrionic."

Duncan acknowledges Mead's great importance and sketches these roots of symbolic interactionism in some detail, but in the end finds Mead to be excessively optimistic and theoretically inconsistent. Despite Mead's extensive considerations of the relationship of art to communication, "he never really tells us how art arises in, and continues to exist in, communication in society, and what likenesses and differences exist between art and the social as categories of experience."

One wonders—What thinker can satisfy Duncan? Who comes closest to the mark by embracing the notions we by now know are crucial for him: symbol, form, context, art, interaction? For his conceptual mentor, Duncan joins a handful of other sociologists (Erving Goffman, Clifford Geertz, Joseph Gusfield) in choosing master symbolist Kenneth Burke. Duncan's dual interest in literary criticism and social theory made Burke a natural choice, for despite the literary apparel of Burke's prose he is at root a social philosopher, interested in "the use of language as a symbolic means of inducing cooperation in beings that by nature respond to symbols."

Burke considers human behavior in terms of drama; these terms begin in theories of action rather than theories of knowledge. Society is a dramatistic process in which hierarchy forms structure through power relationships. When hierarchy has a definite organization it is "bureaucratized" and then there is order in society. It is this bureaucratization of hierarchy resulting in order which makes hierarchy the structure of society. Hierarchy embodies authority, upon which three attitudes may be brought to bear: acceptance, rejection, or doubt. Acceptance begets satisfaction and order; rejection begets alienation and disorder. Langauge allows rejection because of its "peculiar possibility of the negative." Guilt results when hierarchy is rejected; guilt is inherent in society—class conflict is inherent in hierarchy. Guilt compels purification through either mortification (self-sacrifice) or victimization (scapegoating), both of which lead to redemption.

If the function of an act can be explained in terms of hierarchy, guilt, victimization, and redemption, its structure can be discussed in terms of Burke's "dramatistic pentad": Terms of the pentad are act (what was done), scene (when or where it was done), agent (who did it), agency (how it was done), and purpose (why it was done). The pentad is both divided and unified, analogous to the hand, and all components are interrelated in some ratio. For instance, scene and agent reciprocally relate such that social context shapes the behavior of actors who in return determine the scene. Or again, act and purpose manifest their relationship when "the end of action and action itself are congruent," as in the Indochinese war policy of destroying a village in order to save it.

Duncan's debt to Burke is one of both style and substance. Those who object to the religiosity of Burke's language will find little reprieve in Duncan, who likewise adopts something of a transcendent vocabulary. Duncan also resembles Burke in his sometimes maddening pursuit of every turn an idea may take, a dizzying habit of mind to the reader in search of the "point." Nothing comes easy from either of these hybrid thinkers, and the audience is not exempted from sharing the labor of discovery. Duncan and Burke both write as if to omit the slightest implication may squander a diamond in the rough. The density and richness of this sort of writing may account in no small measure for the slight that social and communication theorists have handed both thinkers, despite the fact that as early as 1935 Louis Wirth (Duncan's Ph.D. adviser) introduced Burke to the sociological community via a highly praiseworthy review of *Permanence and Change* for the *American Journal of Sociology*.

Alas, here we are nearly half a century later gathered to witness the resurrection of a work in the Burkean tradition which has received far less than its due. And having said quite enough about most of Duncan's forbears, it remains to explore the story of *Communication and Social Order* as it unfolds both in and between the lines.

Communication and Social Order was more than a decade in the making; Duncan wrote at least five full drafts of the work beginning in the early 1950s, substantially shifting the conceptual center over the years. The seed of the work was no doubt planted even earlier, perhaps as early as 1938 when Duncan fell under the spell of Kenneth Burke, who led him in a Psychology of Poetic Form seminar at the University of Chicago, a fateful day: It was at this time that Duncan initiated what was to become a lifelong correspondence with Burke, much of which pertains to Duncan's long struggle to articulate the position he comes to take in *Communication and Social Order*. The position, as I understand it, comes to this: Social order is inescapably hierarchical, presuming the existence of superiors, inferiors, and equals. Hierarchy begets classes, and the differences between classes allow a form of miscommunication—mystification—which it is the function of the social order to maintain. Yet there seems to be a basic human instinct toward community, synthesis, and equality. And while it is the office of most social forms (as diverse as government bureaucracy and conversational rules for politeness) to uphold the status quo, selected forms such as play and humor provide opportunities for safely challenging the prevailing order. Both play and humor function within frames which metacommunicate the message "don't take this seriously," thus much of the most serious hierarchy-goading information can be communicated while simultaneously being denied. This activity can take the guise of an editorial cartoon, a political satirist, or witticisms about the "boss" traded over a beer, but in any case the effect is a demystification—however passing—of class difference.

When Duncan hits his stride in the present volume—about halfway through—it becomes evident that he has embraced hierarchy as his central image and comic art as his key exemplification, emphases which took years to mature. To understand this process with a view toward fuller appreciation of Duncan's work, a look at extant papers from the decade-long development of *Communication and Social Order* is revealing.

At least three full outlines from various writing stages of *Communication and Social Order* survive, offering special insight into a major thinker at work. Taken together, these outlines (from 1954, 1956, and 1960) display clearly that Duncan labored mightily to find a key image or theme which would ground and unify the work. Three major themes of the book which underwent major transformations during its development were art, comedy, and hierarchy.

As early as 1951 Duncan wrote to Kenneth Burke that "obviously, my own work is a search for some kind of statement of society in terms of communication."[5] Interestingly, this same letter also includes the first of Duncan's many exhortations to Burke to write on the subject of comedy, advice Duncan somewhat later took to heart for himself by making comedy his case study of communication and social order. But in 1951, Duncan was trying to parcel the topic out. He wrote to Burke:

I wish you would turn over in your mind a statement about comedy. It might actually be a purge for our times. And it might take a little of the sanctimonious air away from the way we are all beginning to talk about talk. Mencken, the merry semanticist, is the only one I know who depicts the verbal scramble as a scuffle in a world populated by W.C. Fields and his phonies, or maybe we should begin laughing at some others. At any rate the comic muse should be invited to leave the boys in the back room for a while. But again maybe she is in safer hands there. . .6

This closing amvibalence may provide a clue as to why Duncan was so long in coming to a treatment of comedy himself, while at the same time his frequent urgings to Burke to join the fray suggest the abiding value he placed on serious treatment of the subject.

By 1952, the theme of hierarchy was becoming salient in Duncan's thinking, as it had been all along for Burke. While struggling with an early draft of *Communication and Social Order,* Duncan wrote to Burke that "you are the only one I know who keeps to the central problem: how status arises in and through communication."7 Moving into the thick of contemplation on the subject, Duncan queries:

How are we to keep a pious attitude toward criticism of hierarchy? Weber suggests (and Parsons paraphrases this) criticism is a means-end relationship as the end of reason (over social relationships). Granted, but how do we create and sustain the necessary pieties toward reason. . . . I suppose all you can say is that whatever is conscious, that is whatever is "open to reason," in conditions where reason is a value, will be safe. Yet as Mannheim stresses we must be careful to note who "owns" reason. As you point out, reason is not without its own magic, as in the scientific labs, the professor's office, etc., where there is great authority and the most rigid hierarchy I have known. Even the army was very flexible about transfers from one unit, branch, etc., to another, but the learned professions assume that each professor is making a unique contribution to knowledge, at the same time they assume that the professor alone is competent to judge what others are accomplishing as contributions to knowledge. Here again the only way out of this impasse is open criticism. Suggestion: All theses be passed by boards of critics drawn from various fields and approved at annual conventions of learned bodies. Wow!8

The personal turn and urgent tone of Duncan's musings on hierarchy here make it come as no surprise when he later places the notion centrally. The vision of society here is an open one, one in which all formal institutions are vulnerable to criticism, one in which it is a right if not a duty to "question authority."

Another feature of this especially impressive letter merits note, for here is the first time in Duncan's correspondence with Burke that he links his three major themes of art, comedy, and hierarchy:

On the whole I think that art is the best corrective [for hierarchy]. The more I think about our great clowns and the richness of American laughter the more I am convinced that an open society can remain fairly healthy as long as it subsidizes laughter. Perhaps there is nothing more profound about reason than laughter. At least in the reduction of psychoses attendant to hierarchy laughter is, to use a hierarchical term, the sovereign remedy. I know that it is necessary at times to have tragedy. The *Passions* of Bach are to me the great counterpart of the Greek tragedy (the role of the congregation, the great choruses, etc.). But I think the Christian tradition was so rooted in the notion that the world, when all was said and done, must be written off and we must prepare ourselves here for the next, that it becomes highly unusable as a secular ethic. Confucius, Rabelais, Montaigne, Erasmus, and on a more popular level now, Chaplin, W.C. Fields, Krazy Kat, and the terrible irony of Kafka where he chides himself for trying to make sense out of a hierarchy essentially senseless, strike me as very useful.[9]

The representations evoked by art are the safeguards of equality, hence of democracy, and in Duncan's view it is the art of laughter, not of tears, which opens the true path through the hierarchical maze he takes as given.

Duncan's 1954 outline of *Communication and Social Order*—then titled *Art and Social Hierarchy*—shows relatively scant evidence ·of this art-comedy-hierarchy relationship when compared to the final manuscript. More than half of the fifty chapter heads and subheads of this outline include the word *art,* but *hierarchy* is mentioned only six times (in subheads) and *comedy* is not mentioned at all. Mead, Burke, and Freud are included here, but receive nowhere close to the attention they are given in the final version. The two points here which become most important in *Communication and Social Order*—"mysteries of hierarchy opened to reason through art" and "communication of hierarchy as basic sociological function of art"—are both relegated to minor status in this early outline. At this stage it appears that Duncan is using art as a lens through which to view communication, a position later radically transformed when communication—symbolic interaction—becomes the lens itself.

By 1956 Duncan's focus had changed dramatically. In June of that year he wrote to Burke, by now a monthly correspondent, reporting:

I am deep in hierarchy. All sorts of models of hierarchic action flit through my head. Once you have a scheme it is amazing how it can be turned and looked at in various ways. The trouble is, what does it have to do with experience?[10]

Burke had earlier given Duncan a bit of advice on the question of hierarchy:

Incidentally, as regards the hierarchy bizz, might it add up to this: The old-time reactionaries and conservatives affirmed the great desirability of hierarchy: progressives, liberals, revolutionaries, nihilists, etc., affirmed its evil and variously promised its abolishment; dramatism would simply study it neutrally, as a major "fact."[11]

It is evident that Duncan is closer to finding his center when he can ask:

How can we open the mystifications and the linkages of hierarchy to some kind of method like the Socratic? The only hope I see is comedy, sports, and play, where in the guise of fun we can think about what we must be very solemn about in other phases of action.[12]

An outline of *Communication and Social Process* written in approximately 1956 reflects Duncan's shifting emphasis. "Art" is now dropped from the working title, which reads *Social Hierarchy: A Sociological Essay on the Expression of Social Hierarchy in Symbolic Phases of Communication.* "Hierarchy," rather than gaining mention in one-tenth of the chapter headings as in 1964, now appears in nearly half of them. Conversely, "art," which held a similar high position in the earlier outline, now shows in but one-seventh of the headings. And comedy at last appears, albeit one time only. Duncan is closing in on his goal.

Kenneth Burke played a major role in the development of *Communication and Social Order,* both indirectly as theoretical (one is almost tempted to say "spiritual") mentor and directly as an exceptionally thorough manuscript reviewer. In 1955, Burke wrote:

Started your manuscript some time back, and found it convincing but perhaps a bit too ranging. However, that reservation will certainly be modified if you subsequently come to rest on the building of some asseveration, without giving a poop about any of us. You are too considerate, sir.[13]

While Duncan never seemed to overcome the excessive consideration of his forbears as writ large in his exhaustive presentations of their key ideas, he did, at this point, come to rest on the asseveration that social reality is a *symbolic* construction whose form is hierarchical, whose process is dialectical, and whose most telling expression is to be found in comic art.

Burke's most extensive critique of *Communication and Social Order* survives in the form of a twelve-thousand-plus-word letter written in 1955.[14] While generally supportive, Burke (with characteristic thoroughness) comments on everything from the broadest focus of the work to incidences of awkward sentence structure. Several samples of middle-level criticism should suffice in communicating the flavor of Burke's approach:

Incidentally, another notion is beginning to occur to me. Might the best architecture of a period be towards serenity, or some such, precisely when the best drama is toward bellyache? As per the poet who loves to get himself comfortably settled by the fire and weep bitterly for all mankind.

Maybe our difference (if there is one!) is this: I would approach art in terms of symbol-using. You would approach it in terms of communication. The two greatly overlap, but they are not identical. One may carry out the possibilities of a symbol-system to the point where they interfere with communication, whereas less far-ranging uses of a symbol-system may communicate almost wholly [p. 39].

And:

Here you do use "language" rather than "communication" as your test. My point, then, is that, although language is perfected by communication, one can focus upon its resources without concern with communication and even to the endangering of communication [p. 139].

And gently chiding:

In what Cooley, Mead, Malinowski, Radcliffe-Brown, and now Burke call a *dramatistic form.* Irony indeed. I made up that word as a deliberate trade name of my particular wares. But lo it has thus disparooed, it has flooed the coop of my possession, somewhat as when the trade name "frigidaire" came to apply not just to one company's product but to the similar products of all rival operators, too. But your comment here is the unkindest cut of all. This haint just sociology, bejeez, it's socialization! [p. 317].

And even:

. . . on drunkenness as reducing social differentiation. You might add: "except when it works exactly the opposite way! The trouble with alky friendliness is that it is so often on the verge of ending in a brawl [p. 402].

Burke emphasizes in this review, as he does elsewhere in a brief review for the University of Chicago Press, that "the stuff on comedy and hierarchy is by far the best part of it," an opinion with which most readers of the final product would concur.

It is likewise easy to understand Burke's assessment that "the two main faults in the other sections are surveyitis and scolding [of colleagues]." For someone who worked largely in isolation, Duncan displays extraordinary attentiveness toward other thinkers, a tendency which sometimes obscures his original contributions because of the sheer manuscript space he delegates to friends and foes. Burke urges him to cut, cut, cut:

I think if you could bring yourself to slash into the material in such fashion, you'd have a very effective book. You could leave it as it is and still have something that would pass. But it would be a crime to have put so much work into a book and then to skimp on the week or two still needed to make it a book instead of a sociology clip-sheet. But you could do this work only by the rules I have suggested [e.g. "read the manuscript from beginning to end without a break"]. You'd have to work on it in a situation that allowed for nearly absolute Retreat. For the book as it now stands is too scattered. Let Your Business Rot for One Week.

Abandon Your Love Life for One Week. Just Glumly Revise, being Brutally Willing to Sacrifice.

And you'll have a strong book.

In its present form, it passes, but is not strong.

Naturally, I'd like to see the wavering dialectic cleared up, too. But I consider the cuts more important than the revision. "When in doubt, cut it out."

Readers of this volume may question just how seriously Duncan was able to take Burke's advice, but if *Communication and Social Order* still suffers a bit from "surveyitis," it is not from lack of trying on Duncan's part. Of his six published books, this one is generally considered the most important, and it was certainly his most consuming. None of his other works receives more than passing attention in the Burke-Duncan letters, and while *Communication and Social Order* took well over a decade to come to fruition, four of Duncan's five other books were published in rapid succession during the following seven years: *The Rise of Chicago as a Literary Center* in 1964; *Culture and Democracy* in 1965; *Symbols in Society* in 1968; and *Symbols and Social Theory* in 1969. (*Language and Literature in Society* was published in 1953.) But in 1955, Duncan was

still wraslin' with the problem of structure in my ms. I have enough stuff on comedy and hierarchy to take a stall in the shop you once told me about. I'll label mine Duncan's Patented Hierarchic Cathartic and sell it along with your Symbolic Catharsis. When business falls off we'll do a one cent sale. Attach my nostrum to your package and we're in business.

Sales Problem for the next meeting. . . . who wants to be cured of a hierarchic malady. Awful thought for a man of enterprise. That's the trouble with listening to these long hairs.[15]

"Sales problem" indeed. Duncan may have had a hard time writing *Communication and Social Order,* but he had an even harder time getting it published. In 1956 he wrote to Burke:

Since I last submitted my ms. to the [University of Chicago] Press a new managing editor has been appointed. In my presence he thumbed through my ms. and began a series of negative remarks about it. This whole attitude has been continued. I am sure he has not read it (he never had a chance to until this interview when I took the revised draft for him to see), so there must be policy reasons for his remarks. I just don't get it. The whole thing has become so painful I have written him asking him to send it back to me, for even if he accepted it now I would not have much confidence in any talk with him about changes, etc.[16]

Duncan's publishing tribulations can be understood in part because of his maverick position vis-à-vis both of his "disciplines" of literary art and sociology and in part through the frankly acknowledged fact that writing—to which he was deeply committed—did not come easily to him.

Much of Duncan's early correspondence to Burke includes mention
of this problem. In 1952 Duncan writes that he was scolded by Hayden
Carruth—then managing editor of the University of Chicago Press—
about "my bad expression, although he seems to have a high value for
my ideas. This is a common criticism of my work."[17] Shortly thereafter
he elaborates:

I know I need to write better. The problem is how to write so that you evoke as well as
analyze, or is this simply another way of meeting the old problem of the relationship
between idea and image? Certainly academic lingo is full of ideas, literary of wonderful
images. Good scholarly prose would be which? Or, if combined, how? It beats me.[18]

Duncan recognized that part of the difficulty was some "puzzlement
about whom I address when I write. There seems to be some ideal
audience that you must stick to—the problem in my stage is to create
one—or does one *find* them?"[19] There *was* no ready-made audience for
Duncan's scholarship in this era when communicational and symbolic
approaches to both the social sciences and literature were fledging and
largely fell upon deaf ears. Taking communication as *the* data of
sociation rather than as a means to discover the "real" phenomena of,
say, "psychosis," "social equilibrium," or "class mobility" requires such a
step-function adjustment that the one-eyed man in the land of the blind
faces a formidable pedagogical challenge. Like M. Jourdain, Molière's
bourgeois gentleman, Duncan made much of his realization that we
"speak prose," and as a consequence faced much of the same reception.

All creative thinkers struggle with the constraints of symbol systems,
and Duncan was no exception. "The more you try to write about ideas,"
he averred, "the more you approach the way poets handle words as
your ideal. I am trying to really write. This is very different from
reporting some ideas."[20] So it is, especially to one who recognizes the
critical role of form in the full expression of thought. Ironically this
very thoroughness may have compromised in some measure his ability
to write provocatively. For the most part, Duncan writes in the format
of what Umberto Eco has called a "closed text," which gives the reader
little room to wonder what it is all about. An open text does not satisfy
the reader's "hunger for redundancy," an appetite rather well sated by
Duncan.

There is a poignancy every writer will find familiar in Duncan's
disclosure of self-doubt while writing his book on Chicago literature:

Minna [Mrs. Duncan] tells me that I am very irritable. I tell her that this book is important,
that the future of America hangs on my interpretation of Chicago. Then I think, if it doesn't

it should, because it is about time somebody said something about us out here. And then I get scared about whether I really have the stuff. Then there are other days when I can't seem to believe in what I am doing. These are the worst. Then sweep in other days when heart and head reach over to each other and a moment of glory comes. These are the great moments—but how fleeting. The trouble with writing is that you cannot be ironic about your own work. Irony seems to be one of those fatal contradictions. Perhaps if, like the great aristocrat, you have a great enough audience, it is satisfying. Then I suppose, you could even die in the grand manner.[21]

Despite such periods of doubt, Duncan carried on writing, and must be called prolific by any standards. *Communication and Social Order* was produced somewhat in fits and starts and there were long periods when the manuscript was set aside as Duncan turned to either one of his other books in progress or to a series of real estate ventures which were to make him financially independent. But in 1957 he was back to the project closest in his heart, trying to incorporate the revisions recommended by Burke several years earlier:

I have been reading my Hierarchy ms. once again. I want to spare you too close attention to Part I. It is an awful mess now. Why I did not realize this before I cannot understand. I think it was because I was so busy paying off some kind of score against the profession for not making me a full professor at Harvard. I do not need to feel that way anymore, so all the rambling pages from 1 through 113 can be cut down.[22]

Here Duncan lets it be known that he is revising in response to Burke's complaints about "surveyitis" and "scolding," during a period which ranged from the late 1940s to the early 1960s when he was not formally employed as an academic. (He held a permanent professorial post—at Southern Illinois University—only during the last decade of his life.)

Eventually, *Communication and Social Order* was accepted for publication by Bedminster Press, and the final product bears Burke's influence at every turn. It is virtually impossible to overestimate Duncan's debt to Burke, whom Charles Elkins claims was Duncan's "friend, his critic, his confidant, his father-figure—one of the few with whom Duncan could share his hopes and fears."[23] This is well documented in the Burke-Duncan letters, wherein Duncan continually expresses his admiration and respect, aptly summarized in his imagined dedication to Burke's autobiography in progress: "To Kenneth Burke whose long voyage into the night has brought us nearer to the shores of light."[24]

One theme that pervades Duncan's letters of the 1940s is his astonishment that Burke has not yet received his just due from academicians:

What amuses me about . . . academicians I have talked to about your work is that they insist it is of great importance but they really don't know why because it doesn't fit into any of the bins. So, I have decided to circumvent them by creating a Burkian Bin, called "The Nature of Communication as Evidenced by the Symbolic Act." My strategy is to insist that you are wholly involved in the matter of method, of *how* we can analyze discourse.[25]

This was a bold statement to make during an era when neither Burke's nor Duncan's work was even considered to be "research," let alone *methodological* research. Part of the difficulty, Duncan writes to Burke, may arise from the fact that

your method of writing is based on extension and the small minds will want intension. They want you to do a set piece so that they can use it for practical purposes such as teaching, etc. Instead you like to extend your range of observations throughout as many fields as possible. This allows you to test your ideas against those of creative minds in place of submitting your ideas to the test of merely orderly minds.[26]

This, then, is why:

No specialist can like your work for you are the bull in the world of bins. When you proportionalize what they are essentializing, they simply cannot follow you. That is why I told you that you have a theory of society in your work.[27]

Duncan's view of Burke as a social philosopher is now so widely accepted that it is difficult to appreciate the astuteness of his claim made more than thirty years ago.

Some of Duncan's most engaging prose expresses his utter enchantment with Burke's work. In 1949 he wrote:

A note, struck off in a moment of Burkian euphoria, after delving again into your works, specifically regarding your social act construct (Act, Scene, Agent, Agency, Purpose). Having piled up some 200 pages in my ms. in which I am trying to say something about communicative acts [most likely the seed of *Communication and Social Order*], I admire your pentad more and more. I hope my admiration will become the sincerest form of thanks: a good book.[28]

Along the same lines, Duncan wrote shortly thereafter:

I am so damn glad you are to be out here because I am at the point in my work where I am beginning to personalize The Act. Some days I cozy up with Scene and find Tradition, Memory, Commemoration, etc., everywhere. Other days Purpose lures me into Utopias, Futures, Teleology, Heavens, Ideals, Models.[29]

Duncan found in Burke the sort of provocative writing that he himself strove to achieve. And the years did little to diminish his reverence for the master. In 1954 Duncan wrote:

I cannot tell you how wonderful I think your working out of the various aspects of symbolic expression are. I work in your shadow at every turn, a luminous shadow for me. When I get through with a chunk of work I always feel guilty about how much better you have said what I try to say! That is why I call you a shadow, I guess. The trouble is that I really do not want to get out from it because only when under it does my mind leap about in the most amazing fashion. Freud trails off into the Unconscious, the libido, the Id, but you soar into the light, the conscious, the community of communicants who like the Thelemites are content to be human even though aware of the risks.[30]

Duncan frequently expressed this concern that he was laboring too fully in Burke's shadow, making many tongue-in-cheek references to his "plagiarism." For instance, in 1949 he wrote:

I haven't written to you or about you because I am so busy stealing your ideas in a book I am now writing that it seems almost superfluous to write you as you exist in Andover. With your help, as well as Dilthey, Weber, Lukacz, Collingwood, Dewey, Veblen, Malinowski, Frazer, etc., I hope to get out an extended essay on the nature, function, structure, and relation to power of the *aesthetic act* in American society.

During dry spells I think—what the hell, Burke and Dewey have done this anyway. Why should I simply repeat what good men have done! But then I return to my cheerful thievery. The best I can say as I whistle while I work is well—Burke said this so well that it is even fun to say it again.[31]

Duncan even explains his intermittent correspondence in a 1955 letter accompanying a draft of *Communication and Social Order* by writing: "I think when you look through my ms. you will see why it is I write so seldom. Thus far my work has been so much of a dialogue with you that letters seem superfluous."[32]

Duncan is too modest, for despite Burke's inescapable mark, *Communication and Social Order* emerges from his shadow in at least one very significant way through Duncan's emphasis on the social functions of *comedy*. In contrast to Burke's focus on ritual and tragedy, Duncan calls comedy nothing less than the "rhetoric of reason in society," and his treatment of it is the most original contribution of this work. What makes this so fascinating is knowing how late Duncan came to the subject after his years of urging Burke to take it up. It appears that Duncan took the topic as his own only after Burke had parceled it out to him as a conference paper topic in 1956.

Why comedy? Because laughter "clarifies" where tragedy "mystifies"; because "comedy opens to reason the mystifications of social hierar-

chy"; because "as we laugh together, loneliness and alienation vanish"; because "comedy teaches us that men can endure much if they can endure it in rational discourse with each other." Comedy relieves social tension and serves as a resistance against authority. Comedy strengthens social bonds; thus "all comedy is highly moral." Unlike tragedy, which prepares the victim for sacrifice, comedy prepares him for *dialogue.* "Comedy is ethical because it is rational and rational because it leads to good social relationships." Comedy offers a way of challenging those social hierarchies which are vulnerable to change and enduring those which are not. "Laughter may not be enough to save us," wrote Duncan, "but unless we live under reason and love, what is the use of living at all?"
In a 1963 autobiographical piece, Duncan explained:

The drama of society is for me a comic, not a tragic drama. This is not because I find life a great joke, nor because I think tragedy a great illusion, but because comedy keeps reason alive, demands equality in social relationships, and permits us to re-examine our social relationships so we can change them. It is, in short, for me the typical democratic relationship, and the typical modern expression of art. Perhaps, when all is said and done, I prefer comedy because it seems far more benign than tragedy, and as befits a scholar who grew up in the land of Mark Twain and Lincoln, laughing gods of art and society, comedy seems far more trustworthy in the mundane affairs of life . . . at least in the Middle West, for we are at our best out here when we laugh at each other.[33]

Duncan, the taciturn Scot, finds many of his truest moments as a theorist concerned with the language of laughter, a language which comes closest to allowing the social equality he so passionately championed.

In all, Duncan's vision is profoundly democratic. Kenneth Boulding, in the review cited earlier, reckoned that "Duncan's discussion of the nature of social equality impresses me as being the most profound body of insight into this subject I have ever read." How did this theme of democracy come to pervade Duncan's work? Perhaps, as Charles Elkins has suggested, it had something to do with Duncan's service during World War II as an intelligence officer. It may reflect the subtle effect of the Cold War upon his consciousness. Duncan himself wrote that the period during the late 1930s when he lived and worked at Chicago's famed Hull House "heightened my awareness of social injustice, and forced me to search more deeply into the meaning of art."[34] In any case, democratic egalitarianism is clearly Duncan's ideal social order. "It is only among equals that we find conversation and discussion," he wrote. Only under "the conditions of equality can the self be born." But there is a paradox here, for the natural form of social organization is hierarchy, and hierarchy is comprised of relationships among superiors, inferiors, and equals. Conversation can take place only among equals, yet social systems are maintained by a balance of inequality. This is the fundamental dilemma which we strive to overcome through humor, art, and social play where "the purest form of relationship among equals exists."

The struggle is never easy, especially given the fragile gift of communication through which the battle must be waged. The alternative is the dark world sought by a master manipulator like Hitler, whose "rhetoric of hell" moves Duncan to some of his most fervent prose in this book. Hitler—"the greatest rhetorician of evil known to history"—well understood that the purpose of rhetoric is "to satisfy the longing of people for communion with each other." He understood that symbols find their end in action and he knew the power of art. Duncan laments that "the tragedy of our time" is that it seems only tyrants have exploited the power of art in communication. Indeed, the balance of our future may hang upon this question: "Democratic leaders too can learn to use the arts for benign purposes, but will they?"

Duncan's sociological bent notwithstanding, his theory as it emerges in this book can properly be called *rhetorical,* and not only because he tells us so in several places. Duncan never wavers from his view of symbolic action as the primary data of social reality, a view well stated in an essay on rhetoric written shortly before his death in 1970. Addressing the subject of form and content in social action, Duncan wrote:

The sociodramatic model is not intended to be a metaphor, an analogy, or a fiction, but a *representation* of social relationships which arise in, and continue to exist through, communicative forms studied best in models derived from dramatic form. The way we communicate *is* the way we relate.[35]

Further, Duncan treats extensively of persuasion—the ancient central concern of rhetorical theory—as the means of establishing the sort of identification which offers choice and thus permits the possibility of equality. Also, Duncan's treatment of the audience in his detailed consideration of forms of hierarchical address is among the most extensive in the literature. It is astonishing to note the near total neglect of Duncan by subsequent rhetorical theorists, a state of affairs made no easier by the fact that every one of Duncan's six books has gone out of print. On the brighter side, this should make the republication of *Communication and Social Order* an especially welcome event.

Duncan's treatment of the symbolic function of money and his inspired selection of comedy as an exemplification of his theorizing are among many features which distinguish this work as worthy of sustained attention. And whether talking of money or manners, courtship or comedy, clothes, love, sex, or art, Duncan consistently provides novel insight into the forms and functions of symbolic action. In this time when threats of tyranny and annihilation loom even larger than Duncan could have imagined, his words still speak to these issues, and they do so with both a conscience and a heart.

Having spent some of the better parts of the past year in close quarters with *Communication and Social Order,* if I could send a single message to Hugh Duncan I could hope to do no better than to choose these lines he once wrote to Kenneth Burke:

I have always felt that you were a lonely voyager and there have been times when I sensed that you felt some sort of cold mist closing in about you as you traversed some of the deepest fens. Sometimes I thought this was the way you had to travel to get on with your work; that you would far rather take the risks in the hope of reaching some light, than give up the glory. When we first met it was the wonderful polyphonic quality of your thinking that enchanted me. It still does but now there is something more; the instrumental value of it for saving us from more monsters who know how to use the magic of symbols.[36]

Notes

I would like to acknowledge the invaluable assistance of Kenneth Burke, Charles Elkins, and Charles Mann during the preparation of this essay. Any errors of fact or interpretation are, of course, mine alone.

[1]Kenneth Boulding, "Hugh Duncan's new book *Communication and Social Order,*" *Scientific American* (January 1963).

[2]Hugh Duncan, *Symbols in Society* (New York: Oxford University Press, 1968).

[3]Hugh Duncan, *Symbols and Social Theory* (New York: Oxford University Press, 1969).

[4]Hugh Duncan, "The Need for Clarification in Social Models of Rhetoric," in *The Prospect of Rhetoric,* ed. Lloyd Bitzer and Edwin Black (Englewood Cliffs, N.J.: Prentice-Hall, 1971), p. 150.

[5]Duncan to Burke, 3 March 1951. Unless otherwise indicated, all citations of the Hugh Duncan-Kenneth Burke correspondence refer to letters archived in the Rare Books and Special Collections of Pattee Library at The Pennsylvania State University. Most of Duncan's other papers, including five unpublished manuscripts, can be found at the Morris Library of Southern Illinois University at Carbondale.

[6]Duncan to Burke, 3 March 1951.

[7]Duncan to Burke, n.d., approximately March 1952.

[8]*Ibid.*

[9]*Ibid.*

[10]Duncan to Burke, 14 June 1956.

[11]Burke to Duncan, 27 August 1955.

[12]Duncan to Burke, 11 April 1956.

[13]Burke to Duncan, 17 March 1955.

[14]Burke to Duncan, 27 August 1955.

[15]Duncan to Burke, n.d., approximately December 1955.

[16]Duncan to Burke, 16 December 1956.

[17]Duncan to Burke, 3 January 1952.

[18]Duncan to Burke, 7 January 1952.

[19]Duncan to Burke, 20 June 1951.

[20]Duncan to Burke, n.d., approximately March 1952.

[21]Duncan to Burke, 17 September 1951.

[22]Duncan to Burke, 14 May 1957.

[23]Charles Elkins, " 'Son of a Burke': The Hugh Dalziel Duncan Collection at Morris Library," *ICarbS: Journal of the Morris Library* (in press).

[24]Duncan to Burke, 9 October 1956.

[25]Duncan to Burke, 24 September 1946.

[26]Duncan to Burke, 25 November 1956.

[27]Duncan to Burke, 24 August 1951.

[28]Duncan to Burke, n.d., sometime in 1949.

[29]Duncan to Burke, 10 August 1949.

[30]Duncan to Burke, 15 June 1954.

[31]Duncan to Burke, n.d., sometime in 1949.

[32]Duncan to Burke, 2 February 1955.

[33]"A Letter from Hugh Duncan," *Bedminster Letter* (no. 2, January 1963): 5.

[34]*Ibid.*, p. 4.

[35]Duncan in *The Prospect of Rhetoric,* p. 143.

[36]Duncan to Burke, 7 March 1951.

Contents

———————————

Introduction xxxvii-lii

PART ONE
Symbolic Contexts of Social Experience in Freud, Simmel, and Malinowski

I. *Symbolic Interaction in Freud's Work*
The Importance of Symbols in Freudian Theory 3
Freud's Attempt to Combine Qualities and Quantities in His
    Description of Cathexis 6
Freud's Use of Rhetorical and Dramatic Imagery 8
Freud's Great Contribution to a Sociology of Language:
    Dreams and Communication 13

II. *Simmel's Search for an Autonomous Form of Sociability*
Forms of Sociation Considered as Representative Forms of
    Social Interaction 18
Forms of Sociation Considered as Art and as Play 21
The Purest Moment of Sociability: Equality 23
Coquetry and Conversation as Specific Examples of Pure Forms
    of Sociation 25
Simmel's Contribution to Social Theory Considered in Terms of
    Communication 28

III. *Malinowski's Theory of the Social Context of Magical Language*
The Context of Situation in the Magical Language of the Tribe 34
Language and Social Organization 37
The Relevance of Malinowski's Tribal Context of Situation to
    Communication in Modern Society 40

PART TWO

The Self and Society as Determined by Communication in James, Dewey, and Mead

IV. *Society as Determined by Communication: Dewey's Theory of Art as Communication*
The Problem of Time in Symbolic Analysis 49
James' Pragmatic Approach to Religious Expression: His Views on Human Documents 52
Communication, Art, and Society in Dewey 55
Dewey's Contribution to a Social Theory of Communication 63
Dewey's View of the Social Function of Art 66

V. *Communication and the Emergence of the Self in the Work of George Herbert Mead*
James' Acceptance of Expressive Symbols as Social Data 73
The Emergence of the Self in Communication 76
The Self and the Other in Communication 78

VI. *The Final Phase of the Act: Consummation*
Consummation and Communication: The Aesthetic Moment in Experience 82
The Function of Imagery in Conduct 87

VII. *The Problem of Form in Mead's Theory of the Significant Symbol*
Mead's Theory of the Significant Symbol 92
Problems in the Use of Mead's Concept of Role-Taking 96
The "Organization of Perspectives" and Communication as a Form of Address 100

PART THREE

The Function of Symbols in Society: An Application of Burke's Dramatistic View of Social Relationships

VIII. *Burke's Dramatistic View of Society*
Literature as Equipment for Living in Society 109
The Nature of Symbolic Action in Society 114

IX. *Social Order Considered as a Drama of Redemption Through Victimage*
Hierarchal Identification 121
Redemption and Victimage in Social Order 125
How Victimage Functions in Society 129
The Perfecting of Victimage in Society 131

PART FOUR
Burke's Sociology of Language

X. *The Structure and Function of the Act in the Work of Kenneth Burke*
Social Action as Symbolic Action: A Dramatistic View of Human Relations 143
Logical, Rhetorical, and Symbolic Phases of the Act 147

XI. *A Rhetoric of Motives: Burke's Sociology of Language*
The Socio-Psychological Function of Rhetoric: Identification 154
Identification in Rhetoric 158

XII. *The Rhetoric of Social Order*
Identification and Address 165
Persuasion and Communication 170

PART FIVE
Social Mystification in Communication Between Classes

XIII. *Toward a New Rhetoric: Burke's Analysis of Social "Mystification" in Bentham and Marx*
Jeremy Bentham's Search for a "Neutral" Rhetoric Based on "Reason" 179
Rhetoric and Dialectic in Marxism 181
Marxism Considered as a Rhetorical Critique 185

XIV. *Social Mystification and Social Integration*
Carlyle on Clothes as a Symbol of Social Order: The Rhetoric of Acceptance of Social Hierarchy 190
Doubtful Acceptance of Hierarchy: Irony and Rhetoric 194

XV. *Reason and Hierarchal Disorganization*
The Priority of Rhetoric in Social Relations 202
Diderot on the "Vile Pantomime" of Aristocratic Hierarchy 204
La Rochefoucauld on Courtly Address 207

XVI. *The Rhetoric of Ruling: Communication and Authority*
The Political Public as an Audience: Machiavelli's "The Prince" 212
The Rhetoric of Domination of the Secular World by the Devout
Christian. Gracian's "The Art of Worldly Wisdom" 217

XVII. *Rhetoric as an Instrument of Domination Through Unreason, Hitler's "Mein Kampf"*
Hitler's Theory of Rhetoric as a Means Toward Social Identification 225
The Staging of Appeals to Mass Audiences 229

XVIII. *Social Order Based on Unreason: The Perversion of Religion by the State*
Hitler's Application of Religious Forms to a Political Context 238
Hitler's Rhetoric as Allegory 241
Political Action as Tragic Ritual Drama 245

PART SIX

A Sociological Model of Social Order as Determined by the Communication of Hierarchy

XIX. *Social Order as a Form of Hierarchy*
The Structure of Social Hierarchy Considered in Terms of Communication
of Superiority, Inferiority, and Equality 253
Social Passage 257
The Presentation of Social Roles and Social Roles as a
Form of Hierarchy 262
Manners and Social Order 266

XX. *The Communication of Hierarchy*
Modes of Courtship: Acceptance, Rejection, and Doubt 271
Hierarchal Identification 273
The Dependence of Toleration of Difference on the Communication of
Transcendent Principles of Social Order 278

How Order and Disorder Define Each Other 280
Art Considered as the Guardian of Social Order 282

XXI. *Hierarchal Address*
How Audiences Determine the Character of Hierarchal Appeals 288
A Typology of Audiences Determined by Hierarchal Address 292
The General Public 294
Community Guardians: The Audience as the Conscience of the
   Community 295
Individuals as Audience to Each Other 297

XXII. *A Sociological View of "Inner" Audiences*
Forms of Appeals to Inner Audiences 302
Mortification and Guilt 306
The Social Function of Soliloquy 310

PART SEVEN
Hierarchal Transcendence and Social Bonds

XXIII. *Social Transcendence*
Types of Social Transcendence 315
Social Progression 319
Social Mystification and the Perfection of Hierarchy 321

XXIV. *Equality and Social Order*
Rules as a Principle of Social Order 326
Play and Sociation 328
"Playing Society": The Social Function of the Gentleman 331
Play and Equality 334
Hierarchy and Equality 337
Authority and Victimage 339
The Resolution of Hate and Love Among Equals 343

XXV. *The Establishment of Money as a Symbol of
Community Life*
Mandeville, Marx, and Carlyle on the Transformation of Money
   into a Social Bond 347
The Freudian Symbol of Money 351

The Social Rhetoric of Money: Simmel and Veblen 353
The Shift from the Puritan Ethic of Earning to an Ethic of Spending 355

XXVI. *Money as a Form of Transcendence in American Life*
Spending as Prayer: The American Christmas 358
Spending and Death 360
The Deification of the Businessman 362
American Art and the Dignification of Spending 364

PART EIGHT

The Social Function of Art in Society

XXVII. *Comedy and Social Integration*
The Place of the Comic in Art and Social Theory 373
Comedy and Social Control 376
The Social Function of Irony 380
Comedy and Group Identification 387

XXVIII. *The Comic Scapegoat*
Comedy as Sanctioned Expression of Doubt, Ambiguity, and
    Disrespect 393
Comic Victimage and Social Catharsis 395
Comedy and the Self 402

XXIX. *Comedy as the Rhetoric of Reason in Society*
Comedy and Reason 406
The Social Function of Comic Obscenity 407
Comic Unmasking 411
Comedy and the Purification of Social Order 413

XXX. *Tragic and Comic Sexual Themes Compared*
Sex and Hierarchy in Art and Society 417
Comic and Tragic Communication of Sex 420
Sexual and Social Guilt in Comedy 424

PART NINE
By Way of Conclusion

XXXI. *A Sociological Model of Social Interaction as Determined by Communication*
   The Nature of Symbolic Action in Art and Society 431
   The Structure of the Symbolic Act 433
   The Function of the Symbolic Act 436

Index 439

Introduction

THE BEST we have done thus far in communication theory in sociology is to make vague statements about the reciprocal relationship between society and communication. We have also elaborated biological, physical, mechanical, and, more recently, electronic analogies of communication into models, or "designs," for exercises in research technique. These analogical models are spun out in great detail through elaborate research techniques, which are often not so much a statement of relationship between a hypothesis and data, as an attempt to rephrase old propositions in the new jargon, or to describe how techniques were applied to data selected to fit the technique.

Social acts are now described as events that order themselves through a "tendency to self-maintenance." Social systems are likened to solar systems, and social roles are said to "bring out" possibilities of behavior which fit the "needs and tolerances of the particular patterned structure." In this model of society, attitudes "gear" and "mesh" because "patterned structure" and "integrative patterns . . . bring it about that all the statuses of the society intermesh like a series of interlocking wheels." Communication of expressive symbols is not studied as an enactment of social order, but as a process of cathexis in which meanings are "attached" to objects and persons.

In other analogies, men are likened to dogs, rats, chickens, or pigeons, and we are told that what is true of pigeons in cages is also true of men in society, or, among the more sophisticated technicians, that if men were held like pigeons in a cage then what is true of the behavior of pigeons would be true of men. Such wild analogical leaps from animals and machines to men are often justified on the basis of technique alone. For if (so the argument runs) a certain technique for ordering data about pigeons is "scientific," then the same technique applied to men in society will yield studies of similar "scientific" value. *How* a study is done, not what questions were asked, and the kind of data used, determine its "scientific" value in this kind of thinking.

In the many hundreds of pages of recent sociological theory there is scarcely any indication that communication of significant symbols is anything more than some kind of epiphenomenon of a reality "beyond" symbols. Attitudes do not arise in symbolic acts, or in symbolic phases of action (in which, as heroes, villains, and clowns to each other, we play our parts in a great social drama of social order) but in "expressive reference" contexts, in which attitudes become a "symbolic generalization of cathexis" which functions to maintain "the pattern integrity" of the symbolic system.[1]

And while there is much greater concern with the social function of symbols in Dilthey, Simmel, and Mannheim, and other European students of society, there is a singular lack of congruence between structure and function in their models and images of society. Even Mannheim, who talks at great length about "thought styles"—a concept which he borrows from the history of art—never makes clear just how the structure of "existential" thought functions in communication. The Freudian libido, like the actor in Parsons' system, cathects, but does not communicate. Simmel's forms of sociation emerge, and continue to exist, in social processes that are not determined by the use of symbols in communication, but by social forces that are "like atoms."

Other sociologists find their sociological "facts" in "historical and political reality." Just how one gets at this without symbolic theory and method, or the use of sociological models based on communication, is seldom discussed. Sentences like "What dramatic vision of hell can compete with the events of twentieth-century war?"[2] assume that the "events" of war can be known by means other than a dramatic construction of them, or that they become events in some nonsymbolic realm which does not depend on how they are dramatized by artists in the press, radio, television, literature, cinema, and other arts. What is the source of C. Wright Mills' knowledge of events? How can "events" of war in the past or the present make themselves known to us as social and historical facts, if not through some kind of symbolic construction? How can sociologists, to say nothing of historians, think at all about societal events unless they use models, images, structures—or whatever the forms of our thought are called—of how men *communicate* as they act together in society?

Symbols are the directly observable data of sociation, and, since it is impossible to use symbols without using them in some kind of structure or form, we cannot discourse about society with any degree of precision unless we discourse about the forms social relationships assume in communication. There may be some reality underlying symbols, but all we know about what people do is the meaning of what they say [3] they do. Even Mills admonishes his social scientist: "Always keep your eyes open to the image of man." But where does one find an "image of man"? All we see of man, certainly all we can report of his social activities, are various forms of expression. We no longer need to be told that men exist in history, or society, but to be shown *how* such existence can be studied in some sociological frame of reference.

It will be argued throughout this book that a sociological theory of social action can be created only if we show how *forms,* as well as contents, of symbolic expression are used to create and sustain social order. Following Simmel, we argue that the study of society is the study of forms of sociation. But we argue further—and here our clue is supplied by Mead and Burke—that the data of sociation exist in the various kinds of symbolic expressions men use to enact their social roles in communication with one another. It is not enough to invoke ritual, play, ceremony, festivals, games, or drama as analogies for society unless we make clear *how* these become, and continue to be, *social* forms.

Nor is it of much help to the development of sociological theory to invoke social contexts as "referents" to symbols unless we show just how these referents exist in the symbols. That is, if we say that struggle to attain social order determines social relations, we must show how various significations of social order can be studied as they are used in the communication of such order. As we shall stress in our remarks on social transcendence, authorities use many kinds of symbols to justify their rule. In our view, these justifications ought to be studied in concrete symbolic acts, or in symbolic phases of action. Power always involves persuasion, and whether we persuade under principles of sovereignty, ruling myths, dominant ideas, ideologies, or whether we study ruling ideas of social order as folklore, legitimations, or collective representation, we must study what *kind* of order they involve and above all how this order is expressed in communication.

We must show how social order is expressed, for all we really can observe about order is how it is communicated. We talk, sometimes very grandly, about public sentiments, the people's will, the voice of the people, the leadership principle, the divine right of kings, or the kingdom of God. But when we are asked to point out how these great transcendent images of social order operate, we turn to the various ways in which they are expressed in communication. And social order, we note, always involves people who communicate as superiors, inferiors, and equals, and pass from one position to another. Such communication is always a form of address, a kind of hierarchical rhetoric, in which, as superiors, inferiors, and equals, in passage from one position to another, we justify our rank to ourselves and to others by enacting in various kinds of community dramas the value to some great transcendent principle of social order of the roles we play.

As matters now stand in American social thought, the study of forms of communication is suspect, or tolerated only until social scientists achieve an "intellectual clarity" which science, and usually science based on quantification, is supposed to produce. Men of letters also warn us that using literature or other art works as cultural case histories is false, because art exists "in its own right" and cannot be explained by the culture of an age or country. There is no question about our need for intellectual clarity, and certainly it is true that art cannot be explained by social referents alone. All critics admit that *War and Peace* becomes singularly unclear about the nature of peace (if not of war), and that Tolstoy "distorts" the Russian class struggle in 1800 to produce an art work, not to write social history, just as Freud "distorted" the Oedipus legend and drama to create a model of family interaction, not to write a history of Greek drama.

But when we turn to the sociologist or the aesthete for help in freeing ourselves from the "distortions" of the artist, we find ourselves in the same situation as Freud when he tried to understand why men act as they do from what they said about what they did—or as sociologists do when they must interpret symbolic material in case histories, interviews, or life histories. As anthropologists, psychologists, or sociologists, we join with historians, philosophers, and artists in the realization that our knowledge of human motives is limited by our knowledge of the systems of expressions in which motives are communicated. Even Freud, who hoped all his life to create a mechanical model of mentation, said in 1909: "Dream symbols that do not find support in myths, fairy tales, popular usages, etc., should be regarded as doubtful." Later, in 1917, in his lecture, "Symbolism in Dreams," he is even more explicit.

How do we profess to arrive at the meaning of these dream-symbols, about which the dreamer himself can give us little or no information. . . . My answer is that we derive our knowledge from widely different sources: from fairy tales and myths, jokes and witticisms, from folklore, i.e., from what we know of the manners and customs, sayings and songs, of different people, and from poetic and colloquial usage of language.[4]

Freud is not alone in his belief that understanding society depends on our understanding of symbols. Dilthey argued that speech is the most complete, exhaustive, and objectively intelligible expression of man. He pointed out many times that the exegesis, or interpretation of the remains of human existence which are contained in writing, is central to every method of understanding used in the human sciences. Simmel's forms of sociation are based on many analogies, but he often returns to art form to illustrate his general idea of social form.[5] Kenneth Burke stresses that social interaction is not a process, but a dramatic expression, an enactment of roles by individuals who seek to identify with each other in their search to create social order. George Herbert Mead, too, described such enactments as forms similar to those in play, games, and drama. Our need to stress form in terms of expression and emotion, as well as mechanics and motion, has been pointed out by Talcott Parsons, whose model of man in society is certainly far different from that of Dewey, Mead, or Burke. He says: "Expressive symbolism is that part of the cultural tradition most directly integrated with the cathectic interests of the actor. . . . [Expressive symbols] organize the interaction process through normative regulation, through imposing standards on it."[6]

Dewey, like Mead, Cooley, and Burke, searched for models of society in art, because he believed that art experience is the most characteristically human of all experiences. Dewey and Mead selected the moment of consummation, as found in the experience of art, as the decisive phase of the act. In his own "Rejoinder" to the various essays on his own work collected and edited by Paul A. Schilpp in *The Philosophy of John Dewey*,[7] Dewey is careful to point out that making his theory of instrumentalism synonymous with knowledge reached through science based on quantification is foreign to his whole philosophy.[8] In his summary of Dewey's work, Ratner (who edited much of Dewey's work with his approval) says: ". . . one finds Dewey's best and profoundest exposition of his integral conception of Philosophy, or the nature of intelligence, in his *Art as Experience*."[9]

For Mead, the moment of consummation as found in aesthetic experience was of crucial importance to the study of nature as well as man in society. In the consummatory moment in art, the future (or end) of the act, as well as the past (or tradition), is objectified in expressive forms which bring the end of the act into consciousness. These forms are real because they are public; they are social because they exist in communication. Dewey says: "Literature conveys the meaning of the past that is significant in present experience and is prophetic of the larger movements of the future. . . . The first stirrings of dissatisfaction and the first intimations of a better future are always found in works of art. . . . Factual science may collect statistics and make charts. But its predictions are . . . but past history reversed. Change in the . . . imagination is the precursor of the changes that affect more than the details of life." [10]

Mead argued that art experience must be studied because it tells us much about "the goals toward which our efforts run." Movement into a future, Mead continues, always brings novelty into action. As we press toward our goals we must deal with aspects of the situation that are simply unpredictable. Thus, all action is problematic, and all imagined ends and recalled traditions are hypothetical at best. But this does not mean that the imagined futures, or goals, of human action embodied in art are mere subjective fantasies. They are objective because they are public forms of expression, and instrumental because they are means by which we organize action in a present. For if we do not have clearly expressed goals, either in public symbols of an imagined future or a recalled past which we are striving to recapture, we have no guides and cannot act at all. In short, art *orders* social experience through creating forms which all, artist and public alike, use to communicate so that they *can* act together.

In more recent works in sociology, the search for ways to use art to understand society has shifted from general assertions on the interdependency of society and art, to attempts to create specific descriptions of institutional and community roles. Thus W. Lloyd Warner, in his *The Living and the Dead, a Study of the Symbolic Life of Americans,* says:

The community in which his [Biggy Muldoon, the political leader of Yankee City] rise and fall took place was more than a setting for the drama. The forces acting within it helped to create his personality; they were the all-powerful feelings and beliefs that functioned in his career like Fate in the lives of Greek tragic heroes. Indeed, a good case could be made demonstrating that the flaws in the characters of Greek tragedy and the fates they suffered were no more than the basic precepts and principles of their society, its social logics, operating in the dramas and in the beliefs and values of the audience who watched them. Since Greek dramas are still powerful—for Oedipus Rex can bring tears to the eyes of modern audiences—it seems probable that these same fates and flaws operate in the lives of contemporary men.[11]

The problem now is no longer one of asserting that there is a reciprocal relation between art and society, but of showing *how* this relationship exists. This does not mean there is no more need for theory. There is great need, for until we have a series of *sociological* propositions on the function of art and communication in society, we cannot create hypotheses for dealing with the concrete data of communication in society. Behaviorists are right in their attack on "symbolic interactionists" who keep repeating that symbolic interaction is the characteristic human interaction, yet fail to show *how* symbolic interaction can be studied as a social fact. If we cannot show *how* it affects human conduct, then we must leave the field to those who, within clearly specified limits, are saying some things about conduct that can be verified by other students of society.

We do not answer the behaviorists, or the new school of social mechanists led by Parsons, by criticizing them for the limited range of their observations, their neglect of significant symbols, their naive analogical thinking, or by branding them immoral because they reduce men to machines or animals. That is, we do not answer them as sociologists concerned with rigorous discourse. The only proper answer to behaviorists (of whatever school) is to show how what we say ought to be done in symbolic analysis can be done. For, if we know how symbols ought not to be studied, we must know how they ought to be studied. We ought to be able to communicate clearly just what we mean by saying that sociation takes place in specific forms of communication, and that these forms are created in various expressive systems. And if we argue that the study of one of these expressive systems, art, becomes the study of society, we must indicate what kind of art we are talking about.

The use of symbolic forms of expression to develop theory and method in the human studies is not new. The works of Fustel de Coulonges,[12] W. Robertson Smith,[13] Emile Durkheim,[14] Bronislaw Malinowski,[15] and A. R. Radcliffe-Brown,[16] as well as the work of Weber, Troeltsch, and Tawney, indicate how much social thought owes to the study of symbolic expression in society. But these studies, and, indeed, almost the whole body of sociological thought on the nature of the social bond, are based on religious expression. Art is often used, but only to illustrate "sentiments of attachment" in the expression of the social bond. It is accepted as a kind of conductor (message track in modern jargon) of the underlying reality of religious sentiment as exemplified in the religious rite. Such rites are accepted, in turn, as paradigms for the social bond because it is believed, following Bacon, that religion is the most substantial bond of humanity.

Social mechanists assure us they have escaped the subjectivism of social theory based on symbols by creating "objective" models of sociation that do not depend on individual consciousness. Yet even in the midst of their mechanical images of "geared" motives and moving equilibrium, there are constant references to communication as something more than a kind of cathexis. There is an admission, if not an elaboration, of the fact that men use symbols to "condition" or "motivate" themselves and others. In such views, the symbols men use to motivate themselves serve as triggers to release "forces" whose power is derived from non-symbolic sources in nature, the body, or socio-political laws. And since these "forces" are "beyond" symbols, they can be studied as "processes" in much the same way processes are studied in nature.

But, as Lotze pointed out, *even* in a physical field (mechanical or electronic) interaction cannot be conceived of without reference to points or agents which are internally modified by, and in turn modifiers of, the process which affects them. When we describe mechanical causation we say that the impact of one element on another "communicates" motion, so that the element struck passes from a state of rest (or from one phase) to one of motion (or to another), while the striking element has experienced a change of an opposite character. But even as a description of a physical field, this explains nothing. For, if all that happens in communication is the communication of motion, why does it not pass through the stricken element and leave its state unchanged? Or, in sociological terms, if social forces "affect" the actor, but are not in turn affected by him, then how do we explain the individual, or the creation of symbols used in role enactment by individuals in social interaction? This is *not* simply a "metaphysical problem" which we can thrust aside "to get down to business" as rugged empiricists. The same dilemma haunts Parsons' work. If statuses and roles are "analogous to the particle of mechanics, not to mass or velocity, but are not, in general, attributes of the actor," [17] what are the observable data of role enactment?

Park and Burges, following the tradition of Cooley, Dewey, and Mead, stated that sociology must deal with communication as the prime medium of interaction. But their model of communication was only another variant of mechanism. For, despite all talk about society existing in communication, the symbols which we use to communicate, and the function of art in society, receive small notice. Symbols are but an expression of a reality beyond symbols. This reality is some kind of process in which competition, conflict, accommodation, and assimilation are conceived of as "a constellation of social forces." Thus, while communication is named as the medium of social interaction, the medium itself (the forms of expression we use in communication) is not studied,[18] and we are locked again in the dismal circle in social thought which tells us that social forces determine society because society determines social forces.

Thus the student who seeks to understand society in terms of communication as role enactment must enter a debate whose terms have been set by anthropologists who find their models of sociation in the expression of religious symbols, or by sociologists who find their model in the functioning of a machine. Mechanists are old foes; many battles have been fought with them, and the arsenal of weapons for taking the field against them is well stocked. But sociologists who believe that art, as well as religion, is a constituent social act, have few weapons and certainly few allies—in the arts or in sociology. They must be content for the moment to lead a kind of purgatorial existence in which they are damned by humanists for perverting art, and by sociologists for abandoning science.

To say that what is true of machines is true of men, or that a rational act must be likened to a mechanical act, or that emotion is but another name for motion—this is useful so long as we limit our conclusions to the data used. But when we become "mystics of the machine" and reify our mechanical concepts by treating them as a substance, or a quality of social action, we confuse metaphor and fiction with hypotheses. Even the dedicated behaviorist must admit that he cannot, as a behaviorist, equate quantity and quality in any scientific way.[19] That is, the quantity of somatic discharge cannot be related to the quality of satisfaction or dissatisfaction experienced by the organism in the process of discharge.

But to say that what is true of men in religious worship is also true of men in society also creates many difficulties. We know how easily religious rites, and especially those based on the tragic scapegoat, can be torn out of context and used by the state, or by the church itself, to uphold secular powers whose capacity for corruption is vast indeed. So long as we confuse all authority with supernatural authority, reason in society cannot exist. Too often in the religious rite, those who oppose the gods must suffer and die. Social theory based on such models of the act cannot admit ambiguity, doubt, competition, disagreement, conflict, or opposition, for when society is dominated by religion, those who do not accept authority as they accept God are heretics who must recant or be punished. And, if we follow Durkheim, when men do not accept the god-like authority of superiors they end by living apart from their fellows in a state of anomie whose burden of loneliness and alienation is too great to endure. Such men, in refusing to accept the commandments of their authorities, excommunicate themselves.

It is for such reasons, and others which the text will make clear, that we turn to art, and particularly to comic art, for help in constructing a social theory of communication, and indicating sociological ways of thinking about society in terms of role enactment as a communicative act. We argue that until we can think of ambiguity, doubt, tension, estrangement, and all the ways in which we differ, as well as agree with one another, we cannot think well about democratic, or indeed, *any* society. As we hope to make clear, social order is always defined in terms of disorder, and in the present sad state of affairs in human society, order is at best merely a resolution of struggle between authorities of widely different views who seek to convince us, often by terrible as well as benign means, that their principles alone are the principles of order. Art, we shall argue, is the realm where the expression of doubt, ambiguity, and difference is normal. We shall argue, too, that art gives us forms which make it possible for us to *confront* our differences and thus bring them into consciousness so we can communicate with each other, as well as with our gods.

We do not argue that human society is characterized by communication alone. Animals communicate, machines signal through built-in message tracks, matter readjusts to changes in conditions, organisms respond to stimuli; but whether we call such responses "signals," "signs," "cathexis," or "stimulus and response," we are not talking about communication in the sense of the term as developed in this book. Nor do we argue that art is determined by communication alone. Artists create symbols to express themselves, to name or designate things and events, as they also struggle to make their forms consistent within themselves. And while these are all related to communication, they are by no means subordinated to it. All that we say here is that *from a sociological view* communication is the category of art with which we should be concerned. We argue here that human communication in society is an attempt to create symbols whose use is believed to uphold social order.

Social order is considered here in some detail as a drama of social hierarchy in which we *enact* roles as superiors, inferiors, and equals. We enact roles through communication, and when we enter a group to begin communication, we enter hierarchical relationships which are determined by the consensually validated symbols of the group in which we seek to play our part. No individual is always inferior, superior, or equal. Differential status is common to all societies, and passage from one position to another must be provided if the society is to function well. Thus the study of differential status, so common to democratic society, is necessary to an understanding of any kind of hierarchy, as well as to the satisfaction of our own moral needs as citizens of a democratic commonwealth. For among kings, as among common people, status is won by successful appeals to others who, like the audience of a great drama, determine our success and failure as we play our many roles in society. Status enactment is always a *plea,* a petition, for status is *given,* never taken.

Social order, we argue further, is always a resolution of struggle between superiors, inferiors, and equals. This struggle takes the form of a great community drama in which, through comedy as well as tragedy, the community seeks to ward off threats to the majesty of its transcendent symbols of social integration. Skill in playing hierarchical roles is determined by skill in hierarchical address. The actor in the social drama of hierarchy must please his superiors, inspire his inferiors, and convince his equals. Yet even at best the actor in this drama is never quite successful, and sometimes he fails completely. Thus, no society can survive unless symbolic resources are available for expiating guilt arising out of failures by superiors, inferiors, and equals, to uphold principles of hierarchy believed necessary to the survival of the group.

The failure of our civilization, the pride of men who conquered space but who could not conquer themselves, will someday be subjects for great tragedy and great comedy—if anyone is left to enjoy either. For the next bombs which fall will destroy the world, and all the fair hopes of men will vanish in the dust. Men have lived under terror of annihilation before. The early Christians were convinced, too, that the world was coming to an end. But beyond the dark horror of nothingness there stood the vision of a paradise, a world of beauty and goodness beyond the world of suffering and evil that men knew. What vision do we have as we stand in horror before an impending doom from the skies, haunted by the terrible cries of the victims of Stalin and Hitler?

Our world died in the concentration camps of Hitler, and the slave labor camps of Stalin. The hapless Jews of Europe who shuffled in endless lines to torture and death, so that our "pure Aryan blood" could be purified, were the last victims of the "Master Race." But their doom sealed the doom of their masters. For who can ever believe again in the justice of an Aryan civilization? And now that the same civilization which permitted enslavement, torture, and slaughter has greater power to do evil, the terror of life increases. We see now how fortunate were the early Christians whose last visions in the suffering and pain of torture and death were visions of a paradise beyond the world. We have no paradise. The terrestrial heavens promised us by science and technology have not arrived, and few believe they ever will.

But times of despair can also be times of greatness. For if we can summon up courage to *confront* our evil, to look into the terrible abyss of the human spirit, and to record what we see there, we may yet survive. Or, if we do not, we can at least leave a record which might be of help to others. Men like Hitler and Stalin ruled through social mystification. To argue that economic or political causes made possible their great conspiracies against humanity, would tell us little about why such causes took the form of black tyranny in one nation and of social welfare in another. Hitler never pretended that he was offering his people full bellies and comfortable shelter. On the contrary, he offered them sacrifice and death in struggle against enemies at home and abroad. He created a kind of social drama that we must learn to understand if we are to survive the next "savior" who arises among us—if we are to survive at all.

Authority is always legitimized through reference to social order, but authority must not be confused with superiority or inferiority alone, as it has been so often by those who use tragic ritual or tragic ritual drama for their models of the enactment of social order. Equality, the expression of the will of equals in rules and law, is as universal a form of authority as that based on supernatural legitimation in religion and politics. Without equality, no social order—not even the worst tyranny—can exist. And when there is little equality, reason in society soon withers and dies, the social relationship of friendship cannot come into being, and all relations depending on equality among peers cannot exist. Reason in society depends on free and informed discussion among equals, just as friendship depends on free interchange among equals. Equality is necessary to all institutions and situations where men must agree to bind themselves under rules of their own creation. Without equality, rules cannot function, and without rules, society, and particularly democratic society, cannot exist, because free, open, and informed discussion can take place only between equals. Gods do not discuss; they command.

No social order exists without disorder. In tragic communal rites disorder is exercised through punishment, torture, and death. But there is another kind of communal rite which we use to face disorder. This is comedy, which is a kind of sanctioned disrespect, where we are allowed to express doubt and question over the transcendent principles that those in power uphold in the name of social order. Just as we turn to tragic rites for help in creating models of sociation, so can we turn to comic forms of expression. For in comedy we *uncover* the ambiguities and contradictions which beset us as we seek to act together. And since we are permitted in comedy to discuss openly what we cannot even mention in tragic ritual, comedy offers many clues to the difficulties men find in playing their social roles. The study, then, of art, and particularly comic art, is the proper study of man in society, because it is study of the resolution between order and disorder in society.

This book ends in exhortation. The steps leading to the concluding homily may be summarized as follows: Man as a social being exists in and through communication; communication is as basic to man's nature as food and sex; sociation inescapably involves hierarchy; hierarchy involves incongruities which society solves well or ill (as in war, genocide, or sadism and masochism); until society masters the dynamics of hierarchy as a set of relationships between superiors, inferiors, and equals, all sociation is in a parlous state; art works offer our best clues for the analysis of these dynamics; and finally, students of society must learn how to proceed with such analysis if we are to create a science of human conduct that tells us something about motivation.

In my last book, *Language and Literature in Society* (Chicago: Univ. of Chicago Press, 1953, reprinted by The Bedminster Press of New York, 1961), I said some things about symbols and authority which are now taken up in more expanded form. I indicated there something of my debt to the tradition of Cooley, Dewey, and Mead—a great tradition in American sociology. Much of what I say is taken from the work of Kenneth Burke, who as master and friend taught me how to think of literature as symbolic action. Those familiar with his *Grammar of Motives* and his *Rhetoric of Motives* will see that my debt to him is heavy indeed. I hope to discharge this, not only by repeating what Burke said, but by creating a rigorous sociological statement on the communication of hierarchy that can be used for empiric sociological analysis of symbolic material.

The late Professor Robert Redfield of the University of Chicago was kind enough to read through an earlier version of this manuscript. His death will be deeply felt in American scholarship, for he was in every sense a human scientist. He was also a very gracious and a noble human being. I hope this book will be a fitting, if small tribute to his memory.

And finally I should like to thank my students at Carleton College in Northfield, Minn. who struggled through my first presentation of this manuscript. Emily Bennett, David D. Caulkins, John Fikkan, Betty Forster, Margie Hoover, Mary Jensen, Dean E. Jones, Roger A. La Raus, Barbara L. Mitchell, Patricia L. Riley, Elizabeth A. Tweedy, Jane L. Watson, Marianne Wilkening, and Barbara Will helped me to understand, better than I had been able to understand in the solitary life of a scholar, the complexities in communicating about communication.

H.D.D.

November, 1961

Notes

[1] Talcott Parsons, Robert F. Bales, and Edward A. Shils, *Working Papers in the Theory of Action* (Glencoe, Ill.: The Free Press, 1953), esp. Chapter 2, "The Theory of Symbolism in Relation to Action," by Talcott Parsons.

[2] C. Wright Mills, *The Sociological Imagination* (New York: Oxford Univ. Press, 1959), p. 17. Mills argues that the study of alienating methods of production, enveloping techniques of political domination, international anarchy, the pervasive transformations of the nature of man, and the conditions and aims of his life, is the proper sociological study of man. He rules out the study of symbols in art and communication because art, unlike the social sciences, lacks "intellectual clarity" and "does not and cannot formulate" private troubles and public issues in contemporary society. He assigns no weight to symbols as causal factors in motivation, and shows small concern with the effect of symbolic form on the social content of what form expresses.

[3] "Saying" is not limited to words alone. All the arts of expression are involved in even the most simple acts of communication.

[4] Sigmund Freud, *A General Introduction to Psychoanalysis,* authorized translation by Joan Riviere (Garden City, N.Y.: Garden City Publishing Co., Inc., 1943). This passage occurs near the beginning of Lecture 10, "Symbolism in Dreams."

[5] I have discussed this in some detail in my article "Simmel's Image of Society," which appears in *Georg Simmel, 1858–1918, A Collection of Essays, with Translations and a Bibliography,* edited by Kurt H. Wolff (Columbus: Ohio State Univ. Press, 1959).

[6] Talcott Parsons, *The Social System* (Glencoe, Ill.: The Free Press, 1951), p. 386.

Just how expressive symbols *impose* standards is never made clear by Parsons. His statements on the weakness of sociological theory in dealing with expressive symbols would be much more helpful if he would tell us more about *why* social theory has not been able to deal with expressive symbols.

[7] Paul Arthur Schilpp, ed., *The Philosophy of John Dewey* (New York: Tudor Publishing Co., 1939).

[8] *Ibid.*, pp. 520–521.

[9] Ratner discusses this point in his article on Dewey in Schilpp. In his article on "The Nature of Aesthetic Experience" (which is discussed in Chapter 6 of this book), where he expounds his social theory of art, Mead says in a footnote to the title: "I have not made specific acknowledgements in this article to Professor Dewey, but the reader who is familiar with his *Experience and Nature* will realize that it was written under the influence of that treatise."

[10] John Dewey, *Art as Experience* (New York: Minton, Balch & Co., 1934).

[11] W. Lloyd Warner, *The Living and the Dead: A Study of the Symbolic Life of Americans* (New Haven: Yale Univ. Press, 1959), p. 24. Part V, "Theory and Method for the Study of Symbolic Life" (pp. 445–506) is a discussion of modifications of the theories of Freud, Mead, and Durkheim in terms of Warner's struggle to create working hypotheses from Durkheim's theory of collective representations. Durkheim's collective representations are not derived from art, but from religious rites. I have indicated what I believe to be the fallacies and, for a democratic society, the dangers of confusing the social bond with the religious bond in my article "The Development of Durkheim's Concept of Ritual and the Problem of Social Disrelationships," which appears in *Emile Durkheim: 1858–1917, A Collection of Essays, with Translations and a Bibliography*, edited by Kurt H. Wolff (Columbus: Ohio State Univ. Press, 1959), pp. 97–117.

[12] Numa Denis Fustel de Coulanges, *La cité antique* (Paris: Hachette, 1864).

[13] William Robertson Smith, *Lectures on the Religion of the Semites* (Edinburgh: Black, 1889).

[14] Emile Durkheim, *Les formes élémentaires de la vie religieuse* (Paris: Alcan, 1912).

[15] Bronislaw Malinowski, *Magic, Science, and Religion, and Other Essays*, Selected and with an Introduction by Robert Redfield (Glencoe, Ill.: The Free Press: 1948).

[16] Alfred Reginald Radcliffe-Brown, *The Andaman Islanders* (Cambridge: The University Press, 1922).

[17] Talcott Parsons, *The Social System* (Glencoe, Ill.: The Free Press, 1951), p. 25. The components of interaction are discussed on pp. 3–22 and 24–26.

[18] Basically this was because neither Park nor Burgess believed that symbolic forms *determined* social forms. Society "caused" expression, but *how* we express ourselves, and the resources in various expressive systems for such expression, did not "cause" society. The paradox of deriving our knowledge of society from symbolic expressions which in themselves had nothing to do with determining society did not escape Professors Redfield, Blumer, and Wirth. Mead's "significant symbol" always haunted the Chicago School. It was obvious that art had something to do with society, for art was the domain of the significant symbols, as Dewey and Mead used the term. But the question of how to state *social* categories of art was never resolved. The problem, however, was kept alive. The Chicago School never capitulated to mechanism, as the work of Warner shows, and as this book, by a student of Burgess, Wirth, Blumer, Redfield, Warner, and Burke, should make clear.

[19] But what the behaviorist does not admit is that if we regard men as dogs (which we have learned to control through hunger), it is very easy to reduce men to the level of dogs so that we can control them in like fashion. The German concentration camps and the Russian labor camps are terrible witness to what can be done to men by reducing them to animals. *How* we study men has *moral,* as well as "purely scientific" consequences. If we *regard* men as machines, we are but a step away from *treating* them as machines.

PART ONE

Symbolic Contexts of Social Experience in Freud, Simmel, and Malinowski

1

Symbolic Interaction in Freud's Work

As many have pointed out, Freud's predecessors in the study of men were not the neurologists, psychiatrists, and psychologists from whom he borrowed some of his terms, but the great artists, and especially literary artists, of our civilization. In his early years, as his discussion of the case history of Elisabeth von R. shows, Freud was disturbed over the similarity between his presentation of case histories and the literary form of the short story. He says:

I have not always been a psychotherapist. Like other neuro-pathologists, I was trained to employ local diagnoses and electro-prognosis, and it still strikes me myself as strange that the case histories I write should read like short stories and that, as one might say, they lack the serious stamp of science. I must console myself with the reflection that the nature of the subject is evidently responsible for this, rather than any preference of my own. The fact is that local diagnosis and electrical reactions lead nowhere in the study of hysteria, whereas a detailed description of mental processes such as we are accustomed to find in the works of imaginative writers enables me, with the use of a few psychological formulas, to obtain at least some kind of insight into the course of that affection. Case histories of this kind are intended to be judged like psychiatric ones; they have, however, one advantage over the latter, namely an intimate connection between the story of the patient's sufferings and the symptoms of his illness—a connection for which we still search in vain in the biographies of other psychoses.[1]

In the closing paragraph of this discussion, Freud returns to the problem of symbolization. He tells us that when a hysteric "creates a somatic expression for an emotionally colored idea by symbolization, this depends less than one would imagine on personal or voluntary factors. In taking a verbal expression literally and in feeling the 'stab in the heart' or the 'slap in the face' after some slighting remark as a real event, the hysteric is not taking liberties with words, but is simply reviving once more the sensations to which the verbal expression owes its justification." After quoting Darwin's work on the expression of emotions, in which it is argued that expression originally had a biological purpose, he goes on to say that while constant use has weakened the meaning of such symbols and reduced them to figurative pictures, "hysteria is right in restoring the original meaning of the words in depicting its unusually strong innervations."

The student of human motivation, then, will turn to literature because there he finds "detailed description of the mental processes," and he will study the figures of speech used by those under stress, because they evoke the somatic symptoms of which they are an expression. But what has all this use of literature to do with science? And, if we say that poets know more than anyone else about human conduct, why should we not study poetry rather than psychology to find valid descriptions of behavior? For if hysteria is determined by symbols, then obviously the study of symbols would tell us much about hysteria, since the names given by the hysteric to feelings are all we know in any empiric sense, about such feelings. But at this point Freud drew back: ". . . it is perhaps wrong to say that hysteria creates these sensations by symbolization. It may be that it does not take linguistic usage as its model at all, but that both hysteria and linguistic usage alike draw their material from a common source." [2]

The search for this common source, and the hope that he could represent psychical processes as "quantitatively determined states of specific material particles," subject to the "general laws" of motion conceived of as "quantities in a condition of flow," as he said in his *Project for a Scientific Psychology,* was never abandoned by Freud. But neither did he abandon the use of literature (as well as case histories) to develop his theory. As Jones tells us, and as we know from Freud's speech on Goethe in 1930, Freud admired the poetic and philosophic mind. He did not think of literature as "intuition," "insightful," or as a kind of crude survey of human motives which would soon be refined by social science. [3] To the very end of his life, artists and philosophers were "the few to whom it is vouchsafed . . . with hardly any effort to salvage from the whirlpool of their emotions the deepest truth to which we others have to force our way, ceaselessly groping among torturing uncertainties." [4]

The paradox, then, in Freud's work is that while he refused to study motivation in terms of symbols, he often illustrated what he had studied and conclusions he had reached, through illustrations drawn from symbolic works. His great work, *The Interpretation of Dreams,* is an analysis of language, [5] dream language, whose meaning is elaborated by references to literature, legends, tales, indeed, almost the whole range of verbal expression. Yet while literary forms are used to explain the meaning of a dream, we are told that dream language is typically archaic in nature, and represents a regression to the most primitive mode of thought. This, in turn, can be understood only by the knowledge of the primitive forms of language which psychoanalytic theory can supply.

Perhaps the strongest testimony of Freud's respect for creative writers was his admission that since the "gifts and abilities of the artist are closely bound up with the capacity for sublimation, we have to admit that also the nature of artistic achievement is inaccessible to us psycho-analytically." This, said in 1910 in his book on Leonardo, is repeated several times throughout his works. Thus in the exposition of his work he wrote in 1913, "The Claims of Psycho-Analysis to Scientific Interest," he declares that while the "motive forces of artists are the same conflicts which drive other people into neurosis and have encouraged society to construct its institutions . . ." yet how or why it is "that the artist derives his creative capacity is not a question for psychology." [6]

At times, indeed, Freud's respect for the literary mind is so great that it is hard to distinguish between what is literal and what is metaphor in his use of literary material. He often "discovers" that a literary work like *Hamlet* or *Oedipus Rex* proves or corroborates some aspect of psychoanalytic theory, and then continues to quote the literary work as further proof of another psychoanalytic concept. Thus, he tells us that the ideational contents and memory traces of the experience of former generations, man's archaic heritage, exist in myths, tales, and legends, which are transmitted biologically as well as socially. The individual brings into life at birth not only "dispositions" but symbolic expressions which are hypostasized into a kind of substance. This functions mechanically in the cathexis of the libido. At such times Freud seems almost ready to make communication a category as well as a phase of experience, in line with the tradition of Dewey, Mead, and Burke.

But, as we shall see, he never does. Symbols are modes of expression which have never been individually acquired but are a racial heritage. Such symbols have a fixed meaning, and whether they are found in dreams, mythology, folklore, relation, art, or literature, symbols mean what they do largely because language originated in attempts by men to satisfy their sexual needs. Thus, while it is true that men developed language for communication, this communication was sexual. As time passed, speech was used to accompany work. Men learned to make work agreeable by accompanying their work with rhythmically repeated sounds. Through these rhythms sexual interest was transferred to work. Thus, all words came to possess two meanings, one pertaining to sex, the other to the work which went on as words were uttered. Words became disassociated from their original sexual significance. Because of this a number of rootless words came into existence; they were of sexual origin but had lost their sexual meaning.

FREUD'S ATTEMPT TO COMBINE QUALITIES AND QUANTITIES IN HIS DESCRIPTION OF CATHEXIS

Psychical states are reflections of material elements subject to the laws of motion, in Freud's theory. These elements, called neurones, function mechanically. Nervous excitation is subject to the principle of inertia—that is, neurones tend to get rid of excitation, as when sensory stimulus is followed by motor discharge. Paths of discharge develop for reducing and ending stimulation. Internal stimuli, however, cannot be reduced or ended by simple motor discharge, as when we flee from danger. Mental contents (ideas) replace neurones, and the tendency of neurones to get rid of excitation is replaced by a pleasure–displeasure principle which reflects, in the mind, the mastering of stimuli. Wishes are currents in the mind. They arise from displeasure but end in pleasure, which is reached in the discharge of tension through the motor apparatus of the body.

But there is no orderly progression from tension to motor activity. Orderly progression occurs only when secondary processes of thought replace the primary. Secondary processes employ the reality principle, which is subject to canons of logic and casual inference. On the primary level, the level of pure pleasure principle, thought takes place in a purely mechanical fashion. Ideas are associated through emotional equivalences based on association of ideas with a discharge of tension. Such ideas can be displaced so that the object associated with the discharge of one type of nervous excitation can serve as the object of another. Thus, a snake and a penis are emotionally equivalent. Logical relations of the kind we use in conscious thought are not used. Emotional equivalences are regulated by the tendency toward discharge in pleasure. The pleasure principle makes no distinction between true or false, immediate or remote satisfaction, real or imaginary; it functions like an electric current which, once it is turned on, must run its course.

The Ego, with its secondary processes, is distinguished by a Reality principle, as opposed to the pure pleasure principle. The Ego represents sanity and reason; the Id, the passions. It tests correspondence with reality, interposes a process of thinking, secures postponement of motor discharge, dominates the Id, and defends itself against the Super Ego. At this point Freud's images of the Ego shift from those of the mind as a machine to mind as an agent. The mechanical image of mentation and the functioning of the Id now becomes a *dramatic* image. The Ego becomes a sort of agent in the mind. This agent is depicted like a monarch who must protect himself against enemies without (as the Super Ego), as well as those within (the Id).

When Freud turned to the concrete problems of his patients and attempted to create hypotheses which could be related in some empiric way to what he observed, that is, what his patients said and expressed about themselves, he gave up trying to fit psychological theory into a mechanical model. His speculations on infantile sexuality, mechanisms of defense, and his final statements in *An Outline of Psycho-Analysis* (1940) on the Ego, are expressed in nonmechanical images. The Oedipus complex is a *dramatic* image. The son's longing to sleep with his mother, Freud tells us, "is the subject of the Oedipus complex, which Greek legend translated from the world of childhood phantasy into a pretended reality." The world of childhood phantasy cannot be understood by literal application of the Oedipus legend, for in this there is no castration fear, and Oedipus did not know that it was his father whom he had killed and his mother whom he had married. We know it, Freud tells us, from psychoanalytic theory. Castration occurs in the Oedipus legend, "for the blinding with which Oedipus punished himself after the discovery of his crime, is, by the evidence of dreams, a symbolic substitute for castration." The ignorance of Oedipus, in turn, is a "legitimate representation of the unconsciousness into which, for adults, the whole experience has fallen and the doom of the oracle, which makes or should make the hero innocent, is a recognition of the inevitability of the fate which has condemned every son to live through the Oedipus complex."[7]

Differences from the psychoanalytic view are the result of a "poetic handling of the material." This is not really an "addition of extraneous subject matter but merely a skillful employment of the factors present in the theme." And, finally, those who do not accept the "true" Oedipus theme as a psychoanalytic theme, suffer from a "general lack of comprehension" like that displayed by literary critics whose "lack of comprehension" of the "solution" to the problem of Hamlet [8] by reference to the psychoanalytic version of the Oedipus legend (the "Oedipus complex") showed how ready "is the mass of mankind to hold fast to its infantile repressions." Symbols mean what they do because

> dream-symbolism extends far beyond dreams; it is not peculiar to dreams, but exercises a similar dominating influence on representation in fairy tales, myths, and legends, in jokes and folklore. It enables us to trace the intimate connections between dreams and these latter productions. We must not suppose that dream-symbolism is a creation of the dream work; it is in all probability a characteristic of the unconscious thinking which provides the dream work with the material for condensation, displacement, and dramatization. [9]

Now, displacement and dramatization are very different terms. One is derived from mechanical models; the other, from linguistic. Mind is explained in the mechanical model by topographical imagery; and in the dramatic, by dramatic or forensic imagery. The unconscious is the realm of repressed memories and emotions, but the unconscious is described as a kind of place, and the mind as a place or a number of places, in which ideas move about in space. Instinctual stimuli, or excitation impulses, pass on in three kinds of neurones; those of perception, of memory, and those which are necessary for the retained memories of impressed perceptions to become conscious. But while excitation may flow freely, it may also be inhibited by an organization of neurones, called "the Ego." The uninhibited, free flow of excitation, are "primary processes"; the inhibited, redirected flow are "secondary processes." Primary types of discharge are identified with a Pleasure principle, while the secondary (in which both external and internal stimuli occur) are the Reality principle. The primary processes are basic, for secondary processes are explained by them and not vice versa.

FREUD'S USE OF RHETORICAL AND DRAMATIC IMAGERY

After 1900, Freud's descriptions of psychic function are drawn in forensic, dramatic, and conversational images. When he shifts from structure to function, from the mind as a place to the mind as an agent, his images take on a new life. Nothing could be more dramatic than Freud's notion of a dream that attains expression by stylistic subterfuges designed to evade the inhibitions of a moralistic censor. The Ego with its Id confronts the

Super Ego as an orator confronts an alien audience, whose susceptibilities he must flatter as a necessary step toward persuasion. The joker must make his audience laugh before he can permit himself to laugh at his own joke.

But if the dream "dramatizes," how do we really know what these dramatizations mean? If the dream is a drama, why do we explain it by one form, and not another, of drama? If the dream is a drama based on censorship, what exactly is the role of the censor? If the censor is a mental agent, of what is he an agent? Is the censor analogous to the child seeking to outwit the father, an orator pleading his cause before an audience, or a wit whose hostile remarks to others are permitted because we laugh with pleasure at the way he says them? Is the *form* of the dream that of a picture, a conversation, a courtroom, or what? If the Ego confronts the Id and the Super Ego, how does it do so? If the joker addresses an audience whose authority makes disrespect possible, who (aside from the father) is this authority?

If the secondary processes, where communication takes place, are dependent on primary processes where nervous excitation functions mechanically, how do rhetorical, dramatic, or conversation images help us to think about mechanical process? Freud emphasizes catharsis (in therapy, whereby the patient purges himself through words) but holds that words are but masks (or puns) for libidinal wishes. But even if all expression is a kind of sexual pun, the *form* is still important, because some forms of appeal are successful while others are not. If communication is used as a category to describe the origin and function of attitudes and ideas in others and in ourselves, it must be recognized that communication is always a plea to others to give us the response we need to enjoy ourselves. The other whom I address may be an audience like the one I address when I read to myself something I have just written, but it is always an audience which must be addressed in styles considered proper to the occasion and worthy of response.

When we turn from Freudian theory to his concrete descriptions of conduct, we are much closer to a social view of communication. Freud describes how we hide, deny, or mask what is improper or heretical to powers within the self and society. Whenever we deal with censors who make communication difficult or impossible, wherever there are blocks in communication, Freud's illustrations of repression are very useful. But even here it is not so much Freud's theory of repression, but his remarks on the expression of the repression, which are significant to those seeking to develop a theory of social action based on communication.

By his use of dramatic images, Freud teaches us to think of authority as a resolution of conflict.[10] But his image of conflict is a familial and patriarchal image. His authority is always the father, and while this image is far too limited for social theory, it does not commit us, as does anthropological theory, to think of social action void of ambiguity, doubt, disagreement, and conflict. And in Freud there are comic, as well as tragic, forms of dealing with authority. For the comic Freudian drama in his book on jokes is not only a sexual drama, but a status drama where we strive to relieve the burden of obeying authorities whose commandments we find dull, tedious, boring, and painful.

Freud shows little concern with communication between equals, or from superiors to inferiors. He derives his group psychology from the roles of sons who, deprived of sexual gratification by the monopolistic father, band together in hatred of the father and for their mutual benefit. The genesis of rules, as the expression of mutual consent, and of all relationships of equality are neglected. Until we have much more emphasis on the nature of authority among equals, we will have no social theory to substantiate the reality of democratic forms of relationships. The rise of Hitler showed how little Germans really believed in rules as authority or equality as a social principle, and we now know how well Freud understood the craving for authority. But we need (perhaps indeed for sheer survival) to know much more about the social psychology of equality.

It is not until his book on jokes that Freud really considers communication as a basic category. No one can be content with having made a joke for himself alone. "An urge to tell the joke to someone is inextricably bound up with the joke-work; indeed, this urge is so strong that often enough it is carried through in disregard of serious misgivings. In the case of the comic as well, telling it to someone else produces enjoyment; but the demand is not preemptory. If one comes across something comic, one can enjoy it by oneself. A joke, on the contrary, *must* be told to someone else. The psychical process of constructing a joke seems not to be completed when the joke occurs to one: something remains over which one seeks, by communicating the idea, to bring the unknown process of constructing the joke to a conclusion." [11]

"Everything in jokes that is aimed at gaining pleasure is calculated with an eye to the third person, as though there were internal and unsurmountable obstacles to it in the first person." We are compelled then to tell a joke to someone else because we cannot laugh at it ourselves. When we make the other person laugh by telling him a joke, we use him to arouse our own laughter, as we see when the joker himself follows his audience in laughter at his own story. "Accordingly, telling my joke to another person would seem to serve several purposes: first, to give me objective certainty that the joke-work has been successful; secondly, to complete my own pleasure by a reaction from the other person upon myself; and thirdly—where it is a question of repeating a joke that one has not produced one-self—to make up for the loss of pleasure owing to the joke's lack of novelty." [12]

Passages such as these, in this, the most socially oriented of all Freud's writings, indicate clearly Freud's lack of interest in communication as a psychological category. He uses expressive forms, here jokes, to illustrate what he is talking about, but his illustrations are not used to demonstrate, but to repeat an assertion already made. Throughout the book we are told that in jokes we seek to outwit a censor by masking sexual and aggressive desires which the censor will not allow us to satisfy. Then we are told that we cannot enjoy a joke until a third person is communicated with and enjoys it. The other, as censor or audience, inhibits, and at the same time, releases, desire. We are told over and over again that repression comes from culture; now we are told that discharge of affect, the release of repression (already caused by culture), is made possible by an expressive form, joke-telling, in the culture.

There is nothing implausible about a censor who inhibits and sanctions at the same time. Freud was aware that we seek to please those who censor us. But there is nothing in his *theory* that tells why the approval of the censor is necessary, or why, if all communication is nothing but cathexis and the pleasure in communication simply relief through discharge, we need to communicate at all. On purely logical grounds, or at least on the grounds of logic required for theoretical construction, we cannot say that the data of interpersonal relations, communicative symbols, are determined by cathexis, and then go on to explain that cathexis is determined by the use of communicative symbols. If cathexis is a mechanical process, it cannot be explained by nonmechanical events; and if communication is not mechanical, it cannot be explained by mechanics.

Nor does Freud take into account the success and failure of jokes. A joke, like any expression, has both form and content. We may want to laugh at the haughty policeman who is about to get a pie thrown in his

face, but our degree of laughter is determined by the style in which the pie
is thrown. We may want to laugh at the rich and powerful Baron Rothschild, but we do not laugh at *any* joke about him. It must be, as we say,
a good joke. And even a good joke poorly told no longer arouses laughter
—unless at the would-be joker for ruining a good story. This neglect of form
in Freud indicates clearly how little communication meant to his theoretical
interests. Yet, if symbolic form, the way in which communication takes
place—who communicates, by what means, in what kinds of situations, for
what purpose, and in what kind of action—is neglected, how *can* we
observe interaction unless we reduce it to motion?

Even mechanists admit that form determines content (as content determines form) in their descriptions of social mechanics. When Parsons
and Bales describe social interaction in dimensions of action-space,[13]
where there is an ongoing process which can be "usefully described by
comparison with a hypothetical system in a state of moving equilibrium," [14]
they are explaining social interaction by form. In their theoretical construction, as in any construction, the form of the theory, the model of man
in society, the design of the experiment—call it what you will—determines
what kind of facts can be observed, how they can be ordered, and what
can be concluded about their relevance to social interaction. So long as the
form of social interaction is conceived of in the form of mechanical equilibrium, the social facts observed will be mechanical facts.[15]

But the basic problem for human scientists interested in social communication of how to explain emotion, not as motion but as communication, is
not solved in Freud. Love, hate, envy, jealousy, pride, anger, and shame
arise only in communication with other human beings. The ability to
understand the motives of others and of ourselves originates in our capacity
to *express* feelings, not simply to discharge them. We share with animals
feelings of sex, hunger, and hierarchy; but unlike animals we *name* these
feelings, and in such naming, feeling becomes emotion because it can be
communicated. *How* it is communicated determines whether we will act
together in love, hate, or indifference. Thus, the proper study of motives
is not how we *discharge* feelings but how we *express* them.

FREUD'S GREAT CONTRIBUTION TO A SOCIOLOGY OF LANGUAGE:
DREAMS AND COMMUNICATION

Yet when all this is said, reading Freud is a very stirring experience for the sociologist interested in communication. On page after page there are sentences and paragraphs which fairly cry out for a sociological gloss. Our excitement mounts as we discover a way to think of the *unconscious elements in communication*. For, even while we communicate with others consciously, we are aware of sudden rushes of fantasy, of sharp gusts of passion, of longings and wishes that arise from we know not where and turn, as swiftly as they came, into new forms which seem to carry on a conversation of their own within us. How many times a gesture, a tone of voice, a phrase, carries us back to a past we have forgotten or transports us into a future we envision for the first time.

And in our dreams of the night what poets we all become as we pass into sleep! What dramas of lust, crime, beauty, and horror we stage in our unconscious. And in the terror of the nightmare what anguish we suffer, as we toss and turn in our beds. How often deep guilt, sharp envy, or blinding hate leave their hiding place in consciousness to pass through our dreams of the night and the day. But, we say, these are only dreams. What has all this to do with conscious communication? Even as we ask we know it has a great deal to do with it. We can hide from others the real reason why we suddenly change a course of action, why suddenly a new wish supplants an old; but we cannot hide it from ourselves.[16] This does not mean that we know *why* our wish changes, only that it *does*. To discover *why* and *how* we turn back to Freud—even though we know that his theory is mechanistic and his concern with the sociological aspects of communication is very limited.

He teaches us that symbols in the dream can be analyzed in terms of "condensation" and "displacement." In condensation we "form fresh unities out of elements which in our waking thought we should certainly keep separate. As a consequence of this, a single element of the manifest dream often stands for a whole number of latent dream-thoughts, as though it were a combined allusion to all of them; . . ."[17] In displacement we "create new significant values from elements of slight value. . . ." This is done *"by means of overdetermination"* of what, to the awakened dreamer, is something of slight value. As a result of displacement, the dream-content no longer has any likeness to the nucleus of the dream-thoughts, and the dream produces only a distorted form of the dream-wish in the unconscious.

We can argue that *what* is being condensed or displaced is not necessarily the patriarchal Freudian father, or that symbols, even in the dream, are a communication, an address to someone, but this does not alter the value of Freud's *method* for the sociologist interested in communication and social order. As in any communicative situation, the dreamer is concerned with making successful pleas to authorities he must placate, if he is to fulfill his wish. Freud calls such authority the censor, and even the dreamer, who is "beyond" public communication with real others, must still "outwit" this censor. In his book on dreams, Freud states the relationship between the dreamer and the censor in communicative terms. For so long as the dreamer is trying to outwit the censor, and so long as the Ego is trying to "come to terms" with the Id and the Super Ego, he is communicating and thus falls into the realm of rhetoric.[18]

Even in conscious communication when we address others we do so in the presence (real or imaginary) of *several* audiences. Thus there is not *a* censor, but *many* censors. And even if we address the parent, there is, as Malinowski pointed out, a mother as well as a father. Mead has proposed that we consider address in terms of dialogue between the "I," the "Me," and "They."[19] Burke has pointed out that "the slightest presence of revision is per se indication of a poet's feeling that his work is addressed (if only, as Mead might say, the address of an 'I' to its 'Me')."[20] But even when we admit this, we still must turn to Freud for many clues as to *how* we communicate with authority when such communication is very difficult or blocked. His analysis of the ruses and subterfuges the dreamer uses to say in his unconscious what he cannot say in conscious communication is as important to the sociologist of language as it is to the psychologist.

Even when we think of the difficulties in communicating between superiors, inferiors, and equals as social, and not sexual, problems, and when we are aware of the many subterfuges which must be used in conscious communication, Freud has much to say to us. For his description of the child struggling to communicate with elders is one of our great descriptions of all communication between inferiors and superiors. From Freud we learn what it means to communicate with strange and distant authorities.[21] Freud's teachings can hardly be called "sociological"; neither can they be called "individual psychology." Freud's psychology is a *family* psychology, and in so far as it deals with communication it is communication between parents and children that Freud uses as a model.

When Freud applies his model to the concrete data of his case histories, we suddenly discover that his abstraction of sexual elements and his monistic way of thinking leave much unexplained. In case after case, sexual and status frustrations are so intertwined that it becomes difficult —sometimes, indeed, impossible—to separate them. For if the father and the mother are sexual objects, they are also authorities, *superiors,* who must be appealed to successfully. The child, in turn, is an *inferior,* who must be persuaded to "behave." And both parent and child live within the society of the family, a social group whose members, like those of any social group, must learn to communicate with outsiders.

Close examination of many of the illustrations Freud himself gives of consensations and displacement show that there are often social as well as sexual elements involved. Even the simple "Freudian slips" mentioned in his *Introductory Lectures* and *The Psychopathology of Everyday Life* (and of course, in *Jokes and Their Relation to the Unconscious,* which is the most "social" of Freud's books) are social as well as sexual "slips." When we forget a name because we are fearful about whether we are pleasing a superior, we are suffering social, not "sexual," embarrassment. Here we enter the realm of courtship, which involves us in subterfuges that arise out of the pudencies of courtship among superiors, inferiors, and equals. To the degree the woman is courted, she is courted in forms determined by the *expression* of courtship prevalent in her society.

Whenever the social aspects of communication (the appeals to each other of superiors, inferiors, and equals) become complex and difficult, we are in the realm of neuroses and psychoses. When courtships of superiors and inferiors break down, or become so complex that conscious elements in communication are submerged in the unconscious, we must use Freudian terminology to begin our analysis even though we know that social and sexual courtship are not the same.[22] But even though we begin the exploration of unconscious communication, differences which emerge in our analysis must be analyzed in sociological terms. Until we are able to do this, we will be forced to discount description of communication as a kind of sexual pun with sociological concepts. We can use Freud's wonderful description of communication in the dream, and of communication in the family, as a *source* for the development of a specific sociological approach, but a source is only a beginning. The development of a sociology of language, and specifically of the unconscious aspects of social communication, must be undertaken by sociologists themselves.

Notes

[1] See *Studies in Hysteria,* by Josep Breuer and Sigmund Freud, in *The Standard Edition of the Complete Psychological Works of Sigmund Freud,* translated from the German under the general editorship of James Strachey (London: The Hogarth Press, 1953-), Vol. II, pp. 160–181.

[2] This is the last sentence of his discussion.

[3] The latest expression of this in American sociology is in the work of C. Wright Mills.

[4] See Freud's "Address Delivered in the Goethe House at Frankfurt" in *Standard Edition,* Vol. XXI. In his *Delusions and Dreams in Jensen's "Gradiva,"* his first published analysis of a work of literature which appeared in 1907, he says: "But creative writers are valuable allies and their evidence is to be prized highly, for they are apt to know a whole host of things between heaven and earth of which our philosophy has not yet let us dream. In their knowledge of the mind they are far in advance of us everyday people, for they draw upon sources which we have not yet opened up for science." See *Jensen's "Gradiva,"* in *Standard Edition,* Vol. IX, p. 8.

[5] This is one of our greatest examples of symbolic analysis. See Kenneth Burke, "Freud and the Analysis of Poetry," in *The Philosophy of Literary Form: Studies in Symbolic Action* (Baton Rouge: Louisiana State Univ. Press, 1941). Also reprinted in Vintage Books (New York, 1957) in a revised and abridged edition.

[6] See "The Interest of Psycho-Analysis from the View of the Science of Aesthetics," in *Standard Edition,* Vol. XIII, p. 187. In Vol. III, p. 444, of *Sigmund Freud: Life and Work* (London: The Hogarth Press, 1953), Ernest Jones lists other references to this point in Freud's work.

[7] See Freud's *An Outline of Psychoanalysis* (New York: W. W. Norton, 1949), p. 96n, for this discussion.

[8] This extraordinary attack on literary critics who disagreed with his interpretation of Hamlet is further extended. "The name 'William Shakespeare' is most probably a pseudonym behind which there lies concealed a great unknown. Edward deVere, Earl of Oxford, a man who has been regarded as the author of Shakespeare's works, lost a beloved and admired father while he was still a boy, and completely repudiated his mother, who contracted a new marriage soon after her husband's death." That is, to the extent "Shakespeare" was a psychoanalyst, his interpretations of human motivation were profound.

[9] Sigmund Freud, "On Dreams" in *Standard Edition,* Vol. V, p. 685.

[10] The stress on conflict, and the need for resolving it in some kind of authority, is lacking in Malinowski, as it is in Dewey and Mead.

[11] Sigmund Freud, *Jokes and Their Relation to the Unconscious,* in *Standard Edition,* Vol. VIII, p. 143. See Chapter 5, "The Motives of Jokers—Jokes as a Social Process."

[12] *Ibid.,* pp. 155–156.

[13] See Chapter 3 of Talcott Parsons, Robert F. Bales, and Edward A. Shils, *Working Papers in the Theory of Action* (Glencoe, Ill.: The Free Press, 1953).

[14] *Ibid.*, p. 71.

[15] That is, so long as the theory is consistent. If there is one virtue about the theoretical construction of Parsons, Bales, and Shils, it is that of consistency.

[16] As Freud himself tells us, even the neurotic has a nonneurotic self which regards his neurotic antics in a detached, rational fashion.

[17] Taken from *Freud: Dictionary of Psychoanalysis,* edited by N. Fodor and F. Gaynor, with a Preface by Theodor Reik (New York: Philosophical Library, 1950), p. 51. These quotations are from Freud, and the italics are his.

[18] Freud does not analyze the rhetorical aspects of the unconscious, but is content with saying that *some kind* of communication exists between the Id, Ego, and Super Ego.

[19] This will be discussed in the section on Mead. In Part Six another scheme of address is offered.

[20] "Freud and Analysis of Poetry," Kenneth Burke in *The Philosophy of Literary Form* (New York: Vintage Books, 1957).

[21] But we do not learn from Freud, as we shall argue, how to think about relationships between equals.

[22] Even in societies where there is little sexual inhibition, *how* one courts, the style and form of sexual communication, determines the "honor" of winning the loved one, as we see in Ovid's *The Art of Love.*

2

Georg Simmel's Search for an Autonomous Form of Sociability

FORMS OF SOCIATION CONSIDERED AS REPRESENTATIVE FORMS OF
SOCIAL INTERACTION

S IMMEL TAUGHT that until sociologists isolated a specific form and content of social experience there could be no science of sociology. "Pure sociology," must investigate "societal forms themselves," in hope of creating a grammar of the forms of sociation. "It must, so to speak, abstract a 'pure' element of sociation. It isolates [the element of sociation] inductively and psychologically from the heterogeneity of its contents and purposes, which isolates the pure forms of language from their contents through which these forms, nevertheless, come to life." For, whatever the content of social experience, forms of sociation, such as "superiority and subordination, competition, division of labor, formation of parties, representation, inner solidarity coupled with exclusiveness toward the outside," are common to all. The identification, ordering, and naming of such pure forms of sociation must become the central task of sociology.[1]

What is a "pure form of sociation"? How do we study it? We find social processes such as superiority and subordination, competition, division of labor, formation of cliques and parties, representation by delegation, and many other similar features, in the state, in a religious community, in a band of conspirators, in an economic association, in an art school, and in the family. On the other hand, interests which have an identical content may take form in very different sociations. Economic interest is realized both in competition and in cartels, in isolation from other groups as well as in fusion with them. Religious experience is expressed in unregulated as well as a centralized form of community, although the content of the experience expressed in each form may be quite similar. Sexual relations are expressed as social acts in many different forms of family life.

A sociological image of social interaction must then have both form and content, and must be described not through historical, biological, or economic features, but in the forms of men's social relations. To say, for example, that the strong individualism of early Italian Renaissance political constitutions was the effect of the liberation of economic life from guild and church ties, tells us nothing about the specific social forms of life, the ways in which individuals enacted their social roles in Italian society. For this we must turn to the history of art, which tells us that in the beginning of the Renaissance there was an immense spread of naturalistic and individualistic portrait busts. "Thus the general attention appears to have shifted from what men have in common (and what therefore can easily be relegated into somewhat more abstract and ideal spheres) to what must be left to the *individual*. Attention is focused on the significance of personal strength; the concrete is preferred to the general law that is valid 'on the whole.' " This suggests that the "observed economic individualism is the manifestation of a fundamental sociological change which has found its expression in the field of art and politics as well. It suggests that none of these immediately caused the other." [2]

How must we think of historical change? We begin by noting that historical changes are really changes in sociological forms.

It is perhaps the way in which individuals and groups behave toward one another; in which the individual behaves toward his group; in which value accents, accumulations, prerogatives, and similar phenomena shift among the elements of society—perhaps it is *these* things which make for truly epochal events. And if economics seem to determine all the other areas of culture, the truth behind this tempting appearance would seem to be that it itself is determined—determined by sociological shifts which similarly shape all other cultural phenomena. Thus, the form of economics, too, is merely a "superstructure" on top of the conditions and transformations in the purely sociological structure. And this sociological structure is the ultimate historical element which is bound to determine all other contents of life, even if in a certain parallelism with economics.[3]

Hunger, love, work, religion, technology, art, and reason become factors in sociation only when they "transform the mere aggregation of isolated individuals into specific forms of being with and for another—forms that are subsumed under the general concept of interaction." These forms, originally developed to satisfy such needs, "remove themselves from the services of life that originally produced and employed them" to develop in terms of their own resources as forms. This is true, of course, in all forms of expression. Science is no longer bound to practical tasks but chooses its own objects, shapes them according to its own needs, and as pure science is interested in nothing beyond its own perfection as pure science. So, too, with law, which becomes, as we are told, the science of legal forms which determine in their own right, and not by legitimation through any higher extrinsic agency, how the contents of life should be shaped.[4]

Thus, we cannot say that social form itself determines completely the forms of economic, political, religious, or cultural life. For, however socially determined and permeated every political, religious, and cultural act may be, this social determination is interwoven with other determinations that stem from other sources. The best that a science of sociology can do is to abstract, in a very one-sided way, the structure and function of interaction among individuals as they enact their roles in society to achieve economic, political, religious, and cultural goals. But this limited and abstract sociological view of the forms of interaction, which must be supplemented by other perspectives, is at least a *specific* form of knowledge, and this, in the last analysis, is all we can ask of any study of man.

We need not conclude, then, that because we lack an exhaustive and undisputed definition of the nature of society we cannot create a sociological body of knowledge. Many forms of knowledge have developed on disputed foundations. Scientific propositions in physics and chemistry are useful in research even though the concept of matter is problematical and obscure. Juridical concepts have been created despite constant argument over the nature of law and its principles. Psychology has been able to develop even though we do not really know how the mind functions. Questions on the origin, nature, and development of society must be rephrased as questions on the structure and function of interaction among individuals as they act for, with, and against each other in their social relations.

The forms and contents of reciprocal relations among human beings is, then, the proper concern of the sociologist.

Men regard one another, and men are jealous one of another; they meet in sympathy or antipathy quite apart from all tangible interests; their gratitude for altruistic service weaves a chain of consequences never to be sundered; they ask the way of one another, and they dress and adorn themselves for one another;—these are instances chosen quite at random from the thousand relations, momentary or lasting, conscious or unconscious, transitory or fraught with consequences, which, playing from person to person, knit us incessantly together. Every moment such threads are spun, are dropped and again caught up, replaced by others, woven up with others. These . . . determine all the tenacity and elasticity, all the variegation and unity of this so intelligible and yet so mysterious life of society.[5]

FORMS OF SOCIATION CONSIDERED AS ART AND AS PLAY

What is the nature of these forms, and how do they emerge in social life? First, we note that forms of expression are able to free themselves from the practical needs which originally produced and sustained them. "They become autonomous in the sense that they are no longer inseparable from the objects which they formed and thereby made available to our purposes. They come to play freely in themselves and for their own sale; they produce or make use of materials that exclusively serve their own operation or realization." Science, for example, once devoted to the solution of practical problems, has now become a value in itself. Pure scientists select their own problems and solve them as they see fit. Great jurists tell us we must uphold "government by law, not by men," or that "justice must be done, even if the world perish." Here, lawful behavior, which has its roots in the purposes of social life, has no practical end. The forms of law, legal statutes, are just to the degree they become consistent with other legal forms created and determined by their nature as legal symbols.

But the greatest example of change from the determination of forms by the practical needs of the community, to the determination of these needs by forms which have become values in themselves,[6] is perhaps most extensively at work in the numerous phenomena that we lump together under the category of play. "Actual forces, needs, impulses of life produce the forms of our behavior that are suitable for play. These forms, however, become independent contents and stimuli within play itself, or, rather, play *as* play. There are, for instance, the hunt; the gain by ruse; the proving of physical and intellectual strength; competition; and the dependence on chance and on the favor of powers that cannot be influenced."[7] In play all these forms are lifted out of the flux of life and freed of their inherent seriousness and gravity.

In playfulness and in all forms of play we create themes and events which will increase the playfulness of play. This is what distinguishes the gaiety and symbolic significance of play from mere joking. Play, like art, developed originally out of the realities of life, yet both have created spheres which preserve their autonomy in the face of these realities. This autonomy, in play as in art, still draws its strength from its origin in life, which keeps them permeated with life. When art and play are emptied of life, they become artifice and "empty play." Yet it is not until the forms of play and art are separated from the purposes and needs of the community and become the purpose and means of their own existence as forms that they become true play and art. "From the realities of life [art and play] take only what they can adapt to their own nature, only what they can absorb in their autonomous existence." [8]

In play, individuals free themselves from all other ties. Play exists for its own sake and for the sake of the fascination which, in its liberation from other ties, is created by the game itself. Thus, while we are acting together in economic associations, religious societies, criminal associations, or art cliques we feel there is something more in our relatedness than economic, religious, criminal, or aesthetic activity. This is a feeling "of being sociated," of being together on a social basis. We seek satisfaction for our aesthetic needs at an art gallery, yet we still seek purely social satisfaction in the event. We attend church to worship God, yet we still seek social as well as religious communion with our fellow worshippers. Thus, in the most serious as in the most ephemeral relationship, there is a kind of relatedness which (like play) cannot be explained by anything outside of play itself.

The realm of art, along with that of play, offers other examples of what is meant by a form of sociation. The interpretation of reality in terms of spatial perspectives, of rhythms, and of sounds certainly had its origin in practical needs. But these interpretations have become purposes in themselves in the various arts. They are "effective on their own strength and in their own right, selective and creative quite independently of their entanglement with practical life, and not because of it." A fully developed art form is wholly separated from life. It takes from life only what it can use, as we see when the artist creates images which express sexual relations. The relationship he depicts is a relationship in art, not life. Yet while sex relationships in art are not the same as in life, and while the artist's forms free themselves from the biological reality of sex, they are grounded still in the interest of men and women in satisfying sexual need.

In similar fashion the social "instinct," or whatever we call our need for being with, for, and against each other, becomes a pure process of sociation which we value in its own right. It is no mere accident of language that all men, primitive and civilized alike, place so much emphasis on what they call "good form" in social relationships. In many European languages "society" and "high society" simply designate a *sociable* gathering. We call many associations "societies," but it is not societies of men gathered for special purposes, but only purely social groups, that make up what we call society and are reported as such in the society section of our news-papers. Such "society" is an abstract image in which all contents such as sex, money, or rank are dissolved in the mere play of form. Thus, we can say sociability is the primary sociological category. And we must learn to think of the relation of this play-form to reality as we think of the rela-tionship between art to reality.

Sociability has no objective purpose, no content, no extrinsic results. The success of a social gathering depends entirely on the personalities of those present. But it is only when members of a party subordinate their person-alities to the social demands of the moment that a party "comes off." Amiability, refinement, cordiality—what we call social charm—determine social skill. These have no content beyond that of the social drama itself, just as manners, the ways we greet, talk, and part, have no meaning be-yond that of a purely social expression. Wealth, social position, erudition, fame, rank, age, and sex must if the party is to be a success be subordinated to the demands of sociability. Expression of personal moods of depression, excitement, despondency—*any* of the heights and depths of one's indi-viduality—destroys sociability.

A purely social gathering is regulated in many ways, but in so far as our relations are not determined by external or immediate egoistic interests, the purely social phenomenon of tact regulates our relations with others. The most essential function of tact is to make clear the bounds of social inter-action beyond which the impulses, egocentricity, or intellectual or material desires of the individual cannot go. Thus, a lady who would appear at a small intimate party in the kind of low-cut dress she wears with no em-barrassment at a formal party, would be considered tactless. She would lack, as we say, a sense of what is appropriate to the occasion. From a sociological view, tactless people are antisocial because they militate against the development of interaction within the group on a purely social level.

THE PUREST MOMENT OF SOCIABILITY: EQUALITY

The most profound expression of sociability occurs between equals. Soci-ability between superiors and inferiors, or between members of widely different social classes of status groups, is always limited. Equality makes possible the highest expression of sociability because as equals we eliminate the wholly personal and the wholly objective. Among social equals the democracy of sociability is really played as we play a game or mount a drama on the stage, for sociability creates an ideal social world in which the pleasure of the individual is closely tied up with the pleasure of others. In principle, no one has the right to enjoy feelings which are exactly the opposite of those of others. In sociability such divergencies are not excluded through some superimposed ethical imperative, but by the intrinsic principle of the social form itself. Thus, the world of sociability is the only world in which those with equal privileges can relate without friction.

The democratic world of sociability is an artificial world. It is composed of individuals who desire only to create moments of pure interaction, moments when the stresses of life are transformed into styles of meeting, greeting, and talk, in which we find deep joy in simply being together on a purely social basis. But it is a mistake to think that we are first equal and then sociable. On the contrary, our equality arises in the expression of sociability. For, if sociation is interaction, its purest, that is to say, its most stylized expression, occurs among equals—just as symmetry and balance are the most characteristic elements in artistic stylization. And, inasmuch as interaction is abstracted from sociation through art and play, sociability calls for the purest, most transparent, and most casually appealing kind of interaction: that among equals. Because of its very nature as art and play, sociability creates human beings who are capable of modifying their external and internal significance.

We can formulate the principle of sociability which finds its purest expression among equals as the axiom that each individual should offer the maximum of sociable values (joy, liveliness, humor, etc.) that is compatible with the maximum of values he himself receives. Among equals, social values can be attained by the individual only if others with whom he interacts also gain them. For sociability is a game in which one acts as if all were equal and, at the same time, as if one honored each individual. To some, this characteristic of equality in democracy seems to be a lie or a deviation from reality. But sociability is no more a lie than play, games, or art are lies. The social game becomes a lie only when sociable action and speech are subordinated to some motive outside of sociability itself—just as art becomes a lie when it is used in commercial art to dress up a product which is not fit to be used or even endangers life. "What is perfectly correct and in order if practiced within the autonomous life of sociability with its self-contained play of forms, becomes a deceptive lie when it is guided by non-sociable purposes or is designed to disguise such purposes." [9]

The forms of interaction among men, or at least those which develop into forms of sociation, always develop out of striving to attain serious and practical ends. The desire for domination, for profit in business, for political power, the sudden shifts from love to hate, the terrible ways we wound and kill in war—all are imbued with purposive and practical contents. But in games, these forms take on a life of their own. In gambling, for example, it is not the money alone which motivates the players, for there are many other and more honorable ways to make money. To the person who really likes to gamble, the charm of gambling is in the game, in the purely social aspects of gambling, not in the winning of the stake. For as we know, the double sense of the "social game" (in whatever contest it occurs) is that not only the game is played in a set of social relations (the external structure of its existence), but that through the help of the "social game" people actually "play" society.

COQUETRY AND CONVERSATION AS SPECIFIC EXAMPLES
OF PURE FORMS OF SOCIATION

Playing society can be observed in many contexts. The play-form of eroticism is coquetry, in which eroticism finds its most facile, playful, and widely diffused realization. The body demands sexual release, society depends for its continuance on sexual relations, and the community seeks to regulate sexual relations according to some principle of social order. But as individuals we seek other satisfactions in sex. These exist in art or play, in the common blend of art and play we find in coquetry and flirting, and in all the nuances of sexual approach men and women use in their enactment of masculine and feminine roles in society.

Between individuals the sexual question is simply one of offer or refusal. The feminine coquette dramatizes alternately allusive promises and equally allusive withdrawals. She flirts "outrageously," as we say, to attract the male, but she stops short of decision. She rejects the male, yet manages to leave him with hope that she will yield to further advances. "The coquettish woman enormously enhances her attractiveness if she shows her consent as an almost immediate possibility but is ultimately not serious about it. Her behavior swings back and forth between 'yes' and 'no' without stopping at either. She playfully exhibits the pure and simple form of erotic decisions and manages to embody their polar opposites in a perfectly consistent behavior: its decisive, well understood content, that would commit her to one of the two opposites, does not even enter." [10]

What is the aim and end then of flirting? And how can we explain its profound fascination? What is the element that lifts sex out of sex, so to speak, and is powerful enough to subordinate lust itself to its purpose? How can we explain the great range of erotic symbolization in all forms of art, in primitive [11] as well as highly sophisticated societies? Only by the fact that sociability is as much a need as sex, and that the expression of eroticism in purely social terms is as important to society as the satisfaction of sex on a somatic level. To call the art and play of sex, the social festivities which are organized around courtship, "unreal," "fore-pleasure," or simply "fantasies" which are "superimposed" on the reality of sex, overlooks the deep *social* need which we also satisfy in our sexual roles.

For sexual expression is a communication which always involves a self and another.[12] The woman cannot be a flirt all by herself.[13] As long as the man rejects flirtation, or is a passive victim without any will of his own, who vacillates continually between a half "yes" and a half "no," flirtation has not yet reached a fully developed level of sociability. So long as the man and the woman still hope to win each other sexually, they are not flirting. For the essence of the social aspect of flirting, which is indeed its very essence, is the high artificial play of sex which only dimly reflects the specific erotic motivation in sex. Only when the actors in the drama of flirtation are no longer attracted to each other by lust alone, or are no longer overwhelmed by the fear of lust which coquettish allusions and gestures produce, can the social element of sex occur. This is why coquetry unfolds its charm precisely at the moment when highly stylized forms of sexual communication make it possible for us to leave far behind the reality of erotic desire, consent, or refusal. All the power and drive of sex becomes embodied in the interactions of silhouettes, so to speak, of this power.

In our society, erotic desire leads men and women to withdraw from society. Sex is a "private affair," as we say, and even courtship or the engagement period, are a time of mystery and seclusion from the group. But sexual play, like all play, is done for the audience, as well as for the individuals who compose the cast of the drama or the members of the team. Thus, under the "sociological sign of sociability from which the center of the personality's concrete and complete life is barred, coquetry is the flirtatious, perhaps ironical, play in which eroticism has freed the bare outline of its interactions from their materials and contents and personal features. As sociability plays with the forms of society, so coquetry plays

with those of eroticism, and this affinity of their natures predestines coquetry as an element of sociability." [14]

Conversation also offers many examples of sociability. Indeed, conversation is the most characteristic moment of sociability, for it is the "most general vehicle for all that men have in common." We talk to each other for
many reasons, but at a social gathering we talk merely for the sake of
talking. Talk becomes its own purpose. This does not mean that any kind
of talk satisfies, or that idle chatter is enough. There is, as we say, an art
of conversation which, like any art, has laws of its own. In purely sociable
conversation, the topic is used merely as a means to develop the charm and
attraction of good talk. Other forms in which talk occurs—the quarrel,
argument in law, debates on the issue of the day, gossip, the confessional,
adjudication of disputes through compromise, parliamentary discourse—
are used to attain practical ends in community life.

But in talk, all the forms, the kinds of gestures and expression we use in
"serious" talk, suddenly derive their significance only from themselves,
"from the fascinating play of relations which they create among the
participants," as we see in the "joining and loosening, winning and suc-
cumbing, [and] the giving and taking" which goes on in purely social talk.
For if conversation is to become and remain pleasurable, no content,
idea, or theme can become dominant in its own right. "As soon as the discussion becomes objective, as soon as it makes the ascertainment of a truth
its *purpose* (it may very well be its *content*), [conversation] ceases to be
sociable and thus becomes untrue to its own nature. . . ." Thus, while the
"*form* of the ascertainment of truth or of a quarrel may exist, . . . the seriousness of their contents may as little become the focus of sociable conversation as a perspectivistic painting may contain a piece of the actual, three-
dimensional reality of its object." [15]

The content of sociable conversation is no less important than its form.
The subject of talk must be interesting and fascinating. And as playful
and gay as talk becomes, it cannot become sheer nonsense. Yet all social talk,
however serious, must be subordinated to the purely social demands of the
occasion. At parties we do not talk to decide, judge, or reach a conclusion,
but to socialize, to be with, for, and against one another in the pure play
of sociability. Because of this we change topics easily and quickly; we
"keep the ball rolling," as we say. Talk always presupposes two parties. It
is in every sense an I and Thou relationship in which the meaning of the I
depends on the response of the Thou. "It thus is the fulfillment of a rela-

tion that wants to be nothing but relation—in which, that is, what usually is the mere form of interaction becomes its self-sufficient content." [16]

In social conversation we seek to achieve harmony, a common consciousness of being together at a party, or enjoying each other in terms of the social personality alone. We seek to turn conversation away from too individual and intimate moments because these cannot be shared by others. We resent those whose remarks are so purely personal that they cannot be shared by the group. This is why the telling of stories and jokes is so common at parties. They provide a content in which all can participate alike. The story belongs to all because, unlike the highly personal anecdote, it belongs to no one. It is the individual's gift to the group, a truly social gift because it is given only to enhance the social, and not individual, relation within the gathering. This, perhaps, is why we do not laugh at our own stories until others do, and even then in a more subdued manner than others. We want to increase the warmth and joy of the party because only as we do so can we increase our own.

Perhaps when all is said and done, moments of pure socialization, as in the talk at a party, keep our relations in society flexible and grounded in the interplay of individual consciousness. In religion, politics, war—all the "serious" and practical moments of life—we must commit ourselves deeply, sometimes, indeed, irrevocably, to leaders and causes. The soldier watching his leader for signals which will take him into battle, the priest waiting to declare his conscience to alien inquisitors, the political candidate who must declare his views on segregation, the teacher who must answer to political inquisitors on his religious beliefs, must act out of deeply believed and deeply fixed ideas. In such moments, no man is free, for he is bound by ideals greater than himself which, come what will, he must follow to the end.

SIMMEL'S CONTRIBUTION TO SOCIAL THEORY CONSIDERED IN TERMS OF COMMUNICATION

In Simmel's final image of pure sociability (as at a party) we are bound to the group, but the tragic and real character of these bonds are transformed into a kind of mythological realm, as in dramas of the gods. Like the gods of Olympus or the courtiers in the enchanted palace of the fairy king, we are no longer old, fearful, tired, corrupt, or stupid. We cringe before no stern superiors, nor do we suffer from the cupidity and disloyalty of inferiors. We are free to wander about and talk to whomever we will. Groups form and reform as the party goes on. As the feeling of pure sociality mounts, our pleasure in each other's company increases. We realize that our pleasure has little to do with the presence of powerful, rich, learned, or beautiful people. We are able to express ourselves purely as social beings. As the party develops, there is nothing left in our relatedness but play, a play of sociability which obeys laws of its own form, and whose charm is contained in itself.

Thus, as we see, Simmel's contribution to a social theory of communication is his insistence that we isolate from experience a specific form and content of social experience which is based on the interaction of individual actors who relate to each other through communication to satisfy needs and interests which they cannot satisfy alone. Moments of sociability must not be explained by anything outside of sociability itself. The study of these moments of sociability, their form and content, ought to be, Simmel insists, the central concern of sociologists. For if these forms of sociation are autonomous in whatever context they occur, there must be a specific sociological content which can be studied. Simmel keeps our attention focused on a specifically sociological aspect of experience. He asks: What, really, are we talking about when we talk about a sociology of society?

At first glance, nothing seems better suited to a social theory based on the communication of significant symbols than Simmel's image of sociation: "that being with one another, for one another, against one another, which, through the vehicle of drives and purposes, forms and develops material or individual contents and interests." [17] In his discussion of knowledge, truth, and falsehood in human relations he says: "Human interaction is normally based on the fact that the ideational worlds of men have certain elements in common, that objective intellectual contents constitute the material which is transformed into subjective life by means of men's social relations. The type, as well as the essential instrument of these common elements is shared language." [18] And, as we have seen, he held that conversation was "the most general vehicle for all that men have in common."

Yet, even if we take Simmel's advice not to wait until the theoretical foundations of sociology are firmly established and begin at once to investigate social forms as forms of sociation, we run into trouble. For, despite his many references to art, play, and conversation as illustrations of the forms of sociation, there really is no *model* of social interaction as a social act which arises in and exists through communication. Like Freud, Simmel makes constant use of symbolic material. And, just as Freud used Greek drama to form his model of the Oedipus complex, so does Simmel turn to art for illustrations of what he means by an autonomous form of sociation. But it is very difficult to fashion methodological tools, or to construct a methodology based on communication as the medium in which social forms arise and continue (as Simmel seems to believe they do) out of Simmel's forms.

When we try to apply Simmel's forms to an observable content of sociation such as games, play, or art, we find that his prime image of sociation —the being with-one-another, for-one-another, in-one-another, against-one-another, and through-one-another—is really a spatial and mechanical image. And, despite all his talk about the individual and the extraordinary subtlety of his analysis of the forms of interaction, he *reduces the social process to a natural process.* Individuals are the "bearers of the processes of association," and "are united by these processes into the higher unity which one calls 'society.'" To illustrate how individuals are "united," he turns to physics. "The energy effects of atoms upon each other bring matter into the innumerable forms which we see as 'things.' Just so the impulses and interests, which a man experiences in himself and which push him out toward other men, bring about all the forms of association by which a mere sum of separate individuals are made into a 'society.'"[19]

Within or outside the higher "constellation" called society "there develops a special sociological structure corresponding to those of art and play. . . ." But art and play, it turns out, are merely used as illustrations, just as Freud used art forms to *illustrate,* not to constitute, psychoanalytic theory. "It may be an open question whether concept of a play impulse or an artistic impulse possesses explanatory value; at least it directs attention to the fact that in every play or artistic activity there is contained a common element not affected by their differences in content." Thus the *content* of sociation, the process of sociation, is like the "energy affects of atoms," but the *form* is like art or play. The question immediately arises: How can a form modeled after art or play be applied to a content described in terms of physical nature?

Here Simmel, despite his avowed sociological orientation, joins Freud in a common dilemma. Interaction as a category in social theory cannot be *both* a mechanical or electronic process *and* a form similar to the form of art or play. The gap between nature and man cannot be jumped so long as we assert that *either* nature or man is primary and do not explain how men get from nature to society. In Freud interaction is really based on cathexis, while in Simmel the forms of sociation are really forms of "process." In both schemes communication through significant symbols becomes little more than a signal, and social interaction becomes some kind of "process" or "force" which determines individuals and society.

If the forms of expression in society are objective and real, as Simmel tells us they are, and some meanings are fixed and timeless, as both Freud and Simmel say they are,[20] we expect to be shown *how* forms of sociation are determined by communication, and how in turn, specific forms of sociation determine communication. And, if the forms of art, play, and conversation are models from which we must draw our model of the higher synthesis of sociation itself, then we ought to study the forms of art, play, and conversation for help in constructing our "pure forms of sociation." But just when Simmel ought to show us how to create models taken from art, play, or conversation and how to apply them to social data, he only repeats that forms of sociation are a "process" whose forms must be thought of like art or play.

No one thought more highly of Simmel than Park, who attended Simmel's lectures in Berlin and did so much to make Simmel's work known in America. Yet when Park and Burgess accepted Simmel's theory of communication as "the medium of interaction" and tried to create a model of sociation from Simmel's discussion of forms, they could do no more than make interaction into a process, which was never related in any constitutive fashion to communication at all. Simmel's category of being for, with, and against one another, was reified into social forces described as competition, conflict, accommodation, and assimilation. These new terms changed the appearance, not the body, of the problem. The problem for sociologists is how to distinguish the *data* of being for, with, and against one another and how to analyze this process. We know men compete; but in what kinds of human interaction should we study competition, and, if we study it as sociologists, what is the sociological model proper to our study?

If mind is social, it must arise in and through some kind of expression which is determined by social elements. Expression as communication cannot be a process which somehow passes through one individual to another, for in such passage the individual becomes meaningless. Nor do we solve anything by saying that roles, not individuals, determine socialization. For roles must be internalized before they can be enacted. Theories of "role cathexis" (however disguised) reduce men to automatons, and no matter how brilliantly we spin out our mechanical analogies, they are mechanical analogies still. Roles are *enacted* by individuals who struggle to achieve ends which must be reached in competition and conflict with others who also seek to achieve ends in the great drama of community life.

Structural descriptions of forms of interaction which do not derive from a function to which the structure is related can never become theories of social interaction. So long as we go on spinning out structural descriptions, we are like workmen who spend so much time and effort at building a scaffold that they fail to get their building underway. Simmel keeps repeating that there are forms of interaction; but his forms, subtle and brilliant as they are, never lead us to action in society, only to more elaboration of abstract forms of sociation. The building within the forms—that is, a sociological structure based on some kind of observable data of sociation (such as communication)—is never finished, because it is never begun.

Notes

[1] Most quotations from Simmel will be taken from *The Sociology of Georg Simmel,* edited by Kurt H. Wolff (Glencoe, Ill.: The Free Press, 1950). See "The Study of Societal Forms . . . ," pp. 21–23, for these quotations.

[2] *Ibid.,* p. 15. Simmel's italics.

[3] *Ibid.,* p. 16.

[4] *Ibid.,* p. 42.

[5] Translated from Simmel as given in Howard Becker, *Systematic Sociology on the Basis of the Beziehungslehre and Gebildelehre of Leopold Von Wiese* (Gary, Ind.: The Norman Paul Press, 1950), pp. 24–25.

[6] Or, as Veblen used to say: "Invention is the mother of necessity."

[7] Simmel, *op. cit.,* p. 42.

[8] *Ibid.,* pp. 42–43.

[9] *Ibid.,* p. 49.

[10] *Ibid.,* p. 50.

[11] Accounts of dances in primitive society often depict a kind of sexual teasing and mockery among the dancers. And even the singularly humorless accounts of primitive society by Malinowski and Radcliffe-Brown mention that laughter and joking over sex are very common in primitive society.

[12] Psychoanalysts tell us they pay great attention to the "nature of the fantasy" of those who cannot communicate with real others, but must communicate with others created in fantasy to obtain sexual satisfaction.

[13] When the child flirts with his own image in a mirror, he is "sublimating" his

narcissistic tendencies through the image of another, and not the self alone, according to Flugel.

[14] Simmel, *op. cit.*, p. 51.

[15] *Ibid.*, p. 52.

[16] *Ibid.*, p. 53.

[17] *Ibid.*, p. 43. This image occurs in the *Grundfragen der Soziologie*, Simmel's last explicit sociological statement on the nature of socialization.

[18] *Ibid.*, p. 315.

[19] These quotations are taken from Everett C. Hughes' translation of the "Soziologie der Geselligkeit," which was Simmel's opening speech at the first meeting of the German Sociological Society in October, 1910, in Frankfurt. This was a statement of Simmel's final theoretical position on the nature of his forms of sociation. For Hughes' translation, see *American Journal of Sociology*, LV (November, 1949), pp. 254–61.

[20] In Freud the sexual meaning of symbols was fixed in archaic times; in Simmel the meaning of symbols is created in the "objective process" of sociation. Freud's genetic theory drives us into an infinite regress; Simmel's to a conversion of mind into nature, and communication into process.

3

Malinowski's Theory of the Social Context of Magical Language

M ALINOWSKI, like Simmel, held that speech is a kind of social communion. It "is the necessary means of communion; it is the one indispensable instrument for creating the ties of the moment without which unified social action is impossible."[1] Language must be thought of as a "mode of action," not as an instrument of reflection, for only when we know the situation in which men communicate, and what they are trying to achieve as they communicate (the "context of situation") do we know what their expression means. The conception of meaning as "contained" in an utterance is false and futile, because a statement cannot be detached from the situation in which it is uttered. For each verbal statement has the aim and function of expressing some thought or feeling at the moment it is used in a particular situation, in order to serve common purposes of action, to establish ties of purely social communion, or to express the violent feelings and passion of the speaker.

The context of situation must be stressed if we are to return language to society, and thus recover a sense of how it is determined by society. The philologist who deals only with remnants of dead languages differs greatly from the ethnographer who, deprived of the fixed data of an inscribed language, must rely on the living reality of spoken language. The former reconstructs the general situation, the culture of a past people, from existing statements of their culture, but the ethnographer can study directly the conditions characteristic of a culture and interpret the statements through them. Only the ethnographer's approach is relevant to meaning. The philologist's view is fictitious and irrelevant, because he does not study how language is used in social situations but merely relates words to each other in highly abstract grammatical and lexical schemes.[2]

Neither a word nor its meaning has an independent and self-sufficient existence. The ethnographic view proves that all symbols are relative. That is, words must be regarded only as symbols, and a psychology of symbolic reference must serve as the basis for all science of language. "Since the world of 'things-to-be-expressed' changes with the level of culture, with geographical, social, and economic conditions, the consequence is that the meaning of a word must be gathered always, not from a passive contemplation of this world, but from an analysis of its functions, with reference to the given culture. Each primitive or barbarous tribe, as well as each type of civilization, has its world of meanings and the whole linguistic apparatus of this people . . . can only be explained in connection with their mental requirements."[3]

But, as Malinowski himself asks, if we draw our illustrations of the pragmatic function of language from work situations alone how do we explain narrative and dramatic uses of language? What is the function of songs, sayings, myths, legends, and all the magical and ritual uses of language? And what about the use of language in purely social conversation when the object of talk is not to achieve some practical aim but simply to exchange words as an end in itself? Malinowski argues that his theory of the context of situation can be applied to all forms of expression. "When incidents are told or discussed among a group of listeners, there is, first, the situation of that moment made up of the respective social, intellectual and emotional attitudes of those present. Within this situation, the narrative creates new bonds and sentiments by the emotional appeal of the words. . . . [Thus] the referential function of a narrative is subordinate to its social and emotive function."[4]

But what is the referential function of purely social talk? When a number of natives sit together at a village fire, after the day's work is done, and simply chat, it cannot be said that language depends on what happens at that moment. The meaning of what is said cannot be connected with the behavior of the speaker or the listener. There seems, indeed, to be no purpose to what they are doing, and thus the context of situation seems to be nothing but the words themselves. Inquiries about health, remarks on the weather, hearty agreement with what has just been said—such exchanges are made, not to inform, to connect people to any kind of action, or to express any kind of thought. It cannot be said either that such words establish a common sentiment, for sentiment seldom marks the empty phrases of purely social talk. We do not really think during such talk that those who ask us how we are really care about our health, and we carefully refrain from telling them much about our real state of health.

Yet, in these seemingly purposeless moments of idle chatter and mere sociability "we come to one of the bedrock aspects of man's nature in society." This is his tendency to congregate, to be together, to enjoy the company of other men. All the types of "social sentiments such as ambition, vanity, passion for power and wealth, are dependent upon and associated with the fundamental tendency which makes the mere presence of others a necessity for man." Speech is the "intimate correlate of this tendency, for, to the natural man, another man's silence is not a reassuring factor, but, on the contrary, something alarming and dangerous. The stranger who cannot speak the language is to all savage tribesmen a natural enemy. . . . The breaking of silence, the communion of words is the first act to establish links of fellowship, which is consummated only by the breaking of bread and the communion of food." [5]

Here, Malinowski says, we have a new type of linguistic use: "phatic communion." Words in "phatic communion" are not used to convey the meaning which is symbolically theirs. Nor are they used to transmit thought. And, if we think of them as a mode of action, we must discover in what, and for what purpose, "phatic communion" exists. It consists simply in an atmosphere of sociability, and in the personal communion of the talkers. The whole situation consists in what happens linguistically. Each utterance "is an act of serving the direct aim of binding hearer to speaker by a tie of some social sentiment or other. Once more language appears to us in this function not as an instrument of reflection but as a mode of action." [6] Thus, among savage and civilized man alike, words are often used simply to bring men into a pleasant atmosphere of polite, social intercourse. [7]

But the ethnographer soon discovers there is another kind of language, which is not like the pragmatic language of work or purely social talk. This is magic. The language of magic is sacred; it is fixed, like the language of religious ritual, and it is used for purposes different from those of ordinary life. Magical formulas, sacramental utterances, exorcisms, curses, blessings, and prayers have a creative effect on action because they are believed to set in motion some supernatural or transcendent power. Practical utterances, an order given in battle, a cry for help, are more like signs than symbols; they "trigger" motor phases of action. But supernatural symbols of God, transcendental symbols of community, or legal sanctions, create and sustain attitudes, beliefs, and values necessary to community life.

LANGUAGE AND SOCIAL ORGANIZATION

Meaning, then, is not only the effect of words on human minds and bodies but on the environmental reality as created in a given culture. Man lives in a symbolic environment. Imaginary and mental effects are as important, in this realm of supernatural belief, as the legal effects of a formula are in the use of contracts in society. "There is no strict line of demarcation between the signature on a cheque, a civil contract of marriage, the sacramental vow on a similar occasion, the change of substance in the Holy Eucharist, and the repulsion of bush-pigs by means of a fictitious excrement." Such words are accepted as binding by the members of a society because they are accepted as potentially creative acts. "You utter a vow or you forge a signature and you may find yourself bound for life to a monastery, a woman, or a prison. You utter another word and you make millions happy, as when the Holy Father blesses the faithful. Human beings will bank everything, risk their lives and substance, undertake a war or embark on a perilous expedition, because a few words have been uttered." [8]

Trobriand garden magic is believed to produce fertility. From our view of science there is no connection between the magic spell and garden fertility. But what is very real about the magical words is the manner in which they create and sustain a high degree of morale among the gardeners and give authority to the garden magician to direct the organization and maintenance of the gardens. This magic also is used to control the eating of yams so that they are not eaten up too rapidly and to transform the material substance of food into something which is fit and appropriate for the guardian spirits of the tribe to eat. Thus, no matter how sacred, such symbols are as necessary to action as the simplest word of warning. Without magical language the group could not act because it would have no common and binding symbols which would make the organization of such action possible.

Even in our society the most abstract and theoretical precepts of the chemist or the physicist can be understood only through acquaintance with the processes of chemistry and physics as they are carried out in the laboratory. There is no science whose conceptual forms are not derived ultimately from the practical handling of matter. To argue that civilized or scientific speech is completely detached from pragmatic sources, and thus is very different from primitive speech which is always related to action, is a grave error. Between the primitive uses of words and the most abstract and theoretical there is only a difference of degree. Ultimately, the meaning of all words is derived from bodily experience.[9]

Among Trobrianders the effective change brought about by magical words is profound indeed, although they seem, at first glance, to be without purpose, of no sociological value, and simply a way of talking into a void. But when the magician sits alone in his hut and mumbles over some herbs, the "context of situation" is the production and application of *mana,* the magical force which affects the fertility of crops. "To the Trobriander the magic spell is a sequence of words, more or less mysterious, handed down from immemorial times and always taught by an accredited magician to his successors; it is received by the wielder of the magic from some supernatural agency, or else brought by the first ancestors who came from underground, where they had led an existence in which magic apparently was already in use." [10]

But it is not the genesis so much as the application of the magical rites that concerns the Trobriander. As actually recited in the spell, magical words are distinguished from ordinary usage. They are pronounced according to a special phonology, in a sing-song, with their own rhythm, and are numerically grouped. This creates a weird, strange, and unusual atmosphere during the utterance of the spell. In the linguistic practice of magic there is a specific use of what we call rhetorical devices, such as metaphor, opposition, repetition, negative comparison, imperative, and question-with-answer. All such devices create a clear breach of continuity between the form, as well as the content, of magical and ordinary speech.

The magical spell differs not only in the form of its words but in the social drama of its presentation. The spell must be handled by the accredited magician within an appropriate ceremonial. The magician must be selected, trained, and supported with great care, for he carries on the tradition of a magic which, so it is believed, originated from a divine revelation which occurred during experience such as war or a great community catastrophe. The founders of magic and the original formulators of the spells, who are among the ancestors of the practicing magician, are always thought of as gods, demigods, heroes, or geniuses. "The men who inherited and wielded [magic after them] . . . must have been always men of great intelligence, energy, and power of enterprise. They would be the men successful in all emergencies. It is an empirical fact that in all savage societies, magic and outstanding personalities go hand in hand. Thus magic also coincides with personal success, skill, courage, and mental power. No wonder that it is considered a source of success." [11]

The magical act is not only expressed in a different language from the language of ordinary life, but also by an actor who is believed to be far above ordinary men, and whose skill in expression of the spell is the result of long and hard training. It is also staged with great care. The magical spell is uttered only "in full ritual performance; in teaching, that is, when the accredited magician imparts his knowledge to his successor, and at funerary wakes." It is not proper for laymen to repeat, or even discuss the magical spells, although most of the texts of public magic are well known and comprehensible to the community. And, whenever magicians themselves consented to recite their spells for the ethnographer, they seldom repeated them slowly, piece-meal, or in an ordinary voice, but as a whole. This, too, is the way spells are taught. The magician recites them over and over again to his pupil, who must learn to give them in full. For in the eyes of the Trobrianders and their magicians, it is the formal presentation, the *way* a spell is given, which gives the magical imprint to the language.

In his "Digression on the General Theory of Magical Language," Malinowsky compares the language of childhood with that of magic.[12] All language in its earliest function within the context of infantile helplessness is proto-magical and pragmatic. It is pragmatic in that it works through the appeal to the child's human surroundings; it is "proto-magical" in that it contains all the emotional dependence of the child on those to whom it appeals through sound. Thus, the development of speech in humanity must have, "in its fundamental principles, been of the same type as the development of speech within the life history of the individual." And this, Malinowski holds, is "the only sound scientific approach to the genetic problems of language as also of other aspects of culture." From his earliest days, man uses speech in the conviction that "the knowledge of a name, the correct use of a verb, the right application of a particle, have a mystical power which transcends the mere utilitarian convenience of such words in communication from man to man." [13]

"The child actually exercises a quasi-magical influence" over its environment. He speaks a word, and his needs are satisfied by the adults around him. At the same time his "mastery over reality, both technical and social, grows side by side with the knowledge of how to use words. Whether you watch apprenticeship in some craft within a primitive community or in our own society, you always see that familiarity with the name of a thing is the direct outcome of familiarity with how to use this thing." The same is true of social relationships, for here too the mastery of "social aspect and social terminology runs parallel." [14] Men soon learn that the value of a word, the binding force of a formula, is at the very foundation of reliability in human relations, for the sacredness of words and their socially sanctioned inviolability are absolutely necessary to the existence of social order.

The organizing function of magic on the community can be seen in the effect of the spell on the magician himself, on his retinue and on all those who work with him, under him, and by him. It is this influence of magic on the community practicing it which molds ritual and language, as this in turn molds the community. If the magician were to stop mumbling his incantations a complete disorganization of the work of the whole community would follow. For the magician and his art form the main organizing force in gardening. The magician is the leader who initiates and supervises the successive phases of garden work. He alone wields the *mana* which resides in words. Every member of the community is conscious of each spell being performed. Everyone, even the children, is familiar with the wording of each spell and considers the recitation of the spell as the most important event in tribal activity.

The magician is equally aware of his relationship to his audience. He believes he is uttering his spells for the benefit of the whole community. He voices their hope, pride, and belief in its power. He keeps the traditional charter of the society alive as he reenacts the glory of their ancestors and the greatness of the social principles they personify. In each generation the words of the spell and the staging of the recital are possessed and controlled by the magician in office. He must transmit the content of the spells, and the forms of their enactment, to successors. Thus, the magician, the bearer of the word in primitive society, does not act as a passive receptacle of tradition, but as an actor, or agent, whose proper use of symbols determines the fate of the community.

THE RELEVANCE OF MALINOWSKI'S TRIBAL CONTEXT OF SITUATION
TO COMMUNICATION IN MODERN SOCIETY

In Malinowski, communication is so central to his theory of society that it can properly be called a social theory of communication. The archaic heritage of language, which survives in Freud's theory as libidinal cathexis, and language as a medium in which forms of sociation manifest themselves, as in Simmel, has now been supplanted by a theory in which language becomes an organizing principle of society. Words, and particularly their *mana,* in Malinowski are a constituent, not a residual, part of community life. We seem at last to be on the road to a *sociological* theory of communication, based on the tribal use of words in magic. This is a great step forward in our search for a sociological model of communication, for now we begin to look at the social function of language as a kind of symbolic enactment which affects social organization.

But it is a step the sociologist must take with great caution. For, in subordinating communication to magic, and tribal magic alone, Malinowski reduces language to its purely tribal and collective aspects. The magician has no competitors and thus develops no skill whatever in debate, disputation, argument, and discussion. He does not, like the modern user of symbols, have to persuade audiences whose ear is sought by many (and often very different and deeply hostile) speakers. Nor does he open ends, purposes, and values, to examination or prepare himself to defend the relationship between ends and means in free, open, and informed discussion. The members of the magician's tribal audience know what they want; what they do not know is how to get it, or if they know, they are not sure they can endure the hardships which must be suffered to obtain it. The community goal of gardening is clear to all. What is not clear to the leaders of the community (as to the people themselves) is whether all will work hard enough to insure the survival of the community.

In complex society we possess many corporate identities which are not limited to the single tribal identity which Malinowski found to be so common among the Trobrianders. Successful appeals in our society must destroy old beliefs, offer us passage from old to new, and finally replace the old with the new. We do the first through such symbolic processes as "desanctification," and victimage; the second we do through metaphor (and all kinds of bridging devices) by which we pass from one set of meanings to another; and, finally, we sanctify symbols we believe are necessary to uphold community order. But we do this under conditions where many institutions are in open conflict. Symbols, then, among us, are both positive *and* negative, and the "context of situation" is characterized by bickering, argument, disputation, joking, ridicule, cursing, blessing, obscenity, blasphemy, disagreement, competition, rivalry, conflict, and war. At best, in our society, agreement is a *resolution*, and a precarious one at that, of deep-seated difference, hostility, and hate.[15]

Malinowski's society is an authoritarian society, and his explanation of the function of language is true only to the extent that communication is controlled. As a result, many kinds of communication common to our society do not exist among the Trobrianders. Joking and all forms of the comic, which are used so much in our society, and, indeed, in every society, authoritarian and democratic alike, are not mentioned. Thus, the function of language in disagreement, as well as in agreement—the whole dialectic and rhetorical function—is completely neglected; relationships of the kind we. prize so highly in democratic society—namely, those based on rules which are agreed to by equals, which can be broken at any moment, and which are upheld by umpires agreed to by both sides—are nonexistent. As in Freud's family, there are no equals among the Trobrianders.[16] And, if the tribe is not so patriarchal as Freud's family, neither is it imbued with the hostility and aggression we experience so often in our own lives in modern society.

Nor is there any explanation of the relationship between language and social change. Social organization is discussed as a kind of "charter" whose effects are derived from past myths of origin. But if tradition and the past determine so much of Trobriand life, how are problems in the present met? And if the past determines so much of the present, what is the function of goals, ends, and purpose? The Trobrianders must have goals, if only to organize action in a present. Goals can, of course, be made out of traditions whose "recapture" in a future will insure the well-being of the tribe, but Malinowski tells us little about goals, and we are left to assume that his Trobrianders need no future because they have a past. Thus, we are left with the unsolved problem, common to all genetic theory, of knowing what symbols used in a present mean only by how they were used in a past which can be studied only from what we know in a present [17] which is a residual of a past we can only "recall" but never observe.

Malinowski's past, unlike the single archaic past of Freud or Jung, exists both in the myths of the tribe and the childhood of the adult individual. But he equates the language of the child with the language of magic, and reifies his images of culture into a kind of substance which is both the cause and effect of language. Thus, we hear that "culture defines," "limits," or "determines," what the child does. "The degree to which earliest behavior is molded, the manner in which words and acts are woven into infantile expression, allow tradition to influence the young organization through its human surroundings." [18] Who, or what, "allows" tradition? Culture is not "transmitted" like current in a wire; it is taught in human enactment which is created and staged by individuals within the community who are trained, and who train others, in such cultural presentation. *How* culture is internalized, or taught, not that it *is,* is what we must explain.

In Malinowski's scheme we are never quite sure whether culture is a form, a force, or a process. Malinowski tells us that he is not going to fall, as Durkheim did, into the errors of reifying some kind of Hegelian Absolute which "embodies" itself in the community. Durkheim's simple formula that God is society, "that the substance of the Absolute is nothing but the feeling of dependence which man, intoxicated by the dionysiac influence of a religiously effervescent crowd concretises into sacred entities and sacred beings . . . is to be avoided. In its place there will be a functional 'behaviouristic' account of the acculturization of a 'gradual process of moulding' through the 'traditional mechanisms such as speech, technology, (and) mode of social intercourse.' " By this process of molding is meant "the effect of traditional cultural modes and norms upon the growing organism." Thus, in regard to speech, the individual finds "within his culture certain crystallised, traditionally standardised types of speech, with the language of technology and science at one end, and the language of sacrament, prayer, magical formula, advertisement and political oratory at the other." [19]

But if speech "moulds" a society, who, or what, molds speech? And how does speech mold the individual, or society? If we say "society," we are trapped in a meaningless circle, for so long as we do not define what we mean by society, we cannot use the term to define language. Nor do we break out of the circle of "defining" one unknown by another, by saying, as Malinowski does, that community activity (such as work and speech) run parallel to each other. This brings us back again into all the difficulties of the correspondence theory which Dewey, Mead, and James fought against to develop a psychology which would break down the dualism between a subjective mind and an objective world, in which impressions and things correspond to each other. If language and society run parallel, *how* do we get from one to the other? For, by definition, parallels never meet.

Nor does it help to say that in practical speech men learn meaning by the ease with which they can refer what they are doing to the names they give to their acts. This presumes that we act, and then name what we are doing. But this overlooks the fact that how we name things and acts determines whether or not we do them, and how we feel as we do about them. For, by Malinowski's own admission, the individual "finds within his culture" fixed meanings such as names, which are drilled into the individual (by a process never made clear) who then knows what to do because he knows how things and events are named. Even on the simplest levels of motor activity, we can act together with others only because we communicate with them. Thus, if the referent of a word is an act, it is also another word. We *select* the stimuli we want to respond to, because we attach names to things and events which goad us—and others—to action.

Thus, the greatest flaw in Malinowski's theory of language, and the one that reduces the usefulness of his scheme to a rather elementary level, is his neglect of form in language. He does not seem to realize that *how* a thing is said—the forms of talk, not the forms of experience—is a part of its meaning. For if we say that language affects society (and certainly Malinowski says this about magical language) then we must show what in language itself creates such an effect. Language has many referents in work, play, worship, and civic affairs, but it also has another, and equally powerful referent, in itself as an art of expression. Words, and, indeed, all expressions of form, are *created,* as well as used. And they are created in terms of their own rules by special bodies of men and women called artists who work within the social institution known as art. Until we say something about art, we can say nothing about the internalization within the individual of the traditions and customs which depend, like everything else in society, on how they are communicated.

Malinowski's world is a world without communication, because it is a world without artists. We are told that in

modern art criticism it is customary to regard a work of art as an individual message from the creative artist to his audience, the expression of an emotional or intellectual state translated through the work of art from one man to another. . . . Sociologically [this idea of art] is always incorrect. . . . [for] primitive art is invariably a popular or folk creation. The artist takes over the tradition of his tribe and merely reproduces the carving, the song, the tribal mystery play. The individual who thus reproduces a traditional work always adds something to it, modifies it in reproduction. These small individual quotas, embodied and condensed in the gradually growing tradition, integrate and become part of the body of artistic production. The individual quotas are determined not only by the personality, inspiration, or creative talent of the individual contributor but also by the manifold associations of art with its context. The fact that a carved idol is the object of dogmatic and religious belief and of religious ritual defines to a large extent its shape, size, and material. The fact that a mystery play is an important center of tribal life influences the way in which it is modified and in which it has to be reproduced.[20]

Reduction of art to magic, the artist to the magician, society to the tribe, and communication to a kind of social transmission of traditions which is both cause and effect of society simply violates common sense (to say nothing of canons of theoretical construction). For we know that symbolic action, communication, depends on the *creation* as well as the transmission of symbols. We know that symbols are created in forms whose effects are determined by the principles of art and rhetoric, as well as by the effects of religion, society, God, or the state. We know, too, that symbols are created by men called artists who have established, and who sustain, the institution of art in society. Why then do we not look at art and the men who create it instead of reducing them to magicians, neurotics, or propagandists? For, if we disregard art, we cannot have a social theory of communication, because we have disregarded the observable facts of sociation—namely, the forms in which we express ourselves as we enact our roles in the community.

Notes

[1] Bronislaw Malinowski, "The Problem of Meaning in Primitive Languages," in *The Meaning of Meaning: A Study of the Influence of Language upon Thought and of the Science of Symbolism*, by C. K. Ogden and I. A. Richards (New York: Harcourt, Brace, 1945), p. 310.

[2] Malinowski argues that it would be hardly an "exaggeration to say that 99 per cent of all linguistic work has been inspired by the study of dead languages or at best of written records torn completely out of any context of situation." *Ibid.*, p. 308.

[3] *Ibid.*, p. 309.

[4] *Ibid.*, p. 313.

[5] *Ibid.*, p. 314.

[6] *Ibid.*, p. 316.

[7] It is interesting to note that Simmel found such "superficial" discourse to be characteristic of the most sophisticated society Europe produced; the courtiers of the *ancien régime*, among whom "sociability attained perhaps its most sovereign expression." See *The Sociology of Georg Simmel*, edited by Kurt H. Wolff (Glencoe, Ill.: The Free Press, 1950), p. 55.

[8] Bronislaw Malinowski, *Coral Gardens and Their Magic* (2 vols.; New York: American Book Company, n.d.), Vol. II, p. 53.

[9] This is a shift from Malinowski's earlier position in *The Meaning of Meaning*.

"I am laying considerable stress on this because, in (*The Meaning of Meaning*) I opposed civilized and scientific to primitive speech, and argued as if the theoretical uses of words in modern philosophic and scientific writing were completely detached from their pragmatic sources. This was an error, and a serious error at that." See *Coral Gardens and Their Magic*, Vol. II, p. 58.

[10] *Ibid.*, Vol. II, pp. 216–217.

[11] Bronislaw Malinowski, *Magic, Science and Religion and Other Essays*, Selected, and with an Introduction by Robert Redfield (Glencoe, Ill.: The Free Press, 1948), p. 63.

[12] See *Coral Gardens*, Vol. II, pp. 231–240.

[13] *Ibid.*, p. 233.

[14] *Ibid.*

[15] This point is elaborated in Chapter II, "Literature as Magical Art" in my book, *Language and Literature in Society: A Sociological Essay on Theory and Method in the Interpretation of Linguistic Symbols with a Bibliographical guide to the Sociology of Literature* (Chicago, Illinois: Univ. of Chicago Press, 1953; reprinted by The Bedminster Press, New York, 1961).

[16] Radcliffe-Brown sensed this flaw in the anthropological view of tribal life. In his essay, "On Joking Relationships," he points out how carefully "permitted disrespect" is sanctioned in tribal life. "The alternative to [relations] of extreme mutual respect and restraint is the joking relationship, one, that is, of mutual disrespect and licence. Any serious hostility is prevented by the playful antagonism of teasing, and this in its regular repetition is a constant expressor or reminder of that social disjunction which is one of the essential components of the relation, while the social conjunction is maintained by the friendliness that takes no offence at insult." See A. R. Radcliffe-Brown, *Structure and Function in Primitive Society: Essays and Addresses* (London: Cohen and West, Ltd., 1952), p. 92.

[17] Both Dewey and Mead, and particularly Mead, attacked genetic theories of communication at this point, as the title of Mead's work indicates. See George Herbert Mead, *The Philosophy of the Present,* edited by Arthur E. Murphy, with Prefatory Remarks by John Dewey (Chicago and London: Open Court Publishing Company, 1932).

[18] See Malinowski's article, "Culture," in the *Encyclopaedia of the Social Sciences* (New York: The Macmillan Company, 1937), for his discussion of this. Quotation here is from Vol. IV, p. 642.

[19] See *Coral Gardens*, Vol. II, p. 236, for the quotations in this paragraph.

[20] Malinowski, "Culture," *Encyclopaedia of the Social Sciences*, Vol. IV, p. 645.

PART TWO

The Self and Society as Determined by Communication in James, Dewey, and Mead

4

Society As Determined by Communication: Dewey's Theory of Art as Communication

A MERICAN SOCIAL THINKERS, beginning with Ward and James, pointed out that while it was incontestable that genetic forces determined social interaction, it was equally true that teleological forces affected conduct. In his *Dynamic Sociology* of 1883, Ward argued that all social action involves efforts to attain desired ends, and such ends are present in the mind before action is attempted.[1] He argued, too, that we must think of interaction in society in terms of action, not process, force, or motion. And the kind of action most characteristic of man in society is invention and art.

The intellectual element, though commonly called a force, is not in reality such. It is not comparable with the other true psychic forces. . . . The intellect only guides [psychic forces] in such a manner as to secure maximum results. It also brings other natural forces to their aid and thus increases the effects. The general process by which all this is done is that of *invention*, the product is *art*, and, therefore the faculty may be called the *inventive* faculty, and the phenomena produced, *artificial* phenomena.[2]

Ward, like James and Dewey, argued that a fully developed science of sociology and psychology could develop only if ends, values, and purpose could be studied empirically. It was easy enough to expose the fallacies of theories of human conduct which explained all that man did in the present by what he had done in the past. But from an empirical point of view, the question of how we could know a past was no different from how we could know a future. It was really a question (for the student of society, at least) of how knowledge of the past or of the future could be ordered and demonstrated within some kind of social context. For, if, as Ward taught in his theory of telesis, social ends are present in the mind before action is attempted, what are the social data of such ends? How can we establish hypotheses about ends, values, and purpose, which are "in" the mind?

History, biology, religion, Freudian psychology, and even nineteenth-

century physical science, various as were their conclusions and their methods, were based in a common belief that the past determined the present
and the future. Historians also taught that we could be objective about the
past because the "facts" of the past, the way it "really happened," could be
known. But as attacks on "historical reality" increased, and as the logic
of evolutionary thought came under attack, the question of why knowledge of the past is any less a dramatic reconstruction than knowledge of
the future was raised more frequently. Oakeshott and Croce (among
others) insisted that what we know of the past is really what we know
of the present, and, no matter how we dress up our history and marshal
our "facts" of the past, we are really talking about the present. And, thus,
as Croce insisted, all history is contemporary history.[3]

The argument that the past could become an object of consciousness
while the present and the future could not, because only the past existed
since it had "happened" (and thus could be viewed with objectivity) overlooked the fact that the past, like the future, existed only in symbols. Freud
and indeed all physical and natural scientists, argued that consciousness
could not have any goals outside those determined by instincts or drives.
The future was already fated or determined by the past, and to the degree
one knew the past, he could know the present, and "trends" of the future.
This was not simply a "metaphysical" problem. For (as the work of
Freud, Jung, Sumner, and Malinowski, with their concepts of archaic
heritages, mores, and social charters, make clear) if we assume that a
society was formed in some past moment of origin, then this moment will
be studied as the "representative case" of social order in that society.

Thus, when Malinowski discusses the function of myth in society, he
says: "Myth . . . still lives in present-day life . . . as justification by prec-
edent, [it] supplies a retrospective pattern of moral values, sociological
order, and magical belief. . . . The function of myth, briefly, is to
strengthen tradition and endow it with a greater value and prestige by
tracing it back to a higher, better, more supernatural reality of initial
events."[4] But he never makes clear just how myth functions in solving
problems which tradition has failed to solve.[5] He admits that there are
moments of "sociological strain," and that the power of myth is "constantly regenerated," but we look in vain for any explanation of how this
regeneration takes place, and where we do find reference to social change
in Malinowski, such change, like Hegel's Absolute is both cause and effect.
Historical change "creates its mythology." The obvious question over how

a social process, change, becomes suddenly an agent which can effect itself is never answered, because it is never asked.

Radical European thinkers like Sorel agreed with Ward that we cannot discuss social causation in terms of a past alone. In his writings from 1900 to 1910, Sorel argued that limiting myths to primitive society, and relegating them to the past, was based on a complete misunderstanding of the role of myth in society. In his "Letter to Daniel Halevy," [6] he says "To say that we are acting, implies that we are creating an imaginary world placed ahead of the present world and composed of movements which depend entirely on us. In this way our freedom becomes perfectly intelligible." Thus, Sorel agreed with Malinowski and Durkheim that myths were "collective representations," but he places the power of myth in its depiction, through formed images, of future ends of social acts. This shifts emphasis from a "social bond" to "social myths" which are created and used in a highly partisan manner.

Sorel argued further that the myth must be judged as a means of acting on the present. Any discussion of how myth can be taken literally as future history was, for him, simply nonsense. The power of the idea of a general strike, which was to take place sometime in the future, was that it "embraced all the aspirations of Socialism, and it has given to the whole body of Revolutionary thought a precision and a rigidity which no other method of thought could have given. . . . The question whether the general strike is a partial reality, or only a product of popular imagination, is of little importance. All that is necessary to know is whether the general strike contains everything that the Socialist doctrine expects of the revolutionary proletariat." [7] That is, if we think of social order as a drama of struggle between classes, the vision of the future is as real as the history of the past, indeed, for the proletarian, more real, because it is the means by which he invests action in a present with meaning, and thus creates attitudes necessary to action in the present.

Sorel, and later Mannheim in his *Ideology and Utopia,* judged mythical, utopian, and ideological forms of expression as a means to action in the present. But neither—certainly not Sorel or Burckhardt—believed that the future could be predicted or known in the same way nature can be known in the physical sciences. [8] Constructions of the future would always be provisional at best. Sorel argued, too, that the "truth" of social myths could be determined only by how they helped men act in, not think about, society. The task of the student of society, Sorel believed, was not to spin

out learned theories about economics, history, and philosophy, but to discover ways of thinking about how men *act* in society. We are not, he says,
"on the plane of theories, and we can remain on the level of observable
facts." These facts are the observable forms of expression, the forms of
expression men use to communicate with one another as they act together
to attain desired ends.[9]

JAMES' PRAGMATIC APPROACH TO RELIGIOUS EXPRESSION:

HIS VIEWS ON HUMAN DOCUMENTS

After finishing his *Psychology,* James turned to a study of symbolic action
in his *Varieties of Religious Experience,*[10] which he subtitled "A Study in
Human Nature." He argues at the very outset that the observable facts
of religious experience are its forms of expression, as these are recorded
in literature and in works of piety and autobiography.

I must confine myself to those more developed subjective phenomena recorded in
literature produced by articulate and fully self-conscious men, in works of piety and
autobiography. Interesting as the origins and early stages of a subject always are, yet
when one seeks earnestly for its full significance, one must always look to its more
completely evolved and perfect forms. It follows from this that the documents that
will concern us will be those of the men who were most accomplished in the religious
life and best able to give an intelligible account of their ideas and motives. These
men, of course, are either comparatively modern writers, or else such earlier ones as
have become religious classics. The *documents humains* which we shall find most
instructive need not then be sought for in the haunts of special erudition—they lie
along the beaten highways; and this circumstance, which flows so naturally from the
character of our problem, ... I may take my citations, my sentences and paragraphs of personal confession, from books that most of you at some time will have
had already in your hands, and yet this will be no detriment to the value of my
conclusions.[11]

James rejects Freud's reduction of religious expression to a series of
sexual puns. He argues, as does Burke a generation later, that the observable facts of the content of religious consciousness are the ways in which
this consciousness is expressed. Before we make *any* inferences about religious expression, we must accept it at face value. This requires a study of
religious texts of all kinds, but specifically those which record the religious
experience of individuals in their search for God. "It is true," James explains in the long footnote [12] to his discussion of the connection between
religion and sex, "that in the vast collection of religious phenomena, some

are disguisedly amatory—e.g., sex-deities and obscene rites in polytheism, and ecstatic feelings of union with the Saviour in a few Christian mystics." But when we examine religious expression, we find images of eating, drinking, and even breathing, used as frequently and intensively as images drawn from sexual experience.

Why not, then, he asks, "equally call religion an aberration of the digestive [or respiratory] function, and prove one's point by the worship of Bacchus and Ceres, or by the ecstatic feelings of some other saints about the Eucharist?" The Bible is full of language of respiratory oppression. We "hunger and thirst" after righteousness; we "find the Lord a sweet savor"; we "taste and see that he is good." "Spiritual milk for American babes drawn from the breasts of both testaments," is a subtitle of the New England Primer. Indeed, "Christian devotional literature . . . quite floats in milk, thought of from the point of view, not of the mother, but of the greedy babe." It also abounds in respiratory images. "Hide not thine ear at my breathing; my groaning is not hid from thee; my heart panteth, my strength faileth me; my bones are hot with my roaring all the night long; . . . ." In certain non-Christian countries, regulation and control of breathing is the foundation of religious discipline.

"Religious language," James stresses, "clothes itself in such poor symbols as our life affords, and the whole organism gives overtones of comment whenever the mind is strongly stirred to expression. . . . The plain truth is that to interpret religion one must in the end look at the immediate content of the religious consciousness." The moment we do this, James argues, we see how completely religious and sexual consciousness, *as they are expressed,* are disconnected. "Everything about the two things differs, objects, moods, faculties concerned, and acts impelled to. Any *general* assimilation is simply impossible: what we find most often is complete hostility and contrast." [13] Ascribing religious expression to the mechanics of the body, as by assuming that the chemical contributions to the blood of the brain by the sex organs induce religious ecstasy may or may not be true. Yet, even if true, this mechanical theory tells us nothing about the meaning of religion in human action. This can be found only in the expression, the symbolization, of religious experience.

As American pragmatists who followed James (and more recently European existentialists) discovered, symbolic analysis could not be related to social analysis, until some theory of the act and the function of symbols in the act was developed. This required nothing less than a complete reconstruction of social philosophy. But before reconstruction could begin, much had to be destroyed. James, Dewey, and Mead soon found that they could not make clear what they meant by symbolic expression as a problem-solving process until they made clear how and why they differed from the supernaturalists in theology and the naturalists in biology, as well as mechanists in science who confused scientific knowledge with mathematical knowledge.[14] Obviously, if human conduct in society was determined wholly by God, nature (through evolutionary adaptation), the Absolute, the Idea, or by ideologies and utopias, in some kind of process, then interaction between human beings could be nothing but some kind of manifestation of the laws, divine or otherwise, which determined this process.

It mattered little, from the pragmatic view, what kind of "law" was supposed to determine conduct if we could not study the manifestations of these laws in some kind of concrete manifestation of the operation of the law. And the presumption in biology and the physical sciences of 1875 that nature (as, among theologians, God) operated rationally (that is, according to law) but that man alone acted irrationally, made the scientific study of man impossible. As we have seen, Freud and Simmel, and even Malinowski, seemed to think that when they related man to nature they were being "scientific"—just as the older theologians thought that only when they were relating man to a supernatural being whose truths were revealed, were they being religious.

James had no objection to relating man to nature or to discussing the ends men had in their minds before they acted, but he thought the relationship ought to be demonstrated in terms of human experience. In the very last paragraph of his *Psychology,* he said: "The causes of our mental structure are doubtless natural, and connected, like all our other peculiarities, with those of our nervous structure." But, he warned in the closing sentence, the acts of man in society "have all grown up in ways of which at present we can give no account. Even in the clearest parts of Psychology our insight is insignificant enough. And the more sincerely one seeks to trace the actual course of *psychogenesis,* the steps by which as a race we may have come by the peculiar mental attributes which we possess, the more clearly one perceives the slowly gathering twilight close to utter night."

In Chapter XXVIII, the last chapter of his *Psychology,* James states clearly that he does not believe that "the features of our organic mental structure [can] be explained at all by our conscious intercourse with the outer environment." He asserts, too, that, "taking the word experience as it is universally understood, the experience of the race can no more account for our necessary or *a priori* judgments than the experience of the individual can." He then sums up his position as follows: "On the whole, then, the account which the apriorists give of the *facts* is that which I defend; although I should contend (as will hereafter appear) for a naturalistic view of their *cause.*" That is, for James, the *expression* of emotions and values are the data of the states of consciousness he believes to be the proper study of psychology.

What James is saying in this long footnote on language is that all we know about religious experience is what people have *said* about it. There may be (indeed, there probably is) some kind of religious experience behind the veil of words, but all we can really observe is what religious people say, or what they accept in what others have said, about their religious experience. Thus, when James says that to "interpret religion one must in the end look at the immediate content of the religious consciousness," he means that we must look at religious expression. It may be true, or it may be untrue, that religious experience depends on the sexual organs, the spleen, the pancreas, or the kidneys, but what are the data of such dependence? All materialistic arguments lose their "points in evaporating into a vague general assertion of the dependence, *somehow,* of the mind upon the body." For purposes of a science of society then, how people express themselves about experience, and specifically, religious experience, *is* their experience.[15]

COMMUNICATION, ART, AND SOCIETY IN DEWEY

In recapitulating his own life as a philosopher and as a leader of American pragmatism, John Dewey said he had never been interested only in problems of cognition and knowledge, but in establishing the sphere of values, of human desires and aims, on the same basis and in an analogous form as the system of knowledge. In his early writings on education Dewey searched for ways to train the emotions, as well as the intellect. The good society must have right emotions, as well as right thoughts. In his review in 1893 of Bosanquet's *History of Aesthetic,* he argued that the problem for his generation of students of society would be the reconciliation of emotion and reason in some kind of model of sociation which would break down the false dualism of a mind suffused with thought and emotion, and a matter determined by motion which was independent of man's will.

Dewey pointed out that while all knowledge was based on communication, we know very little about communication.[16] It is only by the naming of events that we make thought and experiment possible. Events when once they are named, lead an independent and double life. In addition to their original existence, they are subject to ideal experimentation: their meanings may be infinitely combined and rearranged in imagination, and the outcome of this inner experimentation—which is thought—may issue forth in interaction with crude or raw events. Language thus becomes the "tool of tools," for without well-developed systems of expression individuals cannot relate, because they cannot act together. In the social studies, then, we need to "discourse about discourse."

In Chapter Five, "Nature, Communication, and Meaning," of *Experience and Nature*,[17] Dewey begins his discussion of symbolic action by pointing out that the character of experience which has been most systematically ignored by philosophy is the "extent to which it is saturated with the results of social intercourse and communication." Because of this refusal to study communication in society, "meanings have either been denied all objective validity, or have been treated as miraculous extranatural intrusions." [18] But this is wrong, for language must be recognized as "the instrument of social cooperation and mutual participation" by which continuity is established between natural events and the origin and development of meanings. Communication is then a naturalistic link which, when properly understood, will do away with the division of experience into two worlds, one physical and one ideal.

But how are we to study communication in society, and what kinds of experience of social cooperation and mutual participation are we to study? We must study art, for the highest (because most complete) incorporation of natural forces and operations in experience is found in art. Normal artistic experience involves bringing to a better balance than is found elsewhere in either nature or experience the consummatory and instrumental phases of events. Art thus represents the culminating event of nature as well as the climax of experience. Art invests experience with meaning, and until we have meaning we cannot communicate and thus can have no social relationships. We cannot study the acts of men in society if we cannot study meanings, values, ends, or purposes, for these determine the kinds of fulfillment which make acting possible because they infuse every phase of the act with a sense of achievement.

Experience in society takes on meaning only when the "precarious, novel, irregular" and the "settled, assured, and uniform" are brought together in union. This is the function of art in society, for "wherever there is art the contingent and ongoing no longer work at cross purposes with the formal and recurrent but commingle in harmony." The distinguishing feature of conscious experience is that "in it the instruments and the final, meanings that are signs and clews and meanings that are immediately possessed, suffered, and enjoyed, come together in one." In sum, art is "solvent union of the generic, recurrent, ordered, established phase of nature with its phase that is incomplete, going on, and hence still uncertain, contingent, novel, particular. . . ." Art is, therefore, unique among the acts of men because it is both instrumental and consummatory. It is instrumental because it liberates men to enjoy new satisfying events. The eternal quality of great art "is its renewed instrumentality for further consummatory experience." [19]

Thus in Dewey we find the function of art in society central to his image of social action. The key to an understanding of society is to be sought in art, because art is the realm of communication in which *completed* acts are expressed. That this expression is only symbolic and, therefore, "unreal," or at least "outside of experience" of the kind open to scientific knowledge—the view held, and still held, by those who confuse science with mathematics—seemed irrelevant to Dewey, as it did to James and Mead. For the future in any description of an act is always symbolic. Even a statistical trend assumes a point of arrival as well as a point of departure, and motion is studied in "fields" which have forms whose beginning and end determine the "path" taken by what is moving. That is, a "tendency" —whether of an instinct or a particle moving in space—must have a "tendency" to arrive at a goal, as well as depart from a point of origin.

By stressing the study of ends in art and arguing that the ends of acts were open to empiric investigation, Dewey rescued the social studies from dependence on definitions of the social taken from religious ritual, physical process, myth and magic, biological evolution, or the social organization of the primitive tribe. The proper study of man was the study of how men communicated, and the representative example to be studied in communication was art.[20] There are, then, in Dewey's scheme, three key terms: communication, society, and art. None of these terms can be defined alone; each depends on the other, and there are many areas of "overlap" in the experience to which these terms apply. Yet if any of the three is to have any theoretical function as an independent variable, it must be capable of definition in its own terms. Unless we do this, one term—either communication, society, or art—becomes dominant, and we are faced again with another version of an Absolute which is both cause and effect of its own manifestations. Dewey understood that it mattered little whether we called our absolutes, God, Nature, Society, Sex, or Mind; they all placed the "laws" of social experience beyond communication, and thus beyond experience.

"Nature, Communication, and Meaning" [21] is probably Dewey's definitive discussion on communication. How is communication defined, and what specific *form* of communication does he select, or create, as his model for the structure and function of communication in society? And what is the nature of the relationship between society *and* communication *and* art? He begins by saying that when communication takes place, "all natural events are subject to reconsideration and revision: they are readapted to meet the requirements of conversation, whether it be public discourse or that preliminary discourse termed thinking." The requirements of conversation are, above all, experimentation with ideas and the ends of action, because naming through symbols makes the "inner experimentation—which is thought—" possible. For where communication exists, "things in acquiring meaning, thereby acquire representatives, surrogates, signs and implicates, which are infinitely more amenable to management, more permanent and more accommodating than events in their first estate." [22]

But if communication liberates "brute efficiencies" and the purely utilitarian phases of conduct for wider contexts in experience, so too does it remove "qualitative immediacies" from the domination of sensation and passion. In communication

qualitative immediacies cease to be dumbly rapturous, a possession that is obsessive and an incorporation that involves submergence: conditions found in sensations and passions. They become capable of survey, contemplation, and ideal or logical elaboration. . . . Even the dumb pang of an ache achieves a significant existence when it can be designated and descanted upon; it ceases to be merely oppressive and becomes important; it gains importance, because it becomes representative; it has the dignity of an office. [23]

Thus, psychic events have language for one of their conditions, just as organic "psycho-physical" actions attain a perceptible character through "their concretion in discourse." Inner dialogue, what we call soliloquy, seems to be locked within the self, but soliloquy is the "product and reflect of converse with others." That is, "social communication" is basic, and soliloquy is derived from it. For "if we had not talked with others and they with us, we should never talk to and with ourselves." Because of the give and take of conversation in society,

various organic attitudes become an assemblage of persons engaged in converse, conferring with one another, exchanging distinctive experiences, listening to one another, over-hearing unwelcome remarks, accusing and excusing. Through speech, a person dramatically identifies himself with potential acts and deeds; he plays many roles, not in successive stages of life but in a contemporaneously enacted drama. Thus mind emerges.[24]

At this point, Dewey realizes that he is perilously close to saying that the structure of discourse is the structure of things, and thus in danger of leading us back into the realist position that a word vouches for, or contains, the reality of its meaning. For, if we say that symbols which arise in conversation determine meaning, then why not, as the realists and medieval rhetoricians did, simply study grammar and rhetoric, the structure and function of words, as the structure of reality itself? Dewey insists that he is not denying the reality of things. The structure of discourse cannot be taken for the structure of things but as "forms which things assume under the pressure and opportunity of social cooperation and exchange." For the import of logical and rational meanings is the consequence of "social interactions, of companionship, mutual assistance, directed and concerted in fighting, festivity, and work." [25]

But if we explain communication by society, how are we to think of society, and how does action in society invent symbols with meaning? This is done through interaction, which is defined as an "operative relationship." Language is a mode of interaction of at least two beings, a speaker and a hearer, and it also presupposes an organized group to which the hearer and the speaker belong and from whom they have acquired their habits of speech. Meaning is thus never personal in a private and exclusive sense. Primarily, meaning is intent; secondarily, the signification of our ability to make possible and fulfill shared cooperation.

If we consider the form or scheme of the situation in which meaning and understanding occur, we find an involved simultaneous presence and cross-reference of immediacy and efficiency, overt actuality and potentiality, the consummatory and the instrumental. A in making a request of B, at the same time makes the incipient and preparatory response of receiving the thing at the hands of B; he performs in readiness, the consummatory act. B's understanding of the meaning of what A says, instead of being a mere reaction to the sound, is in anticipation of a consequence, while it is also an immediate activity of eyes, legs, and hands in getting and giving [an object] to A. [An object] is the thing which it immediately is, and it also is a means of a conclusion. All this is directly involved in the existence of intelligible speech.[26]

Thus *all* things have a phase of potential communicability. The act of striving to bring potential consequences existentially into the world "may be commuted into esthetic enjoyed possession of form." Thus, while communication is instrumental it is also an immediate enhancement of life, enjoyed for its own sake. But even in consummatory moments, as in a purely social greeting, such a moment becomes a social ceremonial with its prescribed forms and rites. In such ceremonies there is an intense feeling of sharing and belonging to a whole. "Forms of language are unrivalled in ability to create this sense, at first with direct participation on the part of an audience; and then, as literary forms develop, through imaginative identification." [27] On both levels, meaning is a method of action, a way of using things in shared consummation. Meaning and interpretation always rest on an imputation of potentiality for some consequence.

Meanings are objective because they are modes of natural interaction: "such an interaction, although primarily between organic beings, as includes things and energies external to living creatures." Scientific meanings were "superadded to esthetic and affectional meanings when objects instead of being defined in terms of their consequences in social interactions and discussion were defined in terms of their consequences with respect to one another. This discrimination permitted esthetic and affective objects to be freed from magical imputations, which were due to attributing to them *in rerum natura,* the consequences they had in the transmitted culture of the group." [28] Thus there is much truth in classic philosophy which assigns objectivity to meanings, essences, and ideas. So long as we attribute meanings to their naturalistic origin in communication or communal interaction, and not to God, the Absolute, or the Idea as Essence, we can follow classic thought.

The function of art, the highest form of communication, is to fix "those standards of enjoyment and appreciation with which other things are compared; it selects the objects of future desires; it stimulates effort." This is true of the individual as well as the community. "The level and style of the arts of literature, poetry, ceremony, amusement, and recreation which obtain in a community, furnishing the staple objects of enjoyment in that community, do more than all else to determine the current direc-tion of ideas and endeavors in the community. They supply the meanings in terms of which life is judged, esteemed, and criticized." The highest form of community life is reached when the instrumental and consum-matory are shared in moments of deep communion. When there is a separation of instrumental and final functions (as in science and "fine" art) the good community cannot exist. "When the instrumental and the final functions of communication live together in experience, there exists an intelligence which is the method and reward of the common life, and a society worthy to command affection, admiration, and loyalty." [29]

In the closing pages of Chapter Nine, "Experience, Nature, and Art," Dewey argues that the separation of the instrumental from consummation makes art wholly esoteric, and science simply a matter of "brute efficiency." There are, he argues, but two alternatives.

Either art is a continuation, by means of intelligent selection and arrangement, of natural tendencies of natural events; or art is a peculiar addition to nature springing from something dwelling exclusively within the breast of man, whatever name be given the latter. In the former case, delightfully enhanced perception or esthetic appre-ciation is of the same nature as enjoyment of any object that is consummatory. It is the outcome of a skilled and intelligent art of dealing with natural things for the sake of intensifying, purifying, prolonging, and deepening the satisfactions which they spon-taneously afford. That, in this new process, new meanings develop, and that these afford uniquely new traits and modes of enjoyment is but what happens everywhere in emergent growths.[30]

If we follow aestheticians who assert that fine art has nothing to do with other activities and products, then it has nothing inherently to do with the objects, physical and social, experienced in other situations. "It has an occult source and an esoteric character." And if the qualities of aesthetic experi-ence is by conception unique, then their signification is hidden and special-ized to a high degree. We hear it said that art is the expression of emotion, with the implication that because it is an expressed form, subject-matter is of no significance except as material through which emotion is expressed. In such a statement emotion

either has no significance at all, and it is mere accident that this particular combina-tion of letters is employed; or else, if by emotion is meant the same sort of thing that is called emotion in daily life, the statement is demonstrably false. For emotion in its ordinary sense is something called out *by* objects, not something existing somewhere by itself which then employs material through which to express itself. Emotion is an indication of intimate participation, in a more or less excited way, in some scene of nature or life; it is, so to speak, an attitude or disposition which is a function of objective things.[31]

The origin of the "art-process" lies in "emotional responses spontaneously called out by a situation occurring without any reference to art, and without 'aesthetic' quality save in the sense in which all immediate enjoyment and suffering is esthetic. Economy in use of objective subject-matter may with experienced and trained minds go so far that what is ordinarily called 'representation' is much reduced. But what happens is a highly funded and generalized representation of the formal sources of ordinary emotional experience." This, too, is all that the phrase "significant form" can mean. It denotes a "selection, for sake of emphasis, purity, subtlety, of those forms which give consummatory significance to every-day subject-matters of experience. 'Forms' are not the peculiar property or creation of the esthetic and artistic; they are characters in virtue of which anything meets the requirements of an enjoyable perception." [32]

The artist does not create forms as a God creates a world. He selects and organizes them "in such ways as to enhance, prolong, and purify the perceptual experience." The fact that some objects and situations afford marked perceptual satisfactions is not an accident; "they do so because of their structural properties and relations." An artist

may work with a minimum of analytic recognition of these structures or "forms"; he may select them chiefly by a kind of sympathetic vibration. . . . [Thus the] tendency to composition in terms of the formal characters marks much contemporary art. . . . At their worst these products are "scientific" rather than artistic; technical exercises, sterile and of a new kind of pedantry. At their best they assist in ushering in new modes of art and by education of the organs of perception in new modes of consummatory objects; they enlarge and enrich the world of human vision. . . . The creators of such works of art are entitled, when successful, to the gratitude we give to inventors of microscopes and microphones; in the end, they open new objects to be observed and enjoyed. This is a genuine service; but only an age of combined confusion and conceit will arrogate to works that perform this special utility the exclusive name of fine art.[33]

In summing up his discussion of art in *Experience and Nature,* Dewey tells us that experience

in the form of art, when reflected upon . . . solves more problems which have troubled philosophers and resolves more hard and fast dualisms than any other theme of thought. . . . In creative production, the external and physical world is more than a mere means of external condition of perceptions, ideas, and emotions; it is a subject-matter and sustainer of conscious activity; and thereby exhibits, so that he who runs may read, the fact that consciousness is not a separate realm of being, but is the manifest quality of existence when nature is most free and active.[34]

Even in the moral sphere, art brings moral goods into consciousness. "As empirical fact . . . the arts, those of converse and literary arts which are the enhanced continuation of social converse, have been the means by which goods are brought home to human perception." [35]

After having placed art as a social category, indeed, almost *the* social category, of experience, Dewey turned to a discussion of art. To say that art was the characteristic human experience was only a beginning. For if art was to be thought of as a constituent part of social reality, what in its form and content made it so? That is, if the social was to be understood by art, the "social" could not be defined until art was defined. The social function of art depended on a specific quality of experience in art, just as the function of social experience in art determined the content and form of art. How to define art as experience, and yet not reduce art to "experience" alone and thus fail to bring out the specific quality of art, was the task undertaken in *Art as Experience*.

DEWEY'S CONTRIBUTION TO A SOCIAL THEORY OF COMMUNICATION

We can agree readily enough that society exists in and through communication, and that the social arts of ceremony, festival, and rite, in which the community or an institution within the community presents itself (as drama is presented upon a stage), determine society. We have been told that social life is not a flow or a process, but has its own plots—that such plots have their own movement toward an ending, and have a particular rhythmic movement of their own with a unique quality pervading throughout. And, finally, we are assured that no experience of any kind is a unity unless it has "aesthetic quality."

But if every experience has such quality and "moves toward a close" and ceases only when the energies active in it have done their "proper work"—how do we observe such energies at work, and what is the specific quality of art experience which produces unity? And if it is the form of art, what kind of art form or forms must we select to study as paradigms of the "social arts"? That is, we must do more than say that experience is aesthetic, just as we do more than say it is economic, political, or cultural. In economic discussion we are asked to describe how the forms of exchange, the market as a social institution, and the specific qualities of various types of activity determine our economic life. What, then, are we to say of art as art, so that when we say art is experience, or an expression of society, we can define art as a constituent part of the experience we have already said it is?

In the chapter of *Art as Experience* [36] called "Having an Experience," Dewey argues that aesthetic quality in experience, the quality that rounds out an experience into completeness and unity, is emotional. The structure taken by emotions in communication is dramatic; emotions are experienced as we experience emotions in watching a play. Yet, as so often happens when he has drawn an analogy between drama, conversation, play, or ceremony, and thought or emotion,[37] Dewey does not go on to tell us why or how the emotions actually function within a dramatic structure. He tells us that emotions are "attached" to events and objects in their movements. They are not, "save in pathological instances," private. And even an "objectless" emotion must attach itself to something beyond itself. It cannot simply be "process."

How do emotions "attach" themselves? How does the dramatic structure of the emotion function in terms of its structure? Unfortunately, these questions are not answered. The emotion becomes an agent in itself. Emotion is a "moving and cementing" force. It "selects" what is "congruous" and infuses with its own tone and color whatever it selects, and thus gives qualitative unity to disparate and dissimilar materials. Thus, we are told again *what* having an experience is like—it is like aesthetic experience—but we are not told *what the specific aesthetic quality of experience* is, nor *how* the forms of emotional expression, based on aesthetic experience, operate.

Dewey tries to meet this difficulty by shifting his functional term from attachment to relationship. An experience has form, because it is not just "doing and undergoing in alternation," but expresses them in relationship. By "relationship" is meant "action and its consequences [as] joined in perception." The ability to invest the present with the consequences or future of this present is characteristic of the artist, as it is of the scientist. The artist thinks as "intently and penetratingly" as any scientific inquirer. A painter must consciously undergo the effect of his every brush stroke, or he will not be aware of what he is doing. Thus, making and forming is artistic when the perceived result of its qualities control how the work is formed. The artist above all other men embodies in himself the "attitude of the perceiver" as he works.

The great question concerning form and content, as Dewey states it, is: Does matter come already constituted, and do attempts to create form in which to embody it in communication follow? Or is the work of the artist an effort to form and shape material so that the form itself will be the real substance of the art work? It is obvious that form and content cannot exist apart from each other. *What* the artist expresses is determined by *how* he expresses it. Form, of course, is not found exclusively in art works. Form is a character of all experience. We arrange events and objects with reference to the ends, purposes, and values we struggle to reach. Art simply "enacts more deliberately and fully" the ways in which we organize unity within a field of perception or experience. Form then is the quality of experience which "carries" experience to its "own integral fulfillment." In this view, therefore, form is not imposed from without, but from within, for it determines the moment of consummation of the act.

But what of the objectivity of form? And what is the difference between the form of, say, a locomotive and an art work? For if we say that the common element between the arts and technology is the organization of energy, what is the difference between the energy of an art work and a machine? Or if we say that the "social arts" such as ceremony, festivals, and celebrations organize the energy of the community, what is the difference between a Founding Day Parade and the processional in a great ballet such as *Graduation Ball*? And, finally, what is the relationship between art and *social* experience? These are some of the questions Dewey realizes he must answer. For those in search of a social theory of communication, the answers in Chapter XIV, "Art and Civilization," of *Art as Experience* are the most important. It is clear by now that Dewey defines art by the social, just as he defines the social by art. But has he defined them as independent variables, or has he really assumed one under the other? And, finally, has he broken out of the vicious circle in cultural theory wherein society determines art because art determines society?

Dewey begins his summation by saying that aesthetic experience is a record and celebration of the life of a civilization, a means of promoting its development, and is also the "ultimate judgment upon the quality of a civilization." Art is produced by individual artists, the content of whose experience has been determined by the cultures in which they live. Art functions in many ways to create and sustain community life. Its greatest function is to create and transmit the meaning of community life in imaginative forms which make social experience possible. Even religion and law depend on art to clothe them with dignity and majesty: the Magna Carta, the great political stabilizer of Anglo-Saxon civilization, affects us through imagination, not by its literal contents.

Art also transmits custom because it dramatizes the meaning of custom so that we learn to enact, not simply to "perceive," our cultural roles. But it also creates forms that *are* custom; for customs are more than uniform external modes of action—they are saturated with story and transmitted meaning. All art in some way is a medium of such transmission. Thus, culture, and the continuity of culture in passage from one civilization to another, as well as within the culture, is conditioned by art "more than by any other thing." For what, after all, are the monuments of the past but aesthetic monuments? What would we know of the past if it were not for song, dance, architecture, poetry, and all the arts which were used to communicate rites and ceremonies to create what Durkheim called the "collective representations" which compose our social bonds? We would know nothing, and the events of the past "would now be sunk into oblivion."

The arts which primitive peoples used to transmit their customs and institutions were communal arts and were the source out of which all fine arts have developed. Patterns applied to tribal weapons, tools, and utensils were marks of tribal union. Rite, ceremony, legend, tale, narrative, and myth bound the living and the dead in common partnership. These were aesthetic, but they were more than aesthetic. Magical rites were more than a way of commanding forces of nature to do the bidding of the tribe. Communal modes of activity in rites and ceremonies united practical, social, and education experience in a harmonious unity characteristic of aesthetic form. They introduced social values into experience. The aesthetic strand in experience was ubiquitous and constitutive because without it there could be no society and hence *no* experience.

DEWEY'S VIEW OF THE SOCIAL FUNCTION OF ART

Art is the ideal form of communication because it gives us experience of the *qualities* of relationships. Communication through speech, oral and written, is the familiar and constant feature of social life. It is the foundation and source of all activities and relations that are distinctive of internal union of human beings with one another. The artist creates forms which make possible *participating in community life*. Participation is possible because I can anticipate the response of others, who, in turn, can anticipate my response. But this sympathetic projection arises *in* communication, and such communication is dependent on forms of expression. Art conveys the meaning of the past that is significant in present experience and is prophetic of the larger movements of the future. The first stirrings of dissatisfaction and the first intimations of a better future "are always found in works of art." Factual science may collect statistics and make charts. "But its predictions are, as has been well said, but past history reversed. Change in the climate of the imagination is the precursor of the changes that affect more than the details of life." [38]

The function of art in society, Dewey concludes, is "by disclosure, through imaginative vision addressed to imaginative experience . . . of possibilities that contrast with actual conditions." The excitement of the aesthetic moment in experience occurs when a "sense of possibilities that are unrealized and that might be realized" floods our consciousness. As Shelley said, "The imagination is the great instrument of moral good, and poetry administers to the effect by acting upon the causes." Art is, therefore, not simply the communication of moral ideas already formed in religion, or in ethical discourse. "The moral prophets of humanity have always been poets. . . . Uniformly, however, their vision of possibilities has soon been converted into a proclamation of facts that already exist and hardened into semi-political institutions. Their imaginative presentation of ideals that should command thought and desire have been treated as rules of policy." [39]

In the last sentence of *Art as Experience,* Dewey places the function of art in purpose. "Art has been the means of keeping alive the sense of purposes that outrun evidence and of meanings that transcend indurated habit." To do this the artist must be able to experiment with his forms. His audience, in turn, needs the disclosures of the possibilities of action, because without them social action in new, novel, and emergent kinds of experience is impossible. The union of the possible and the actual in art *remakes* impulsion, because art is a mode of prediction which "insinuates possibilities of human relations not to be found in rule and precept, admonition and administration." [40]

Dewey's great contribution to a theory of communication is that he makes the experience of art central to his theory of society. He makes clear that the study of communication must involve the study of art. He rejects resolutely any kind of supernaturalism which assigns dignity to man because of his derived dignity from God. At the same time, he will not surrender man to a nature whose laws are not determined by the creative imagination of man. He finds the dignity and worth of man in human nature itself, in the relationships, actual and potential, of human beings in their natural social relationships. He argues that a foundation within man and nature is a much better basis for knowledge and the good life than one outside the constitution of man and nature. He turns to art in experience as the kind of experience which allows us to reintegrate human knowledge and activity in the general framework of reality and natural process.

By making the consummatory moment in art experience characteristic of the way in which the future invests the present, as well as the past, with meaning, he raises the study of art to central importance in the social studies. For if art is the depiction of possibilities in action, and we cannot know the meaning of an act until we know what is the assumed end of the act, then only in art can we study the ends of acts. This view equates art with religion and history as a source of knowledge of human conduct in society. For if we must know the past to understand the present, we must also know the goals which determine how we organize action in the present. As Dewey stresses, traditions and goals arise in communication; they are not "supplied" to it by mind or nature alone. Action is always problematic. We do not solve problems in reflection and then act, but in action where we resolve tension, anxiety, ambiguity, and conflict by investing action with a sense of fulfilling ends.

Yet there are many difficulties in using Dewey's work to create a model of social action based on communication. He tells us *what* communication and communication as art in society do, but he tells us very little about *how* they do it. His use of art is descriptive, not analytic. He uses art to illustrate, not to define, propositions about communication in society. Of the two variables—society and art—society is the more important. He is singularly vague on the specific nature of the art experience as art. We are warned continually against turning to aesthetic canons of "fine art" for clues to the experience of art as art, because this takes art "outside" experience. We are constantly referred to the social context of art. This, on close analysis, is a context whose reality is not distinguished by art, but by society—and a society characterized by a kind of interaction determined by communication whose highest form is an art which we have not defined. Thus, he makes society both an environment in which action "occurs" and an agent who determines what happens in the environment.

To say, for example, that investing the present with its future as a moment of enjoyed consummation is characteristic of art, disregards the use of the future as Utopia, heaven, hell, ideology, trend, etc., in religious, political, and, indeed, all thought and expression. Even a scientist must assume a "perfect" solution to his problem before he begins his experiment. He does not build his laboratory, order supplies, hire technicians, and draw up his budget after, but *before,* he begins his experiment. Priests teach us to face decay and death, the basic tragedy of humanity, by placing a meaningful future in heaven or hell before us. Economists create models of a "perfect" market against which to measure the "workings" of a present market. All such fictions, as Hans Vaihinger called them, are used to organize action as in a present. But when we ask of Dewey just what the specific difference is between any fiction and the ends of action depicted in art, we get no answer.

How can we use the term "art," which has not been defined, to help us understand what we need to define? If society is determined by art, what is the *form* this determination takes; and if society determines art, just *how* does this happen? A close reading of *Art as Experience* indicates that Dewey has not created a *functional model* of art in society which the sociologist can use to think about art as a determinant of society, and about society in turn as a determinant of art. We are told that men relate through communication and that the symbols we use to communicate are brought to their highest form of perfection in art, but until we know how this occurs we cannot construct a model that will be of much value to rigorous thinking about the interdependency of communication and society.

Dewey tells us that art is the characteristic form of human experience, but he never tells us what *form* of art—either as it actually exists in art, or as a fiction of his own drawn from art—can be used to think about social aspects of experience. When he discusses intellectual activity, he uses conversation as his model. Perception is discussed in terms of painting; emotional activity in terms of drama. When he discusses rhythm and harmony in the act, he turns to music. Unlike Freud who selected *one* model of art, namely, the Oedipus drama, to create his model of family interaction, Dewey selects no specific form and thus fails to create a congruent model which we can use to understand how society arises in, and continues through, communication. His statements on art in society constitute a program, not a systematic body of propositions which can be used to create hypotheses about the function of art in society.

Notes

[1] Lester F. Ward, *Dynamic Sociology,* 2 vols. (New York and London: D. Appleton and Company, 1883). See Vol. II, Chapter XI, "Action." In the section "Dynamic Action" (Vol. II, pp. 376–385) he discusses this point. Ward's italics.

[2] *Ibid.,* p. 100.

[3] These points are discussed by R. G. Collingwood in his *The Idea of History* (Oxford: Oxford Univ. Press, 1946). He argues that if we can know a present, we can also know a past, because the mind which knows the present is the same mind which knows the past, and the experience we have of a present has much in common with the experience of the past because we reconstruct both in our minds by becoming conscious of our own reconstruction. The same argument could be upheld, with equal logic, about our knowledge of the future.

[4] Bronislaw Malinowski, *Magic, Science and Religion, and Other Essays,* Selected, and with an Introduction by Robert Redfield (Glencoe, Ill.: The Free Press, 1948), p. 122.

[5] That is, he never questions the *failure* of tradition, or *conflicts* among institutions which interpret tradition in different ways.

[6] Sorel used this as an introduction to his 1908 edition of his *Reflections on Violence.* Quotations here are taken from the authorized translation by T. E. Hulme (London: George Allen and Unwin, Ltd., 1915).

[7] *Ibid.,* p. 136.

[8] If we knew everything about the future there would be no incentive to act, and we should all die of boredom or of anguish over our knowledge of what was in store for us. Thus, knowledge of the future would destroy, not create, incentives to act.

[9] Sorel, like Burke, held that the symbolic realm of what he called "myth" was real, concrete, and observable, while the nonsymbolic realms of economics, political, and philosophical "laws" were highly inferential. His discussion of the proletarian strike (Chapter IV of the *Reflections*) deals with this point.

[10] This book grew out of the Gifford Lectures on Natural Religion given at Edinburgh in 1901–1902.

[11] *Varieties of Religious Experience* (New York: Random House, Modern Library Edition, n.d.), p. 5.

[12] *Ibid.,* p. 12.

[13] *Ibid.*

[14] Peirce warned against this tendency, as did James, Cooley, Dewey, and Mead.

[15] In his study, *The Use of Personal Documents in Psychological Science* (Social Science Research Council, New York, 1942, Bulletin No. 42), Gordon W. Allport, while praising *The Varieties of Religious Experience* as a "masterpiece of descriptive science," seems to miss this point, and the discussion of it by James. The "orginal states" of religious experience to which Allport refers (see p. 6) are the verbal expres-

sions of these states, and, as James makes clear in his discussion of language, the means available for expression ("Religious language clothes itself in such poor symbols as our life affords, . . .") will determine the kind of religious experience the individual will have. This is central to *any* theory and methodology of symbolic analysis.

[16] This statement is repeated, with slight variation, by many social scientists. What should be said is that *social scientists* do not seem to know much about communication—which is another way of saying that communication is not amenable to techniques which are held to be proper to the science of sociology. Literary critics, from Aristotle to Kenneth Burke, have said a great deal about communication. Ignorance among social scientists of this rich heritage of "discourse about discourse" should not be condoned. The somewhat ridiculous swagger of those like Mills, who assert that sociology can tell us more about human conduct than great art, if not checked, will soon make ignorance a virtue. Sociologists would do better to produce some of the knowledge they say they know how to produce than to castigate others for producing knowledge in the "wrong" way. Freud, for all his dogmatism, was very careful to keep the mind of the analyst open to literature and art, as well as to science.

[17] John Dewey, *Experience and Nature* (New York: W. W. Norton, 1922).

[18] *Ibid.*, p. 166.

[19] See Chapter 9 for discussion of these points.

[20] In Dewey's early writings there is little about communication or art as a determinant of judgment. That is, he is content to talk about adjustment, consciousness, reconstruction, habit, as "functionally active" without telling us the *medium* or the means by which all this takes place. In his later work, he turns to communication, and to art as the ideal type of communication, to illustrate the function, as well as the structure, of the relationship between the self and its environment.

[21] Both Malinowski and Mead refer to *Experience and Nature* as a definitive statement for them of how to think about symbols and society. In the footnote to the title of his article "The Nature of Aesthetic Experience," Mead says: "I have not made specific acknowledgments in the article to Professor Dewey, but the reader who is familiar with his *Experience and Nature* will realize that it was written under the influence of that treatise." At the end of Chapter Five, Dewey quotes approvingly from Malinowski's supplementary essay in C. K. Ogden and I. A. Richards, *The Meaning of Meaning* (New York: Harcourt, Brace, 1945).

[22] This estate is that of "brute efficiencies and inarticulate consummations" which are "liberated" from local and accidental contexts in communication.

[23] Dewey, *op. cit.*, p. 167.

[24] *Ibid.*, p. 171.

[25] *Ibid.*

[26] *Ibid.*, p. 181.

[27] *Ibid.*, p. 184.

[28] *Ibid.*, p. 189.

[29] This is the last sentence of Chapter Five, to which there is appended a long footnote in praise of Malinowski's essay (in *The Meaning of Meaning*) on the meaning of meaning in primitive society.

[30] Dewey, *op. cit.*, p. 389.

[31] *Ibid.*, p. 391.

[32] *Ibid.*, p. 391.

[33] *Ibid.*, p. 392.

[34] *Ibid.*, pp. 392–393.

35 *Ibid.*, p. 432.

36 *Art as Experience* (New York: Minton, Balch & Company, 1934), pp. 25–36.

37 Dewey's dominant image of how thought arises in experience is an image of conversation; his image of how emotion arises in experience is a dramatic image.

38 *Art as Experience*, pp. 345–346.

39 *Ibid.*, p. 348.

40 *Ibid.*, p. 349.

5

Communication and the Emergence of the Self in the Work of George Herbert Mead

JAMES' ACCEPTANCE OF EXPRESSIVE SYMBOLS AS SOCIAL DATA

THE OPPOSITION in European social thought between the individual and society was more than a difference in social theory. Durkheim, Le Bon, de Tocqueville—indeed, almost every European social philosopher —believed that the individual, when left to himself, is reflective and rational.[1] He is beset by emotional obsessions and irrationalities only in association with others. Thus, we hear of the psychology of the crowd, the instincts of the masses, the rule of mobs, the apocalyptic myths of the proletariat, etc. Strong authority, and usually the authority of the individual, is needed to curb the irrational yearnings of the people who, once in direct association with each other in large groups, easily succumb to "mass suggestion." For the crowd, mass, or the public mind could never rise above unreason. Men in groups were like herds, alone they were like gods. . . . This view, as Dewey, Cooley, and Mead were quick to point out, made democracy impossible because it equated democracy *by definition,* with unreason.

Cooley and Mead[2] argued that the locus of reason was in interaction *between* the self and society. We do not have selves and then form societies, but we form and develop a self in the give and take of social relations. Thus, the social bond must be described in terms of what goes on between individuals *within* society. The data of this interaction is language, and the representative human form of communication in society is art. Art, unlike religion, invoked no supernatural power to substantiate its reality,[3] and thus the artist was of importance to the sociologists because he was seeking to develop communication among men, not with God. The truth of art was a social truth, for, whatever the artist intended, the symbols he created became the symbols men used to communicate, and thus the "truths" of art were always tested in experience. Man became an agent who determined, as well as who was determined by, his environment, because his environment was symbolic as well as spatial, or material, or supernatural. And whatever else was said about language, it was generally agreed that man created his own speech and determined its laws.

James argued in *The Will to Believe* and *Varieties of Religious Experience* that human action is a matter of ends, purposes, goals, and ideas, as well as instincts, drives, discharges, and impulsions. The "pull of the future" was as real as the "push from behind." He championed mysticism as a social fact, and warned positivists and agnostics alike that "a rule of thinking which would absolutely prevent [us] from acknowledging certain kinds of truth if those kinds of truth were really there, would be an irrational rule." That is, James argued, if science does not recognize religion and art as social facts, because science has no methods for dealing with the data of religious or aesthetic experience, then we need a new science. In *Varieties of Religious Experience* he tries to show *how* men of religion think and act on the basis of how they describe their own actions. What a man said, or how he agreed with what others said, about his experience of the living God, as well as on what occasion, and with what effect, seemed to James as much of a social fact as how many Americans migrated from farms to cities in 1900.

Dewey distrusted James' mysticism because, as he said in his essay on the subject in the psychology of James,[4] absolutes, whether of God or nature, tended to make the subject residual to the object. In his article of 1910 on William James,[5] Dewey tells of the dilemma faced by James in his search for a psychology and a philosophy which would deal with the observable facts of community life. After Darwinism won its decisive victory in America (about 1870), and Spencer became the guide and philosopher of an aggressive and militant group of thinkers in England and America, positivists and materialists simply replaced older religious and philosophical dogmas with new dogmas, spoken in the name of science, to the effect that there could be no rational inquiry, and hence no knowledge, of all that was vague and mystical, because this was beyond the realm of facts verifiable by the senses. This scientific philosophy, whether materialistic, agnostic, or positivistic, defined science as a *way* of knowing and argued that what could not be known by certain techniques—usually quantitative—could not be known at all.

James objected to this, not because it was scientific—after all, James was a graduate of the Harvard Medical School, and, like Freud, a trained physiologist—but because the positivists were not telling us what we needed to know, and because their faith in positivistic science was not being justified by work significant enough to demonstrate the efficacy of their faith.[6] He also stressed that the *observable* facts, and the facts of religious life to which we must return for validation, are the ways in which men express their religious life. To positivists, expressive forms could be understood only through what they called introspection. Even Dewey referred to James' "introspective method," although he is careful to add in his summation of James' method that "most of what had been called introspection, and that had brought the method into disrepute, was not introspection at all, but simply the spinning out of certain ready-made ideas. With William James, introspection meant genuine observation of genuine events."[7]

But as both Dewey and Mead tell us, the escape from materialism and positivism offered by German idealism in the guise of neo-Kantianism and Hegelianism seemed equally dangerous. James' training in the methods of natural science made him uneasy with systems based on so much respect for concepts that brute facts and the concrete experience of the living individual were overlooked. German idealism shared with positivism an "absolutistic" tendency (what James called a "block universe")—a world all in one piece. In this world there was no place for novelty, change, adventure, ambiguity, creation, choice, and freedom. It was a world, in short, which was entirely lacking in distinctive individuality, and which, as the system spun on in thought, soon banished the individual to a "manifestation" of the Idea—whether God, the State, Society, the Tribe, or Culture. Thus, it made little difference to James whether the unity to which the acting individual was sacrificed was called Matter or Thought. The acting individual was sacrificed, and this was unacceptable to James, as it was to Cooley, Dewey, Mead, and later, Burke.

But what was the *via media* between positivism and German idealism, between natural science and the ideal interests of art, morals, and religion? Admitting that symbolic phenomena were facts of sociation, how did one deal with them so that what was said about symbols in art, religion, or morals could be verified by others? That is, *what was the symbolic data of sociation, how could it be thought about, and, finally, how could conclusions reached about symbolic action be demonstrated?* James tried to answer such questions in his *Varieties of Religious Experience.* Unlike Freud (and many sociologists), James does not create his own case histories and then "discover" that they "substantiate" his theory, nor does he use religious documents simply to develop concepts. He wanted to get at the facts of religious experience. These he found in the self-reported religious experience of devoutly religious people describing their most acutely religious moments. The records of religious experience, as expressed by those who had such experience, would disclose "the feelings, acts, and experiences of individual men in their solitude, so far as they apprehended themselves to stand in relation to whatever they may consider the divine." [8]

THE EMERGENCE OF THE SELF IN COMMUNICATION

Mead believed that the data of symbolic interaction offered sociologists their greatest clue to an understanding of society. Dealing with experience from the standpoint of society, for Mead, meant from the standpoint of communication as necessary to the social order. His social data are taken from the field of communication because it is only in the experience of communication that we can *observe* both the self and society in action.[9] He does not, like Freud, use expressive material to "illustrate" the functioning of a psyche whose reality is not determined (although it is illustrated) by symbols. For Mead, communication is not a residual, but a constitutive, category. We act as we do because we communicate, not because we have drives or ideas first and then come together to express them. The self and society originates and develops *in* communication.

The fundamental fact of sociation, and that which distinguishes men from animals, is not communication but the ability of men to become objects to themselves through the use of symbols [10] which men themselves *create*, as well as *use,* in communication. The individual experiences himself as a self, not directly, but indirectly, from the standpoints of other members of the same group or from the standpoint of the social group as a whole to which he belongs. He becomes an object to himself by taking the attitudes of other individuals toward himself within a social world in which both he and they are involved. He can take these attitudes because what he says to others can mean the same to himself as it does to them. For when he speaks he hears his own words, and thus learns what words mean because he can observe how they affect others, as well as how they affect him.[11]

How does this happen? How does the self develop in communication? And how do the different kinds of communication affect the development of the self? The first kind of conversation is the conversation of gestures which we see going on between animals who are involved in some sort of cooperative activity. The beginning of the act of one dog is a stimulus to the other to respond in a certain way, while the beginning of this response becomes, in turn, a stimulus to the first to adjust his action to the oncoming response. The same is true of two boxers, each of whose feints determines the position of the other. Conduct—even on the level of gestures—with reference to others goes on in communication whose meanings depend on the relation of the gesture of one organism, in its "indicative capacity as pointing to the completion of or resultant of the act it initiates (the meaning of the gesture being thus the response of the second organism to it as such, or as a gesture)." [12]

The meaning, then, of a gesture by one organism is found in the response of another organism to what would be the completion of the act of the first organism which that gesture initiates and indicates. Thinking always implies a symbol which will call out the same response in another that it calls out in the thinker. A person who is saying something is saying to himself what he says to others; otherwise, he does not know what he is talking about. But the "response" we call out in others, as in our self, is based on what we think (or imagine) the end will be, as well as what we perceive in the beginning of the act.[13] For the beginning, the stimulus, or in social action the "attitude," [14] is understandable only because we know what kind of response such stimulus produces or what kind of fulfillment a certain attitude will bring.

All symbols are universal because all meaning is social, and the social meaning of a symbol precedes individual meaning. The individual is born *into* a society, he does not create it.[15] It is impossible to say anything that is absolutely particular. For there to be meaning in communication, symbols must mean the same to the speaker and the listener. As we see in conversation, play, games, and drama, actors can act together only because they possess symbols which have meanings common to all. And for there to be social relations at all, meanings of symbols must endure. We must be able to hold on to common meanings. That is, just as we are able to create rules for a game that will be used over and over again and will not have to be created each time the game begins, so must we be able to fix and hold on to meanings over a period of time. If we had to create and fix meanings every time we acted, society could not exist.

These universal symbols derive their meaning from the organization of the social group to which the individual belongs. A game has rules, a drama has a plot, a society has festivals and ceremonies. In all games (as in all such organized social acts) there is a regulated procedure embodied in rules. The individual must assume the various roles of all the participants in the game (the "generalized other") and act in terms of how he assumes they will act. As he plays his own position, the player guides himself by his ability to arouse within himself responses and attitudes that arise in those who play other positions. Players on a team are related in an organic and unitary fashion. The responses of the players are predictable in terms of rules which all know and agree to. When conflict arises, the umpire is given power to make decisions which preserve the organic quality of the relationships between the players in the contest. He is the actor whose role personifies the "generalized other." In him, universal and highly abstract rules come to life in action. The umpire does not *create* rules, he *applies* them. He carries out rules already made by the various institutions empowered by the sports world to change old rules and make new ones. He subordinates himself to the game, holds himself aloof from players and spectators alike, and seldom argues or enters into long discussions with players or their managers. He can dismiss anyone from the playing field. He personifies the weight and importance of rules which are believed necessary to the organization of the game as a whole.

In play, and especially in the play of small children or the random spontaneous play of adults, there are no such fixed rules, just as there is no umpire. The child plays one role after another. Whim, mood, and make-believe dominate the play. What the child is at one moment does not determine what he is at another. The players themselves must settle disputes, just as they must determine how they are to play together. Often far more time is spent in arguing about how the game is to be played than in playing the game itself. There is no set of rules which makes common action possible. The individual player uses other players as an audience to reflect his glory, as the child does the mirror before which he plays make-believe, or as he uses elders as an audience before whom he "shows off." He does not take into account the attitude of the group as a whole toward himself, nor is he deeply involved in the attitude of others beyond their response, inattention, or rejection.

To become conscious of his self, the child must learn to take the attitude of others (who are, of course, different and indifferent and who hate as well as love). And to gain the responses of others, even, indeed, to make them agree to be an audience to him, he must learn how to please those whose responses he wants. He soon learns that individuals are bound to groups and act in terms of what they consider to be principles of group survival. His parents do things because they are "good for the family"; his playmates accept certain rules because that is the way the game has "always been played." Thus, it is only by taking the attitude of individual and general others into account that he can exist within the group, and get the kind of responses he needs to stimulate himself to relate to others.

It is the child's ability to take roles, not simply to talk to himself or to "think," which determines his development. That is, the basic *form* of communication as a social act, whatever its content, is histrionic. When the child talks to himself he addresses himself in roles.

In the play period . . . the child in one role addresses himself naively in another role. These roles are not at first organized into a personality, the child simply passing from the one into the other as the conduct in one calls out a response in the other. In more consecutive play, especially of two or more children, the tendency to take other parts comes in to stimulate and control the execution of the part assumed. Thus a child will stop and applaud himself and then resume his performance. If the play becomes a consecutive whole, the tendency to take all the parts at the appropriate moments is present in the attitude of the individual child, controlling his entire conduct. The child becomes a generalized actor-manager, directing, applauding, and criticizing his own roles as well as those of the others.[16]

The means by which we become objects to ourselves, thus becoming not only conscious but self-conscious and thus human, is through acting together in forms similar to the way actors on a stage mount a drama. As the child strikes a pose or as the adult "takes an attitude" they are like actors on a stage playing before an audience. Actors do not know how a gesture will "go over" before they strike it. They learn from the responses of other actors and the audience the meaning of what they have just done. Certain interpretations of parts have become accepted because they aroused good response from the audience and stimulated other actors to the kind of response which keeps the play going. But when these traditional interpretations are no longer relevant to the interests of audiences or fail to inspire other actors, new roles must be developed. For the actor is always bound to his audience, just as the audience is always bound to the actor, to dis-cover what roles mean.

That is why the drama is of such vast importance in human society. "It has picked out characters which lie in men's minds from tradition, as the Greeks did in their tragedies, and then expressed through these characters situations which belong to their own time but which carry the individual beyond the actual fixed walls which have arisen between them, as mem-bers of different classes in the community."[17] The development of this type of communication from the drama into the novel has historically something of the same importance as journalism has for our own day. The novel presents a situation which lies outside the immediate experience of the reader in a form which makes it possible for him to enter into the attitudes of the groups in the situation.

Notes

[1] That is, to the degree that man is rational, his chances of rationality are far greater when he is alone with his thoughts.

[2] "The point of approach," Mead states in the first paragraph of *Mind, Self, and Society* (Chicago: Univ. of Chicago Press, 1934), "which I wish to suggest is that of dealing with experience from the standpoint of society, at least from the standpoint of communication as essential to the social order." As Mead pointed out, even Watson and his behaviorists argued that language was the prime source of motivation. Imagery and consciousness did not exist, according to Watson. Thought was lan-guage, language was action, and the scientist must observe conduct as it takes place without reference to inner experience or consciousness as such. Conduct, "as it takes place," as Mead pointed out, is communicative or symbolic.

[3] "Beauty" is sometimes used in aesthetic discussion as theologians use God, that is, as a power beyond reason whose truths are "revealed" in moments of aesthetic ecstasy. And there are aesthetic myths, just as there are political and religious myths.

[4] John Dewey, "Vanishing Subject in the Psychology of James," *Journal of Philoso-phy*, XXXVII (October 24, 1940), pp. 589-599. This was reprinted in *Problems of Men* (New York: Philosophical Library, 1946).

[5] Published in *The Independent*, Sept. 8, 1910, under the title "William James," and reprinted in *Character and Events*, 2 vols. (New York: Henry Holt and Company, 1929).

[6] In reply to Taine's famous dogma that vice and virtue are products like vitriol and sugar, James said: "When we read such proclamations of the intellect bent on showing the existential conditions of absolutely everything, we feel—quite apart from our legitimate impatience at the somewhat ridiculous swagger of the program, in view of what the authors are actually able to perform—menaced and negated in the springs of our innermost life. Such cold-blooded assimilations threaten, we think, to undo our

soul's vital secrets, as if the same breath which should succeed in explaining their origin would simultaneously explain away their significance, and make them appear of no more preciousness, either, than the useful groceries of which M. Taine speaks." *Varieties of Religious Experience* (New York: Random House, Modern Library Edition, n.d.), p. 11.

⁷ *Character and Events*, Vol. II, p. 115. For full discussion of this article see "William James," originally published in 1910 and reprinted in *Character and Events* as Part II of the section on William James.

⁸ James, *op. cit.*, p. 32. James is very careful to disavow any sympathy or personal identification with mysticism. "Whether my treatment of mystical states will shed more light or darkness, I do not know, for my own constitution shuts me out from their enjoyment almost entirely, and I can speak of them only at second hand." But he does not argue that because he has little personal involvement or commitment to mysticism that he is therefore *more* objective than the true believer. On the contrary, he thinks that being "outside" a subject is a handicap, not a help, to objectivity. "But though forced to look upon the subject externally, I will be as objective and receptive as I can. . . ." (See page 370.)

⁹ As we shall see, social action in Mead is action in time, as well as in space. While few American students of society have said more than Mead about how we perceive objects in space, he relates action in space to action in time, and thus grounds his theory of action in temporal as well as spatial duration. As we shall see, time for Mead is a present time, but this present has a past and a future. Thus, while he does not deny the past, and certainly upholds the future, they are the pasts and futures of a given present. In this sense, Mead's sense of time, like Burke's, is dramatic, *not* mechanical.

¹⁰ Thus, it is not the eye (how we perceive others) but the ear (how we hear others) that determines how we think about ourselves and others as persons. We cannot see our own eye, thus we can never become self-conscious of how we perceive our world. So, in all theories of cognition based on models of perception fashioned on the act of seeing, *self*-consciousness is very difficult to account for.

¹¹ In his discussion of the self in *Mind, Self, and Society*, Mead says: "Man's behavior is such in his social group that he is able to become an object himself, a fact which constitutes him a more advanced product of evolutionary development than are the lower animals. Fundamentally it is this social fact—and not his alleged possession of a soul or mind with which he, as an individual, has been mysteriously and supernaturally endowed, and with which the lower animals have not been endowed—that differentiates him from them." (See footnote to page 137.)

¹² Mead, *op. cit.*, p. 145.

¹³ That is, meaning always involves an assumption about the kind of communication involved in a certain kind of action.

¹⁴ "Attitude" in Mead's work means an "incipient act."

¹⁵ That is not to say that the individual cannot create or change a society, but simply to point out that communication in society has been going on long before the individual entering a society begins to communicate in it. The problem for Mead is *how* the individual internalizes the meanings which exist "outside" of him in his society.

¹⁶ George Herbert Mead, *The Philosophy of the Act* (Chicago: Univ. of Chicago Press, 1938), p. 374.

¹⁷ *Mind, Self, and Society*, p. 257.

6

The Final Phase of the Act: Consummation

WHAT IS PECULIAR to aesthetic experience, Mead argues, is its power "to catch the enjoyment that belongs to the consummation, the outcome, of an undertaking, and to give to the implements, the objects that are instrumental in the undertaking, and to the acts that compose it something of the joy and satisfaction that suffuse its successful accomplishment." The artist attempts to "interpret complex social life in terms of the goals toward which our efforts run." It is not simply because of its capacity to envision a future that art affects a society—religious, political, educational, hygienic, and even technical acts establish goals in a future to direct their activity in a present. The peculiar quality of aesthetic experience is the appreciation and satisfaction of a sense of the finalities of action which it gives us. Other forms of experience "do not carry with them the satisfactions that belong to finalities." [1]

This is because other acts are "infected by the interest which belongs to the fashioning of means to ends, to the shaping and testing of hypotheses, to invention and discovery, to the exercise of artisanship, and to the excitement of adventure in every field. It is the province of action, not that of appreciation." Our affective experience may be divided, roughly, between doing and enjoying and their opposites. Our experience of emotion and interest, of pleasure and pain, of satisfaction and dissatisfaction, of the final states of affect, "that which attaches to finalities," are found in their most characteristic form in the harmony of emotional tones we experience in aesthetic states of consciousness. In such movements the clash of interests and impulses are resolved. A great stanza of Whitman's verse resolves the conflicting interests of the democratic community because as we read it we recover a sense of the final transcendent moment of democratic communion. This "recovery of the sense of the final outcome in partial achievement" is the function of art in society.[2]

Intellectual experience fails to give us this harmonious sense of finality, of completion of the act. "In the fashioning of means into ends, in the use of tools, and the nice adjustment of people and things to the accomplishment of purposes, we give attention only to that which forwards the undertaking; we see and hear only enough to recognize and use; and pass from the recognition to the operation; . . ." But in aesthetic appreciation "we contemplate, and abide, and rest in our presentations." The artisan who stops to sense the nice perfection of a tool or a machine "has interrupted its use to appreciate it, and is in an aesthetic mood. He is not interested in its employment, he is enjoying it." The statesman who turns from the writing of his speeches and the organizing of a campaign for a better life for children to "the picture of their healthful and joyous life, is for the time being no longer in action. He is savoring the end that he is fashioning into practical politics." [3]

When anyone stops in the midst of his work "to feel the surety of his colleagues, the loyalty of his supporters, the response of his public, to enjoy the community of life in the family, or profession, or party or church, or country, to taste in Whitmanesque manner the commonality of existence, his attitude is aesthetic; . . ." In the arts the aesthetic attitude appears in "appropriate decoration, that which infuses the spirit of the meaning of the instrument into its structure and adornment, that which informs our equipment and immediate effort with the significance and splendor of their accomplishments." The aesthetic attitude adds distinction to utility, and "poetry to action." In community life it dignifies the commonality of existence in festivals and solemn concourses. Without these we would not know what common action means because we could not experience the emotions which only the finalities of action evoke. [4]

But while the aesthetic attitude "which accompanies, inspires and dedicates common action" finds its moment of ideal finality in future achievement, "the material in which its significance and beauty is fashioned is historic." For "all the stuff with which the most creative imagination works is drawn from the storehouses and quarries of the past." All history

is the interpretation of the present, that is, it gives us not only the direction and trend of events, the reliable uniformities and laws of affairs, but it offers us the irrevocableness of the pattern of what has occurred, in which to embody the still uncertain and unsubstantial objects we would achieve. We import the finalities of past victories and defeats into the finalities of the uncertain future. The solidity and definiteness and clarity of our undertakings are the donation of the past. [5]

The perfection of art is reached in what we call the fine arts, but the aesthetic attitude "involves the creative imagination and aesthetic appreciation of the least artistically endowed. . . ." But the aesthetic attitude can develop only when the enjoyment of the ultimate use of goods and services are "suggested by the intermediate steps in their production, and flow naturally into the skill which constructs it." The capacity and the opportunity to follow through to completion what we are making creates joy in work. Aesthetic joy becomes community joy because art "belongs to the co-ordinated efforts of many, when the role of the other in the production is aroused in each worker at the common task; when the sense of team play, esprit de corps, inspires interrelated activities. In these situations something of the delight of consummation can crown all intermediate processes." [6]

Such delight is absent from most labor in modern competitive industrial society. When the ends of work are too far removed from the task in hand because of specialization of labor and because of difficulties of communication between widely separated and different publics, "the imagination leaps to the ultimate satisfactions which cannot be fused with the uninteresting detail of preparation, and day-dreaming supervenes and cuts the nerve of action." [7] The imagination is deprived of its normal function. For in normal aesthetic experience "delight in creation is the recovery of the sense of the final outcome in the partial achievement," and it is this which "gives assurance to the interest of creation." [8] In day-dreaming we try to make up for the absence of any connection between means and ends by leaping to an end that is not expressed in terms of means.

In aesthetic enjoyment of the work of great artists, "what we are doing is capturing values of enjoyment there, which fill out and interpret our own interests in living and doing. They have permanent value because they are the language of delight into which men can translate the meaning of their own existence." [9] But community life must be so organized that those who can import such aesthetic experience into activity can help other members of the community to attain the same kind of experience. We must strive to make work meaningful, as well as efficient. Work must become more than labor; it must become art. Art, in turn, must become more than a substitute for reverie; it must be honored as a means of experiencing the joy of common effort which comes only when the end of such effort is felt and understood in the means we create to achieve our ends. In one sense, of course, art is a means, the means used by the community to interpret ends so it can select means necessary to such ends. For men must know what ends are before they can stimulate themselves to attain the ends.

The delight of art in community life will come only from shared effort. Aesthetic joy, like all joy, must be earned. "It is silly and inept to offer hopeless counsels of perfection, to undertake by the spread of so-called culture to replace the consummatory objects in men's reveries by the imagery of great artists, or to replace machine production by medieval artisanship." [10] Aesthetic imagining is not the same as reverie. The machine industry is not necessarily hostile to art. Any work becomes art so long as we have a sense of the whole which we are completing in our work. True, one cannot say that aesthetic delight has been normal in community life, and it may be that vast changes in society must occur before aesthetic delight is shared by many. But this is not the fault of art, but of the value men have placed on art. Just so far as we can endow men with the gift of artisanship, give them creative impulse of any kind, and provide them with an opportunity for expressing their creative impulses, we will give them opportunity for aesthetic delight and thus bring joy back into work.

Art performs its social function when it interprets experience to the individual as the shared experience of the community of which he feels himself a part. The imagery in art enjoyed by the community may be nothing more than unsatisfied animal impulses of sex or hate, or of lust for money and power. But in so far as art gives us an opportunity to identify with a town, a class, a city, a nation, or all men everywhere, it gives men the gratification of experience as shared by the community to which he belongs. Such forms of art are the "determining forms which interpret his social experience." Without such forms we could not share experience because we could not take the roles of others.

Through art forms we "externalize reverie" and depict ends in conduct which deepen and enlarge shared experience. The power of art, popular and fine art alike, is its capacity to break down the walls that separate men. Through art we are able to take the role of others, and thus break down the unrecognized and unconscious pressure of the isolated individual in modern society. "The isolated man is the one who belongs to a whole that he yet fails to realize. We have become bound up in a vast society, all of which is essential to the existence of each one, but we are without the shared experience this should entail." [11] The hunger and yearning of isolated men for some kind of identification with each other is being satisfied through popular art forms such as the newspaper and the motion picture.

These popular arts "spread the pattern of men's reveries before our outward eyes. . . . With marvelous exactness they have copied the type of happening, and the sort of imagery, that run behind the average man's eyes and fill up the interstices of overt conduct, and they emphasize and expand what is needed to render the reverie vivid and concrete." They do this by depicting news in dramatic form; editors themselves call their depictions "human interest" stories. There are certain sections, like the reports of the stock market, in which quantified facts are simply reported, but outside of these "the enjoyability, the consummatory value, of the news bulk in value on the market. The reporter is generally sent out to get a story, not the facts. . . . It is this realm of the reverie—of imagined enjoyable results—which dictates the policy of the daily press." [12]

The film intensifies our experience of visual imagery by creating forms which make possible the organization of highly volatile reveries. "Our visual images are slight, incomplete, and not readily controlled. We do our thinking in the form of conversation, and depend upon the imagery of words for our meanings. It is only at the favored moments that vivid pictures of the past throng the imagination. Visual imagery operates largely in filling our perception, rather than in satisfying the inward eye, which was the bliss of Wordsworth's solitude." The visual image "does not lend itself readily to shared experience." The movie "has no creative audience such as have been the inspiration of the moving speeches of great actors. Under the power of an orator one is in the perspective of the whole community." In the movie the individual sees the pictures in his own perspective. The isolation of the members of a compact audience at a movie "is in crying contrast with the shared response of those that, each at his own breakfast table, read the morning press." [13]

The reveries produced by such an art as the motion picture provide us with imagery of common values, the common consummatory experiences, as well as with compensations for our defeats, our inferiorities, and our unconfessed failures. The average film brings to light the hidden unsatisfied longings of the average man and woman, and these, we discover, are very immediate, simple, and primitive. But this is not without its value to society. The "unwittingly confessed defeats of men are not of the wide and generous impulse. It is that which is rather primitive in us that is repulsed in modern society." The man who finds sidesplitting humor in the near-disasters of Charlie Chaplin "is presumably finding compensation for some repressed primitive tendencies to inflict suffering and pains upon his enemies." But this is not a reversion to barbarism; it is rather "a catharsis, in an Aristotelian phrase, than a revolution." [14]

Genuine aesthetic effect is produced in the movies only when "the pleasure in that which is seen serves to bring out the values of the life that one lives." This is why salacious movies are not art. "They are not the cause of finding meaning and pleasure in other things, nor are they informed with the meaning of that which leads up to their enjoyment. They blot out all but the immediate response." [15] The inchoate phenomenon of the human reverie, which the press and the movies have projected before us, are not purely private affairs. Art that is too private is subject to disintegration. Even the most subjective art, such as James Joyce's *Ulysses,* passes into the universal meanings of common discourse and cooperative effort. Out of this rise the forms of universal beauty,

the intuitions of the inventor, the hypotheses of the scientist, and the creations of the artist. It is that part of the inner life of man which cannot be given its implicated meanings because of the incompleteness of social organization. It marked man's isolation within society. We have decried its vulgarity when the daily press and the movie films have stripped off its privacy. It is better, however, to live with our problems than to ignore them.[16]

THE FUNCTION OF IMAGERY IN CONDUCT

Mead makes the aesthetic moment necessary to experience by making it a part of what he calls "the philosophy of the act." In "The Reflex Arc Concept in Psychology," Dewey had argued in 1896 that the stimulus is actually a stimulus to the organism in virtue of the implicit response or interest which sensitizes the organism to those features of the world capable of furthering the release of the response itself. What the organism is attentive to is a function of its impulses seeking expression, not simply a discharge. We are more than organisms, we are actors who seek to create environments which will satisfy our heart's desire, not simply to adapt or to adjust to our environment. *How* ends or values infuse action and *how* the future of an act determines the present were the problems Mead faced in his discussion of consummatory moments as found in aesthetic experience.

In 1900 Mead argued that modern philosophy could reconcile its conflicting schools only by some conception of the act, and man as an actor in society. As a philosopher his deepest concern with the act was in how we know the world as we act within it. But his first concern, and the task which was central to his whole view, was in how to describe the act so that what he said could be tested in social experience. We have already seen how much he relied on aesthetic experience for his description of one phase of the act, the moment of consummation. By 1900, the "Chicago school of thought," as James called it,[17] had brought art back into experience and seemed ready to concern itself with how art *determines* experience. In Mead's work this was done first in his description of the stages of the act and, at the very end of his life, in what he called his "philosophy of the present."

All perception, Mead held, involves not only an immediate sensuous stimulation but an *attitude toward this stimulation*. This attitude is the reaction of the individual to the stimulation he has received. In so far as the perception does not pass immediately into motor activity, the reaction appears in consciousness as an attitude. This attitude is accompanied by imagery which is taken from past experience in which the responses have been carried out, and by imagery of the hypothetical result of the performance. An attitude thus becomes an incipient act. A perception must be thought of as an act, not as a presentation of some kind of material. We see our environment in terms of acting within it to satisfy ends we value. We accept and reject stimuli in terms of the kind of response our imagery of ends have made us want. All action, and all thought and imagery arising within action, is problem solving. We are trying to resolve the conflicts and difficulties which arise out of the lack of adjustment between the individual and his world.

An act has a beginning, a middle, and an end, and it exists in time as well as space. That is, even though we move through space we move too in time. Acts have duration as well as extension. And as we move through space and in time, as we try to act in a present, we are aware of a past and a future. "A living individual is one that lives in the future." But we are not living in a future and we do not set up hypothetical ends in imagery simply to act, but to act in accordance with certain values. We want to achieve ends, and we select the kind of images we need to reach such ends. Thus, while we recall pasts, we do so to act in a present which we are organizing in terms of images of a future. Imagery, then, is not confined to memory. "Whatever may be said about its origin in past experience, its reference to the future is as genuine as to the past. Indeed, it is fair to say that it only refers to the past in so far as it has a future reference in some real sense." [18]

Imagery takes place within the individual, since by its nature it is divorced from the objects that would give it a place in the perceptual world, although it has representational reference to such objects. This reference is found in the attitudes (evoked by symbols of the completion of the act) which are taken toward the various stimuli which initiate the act. These attitudes are brought into harmony through the reorganization of the contents of the stimuli. Into this reorganization enter the images of the completion of the act. These images may be based on any of the senses, but in so far as they enter communication, they are predominantly vocal. The purpose of the reorganization of images into some kind of harmony is to act as a kind of preliminary testing of the success of the reorganized end in action.

But, while values are hypothetical, this does *not* reduce them to mere means, any more than (in democratic society, at least) diverse points of view weaken truth. In our society we believe that we understand our own conduct better when we are able to see ourselves as others see us. It is not the many differences among people and the great variety of various traditions and Utopias from which we must choose our past and future, but the lack of organization of them, that makes action difficult. In symbolic reconstruction we mark out and define the future field and objects which make the environment. The objective of social action, while it has no existence apart from individuals, is determined by the symbolic processes of the group.

Thus, for Mead, imagery of the future determines the act because it *organizes* (if only hypothetically) action in the present. He opened his last work, *The Philosophy of the Present,* which he was working on at his death, thus: "The subject of this lecture is found in the proposition that reality exists in a present. The present of course implies a past and a future, and to these both we deny existence." Social experience is a process continually passing into the future. This passage has, in consciousness, a succession of past and future, but the present in which we act is the only moment when both are involved. Even in nature the object of perception is the existent future of the act. The food is what the animal will eat; his refuge is the burrow where he will escape from his pursuer.

In so far as there are social acts, there are social objects. A social object is the character or the form of an act, and it is the form of the act which controls the expression of the act. The form of those acts determining social action does not exist completely in the existence of any single individual. The rules of a game, the forms of great community ceremonies, in which each individual plays a position or takes a role, are like great dramas. The individual actor can play only his own role, he cannot be the whole show. But he must be able to internalize within himself the ways in which others will play their parts, for only then will he know how to play his own. It is therefore only by our capacity to symbolize the future of our acts as completed acts that we are able to organize action in a present, under the assumption that what we do now is justified because it will lead to a desirable end.

Problems in playing our roles in a modern world do not arise out of the confusion of perspectives. Nor, on the other hand, can we assume that we gain in understanding simply by becoming acquainted with an indefinite number of perspectives. We must overcome distances of space and time and the barriers of language, convention, and status so that we can take the roles of those who are involved with us in the common undertakings of life. Our only hope is our curiosity, which may be called "the passion of self-consciousness." This teaches us that "we must be others if we are to be ourselves. Our best hope of becoming conscious of others is in art. The modern realistic novel has done more than technical education in fashioning the social object that spells social control. If we can bring people together so that they can enter each other's lives, they will inevitably have a common object which will control their common conduct." [19]

Notes

[1] George Herbert Mead, "The Nature of Aesthetic Experience," *International Journal of Ethics*, XXXVI (1926), p. 384. Unless otherwise specified, all quotations are taken from this article.

[2] *Ibid.*, p. 385.

[3] *Ibid.*

[4] *Ibid.*

[5] *Ibid.*, p. 386.

[6] *Ibid.*, p. 387.

[7] *Ibid.*

[8] *Ibid.*

[9] *Ibid.*

[10] *Ibid.*, p. 388. This was, of course, the argument of the Chicago school of architecture, headed from 1880 to 1890 by Louis H. Sullivan and later by Frank Lloyd Wright, whose lecture in 1901 at Hull House on "The Art and Craft of the Machine" signalized in American architecture the beginning of a new world order of design.

It is also Veblen's argument. Men, he says, "like to see others spend their life to some purpose, and they like to reflect that their own life is of some use. All men have this quasi-aesthetic sense of economic or industrial merit, and to this sense of economic merit, futility and efficiency are distasteful. In its positive expression it is an impulse or instinct of workmanship; negatively it expresses itself in a depreciation of waste." ("Instinct of Workmanship and the Irksomeness of Labor," *American Journal of Sociology,* Vol. IV, September, 1898.) This quotation is taken from *Essays on Our Changing Order,* edited by Leon Ardzrooni (New York: The Viking Press, 1943), p. 78. Veblen is concerned with the *pathology* of workmanship in American society. He thus serves as a corrective to Dewey and to Mead, whose vision of the democratic commonwealth is often blind to the darker sides of democratic culture.

[11] Mead, *op. cit.,* p. 389.

[12] *Ibid.* From 1890 to 1930 in Chicago, poets, novelists, and all kinds of literary artists worked for the press. Indeed, the relationship between the newspaper and literary art was so close in Chicago that newspaper experience was considered the best kind of training for literature.

[13] Mead, *op. cit.,* p. 391. Mead obviously wrote before the rise of Hitler, and while he pays tribute to Freud he does not share his tragic sense of life.

[14] *Ibid.*, p. 392.

[15] *Ibid.*, p. 393.

[16] *Ibid.*

[17] In his letter to Mrs. Henry Whitman, of October 29, 1903, James writes: "Chicago University has during the past six months given birth to the fruit of its ten years of gestation under John Dewey. The result is wonderful—a *real school,* and *real Thought.* Important thought, too– Did you ever hear of such a city or such a University? Here [Harvard] we have thought, but no school. At Yale a school, but no thought. Chicago has both. . . ." See *The Letters of William James,* edited by his son Henry James, two vols. in one (London: Longman's, Green and Co., Ltd., 1926), Vol. II, p. 201.

[18] "The Function of Imagery in Conduct," in *Mind, Self, and Society,* p. 344. For Mead the future, or what Ward called the "telic factors," was far more important than the past. Thus, Mead's social psychology represents a sharp break from genetic psychologies which grounded motives in man's past.

[19] This is among the closing sentences of "The Genesis of the Self and Social Control" as given in the edition of *The Philosophy of the Present,* edited by Arthur E. Murphy (Chicago and London: Open Court Publishing Company, 1932), p. 194.

7

The Problem of Form in Mead's Theory of the Significant Symbol

Few social theorists have made communication so central to their systems as Mead. Indeed, it may be said that his theory of society is based on a theory of communication. Even our knowledge of external nature is determined by our social experience in communication. Animals, as well as human beings, do not respond to stimulus, but communicate in a "conversation of gestures." Thought itself is described as "inner conversation" and the mind an "inner forum." Mind, self, and society are born in communicative acts. We become selves because we can take the role of others toward ourselves. We become moral selves when we take the general attitudes of the community toward ourselves. When we do this, our "I" becomes a "Me," and we begin to see ourselves as others see us. Even the act of feeding by an animal, which involves the stages of perception, manipulation, and consummation, is a kind of dialectic between the animal and his environment. The highest capacity of man is his ability "to take the role of the other."

As we read Mead we leave a world of "process" where self "arises" in the "continuity" between man and nature. Man does not "organize his perspectives," nor do we hear about basic human "drives toward self-consistency or self-realization." Mead rejects all mechanical models of sociation. And, if his concept of the "generalized other" sometimes comes perilously close to Durkheim's "collective representations," which are both cause and effect of society, Mead points out that it is not the existence of "collective representations," but the fact that they arise in role-taking, that makes them social. This explanation, he argues, must be sought in language, for how men communicate determines how they relate. His work, and certainly his teaching, in social philosophy and psychology is the record of a search for a model of sociation based on communication.

To accompany Mead on this search is one of the most rewarding experiences in modern social thought, for Mead faces the questions which must be faced if we are to construct a model of sociation which will make possible some kind of empiric investigation of how communication determines society. In bringing knowledge, emotion, and reason into an act carried on by an actor who takes roles and is able to internalize the attitudes taken by others who play different roles, he removes us from a sterile mechanical world, where communication is reduced to signaling and man responds but does not relate. And finally Mead makes us respect symbols as the observable facts of sociation. Mead's description of the act in terms of significant symbols, an act whose beginning is determined by imagery of its end, places symbols *within* the act. In doing so he returns symbols to "reality" and "experience."

Mead's argument that mind, self, and society arise in the communication of significant symbols has found few followers within the ranks of American sociologists. And, indeed, with the rise of the Harvard mechanists led by Parsons, Mead's search for a model of sociation based on language is even more remote from the concerns of sociologists in 1961 than it was in 1931. There are many reasons for this, but the neglect of symbolic analysis stems largely from the confusion of science with quantification. Those who believe this to be the true path of sociology accuse Mead, and those who try to follow in Mead's steps, of believing strongly in the social efficacy of symbols without being able to demonstrate how this efficacy is manifest, or at least manifest in ways open to any kind of rigorous discourse.

Those who try to create models for the study of symbolic interaction in society no longer have to defend the "reality of the unseen," as James did in *The Varieties of Religious Experience* in 1902. All now admit that there is something called "symbolic behavior," and Mead's placement of value as the consummatory imagery which affects every stage of the act is generally accepted. Even mechanists admit that we do not act at random but within "fields" whose boundaries are set by values, goals, and purposes. That is, we must have some idea of what we want before we try to get it. Interaction, whether determined by cathexis, learning "process," or "patterned response," is a basic image in contemporary social thought. The problem is then no longer *whether* to study symbolic interaction in society, but *how* to study it. Students of society are agreed that we ought to be studying values, ends, and goals in action, but, again, how this is to be done is one of the crucial problems in contemporary sociology.[1]

The problem of how to study symbolic action is one of how to construct *models of symbolic interaction* which can be applied to the observable data of communication. And if symbolic interactionists (as the followers of Mead are sometimes called) can accuse the mechanists of having a technique but no model, the mechanists, in turn, can accuse Mead of failing to construct a model which will serve as a support for a functional description of symbolic action. There is no question that there is a good deal of confusion in Mead's use of models of symbolic action. And until this confusion is pointed out and cleared up, it will be difficult to construct hypotheses based on Mead's views on symbolic action. As great as is Mead's contribution—and it is very great indeed—we must stop repeating what Mead said and get on with the task of creating hypotheses which we can apply to the concrete reality of communication in society.

Mead's image of how the self arises in communication has four phases. First, there is the image of conversation. On the simplest level, both among men and animals, there is the conversation of gestures.

Meaning arises and lies within the field of the relation between the gesture of a given human organism and the subsequent behavior of this organism as indicated to another human organism by that gesture. . . . In other words, the relationship between a given stimulus—as a gesture—and the later phases of the social act of which it is an early (if not the initial) phase constitutes the field within which meaning originates and exists. Meaning is thus a development of something objectively there as a relation between certain phases of the social act; it is not a physical addition to that act and it is not an "idea" as traditionally conceived.[2]

The conversation of gestures is a triadic relationship. "A gesture by one organism, the resultant of the social act in which the gesture is an early phase, and the response of another organism to the gesture are the relata in a triple or threefold relationship of gesture to first organism, of gesture to second organism, and of gesture to subsequent phases of the given social act; and this threefold relationship constitutes the meaning with which meaning arises, or which develops into the field of meaning."[3] On this level, awareness

or consciousness is not necessary to the presence of meaning in the process of social experience. A gesture on the part of one organism in any given social act calls out a response on the part of the other organism which is directly related to the action of the first organism and its outcome; and a gesture is a symbol of the result of the given social act of one organism (the organism making it) in so far as it is responded to by another organism (thereby also involved in that act) as indicating the result. The mechanism of meaning is thus present in the social act before the emergence of consciousness or awareness of meaning occurs. The act or adjustive response of the second organism gives to the gesture of the first organism the meaning which it has.[4]

On this level of communication there are no symbols, according to Mead, because symbolization

constitutes objects not constituted before, objects which would not exist except for the context of social relationships wherein symbolization occurs. Language does not simply symbolize a situation which is already there in advance; it makes possible the existence or the appearance of that situation or object, for it is a part of the mechanism whereby that situation or object is created. The social process relates the responses of one individual to another. . . . Meaning is thus not to be conceived, fundamentally, as a state of consciousness, or as a set of organized relations existing or subsisting mentally outside of the field of experience into which they enter; on the contrary, it should be conceived objectively, as having its existence entirely within this field itself.[5]

The conversation of gestures is not significant below the human level, because it is not conscious. By this Mead means that it is not self-conscious, not that there is no consciousness of feelings or sensations. In the conversation of gestures, the animal does not indicate to himself what he is indicating to others. His gesture is not symbolic because the response of another organism to it does not indicate to the organism making the gesture what the other organism is responding to. The essential steps by which we attain self-consciousness are two-fold. We learn to take the attitude of individual others toward us, and finally, we learn to take the attitude of a whole community (the "generalized other") toward ourselves.

In early play, the child is continually enacting roles. He plays at being a parent, a teacher, a preacher, a grocery man, a policeman, a pirate, or an Indian. It is a period of endless imitation and make-believe, in which, as Froebel recognized, "the child is acquiring the roles of those who belong in his society." This takes place, not through simple imitation, but because the child "is continually exciting in himself the responses to his own social acts." Since the infant must depend on the responses of others to his own social stimuli, he "is peculiarly sensitive to this relation." Having "in his own nature the beginning of the parental response, he calls it out by his own appeals. The doll is the universal type of this, but before he plays with a doll, he responds in tone of voice and in attitude as his parents respond to his own cries and chortles." [6]

The next stage in the child's experience of communication as a social act is the game.

The play antedates the game. For in a game there is a regulated procedure, and rules. The child must not only take the role of the other, as he does in play, but he must assume the various roles of all the participants in the game, and govern his action accordingly. If he plays first base, it is as the one to whom the ball will be thrown from the field or from the catcher. Their organized reactions to him he has imbedded in his own playing of the different positions, and this organized reaction becomes what I have called the "generalized other" that accompanies and controls his conduct. And it is this generalized other in his experience which provides him with a self.[7]

PROBLEMS IN THE USE OF
MEAD'S CONCEPT OF ROLE-TAKING

The fourth and basic image in Mead's description of how the self and society emerge in communication is that of role-taking. "Taking the role of others" is the characteristic human act in communication, for only in role-taking do we take into account the attitudes of others toward us and toward the situation we share. Attitudes are incipient acts, just as moments of consummation are completed phases of the act. That is, we *act* in roles. The image we have of the way we understand another human being is based on the way he acts, not the way he thinks, discharges affect, or adjusts to his environment. We must be others to become ourselves, and we get to others "by playing at" being another. The self realizes its own role at the same time it realizes the character of other persons who are enacting their roles.

When we try to make a cohesive definition of Mead's role concept, as he uses it in his own writings, we soon discover that he does not use role in the ordinary sense of the word, nor does he make clear the sense in which he uses it. Role is a term taken from drama. It is a part, or character, performed by an actor in a drama; hence, a part or function taken or assumed by anyone (as, the role of philanthropist). The words "part, office, duty" are synonyms. "Office" is the term applied to any prescribed service or form of worship, as when we speak of the "office of the mass." It is also applied to public roles which have become fixed by long tradition, so that we distinguish between how the individual must play his official role and what, as an individual, he adds to the role. As the proverb [8] puts it: "He that puts on a public gown must put off a private person."

Anthropologists often use role concepts, in one guise or another, as indeed do all students of society, when describing men as "acting" together. Thus, in his *Study of Man,* Ralph Linton defines role as "the dynamic aspect of a status. The individual is socially assigned to a status and occupies it with relation to other statuses. When he puts the rights and duties which constitute the status into effect, he is performing a role." He then goes on to say:

Role and status are quite inseparable, and the distinction between them is only of academic interest. . . . Every individual has a series of roles deriving from the various patterns in which he participates and at the same time *a role,* general, which represents the sum total of these roles and determines what he does for his society and what he can expect [9] from it. . . . Although all statuses and roles derive from social patterns and are integral parts of patterns, they have an independent function with relation to the individuals who occupy particular statuses and exercise their roles.

Linton then adopts Mead's image of role-taking in the game.

Status and role serve to reduce the ideal patterns for social life to individual terms. They become models for organizing the attitudes and behavior of the individual so that these will be congruous with those of the other individuals participating in the expression of the pattern. Thus, if we are studying football teams in the abstract, the position of the quarterback is meaningless except in relation to the other positions.

But we must recognize that a status which will be congenial for one may not be for another. Conflict and differences among "social patterns" are met by societies through the development of two types of status, the ascribed and the achieved. Ascribed statuses are those assigned to individuals

without reference to their innate differences or abilities. They can be predicted and trained for from the moment of birth. The *achieved* statuses are, as a minimum, those requiring special qualities, although they are not necessarily limited to these. They are not assigned to individuals from birth but are left open to be filled through competition and individual effort. The majority of the statuses in all social systems are of the ascribed type and those which take care of the ordinary day-to-day business of living are practically always of this type.[10]

The functioning of societies, Linton continues, "depends upon the presence of patterns for reciprocal behavior between individuals or groups of individuals. The polar positions in such patterns of reciprocal behavior are technically known as *statuses.* . . . A *status,* in the abstract, is a position in a particular pattern." [11] And, further, a "status, as distinct from the individual who may occupy it, is simply a collection of rights and duties." The relation between any individual and any status he holds "is somewhat like that between the driver of an automobile and the driver's place in the machine. The driver's seat with its steering wheel, accelerator, and other controls is a constant with ever-present potentialities for action and control, while the driver may be any member of the family and may exercise these potentialities very well or very badly." [12]

Thus, in Linton, role is not a dramatic concept, and certainly it has little to do with communication. Granted that there are "patterns of reciprocal behavior," how do we observe them? And if society is to be likened to an automobile, or any kind of mechanical process, how do machines interact and how does their "behavior" become reciprocal? Machines don't talk, they signal. [13] And if all statuses and roles "derive from social patterns" (which are not determined by communication), what is the source of the "pattern"? Linton answers none of these questions, for his use of the role concept suffers from a fault common to much sociological theory. This fault is the failure to describe structure and function as occurrences within the same field, or, put more simply, mixing images of structure and function so badly that we cannot relate them coherently in our thinking. The individual who takes the role of the other, as in a football game, and who, at the same time, is like the driver of an automobile, simply cannot be related. The construction of hypotheses on the structure and function of the act as determined by communication is possible only when structure and function are images *of the same kind of experience.*

Mead's basic image of the role is not dramatic. His favorite image of role-taking is that of the game, and particularly (as befits a good Chicagoan) of the baseball game. But here it is not the conversation of the players but their *gestures* that he describes. He also uses the term "role" in a mechanical context, as in the section on the process of the mind in nature entitled "The Mechanism of Role-Taking in the Appearance of the Physical Object." [14] Here we are told that the "effective occupation of space involves not simply different degrees of effort in reacting to things but also an experience of the resistance which the object itself offers to these efforts." This implies, Mead continues, "the identification of the individual organism with the object, for resistance which finds its expression in the kinaesthetic experience of effort can appear only in so far as this effort is located in the object." [15]

How does this identification occur, and how do we "feel our way" into the object? Mead begins by pointing out that it is the transfer of the experience of the subject to the object which is important. In Lipps' doctrine of *Einfuhlung,* which Mead mentions in corroboration of his own theory, we project ourselves into the object through aesthetic personification, as when we say we feel we are carried up, or uplifted, by a Gothic tower because the Gothic tower has an upward impulse. In this theory of aesthetic sympathy, Lipps and other German students of aesthetics assumed that the mind conceives of the experience of the other individual as if it were his own, that we live through the psychic states which a lifeless object would experience if it possessed a mental life like our own, and also that we inwardly participate in the movements of an external object. We also conceive of the motions which a body at rest might make if the powers which we attribute to it were actual. We then transfer the aesthetic attitude, which is the result of our own inward sympathy, to the object and speak of the solemnity of the sublime, the gaiety of beauty, etc.

Mead takes his cue from this doctrine of aesthetic sympathy, but generalizes the specific aesthetic content of this sympathy into what he calls a "wider statement." This is to the effect that the

self does not transfer its kinaesthetic sensation to the object but that, through the tendency to push as a physical thing against one's own hand in the role of another individual, one has become a physical object over against the physical thing. Such a development of the physical over against the physical self is an abstraction from an original social experience, for it is primarily in social conduct that we stimulate ourselves to act toward ourselves as others act toward us and thus identify ourselves with others and become objects to ourselves. The identification lies in the identity in the conduct of others toward ourselves with that conduct toward ourselves which we have tended to call out in our own organism. The child by his cry has called out a tendency in his own organism to soothe himself. The identity in kind of this with the sympathetic response of the parent is the identification of the child with the parent.[16]

Thus, says Mead, our earliest objects are social objects, and "all objects are social objects." In later experience, social and physical objects become differentiated, "but the mechanism of the experience of things over against the self as an object is the social mechanism." The identity in the response of a thing, and in the response which we call out in ourselves in acting upon a physical thing,

is given in embracing or grasping or fingering a thing. The thing presses against us as we press against ourselves. We pass on into the thing the pressure which we exert against it in grasping it, and this is something more than the appearance of its surfaces in our experience plus the effort we exert in pressing. The something more is the location of the act of pressing in the thing, over against our own response, and this capacity for location of the act within the thing by our own action against it is what has passed over to our physical conduct from social conduct—passed over by way of abstraction, for the social object is also physical. Out of it arises in experience a physical self, also an abstraction from a social self. In sum, we are conscious of an object because in the act in society we can arouse a response of resistance in our own organism which is also the reaction of the object upon us.[17]

The tendency, then, to take the role of the other applies to physical as well as social objects. But what does Mead really mean when he says that we take the "role" of a stone? That is *how* do we do this? What exactly is the "mechanism" of role-taking? Mead answers by saying that the mechanism functions through symbols. "The mechanism of putting content into the object is that of symbolism; the things which stand for a later stage of the act play into the earlier stage; the ultimate act of driving in a nail is for us the meaning of the hammer. Meanings of things are resultants that control the present act; ends of the act present in the ongoing process."[18] In another passage Mead says: "We talk to nature; we address the clouds, the sea, the tree, and objects about us." An engineer who is constructing a bridge,

is talking to nature in the same sense that we talk to an engineer. There are stresses and strains there which he meets, and nature comes back with other responses that have to be met in another way. In his thinking he is taking the attitude of physical things. He is talking to nature and nature is replying to him. Nature is intelligent in the sense that there are certain responses of nature toward our action which we can present and which we can reply to, and which become different when we have replied.[19]

Now this is singularly elusive reasoning for a tough minded pragmatist. If a thing exists because we can take its role, and if it is a physical thing because it cannot take our role into account, and if this role-taking is described as a mechanism in the social process, what has happened to the private phase of the individual experience Mead himself has taken such great pains to describe as the "I," or the subjective self where the inner drama of role-taking goes on? And what has happened to the positing of language as the principle of social organization as well as of social beings? For if existence of the thing, as of the self, is not just being known but *addressed* as an actor playing a role addresses others, how is this possible in "mechanisms" of a social process?

THE "ORGANIZATION OF PERSPECTIVES" AND COMMUNICATION AS A FORM OF ADDRESS

Mead's world, despite all his talk about action, is not a world where address—that is, the *forms* in which we address each other—determines how we relate to each other. But the decisive element in communication as a social act is the act of address, and the moment of consummation (which in Mead's system characterizes the social quality of action) is a moment in address, as in the drama, *not* "an organization of perspectives," as in looking at something in our environment. We do not organize perspectives in a conversation or in dialogue on the stage; we organize attitudes. That is, in the world composed of perspectives, or process, the individual cannot act, but must be acted upon. Mead argues that the "I" is necessary to account for the expressive forms in society which make possible communication, and that the "Me" cannot exist with an "I." But to say that the "I" is necessary to account for the "Me" on a purely heuristic basis is not the same as saying that the "I" has the same kind of real existence he has given to the "Me," or to "society" which is prior to the "I."

Mead deals very sparingly with the capacity of human beings to take the role of others. He keeps repeating that mind, self, and society arise and develop in the communication of symbols. And, as we have seen, he refers constantly to aesthetic experience, the experience of consummation, as the characteristic social moment, the moment when action is infused with value, and thus makes it meaningful. But his account of symbolic action in art does not justify the use of the term. That is, he has not *demonstrated* how the aesthetic moment of consummation may be used in a model showing how the end of the act infuses the imagery which accompanies stages of perception, and manipulation, with values. Actually, there is very little discussion in Mead of art. To assume that consummation can be understood by analogies taken from aesthetic experience, *without* describing what kind of aesthetic experience (i.e. its form and content) he is talking about, makes the construction of hypotheses very difficult.

It is not enough to be *told* that art and aesthetic experience offers us models of how the self and society arise in communication, we must be *shown specifically what is meant by an act in which we take roles.* In Mead's description we enact roles in models of the act taken from play and games, but the forms in which thought emerges are not those of the game, but conversation. In all these statements of Mead there is a presupposition that we are determined by others—that is, we *are* the others of a team, a group at play, another in conversation, or the gesturing individual—*before* we are selves. To say that meaning is the contribution of the other assumes that the other is the same as the self. That is, if the "I," the subjective self, is the locus of the emergent, the novel, the creative, so must be the "I" of the other. His "I" must be as much a locus of novelty and emergence as mine.[20]

Thus, while Mead assures us that he has rejected all *a priori* entities, all idealistic speculation, and all mechanistic theory of motivation, he has really exchanged these for some absolutes of his own. The Absolute he smuggles in varies from biological to aesthetic categories. Man takes the roles of others because of the construction and function of the brain; man also takes the role of others because of his histrionic tendencies. And, finally, man also takes the role of others because the mechanism of the social process precede those of the individual. So long as these ideas are used to construct hypotheses which are applied to data, there can be no quarrel. But when such ideas as "social process" are found to be both cause and effect, and the concept of role-taking is applied to things as well as persons, we have not abandoned absolutes but simply given them new names. At least religious styles of thought assign man a place as an actor who determines, as well as is determined by, his God. In religious thought and experience, communication reaches its ultimate moment in the address of God in prayer. We may not agree with this ultimate, but at least it is a moment of communication. In behavioral psychology, and all "sciences" of man based on mechanical models, communication and role-taking cannot be considered as moments of address by actors, but only signals by "message centers."

Mead's "generalized other" is a curiously benign other. In the dialogue between the "I" and the "Me," or between the "I" and the "generalized other," the group or the community, there seems to be no deception, no hate, no indifference. But is there really much justification, logical *or* moral, for such equating of the "moral" with the "social"? [21] For a generation living with the terrible memories of the torture and murder in Hitler's death camps and the torture and murder of Negroes in our own country, Mead's world of benign others who, if they can only be reached, will help the individual to realize himself to his fullest capacity, seems a utopian dream. It certainly was not the society shared by Veblen, Mead's colleague at the University of Chicago, nor Louis H. Sullivan, the great American architect, who was also in Chicago at the same time as Mead.[22]

Mead's assumption that an increase of knowledge would bring an increase of virtue does credit to his heart if not to his head. His extraordinary optimism and deep belief in human perfectibility were evidently a matter of choice. It was by no means the prevailing attitude among the artists and intellectuals of Chicago during Mead's life in the city. Few cities in the world were rocked by more violence. Life in Chicago slums and the struggle of the workers for a fair share of business profits supplied themes for Upton Sinclair's *The Jungle,* the *Uncle Tom's Cabin* of wage slavery, which became a sensation overnight in 1905. No city in the world was studied so closely, written about so much, and exposed so openly as Chicago. Yet in the midst of all this exposure of the dangers of a democratic society, Mead was consistently optimistic. Not even the First World War shook his complacency in the world he saw from the University of Chicago.

Mead assumed without much question that an increase in knowledge would bring an increase in good.

Anthropology and all the comparative social sciences have been making it easier and easier for us to put ourselves in the places of those far removed from us by social caste, economic status, race, and differences of culture and civilization. They bring us nearer the emotional attitude which has been the inspiration of the universal religions, that of regarding every man as our neighbor. In fact, we may regard as paramount the results of the physical and social sciences in bringing the members of the whole human community on earth into such close social relations, and into such intimate comprehension of one another, that the toleration of the evils of misery, of disease, of war, and ignorance, which spring from the isolations of communities from one another, becomes increasingly possible. . . . Men in human society have come into some degree of control of the process of evolution out of which they arose . . .[23]

How incredible this sounds in the time of Buchenwald and Hiroshima!

But the most serious flaw in Mead for the student who seeks to create a sociological model of communication is his failure to create a consistent model of the act. Few have said more than Mead about communication, and certainly his concept of communication as the process in which the self and society emerge is one of our great contributions to social thought. No American social philosopher has related art to communication more than Mead. But, despite Mead's use of aesthetic categories of experience and his placement of the consummatory moment in the act, he never really tells us how *art* arises in, and continues to exist in, communication in society, and what likenesses and differences exist between art and the social as categories of experience.

We have already spoken about the lack of consistency in his images of the act in society and his failure to develop a clear model of the act as it functions in communication. The source of the fault lies not, as some sociologists seem to think, in his use of art, but in his bad use of it. That is, when we are told that the act is to be understood through art, and yet art is never analyzed to show how it produces the social effects it is supposed to produce, or how it can be used to create a model of the act which, while derived from an art we have not yet defined, can yet be used to understand society, we are left hanging in the air. It does us little good to know that the consummatory phase of the act is like aesthetic phases of experience, if we are not told something about the form and content of aesthetic experience. For if the kind of experience we have in art determines certain phases of social action, then we ought to know what constitutes art as experience and how such experience affects society.

Mead's "I," the subjective self whose dialogue with its "Me," and the "generalized other," create the conditions from which the individual emerges in society, seems to arise from two sources—nature and art. To create his "Me," Mead turns to nature, while for his "I" he turns to art. Then occur highly dexterous sleight-of-hand operations in which nature is explained by art, which in turn explains nature. That is, whenever Mead talks about the self he turns to a discussion of imagery, and particularly of imagery of a future, but when he talks about society he turns to images of process, of environment, adaptation, and response. He is, he tells us, developing a behavioristic psychology "which is planting communication, thinking, and substantive meanings as inextricably within nature as biological psychology has placed general animal and human intelligence. . . ."[24]

But if Mead, like Hume, denies the self a spiritual substance and defines it in terms of tendencies to act, and defines the act, in turn, as symbolic, he must be careful not to give the self a substance in nature which, if not spiritual, is no less mystical. And, if the self is to be saved from being reduced to "nature," then we must show *how* it arises in symbolic experience. This leads us into religion or art, the great symbolic structures of society. The works of Durkheim and his followers teach us something about the pitfalls of finding the sources of society in religious expression. For if models of society are taken from religion, communication as well as society must be subordinated to religion, and art (the creative source of communication) subordinated to nothing more than a communication of religion. But we know that aesthetic experience is an experience which exists in its own right, and we know that if any institution is concerned with the creation and use of the symbols by which we communicate, it is art. Why not, then, turn directly to art to find clues for ways to create a model useful for ordering the only social facts we really can observe, namely, how we express ourselves as we enact our roles in society?

Notes

[1] The Harvard Laboratory of Social Relations cannot be accused of neglecting the study of values, as the *Selected Biography on Values, Ethics, and Esthetics in the Behavioral Sciences and Philosophy, 1920–1928* (Glencoe, Ill.: The Free Press, 1959), makes clear. Unfortunately, this bibliography is very weak in the field where the best thinking of our time on the function of symbols in society has been done. This is in literary criticism. Kenneth Burke's *Permanence and Change* (Los Altos, Calif.: Hermes Publication, 1954), and *Attitudes Toward History* (Los Altos, Calif.: Hermes Publication, 1959) are not mentioned. Arnold Hauser's *Social History of Art* (London: Routledge & Kegan Paul, 1951) is not mentioned. Despite the mention of aesthetics in the title, this bibliography is not a very reliable guide to the sociological study of art and aesthetics. Such neglect of art, and particularly of literary criticism, limits its value as a tool for the study of how values arise in communication, and thus in society.

[2] George Herbert Mead, *Mind, Self, and Society* (Chicago: Univ. of Chicago Press, 1934).

[3] *Ibid.*, p. 76.

[4] *Ibid.*, pp. 77–78.

[5] *Ibid.*, p. 78. In a footnote to this passage we read: "Nature has meaning and implication but not indication by symbols. The symbol is distinguishable from the meaning it refers to. Meanings are in nature, but symbols are the heritage of man."

[6] *The Philosophy of the Present* (Chicago and London: Open Court Publishing Company, 1932), p. 186. Mead adds: "This has been denominated imitation, but the psychologist now recognizes that one imitates only in so far as the so-called imitated act can be called out in the individual by his appropriate stimulation. That is, one calls or tends to call out in himself the same response that he calls out in the other."

[7] *Ibid.*, p. 186.

[8] Proverbial lore sums up this distinction in different ways. "When God gives a man an office, He gives him brains enough to fill it" (German proverb). "Fortune often redresses the eminence of an office by the inferiority of the office-holder" (Baltasar Gracian, *The Art of Worldly Wisdom*, CLXXXII). In *King Lear*, Shakespeare sums up the bitterness of all those suffering from the weight of power in office. "Thus hast seen a farmer's dog bark at a beggar? And the Creature run from a cur? There thou might'st behold the great image of authority: a dog's obeyed in office" (Act IV).

[9] It should be noted that Linton does not mention Mead in a footnote, or even in the bibliography!

[10] See Chapter VIII, "Status and Role," in *The Study of Man* (New York and London: D. Appleton-Century Company, 1936) for Linton's discussion of this. The quotation given here occurs on p. 115.

[11] *Ibid.*, p. 113.

[12] *Ibid.*

[13] A machine's signals have to be set by some one. Linton's confusion in using Mead's role concept is not unique. The conception of the social bond as arising in, and existing through, communication of significant symbols has not been reduced to hypotheses which can be tested in symbolic data. Not all of this failure can be ascribed to the ineptness of American social scientists in thinking about role-taking. Some of the confusion in Mead's writings may be the result of student editing, for the three large volumes of the work of Mead are taken largely from students' notes, unpublished manuscripts, and notes taken from Mead's papers after his death. But even in the essays, articles, and lectures which Mead himself published, there is no consistent development of his concept of role-taking.

[14] See George Herbert Mead, *The Philosophy of the Act* (Chicago: Univ. of Chicago Press, 1938), pp. 426–442.

[15] *Ibid.*, p. 427.

[16] *Ibid.*, pp. 428–429.

[17] *Ibid.*, p. 429.

[18] George Herbert Mead, *Mind, Self, and Society* (Chicago: Univ. of Chicago Press, 1934).

[19] *Ibid.*, pp. 184–185.

[20] Paul E. Pfuetze, in *The Social Self* (New York: Bookman Associates, 1954), offers a very good exposition, comparison, and criticism of the concept of the social self in the writings of Mead and Martin Buber. It is by far the best commentary on Mead. Pfuetze argues that the corrective to Mead's "social positivism" is religion, while I argue here that it is art. This difference does not in any way affect the cogency and usefulness of Professor Pfuetze's criticism.

[21] This is Professor Pfuetze's point, and one that he deals with so trenchantly that the reader is referred to his discussion, "The Validity and Value of the Social Self," which is Chapter V of Pfuetze's *The Social Self*.

[22] See Sullivan's *Democracy: A Man-Search* (Detroit: Wayne State University Press, 1961), where he links the crucifixion of Christ to money-changers (in their modern counterpart, the business man). In Thorstein Veblen's *The Higher Learning in America: A Memorandum on the Conduct of Universities by Business Men* (New York: B. W. Huebsch, 1918) the business man (certainly the "generalized other" of Chicago from 1890 to 1930) is cunning, shrewd, and predatory. When he is not higgling the market for all it will bear, he is engaged in swinish bouts of eating and drinking which will leave "those characteristic pathological marks that come of what is conventionally called 'high living'—late hours, unseasonable vigils, surfeit of victuals and drink, the fatigue of sedentary ennui. A flabby habit of body, hypertrophy of the abdomen, varicose veins, particularly of the facial tissues, a bleary eye and a coloration suggestive of bile and apoplexy—when this unwholesome bulk is duly wrapped in a conventionally decorous costume it is accepted rather as a mark of weight and responsibility and so serves to distinguish the pillars of urban society." (See note on page 243 of *The Higher Learning*.)

[23] Mead, *The Philosophy of the Act*, p. 511.

[24] See "The Objective Reality of Perspectives," in *The Philosophy of the Present*, p. 162.

PART THREE

The Function of Symbols in Society: an Application of Burke's Dramatistic View of Social Relationships

8

Burke's Dramatistic View of Society

K ENNETH BURKE holds that while expressive forms are part of a communicative context which is not wholly verbal, they do have a nature of their own. When discussing them as modes of action, "we must consider both this nature as words in themselves and the nature they get from non-verbal scenes that support their acts." A theory of communication in society must therefore be a theory of language, and a theory of how language functions in society; the identification of the "substance of a particular literary act by a theory of literary action in general." This involves a definition of "literary act" and "communicative context." For if we say that society arises in and through communication, we must define what we mean by "society," and by "communication."

There are, Burke points out, many ways to talk about society. For Aquinas, the principle of society existed in the supernatural power of God; for Marx, in the ownership of productive resources; for Darwin, in a nature where organisms were determined by their struggle for survival; for Max Weber, in the structures of authority. Such monistic views no longer serve our purposes, not because they are wrong but because we need a *general* theory of symbolic action in society, as well as a social theory of communication. We need, too, propositions about symbols concrete enough to be tested by observation of symbols as they are used in communication. The problem we face is how to consider words "as acts upon a scene," so that we avoid the "*excess* of environmentalist schools which are usually so eager to trace the relationships between act and scene that they neglect to trace the structure of the act itself."

Analysis of social acts must take full account of complexities and ambiguities. We cannot say that recent behavioristic accounts of conduct are false, for man inhabits space and is therefore determined by laws of motion. The real question is: How *representative* of human acts and for our purposes here, of symbolic action, is such theory? What kinds of conduct does it neglect; what kind does it include? Obviously, we cannot answer these questions, and cannot generalize from any specialized view, unless we have a general theory of communication as symbolic interaction. We have enough analogies of man as a primitive, a child, a machine, a buyer and seller, a rat, etc., but we lack sociological ways of thinking of man as he relates in communication to other men in anxiety, doubt, confusion, love, hate, fear, despair, and hope. For this is our *human* condition. We do not need theories of authority *beyond* doubt and rejection, but of how authority is achieved *in* doubt and rejection. We must think of authority (and certainly democratic authority) as a resolution of contending voices through some kind of social transcendence which is not revealed by supernatural powers, determined by "social forces," but open to reason and unreason, in discussion and debate. In democratic society, authority is achieved only when differences are recognized, inspired, indeed *goaded,* to intense and self-conscious expression, and *then* resolved. When differences are avoided and when ways of expressing differences openly are minimized, *not* maximized, democracy wanes and dies. When disagreement becomes heresy, democracy cannot exist.

In one of his early discussions on literature in society, "Literature as Equipment for Living," [1] Burke proposes that we begin thinking about the function of literature in terms of proverbs. "Examine random specimens of proverbs and you find no 'pure' literature because they are designed for consolation, vengeance, admonition, exhortation, and foretelling —all ways of charting conduct so we can act successfully." Proverbs are "*strategies* for dealing with *situations.* In so far as situations are typical and recurrent in a given social structure people develop names for them and strategies for handling them. Another name for strategies might be attitudes." [2] In this view an art work is the "strategic naming of a situation." It singles out a pattern of experience that is sufficiently representative of our social structure, that recurs sufficiently often *mutatis mutandis,* for people to "need a word for it" and to adopt an attitude toward it. [3]

The rise of the once humble businessman to power is such a representative act in our society, perhaps even *the* representative American act. Following Burke, we would codify the various strategies artists develop for naming business relations. We begin by examining proverbial expression— attitudes toward business expressed in slang, the cant and jargon of business apologist, as well as in art proper. This examination does not require insight because we deal with existing facts (the documents of art and all expression), facts which exist independently of the analyst, and facts whose function in society can be checked by sources independent of art. We have the novels of Mark Twain, Howells, Dreiser, Lewis, Herrick, the aphorisms of Franklin, Howe, and Haskins, the business "gospel" of Bruce Barton, the success stories of Lorimer, and even juvenilia on the boy businessman in Horatio Alger, Jr. We have the business buildings of Root, Burnham, Adler, Holabird and Roche, Sullivan, Wright, and Mies van der Rohe. We find business cursed by interests whose power it threatens, blessed by those it upholds, and doubted by others who think the relations between business and society should be open to inquiry. How business defends itself, how it attacks its enemies, how it seeks to silence doubts, the strategies and tactics of struggle for power is *not* a matter of inference, but a communicative act, and, therefore, an existent symbolic act.

Social categories for the analysis of art and all communication in society must cross the categories of modern specialization. What would such sociological categories be like?

They would consider works of art as strategies for selecting enemies and allies, for socializing losses, for warding off evil eye, for purification, propitiation, and desanctification, consolation and vengeance, admonition and exhortation, implicit commands or instructions of one sort or another. Art forms like "tragedy" or "comedy" or "satire" would be treated as *equipments for living*, that size up in various ways and in keeping with correspondingly various attitudes. The typical ingredients of such forms would be sought. Their relation to typical situations would be stressed. Their comparative values would be considered, with the intention of formulating a "strategy of strategies," the "over-all" strategy obtained by inspection of the lot.[4]

We accept, reject, and doubt reigning symbols of authority. Acceptance, as when we make an authority's commands our duty, is the most rewarding adjustment to authority. But when incongruity between means and ends becomes so great we cannot act, or suffer greatly when we do act, we reject authority. When doubt and question are still subject to reason, and we still believe that authority is capable of correction, we are skeptical but not rebellious. When we *must* reject reigning symbols we are alienated, and if such dispossession (either material or spiritual) increases, we pass into despair and madness, or crime and war. In their search for a place in the social order men enroll in many groups and thus obtain a social and psychological identity. In our complex society no one is a member of only one institution. The individual must identify with many institutions. Sometimes these institutions are in harmony, sometimes in conflict, with each other.

In times of transition shifts in allegiance to symbols of authority are common. Problems of identity, not simply the need to belong but with whom to belong, become crucial. When men cannot act under one set of names they must choose others; *how* such choices are made is revealed in the symbolic phases of the struggle for new meanings. Identity is expressed as a glory, a mystical moment of belonging in which we commit ourselves to act under a certain name. These inner "mysterious" moments must be expressed to become acts or attitudes, which are incipient acts. Thus, identification is always dependent on objectification through communication.

Style itself is an aspect of identification. Styles evoke a hallowed past, or a cherished future, as we try to act well in the present. Even a materially dispossessed immigrant or a poor youth may "own" privilege vicariously by adopting the style of a privileged class. Thus a Polish immigrant buys an "American Colonial" house, or a high school boy borrows expensive adult clothing and a car to "date" his girl (who in turn boasts symbolically by wearing clothes borrowed from older sisters and her parents). Such "symbolic boasting" is a clue to social identification; it tells us to whom people *want* to belong.

Human relations, Burke argues, are analyzed best in terms of drama. "Men enact roles. They change roles. They participate. They develop modes of social appeal." People are not animals, or machines, nor do they "relate" in configurations.[5] They relate as actors playing roles to achieve satisfactions which only other human actors can give them. They do so through communication which, like struggle in the drama, involves both competition and cooperation. The difference between symbolic and social drama is the difference between imaginary and real obstacles, but, to produce effects on audiences, symbolic drama must reflect the real obstacles of social drama. Conflict must then be resolved in the symbolic realm by the expression of attitudes which make conformity possible. All such expression, like prayer, is an exhortation to the self and to others. It is a preparation for social action, an investment of the self with confidence and strength.

If the structure of social action is dramatic, what is the social function of this structure? As Burke tells us in his *Attitudes Toward History,* the symbolic expression of social structure is an expression of authority. We create and sustain social order through a distribution of authority. Authorities embody their power in roles whose enactment is held necessary to community survival. There are many kinds of institutional orders, and every institution struggling for power believes, indeed, *must* believe, that its values are very necessary to community well being. But whatever its values, any institution seeking to dominate a society must perform seven basic functions.[6] It must govern, serve, defend, teach, entertain, cure, and create and sustain symbols of integration great enough to overcome the disintegrative forces of fear and weakness. Only very powerful institutions perform one or more of these functions, but a well-rounded community life requires them all. Institutional allocation of these functions vary from time to time, and from one society to another. Thus, curing ills may be done by magicians, priests, doctors, or artists.[7] Symbols of integration may be created and controlled by the church, the army, the state, or the school.

Old and powerful institutions create and sustain their power through dramatic enactment in community presentations, as in the many Christian dramas of salvation. The Passions of Christ, the Fall of Adam, the struggle between God and the Devil in *Paradise Lost* are dramas of Christian order which are assumed (by Christians at least) to be dramas of social order. The Fall of Adam is the fall of man; the sufferings of Christ are the sufferings of men. Principles of institutional order become principles of social order. Common to all communication of order must be a central drama, a "ritual drama" which is held sacred because society is created and sustained through its enactment. Such dramatic enactment does not "reflect" social structure, but *creates* it. When the devout Christian eats bread and drinks wine during communion service, he creates Christian fellowship. Christians do not go to communion simply to be with other Christians, but to reenact their Christian fellowship in the act of communion.

Religious ideas of order assume God as both creator and ruler. God's problem is man's disobedience. Yet if man is to be free he must be allowed choice between good and evil. God's rule is manifest in a covenant which implies that it is possible (indeed, probable) that it will be broken. Rewards (heaven) for those who obey, punishment (hell) for those who disobey are described. Commandments are both positive and negative ("thou shall" and "thou shalt not"). Disobedience comes from the senses and the imagination, obedience from faith and reason; we must therefore fortify the senses to keep them subordinate to faith and reason. Men sin through disobedience, not through ignorance, for man once knew grace in the Garden of Eden, and grace of God can be seen again if we but open our hearts and mind to Him. The tragedy of man is that he knows God, yet disobeys His laws. Only in humbling himself before God, in patience, repentance, and sacrifice will he be redeemed. But the burden of human sin is too heavy for mortal expiation. Thus emerges the sacred victim, and the principle of victimage becomes fixed in religious ritual.

Now a devout Christian does not think of this as a narrative subject, like all narrative, to aesthetic norms. He thinks his drama is the actual drama of the human soul, and until we understand the Fall and redemption by vicarious atonement, as told in the Bible, we cannot understand human motives. The Edenic myth is not, then, true or false from a historic view, but true in principle (Christian principle, that is) for it represents the spiritual voyage each man must make and the kind of ritual a society must uphold, if there is to be order within the individual and in social relations. An artist, in turn, may argue that since the myth of Creation, Eden, and the Fall *is* an art form, it is subject to the laws of such form. Stories are told in certain ways, and the way selected will determine social expression of the ritual. And he will argue, as Burke does, that only when we analyze carefully the ways in which language is used do we know what terms ascribed to God nature, or society, really mean. For, if God determines language, He, in turn, is determined by His own creation, for it is through language and other expressive symbols, that men communicate with Him.

THE NATURE OF SYMBOLIC ACTION IN SOCIETY

Burke's system, which he calls "Dramatism," is distinguished from Mead's and others' by its grounding in symbols themselves. He does not tell us simply *what* symbols do in communication, but *how* they do what he says they do. That is, he *begins* where others like Mead and Malinowski *end*. As we plunge into his work, we feel at once that here, for the first time in American social thought, is a discussion of *how* symbols operate as symbols in communication and how communication, in turn, affects social order. Burke does not explain symbols by something outside of symbols, such as God, sex, nature, mind, society, environment context of situation, taking the role of the other, collective representations, or cathexis. Instead, he argues that if we regard man as a symbol-using animal we must stress symbolism *as a motive* in any discussion of social behavior. That is, the kind of symbols we have, who can use them, when, where, how, and why

—these do not "reflect" motives, they *are* motives.

This is not all that interests Burke about symbols. Our leading question—How can we create a sociological model of society based on communication?—limits our analysis of Burke's work. What follows is but *one* aspect of Burke's work, and is in no way to be considered an analysis of all his work. Burke's concern with the philosophical, aesthetic, and moral aspects of language must be understood if we are to understand his specific sociological concerns, but since our task here is the creation of a sociological model of communication, we stress elements in Burke's work that will help in this task.

"Human conduct," Burke states, "being in the realm of action and end (as contrasted with the physicist's realm of motion and position) is most directly discussible in dramatistic terms. By 'dramatistic' terms are meant those that begin in theories of *action* rather than in theories of *knowledge*." [8] Terminologies based on the observation of sensory perception, of how we move in a world or how we perceive it, cannot be used to describe social acts as communicative acts. Thus, for Burke, theories of conditioning are not theories of social action, because they tell us little about the specifically human interaction in society—however much they tell us about motion in space. This does not mean that Burke regards action in society as *purely* symbolic. On the contrary, he takes great pains to relate symbols to biological, social, and psychological needs. It is the *reduction* of symbols to things outside of symbols which he argues against. [9]

"Man," he says, "being generically a biological organism, the ideal terminology [for talking about human behavior] must present his symbolic behavior as grounded in biological conditions." But to say that it must be grounded in biology is not to say that we can explain the *human* experience of biological functioning *without* reference to language. Property is a necessity in a purely biological sense, and in sociology we use ecological concepts to describe the kinds of mechanical balance characteristic of a sub-verbal, extra-verbal, or non-verbal community. "Balance" may be of many kinds. We may study the balance of traffic, food resources, breeding grounds, play space, etc., to show how purely spatial patterns emerge out of the adaptation of one creature, or one thing, to another. But though man as a biological organism requires property in a purely biological sense, and we can study property from a purely mechanical view, man, because of his nature "as a characteristically symbol-using species . . . can conceptualize a symbolic analogue of [property]." [10]

Such analogues exist in terms like "rights" and "obligations." It is true enough that food and shelter are not, or at least not in their rudimentary sense, "rights" but "necessities." Yet men use symbols to possess property which they claim through "rights" that have little to do with biological needs. The idea of rights in nature, as such critics as Jeremy Bentham, Karl Mannheim, and others have pointed out, is a metaphysical subterfuge for "sanctioning in apparently biological terms a state of affairs that is properly discussed in terms specifically suited to the treatment of symbolism as motive." "Rights" are not in "nature"; they are "a result of man-made laws, which depend upon the resources of language for their form." [11]

What we often do with property rights, and, indeed, all social rights, is to ascribe them to nature [12] and then derive them from it. Such a mode of sanction seems persuasive "only because 'nature' itself [is] being perceived through a terministic fog that took form by analogy with socio-political principles then current." [13] The role of symbols in shaping men's views on the ownership of money and land is seen too in the division of labor, and the handing down of property. Here there are not only abstract rights, but specific rights for certain classes or conditions of people which are determined by age, sex, family membership, skill, conquest, religion, or ownership. Thus even "natural law" or "universal law" has localized and specific applications, indeed, can only be understood in terms of how it functions at a given time and place.

There must be some kind of order among these "rights" if the society in which they exist is to function at all. This order is not some kind of "equilibrium" or "balance" or "regularity," but an enactment of authority, a "mutuality of rule and service" which takes a hierarchical form in some kind of social ladder. *Why* certain characteristics determine hierarchical position, and *how* the acceptance of these characteristics determines social bonds, can be determined only by the study of the terms men use to invest a system of hierarchy with powers which are supposed to guarantee order. "Thus the purely *operational* motives binding society become inspirited by a corresponding condition of *Mystery*." We call these mysteries by various names. Sexual "glamour" (the "sweet mystery of love") is one of these. The "divine right" of kings, "the voice of the people is the voice of God," or "God, the Father, Son, and Holy Ghost," are others. But whatever we call them, they are, in the last analysis, the "ultimate conditions" of our social bonds, the "glories" we live by. [14]

Mystery springs from difference and strangeness. "Owing to their different modes of living and livelihood, classes of people become 'mysteries' to one another." Men and women become mysteries to each other simply through differences which they uphold, and even accentuate—through modesty, coyness, and all the arts of sexual courtship. We do not seek in sexual courtship (or any other kind of courtship) to *obliterate* the mystery of difference and strangeness, but to *enhance* it as a condition of social order. The tension caused by sexual or social difference is the basis for the pleasure we feel when we reach the other *in* his difference, *through* his difference. [15] We experience such moments of resolution in moments of social communion, and these great moments intensify our social bonds.

We have many studies of priestly stress upon mystery. The simplest case seems to be found in the primitive tribe where all classes and status groups derive their *mana* from their power to create and sustain social order. Tribal priests accentuate the differences, the Mysteries of different classes in the tribe, because these differences are held necessary, *not* inimical, to tribal cohesion. All such differences are considered a *distribution* of authority which favors some at the expense of others. In complex societies "the normal priestly function of partly upholding and partly transcending the Mysteries of class, is distributed among many kinds of symbol-users (particularly educators, legislators, journalists, advertising men and artists)." [16] The priestly stress upon Mystery, which "attains its grandest expression in the vision of a celestial hierarchy loosely imagined after the analogy of a human social order, becomes secularized and distributed among these other roles, each of which treats the social Mystery after its own fashion." [17]

Thus, the educator has rituals and ceremonies where cap, gown, and Gothic are used as insignia of the majesty and splendour of learning; legislators gain respect for themselves through arousing respect for the august body of which they are members; businessmen (with the artist's help) surround a system of social values with "glamor," as they find ways to transform the austere religious passion of the holy day into a holiday where we are exhorted not to pray but to spend our way into heaven. In all such symbolic undertakings, journalists and commercial artists in the advertising world make a good team, "since the one group keeps us abreast of the world's miseries, and the other keeps us agog with promises of extreme comfort, the two combining to provide a crude, secular analogue of the distinction between Christus Crucifixus and Christus Triumphans." [18]

But as powerful as is the social drama, we must be careful not to reduce mystery in general to hierarchal mystery in particular. "Though we would stress the element of Mystery arising from the social hierarchy, we must recognize that there are other mysteries, other orders." There are "the mysteries of dream, of creation, of death, of life's stages, of thought (its arising, its remembering, its diseases). There are the mysteries of adventure and love. (As property is part natural, part doctrinal, so love is part natural, part courtesy.)" Sociological analysis of such powers must deal with the linkage between them and social glamor, the moment when social bonds are infused with a deep sense of communion. For "social mystery gains in depth, persuasiveness, allusiveness and illusiveness precisely by reason of the fact that it becomes inextricably interwoven with mysteries of these other sorts, quite as these other mysteries must in part be perceived through the fog of the social mystery." [19]

We see this clearly in our sexual responses. To *reduce* sex to status, as the sociologist sometimes does, or status to sex, as Freud does, is fallacious. Our sexual reactions are *both* sexual and status reactions, just as our social reactions are *both* social *and* sexual.[20] The glamorous woman of *Harper's Bazaar*, or any magazine of high fashion, seldom appeals to us through her nudity but through her style in covering her body with "elegant" clothes. Thus even the fundamental biological drive of sex relies on the communication of hierarchy for its expression. Proper sociological analysis will then seek to distinguish the *proportions* of social and biological satisfactions in the sexual act.[21]

Notes

[1] This is included in *The Philosophy of Literary Form* (New York: Vintage Books, 1957), which is a revision and abridgement of the edition of 1941 published by Louisiana State University Press.

[2] *Ibid.*, p. 256. Burke's italics.

[3] *Ibid.*, p. 259.

[4] *Ibid.*, p. 262.

[5] The image of configurations, like all pictorial images, is really not much better than mechanical images. Pictures, like machines, don't talk. The unconscious pictorial imagery of myth (Jung's archetypes), as well as visual dream symbols, are still subject to verbal imagery for they are reported in talk, analyzed in talk, and communicated

in words which have their conventions of expression determined purely by their nature as words. Thus, like the mathematician, the analyst is bound by the nature of his symbols.

⁶ These are discussed by Kenneth Burke in his article "The Seven Offices," *Diogenes*, No. 21 (Spring, 1958), pp. 68–84.

⁷ Art is now used for therapeutic purposes. The "efficiency" of comedy for health (a laugh a day keeps the doctor away) has long been recognized, as in Robert Burton's *Anatomy of Melancholy*, first published in 1621.

⁸ Kenneth Burke, *Permanence and Change: An Anatomy of Purpose*, rev. ed. with new preface and appendix (Los Altos, Calif.: Hermes Publications, 1954). This quotation is taken from the essay in the appendix entitled "On Human Behavior Considered 'Dramatistically.' " See page 274.

⁹ Obviously, the reduction of things to symbols alone is equally false. No matter how much symbolism surrounds the act of giving birth to a baby, the completed act is very different from the symbolic phases of the act. No matter how many poems we write about motherhood, the real act of motherhood cannot be explained as a social act purely in symbolic terms. In Burke's thought there are few "either-or," but many "both-and" propositions. He seeks proportions, not essences, in his search for a model of the act. As we shall see, he expands Mead's triadic model of the act (perception, manipulation, consummation) to a pentad (act, scene, agent, agency, and purpose). Mead's triad explains how we perceive the world; Burke's pentad accounts for how we act in society, in so far as action is determined by communication.

¹⁰ Burke, *op. cit.*, p. 275.

¹¹ *Ibid.*, p. 276.

¹² We may also ascribe them to God, the state, or a socio-political order.

¹³ Burke, *op. cit.*, p. 278. Nature "red in tooth and claw" and other descriptions of "nature" are evidence of the fact that man depicts "nature" through the lens of his socio-political, theological, and psychological concerns. This does not deny that man has a biologically conditioned nature, but that this "nature" in so far as it relies on communication between separate beings for its satisfaction, *even on a purely biological level as in hunger and sex,* must be analyzed in symbolic, as well as physical, terms. This has been a truism in sociology since Sumner's day. But *how* symbols, the *expression* of sex and hunger, affect their nature as social acts had not yet been studied by American social scientists. From them we learn *what* "society" or "culture" does, but very little about *how* it does all the things it is supposed to be doing.

¹⁴ In the presidential campaign of 1960 we heard that Senator John F. Kennedy attracted "touchers" and "squealers"—women who broke through police barriers to touch Senator Kennedy, and others, somewhat younger, who jumped and "squealed" when he presented himself to them. Experienced journalists, little given to sentiment, described the Kennedy campaign as "catching fire" because "an indescribable aura" (which is then described in thousands of words) emanated from Kennedy. Thus we read: "They have a word for it in India: This thing between Sen. John F. Kennedy and the shouting, shoving boys and girls and men and women who break police lines to grasp the senator's hand or merely touch him. . . . In India it is called 'darshan.' It means an electric, mysterious rapport between a leader and the people, born out of a deep emotional feeling that he grasps—better than they themselves—their profoundest aspirations and their deepest needs." Chicago *Sun Times*, October 31, 1960, p. 8.

¹⁵ Gallants like Casanova tell us that sexual pleasure depends on the effort involved in the pursuit of the sexual partner. Romantic love, as De Rougement points out,

enhances sex because it pits sex against suffering and death, as in the Tristan and Isolde myth.

[16] Kenneth Burke, *op. cit.*, p. 276.

[17] *Ibid.*, p. 277. Burke's use of the term "Mystery" is no more hazy than the Dionysiac "Social Bond" of Durkheim, the moment of "pure socialization" in Simmel, or the mystical mechanics of the "social equilibrium" of Parsons. And, unlike most social scientists, Burke is careful *not* to *ascribe* effects to his social moment of "mystery" and then *derive* the same effects he has already ascribed.

[18] *Ibid.*, p. 277. I have discussed this in "Literature as Magical Art," which is Chapter II of my *Language and Literature in Society* (Chicago, Ill.: Univ. of Chicago Press, 1953; reprinted by The Bedminster Press, New York, 1961).

[19] Kenneth Burke, *op. cit.*, pp. 277–278.

[20] Our social reactions are a fusion of many other reactions too. Religion, art, and politics are but three of these. Here, as in so many other places in his work, Burke warns us that *proportional* and not essentializing propositions must be used because they tell us *more* about the single "essence" we are studying.

[21] As we shall point out later in our discussion of the communication of sex in society, much of what passes for analysis of "sexual determinants" in society is really a discussion of hierarchy. Sadism, masochism, fetishism, and many of the perversions display an extraordinary *social* content. Sexual satisfaction is reached *through* social symbols, and thus depends on communication as well as biology. In the chapter "The Naked and the Nude" of his *The Nude: A Study in Ideal Form* (New York: The Phaidon Press, 1956), Kenneth Clark says: "It is widely supposed that the naked human body is in itself an object upon which the eye dwells with pleasure and which we are glad to see depicted. But anyone who has frequented art schools and seen the shapeless, pitiful model that the students are industriously drawing will know this is an illusion. The body is not one of those subjects which can be made into art by direct transcription—like a tiger or a snowy landscape." (p. 65)

9

Social Order Considered as a Drama of Redemption Through Victimage

M YSTERY," in Burke's terminology, is used to denote the deep moment of communion when we identify with each other so closely that, as we say, "we are one." But there are opposite moments, moments of profound social disrelationship, which Burke describes under the term "guilt." Guilt arises out of *negation* of the principles of social order, and their expression in hierarchy. We believe we should be identifying with such a principle, but we are not. Our sin is a sin of disobedience. There is another type of disrelationship which Burke calls "hierarchal embarrassment." The specialist in one field "is not 'guilty' with regard to the specialist in another field; he is *embarrassed*. He doesn't know exactly how much to question, how much to take on authority, how much to be merely polite about." [1]

The most profound example of hierarchical tension, Burke argues, "is in the theological doctrine of Original Sin." " 'Original sin' is categorical guilt, one's 'guilt' not as a result of any personal transgression, but by reason of a tribal or dynastic inheritance." We see this in *Huckleberry Finn,* where the curse of being a Negro and a slave is laid upon Jim before Huck and Jim run away together. On their wonderful voyage together Huck is embarrassed because he does not know how to act toward Jim as an individual. When he acts in terms of Jim's tribal guilt as a Negro slave he is thrown into deep conflict because Jim's "tribal guilt" and his capacity for love and nobility in friendship far surpasses Huck's. That is, by the principles of the white social order, Jim is superior.[2]

Thus what seems at first glance to be simply a theological concept is found to be, Burke says, a paradigm for certain aspects of all social disrelationships. There is no society without *some* idea of original sin, which is expressed socially by branding some group as the categorical "cause" of disrelationships. What sociologists call stereotypes function in this way. Jews, Negroes, and minority groups are branded as evil *before* they act at all. Heretics are damned to eternal punishment *before* they are born. Like Adam, who sinned because of his generic human nature, the target of prejudice sins because of a tribal, dynastic, or familial nature. The concept of "original sin" seems, in its formal mode of generalization, to fall outside the disrelationships of social rank, but the "context of situation" prevailing at the time when the idea was developed will show clear evidence that concepts of sin have deep social roots.

Burke relates the religious concept of original sin to what he calls the "hierarchal psychosis." The hierarchal principle is a principle of order,[3] but of *developmental* order. That is, ranks, grades, classes, status groups, and all other forms of social hierarchy, do not simply follow one another, they *grow out of one another* in terms of some great life-giving hierarchal principle whose power is felt as deep moments of social solidarity when the commandments, under which our hierarchy is organized, are obeyed lovingly. Thus, education ends in "wisdom," the state in "justice," the family, or at least, the mother, in "love," the church in "God." The "way" toward these ultimates is considered a way toward an ideal future whose radiance and glory invest the present with meaning. But when the enactment of hierarchy becomes so dogmatic and the stages of development so rigid that doubt, question, or creation of new hierarchies are no longer possible, and, indeed, are *punishable,* we enter the realm of hierarchal psychosis.[4]

Between the poles of deep communion (which might be called a kind of hierarchal euphoria) and complete alienation, there are, of course, many gradations. Pyramidal magic—the magic of hierarchy—is inevitable in social relations, and it is not the individual, but his hierarchal office which contains and generates the charisma of a hierarchal order. Thus, when we hear slogans of "complete equality" or "equal shares in the land," we may be sure that in the new system in which all are to be equal, some social offices will soon develop which will be "more equal than others."[5] Thus, the *principle* of equality is used to sustain inequality. Even as old hierarchies are toppled, or when there are shifts in power within a single community or institution, some kind of hierarchy soon emerges. Democracies and tyrannies alike order social relations[6] in some system of rank, grades, or classes.

Hierarchies always function as a progression from a lower to a higher, with a corresponding descent from the higher to the lower. There is a way up, and a way down. But there are also landing stages, plateaus, where we pause in our ascent or descent. Burke's favorite image of hierarchy is taken from Coleridge who, in speaking of the intellectual journey he intends to take in the essays published in *The Friend,* says:

Among my earliest impressions I still distinctly remember that of my first entrance into the mansion of a neighboring baronet, awefully known to me by the name of the great house, its exterior having been long connected in my childish imagination with the feelings and fancies stirred up in me by the perusal of the *Arabian Nights' Entertainments.* Beyond all other objects, I was most struck with the magnificent staircase, relieved at well-proportioned intervals by spacious landing-places, this adorned with grand or showy plants, the next looking out on an extensive prospect through the stately window, with its sidepanes of rich blues and saturated amber or orange tints; while from the last and highest the eye commanded the whole spiral ascent with the marble pavement of the great hall; from which it seemed to spring up as if it merely used the ground on which it rested. My readers will find no difficulty in translating these forms of the outward senses into their intellectual analogies, so as to understand the purport of The Friend's landing-places, and the objects I proposed to myself, in the small groups of essays interposed under this title between the main divisions of the work.[7]

Burke then quotes a passage from Coleridge's *Anima Poetae* (selections from Coleridge's notebooks) as an illustration of how Coleridge equates his dialectical method with the image of a staircase which is clearly equated in Coleridge's own mind with the principle of social distinction. The effect of the principle of hierarchy, the glamor of a class society headed by a landed aristocracy, is quite explicitly described in the image of "the mansion . . . awefully known to me by the name of the great house. . . ."[8] The form of hierarchy Coleridge prized is reflected again in the images he used to describe good thought. "The progress of human intellect from earth to heaven is not a Jacob's Ladder but a geometrical staircase with five or more landing-places. That on which we stand enables us to see clearly and count all below us, while that or those above us are so transparent for our eyes that they appear the canopy of heaven. We do not see them, and believe ourselves on the highest."[9]

Burke makes clear that he does not want the "hierarchal motive" to be thought of simply as a synonym for "prestige." His concern is not so much with any one term "as with the question of *companion-terms.*" This is because too "often, the argument over some terms conceals the really important matter: the way in which (with the given terministic system) the one term is *modified* by *other terms.* He refers to the example of his *Attitudes Toward History*[10] where he found himself pairing antithetical terms, as when he speaks of "bureaucratization of the imaginative," or the use of organizational devices to put ideas into action. By such pairings we expose contradictions and ambiguities which monistic styles of thinking often miss. Thus, a system of thinking like Idealism, which explains action by ends, ideals, purpose, or spirit, which are materialized in history or nature, should be modified at once in our thinking by pragmatism, which derives ends from the nature of the means available.

We must think in the same "antithetical" manner about authority. All systems of authority involve acceptance and rejection, or some otherwise qualified relation to authority. [11] The three modes of attitudes toward authority are acceptance, doubt, and rejection. There are few pure states of acceptance, or rejection, or doubt. At best, there is a resolution in favor of one, but the other two, while subdued, are not banished. Thus, any study of motives in the concrete acts of men in society must go far beyond the acceptance of authority in the pure act of communion (as when the master's commands become the servant's duty) as the paradigm for the study of *all* social action. For it is precisely at the point where there *is* great ambiguity in action that the springs of action are exposed. We discover the true nature of authority only when we look for acceptance, rejection, and doubt and their *resolution* through transcendence in some principle which is "above the battle." But the battle, though resolved momentarily, continues nonetheless.

Hierarchy and bureaucracy imply each other. "Logically, you can't have a Hierarchy without, by the same token having a Bureaucracy (in the sense of 'organization')." The practical need of some kind of form in which the distribution of authority is clearly marked in official organization is matched in art and in scientific laboratories by the notion of *steps*. Unless processes "*proceed in a 'proper' order,* their nature as efficacies is impaired." [12] Thus, whatever the activity we are engaged in, there is necessarily a mode of order, and this order, in whatever context, is "not merely *regular* but *ordinal* (with canons of first, second, third, etc.— canons ranging from absolutes in pope and king, down to purely pragmatic conveniences in *some moments of localized free enterprise*)." [13] And, of course, whenever we say that method determines knowledge, as we do in science, we at once put various methods and techniques into some kind of hierarchy. [14]

Burke sums up the first three sections of his essay on human behavior considered from a dramatistic point of view, by saying

(1) Man's specific nature as a symbol-using animal transcends his generic nature as sheer animal, thereby giving rise to property, rights, and obligations of purely man-made sorts; [15] (2) the necessary nature of property in a complex social order makes for "embarrassments" of social mysteries in men's relations to one another, thereby giving rise to attitudes that pervade areas of thought not strictly germane to it; (3) the terms of "Bureaucracy," "Hierarchy," and "Order" all touch upon this realm of social mystery, because of their relation to Authority, and to canons of Propriety.[16]

There are now two other moments in social interaction which must be considered. These are redemption and victimage, or the ways by which we deal with failure or threats of failure in social organization.

REDEMPTION AND VICTIMAGE IN SOCIAL ORDER

A purely social terminology of human relations must deal with the problem of guilt as a failure in society to provide means of expiation of guilt. That is, it must show how the principle of guilt is matched by a corresponding cancellation of such guilt. Transgression of social order must be defined clearly by those who would rule us, but they must, at the same time, make clear how we can absolve ourselves of such guilt. Burke argues that such absolution is "contrived through *victimage*." This involves the "choice of a sacrificial offering that is correspondingly absolute in the perfection of its fitness." Thus, we must assume that "insofar as the 'guilt' were but 'fragmentary', a victim correspondingly 'fragmentary' would be adequate for the redeeming of such a debt, except insofar as 'fragmentation' itself becomes an 'absolute' condition." [17]

Victimage is the means by which we cleanse the group of tribal or "inherited" guilt. Given such guilt in a society, it follows, Burke says, by "the ultimate logic of symbols, that the compensatory sacrifice of a ritually perfect victim would be the corresponding 'norm.' Hence, insofar as the religious pattern (of 'original sin' and sacrificial redeemer) is adequate to the 'cathartic' needs of a human hierarchy (with the modes of mystery appropriate to such a hierarchy) it would follow that the promoting of social cohesion through victimage is 'normal' and 'natural.' " [18] The sacrifice of the ritually perfect victim, in so far as it affects social order, can then be thought of as a kind of purge. The victim, of course, must be prepared for his ritual role, for only a powerful victim can effectively purge the community of great evil.

The killing of Jews by Hitler's Germans is a recent example of how the ritually perfect victim is selected, prepared, and sacrificed to purge the community of corruption and weakness. Medieval Europe offers other examples of the ways in which victimage develops when it is formed into a great community drama. Burke suggests that "if the great pyramidal social structure of medieval Europe found its ultimate expression in a system of moral purgation based on two 'moments' of 'original sin' and 'redemption,' it would seem to follow that the 'guilt' intrinsic to hierarchal order (the only kind of 'organizational' order we have ever known) calls correspondingly for 'redemption through victimage.'" Burke hastens to add that he is saying that this is not the way a society ought to work, and it would be a grotesque misinterpretation of the spirit of Burke's life and work to think that he is resigned to the spectacle of Hitler's human slaughter houses.[19]

Redemption through victimage, Burke argues, characterizes the "great religious and theological doctrine that forms the incanabula of our culture." Thus Burke joins Durkheim, Tocqueville, and Weber in his insistence that the study of religious life is crucial to any understanding of social life.[20] Burke believes the feudal *enactment* of redemption through victimage to be one of the great ritual dramas whose form still determines how we play our roles in society. The dramas of guilt and redemption which characterized feudal Europe affect our science and technology, just as they have affected the function and structure of all modern literature, religion, and political life. Not only literary plots but "plots," or structures, of many community acts depict a struggle between good and bad elements. When this struggle is personified (and it usually is), we have the hero and the villain, or, in common speech, the "good guy" and the "bad guy." Even in the "science" of psychology, or at least in Freudian psychology, we have a struggle between the father and the son for the mother. The resolution of such struggles is achieved through punishing the villain in the name of some great transcendent principle. Only then does the suffering and death of the sacrificial victim purge us of guilt—in literature, religion, and now, as we have discovered to our horror, in the actualities of political life.

Community redemption through victimage was also common in classical Greece. Here redemption was achieved through a union of art and religion. "We take it," says Burke, "that Greek tragedy, being a typically civic ceremony, was designed for the ritual resolving of civic tensions (tensions that, in the last analysis, are always referrable to problems of property). And, noting that in tragedy (as also in Aristophanic comedy) the principle of victimage plays so essential a role, we began to ask ourselves whether human societies could possibly cohere without symbolic victims which the individual members of the group share in common. . . .[21] We are offering the proposition that . . . here (in the civic enactment of redemption through the sacrificial victim)" is the very center of man's social motivation. Any scheme that shifts the attention to other motivational areas "is a costly error, *except insofar as its insights can be brought back into the area of this central quandary.*" [22]

The principle of victimage takes many forms. The brutal example of Hitler's victimage of the Jews is now our classical example of placing a people beyond redemption (there was nothing a Jew could do to save himself), and thus making them *total* victims. When we consider, as Burke says, "*both* the rationale behind the doctrinal placement of the Crucifixion *and* the pattern of Greek tragedy (nor should we forget the other great line from which the doctrines of our culture are derived, in this instance the lore of Azazel)," we see how profound the motive of victimage may be. When we reflect on the social use of the drama of Christ's Passion, the civic dramas of ancient Greece, and the scapegoat drama (the "lore of Azazel") we have evidence enough that the principle of victimage exists in many societies.[23] The question shifts then from whether there is a principle of victimage, to whether rituals of victimage "are the 'natural' means for affirming the principle of social cohesion above the principle of social division." [24]

We cannot disregard the ritual scapegoat or treat it as "natural" only among savages, children, political spell-binders, and war leaders. Nor should we disregard the "scapegoat principle" as unimportant because it is merely a literary "device." If Hitler's death camps teach us anything, it is that we must watch constantly for the emergence of the scapegoat. Burke warns us—especially those who are content to dismiss the scapegoat as a "necessary illusion" of savages, children, and the masses—that if we are to survive we must spread the "naturalistic lore that will immunize mankind to this *natural* weakness." For we do not go to war and *then* discover our scapegoat. On the contrary, it is only because we make our enemies scapegoats that we torture and kill so often and with such relish. For such killing is a purgation, a cleansing of the community, and thus of the self as a member of the community.

Those who argue that the scapegoat is but an illusion of primitives, children, and the masses seem to feel that development of the scientific point of view will make it unnecessary to solve social problems by the use of ritualistic victims—symbolic or real. Thus we hear of the "crude social insights" of the artist, such as Shakespeare or Sophocles, which will be "refined" by the advancement of social science. Or we hear that the Christian drama is of interest as a study in superstition or illusion.[25] And even when we do face the scapegoat in our society, we do so in a highly fragmented fashion. In place of great community dramas of redemption, in which we face our devils as we call on God, Wisdom, and Justice, to protect us from them, we hope to keep the devil on the run by casting him in many different and minor roles. We believe that when we break up threats to security, and deal with them as isolated fragments, we can deal with them more easily.

As Burke describes it, we say: "Let one fragment of the curative victim be in the villain of a Grade B motion picture, let another fragment be in a radio fool, another in the corpse of a murder mystery, another in the butchery of a prizefight, another in a hard-fought game, another in the momentary flare-up of a political campaign, another in a practical joke played on a rival at the office. . . ." But while this fits our highly diversified publics, it is fragmentary—"and to this extent, there would seem to be something curative in a victimage correspondingly fragmentary." But such fragmentation in the specialized victim makes for triviality and reduces the efficacy of the victim. The curative elements in such triviality can easily "add up to a kind of organized inanity that is socially morbid." [26]

The inanity of our petty scapegoats can only be overcome by some kind of "total" victim. [27] This would be simple enough if people were devout in the full religious sense of the term, for in "the pious contemplation of a perfect *universal* god, there might be the elements of wholeness needed to correct the morbidities of fragmentation." And, whatever we say about Greek tragedy, [28] the classic purity of ritual sacrifice stands in stark contrast to the complicated tangles of intrigue which limit the appeals of much of our art. This does not mean that we ought to return—even if we could!—to religious myths as community myths. But we can use such examples to light up the curious, inadequate and horrible ways in which we employ the principle of victimage. And when we turn to pure expression of religious myths we learn much about the perversions of religion [29] when it is secularized by those who disclaim religion (as do the Soviets) yet use its forms for their own purposes (as in the "purge"trial).

HOW VICTIMAGE FUNCTIONS IN SOCIETY

What would the curative "total" victim be like in our society? How can we overcome the terrible secular use of the scapegoat in modern society? Burke suggests "that the kind of victimage most 'natural' to [our situation] would be some variant on the Hitlerite emphasis." Hitler "put emphasis on the idea of the total cathartic *enemy;* perhaps we can develop ways of putting such emphasis on the total cathartic *friend*." For the terrible lesson we learn from Hitler is that here "was an apparent absolute means of redemption: through the sacrifice of a speciously 'perfect' victim, the material embodiment of an 'idealized' foe." In religion we have the friendly savior, the Christ, who suffers and dies for us, and whose earthly vicars create dramas of vicarious atonement in which we purify ourselves.

As he concludes his essay on Dramatism, Burke returns to his original point about hierarchy, namely, that social order *as such* "makes for a tangle of guilt, mystery, ambition ('adventure') and vindication that infuses even the most visible and tangible of material 'things' with the spirit of the order through which they are perceived." Thus man as symbol-using animal "must perceive even his most 'animalistic' traits dimly through the symbolic fog arising from the social order of which he is part." All of us in the social sciences, empiricists, naturalists, positivists, behaviorists, operationalists, and psychologists alike give "a specious reality to the purely non-symbolic aspect of material property (in things and methods)" [30] when we *disregard* the ways in which property and things are experienced in communication as symbolic acts.

The laboratory, the study, the office, wherever the man of reason works, is as much inhabited by a spirit as any temple. Such spirits are related to some kind of wider authority from which they derive their authority. And "unless such a motive is conceived essentially in terms of pyramidal structure (with its corresponding modes of guilt and redemption), it is hard to see how one can get a wholly relevant terminology for the charting of social behavior." This does not mean that we must deny the "tremendous motivational importance of all the new properties which modern technology has produced, and the importance of techniques for the management of these . . ." but the ideal social terminology must be designed, first of all, to perceive how man's relation to his properties is *symbolically* constituted.[31] The structure of authority in science, as it is in any institution, is a symbolic structure. How things and processes are *named* and *communicated* determines research, as it does prayer or making love.

When we pass from consideration of the general ritual of redemption through the scapegoat in religion, to its many secularized counterparts in our society, we find many variants of mortification. Mortifications arise when we do not want to (or cannot) cross certain social barriers. Such resignation is sacrificial in attitude, as we see among ascetics who *organize* mortification into a program for defeating the power of the senses over the spirit. "A gallant excess of self-control thus becomes organized into a strategy for living, that attains its grand rationale in a cult of the 'dying life.'" Mortification thus becomes not a repression or an inhibition, but a freeing of energy for a higher life, a life beyond death and thus beyond the senses.

There are, of course, other and opposite strategies, as we find in an artist like Henry Miller. Here one denies the senses nothing, following Blake's saying that excess is the road to wisdom—here the wisdom of art. And, if mortification in religion is a scrupulous and deliberate limitation of the self, its antithesis in art is a scrupulous and deliberate expression of the self; as in Rabelais' rules for the Abbey of Thelma, whose motto was: "Do What Thou Wilt." Both the ascetic and the "deliberate" voluptuary discipline the senses to produce desired states of consciousness. And, even though mortification seems far more individual than social, we know that certain requirements for the maintaining of a given social order attain their counterparts, indeed, *must* attain their counterparts, in the requirements of an individual conscience. It is only when the *principle* of these requirements is scrupulously carried to excess that mortification occurs.

Burke illustrates this by reference to monogamous marriage. If "conditions of private property call forth corresponding ideals of monogamistic love, and if the carrying-out of such ideals, to be scrupulously complete, requires that one should not trespass upon the property of another's wife, then by the rules of 'mortification' one should voluntarily punish whatever 'senses' are thought to make such trespass seem desirable." Such ways of thinking become institutionalized in vows of chastity taken for reasons of piety. "But it seems likely that psychogenic illnesses can often be disguised variants of the same motive, though without the conscious code of discipline; for they would be, as it were, the carrying-out of judgments pronounced, willy-nilly, against the self."[32]

Crime, too, may be regarded as springing from similar social motives. The criminal turns against others as the ascetic turns against himself. As criminologists have pointed out, the attitude of criminality often precedes the actual committing of a crime, "so that the crime is in effect the translation of a vague, unreal, and even mysterious sentiment into the conditions of something really here and now." That is, we think of crime as an enactment, a communication, an address to some power, whose audience is necessary for personal salvation. Such audiences can range from those born in sheer fantasy, to the most public crime of the "shoot-out" with police, FBI agents, deputies, and the public (with publics not present represented by reporters) as audiences.

THE PERFECTING OF VICTIMAGE IN SOCIETY

Burke proposes, as models for social and private mortification, the religious concepts of "original sin" and "actual sin." "Original sin" corresponds to the categorical tribal, or familial, "guilts" implicit in social order; while the temptation to "actual sin" is a kind of casuistry for the "reduction of such generic motives to individual criminal impulses with regard to unlawful encroachment upon property and persons." Thus, under certain conditions,

the *categorical* motive may serve as a matrix for a corresponding *personal* motive. That is, in so far as the notion of an absolute generic or "tribal" guilt is not adequately matched by a correspondingly absolute means of cancellation, crime becomes another partial "solution." [33] Indeed, it even serves to organize the life of the criminal. The hunted or undetected criminal finds danger everywhere, and thus must prepare to meet it at any moment.

But war, which far transcends the individual violence of the criminal, is the most common form of community victimage. Warfare, "in its nature as 'imagery' (a nature reenforced by the pronouncedly pyramidal design of military hierarchy) can readily be so much more 'cathartic' in its promises than its deliveries." For, the dialectic of antithesis contributes spontaneously "to his (the enemy's) ritual role (in which) by his sacrifice all evils would be redeemed." In this sense all wars are conducted as "holy" wars. The enemy must be defeated, not only to gain more "living space," "customers," "workers" or any of the alleged "rational" reasons for war, but because his defeat and punishment will relieve us of our guilt and fear. At the same time, as we wound and kill our enemy on the field and slaughter his women and children in their homes, our love for each other deepens. We become comrades in arms; our hatred of each other is being purged in the sufferings of our enemy.

The most subtle and most baffling effects of hierarchy are the "ways whereby the very existence of a hierarchy encourages undue acquiescence among persons otherwise most competent to be its useful critics." [34] Here enter all the variants of "going through channels." Army officers soon learn that "the army does not wash its dirty linen in public." Professors discover that it is wise not to criticize their school in public. Grade school teachers are told that the principal must be informed about parents' criticism. "Going through proper channels," the *way* we communicate in a hierarchy, often becomes as powerful as *what* we communicate. Hierarchal decorum is justified by the "mystery" of hierarchy, yet why is it "better" to hold a fork one way and not another? The answer is simple enough: "Because the best people do it." And why are they the best? What is the basis for the mystique of the hat Mrs. High Society wore at her last party? All we can say is that it is an insigne of glory, the glory of rank which bursts into splendor in the acts of those at the top of the social ladder.

When hierarchal manners become ritual and the ritual becomes sacred, "hierarchal psychosis" can easily occur. For as new problems arise—such as the emergence of an adolescent world with interests and values of its own—traditional hierarchal manners simply no longer work. They are, as we say, "irrelevant" to the problems of a new generation. At worst their irrelevance becomes a profound threat to the society as a whole. Burke offers as a specific example the tendency to encourage wasteful teaching of the humanities. "A mere glance at a typical list of doctoral theses is enough to make clear the kind of elegant irrelevancies (with question mark after the 'elegant') that are being encouraged. This adds up to a vast subsidizing of inaccuracy such as might have been welcomed in less exacting times, but is almost insupportable now. The purpose seems to be to teach the acquiring of insignia so full of false promises that they are questionable even as insignia." [35]

When considering the ways in which we redeem guilt, we note that it is something like the payment of ransom. We "pay" for our "release," and as befits a society rooted in property and money, the "material means of livelihood provide analogies for the building of purely 'spiritual' concepts and ideas." And, for purposes of analysis, it seems sufficient to show how "the conception of guilt and redemption reflected certain past habits of the society with regard to the exchange of material property." Burke admits that this way of thinking about redemption can be very useful, but he goes on to say: "We would remind the reader that the present 'Dramatistic' treatment requires the addition of an important intermediate step between the 'material' field from which the image is borrowed and the 'spiritual' field to which it is applied as a 'fiction.' This intermediate step involves a kind of 'perfecting' or 'absolutizing' of the notion or relation from which the analogy is borrowed." [36]

As soon as an act is brought within the realm of symbols, attempts are made by those in power over the symbols to universalize meanings which begin on a purely local level.[37] This tendency is strengthened by the logics of symbols as symbols, and by the ways we use them in society. When we ask a partner in discourse to define his terms he searches for universals, terms which will maximize the power of his meanings to fit the arguments we bring against him and any we may bring in the future. Thus, individual acts are conceived, not just after a limited or specific analogy, but "*in terms* of a corresponding perfection." The most highly developed type of this kind of thinking about hierarchy, and all human conduct, is the theological notion of God as the *ens perfectissimum*. Here the "logic of ultimates," implicit in all symbolism, finds its purest expression and thus may serve as a model for the way in which all ultimates function in symbolic expression.

Because of this tendency of symbols to become refined and perfected in discourse (that is, to reach "ultimates" or universals), it is very dangerous to assume that the "naturalness" of analogies is enough to account for their persuasiveness, "as with the anthropomorphic notion that God, like Shakespeare's Shylock, wants vindicative satisfaction for default in a bargain." In place of this, we should watch for "ways whereby 'ultimate' motivations come to be implicit even in the world of contingencies." Thus, when searching "socio-anagogically" [38] for the "spirit" in *things,* we may begin with simple correspondence. We may note "that regulated grass on a college campus, besides its nature as sheer grass, has a social role as insignia, standing for a certain order of promises and distinctions connected with the discharging of certain moral and academic obligations." [39]

In holy orders, social distinction and the symbols of such distinction become so interwoven with divinity that the vestments themselves of the priest inspire awe and wonder. Who knows whether the priest is a holy man? And who knows whether the majestic scholar, wending his way in mortar board, hood, and gown to the chapel on Convocation Day, is a wise man? We cannot *see* the holiness of the priest or the wisdom of the scholar. What we do see is a drama of hierarchy wherein rank is infused with a principle of hierarchal order that, by reason of its nature *as a principle,* is "perfect" because it is an "ultimate." The dangers of this strange power of hierarchy are obvious to those who must keep the spirit of holiness or wisdom alive as spirit. Churchmen are aware that Christ has been taken out of Christmas by businessmen; scholars are painfully aware of the incongruities in the "solemn concourses" of Gothic ceremony which reduce the search for wisdom in a democratic society to a ritual taken from a feudal past. But the tendency of hierarchal expression to perfect itself by relating rank and grade to a procession toward some kind of godhead which ends in a moment of mystery seems indigenous to every kind of social order.

To control the interweaving of hierarchal motives with motives of guilt, wonder, adventure, and victimage we must learn to *confront* the mysterious power of hierarchy. If we can do this, it may be possible to make conscious use of hierarchy for good ends. All magic is not black. All manners are not ritual. But we admit sadly that the enemies of democracy often possess great skill in hierarchal enactment. Within one short generation the German people—the great German people who gave us Goethe, Beethoven, Mozart, Kant, Einstein, Freud, and Marx—turned to Hitler, Goering, Goebbels, and Himmler. As their black magic wove its spell, the German community surrendered to the "principle of leadership." The awesome power of hierarchy to perfect itself, first in symbols, and then in action, soon became manifest. To the amazement and horror of the world, the descendants of Goethe and Mozart became willing accomplices to the crimes of Hitler and Goebbels. The purification of the German race was a holy duty; the lowest Nazi beating a Jew to his knees in the streets acted under the hierarchal glamor of a party that was "cleansing" the community of its evils.

It is always very tempting, as Burke warns us in the closing lines of his essay on human behavior, to use hierarchal mystification. And it is easy, far too easy, to fall under the sway of hierarchal magic. As scientists and scholars dedicated to the study of human society, who work within institutions where doubt and question are considered ways to wisdom (where doubt is *institutionalized*), we yet place the same categorical value on rank and office as do other institutions. How often we find the largest office, the best secretaries, and the largest sum of money allotted to the dean or to those "in charge" of the research project, while those who do the research work in poorly ventilated basements.[40] The dean in his office, surrounded by busy secretaries who carefully sort out those who seek conference with him, upholds the majesty of office. This is done in the name of the hierarchy, whose "mystery" is felt by all scientists and humanists alike in the "community of scholars."

How can we overcome, or at least become conscious of, the dangers of hierarchal mystification? Only by aiming "at the kinds of contemplation and sufferance that are best adapted to the recognition and acceptance of a social form inevitable to social order." That is, what *kind* of social order will result from what *kind* of hierarchy. This will not be done simply by "debunking" or "unmasking" hierarchal mystifications. People habituated to mystification cannot be expected to stop and think about it, and yet when a social order is wholly and constantly unmasked, no social cohesion is possible.[41] Thus far in human history, fluctuation between mystification and unmasking has characterized hierarchal action, as we see in the public relations "build up" and the compensatory "character assassination" (done also by public relations men who are skilled in public relations in reverse).

Burke's final plea is for education in the relation of hierarchal means to good community ends. Thus, if we say that a university should be a community of scholars in the pursuit of wisdom, we must study how to enhance the role of the scholar and honor wisdom. Wild fluctuations between mystification (usually Gothic or Classical) in the "solemn concourses" of academic pageantry, or a "debunking" of the intellectual as an impractical "egghead," do little to honor wisdom. "Fluctuation between one extreme and the other seems to be the usual way in which society considers individual persons enacting roles in the social order (and, at times of radical upset, certain of the categorical roles themselves undergo such fluctuation). But might it not be possible that, were an educational system designed to that end, this very fluctuancy could be intelligently stabilized, through the interposing of method?"[42] This is the clue to Burke's intentions in writing *A Grammar of Motives*[43] and *A Rhetoric of Motives*.[44] To these we must turn for Burke's statement of how to study what we ought to study in society.

Notes

¹ Kenneth Burke, *Permanence and Change: An Anatomy of Purpose* (Los Altos, Calif., Hermes Publication, 1954), p. 278. The section of this essay "On Human Behavior Considered 'Dramatistically,'" is entitled "The Hierarchal Embarrassment." Weber's use of the term "charisma" has something in common with Burke's use of "mystery." Another word in common usage, "glory," is in the same lineage as "mystery," "glamor," and "charisma."

² Much of the humor of *Huckleberry Finn* is based on incongruities and embarrassments in hierarchical relationships. Huck's soliloquies expressing puzzlement over Jim's capacity for love are some of the greatest scenes in the book. He keeps "discovering," to his astonishment, that a Negro slave can miss his family and love his daughter. At each such discovery Huck's chagrin and shame deepen.

³ Burke makes clear that hierarchy is not just a *social* principle. "The hierarchic principle itself is inevitable in systematic thought. It is embodied in the mere process of growth, which is synonymous with the class divisions of youth and age, stronger and weaker, male and female, or the stages of learning, from apprentice to journeyman to master. . . ." See p. 141 of his *A Rhetoric of Motives* (New York: Prentice-Hall, Inc., 1953) where he discusses the principle of hierarchy in the section entitled "A Metaphorical View of Hierarchy," pp. 137-142.

⁴ The idea of "inner contradiction" also applies here.

⁵ *Animal Farm* (New York: Harcourt Brace and Company, Inc., 1946), by George Orwell, is wonderful satire of how tyrants mask inequality under slogans of equality. On Manor Farm "all animals are equal but some animals are more equal than others."

⁶ Since so much of my own contribution to this book is about hierarchy, and is based so much on Burke's work, elaboration of my point of view on the structure and function of hierarchy as a communicative act, in the following chapters, makes it unnecessary to go into greater detail here.

⁷ Quoted from Burke, *Permanence and Change*, pp. 279–280.

⁸ Coleridge deepens the hierarchal glamor of this image by referring to the *Arabian Nights*, a book which moved Coleridge to "dread and intense desire" as a child, where hierarchy itself is used to arouse wonder. Few collections of tales exploit the glory and mystery of rank more than the *Arabian Nights*, where the Caliph, like a god descended from heaven, dresses as a beggar to mingle secretly in the night with the people of Baghdad. Where differences in rank are so great that the great can mingle with their people only in disguise, communication between classes becomes a kind of conspiracy. This enhances the wonder and mystery of the hierarchal principle which makes such concealment "necessary."

⁹ Burke, *op. cit.*, p. 281. Students of sociology of knowledge could benefit from this clue to the importance of *forms*, as well as the *content*, of thought in relation to the *form* of hierarchy followed by a thinker in his ascent to truth.

¹⁰ Kenneth Burke, *Attitudes Toward History*, revised edition with a new introduction and appendix (Los Altos, Calif.: Hermes Publications, 1959). Burke frequently "pairs opposites" to create contrasts which throw into violent relief whatever differences exist between the twosome. He then fills in between the opposing terms.

¹¹ This is what Burke's *Attitudes Toward History* is about. It could easily be called

"Attitudes Toward Authority." The first section, "Acceptance and Rejection," describes the way we accept, reject, and doubt authority; the second, how authority must merge and divide its power to reach a final synthesis; the third, "The General Nature of Ritual," shows how routine often becomes ritual, and, in turn, how ritual can become routine; the fourth section is a "Dictionary of Pivotal Terms," which is a typology of the ways in which we adjust to authority. Thirty-three of these are described, ranging from alienation to transcendence. The "Appendix" (to the revised edition) contains Burke's essay, "The Seven Offices," which is a typology of the *functions* of authority from an "official" point of view. "The basic offices . . . that people perform in their relations to one another, are: Govern, serve, provide for materially, defend, teach, entertain, cure, pontificate (that is, minister in terms of a 'beyond')." (See pp. 353–376.) For those with little humanistic training, *Attitudes Toward History* and *Permanence and Change* are the most comprehensible of Burke's books. They should be read in the revised editions.

[12] This is also true of magic, where efficacy shifts to *how* the spells are uttered. That is, the ability of the magician to achieve ends desired by the community is not questioned but his performance of the magic is.

[13] Burke, *Permanence and Change*, pp. 282–283. Burke's italics.

[14] As matters stand now in American social science, it is *how* something is said, not the importance of what is said, that determines the scientific virtue of a statement. As any candidate for the doctorate soon learns, and adult scholars who submit papers for publication soon discover, those who avowedly care only for the "facts" have many notions—often very rigid notions—about how "facts" ought to be and ought not to be gathered, ordered, and presented. It is often not the degree of inference which is questioned or the highly arbitrary manner in which meanings are assigned to the "facts" but the way in which they are manipulated that determines the "scientific" validity of a study.

[15] That is, man attaches *names* to acts and things, and these names, or symbols, are manipulated *as symbols*.

[16] Burke, *op. cit.*, p. 283.

[17] *Ibid.*, pp. 283–284. Victimage and the scapegoat have much in common, but the scapegoat, as derived from religious institutions and primitive tribes, is extended by Burke to a general concept of victimage which ranges from the *symbolic* victim, as the villain in a play, to the actual victim, as the Jews in Hitler's Germany.

[18] *Ibid.*, p. 284.

[19] The *fact* of victimage, so terribly obvious in our time, must be accepted and studied. Any social theory that does not take into account the terrible fact that men "need" each other to satisfy their hate, as well as their love, becomes singularly irrelevant to a generation that has lived in the world of Hitler. For if the depression was the spiritual and intellectual crisis of the second generation of American sociologists, the death camps of Germany and the slave labor camps of Russia are ours. The social bond, we have discovered to our horror, depends on hate as well as love. The easy optimism of Cooley, Dewey, and Mead seems grotesque against the horrors our generation has witnessed in these death camps and slave labor camps, to say nothing of *two* world wars within twenty years.

[20] Burke, it should be noted, does not apply religious forms of expression to social life without taking into account what happens in the secularization of the feudal religious drama. And while we can construct useful analytic models of some forms of sociation out of religious experience, we must not confuse our model with the real

structure of social experience. The religious bond, while social, cannot be used to characterize *all* social bonds, any more than social bonds can be used to explain religion. But in so far as we live in a hierarchy where guilt is commonly experienced and redeem our guilt through victimage, we can learn much from religious forms of experience.

[21] Burke, *op. cit.*, p. 285. Burke describes four functions of language—expression, communication as exhortation, designation as naming, and self-consistency or development of form. In his recent writings on "poetic motives," which are now being prepared for publication, he is concerned with what is characteristic of language *as* language, as well as characteristic of it as a means of sociation. Such an approach is the *only* way to avoid ascribing language to society and then deriving it from society.

[22] *Permanence and Change*, p. 285. Burke's italics. In his discussions on Aristotle, Burke points out that the social effects of art are discussed in the *Politics*. The idea of catharsis, what Burke calls the stylistic cleansing of the audience, occurs in the *Politics*. Aristotle refers to the *Poetics*, which, he indicates, contains his basic discussion of catharsis, but this passage has been lost, and what we know of Aristotle's theory of catharsis comes from his social discussion of art.

[23] *Encyclopedia of Religion and Ethics*, ed. by James Hastings (Edinburgh, Scotland: T. and T. Clark, 1908). See the Index under "Scapegoat, Scape-Animal." Frazer's volume *The Scapegoat* in *The Golden Bough* (London: Macmillan and Co., 1911–1915, 12 vols.) describes many of them. The description and codification of modern scapegoats—the most terrible known to history—has not yet been undertaken.

[24] Burke, *op. cit.*, p. 286.

[25] Yet the *forms* of religious redemption through victimage still linger in Russia. We call their trials "purges." Thus, we see that in a society that disavows religions, the *forms of religion* are used to further nonreligious ends. Nonreligious institutions adopt religious forms to their own purposes—as in our society where the Nativity and the Resurrection (and now the burial of the dead) have been taken over by the business community.

[26] Burke, *op. cit.*, p. 287. Television has added new dimensions to the portrayal of these symbolic victims. Most notable, and certainly the most popular, is the Western "bad guy" who is beaten, shot, hanged, and tortured for the edification of millions daily and nightly on television. In such mass communication we see again the power of civic drama, the hunger for such drama, and the need for the community scapegoat. His suffering and death cleansed and purified the West, and thus, pioneer America. And in a time when we cannot grapple directly with our community villains, it is a great relief to do symbolically what we cannot do in reality.

[27] Perhaps our current "sick humor" is but a way of *confronting* the inadequacy of our cures. What the sick joke seems to be saying is, "At a time when the world is threatened with complete disaster, and with the memory of the bestiality of man fresh before us from two wars, slave labor, and concentration camps, we are told that it is 'normal' to love one another. This (to the sick humorist) is simply incredible, so, to show how phony these slogans of love are, we will depict their *opposites* in stories about how brothers eat each other, children burn their parents to death, etc." As we laugh at "sick" jokes, we *confront* the terrible ways in which we use each other as things. In such jokes there is a complete *reduction* of humanity to absurdity because the human being has become a thing. "Sick humor" often passes beyond comedy to become grotesque, just as the dream shifts to a nightmare.

[28] This is also true of comedy, for, in much of our symbolization of the scapegoat

in art, the clown takes on the burden of the victim. Shakespeare, Mozart, and Verdi wrote their great comedies at the *end* of their lives. Their final statements as artists were comic, not tragic. This will be discussed in later chapters on the comic.

²⁹ Burke mentions the Sunday paper as a prime example of the secular perversions of religious ritual drama in a capitalistic society. Here, on our holy day of rest, when we are supposed to be (as a Christian community) devoting our thoughts to the pacific and brotherly aspects of our common lives, we publish the biggest paper of the week, filled with stories and reports on the "materialistic, operational, administrative, and technological" aspects of our society. The great symbol in the Sunday paper is not a symbol of God, brotherhood, charity, or love, but of money. As materialistic as are the pages of news stories, they are nothing compared to the direct expression of money in the Sunday advertising sections. What is on "sale," where, and when, makes up the bulk of the paper. Thus, Sunday, which should be a day of purgation from too much materialism, becomes the day when the goads of materialism (buy! buy!) are felt the most.

³⁰ Burke, *op. cit.*, p. 288.

³¹ *Ibid.*, p. 289.

³² *Ibid.*, p. 290.

³³ *Ibid.*, pp. 290–291. Deep belief in a principle of absolute evil, as in the form of the Devil, the "Prince of Darkness," also serves to organize our lives. As many have pointed out, an important ingredient of unity in the Middle Ages (and on the American Frontier) was the symbol of a *common enemy*, the Devil. The dramatization of the Devil—he was always the villain in the mystery plays, and the antagonist in the camp meeting revivals where "driving out devils" took the form of jerking, rolling, barking, and wild dancing—*unified* hostile and warring sects and factions in the community. On the Devil and his nefarious work all could agree, and this common enemy did much to create consensus in the Puritan community.

³⁴ *Ibid.*, p. 291. It is certainly exasperating to the superior who finds himself surrounded by "yes-men." The Hollywood executive who issued orders to the effect that his underlings were not to say "yes" before he had finished his sentence, and all variants of our humor over the "yes-man," indicate how difficult it is for inferiors to play a role as "loyal opposition" to a superior, in the pyramidal form of hierarchy common to modern bureaucracy—public and private alike.

³⁵ *Ibid.* In moments of candor, scholars admit that when method and technique, and not the *problems important to an age,* are held to be the proper end of study, there is great danger of irrelevancy, or what Burke calls "inaccuracy." Thus, when we should be studying the rise and fall of dictators, how they stage their drama of power, what means of communication they use, where, when, and for what purpose, we select instead problems that are amenable to techniques considered "proper" to the subject by those in power over the subject. How little German historians, the greatest in Europe, seemed to know about the history of their own time! Many books were written in Germany on how to study the history of the past, few on how to study the present. Indeed, it was believed by many that *only* the past could be studied "objectively."

³⁶ *Ibid.*, p. 292.

³⁷ American political campaigns offer many examples of this. The local candidate for township engineer assures us that his party will save the city, which in turn will save the nation, which in turn will save the free world, until finally we are saving Christian civilization by voting the local surveyor into office. Such "mountings"

always end in God, and thus, by inference, if we vote for the candidate, we vote for God.

[88] This is Burke's term for his sociological technique of symbolic analysis.

[89] *Ibid.,* p. 293. University of Chicago students of the thirties will recall the attempts to make grass grow *in the cracks* between the slate walks on the Quadrangle. As Veblen (who watched the "monastic real estate" of the University of Chicago campus develop) pointed out, the development of the clipped lawn, and the banishing of the munching cow to the meadow, was an early indication of "conspicuous consumption" in the Middle West. Veblen's work, especially *The Higher Learning,* is filled with illustrations of the pathologies and incongruities common to these "simple correspondences."

[40] Veblen, who had a keen eye for such incongruities, has recorded many of the strange results of "hierarchal psychosis" in academic life in *The Higher Learning in America: A Memorandum on the Conduct of Universities by Business Men.*

[41] As Burke points out, the unmaskers soon develop hierarchies of their own. "While leading you to watch his act of destruction at one point, the 'unmasker' is always furtively building at another point, and by his prestidigitation he can forestall accurate observation of his own moves." (*Permanence and Change,* p. 294.) The creation of bureaus to study ways of getting rid of bureaus is common in our government. How often in academic life we find ourselves about to organize a committee to consider reducing the number of committees!

[42] *Ibid.,* p. 294.

[43] Kenneth Burke, *A Grammar of Motives* (New York: Prentice-Hall, Inc., 1945; reissue, George Braziller, Inc., New York, 1955).

[44] Kenneth Burke, *A Rhetoric of Motives* (New York: Prentice-Hall, Inc., 1950; reissue, George Braziller, Inc., New York, 1955).

PART FOUR

Burke's Sociology of Language

10

The Structure and Function of the Act
in the Work of Kenneth Burke

SOCIAL ACTION AS SYMBOLIC ACTION:
A DRAMATISTIC VIEW OF HUMAN RELATIONS

THE CLOSING LINES of Burke's essay, "On Human Behavior Considered 'Dramatistically,'" make clear that on both moral and scientific grounds "interposing of method" is a necessity. His method, as he tells us many times, is concerned with the analysis of language, and unless we understand his views on how language affects human relations we cannot understand his work. He is not interested in "forms of experience" [1] but in *"forms of talk about experience."* We need, Burke argues, to become more conscious of the structure and function of language as a social instrument. In place of more discourse about how we think, we need more on how we communicate and, finally, on *all* the forms of expression which are involved in communication. For if we say that society arises in, and exists through, the communication of significant symbols, we must develop theory, method, and technique to show *how* language does all the things we say it does.

Burke's search is a search for *method.* He is *not* interested in repeating what has been said many times before—most recently in America by Dewey—that art belongs to experience or is determined by society. Nor is he content simply to point out the fallacies of those who find their social "reality" in some kind of process beyond symbols, which must be studied through analogies drawn from the sciences of nature. Nor does he use history to construct vast syntheses of the "meaning" of art among people who lived far away and long ago. Instead, he asks simply: "What is the *function* of art in society?" As we have seen, he argues that art is a form of symbolic action concerned with motives of guilt, redemption, hierarchy, and victimage. [2] This is *what* art does, its "social" function. *How* it does these things is the next step, and from the view of the human scientist the most important step, in Burke's thought.

Many questions face the sociologist seeking to create a model of sociation based on language, and while Burke's concerns range far beyond sociology, his model of symbolic action as a kind of dramatic action is of great significance. Like Mead, Burke argues that language determines society. It *orders* experience because it creates the forms which make possible the communication of experience. He accepts Dewey's and Mead's theory that the imagery of the end of an act, its "consummatory moment," determines how we form our attitude toward what we are about to do, and how we regard what we are doing, as we pass into the motor phase of the act.[3] But for Burke this is only a first step. He wants to show *how* this consummatory moment arises in symbolic action. This can be done, he asserts, only if we relate art to action in society. In short, not how we "know" the world, as the scientist knows it, but how we "act" in it, is the proper study for the sociologist.[4]

Burke's argument that we act in terms of language, as well as biology, physics, economics, politics, or God, is not new. But the *way* he faces language as a social fact is very new. He argues that our greatest body of observable social "facts" are not derived from what people do, but what they *say* about what they do. Whatever we say about symbols, we must admit, Burke argues, that statements about symbols have reference to the *observable* facts of meaning in human sociation. Reports about what is supposed to be going on in the extra-symbolic realm of the body, space-time, socio-economic processes, or in the mind of God, are at best highly inferential. The "nature" of the biologists and the physicists, the "social forces" of the economists, the "mind of God" of the theologians, and the "forms of thought" of the philosophers must be tested (by the sociologist, at least) in terms of their use in communication. How, Burke asks, have the various systems of social thought relied on language, and how have they made use of the resources of all forms of symbolic expression?

When we explain social motives by biology, physics, history, economics, politics, or other "realities" which are "beyond" symbols, there is a very high percentage of inference or interpretations—even in a statement we are content to call "factual." As Burke points out about political history: "We can but infer what the diplomat did"; what we usually do is to cite some report which tells us what he did. And even if we talk directly to (or, as we say, "interview") the diplomat about what he did, we must rely on what he says he did. For obviously what he did, he did in the past, and while he was doing it he did not stop to talk about it, so all we can really study about the diplomat's activity, is what he says about it. The fact that we have talked directly to the man who really performed the act we are trying to study does not obviate the fact that we are studying his act in terms of his expression of it.[5] And he, like ourselves as students, must have learned to express himself about action (others' as well as his own) from the body of expression common to his society. Thus his statement is not wholly "subjective," for if it were, we could not communicate at all.

Sociologists think of the nonsymbolic realm as clear, while the symbolic realm is hazy and "subjective." But if we use words as data—and certainly in the human studies we use them a great deal—it matters little what our attitude toward their vagueness or subjectivity may be. We must prove that what we say about an event, described in words, can be shown to exist in the words themselves.[6] For if we do not, then we are in the realm of inference, not fact. But if we stick to the observable facts in words (or other symbols), we can argue that there is a sense in which we get our view of acts as facts from our sense of symbols as facts, rather than *vice versa*. But when we ground our proof in symbolic facts, we must make clear what inference or interpretation has been added to the words or symbols themselves, and we must *demonstrate* why what we say exists in symbols can yet be explained only by nonsymbolic factors.

Failure to do this occurs most commonly in American sociology when an *ascription* of motives is made to some such "social force" as "equilibrium," "patterned structure," "consentient sets," "structural processes," and the like, and then *derived* from it. Thus, in ecological studies we ascribe certain characteristics to a "territorial base of the community," and then later derive effects from the ascriptions we have made to the territorial base —as when we say that certain things happen to people in a neighborhood because of the things that are characteristic of "that kind" of neighborhood. Or, again, in the studies of bureaucracy we ascribe qualities to the "structure" of the bureaucracy, and then a few pages later derive "functions" from the ascriptions we have made to the structure.[7] Thus we hear in the early pages of such studies that bureaucratic roles are "seeking equilibrium," and then in later pages, that "it can be derived from the tendency of bureaucratic roles to seek equilibrium." This is like saying that since rain is a quality of raining, rain is caused by raining.

Now, in so far as we deal with bureaucratic relationships as social, we deal with social *meaning*. Structures do not act; people act. Bureaucracies have no purpose, end, or value that can be examined apart from the actions of people who are trying to achieve the ends ascribed to them. In even the most traditional social office, such as that of the priest, the vestments of the priest gain their holiness from the kind of enactment in which they are worn by the priest. The "Priest and the Victim on the Cross and in the Mass, are one and the same person." Thus, the mass is not a sacrifice, "but another *enactment* of the one supreme sacrifice on Calvary." For when "Our Lord came, He became at one and the same time *Priest* and *Victim*. He became both the Offerer and the One Who was offered. No longer were the priest and victim separate as they had been before [in the time of sacrifice and the scapegoat]." So speaks Bishop Fulton J. Sheen in his description of the mass as a holy drama.[8]

The "structure of bureaucracy," the hierarchically arranged, continuously functioning offices, which "determine," or "structure," the behavior of occupants by "channeling" their actions through general rules which are "obeyed" impersonally, cannot be observed, but only inferred. What we do observe is people acting together as superiors, inferiors, and equals, as they pass from one position to another because of death, changes in authority, the need to meet new problems, or profound changes in the society in which the bureaucracy exists. But all this is done through, and can be observed only in, communication. Even the most rigid rule exists only as it is communicated. *Where* it is communicated, by *whom, when, how,* and for what *purpose,* determine its meaning. Rules, then, are observed in communication; communication, in turn, arises in the enactment of roles; roles are enacted in hierarchal dramas; and hierarchal drama creates social bonds because it creates and sustains social order.[9]

Burke wants us to think about the structure of social action in terms of dramatic plot, because the concept of plot makes possible the use of the observable data of sociation, namely, expressive symbols. A "dramatistic" concept *reduces* the amount of inference necessary in sociological study. A "dramatistic" study of a bureaucracy regards the institution under study as a stage, upon which certain kinds of action are performed, by actors who use means and instruments of a certain kind to achieve certain purposes. The data used in this method are the expressive symbolism of the action viewed (in the sociological perspective of this study) as a hierarchal enactment. The location of the office, how it is arranged, how people enter, how they move within, how they leave, are spatial studies (even studies in motion). The meaning of these movements can be understood only as a dramatic plot in which people seek to establish *social* (not *spatial*) relations through a dramatization of status.

LOGICAL, RHETORICAL, AND SYMBOLIC PHASES OF THE ACT

An act, as Burke describes it, is a certain *kind* of act. It is performed by certain kinds of *people,* with certain *instruments* or *means,* and for certain *purposes.* These elements—Burke calls them Act, Scene, Agent, Agency, Purpose—are the structure of the act whose function has already been discussed in terms of guilt, redemption, victimage, and hierarchy. "In a rounded statement about motives, you must have some word that names the *act* (names what took place, in thought or deed), and another that names the *scene* (the background of the act, the situation in which it occurred) : also, you must indicate what person or kind of person (*agent*) performed the act, what means or instruments he used (*agency*), and the purpose." This dramatistic pentad of terms is to be thought of as a "generating principle" which allows us to "inquire into the purely internal relationships which the five terms bear to one another, considering their possibilities of transformation, their range of permutations and combinations—and then to see how these various resources figure in actual statements about human motives." [10]

Burke makes clear that he is not interested in abstract discussion on the structure of his dramatistic model, but in the application of five terms to the analysis of symbolic action in society. He does not want to think of human motives "apart" from, "beyond," or "outside" of language. Nor would he "make the mistake of thinking that the lore of human foibles stops with the depicting of different personal types in fictions," for there is also "the *categorized* lore of human foibles, as we find it expressed in proverbs or in moral philosophy. Generalizations about human ways are as essentially humanistic as is the depicting of some particular person acting in some particular way; and they are needed to complete the act of humanistic contemplation. And all this comes to a head in the contemplation of men's linguistic foibles, which can so drastically transform their ways of life." [11] That is, proverbs are intended to be used. They express, as Gracian said, the art of worldly wisdom.

But, as Burke points out, serious consideration of language in social life requires both an *attitude* and a *method.* The attitude, however, must be grounded in the *systematic development of the method.* The method, in turn, "would involve the explicit study of language as the 'critical moment' at which human motives take form, since a linguistic factor at every point in human experience complicates and to some extent transcends the purely biological aspects of motivation." Thus, Burke's Dramatism, while a method of symbolic analysis, is, he insists, "both a gymnastic of ideas and a clinic of ideas,"and one "which would assist health by aiming always at the first without forgetting the claims of the second." [12] Burke makes no pretense whatever to be above the battle, or to view the world from a godlike realm of "pure knowledge." His Dramatism is a theory of action which he struggles to reduce to a methodology so it can be tested by concrete application to forms of expression.

There are, Burke argues, two attitudes which make the social study of language difficult. The first is "debunking" which reduces language to a "reflection" of interests, the second an "uncriticized scientism, which is *too evasive of the dramatistic to make even an adequate preparatory description* of linguistic forms." [13] That is, if we turn away from symbols *in principle,* as we do in so much sociological and psychological research, we cannot be expected to say much about communication. For if we are to study communication we must develop terministic equipment that makes such study possible. The lack of this becomes painfully obvious when we examine contemporary studies in sociology. Here we find knowledge about the "structure" of social institutions founded on everything except *how men communicate within the institutions.* For in such studies, as in behavioral studies in general, the technique (*not* the methodology) determines their sociological virtue, and "official" sociological techniques, as developed by American sociologists of the second generation, cannot be applied to symbolic behavior, since they were never designed for such analysis in the first place.

Burke's claim that American social scientists have closed their minds to communication as a symbolic experience is true of the second generation only. It was not true of the original Chicago school, the founders of American sociology. Nor has it been true of social anthropologists such as Sapir, Whorf, Redfield, Warner, or Kluckhohn. [14] But Kluckhohn himself, who has done as much as any contemporary social scientist to relate symbolic analysis to social analysis, is the first to admit that anthropologists are at fault for having made few attempts to specify the steps really taken in their analysis of symbolic action. For, despite constant references to "patterns," "configurations," "structure," and "contextualism," no one has made clear just how any of these structures arise in society and what methodological justification exists for applying them to the data of communication.

And, obviously, if our image of society is that of a "configuration," there is little we can say about language, because "configurations" don't talk.

American sociologists of the present (third) generation have no theory of symbolic action. In American sociology, communication is now studied as "mass communication," and this is not a study of interaction as a symbolic act, but as a mechanical process. Thus we read of "paths along which influence flows," and communication is defined as some kind of "mechanism" through which "human relations exist." "Empiric studies" discuss the "element of feedback" of "messages." Bales tells us even "if the top man [in a small group] is initiating most of the action, he still has to expect that he will receive a 'feedback of reactions,' of both a positive and a negative sort, that will tend to equal the amount of action he initiates." [15] T. M. Newcomb's discussion of communicative acts reduces the act to mechanistic patterns, as we see in such phrases as "if A has a positive cathetic orientation toward B and a negative orientation toward X, and if A judges that B's orientation toward X is positive, the situation is one of imbalance or strain. Hypothetically, the strain of perceived nonconsensus, or discrepancy, serves as an instigation to communication—the process by which, ordinarily, consensus is increased." [16]

Burke's claim that language is rejected *in principle,* as a proper study for the social scientist, is only too true. Yet, as Cooley, James, Mead, Dewey, and Burke stress, until we discuss the end, purpose, goal, or value—what is generally called the consummatory moment in the act—we are discussing not *human,* but *physical,* interaction. There is no way for a behaviorist to include purpose, *as a symbolic expression in communication,* in his scheme at all.[17] Very often behavioral statements of conduct smuggle in concepts of purpose disguised as "goal oriented activity," "equilibrium," or "tension reduction." For even a behaviorist cannot quite equate random motion with human motivation, or a boundless "field" with what he calls "structural" human acts.

But what Burke is saying, and what he has a right to say, is that when we *rule out* symbolic expression as *improper* to the study of society, we make dogma do the work of reason. And when we *reduce* communication to signalling because we have developed techniques for studying "messages," we are making technique do the work of inquiry. Or, when we say, as Blumer did, that we know that such a study as *The Polish Peasant* is "unscientific," without at the same time making clear our model of "scientific" study, we simply do not make sense. For how can we know the validity of an inquiry, if we cannot define validity? [18] In sum, if we do not think the study of communication as a symbolic experience to be of value to social science, or if we follow dedicated positivists and mechanists [19] who tell us they alone are guardians of "right" method, then *any* attempts at symbolic methodology will be condemned as "unscientific."

Burke conceives of his method of symbolic analysis, as grounded in a statement about the "grammatical principles of motivation," to be broad enough to include every kind of ambiguity. Thus, his grammar is not a monistic *reduction* (like Freud's) of all motives to one single drive, but an expanded model of action which describes several grounds for motives. He seeks not to *avoid* ambiguity, doubt, question, incongruity, and contradiction, but to *include* them in his theory of the act. In the development of his work he sought "to formulate the basic stratagems which people employ, in endless variations, and consciously and unconsciously, for the outwitting or cajoling of one another. . . ." He noted that all such devices "had a 'you and me' quality about them, being 'addressed' to some person or to some advantage." These he classed under the heading of "Rhetoric." But there were other notes, concerned with modes of expression and appeal in the fine arts, and with purely psychological or psychoanalytic matters. These were classed under the heading of "Symbolic." [20]

Thus, while the *Grammar* comes first in Burke's trilogy, it came last in the development of his theory of the structure and function of the symbolic act in society. This was because he discovered that his project "needed a grounding in formal considerations logically prior to both the rhetorical and the psychological." This, of course, we all discover when we talk about the "act." We soon find that we must define just what we mean by "act," and we must (as symbol analysts) talk about the act in terms of structure and function in communication. And, finally, the structure of the act must be the structure of a function in the same field, and thus each element must be defined in terms of the other. A grammar of motives dealing with motives as they arise in symbolic phases of action, must be capable of explaining the function of symbols in various kinds of acts. The kinds of acts best suited to developing a Grammar, Burke believes, are those found in theological, metaphysical, and juridical expression, while the methods and forms of art best illustrate the Symbolic of Motives, and finally, a Rhetoric of Motives "comprises observations on parliamentary and diplomatic devices, editorial bias, sales methods and incidents of social sparring." [21]

A Grammar of Motives is important to the sociologist, but *A Rhetoric of Motives* is of peculiar significance since it contains a theoretical and methodical statement of how social order arises in and continues through communication.[22] The *Rhetoric* considers the

> ways in which individuals are at odds with one another, or become identified with groups more or less at odds with one another. Identification is affirmed with earnestness precisely because there is division. Identification is compensatory to division. If men were not apart from one another, there would be no need for the rhetorician to proclaim their unity. If men were wholly and truly of one substance, absolute communication would be of man's very essence. It would not be an ideal, as it now is, partly embodied in material considerations and partly frustrated by these same conditions; rather, it would be as natural, spontaneous, and total as with those ideal prototypes of communication, the theologians, angels or "messengers." [23]

Notes

[1] Burke places himself in the Kantian lineage. "Our five terms (of Dramatism) are 'transcendental' rather than formal (and are to this extent Kantian) in being categories which human thought necessarily exemplifies." Kenneth Burke, *A Grammar of Motives* (New York: Prentice-Hall, Inc., 1945), p. 317.

[2] The increase in power and range in this model of the symbolic act is obvious when we turn back to Cooley, Mead, and Dewey, who, despite all their talk about symbolic action, tell us little about how art and language do all the things they are supposed to do. This is far less true of Mead than of Dewey and Cooley, for Mead at least places the "aesthetic moment," as he calls the moment of consummation, within the act as a *communicative* act. And certainly no one struggled more to define the act as a social act than Mead; but, as we have said in our discussion of Mead, there is very little discussion in Mead of the communicative act in terms of art.

[3] He accepts Mead's philosophy of the act. "Particularly in his remarks on attitudes as incipient acts, on modes of identification, on personality and abstraction, on the relations between the biological and the social, and on thought as gesture, his writings seem to map out the field of discussion for forthcoming years. . . ." This is taken from Burke's review of Mead's work in *The New Republic*. This is reprinted in *The Philosophy of Literary Form: Studies in Symbolic Action* (Baton Rouge: Louisiana State Univ. Press, 1941). (The version reprinted in the Vintage Paperback of 1957 is abridged.) Burke has a very high regard for Mead's work. "It is a great loss to the quality of discussion in America that the volumes were not publicly available during the period of upheaval and recasting that went with our attempts to refurbish our individualism for collective necessities after 1929." (See pp. 380–382.) It is still a great loss that so little secondary literature on Mead has emerged in American sociology—or anywhere else.

[4] That is, Burke is interested not only in how the act determines how we perceive or "think about" the world as we prepare to act, but also how we exhort others and ourselves to act in it.

[5] We learn to express ourselves according to the accepted ways of doing so in our society. Yet we still hear sociologists complaining that interviews sound like stories. If a delinquent does not learn to *describe* his delinquency from stories, television dramas, etc., how does he learn to describe it?

[6] This point and other points mentioned here are elaborated in Burke's discussion on "socio-anagogic" technique. Here it is enough to point out that it is not the data of our case histories, interviews, etc., that are "objective." We impute meanings to responses, and *then* order them in terms of what we consider proper method and technique. We all know that this is often done in a highly arbitrary fashion (and by the *same* investigator who devised the schedules he analyzes). It is the way symbolic data are manipulated, in various processes of quantification, that makes it "scientific" for many sociologists. But, however it is manipulated, proper use of data will be determined by the nature of symbols as they are used in communication, not by the way they are ordered to suit a prescribed technique.

[7] That is, we suddenly make a verb out of a noun. This is easier to do in history because there is a great span of time between our ascription to "nature," "society," "class-struggle," "manifest Destiny," or "freedom" and our derivations. Such time-spans also involve many pages of description. But whether our drama extends through a thousand years or through one single day, its form and content is still determined by the resources of symbols. Historical time is *dramatic* time and, therefore, subject to the laws of dramatic development, or it is spatial time and subject to physical laws of development. Obviously, these two kinds of time cannot be mixed.

[8] *This Is the Mass* (New York: Image Books, 1959), pp. 18–19. Vestments, like relics under glass, must be made part of intense and frequent dramatizations of their power, in order to retain their glamor or mystery. This is not meant to "deny" the specifically religious nature of worship, but to stress that even religion depends for its effect on communication and is, therefore, dependent on the resources of the symbols used in communication.

[9] That is, that while there is a structure to bureaucratic relationships, as there is to every relationship, Burke argues that this structure depends as much on *how* this structure functions in communication as upon the interests which the structure is supposed to "serve." And whatever we say about interests, it is their expression, not their "reality" we study. Bureaucratic "interests" are inferred, bureaucratic roles and their enactment are observed.

[10] Burke, *op. cit.*, pp. xv–xvi. Burke's italics and parentheses.

[11] *Ibid.*, p. 319. The categories of social experience expressed in the proverb exist on an almost purely social level. They are the "current coin" of communication, used to deal *generally* with situations in which we must act. A proverb like "Time is money," or "Waste not, want not," is not "subjective" or "individual," but objective and social. The opposite of the proverb is the dream, where symbolic action is enigmatic, or the soliloquy, in which the burdens of a society are expressed as individual burdens.

[12] *Ibid.*, p. 318.

[13] *Ibid.*, p. 319.

[14] Kluckhohn's essay, "The Personal Document in Anthropological Science," in *The Use of Personal Documents in History, Anthropology, and Sociology*, by Louis Gottschalk, Clyde Kluckhohn, and Robert Angell (New York: Social Science Research Council Bulletin, N. 53, 1945), and his remarks on methods of symbolic analysis, as in "Common Humanity and Diverse Cultures," in *The Human Meaning of the*

Social Sciences, ed. by Daniel Lerner (New York: Meridian Books, 1959), indicate the concern of American anthropologists with symbolic behavior. *The Living and the Dead* by W. Lloyd Warner (New Haven: Yale Univ. Press, 1959) is subtitled *A Study of the Symbolic Life of Americans.* His section, "Theory and Method for the Study of Symbolic Life," is one of the few attempts in American social study to relate theories of symbolic analysis to a concrete case. Many American sociologists talk about "message tracks," communication, and signalling as the same thing.

[15] Quoted from *Sociology Today: Problems and Prospects,* edited by Robert K. Merton, Leonard Broom, and Leonard S. Cottrell, Jr. under the auspices of the American Sociological Society (New York: Basic Books, 1959), p. 566.

[16] *Ibid.,* p. 282. See also, T. M. Newcomb, "An Approach to the Study of Communicative Acts," *Psychology Review,* 60 (1953), pp. 393–404. There is nothing "wrong" with such studies in so far as they are careful to state conclusions derived from the data which are used in the study. What is wrong is the high degree of inference used and the very narrow range of conduct which is opened to observation by their use.

[17] The index of *Sociology Today* which, as the title indicates, was written "under the auspices of the American Sociological Society," contains *no* index reference to symbols, and only two references to "communication." The study of communication approved officially is "mass communication." On p. 197 we are told that "the sociological study of art is comparatively new. . . ." What this statement means only those privy to the "higher sociology" know. The social, if not the "sociological" study of art is very old. Every major writer on art, from Aristotle to Burke, has said something about the reciprocal effects of art and society. As sociologists we ought not to confuse our ignorance of a subject with the state of learning in a field of study. What sociologists are really saying is: "There is a 'right' way (i.e., a right 'sociological way') to study art. Art has not often been studied this way, hence there is very little of value in the sociology of art." Now this assumes two things: one, that our "right" way can really be described (that is, that it is more than a pious hope); and two, that our "right" way is right. And whatever we say as sociologists, few would be willing to argue that our judgment of sociological method is based on highly significant results. All sociological discussions of method and technique in symbolic analysis are based on "ideal" methods and techniques which exist only in the minds of sociological dogmatists, not in actual research.

[18] There is an interesting discussion of this point in *Critiques of Research in Social Sciences: I: An Appraisal of Thomas and Znaniecki's The Polish Peasant in Europe and America* (New York: Social Science Research Council, Bulletin 44, 1939), especially in Part Two.

[19] It is the positivists and the mechanists who now dominate American sociology.

[20] Burke, *op. cit.,* p. xvii.

[21] *Ibid.,* p. xviii.

[22] Burke's sociological interest in social order pervades all his work. His early works, *Permanence and Change* and *Attitudes Toward History,* contain many useful observations on social order, but it is in his later works, notably the *Grammar, Rhetoric,* and the forthcoming *Symbolic,* that he creates a tightly knit body of theoretical and methodological propositions which sociologists interested in communication can use to great advantage.

[23] Kenneth Burke, *A Rhetoric of Motives* (New York: Prentice-Hall, Inc., 1950), p. 22.

11

A Rhetoric of Motives:
Burke's Sociology of Language

THE SOCIO-PSYCHOLOGICAL FUNCTION OF RHETORIC: IDENTIFICATION

THE KEY TERM for rhetoric in Burke's usage is not persuasion, but *identification*. "Traditionally, the key term for rhetoric is not 'identification,' but 'persuasion.' Hence, to make sure that we do not maneuver ourselves unnecessarily into a weak position, we review several classic texts which track down all the major implications of that term. Our treatment, in terms of identification, is decidedly not meant as a substitute for the sound traditional approach. Rather, as we try to show, it is but an accessory to the standard lore. And our book aims to make itself at home in both emphases." [1] And since identification and persuasion imply an audience, a third aspect of rhetoric—its nature as *addressed* to others and the self—rounds out Burke's scheme for a rhetoric of motives in the triad: identification, persuasion, and address.

What does Burke mean by identification? How does he fit the traditional concerns of rhetoric into his analysis of identification? The answer to both these questions is conditioned by the fact that Burke's *Rhetoric* is grounded in *method*, the application of traditional rhetorical devices to symbolic action considered as a process of identification. This does not mean that he is not interested in the philosophy and the morality of rhetoric, but he seeks to ground these in *methods* of analysis which are derived from the function of persuasion *as* identification in communication. This social emphasis, the description of persuasion *as* identification, is derived from the aspects of persuasion found in "mystification," "courtship," and the "'magic' of class relationships." The development of this method involves a recasting of the classical idea of clear persuasive intent in rhetoric. For Burke, rhetoric promotes social cohesion by making it possible for men to act "rhetorically upon themselves and others." In Burke's approach, and specifically in his sociology of language, analysis is designed to "throw light on literary texts and human relations generally." [2]

Rhetoric can do this, Burke argues, because it is *"rooted in an essential function of language itself, a function that is wholly realistic, and is continually born anew; the use of language as a symbolic means of inducing cooperation in beings that by nature respond to symbols.*"[3] "Inducing cooperation" through rhetoric must not be confused with inducing cooperation through magic. The "use of words by human agents to form attitudes or to induce actions in other human agents, is certainly not 'magical.'" For if you are in trouble and call for help, "you are no practitioner of primitive magic. You are using the primary resource of human speech in a thoroughly realistic way." But neither can a call for help be considered a "signal" and thus reduced to a "science," in the strict meaning of science today, as a "semantic" or "descriptive" terminology for charting the conditions of nature from an "impersonal" point of view, regardless of one's wishes or preferences. A call for help is very biased; "it is the most arrant kind of 'wishful thinking'; it is not merely descriptive, it is *hortatory*. It is not just trying to tell people how things are, . . . it is trying to *move people*."[4]

But if rhetoric cannot be thought of as magic, nor as science (that is, as the scientific view which reduces language to semantics which can be studied by techniques developed in the sciences of nature) how then can we think of rhetoric, and what examples, or cases, can we study? The answer to this makes up the first section of Burke's *Rhetoric*. This is called "The Range of Rhetoric." This is followed by a section, "Traditional Principles of Rhetoric." The third and final section, entitled "Order," is a statement of rhetoric in terms of hierarchal address, which we usually think of as "courtship." "The Range of Rhetoric" attempts to illustrate the main aspect of rhetoric: "its use of *identification*." Burke argues that he can "place in terms of rhetoric all those statements by anthropologists, ethnologists, individual and social psychologists, and the like, that bear upon the *persuasive* aspects of language, the function of language as *addressed,* as direct or roundabout appeal to real or ideal audiences, without or within."[5] But to do this he must first ground rhetoric in its sociopsychological function of identification.

Men use rhetoric, Burke argues, to *persuade* others (and themselves), through *address*, to *identify*. How is this done? In his discussion of *Samson Agonistes,*[6] Burke shows how a poem of violence, suicide, and slaughter can be used as a tract for our times, where brutality, torture, and murder characterize the imagery of our art (to say nothing of the daily reality of our lives). Milton's poem, a poem of "righteous ferocity," "is no mere evidence of a virtuoso's craftsmanship, it is not sheer poetic exercise, as with a versatile playwright able to imagine whatever kind of role the exigencies of plot happened to require." On the contrary, "it is almost a kind of witchcraft, a wonder-working spell by a cantankerous old fighter-priest who would slay the enemy in effigy, and whose very translation of political controversy to high theologic terms helps, by such magnification, to sanction the ill-tempered obstinacy of his resistance." [7]

Such use of literature is, then, wholly in the realm of ritual and magic. But the ritual power of the poem (or any expressive poem) comes, in a large part, from the resources of language, as form, not from something beyond language, such as the tribe, social process, work, sex, or God. Nor does he give much value to interpreting the figure of Samson purely as a rationalization in the psychoanalytic sense. We must take the poem, and any symbolic expression, at face value. "If two statements, for instance, one humorous and the other humorless, are found to contain the same animus against someone, we are not thereby justified in treating them as the same in their motivational core." For, whatever the source of instigation, the two statements may have different ends. The "humorless statement may *foretell* suicide, and the humorous one may be the very thing that *forestalls* suicide." [8]

That is, a motive "introduced in one work, where the context greatly modifies it, and keeps it from being drastically itself, may lack such important modifications in the context of another work." Broad, sweeping statements about the "gist" of the context, with everything reduced to a "rationalization" of it, or described as mere concealment, will not lead to a sound methodology in symbolic interpretation. It is the proportions of the modifications in themes which we must analyze as we pass from one context to another. We must take the motivation of Milton's poem at face value, "considering the aggressive and theocratic terms just as significant in the total recipe as the reflexive terms are. Whether there are gods or not, there is an *objective* difference in motivation between an act conceived in the name of God and an act conceived in the name of godless Nature." [9]

We must understand that expression of the desire to kill a person in a symbolic work, such as Milton's poem, is a "desire" to *transform the principle* which that person *represents*. Thus, when the old rancher who will not allow newcomers to take up land for farming, is killed by the young pioneers, it is not a "father figure" who is being killed, but a principle of holding land, and a way of life which must be *transformed*, if the new life is to become possible. In such transformations the *principles* of the "shoot-out" are really not warlike at all. The battleground of the fight is the West, the new America which must be settled, and thus, even though soaked in blood, the battleground itself *transcends* the factions struggling over it. We watch for such transcendencies in symbolic expression, for they are ultimate clues to final values—the values, which, as we say, transcend "life itself." Rhetorical transcendencies of this type are common in religion, as well as art, as we learn from Christianity, which teaches us that in death there is life eternal.

How do we track down the ways in which final values are expressed? Is there a *method* we can use to analyze and codify the kinds of transformations necessary in the process of identification? Burke suggests that "we may stress the respects in which many different kinds of imagery can perform the same function. One may prefer imagery of the Upward Way and Downward Way, or of the Crossing and Return, or of Exile and Homecoming, or of a Winding-up and an Unwinding, or of Egresses, or of a Movement Inward and a Movement Outward, or of seasonal developments, or of various antitheses, like Day and Night, Warmth and Frigidity, Yes and No, Losing and Finding, Loosing and Binding, etc. . . ." Such pairs "are not merely to be placed statically against each other, but in given poetic contexts" which usually "represent a development *from* one order of motives *to* another. Such terms, here selected at random, suggest different families of images in terms of which the processes of transformation in general might be localized, or particularized." [10]

As these images of symbolic transformation imply, where we are going, what we are transforming to, is as important in determining identification as what we have transformed from. That is, "if there is [an] ultimate of *beginnings,* whereby theological or metaphysical systems may state the essence of mankind in terms of a divine parenthood or an originating natural ground, there is also an ultimate of endings, whereby the essence of a thing can be defined narratively in terms of its *fulfillment* or *fruition*.[11] In foretelling the end of a character, as when we say, "he will come to no good end," we invest the present actions of the character with his "doom," or fate, and *then* watch him progress toward this "inevitable" destiny. Thus, in symbolic works which are determined by narrative form, the end determines the beginning [12] and thus the whole act.

From this point of view, the imagery of slaying (of the self or another) is a kind of birth as well as a death. As we kill off the old, we are born in the new. For "the killing of something is the *changing* of it, and the statement of the thing's nature before and after the change is an identifying of it." In Burke, identification is born in strife, and only categories which pair peace and war, love and hate, cooperation and hostility, are useful in the study of identification. This is why Burke selects anecdotes of killing as his "representative cases" in the first pages of his *Rhetoric.* "We begin with an anecdote of killing, because invective, eristic, polemic, and logomachy are so pronounced an aspect of rhetoric. But we use a dialectical device (the shift to a higher level of generalization) that enables us to transcend the narrow implications of this imagery, even while keeping them clearly in view." [13]

Thus Burke argues that it is precisely because rhetoric is *"par excellence* the region of the Scramble, of insult and injury, bickering, squabbling, malice and the lie, cloaked malice and the subsidized lie" that it is useful in the study of identification.

We need never [if we follow his view of rhetoric] deny the presence of strife, enmity, faction as a characteristic motive. . . . We need not close our eyes to their almost tyrannous ubiquity in human relations; we can be on the alert always to see how such temptations to strife are implicit in the institutions that condition human relationships; yet we can at the same time always look beyond this order, to the principle of identification in general. . . . [14]

IDENTIFICATION IN RHETORIC

But while we recognize killing and victimage in rhetoric, identifications in the order of love are also characteristic of rhetorical expression. Here we find resources of appeal "ranging from sacrificial, evangelical love, through the kinds of persuasion figuring in sexual love, to sheer 'neutral' *communication* [15] (communication being the area where love has become so generalized, desexualized, 'technologized,' that only close critical or philosophic scrutiny can discern the vestiges of the original motive)." That is, while Burke is thoroughly determined to create a methodology which will include hate, war, and death as characteristic of human action, he does so for a humane purpose. If we follow his theory of rhetoric as identification and his methodology of analysis of rhetoric as a symbolic resolution of hate and love, "we can treat 'war' as a *'special case of peace'*—not as a primary motive in itself, not as *essentially* real, but purely as a *derivative* condition, a *perversion.*" [16]

The concept of identification must not be confused with the idea of being identical or the same. "A is not identical with his colleague, B. But in so far as their interests are joined, A is *identified* with B. Or he may *identify* himself with B even when their interests are not joined, if he assumes that they are, or is persuaded to believe so." Burke is anxious to avoid categories which do not recognize the individual. "In being identified with B, A is 'substantially one' with a person other than himself. Yet at the same time he remains unique, an individual locus in motives. Thus he is both joined and separate, at once a distinct substance and consubstantial with another." This, Burke insists, is the crux of his whole system.

To identify A with B is to make A "consubstantial" with B. Accordingly, since our *Grammar of Motives* was constructed about "substance" as key term, the related rhetoric selects its nearest equivalent in the areas of persuasion and dissuasion, communication and polemic. And our third volume, *Symbolic of Motives*, should be built about *identity* as titular or ancestral term, the "first" to which all other terms could be reduced and from which they could then be derived or generated, as from a common spirit. The thing's *identity* would here be its uniqueness as an entity in itself and by itself, a demarcated *unit having its own particular structure*.[17]

Thus, Burke begins his system with acting (that is, communicating) individuals who are at odds with one another and who become identified with groups "more or less at odds with one another." He seeks ways in which to *confront* the implications of division, not to explain them away, or to disregard them, or to reduce them to an "abnormal" condition of loving cooperation. Nor does he, like Mead, make the category of the "social" prior to that of the individual. And when he does evoke the "social" as a category, his image of society is not that of absolute and perfect communication. The purpose of the *Rhetoric,* and the application of his "socio-anagogic"[18] method of symbolic analysis, "must lead us through the Scramble, the Wrangle of the Market Place, and flurries and flare-ups of the Human Barnyard, the Give and Take, the wavering line of pressure and counterpressure, the Logomachy, the onus of ownership, the Wars of Nerves, the War."

The human "Scramble" has its peaceful moments: "at times its endless competition can add up to the transcending of itself. In ways of its own, it can move from the factional to the universal." Ideal culminations of the "Scramble" or, what is so familiarly called the "rat race," are often "beset by strife as the condition of their organized expression, or material embodiment."[19] Even our capacity to abstract and universalize is used to develop partisan weapons. "For one need not scrutinize the concept of 'identification' very sharply to see, implied in it at every turn, its ironic counterpart: division. Rhetoric is concerned with the state of Babel after the Fall. Its contributions to a 'sociology of knowledge' must often carry us far into the lugubrious regions of malice and the lie." [20]

Identification, while expressed in symbols and determined by success or failure in persuading audiences to our point of view, has extrasymbolic roots. One of these is property. "Metaphysically, a thing is identified by its *properties*. In the realm of Rhetoric, such identification is frequently by property in the most materialistic sense of the term. . . . Man surrounds himself with properties in goods, services, and in status, position, and rank, to establish his identity. But however ethical a man's rights may be, it often happens that his rights come into conflict with the rights of others. Indeed, from a socio-psychological view, it seems that only when others want something do I want it (and *vice versa*). That is, competition for property creates the value of the property. And since such competition, in so far as it depends on communication, is rhetorical, we can expect the symbolization of property "rights" to be specialized and "perfected" to such degree that property rights soon come in conflict with other rights, such as religion, the state, art, or education, which, in turn, are busy perfecting the expression of their "rights."

In all such struggles, especially when we are in opposition to those who think their rights to be "natural rights," we discover many types of identification. If we are scientists, we are quick to point out that religious institutions identify their causes and their property with a supernatural God. Men of God, on the other hand, are quick to point out that scientists identify themselves with a "Godless" state which is preparing for war. Thus, "however 'pure' one's motives may be actually, the impurities of identifications lurking about the edges of such situations introduce a typical Rhetorical wrangle of the sort that can never be settled once and for all, but belongs in the field of moral controversy where men properly seek to 'prove opposites.'" By "proving opposites" Burke means using rhetoric to argue that two ends, really opposed, are the same after all. Thus, when we defend "pure science" yet accept large military grants for research in atomic warfare, it is only the devout scientist, or the blind specialist, who believes that "pure" science can remain "pure" when supported by those devoted to slaughter of their own kind.

As Burke says, "The fact that an activity is capable of reduction to intrinsic, autonomous principles does not argue it is free from identification with other orders of motivation extrinsic to it. Any specialized activity participates in a larger unit of action. 'Identification' is a word for the autonomous activity's place in this wider context, a place with which the agent may be unconcerned. The shepherd, *qua* shepherd, acts for the good of the sheep, to protect them from discomfiture and harm. But he may be 'identified' with a project that is raising the sheep for market." It is quite possible to concentrate on one particular integrated structure of motives, but we are "clearly in the region of rhetoric when considering the identifications whereby a specialized activity makes one a participant in some social or economic class." [21]

Burke illustrates this by describing what has happened to college study of literature and the fine arts, where there is great stress on the pure autonomy of the humanistic "spirit." Such stress "is a round-about identification with a privileged class." Study in the liberal arts "may enroll the student stylistically under the banner of a privileged class, serving as a kind of social insigne promising preferment. As Burke points out, Veblen has explored the rhetoric of such identifications (notably in his writings on higher learning in America). Veblen shows how institutions, ostensibly dedicated to learning, find themselves forced by the exigencies (that is, the *rhetoric*) of pageantry, parade, and ceremonial discourse in a business community, to make learning either decorative and genteel, or practical and vocational. To have studied the fine arts (the "true, the good, and the beautiful") was a sign of ability to waste time and money, and thus, says Veblen, identified one with a genteel class beyond "vulgar" concern with profit and loss.

The rhetorical principle of identification teaches us then, that whenever an autonomous principle is advocated we must search at once for ways in which it is used for purely partisan purposes. This does not deny the value, or indeed, the truth of the principle.

In particular, as regards the teaching of literature, the insistence upon "autonomy" reflects a vigorous concern with the all-importance of the text that happens to be under scrutiny. This cult of patient textual analysis (though it has excesses of its own) is helpful as a reaction against the excesses of extreme historicism (a leftover of the nineteenth century) whereby a work became so subordinated to its background that the student's appreciation of first-rate texts was lost behind his involvement with the collateral documents of fifth-rate literary historians.[22]

But the greatest resistance to the questioning of "purity" in specialized studies and activities comes now from the "liberal apologists of science," not from students of literature. Theologians admit that in corrupt times there is a corresponding corruption in the church. Science, we see now, is no longer without sin, as "those specialists whose technical training fitted them to become identified with mass killings and experimentally induced sufferings in the concentration camps of National Socialist Germany" remind us. The American liberal scientist is horrified at implications that what happened in Germany might happen here. He is

disinclined to consider such possibilities because applied science is for him not a mere set of instruments and methods, whatever he may assert; it is *good* and *abso-lute,* and is thus circuitously endowed with the philosophic function of *God* as the grounding of values. His thinking thus vacillates indeterminately between his overt claims for science as sheer method, as sheer coefficient of power, and his covert claims for science as a substance which, like God, would be an intrinsically *good* power.[23]

Thus we see that through the resources of identification, rhetorical motives can operate "without conscious direction by any particular agent." Classical rhetoric emphasizes the element of explicit design in rhetorical communication. "But one can systematically extend the range of rhetoric, if one studies the persuasiveness of false or inadequate terms which may not be directly imposed upon us from without by some skillful speaker, but which we impose upon ourselves, in varying degrees of deliberateness and unawareness, through motives indeterminately self-protective and/or suicidal." Such identifications Burke calls "ingenuous and cunning." They may be thought of as the "psychopathology of identification." (These are discussed fully in his analysis of hierarchy and social order, which is the final section of the *Rhetoric.*)

Burke suggests, in his discussion of identification, that the psychologist's concept of "malingering" to designate the ways of neurotic patients who are not really sick but persuade themselves that they are so they can gain the attention of an audience significant to them, is appropriate to some aspects of rhetoric. When the feigned illness becomes habitual, it is very real—to both the patient and his audience. "Similarly, if a social or occupational class is not too exacting in the scrutiny of identifications that flatter its interests, its very philosophy of life is a profitable malingering (profitable at least until its inaccuracies catch up with it)—and as such, it is open to either attack or analysis. . . ."[24] For rhetoric is both a weapon of attack (as in the Philippics of Demosthenes) and an instrument of analysis (as in Aristotle's treatise on the "art" of rhetoric).

Notes

[1] Kenneth Burke, *A Rhetoric of Motives* (New York: Prentice-Hall, Inc., 1950), p. xiv. The second part of the *Rhetoric* deals with the traditional principles of rhetoric as persuasion.

[2] *Ibid.*, p. xiv.

[3] *Ibid.*, p. 43. Burke's italics.

[4] *Ibid.*, p. 41. Burke's italics.

[5] *Ibid.*, pp. 43-44.

[6] Burke is *not* saying that Milton's *Samson Agonistes* can be interpreted *only* in terms of rhetoric. He is very careful to point out that one "can read it simply *in itself*, without even considering the fact that it was written by Milton. It can be studied and appreciated as a structure of internally related parts, without concern for the correspondence that almost inevitably suggests itself: the correspondence between Milton's blindness and Samson's, or between the poet's difficulties with his first wife and Delilah's betrayal of a divine secret." (*Ibid.*, p. 4.) But this is not the task of the sociologist, and those who inveigh against the "sociological reduction" of literature to "communication" would serve the cause of the humanities better by showing us, not what is wrong with the sociological approach, but on what "right" methodology the aesthetic approach is based.

[7] *Ibid.*, p. 5.

[8] *Ibid.*, p. 6. This is Mead's point, too.

[9] *Ibid.*, p. 6. "Naming" is a function of language too (as are expression, communication, and the attempt to create self-consistent forms), but here Burke is concerned with how meaning is used to create identification.

[10] *Ibid.*, p. 11. Burke's systematic statement, in his "Theory of the Index," as he calls this technique of symbolic analysis, will be considered later. Here we try to describe the general principles on which his method and technique rest, but we must understand that Burke's theory, method, and technique are based on the analysis of *concrete forms of expression which exist in given texts.* Thus, he avoids the vague historicism of Simmel, and the high levels of abstraction in the writings of sociologists like Parsons.

[11] *Ibid.*, p. 13.

[12] We have already discussed how Dewey and Mead (particularly Mead) made use of this principle. As Mead put it, the image we have of the future serves to organize what we will do in the present. But Burke, unlike Dewey and Mead, *creates a method for analyzing the ways in which ends and values actually are used in symbolic expression.*

[13] Burke, *A Rhetoric of Motives*, p. 20.

[14] *Ibid.*, p. 19.

[15] Or, as we say in sociology, "mass communication," which is not the study of identification, and certainly not of *symbolic* action.

[16] Burke, *op. cit.*, p. 20. Of course, it can be argued that these terms can be reversed with equal logic—that is, peace can be treated as a special case of war, as when we say "and then peace broke out"—but from a rhetorical point of view, war is an attempt *to induce* an enemy to cooperate. Burke rejects views which regard friendly and ethical motives as a "kind of benign fiction" for harnessing our "natural" drives

of vengeance and murder. That is, he refuses to believe that we should use our minds to prove that we do not have minds.

[17] Burke tells us in the Introduction to his *Rhetoric* that these passages on identification are the key to the book. The slogan for his *Rhetoric* which he offers is: "In identification lies the source of dedications and enslavements, in fact, of cooperation." (*A Rhetoric of Motives*, p. xiv.)

[18] A method of analysis whereby we expose the identifications of symbols with judgment of status.

[19] Burke, *op. cit.*, p. 23.

[20] *Ibid.*

[21] *Ibid.*, pp. 27–28.

[22] Ibid., p. 28. Burke stresses, too, the *methodological* value of emphasis on autonomous fields. Arguments over autonomy force us to define the range and relevance of our observations. This way of thinking, Burke says, "is particularly needed now, when pseudoscientific thinking has become 'unprincipled' in its uncritical cult of 'facts.' "

[23] *Ibid.*, p. 30.

[24] *Ibid.*, p. 36.

12

The Rhetoric of Social Order

IDENTIFICATION AND ADDRESS

Rhetoric designed for use is designed for specific audiences, and whenever we assume that "low" or "prejudiced" audiences must be addressed in terms of their own "distortions," it is easy to become cunning and disingenuous in our address. A common example of rhetorical cunning is the use of terms so vague or so general that they cannot be criticized because the critic cannot find any meaning in them. Cunning and disingenuous rhetoric may be used in all honesty, as when a politician believes that to save his community he must cajole and even lie to his constituents. Yet such "persuasive identifications of Rhetoric, in being so directly designed for *use,* involve us in a special problem of *consciousness,* as exemplified in the Rhetorician's particular *purpose* for a given statement." [1]

The paradox in all address is that, whatever our motive in addressing another, and however great our skill in address, he alone can give us success. We cannot force but must persuade an audience to respond to us. It is because of this, as Burke points out, that there is a peculiar kind of *anguish* [2] in communication. Stendhal's Julien Sorel and the scrupulous criminals of Gide seem to exist under an aesthetic of pure expression. They have little regard, indeed, even scorn for communication, yet they are constantly involved with the effect of their poses on audiences within the self, as well as within society. The hermit in his cell seems "beyond" communication, and so he is, but only with men, not with God. For God is the audience, an *ultimate* audience, whom he addresses. *How* he addresses his God will determine the success of his plea for salvation.

While Burke places the individual under the head of Symbolic, and the social under that of Rhetoric, he is careful to stress that such categories as "individual" and "society" meet in rhetoric when we consider the relationship between the speaker and his audience. Even Freud, who does not make communication a category, often uses rhetorical images to describe the action of the psyche.

[W]hat could be more profoundly rhetorical than Freud's notion of a dream that attains expression by stylistic subterfuges designed to evade the inhibitions of a moralistic censor? What is this but the exact analogue of the rhetorical devices of literature under political or theocratic censorship? The *ego* with its *id* confronts the *super-ego* much as an orator would confront a somewhat alien audience, whose susceptibilities he must flatter as a necessary step toward persuasion. The Freudian psyche is quite a parliament, with conflicting interests expressed in ways variously designed to take the claims of rival factions into account.[8]

Thus, in Burke's argument, rhetoric explains psychology as much as psychology explains rhetoric.

For Burke, Freud's *Jokes and Their Relation to the Unconscious* is conceived in rhetorical terms, with speaker and hearer as partners "in partisan jokes made at the expense of another." If we internalize these roles, we get a complex individual of many voices. From the standpoint of rhetoric, this may be thought of as a "parliamentary wrangle which the individual has put together somewhat as he puts together his fears and hopes, friendships and enmities, health and disease, or those tiny rebirths whereby, in being born to some new condition, he may be dying to a past condition, his development being dialectical, a series of terms in perpetual transformation." A man becomes his own audience when he cultivates certain ideas as images for the effects he hopes they may have upon him. When the "I" addresses its "Me" (in Meadian terms) the "I" is as much in the realm of rhetoric as the orator addressing a public audience.

In traditional rhetoric the external audience is stressed, and since the audiences of Aristotle's Athens were small groups who met frequently in face-to-face situations, it was possible for Aristotle to list typical beliefs and methods of appeal to such a familiar and well-understood audience. "But a modern 'post-Christian' rhetoric must also concern itself with the thought that, under the heading of appeal to audiences, would also be included any ideas or images privately addressed to the individual self for moralistic or incantatory purposes." In our world we become our own audiences, "in some respects a very lax one, in some respects very exacting, when you become involved in psychologically stylistic subterfuges for presenting your own case to yourself in sympathetic terms (and even terms that seem harsh can often be found on closer scrutiny to be flattering, as with neurotics who visit sufferings upon themselves in the name of very high-powered motives which, whatever their discomfiture, feed pride)." [4]

The internalization of motives through address to the self, the ways in which we try to form the self in accordance with the communicative norms of the group significant to us, indicate how the rhetoric of identification becomes a prime element in socialization. To act persuasively upon the self we select images and ideas that will form the self into the kind of self we want to be. Education and all forms of indoctrination do this from without. The individual completes the process from within. When he fails to tell himself (as his own audience) what the various kinds of rhetoric in his society have told him, his persuasion is not complete. "Only those voices from without are effective which can speak in the language of a voice within." Perhaps, Burke suggests, when we understand hysteria better we will begin to analyze it as rhetoric, an attempt to communicate to the self and others something which cannot be communicated at all except through the "rhetoric of hysteria." [5]

In the closing pages of his section on identification, Burke suggests that one of the great ironies of modern social thought is that precisely at the time when the term "rhetoric" has fallen into great neglect as a form of symbolic analysis and into disrepute as a mode of appeal, writers in the social sciences have been making good contributions to the "New Rhetoric." [6] Cross culture studies have thrown much light on classical approaches to rhetoric. But the combining of traditional and modern anthropological theories of communication in this "New Rhetoric" based on identification, persuasion, and hierarchy has not been easy. Burke tells us that while he was strongly influenced by anthropological inquiries into primitive magic, he did not clearly discern the exact relation between the anthropologist's concern with magic and the literary critic's concern with communication until he had systematically worked on his *Rhetoric* for years. Prior to this discovery, though he persisted in "anthropological hankerings," he did so with a bad conscience; and "he was half willing to agree with literary opponents who considered such concerns alien to the study of literature proper." [7]

Modern literary critics have absorbed anthropological views on language as magic, but anthropologists and other social scientists are not yet aware of the basic tenets of rhetoric. [8] And so long as we regard magic as an early form of bad science, we are left only with a distinction between bad science and good science. Scientific knowledge is thus presented as a terminology that gives an accurate and critically tested description of society, while magic is treated as antithetical to such science.[9] "Hence magic is treated as an early uncritical attempt to do what science does, but under conditions where judgment and perception were impaired by the naively anthropomorphic belief that the impersonal forces of nature were motivated by personal designs." In this view we confront "a flat choice between a civilized vocabulary of scientific description and a savage vocabulary of magical incantation."[10] To avoid this, Burke proposes that distinctions be made between poetic, scientific, and rhetorical language. "Whereas poetic language is a kind of symbolic action, for itself and in itself, and whereas scientific language is a preparation for action, rhetorical language is an inducement to action (or to take a certain attitude, attitude being considered an incipient act)."[11]

As Mead and Burke stress, the future in which we will act is an image. As a goal, vision, or ideal, it cannot be studied as the biologist studies bacteria, nor can it be tested by a knowledge of "approximately" equivalent conditions in the past. When "you turn to political exhortation, you are involved in decisions that necessarily lie beyond the strictly scientific vocabularies of description." What then are we to do in our search for understanding of human motives in rhetoric? One solution is to say that since political rhetoric cannot be studied as a science, we must study it as a kind of primitive magic. But this approach to rhetoric as "word magic" gets the whole subject turned backwards. The magical use of symbols to affect nature and all natural processes by incantations and rituals *"was a mistaken transference of a proper linguistic function to an area for which it was not fit."* The real use of language in address, its function *to induce action in people,* "became the magical use of addressed language *to induce motion in things"*—things, which by nature are alien to purely linguistic orders of motivation. Thus, Burke concludes: "If we begin by treating this *erroneous* and derived magical use as *primary,* we are invited to treat a *proper* use of language (for instance, political persuasion) simply as a vestige of benightedly prescientific magic."[12]

Between magic and science there are other categories of human experience. These exist in religion and art. Treating art, religion, and language in terms of flat dialectical opposition to modern technology tells us little about how we, in America, order social effort in terms of our most powerful symbol, money. Rhetoric in America must establish social identifications, in a life highly diversified by money, with the great division of labor and social status which money serves to rationalize.[13] In view of this,

Burke holds, much more understanding—even of primitive life—can be gained if we confront the term "magic" with the term "rhetoric." One comes "closer to the true state of affairs if one treats the socializing aspects of magic as a 'primitive rhetoric' than if one sees modern rhetoric simply as a 'survival of primitive magic.'" For once we emend the anthropological analysis of magic, based on the theory that magic was used to produce linguistic responses in kinds of beings not accessible to the linguistic motive, there is much to be gained.[14]

Anthropologists, as well as other social scientists, must learn to confront *explicitly* the rhetorical ingredient in their fields of study.[15] The rhetorical approach is a *functional* approach, but not the kind of functional approach common to those who talk vaguely about "magic," "witchcraft," and "consensus" as "integrating forces." Rhetoric involves identification, and the relationship of identification to order in society (hierarchy) brings us into the realm of *human* interaction, where both a future and a past come into existence only as we act together in a present. The propositions of "scientific realism" can tell us nothing about a future, in so far as this future is determined by language. The study of language as rhetoric, whether it is science or not, tells us what we need to know, namely, what kind of goals men select to stimulate themselves and others to act.

The use of rhetoric as *identification* and its nature as *address* must be considered together. Identification implies division, and rhetoric involves us in acts of socialization which are attempts to resolve the divided and contending voices which arise out of this division. Since identification is obtained through property, and property gives rise to conflict, and the ultimate of conflict is war and murder, Burke tells us that we must consider how the imagery of division and conflict "can figure as a terminology of reidentification . . . in transformation and rebirth." When we approach the border between identification and division, we come always upon the war of words, "avowed as in invective, unavowed as in stylistic subterfuges for presenting real divisions in terms that deny division"[16] (as when a political leader like De Gaulle tells France his rule will be above politics).

The relationship between identification and persuasion is very close. The speaker persuades through stylistic identification, in which he tries to identify himself with the listener's interests; and the speaker in turn draws on identification of interests to establish rapport between himself and the audience. It is difficult, as Burke says, to think about identification without, at the same time, thinking about persuasion, and it is equally difficult to distinguish between communication, identification, and address. And since beings unequal in status, strange to each other and often deeply hostile, must yet find cohesion in the magic and glamor of some great transcendent social bond (which alone can hold disparate and strange beings together), the study of *how men court each other* in the name of the transcendent social bonds will tell us much about the function of rhetoric in society.

PERSUASION AND COMMUNICATION

Identification occurs in communication when speaker and hearer reach deep communion. Persuasion is the means by which this is achieved. "You persuade a man only in so far as you can talk his language by speech, gesture, tonality, order, image, attitude, idea, *identifying* your ways with his." [17] This is done through evoking in the audience a sense of collaboration with the speaker. In great moments of rhetoric the audience feels that it is participating creatively in the assertions of the speaker. [18] Rhetoric thus becomes an inducement to action, when by action we mean *both* incipient action (as in the formation of attitude) and fully developed action (as in motor phases of the act). As Augustine tells us, rhetoric must bring men "not merely to know what should be done, but to do what they know should be done." [19]

Persuasion involves choice, for only in so far as man is free can he be persuaded. When a man must do something, either because he is forced to, or believes that his act is "fate," rhetoric cannot be used. But even when an individual cannot act freely, rhetoric may be used to affect his attitude. Criminals awaiting execution, soldiers waiting to go into fire, the man who knows his life is slowly ebbing away—these cannot choose to avoid death. What they can choose is what attitude to take toward what they must do. Cicero and Augustine believed the ultimate function of persuasion in rhetoric to be the creation of attitudes which would "bend" or incline men to act in certain ways. Thus, while there is the obvious function of rhetoric as a goad to action, there is also another function—the creation of attitudes and states of mind.

In the creation of states of mind we enter the realm of the poetic, "the study of lyrical devices," which can be classed under the head of rhetoric when these devices are considered for their power to induce or communicate states of mind to readers, even though the kinds of assent evoked have no overt, practical outcome. Thus even in the most subjective kind of discourse there is an element of address. In lyrical discourse we address the self, or an ideal other, who may not exist, but is created through the power of rhetoric. For audiences not only exist but *are created by rhetoric.*[20] Needs and interests exist, it is true, yet the *forms* of satisfaction, the *ways* in which these needs will be satisfied is a matter of communication in general, and of rhetoric, the art of persuasion, in particular. The forms of rhetoric, considered as inducements to action, must be understood, therefore, in terms of the character of the audience and the purpose of the speaker.

Classical orators recognized three basic uses of rhetoric—the oratory of political assemblies, the oratory of law courts, and oratory designed to instruct or to inspire men to virtue. Thus, as De Quincey points out in his essay on rhetoric, the art of rhetoric in classic times designated the whole cycle of accomplishments that prepared a man for public affairs. Rhetoric also prepared a man for private life, for, by Quintilian's time in Rome, rhetoric was considered the key to the education of a gentleman. Even poetry was admired, not so much for lyrical as for rhetorical qualities.[21] On almost every level of life—from the "Art of Cheating" (as perfected by some of the Greek Sophists) to the highest intellectual and moral reaches of the soul—rhetoric was held indispensable. For, so believed the ancients, men could be persuaded to good or to evil. How men communicated determined how they lived.

We are taught that scientists create and use instruments that give them control of nature and society, but the Greeks and Romans, as well as the Christian rhetoricians led by Augustine, thought such control (or at least, social control) could be achieved in the science or art of language. This science had nothing in common with our "science" of content analysis (which reduces a symbolic text to spatial or temporal units which can be studied by the same techniques we use to study matter). Aristotle agreed with modern behaviorists in their belief that we must study nonverbal factors if we are to understand communication, but for Aristotle this factor, the factor extrinsic to symbolic expression in rhetoric, is the *audience* and not nature, environment, or social forces. "Audience analysis" must, therefore, include the character of the scene in which persuasion was attempted and the character of the audience addressed by the speaker.

And, as we learn from Aristotle's attempt to create a science of language through the study of rhetoric, if we relate language to action we must state clearly what we mean by the term "action." This Aristotle does when he tells us that to understand why a man acts as he does, we must know "who acts, what he is doing, with respect to what or in what, sometimes with what, as with what instrument, and with what result (as that of preservation, for instance), and how, or whether softly or violently." [22] Or, as Burke says in his *Grammar of Motives,* any complete statement of why men act as they do must offer some kind of answer to five questions, namely, what was done, when or where it was done, who did it, how he did it, and why. Aristotle argues that we must develop a universal model for appraising the structures of *all* acts, whatever their motive. Burke argues, too, that only a structural and functional theory so broad it will admit of no exceptions (as he proposes in his Dramatistic Pentad of Act, Scene, Agent, Agency, Purpose) must be created. [23]

Thus Burke, following Aristotle, argues that even extrinsic considerations of language can be derived from persuasion as a generating principle, for "an act of persuasion is affected by the character of the scene in which it takes place and of the agents to whom it is addressed." Rhetorical analysis of persuasion should not be confused with the modern public relations analysis of how to appeal to timely interests (as when the election of the President of the United States is used as a "pitch" to sell ice boxes). But neither, as Aristotle, Cicero, Quintilian, Augustine, and now Burke warn us, will a theory of rhetoric be of any value unless it can be applied to the affairs of men in society. Classical rhetoricians are much more concerned with *how* to persuade than with the abstract principles of persuasion. They *assumed* that everyone knew that language, motives, and society could not be separated. Thus, for them, the argument was not *whether* language served to create and sustain social bonds,[24] but *how* it did so.

While Aristotle and Cicero were sensitive to how audiences affected the success of persuasion, they took their audiences more or less for granted. The classical rhetoricians were not involved with the peculiarities, the "interests," the "unconscious motives," the ideologies, or any of the great questions concerning audiences which haunt those who must appeal successfully to the varied and extensive audiences of our time. But this does *not* mean that Aristotle and his followers were unaware of the power of nonrational appeal. Aristotle argued that the one legitimate means open to the orator is reasonable argument, but, since man is a creature of passion and emotion and audiences are sure to be swayed by emotion, the speaker has to reckon with emotion and learn how to deal with it. Thus it is not the neglect of passion and emotion, but the attempt to understand them *as a means to reason,* that distinguishes Aristotle's analysis of rhetoric.[25]

Thus, when Aristotle discusses fears, he is careful to define what they are, their causes, the conditions under which men fear, and the classes of people who are without fear. But this analysis of fear is not done in the spirit of a science which seeks to measure how fear inhibits salivation or appetite, but of a science of rhetoric which can teach us to move men to good acts. Accordingly, Aristotle says,

when it is desirable that the audience should fear [that is, when it is necessary to make men fear evil], the speaker must bring them into the right frame of mind so that they shall take themselves to be the kind of people who are likely to suffer. He must argue that others greater than they have suffered; and must point out that others like them (in a like situation) are suffering, or have suffered, at the hands of people from whom they did not expect, and at times when they thought themselves safe.[26]

But Aristotle is careful to stress that he advocates arousing fear because fear leads to deliberation and thus opens the mind to rational appeals. Fear, he states,

is experienced by those who think themselves likely to suffer, and to suffer from particular persons particular things at particular times. People do not expect suffering when they are, or think they are, in states of great prosperity—conditions that make them insolent (prone to outrage), contemptuous (prone to slighting), and bold (reckless); such types of character as result from wealth, bodily strength, abundance of friends, power. Nor, on the other hand, do men expect suffering when they think they have already suffered the last extremity of horror, and are become callous to the future, like culprits who have been flogged until they are done for. *If there is to be the anguish of uncertainty, there must be lurking hope of deliverance; and that this is so would appear from the fact (a sign of this is) that fear sets men to deliberating. Accordingly no one deliberates about things that are hopeless.*[27]

Burke summarizes the purely traditional evidences of the rhetorical motive as "persuasion, exploitation of opinion (the 'timely' topic is a variant), a work's nature as addressed, literature for use (applied art, inducing to an act beyond the area of verbal expression considered in and for itself), verbal deception (hence, rhetoric as instrument in the war of words), the 'agonistic' generally, words used 'sweetly' (eloquence, ingratiation, for its own sake), formal devices, the art of proving opposites (as 'counterpart of dialectic')." To these he adds, for the purposes of establishing a "New Rhetoric," Malinowski's concept of "context of situation," especially when considering the semiverbal, semiorganizational kinds of tactics one might classify as a "rhetoric of bureaucracy." [28] He then discusses the forms of appeal used by rhetoricians, the analyses of rhetorical devices made by the masters of rhetoric, and then discusses how writers like Bentham, Marx, Carlyle, Empson, Veblen, Diderot, La Rochefoucauld, De Gourmont, Pascal, Machiavelli, and Dante used rhetoric, and how what they thought about rhetoric can be used to create a "New Rhetoric" based on the social function of language.

Notes

[1] Kenneth Burke, *A Rhetoric of Motives* (New York: Prentice-Hall, Inc., 1950), p. 36.

[2] Communication is an act of love and hate, but love looms larger than hate, because so long as we require an audience we cannot destroy it (as we kill an enemy in war), or be indifferent to it (as we are to strangers whose response means nothing to us). Thus, there must be some kind of *regard* for our audience.

[3] Kenneth Burke, *A Grammar of Motives* (New York: Prentice-Hall, Inc., 1945), p. 38.

[4] *Ibid.*, pp. 38–39. As we shall point out later, "feeding pride" is a highly social motive whose power can equal and, indeed, sometimes surpass that of hunger or sex. It is, so to speak in biological terms, a hierarchal "drive."

[5] *A Rhetoric of Motives*, p. 39. And Burke adds that in hysterical communication we confront "an ultimate irony, in glimpsing how even a catatonic lapse into sheer automatism, beyond the reach of all normally linguistic communication, is in its origins communicative, addressed, though it be a paralogical appeal-that-ends-all-appeals."

[6] Modern tyrants have made uses of rhetoric that make Machiavelli's "cynicism" seem almost innocent and parochial.

[7] *Ibid.*, p. 40. Such studies have been interpreted in terms which, as Burke points out, conceal their true relation to earlier work. There is a great deal of smuggling into the social sciences of work already done in the humanities. Images, ideas, and concepts which have long been part of the traditional lore of the philosophy, criticism, and history of art are being disguised in sociological jargon, and then paraded as some kind of discovery. The justification for this is that since we must rationalize sociological terminology, whatever is said by sociologists will be better said in some kind of "official jargon." This may enroll the sociologist who uses such jargon as "official," but it places him beyond communication with those who are not bemused by sociological "science."

[8] This is not altogether a matter of choice, for whenever we talk about the manipulation of men's beliefs we are in the realm of rhetoric, and the more we know about rhetoric, the better students we become of men in society. The danger now is that in using rhetorical concepts, without knowing that we do so, we simply repeat in some kind of new jargon what has been said before—and often said better.

[9] Sociologists such as Mills are now beginning to do this in fields outside of anthropology. For "magic" they substitute "art," which is discussed—when it is discussed at all—as a kind of crude sociology filled with "insights." This repeats the error, in different guise, of sociologists who treated religion as a crude step toward "society."

[10] *Ibid.*, p. 41.

[11] *Ibid.*

[12] *Ibid.*, p. 42.

[13] This was not true of traditional rhetoric. The lack of money, technology, and mass audiences in classical society creates many difficulties in the application of classical principles of rhetoric to our society.

[14] This emendation is already under way in anthropology, if not in sociology. The modern anthropologists, at least those of the "functional school," such as Kluckhohn and Warner, study a system of symbolic expression, such as witchcraft, to discover how it affects society, *not* how it affects "nature," or the individual's "perception" of his world.

[15] Kluckhohn and Parsons agree that this should be done, but this view has not yet seeped down into the middle and lower ranks of American social scientists whose imagery of social action is formed on images of motion in space, not action in society.

[16] Burke, *op. cit.*, p. 45.

[17] *Ibid.*, p. 55.

[18] This is what is meant by saying there is "tension" or "resonance" between speaker and audience.

[19] Quoted from Burke, *A Rhetoric of Motives*, p. 50. This difference was well illustrated by Adlai Stevenson, twice defeated candidate for the presidency of the United States. "Ex-candidate Adlai Stevenson, trying to describe the difference between himself and the man he was introducing, candidate Jack Kennedy, put it poignantly. 'Do you remember that in classical times when Cicero had finished speaking the people said, "How well he spoke"—but when Demosthenes had finished speaking the people said, "Let us march"?'" (*Time*, November 14, 1960.)

[20] Businessmen assume they must create markets for their goods and services by "carving out a piece" of an established market or by creating a new one. This is done through commercial rhetoric, or what we call advertising, and the market is thought of by commercial rhetoricians as an audience which must be persuaded to buy. The teen-age audience is a notable example of the creation of a new buying audience in our time. And our modern commercial rhetoricians know that even when an audience "exists" it must still be won over to one point of view, in competition with other rhetoricians who uphold different views.

[21] Virgil was greatly admired for his rhetoric. Shakespeare's and Racine's audiences enjoyed the rhetorical qualities of drama. Pulpit oratory, what we might call sacred rhetoric, has always been a powerful force in religious life. Prayer, even silent "inner" prayer, is highly rhetorical, for when we beseech supernatural powers we attempt to persuade them to give us what we demand by "pleasing" or "placating" them. And, above all, we must be sure our prayers are "heard," that is, that God is paying attention to us. In this strictly rhetorical view of prayer as beseechment, we do not "demand" God's attention, nor do we have a "right" to it, but must *win* it.

[22] *Nicomachean Ethics*, Book III, 1111a. See *The Nicomachean Ethics of Aristotle*, translated by D. P. Chase (New York: E. P. Dutton & Co., Everyman's Library, 1930), p. 47.

[23] By this he does not mean that there will be no difference in emphasis in the

element of the pentad stressed by various students of society. There will always be disagreement about the purposes behind a given act, or about the character of the person who did it, or how he did it, or in what kind of situation he acted. Finally, Burke continues, men may advocate totally different words to name the act itself. But they must do so, he argues (as does Aristotle), in terms of a scheme that involves analysis of who did what, when, where, how, and why.

[24] *Whether* language thus serves is still argued among American sociologists. In some quarters it is actually held that it does *not* do so, or that if it does there is no way it can be studied. This view was not shared by Hitler and Goebbels, as we see in *Mein Kampf,* in which Hitler told us how oratory affected mass publics, and then went on to practice what he preached.

[25] Hitler's concern with rhetoric is exactly the opposite. He studies how we can *decrease* the effects of reason upon an audience. He is very explicit about this, so much so that his work should be studied as a manual of nonrational kinds of persuasion. We note, too, that Hitler, like Aristotle, seemed in little doubt about his audience, the great mass audience of the modern state. Certainly we cannot argue against his incredible success as an orator before such audiences. Hitler's only peer in oratory (fortunately for us) was Churchill. The powerful speeches of these leaders did not *prepare* men to act, but *moved* them to action—sometimes indeed when they were not prepared. Hitler made it clear that he wanted action, not reflection, as the result of his speeches. The masses must be taught to "will," not to "reason." Yet book after book comes out "explaining" Hitler in light of everything except what his closest associates tell us was his greatest gift—oratory. The same is true of Churchill. There is no treatment of either as rhetorician.

[26] Lane Cooper, *The Rhetoric of Aristotle: An Expanded Translation* . . . (New York: Appleton-Century-Crofts, Inc., 1932), p. 110. This excellent edition, "with supplementary examples for students of composition and public speaking," contains much that is relevant to the interests of sociologists.

[27] *Ibid.,* p. 110. My italics.

[28] Burke, *A Rhetoric of Motives,* pp. 64–65. The "New Rhetoric" will be an "*extension* of rhetoric through the concept of identification."

PART FIVE

Social Mystification in Communication Between Classes

13

Toward a New Rhetoric: Burke's Analysis of Social "Mystification" in Bentham and Marx

JEREMY BENTHAM'S SEARCH FOR A "NEUTRAL" RHETORIC BASED ON "REASON"

B ENTHAM is not simply "debunking" authority, nor is he setting out from a partisan basis, like Marx or Veblen, to "deglamorize" his opponent's way of "clothing" his power with "respect and veneration." He is trying to create ways to discount the power of authority by analyzing how authority is communicated, in terms of a principle of rhetoric which states how authority *ought to be* communicated. "With reference to any proposed measures having for their object the greatest happiness of the greatest number, the course pursued by the adversaries of such measures has commonly been, in the first instance, to try to repress altogether the exercise of the reasoning faculty by invoking authority in various shapes as conclusive regarding the measure proposed." [1]

Appeals to authority by those seeking to repress "rational legislation" are of four kinds. First, there is the appeal to some higher authority in order to show that discussion is useless (Fallacies of Authority). Second, fearful visions of danger are evoked, "to repress discussion altogether, by exciting alarm (Fallacies of Danger)." [2] When neither of these stratagems works, attempts are made to postpone debate indefinitely (Fallacies of Delay). When all these fail, an attempt is made to throw the issue into complete confusion (Fallacies of Confusion). Each fallacy is divided into subcategories. There are six typical fallacies of authority, five fallacies of danger, five fallacies of delay, and fourteen fallacies of confusion. Knowledge of these rhetorical fallacies, Bentham hoped, would reform legislation. The day would come when "any legislator anywhere who is so far off his guard as through craft or simplicity to let drop any of these irrelevant and deceptious arguments will be greeted not with the cry of 'Order! Order!' but with voices in scores crying aloud 'Stale! Stale! Fallacy of Authority! Fallacy of Distrust!' and so on."

Burke, like Hume, points out that a genuinely neutral vocabulary would defeat its own ends; "for there would be no act in it. It would give full instructions for conditioning—but it could not say to what one should condition." Nor does it even follow, as so many scientists believe, that a neutralized vocabulary cannot be used to communicate purposes which are "beyond reason." Thus in our society, where money is so powerful, we often hear it said that a mortgage "must" be foreclosed, a certain interest charged, a loan made, or money spent on roads (but not schools) because "that is the way money is put to work." [3] In the pursuit of making such workings more efficient ("rationalizing the market"), a "neutral" vocabulary of money eliminates the many "censorial weightings that go with the many different philosophic, religious, social, political, and personal outlooks extrinsic to the monetary motive." Bentham's social outlook was that of the utilitarians, who held that the greatest happiness of the greatest number must determine judgment of public issues. But so too does the modern American businessman hold that mass production justifies the power of money in our society. Thus even Bentham's principle of social utility can easily serve as a rhetorical cloak for the use of money.

Another difficulty in the search for "neutral" vocabularies is that many of the rhetorical and linguistic devices discussed as "fallacies" are *natural* to men as communicators. For in community affairs (and even when we address ourselves), we communicate to evoke action, not only to prepare for it or to reflect on it. Even at best there is no such thing as a "perfect act" (or, if there is, only God can perform it). And, as Aristotle is careful to point out, there are objections to any position taken in rhetoric. For to act at all we must *believe* one course of action to be better than another. We can only do one thing at a time, just as when we speak we can only take one position at a time. Therefore, *by the very nature of discourse,* the complaints of the opposition that we are not taking everything into consideration, are always just complaints.

Even when we "appeal to reason," we often spend far more time in showing what is *not* reasonable about our opponents' views than in describing carefully just what is reasonable about ours. We also create attitudes toward a point of view considered rational by irrational means. In teaching we sometimes indoctrinate students with an attitude long before we give them any rational basis for holding to the attitude. A slight gesture, a quizzical look, a shadow of irony in our voice warns the student that there is a "right" and a "wrong" way to think about the subject. And the student, at best insecure, uneasy, and puzzled, watches furtively for the "right" way into the subject which he must learn in terms of the teacher's learning if he is to get good grades. With such a dependent audience it is easy for the teacher to *suggest* that "proofs" of his view exist, without at the same time demonstrating just what they are. It is only when the teacher grounds his position in reason by showing carefully all the steps involved in his argument that he makes it possible for the student to think critically. This frees the student from his limitations, because it teaches him how to think about his limitations.

Bentham's reliance on reason, and the implementation of reason by a "neutral" vocabulary of human motives, seems alien and remote to our time. Yet, even today, in an age of unreason, the vision persists of a "rational" vocabulary which will allow us to "unmask" ideologies. But when we analyze these attempts to use rhetoric to unmask rhetoric we discover that there is no "rhetoric beyond rhetoric." When men communicate they are bound by the resources of language. And, just as we ask of those who propose a planned state who is to plan the planners, so we must ask all seekers of "purely denotative" vocabularies to explain how we could move men to act if we remove all exhortation from language. Burke argues that it would be better to accept language as action and study how it is used, and thus learn how to use its highly dramatic qualities for good ends.[4] Instead of trying to remove the emotional and dramatic qualities from language, let us accept them for what they are—ways to evoke action— and study *how* this is done.

RHETORIC AND DIALECTIC IN MARXISM

Karl Marx, like Bentham, was heavily involved in exposing what he considered to be fallacies in the use of rhetoric. But, unlike Bentham, Marx was not concerned with creating a science of rhetoric, but in carrying out a program of social action.[5] He studied rhetoric to expose the conscious and unconscious deceptions of his opponents. A non-Marxist terminology expressed an "ideology"; a Marxist terminology expressed the dialectic of history. Thus, while the Marxists, like all who communicate, have a rhetoric and use all the arts of persuasion, they argue that their rhetoric is grounded in a dialectic. The rhetoric is symbols; the dialectic, since it is concerned with nonsymbolic orders of social motives, is equated with "science." An art of rhetoric in keeping with this "science" would, as Burke stresses, "be grounded in 'science' (or 'dialectic') in so far as it took its start from the experience of natural reality, while being rhetorical in proportion as its persuasiveness helped form judgments, choices, attitudes deemed favorable to Communist purposes."

The main principles of Marxism as a theory of rhetoric are stated clearly in *The German Ideology* by Marx and Engels. Here it is argued that ideas do not determine social relations but are derived from them. Property and the division of labor create a ruling class with its own set of ideas. The symbol specialists of such a class confuse the function of consciousness, spirit, and idea in human society, because their thinking is infused with ideologies. What is meant by an ideology? Burke distinguishes seven variants of the term. One, the "study, development, criticism of ideas, considered in themselves (as in a Socratic dialogue)." Two, a "system of ideas, aiming at social or political action" (Pareto's sociology, or Hitler's *Mein Kampf*). Three, any "set of interrelated terms, having practical civic consequences, directly or indirectly" (a businessman's code of fair practices might be a good instance). Four, myths created "for purposes of governmental control" ("ideology" would here be an exact synonym for "myth of the state"). Five, a "partial, hence to a degree deceptive, view of reality, particularly when the limitations can be attributed to interest-begotten prejudice" (for instance, a white Southern intellectual's "ironic resignation" to a *status quo* built on "white supremacy"). Six, "purposefully manipulated overemphasis or underemphasis in the discussion of controversial political and social issues." Seven, "an inverted genealogy of culture, that makes for 'illusion' and 'mystification' by treating ideas as primary where they should have been treated as derivative." [6]

The seventh definition is the Marxian definition, and for survival in the War of Words (where shooting wars begin), it is important for us to know just how Marx and Engels conceived of ideologies. For, as we shall see, Marx explores the problem of ideology from both a sociological and a rhetorical view. The schools and social movements selected for criticism in *The German Ideology* are considered "ideologies," which can be exposed only by "objective" Marxism. "The chief defect of all materialism up to now . . . is that the object, reality, what we apprehend through our senses, is understood only in the form of the *object* or *contemplation;* but not as *sensuous human activity,* as *practice,* not subjectively." [7] Thus, philosophers, priests, jurists, all intellectuals become specialists in symbols and ideas. Their separation from manual workers and the degradation of manual labor leads them to place a high value on "ideas" reached through contemplation and the manipulation of symbols as such, because they live in a society which honors, and, indeed, deifies symbolic manipulation.

And, since these intellectuals, or "ideologists," are bound to the ruling class, their job is to perfect and systematize the ideas of this class. The ideas of the ruling class become the ruling ideas of a society because this class controls the main channels of expression and communication. Once the ideas of the ruling class are fixed in art, literature, and religion they seem impervious to changes, even in the society which produced them. Thus, even though the economic base of society changes (with corresponding changes in the class structure), ideas and forms of expression which have little to do with new social needs continue to prevail. Marx argues in his discussion of the "Mystery of the Fetishistic Character of Commodities," in *Capital*,[8] that "the mystery of the commodity form [ideas about commodities] is simply this, that it mirrors for men the social character of their own labor, mirrors it as an objective character attaching to the labor products themselves, mirrors it as a social natural property of these things."[9]

In further search for some way to explain the "mystifications" or "social hieroglyphics" of value in capitalism, Marx turns to analogies drawn from religion. After again asking how it is that money (which has "nothing whatever to do with the physical properties of commodities or with the material relations that arise out of these commodities") becomes a "transcendent or social thing" (that is, a social symbol), Marx tells us that we must "enter the nebulous world of religion" to understand the operation of symbols like money. In religion

the products of the human mind become independent shapes, endowed with lives of their own, and able to enter into relations with men and women. The products of the human hand do the same thing in the world of commodities. I speak of this as the *fetishistic character* which attaches to the products of labor, so soon as they are produced in the form of commodities. . . . The foregoing analysis has shown that this fetishistic character of the world of commodities is the outcome of the peculiar social quality of the labor which produces commodities.[10]

And to emphasize clearly that expression of value in money is purely rhetorical, Marx says: "Value changes all labor products into social hieroglyphs. Subsequently, people try to decipher these hieroglyphs, to solve the riddle of their own social product—for the specification of a useful object as a value is just as much a social product as language is." Bourgeois "mystifications" are then seen to reside in the power of symbols to endow things and relationships with the glory of the ruling class, which they represent. Money becomes "objective"—what the philosophers call a "thought-form"—because it "expresses the relations of production peculiar to one specific method of social production, namely commodity production." The only way to dispel the "mystery of the world of commodities, all the sorcery, all the fetishistic charm, which enwraps as with a fog" [11] labor products, is to compare the social relations of labor in capitalism with labor relations in other societies. In feudal society, for example, we see that "social relations between individuals at work appear in their natural guise as personal relations, and are not dressed up as social relations between things, between the products of labor." [12]

In *The German Ideology,* Marx and Engels discuss three common characteristics of all ruling-class mystification. Following Burke's analysis we note:

(1) The thinker separates the ruling ideas from the ruling class, and by thus dealing with ideas in their "pure" form, concludes that the ruling force of history is "ideas" or "illusions"; (2) the ideas are arranged in a developmental series, with a "mystical" connection among them (this is done by treating the successive ideas as though they were "acts of self-determination" on the part of the divine, absolute, or pure Idea); (3) the "mystical appearance" can be removed by putting progressively "self-consciousness" in place of "the self-determining concept"; or it can be made to *look* thoroughly materialistic (despite its underlying principle of "mystification") if it is transformed into a developmental series of persons, thinkers, philosophers, "ideologists," who are said to be the historical representatives of the "concept." [13]

From a rhetorical point of view, the question we ask of Marxism is whether there are any principles of symbolic development in society which can be applied outside of the specific goals of Marxism. And from our bias in favor of democracy, we ask whether it is possible to discount the Marxist dialectic and still preserve something of value for symbolic analysis. Burke argues that Marxism does offer us a tool for analyzing how an "Idea" becomes accepted as a universal "self-developing organism." And if we are to use this tool properly, we must do more than accuse the Marxists of being "ideologists." For when we do this we have admitted that ideologies do affect social relations, and must therefore be able to say in what way their creation and use conform to, or go beyond, the analysis made by Marx and Engels, who (whether or not we agree with them) *have* created methods for analyzing ideologies.

MARXISM CONSIDERED AS A RHETORICAL CRITIQUE

In his analysis of Marx's rhetoric, Burke asks us to imagine an "ideologist" who is inspecting the documents of his civilization to discover how ruling ideas developed, so that he can work out an explanation which will fit all such developments. If he adopts the Hegelian method, which Marx adopted but with a complete reversal of historical cause and effect [14] (and which, because of this reversal, Marx attacked as bourgeois mystification), our ideologist will subsume the various ruling ideas under some general title such as Spirit, Consciousnes, Historical Destiny, or *die Idee*. "Hence he can look upon the succession of 'ruling' ideas (like 'honor,' 'loyalty,' 'liberty') as though each were the expression of the one Universal Idea (his title for the lot, which he uses not just as a summarizing word, but as a 'sub-ject' in the strict philosophic sense, that is, an underlying basis, a sub-stance, of which any step along the entire series can be considered as a property, or expression)." [15]

Our ideologist can then assign some direction to the series of ruling ideas, such as the achievement of freedom, or reason, as the development of self-consciousness. He then treats these ultimates as the essence, the goal which determines every step, even the very first step where the end is discovered to be latent in the beginning. Thus, the Idea becomes a creative principle, a generating force, operating within the entire range of the act. Each step along the way becomes a limited expression of the great "Universal Idea," and its qualities are determined by its place in the series progressing toward the final Goal. Thus, "within the limitations of its nature, each stage would represent the principle of total development (as bud, flower, and seed could each, at different stages in a plant's growth, be called successive momentary expressions of a single biologic continuity)." [16]

And, just as bud, flower, and seed contain the "principles of growth," so, too, can the "Absolute Idea" become a universal self-developing organism. "Its successive stages make a dialectical series, as shifts in the nature of property, production, and rule make for shifts in the ruling ideas; but these ruling ideas are considered 'purely' (as manifestations, not of particular ruling classes, but of the 'Absolute Idea'). Nature, history, and society are but concrete expressions of this Idea. All material relations in history, and the social relations of men, are interpreted as products of this Universal Spirit, manifesting itself in the empirical world."[17] The empirical world, it is true, seems to contradict the unity of the Absolute Idea, for the world, both that of nature and men, is a world of conflict.

But those under the spell of the "Absolute Idea" do not consider ideas as weapons shaped for battle and subject to change as the battle continues, but as "moments" or stages in a progression toward the fulfillment of the "Universal Idea" which underlies all historical development. Thus, in Simmel we read that conflict is but a way to achieve unity, a "higher" unity because it inspires individuals to greater exertion and sets boundaries (social as well as material) to group life so we know where we belong, and can therefore identify our selves with other selves. From the empyrean heights of Simmel's Absolute—society—the struggles of men far below are but steps on their way to an Absolute of Sociation. "The disappearance of repulsive (and, considered in isolation, destructive) energies does by no means always result in a richer and fuller social life (as the disappearance of liabilities results in larger property) but in as different and unrealizable a phenomenon as if the group were deprived of the forces of cooperation, affection, mutual aid, and harmony of interest."[18]

Hegel's "Absolute Idea" seems almost absurd to those of us raised in a pragmatic tradition. But, Burke warns us, "once you begin to follow the logic of Marx's critique, you see that most people differ from Hegel, not in being immune to such thinking, but in being immune to its *thoroughness*. Marx shows how this position generates a whole *set* of beliefs."[19] Hegelian forms of thought are commonly used, whether we admit it or not. Few are willing (or able) to carry their idea of country to philosophic heights of the Absolute Spirit. Yet in view of the Second World War and the German slaughter of over six million Jews, it would be very dangerous to overlook the fact that people *are* motivated by ideologies (as we now admit, for even the popular press describes it as an "ideological war").

It is precisely because we do not know an end that it moves us so deeply. "We think we actually understand things only when we have traced them back to what we do not understand and cannot understand —to causality, to axioms, to God, to character"—as Simmel (himself a profound voyager into the realms of the Absolute Spirit) reminds us. The ideologist finds security in "pure" manifestations of ideas. In sociology this leads to the use of what Burke calls "over-all-god-terms" such as "consciousness" or the "human essence." Yet, when we turn our eyes away from these "god-terms" to the lives men actually lead, we find these "pure" spirits manifesting themselves in conflict over such material things as property. Where idealists (Hegelian or otherwise) discover unity, we see nothing but disunity, division, and conflict.

Marx, at least, *begins* his analysis of society with what Burke calls the principle of division. On the purely rhetorical level, Marx and Engels warn us to look for "mystification" (what Marx calls "social hieroglyphs") at any point where "the social divisiveness caused by property and the division of labor is obscured by unitary terms (as with terms whereby a state, designed to protect a certain structure of ownership, is made to seem equally representative of both propertied and propertyless classes)." [20] This does not mean we must "accept" Marxism. In our search for a model of sociation based on communication as rhetoric, we note simply the value of the admonition "that private property makes for a rhetoric of mystification, as the 'ideological' approach to social relations sets up a fog of merger-terms where the clarity of division-terms is needed." [21]

Burke makes clear that his analysis of *The German Ideology* is not a complete summary of the work. "For our present purposes we are concerned only with the ways in which its analysis of 'ideology' becomes a contribution in rhetoric." He raises many questions about the validity of the Marxian dialectic which ends in a classless society.

We might question whether, by Marx's own theory, private property could possibly be abolished in a technological society marked by division of labor; we might expect no more than changes which produce a structure of ownership better suited to the conditions of modern industrial production. With the means of production "owned" by the state, private property might arise secondarily, through the diversity of ways in which different individuals and classes of workers participated in the economic process and derived rewards from it. . . . Maybe yes, maybe no.[22]

Thus, if we use Marx's analysis of the rhetoric of ideology against Marx himself,[23] we can show how shifts from ownership of property to "ownership" of jobs, offices, and rank, with all the "rights" and prerequisites which go with such control, might produce *greater*, not *less*, social stratification. The happy worker depicted by Marx and Engels in *The German Ideology* ("shifting from job to job like a Jack-of-all-trades, as the mood strikes him, hunting in the morning, fishing in the afternoon, rearing cattle in the evening, and criticizing after dinner, without ever becoming hunter, fisherman, shepherd, or critic") [24] certainly has not found a home in Soviet Russian industry. Every step in the development of Soviet industry takes the independent worker farther and farther from a society free of the "division of labor (and with the separation of property that goes with it, and the disparate states of consciousness that go with that)" as Burke points out.[25] For, if capitalism breeds "corporation men," Soviet Socialism breeds "bureaucratic men" who find their prototype in the "committee man" led by the Commissar.

Of the three formal ways of talking about human motives—generic, specific, and individual—Burke places the treatment of ideas in terms of class conflict under the specific. Marx "stresses the specifically *class* motives of ideology." The materialistic critique of Spirit is "the analysis of it as a rhetorical device, and [thus] the dialectical symmetry behind the Marxist terms of analysis seems to involve the approach to generic and individual motives through the specific." In sum, Burke tells us, Marx teaches us that ideology is equatable with illusion, mystification, "discussion of human relations in terms like absolute consciousness, honor, loyalty, justice, freedom, substance, essence of man—in short, that 'inversion' whereby material history is derived from 'spirit' (in contrast with the method of dialectical materialism whereby the changing nature of consciousness would be derived from change in material conditions)."[26]

Notes

[1] *Bentham's Handbook of Political Fallacies*, revised, edited, and with a preface by Harold A. Larrabee (Baltimore: The Johns Hopkins Press, 1952), p. 17.

[2] Bentham illustrates this in his discussion of the "Official Malefactor's Screen," a device whereby those opposing a discussion of official wrong-doing assert: "Bring us into contempt, you bring Government into contempt, and anarchy and civil war are the immediate consequences." (*Handbook,* p. 103.)

[3] Money at "work" is money making profit, or more money. Bob Hope's definition of a banker as a man who will lend you money only if you prove you don't need it illustrates the paradox of capitalism when dominated completely by businessmen. As risks are narrowed, the rich get richer and the poor get poorer. Nonprofit financing is "deficit financing," and no businessman prospers by learning to give money away. Yet it is only by spending money on "nonproductive" and "nonprofit" community services that conditions favorable to a capitalistic use of money can exist at all. But how can the business community, which trains men to make profit, also train men to administer nonprofit enterprises? Perhaps this explains some of Dwight Eisenhower's problems in running the government. He recruited men trained to earn a profit to run institutions that spent what others earned.

⁴ This is, of course, the opposite view from that of Hitler, who studied how to use language for evil ends.

⁵ In Thesis XI of his *Theses on Feuerbach*, Marx says, "The Philosophers have only *interpreted* the world differently, the point is, to *change* it." See Karl Marx and Friedrich Engels, *The German Ideology*, edited and with an introduction by R. Pascal (New York: International Publishers, 1947), p. 199.

⁶ Kenneth Burke, *A Rhetoric of Motives* (New York: Prentice-Hall, Inc., 1950), p. 104.

⁷ Marx and Engels, *op. cit.*, p. 197.

⁸ See Karl Marx, *Capital,* translated from the fourth German edition by Aden and Cedar Paul in 2 vols. (New York and London: E. P. Dutton, Everyman's Library, 1946).

⁹ *Ibid.*, Vol. I, p. 45.

¹⁰ *Ibid.*, Vol. I, pp. 45–46. It is interesting to note that Marx turned to religious expression for his examples of mystifications. In this, at least, Marx and Freud agreed.

¹¹ *Ibid.*, Vol. I, p. 50.

¹² *Ibid.*, Vol. I, p. 51.

¹³ Burke, *op. cit.*, p. 107.

¹⁴ That is, where Hegel made the "Absolute Idea" the cause of social change, Marx made social changes in forms of production, etc., the cause of the "Absolute Idea."

¹⁵ Burke, *op. cit.*, p. 106.

¹⁶ Mead uses this principle in his description of how the future is used to organize action in the present, as well as to determine the past we select to legitimize the present.

¹⁷ Burke, *op. cit.*, p. 106.

¹⁸ Georg Simmel, *Conflict and the Web of Group-Affiliations* (Glencoe, Ill.: The Free Press, 1955), p. 18. In his speech "Germany's Inner Transformation," delivered in Strasbourg in November, 1914, Simmel discovered (as did so many German intellectuals) that the Absolute Spirit had found its home in Germany (just before his death Simmel expressed doubts over this identification). As Wolff says in his introduction to his translation of Simmel, Simmel lost interest in the war as a manifestation of the Absolute Spirit in Germany, although his confidence in the Absolute Spirit never wavered. About eighty days before his death, Simmel wrote "for the very sake of Germany and Europe one must free oneself . . . and stand above . . . in the redeeming sphere of the spirit. . . ." *Georg Simmel, 1858–1918, A Collection of Essays, with Translations and a Bibliography,* edited by Kurt H. Wolff (Columbus: Ohio State Univ. Press, 1959), p. xxii.

¹⁹ Burke, *op. cit.*, p. 107.

²⁰ *Ibid.*, pp. 108–109.

²¹ *Ibid.*

²² *Ibid.*

²³ Karl Mannheim does this in detail in his *Ideology and Utopia*, translated from the German by L. Wirth and E. Shils (New York: Harcourt, Brace and Company, 1936).

²⁴ This is Burke's summary of the worker depicted in *The German Ideology*. See *A Rhetoric of Motives*, p. 109.

²⁵ *Ibid.*

²⁶ *Ibid.*, p. 110.

14

Social Mystification and Social Integration

CARLYLE ON CLOTHES AS A SYMBOL OF SOCIAL ORDER:
THE RHETORIC OF ACCEPTANCE OF SOCIAL HIERARCHY

THOMAS CARLYLE found his examples of social mystification not in politics and economics, but in clothes.

> All visible things are emblems; what thou seest is not there on its own account; strictly taken, is not there at all: Matter exists only spiritually, and to represent some Idea and *body* it forth. Hence Clothes, as despicable as we think them, are so unspeakably significant. Clothes, from the King's mantle downwards, are emblematic, not of want only, but of a manifold cunning Victory over Want. On the other hand, all Emblematic things are properly Clothes, thought-woven or hand-woven: must not the Imagination weave Garments, visible bodies, wherein the else invisible creations and inspirations of our Reason are, like Spirits, revealed, and first become all-powerful;—the rather if, as we often see, the Hand too aid her, and (by wool Clothes or otherwise) reveal such even to the outward eye? [1]

For Carlyle, clothes are like metaphors. This metaphorical quality of clothes, their ability to stand for something other than what they are, is characteristic of all symbols. "Examine Language; what, if you except some few primitive elements (of natural sound), what is it all but Metaphors, recognized as such, or not longer recognized; still fluid and florid, or now solid-grown and colourless? If those same primitive elements are the osseous fixtures in the Flesh-Garment, Language,—then are Metaphors its muscles and tissues." True, there are "sham Metaphors," which are like "superfluous show-cloaks," but whatsoever "sensibly exists, whatsoever represents Spirit to Spirit, is properly a Clothing, a suit of Raiment, put on for a season, and to be laid off. Thus in this one pregnant subject of Clothes, rightly understood, is included all that men have thought, dreamed, done, and been: the whole External Universe and what it holds is but Clothing; and the essence of all Science lies in the Philosophy of Clothes." [2]

The power of clothes as a kind of social rhetoric is best understood when we try to imagine what would happen if some august body were to become naked in the midst of a great and awesome ceremony.

What would Majesty do, could such an accident befall in reality; should the buttons all simultaneously start, and the solid wool evaporate, in very deed, as here in Dream? *Ach Gott!* How each skulks into the nearest hiding-place; their high State Tragedy . . . becomes a Pickel-herring-Farce to weep at, which is the worst kind of Farce; . . . the whole fabric of Government, Legislation, Property, Police, and Civilized Society, *are dissolved,* in wails and howls. . . . Lives the man that can figure a naked Duke of Windlestraw addressing a naked house of Lords? Imagination, choked as in mephitic air, recoils on itself and will not forward with the picture.[3]

For whoever would reduce the "solemnities and paraphernalia of civilized Life, which we make so much of, [to] nothing but so many Cloth-rags," is either "the malignest of Sansculottists, or . . . the maddest. . . ." Those who believe that any radical return to the days of the French Revolution ("the boundless Serbonian Bog of Sansculottism") where everybody was "Hail fellow well met," simply court social chaos. *"Society in a state of nakedness"* is nothing but anarchy. "Should some sceptical individual still entertain doubts whether in a world without Clothes, the smallest Politeness, Polity, or even Police, could exist," let him recall the terrible days of the Revolution "where not only armies but whole nations might sink!" And even aside from such vast problems of social polity, what would we, as good burghers, do without places to carry money? "Are we Opossums; have we natural Pouches, like the Kangaroo? Or how, without Clothes, could we possess the master-organ, soul's seat, and true pineal gland of the Body Social: I mean, a Purse?"[4]

But if a naked society would be anarchy, a society wholly determined by clothes (the "Dandiacal Body") would bog down in "that primeval Superstition, *Self-Worship*." For a dandy

is a Clothes-wearing Man, a Man whose trade, office, and existence consists in the wearing of Clothes. Every faculty of his soul, spirit, purse, and person is heroically consecrated to this one object, the wearing of Clothes wisely and well: so that as others dress to live, he lives to dress. . . . a "divine Idea of Cloth" is born with him; and this, like other such Ideas, will express itself outwardly, or wring his heart asunder with unutterable throes. . . . like a generous, creative enthusiast, he fearlessly makes his Idea an Action; shows himself in peculiar guise to mankind; walks forth, a witness and Living Martyr to the eternal worth of Clothes.[5]

For, as silly as the Macaronic Dandy can become, he makes far better sense than those who argue that men without clothes would be free of all social distinction and thus able to live in some kind of Edenic brotherhood.[6] He, at least, understands that clothes "gave us individuality, distinctions, [and] social polity, [and thus] have made Men of us." Man in himself is weak, the feeblest of bipeds; he gains powers by his capacity to wear clothes and to devise tools with which he fashions clothes. "Man is a Tool-using Animal . . . without Tools he is nothing, with Tools he is all." It is a great mistake to laugh at the Dandy because he is "Poet of Cloth." He represents a spiritual principle, a mystic significance. This is his social being, his presentation of himself to others. He asks of us only that we become an audience to him. He solicits nothing, "simply the glance of your eyes. Understand his mystic significance, or altogether miss and misinterpret it; do but look at him, and he is contented." [7]

The devotion of the Dandy to clothes, and his highly developed social sense, is another melancholy instance of the fragmentation of the religious principle. The "Religious Principle, driven-out of most Churches, either lies unseen in the hearts of good men, looking and longing and silently working there towards some new Revelation; or else wanders homeless over the world, like a disembodied soul seeking its terrestrial organization—into how many strange shapes, of Superstition and Fanaticism, does it not tentatively and errantly cast itself. . . . Sect after Sect, and Church after Church, bodies itself forth. . . . Among the newer Sects of [England] . . . is that of the *Dandies*." [8] These "Poets of the Cloth" must not be thought of as a secular sect, for to the "psychologic eye" their "devotional and even sacrificial character plainly enough reveals itself." And, while it is true dandies end in fetish worship, or worse, worship of the self in a mirror, their martyrdom, their poetry, and their highly developed sociability teach us that the religious principle lives in man in society, however perverted its forms become.

The Dandy is sad witness to the fact that all Symbols "are properly Clothes; that all Forms whereby Spirit manifests itself to sense, whether outwardly or in the imagination, are Clothes; and thus not only the parchment Magna Charta, . . . but the Pomp and Authority of Law, the sacredness of Majesty, and all inferior Worships [Worthships] are properly a Vesture and Raiment; and the Thirty-Nine Articles themselves are articles of wearing-apparel [for the religious idea]. . . ." [9] Even those who stand in such contrast to the "Dandiacal Body," the poor, or, as Carlyle calls them, the "Drudge Sect," live under the symbol of clothes. They follow the "Dandiacal Sect" in their grand principle of wearing a peculiar costume, the rags of the beggar, and bind themselves by the two monastic vows of poverty and obedience (if not chastity).

"Drudgism the Negative, Dandyism the Positive: one attracts hourly towards it and appropriates all the Positive Electricity of the nation (namely, the Money thereof); the other is equally busy with the Negative (that is to say, the Hunger), which is equally potent." [10]

Burke believes that "Carlyle's enigmatic symbol may contribute as much as Marx toward indicating a relation between mystification and class relationships." [11] He suggests further that we read *Sartor Resartus* and *The German Ideology* together, since both deal with the "mystifying condition" in social inequality, and "this condition can elicit 'God-fearing' attitudes toward agents and agencies that are not 'divine.'" The views of Marx and Carlyle *taken together,* "can put us on the lookout for expressions that both reveal and conceal such an aspect of 'consciousness' as is the way with symbols (for the dictionaries tell us that 'mystery' is related to *muein* which, accented on the second syllable, means 'to shut the eyes')." Carlyle, more than Bentham or Marx, *accepts* mystification as a necessary part of social order because mystification creates a state of mind, reverence, which is necessary to social life.

Carlyle is not interested in "exposing" the mystery of clothes, but in teaching us to accept their mystery as a *way* to higher truths. Thus, toward the end of *Sartor Resartus,* he asks: "Have many British Readers actually arrived with us at the new promised country; is the Philosophy of Clothes now at least opening around them? Long and adventurous has the journey been; from those outmost vulgar, palpable Wollen-Hulls of Man, through his wondrous Flesh-Garments, and his wondrous Social Garnitures; inwards to the Garments of his very Soul's Soul, to Time and Space themselves! And now does the Spiritual, eternal essence of Man, and of Mankind, bared of such wrappages, begin in any measure to reveal itself? Can many readers discern, as through a glass darkly, in huge wavering outlines, some primeval rudiments of Man's being what is changeable divided from what is unchangeable?" [12] Clothes, then, like all symbols of rank for Carlyle, are what he calls a "Bridge" to the divine.

Clothes instill reverence for rank and uphold principles of hierarchy, but this is not their prime function. Clothes both reveal and conceal the Mystery of the Divine spirit in Man. We must learn then to distinguish between clothes as a social expression of rank, as an end in themselves (as in the Dandiacal Body), and finally as emblem of man's spiritual nature. In his summary of Carlyle's way to divinity through clothes,

Burke says: "In ultimate reality, all men are united—and it is by reason of this ultimate union that the different classes of men can communicate with one another." Hence, if we follow Carlyle and believe that "the world's 'Clothes' symbolize this profounder, divine order, we must reverence them too, insofar as they are representative of it." If we do so, we can "restore with a difference the reverence for 'Clothes' (i.e., the 'garments' of nature and the social order both)" that Carlyle seems to deny when he tells us that reverence for clothes must be more deeply directed beneath the pageantry of social distinctions. "In particular, we can restore reverence for that major class distinction, between ruler and ruled (a pattern of thinking which could then, presumably, be reproduced in miniature, where lesser hierarchic differences were concerned). We should revere a true king (hero) because he really does rule by divine right." [13]

DOUBTFUL ACCEPTANCE OF HIERARCHY: IRONY AND RHETORIC

Superiors sometimes doubt their majesty, just as inferiors sometimes doubt their loyalty. Superiors doubt also the loyalty and honesty of their inferiors, as inferiors doubt the majesty and wisdom of their superiors. Between two poles of suspicion, hate, and hostility, or acceptance, love, and loyalty, there is also a kind of ironic and joking adjustment of one class to another. This does not mean that there is no mystery or what we have called social mystification. The glamor and mystery of the social order is upheld, but with a good deal of playfulness, which passes easily into doubt and irony. Since inferiors are far less powerful than their superiors, they must learn to use "harmless" symbolic devices to "tell off" superiors whose demands are too great, or who fail to uphold the "divinity" (and its secular expression in dignity) which must hedge all kings, great and small alike.

Burke proposes that we think of social courtship in terms of sexual courtship. He argues that while the "mystery of sex relations," which leads to the rhetoric of courtship, is grounded in the communication of beings *biologically* estranged, it is greatly accentuated by the purely *social* differentations which, under the division of human labor, can come to distinguish the "typically masculine" from the "typically feminine." *Any* pronounced social distinction creates conditions for "mystery," just as very pronounced separation of the sexes, and the social stress on sexual modesty, increases sexual tension. And when such a powerful need as sex can only be satisfied through the satisfaction of an equally powerful need for status, intense feelings and emotions are easily aroused.[14]

We are so accustomed to the language of sexual courtship and the depiction of courtship between different classes of people in the "love story" that we forget the function of hierarchal rhetoric in these appeals. The love story often depends for its power on hierarchal mystifications, as much (if not more) as on sexual or romantic appeals. For, in so far as the hero and heroine of a love story *communicate* they do so through symbols charged with hierarchal significance. Some literary classics depend almost wholly on hierarchal mystification for their appeal. *Moby Dick* and *Huckleberry Finn* are stories of hierarchy. *Huckleberry Finn* draws constantly from conscious and unconscious wells of "mystery" and strangeness in relationships between white and Negro, children and adults, rich and poor, gentlemen and bums, Christians and infidels, drunken murderers and law-abiding citizens.[15]

Since the rhetoric of sexual courtship has been codified to a far greater degree (in our time, at least) than any other form of courtship,[16] there is much to be learned from it. Hierarchal "mystery" requires a corresponding rhetoric, "in form [as Burke suggests] quite analogous to sexual expression: for the relations between classes are like the ways of courtship, rape, seduction, jilting, prostitution, promiscuity, with variants of sadistic torture or masochistic invitation to mistreatment. Similarly, there are strong homosexual analogies in 'courtly' relations between persons of the same sex but of contrasting social status."[17] And, similarly, intercourse between social classes, like sexual appeals between men and women are carried on with all kinds of subtle variations of modesty. We connect modesty with sex, but we forget (as befits free citizens of a democracy) all the pudencies of *social* intercourse. And, whatever we say about the familial cluster of motives, they cannot be explained solely by sex. Our first sense of "difference" and the basis for our earliest experiences of the "mystery" of authority is age, which we are taught is a qualitative as well as a quantitative difference. Age is prior to sex, just as the glamor of "old" families, ancestor worship, and many aspects of lineage through blood is prior to sexual glamor.

Novelists, such as Kafka, use hierarchal themes as mysteries in themselves, just as they are used in "mystery stories," where the superior chases the inferior, the inferior outwits the superior, until finally the superior "closes in" on the hunted inferior, the criminal, and kills him "in the name of the law" (the principle of social order). Kafka's novels, says Burke, "are fanciful delving into the mystery of bureaucracy and the rhetoric that goes with it." And just as we have matched Marx's rejection of capitalistic class mystification with Carlyle's acceptance of it, so might we match Kafka's satire on Celestial Hierarchy with writers such as Gregory the Great, John of Damascus, and Dionysius the Areopagite, who minutely describe the angelic bureaucracy in which each angel is an interpreter of those above. "Indeed," as Burke tells us, "hierarchy" is the "old, eulogistic word for 'bureaucracy,'" with each stage employing a rhetoric of obeisance to the stage above it, and a rhetoric of charitable condescension to the stage beneath it, in sum a rhetoric of courtship, while all the stages are infused with the spirit of the Ultimate Stage, which sums up the essence implicit in the hierarchic mode of thought itself, and can thus be 'ideologically' interpreted as its 'cause.' In Kafka this same mystery of class distinctions is all-persuasive, while the Ultimate Bureaucrat, ever Above and Beyond and Behind, is a vague dyslogistic but always mysterious mixture of God and Mr. Big." [18]

Courtship, sexual *or* social, brings us immediately into the realm of persuasion. We cannot "make" or force the other to give us honor, reputation, love, or hate. We cannot even make him attend to us, unless he wants to do so. *All* appeals to others are a kind of courtship, and the variations in the expression of such appeals are legion. They range from the repressed appeals of the dream to the highly contrived stylistic appeals of foreign diplomats at the United Nations. In such appeals we are highly conscious of class differences, even as we hope to transcend the differences we recognize. As an example of the analysis of this kind of appeal, Burke selects William Empson's *English Pastoral Poetry*,[19] in which "typical social-stylistic devices whereby spokesmen for different classes aim at over-all dialectic designed to see beyond the limitations of status," [20] are examined.

Empson selects Gray's *Elegy* as an example of what he means by being conscious of the faults of a class and yet not wishing to abolish or alter the social conditions which sustain the class. Thus, when Gray writes

> Full many a gem of purest ray serene
> The dark, unfathomed caves of ocean bear;
> Full many a flower is born to blush unseen
> And waste its sweetness on the desert air.

he means, Empson tells us, that

eighteenth-century England had no scholarship system or *carrier ouverte aux talents*. This is stated as pathetic, but the reader is put into a mood in which one would not try to alter it. . . . By comparing the social arrangement to Nature he makes it seem inevitable, which it was not, and gives it a dignity which was undeserved. Furthermore, a gem does not mind being in a cave and a flower prefers not to be picked; we feel that the man is like the flower, as short-lived, natural, and valuable, and this tricks us into feeling that he is better off without opportunities.[21]

The sexual suggestion of *blush* brings in the Christian idea that virginity is good in itself, and so that any renunciation is good; this may trick us into feeling it is lucky for the poor man that society keeps him unspotted from the World. One tone of melancholy claims that the poet understands the considerations opposed to aristocracy, though he judges against them; the truism of the reflections in the churchyard, the universality and impersonality this gives to the style, claim as if by comparison that we ought to accept the injustice of society as we do the inevitability of death.[22]

In its most profound reaches, the poem seems to speak "one of the permanent truths; it is only in degree that any improvement of society could prevent wastage of human powers"; and the best anyone can do is to accept this; yet in doing so he need not prostitute himself. For so long as he is prepared to waste himself, rather than "give in" to the system, and so long as he chooses to *confront* the evils of the aristocracy, he preserves his honor.

Burke points up another step, a step in rhetorical analysis, which might be taken in the analysis of the social referents of the poem. The tone of humility may be construed as a modest bid for preferment. "The sentiments expressed are thus a character reference, describing a person doubly reliable, since he doesn't protest even when neglected. In an imaginative way the poem answers such questions, if interviews and questionnaires were capable of such subtle discourses, rather than supplying merely such entries as would fit a punch card." La Rochefoucauld, like Hume, pointed out that humility is often a mask of pride. Thus, he says in Maxim 254: "Humility is often merely feigned submissiveness assumed in order to subject others, an artifice of pride which stoops to conquer, and although pride has a thousand ways of transforming itself it is never so well disguised and able to take people in as when masquerading as humility."

Carlyle and Marx analyzed social rhetoric in terms of their deep (though very different) belief in a "right" and "ideal" class system. Empson is more concerned with how we enact our social roles when we cannot identify our social order with the mysteries of first and last things, as the Christians called the great moments on the way to God. When we lack deep belief and must take a social order seriously (if only to stave off total disintegration, as we sometimes do in national affairs), we act in embarrassment, or even worse, in absurdity. As Burke says, "Where there is wealth and poverty, there is awkwardness." There is always a sense of incongruity when a rich man speaks in praise of wealth, a rich man speaks in praise of poverty, a poor man speaks in praise of wealth, or a poor man speaks in praise of poverty. Such awkward moments in communication, if attenuated, give rise to social pudencies which are as intense and various as the expression of sexual modesty.

One expression of this is what Empson calls "comic primness," [23] or "prim irony." This is an attitude taken by a superior who has some doubts about the social order whereby he enjoys his privileges. But since the superior can enjoy them without too much distress, he resigns himself (after some misgivings) to his society, in a state that is "apologetic, but not abnegatory." Inferiors also use irony, as when in ironical humility the inferior seems to say to his superior: "I am not clever, educated, well born, handsome, or brave, and I admit I should try to emulate your greatness, but there is no use in my trying because your virtues are simply beyond the reach of any mortal." In this way the inferior denies the reality of his master's virtue, while at the same time he upholds his own lowly standards. In making his master, Don Quixote, too good for the world, Sancho Panza makes his own world more real. (Yet Sancho pays a price too, for some dark corners of Sancho's world are brought into bright relief by the gleaming purity of his master's ideals.) [24]

Veblen's distinction between "pecuniary" motives and the "instinct of workmanship" is another aid to reflection on the rhetoric of ironic appeal. Veblen, like Marx, attacks the mystifications of money. These he finds based in the "predatory and animistic habit of mind" common among businessmen, whose "canons of pecuniary decency are reducible . . . to the principles of waste, futility, and ferocity." He asserts that he is trying to create a scientifically "neutral" vocabulary. He has, he tells us, no intention to "extol or depreciate, or to commend or deplore any of the phenomena" which is characterized as "invidious." The term is used "in a technical sense, and is defined as 'the discrimination enjoined by the canons of status'" which proceed "not on the ground of visible efficiency" but on "distinctions of status . . . based on putative worth transmitted by descent from honourable antecedents." [25]

We soon discover that Veblen's mask is a poor disguise for deep suspicion and hatred of the businessman. Veblen's invective against the businessman lacks the weight of Engels' attack in Chapter XII ("Attitude of the Bourgeoisie") of his *Condition of the Working Class in England,*[26] where the good burghers of England (as well as the aristocracy) are depicted as immoral monsters. But where Engels makes the businessman a villain, Veblen makes him a buffoon. He reduces the businessman to a kind of low, cunning clown, whose vulgarity and coarseness prevent him from suffering from the repeated exposure of his predatory greed. This is done in what Burke aptly calls "deadpan satire." In this kind of rhetoric, we pretend that we are simply incapable of *any* emotion over what we have seen, because what we have seen is so senseless that it is beyond emotion,[27] or that we still are in shock over what we have just seen. All we can do is report, quite literally, what we have seen with an air of astonished wonder.

Thus, Veblen pretends that he is just "reporting" or "recording" the antics of businessmen, and professes to pass no moral judgment on them. And while he talks constantly of how businessmen and their wives style themselves to communicate their real or imputed wealth ("conspicuous consumption") he pretends that his analysis is nondramatic. We end, then, as Burke says, with "rhetorically dramatizing in the name of the non-dramatic." [28] And, as in La Rochefoucauld, we end with a class addressing only itself, because only among this one class—in Veblen, the business community, in La Rochefoucauld, the Court—are the values communicated taken seriously enough. For Veblen's worker, whose "instinct for workmanship" is often mentioned, is never described.[29] He does not function as an audience, but as a kind of god. Like the celestial bureaucrats of Kafka, he is so busy doing the actual work of the technological paradise he inhabits that he cannot waste time on the antics of the businessman.

From the view of a New Rhetoric, Veblen's greatest contribution is his analysis of emulation as a kind of vicarious identification.[30] As he refines and sharpens his imagery of "pecuniary canons" in taste, education, business, dress, family life, and religion—even if we cannot accept his categorization of money as "predatory"—we discover many new ways in which money functions in our society.[31] We know that money, unlike any past symbol of status, cannot function in its own right. It is purely symbolic, an abstract form that quite literally transcends the materially real. As money is used to create membership in a higher class through vicarious identification, we see that money must always be transformed into something which is not money, to retain its power as a symbol of life. Veblen's ironic drama of these transfigurations by businessmen for an audience of businessmen, has given us some of our greatest understanding of the rhetoric of money, in a society where, as we say, "money talks."

Notes

[1] Thomas Carlyle, *Sartor Resartus—On Heroes and Hero Worship* (New York and London: E. P. Dutton & Co., Everyman's Library, 1954), p. 54.

[2] *Ibid.*, p. 55.

[3] *Ibid.*, p. 46.

[4] *Ibid.*, p. 48.

[5] *Ibid.*, Chapter X, "The Dandiacal Body," pp. 204–205.

[6] Carlyle did not agree with Bentham, whom he accuses of "mechanising the world." Bentham, Carlyle said, tells us: "Well then, this world is a dead iron machine, the god of it Gravitation and selfish Hunger; let us see what, by checking and balancing, and good adjustment of tooth and pinions, can be made of it!" He continues: "It seems to me, all deniers of Godhood, and all lip-believers of it, are bound to be Benthamites, if they have courage and honesty. . . . That all Godhood should vanish out of men's conception of the Universe seems to me precisely the most brutal error, . . . that men could fall into. . . . One might call it the most lamentable of delusions,—not forgetting Witchcraft itself! Witchcraft worshipped at least a living Devil: but this worships a dead iron Devil; no God, not even a Devil!—Whatsoever is noble, divine, inspired, drops thereby out of life." *Sartor Resartus—On Heroes and Hero Worship*, pp. 400–401.

[7] *Ibid.*, p. 205.

[8] *Ibid.*, p. 206.

[9] *Ibid.*, p. 203.

[10] *Ibid.*, p. 215. Carlyle prophesied that the two classes would soon be in conflict. Carlyle and Marx, so far apart in their social beliefs, agreed in their expectation of class war in England.

[11] Kenneth Burke, *A Rhetoric of Motives* (New York: Prentice-Hall, Inc., 1950), p. 123.

[12] Carlyle, *op. cit.*, p. 201.

[13] Burke, *op. cit.*, p. 122. In his book, *On Heroes, Hero-Worship, and the Hero in History*, Carlyle discusses as heroes the following: gods, prophets, poets, priests, men of letters, and kings.

[14] An example is the adolescent years, when the "mystery" of sex (latent during childhood years) demands expression at the same time as the "mystery" of status engrosses the individual, whose sexual role must be enacted in terms of his social role. Burke, *op. cit.,* p. 115.

[15] Novels of society life, from those of Disraeli to Edith Wharton and Henry James, depend heavily on the mystery of class distinctions as expressed in dress, furniture, architecture, landscape art, speech, and manners.

[16] In La Rochefoucauld, courtship is not a sexual but a status concept, and the pudencies of courtship are social, not sexual. His *Maxims* are a codification of courtly rhetoric. In his *Art of Worldly Wisdom* Gracian does not discuss sex.

[17] Burke, *op. cit.,* p. 115.

[18] *Ibid.,* p. 118. Burke's device of bringing together opposing rhetorics on the same context of experience (here, heaven) is one of his most effective analytic tools. Freud does the same in his interpretation of dream symbols when he inverts the manifest statement of meaning by opposing it with a quite opposite meaning.

[19] The British publisher's title, *Some Versions of Pastoral,* has been used in the paperback edition (New York: New Directions Press, 1958).

[20] This is Burke's summary of Empson's work. See Burke, *op. cit.,* p. 124.

[21] William Empson, *Some Versions of Pastoral,* p. 4.

[22] *Ibid.,* p. 5.

[23] See Empson's discussion of *The Beggar's Opera* in *Some Versions of Pastoral* for his treatment of the comic in social relationships.

[24] Irony is often double-edged.

[25] These quotations are taken from *Thorstein Veblen and His America* by Joseph Dorfman (New York: The Viking Press, 1934), p. 158. Veblen joins Bentham in his search for a neutral "objective" vocabulary of motives; but Veblen is much more concerned with exposing the evils of business enterprise and the perversions of financial, not political, symbols.

[26] Where Engels states flatly: "I have never seen so demoralized a social class as the English middle classes. They are so degraded by selfishness and moral depravity as to be quite incapable of salvation." (This is the first sentence of the second paragraph of Chapter XII.) To buttress this view, he invokes Carlyle's "wonderful description of the English middle classes, in which he paints a vivid picture of their revolting greed for money" (in *Past and Present* published in 1843). See Fredrich Engels, *The Condition of the Working Class in England,* translated and edited by W. O. Anderson and W. H. Chaloner (Oxford, England: Basil Blackwell, 1958).

[27] Adolescents who "play it cool" are highly expert at this kind of satire.

[28] Burke says that Veblen's stylistic devices remind him of the "wag who, having called his enemy a son of a bitch, went on to explain: 'I want it understood that I employ the expression, not as an oath, but in the strictly scientific sense.' " See *A Rhetoric of Motives,* pp. 127–133, for his discussion of Veblen.

[29] Like Marx's worker, he lurks in the background as a kind of unseen hero.

[30] Here, as with Marx, we can admit the limitations of Veblen's views, and yet benefit from his analysis of the rhetoric of money.

[31] Burke argues, however, that Veblen's analysis of money as a symbol, is really rhetorical, not "economic."

15

Reason and Hierarchal Disorganization

CLASS RHETORIC involves many kinds of identifications and takes many forms. In summing up his discussion of Marx, Carlyle, Empson, and Veblen, Burke says: "All told, we might say that where Empson deals with the courtship of classes, Carlyle with their marriage, and Marx with their divorce, Veblen deals with one class and its fascinated appeal to itself." After examining such variations in class rhetoric, Burke turns again to the more fundamental question of how to establish a general principle of social rhetoric. That is, can we say that there is anything about the dialectical or linguistic function of class rhetoric which is natural to man as a symbol-using animal? And is it possible to create a typology [1] of the kinds of identification that occur in the courtship of one class by another?

Burke distinguishes three orders of class rhetoric. One: There "is the realm of accident, mechanical association, response to signs as signs, 'magical' in the sense that it begins in infancy; it is related to Carlyle's pageantry of 'Clothes,' as a child gets a 'mysterious' sense of class distinction through such appearances long before understanding their occupational logic. Two: There are *analogizing* associations, where terms are transferred from one order to another. Thus a business culture may become much exercised over a work's 'value' as an estheticized equivalent of 'price.' Three: There are distinct, specialized expressions, *all derived from the same generating principle, hence all embodying it,*" [2] as when we say, like Ruth Benedict, that a total culture is "Appolonian" or "Dionysian," and then "discover" these traits in the specialized and local activities of the community.

But what is involved when we say, as Burke does, that the laws of symbols are prior to economic and political laws? If we take this view our argument must run, Burke tells us, something like this:

Man, *qua* man, is a symbol user. In this respect, every aspect of his "reality" is likely to be seen through a fog of symbols. And not even the hard reality of basic economic facts is sufficient to pierce this symbolic veil (which is intrinsic to the human mind). One man may seek to organize a set of images, another may strive for order among his ideas, a third may feel goaded to make himself head of some political or commercial empire, but however different the situations resulting from these various modes of action, there are purely symbolic motives behind them all, ... For the human mind, as the organ of a symbol-using animal, is "prior" to any *particular* property structure—and in this sense the laws of symbols are prior to economic laws. Out of his symbols, man has developed all his inventions.[3]

And if this is true, then, Burke continues, "why should not their [inventions'] symbolic origin remain concealed in them? Why should they not be not just *things*, but *images* of 'ideas'?" Thus in response to the Marxian distrust of ideology, and the Marxian reversal of the Hegelian relationship between the Idea and matter, we can assign a definite function to the positions of Hegel and Marx in a scheme which will include both.

Given an economic situation there are ways of thinking that arise in response to it. But these ways of living and thinking, in complex relationship with both specific and generic motives, can go deep, to the level of *principles*. For a way of living and thinking is reducible to terms of an "idea"—and that "ideal" will be "creative" in the sense that anyone who grasps it will embody it or represent it in any mode of action he may choose. The idea, or underlying principle, must be approached by him through sensory images of his cultural scene. But until he intuitively grasps the principle of such an imaginal cluster, he cannot be profoundly creative, so far as the genius of that "idea" is concerned. For to be profoundly representative of a culture, he will imitate not its mere insignia, but the principle behind the *ordering* of those insignia.[4]

But the simple arrangement whereby each rank is superior to an inferior, and whereby inferiors in turn are bound to a superior, is not what gives hierarchal order its greatest power. The hierarchal principle in the social, as in any other realm, must work both ways at once. Each rank must accept the principle of gradation, and this acceptance, in universalizing the principle, makes "a spiritual *reversal* of the ranks just as meaningful as their actual material arrangement." For though the actual operation of any hierarchy breeds exclusiveness between ranks, and snobbishness (if not worse) between "insiders" and "outsiders," the *principle* of hierarchy is not exclusive. All can share, and share alike, in the social values which a given hierarchy upholds. Burke illustrates this by reference to the Christian doctrine in which the first shall be last and the last shall be first. Here, all that is important is the principle of hierarchy as such, for the state of first and last things is the heavenly state, and this is the realm of principle, a pure Christian society which existed before the world began, will exist after the world ends, and finally is a world which exists "outside" of time.

The Christian drama of hierarchy is highly perfected, and whether we are Christians or not we should study Christianity as an "ideal" statement of social order. Such a hierarchy shows us how the "naturalness" of social grades rhetorically reinforces the protection of privilege. "Though in its essence purely developmental, the series is readily transformed into rigid social classifications, and these interfere with the very process of development that was its reason for being." And this leads all too easily to mystifications which hide differences and divisions within the hierarchy. The final or culminating stage of the hierarchy comes to represent the whole meaning of the system. And since those on top who control the final expression of the hierarchy enjoy exalted rank, with all its glory, power, and privilege, it is natural that they should do everything to keep such power in their hands. This is done in the name of "purifying the principles" on which the hierarchy rests. But when inferiors do not think their superiors' privileges are being used to uphold the principles of hierarchy, love and obedience turn to ironic obedience or open disobedience. At this stage, as Burke says, "each class would deny, suppress, [and] exorcise the elements it shares with other classes. This attempt leads to the scapegoat (the use of dyslogistic forms for one's own traits as manifested in an 'alien' class)." [5]

DIDEROT ON THE "VILE PANTOMIME" OF ARISTOCRATIC HIERARCHY

Adjustments to the hierarchal mystifications of those in power take many and varied forms. Every fully developed society creates characteristic ways for attempting to reduce the burden of hierarchal mystifications to manageable proportions. Burke reviews some of these in the work of Diderot, La Rochefoucauld, De Gourmont, Pascal, Machiavelli, Dante, and the rhetoricians of the Middle Ages. In Diderot's *Neveu de Rameau,* as in La Rochefoucauld's *Maxims,* courtly positions of pantomime, "the dance of hierarchy," so to speak, are used to explore the mystifications of courtship in much the same way that Carlyle used clothes. In the inner dialogue between "Moi" and "Lui" in Diderot's *Neveu de Rameau* "Him" voices sensuality, question, doubt, and pride (the aristocratic vices); "Me" speaks for the world, the "honest man" who leads a prudent life. Both share an image of man in society as a courtier who "spends his life taking and holding poses."

For "Him" the aristocratic world has many faults. "What a devil of a system! Some men enjoying a superabundance of everything, while others have a stomach as insistent as theirs, a hunger that renews itself like theirs, and nothing to get their teeth into." The worst of this "is the constrained attitude that want imposes on us. The needy man doesn't walk straight like his fellows; he jumps, he crawls, wriggles, creeps along; he spends his life taking and holding poses." "Me" chides "Him" for his arrogance in acting like a god who contemplates "the varied pantomime of the human race. . . ." "Him" disclaims any such lofty motive. He is a comedian, not a god. "I stick to the earth. I look around me; and I take up my poses, or I amuse myself watching the poses others take up." As "Him's" humor deepens he begins to imitate the sycophant, the suppliant, the time-server, and all the obsequious gestures of the high court of France.

"Him" bursts into mockery as he begins his imitations,

with his right foot forward, his left drawn back, his back bent, his head raised, his eyes apparently fixed on other eyes, his mouth a little open, his arms stretched out towards some object, he awaits an order, he receives it; he is off like a dart, he comes back, he has done his errand and gives his account of it. He attends to everything; he picks up things that fall; he puts a cushion or a footstool under someone's feet; he holds a saucer; he draws up a chair; he opens a door; he shuts a window, draws curtains; he watches the master and mistress; he stands motionless, arms dangling, legs together; he listens, he seeks to read faces; and then adds: "That's my panto-mime, and it's about the same as that of all flatterers, courtiers, lackeys and beggars. . . . I see a prelate as Pantaloon, a president as a satyr, a monk as a hog, a minister as an ostrich, and his chief secretary as a goose." [6]

"Me" replies that while obsequiousness and flattery are necessary for beggars there is "no one who is not acquainted with some steps" in this dance. "Him" replies that only the Sovereign himself "walks straight" while all "the others take up poses." But here even "Me," who represents the world, demurs: "The Sovereign? You can't be too sure about that; don't you think he sometimes has by his side some little foot, some little cluster of curls, some little nose that compels him to do a bit of play-acting?" For whoever "needs somebody else is poor and takes up a pose." Even the king takes a pose before his mistress, and before God; he performs his pantomime steps. The minister performs as courtier, flatterer, lackey, or beggar before his king. The crowd of climbers assume your pose as they perform before the minister, in a hundred ways, each one viler than the other; so does the abbé in his bands and his long gown, once a week at least before the official who controls the list of livings. I tell you, what you call the beggars' pantomime is the way the whole world goes.[7]

"Me" points out to "Him" that he is reducing *all* hierarchal relations to the image of an obsequious pantomime. "But, according to you . . . there are many beggars in this world; and I know no one who is not acquainted with some steps of your dance." "Him" has already refused to admit that the king does not "walk straight." Now it is "Me" who refuses to "debunk" all hierarchy as simply an empty pantomime. There "is one being who has no need to play your pantomime. That is the philosopher, who has nothing and who asks for nothing." "Him" raises doubts over such a radical solution to the evils of courtly hierarchy. He doubts whether living like Diogenes in his tub is a good way to avoid cringing, degrading, and prostituting one's self before the mighty. He doubts too that even Diogenes existed without "playing the pantomime." What about sex, "Him" asks "Me" as he continues to extol the virtues of Diogenes. Even Diogenes, whose organs were not "very rebellious," must have "played the pantomime" before Lais and Phryne (if not before Pericles). For women, like princes, must be courted. And to make his point, "Him" then begins to imitate a coquette's walk. He "tripped along carrying his head high, flirting with a fan, waggling his backside; it was the funniest and most absurd caricature of our little coquettes."

"Him" finally admits that he must go on cringing before his superiors. "I need a good bed, warm clothes in winter, cool clothes in summer; rest and money and many other things; and I'd rather owe them to someone's kindness than acquire them by hard work." "Me" accuses "Him" of being an "idler, a glutton, a base and grovelling soul." "Him" admits this. "Me" concludes sadly that a man will continue to grovel and cringe. "The good things in life have their price, no doubt; but you don't know the price of what you are sacrificing in order to obtain them. You play your base pantomime, as you always have done and as you always will do." And thus man, "a mixture of fineness and baseness, of good sense and folly," turns to courtly hierarchy, with all of its baseness, because, for all its faults, aristocracy at least has style. "Him" closes by admitting that his wearing a priest's skull-cap and bands is not over grief at his wife's death or out of repentance for his sins, but a way of carrying his beggar's "bowl about on my head." What concerns him at the last is what has really concerned him throughout the dialogue. This is art—here, the opera. For art is the realm of style, of beautiful form, like the Court, where obsequiousness, base as it is, yet is played in wonderful and brilliant pantomime.[8]

LA ROCHEFOUCAULD ON COURTLY ADDRESS

Diderot finds the evil of aristocratic courtship in obsequiousness. As "Me" talks, "Him" dances in caricature the various kinds of courtly abasement mentioned in their dialogue. La Rochefoucauld, one of the great courtiers of the court of Louis XIV, finds the fatal flaw in courtly rhetoric not in the debasement of the inferior, but in the arrogance and pride—what he calls "self-love" of the superior, typified in his time by the courtier. He argues that despite all the devotion paid to princes in the great pantomime of the court, such devotion is really devotion to the self. In social address we are like courtiers who know their own majesty and hold audience to enjoy it more fully. Like all self-idolaters we enjoy others only when they pay homage to us. Society thus becomes a pact between arrogant proud selves who serve as audiences to others only because they need audiences to feed their own insatiable pride.

Under the goad of self-love we pay almost any price to satisfy our pride. "A man would rather say evil of himself than say nothing." (Maxim 138) [9] Even humility is "often only a feigned submission which we use to subject others, an artifice of pride which stoops to conquer, and although pride transforms itself in a thousand ways, it is never so well disguised and more able to deceive than when masquerading as humility." (Maxim 254) But the great, too, are dominated by self-love. "The clemency of Princes is often nothing but policy designed to win the affections of the people." (Maxim 15) "This clemency which men call virtue, arises sometimes from vanity, sometimes from idleness, sometimes from fear, and almost always from all three combined." (Maxim 16) For, when all is said and done, pride "is much the same in all men, the only difference is the method and manner of showing it." (Maxim 35)

Even though we are interested only in ourselves, we need each other, if only as audiences to our majesty. The paradox of self-love, then, is that to enjoy ourselves we must become conscious of the self, yet this can be done only when we address others who love only themselves. In address the self becomes an object to its self, and thus we become self-conscious. As we address others we hear ourselves speak, just as when we bow and greet others we see responses to our gestures and feel the power of the emotions which are evoked by expression of these hierarchal gestures. For, "in all walks of life we affect a part and an appearance to seem what we wish to be. Thus the world is composed merely of masks." (Maxim 256) Whatever we "really are," we become the part we play. We make our masks, but they in turn make us.

The final irony of the courtier's lot is that even the great courtiers who strut about in gaudy clothes and lord it over common folk, must solicit office and dignities from their king, as avidly as inferiors solicit favors from them. Superiors and inferiors alike must live in constant abasement, for this is what upholds the principle of kingship. "Kings do with men as with pieces of money; they make them bear what value they will, and one is forced to receive them according to their currency value, and not at their true worth." (Maxim 603) Thus the proud, arrogant courtier who loves only himself and uses others only to satisfy his vanity, must submit himself to superiors, who, he knows, love only themselves and seek continual flattery and praise—even for their crimes.

The courtier is condemned to play his part before an audience of courtiers who despise and hate him as much as he hates and despises them, because of his nature as a social being. For, of all beasts of prey, man is the only sociable one. He can enjoy his lusts and his need for violence, torture, and war only through being "sociable." To enjoy war he must have enemies who are willing to fight, and thus he must learn to persuade others to fight. For just as we cannot enjoy love unless our love is addressed to someone, neither can we enjoy hate unless there is an audience whose response heightens our enjoyment of hate. Man needs hate as well as love, and he can satisfy love and hate only in society, because only in society can he find the audience he needs to express in reality what, as an individual, he must keep hidden in fantasy or must hide in guilt.

The anguish of the courtier who must learn to please those he hates and despises, only deepens with age. For as he grows older he learns more about his favorite subject—himself. Both reason and self-love teach him much about the extravagance, baseness, and corruption of his sentiments and affections. And while it is true that numerous discoveries are made in the realm of self-love, much unknown territory still remains. The anguish and torment of self-love forces man to study himself. Why does man suffer such torment? Perhaps the best we can say is that in "order to punish man for his original sin, God has allowed man to deify his self-love, so that he may be tormented by it in all the actions of his life." (Maxim 509)

The courtier does not, however, turn to God, but to society to transcend the miseries of self-love. In the world of the court, the most powerful law is the law of decorum. "Decorum is the least of all laws, but the most obeyed." (Maxim 447) The power of passion is not in how it is felt, but in how it is expressed. "Love, as agreeable as it is, pleases more by the way it is expressed than by its own nature." (Maxim 501) We can stand any amount of flattery, provided it is done in good style. "We believe, sometimes, that we hate flattery, but what we dislike is only the way it is done." (Maxim 329) Love, like so many other acts, is but a mask after all, and like all masks soon supplants reality. For it "is with true love as it is with ghosts—everybody talks about them, but few have seen them." (Maxim 760) All we really know of emotions is how they are expressed. "Each of the emotions has its own tone of voice, gestures, and expressions, and this harmony, good or bad, pleasant or unpleasant, is what makes people agreeable or disagreeable." (Maxim 255) And, finally, merit and goodness depend on expression for their effect. "There are some persons who only disgust with their abilities; others who please even with their faults." (Maxim 155). For, say what you will, the "world oftener rewards the appearance of merit than merit itself." [10]

Only reason, as weak as it is against the passions, leads to understanding of the social order. But this kind of reason is not born in the laboratory, or through the solitary thinker who seeks to discover laws of nature, but among men and through conversation in society. For, as Montaigne says: "The most fruitful exercise of the mind . . . is intercourse with others," as in the salon life of Paris. In these intimate groups of aristocrats and intellectuals, conversation was considered a *method* for arriving at truth. A conversational tone was not, as among us, considered superficial or careless. Talk could be searching and serious because those who gathered in the salons regarded each other as equals in a search for truth. "Trust contributes more to conversation than does wit." (Maxim 421) Talk was guided by the leader of the salon. The highest purpose of such talks was to think better about human nature in its social aspects. The highest wisdom for the salonier was wisdom about human relationships, and the proper use of reason was the study of how men relate, as well as how they ought to relate, as they play their roles in society.

The highest relationship in La Rochefoucauld's hierarchy of courtly relationships was friendship. Friendship originates in self-interest, and is always endangered by self-love. For we cannot deny that we find some pleasure in the misfortunes of our friends. But true friendship transcends self-interest and the pride and abasement of courtly relationships, because friends must be equals. And since only equals can really talk to each other, it is through friends that we learn to know ourselves, and to bring reason to bear upon life. Intellectual concord, the pleasure of good talk, search within the self guided in discussion with friends, and, indeed, all the moral and intellectual virtues of the soul are possible only among friends. That is why the surest sign of a gentleman is his desire to live openly with his own kind.

But the greatest act of friendship is not to discover our own faults— we must not use a friend only as a confessor or as an audience—but to help friends to discover theirs. This requires great spiritual and social discipline, for it is easy enough to forgive friends for defects which do not affect us. It is easy, too, to persuade ourselves that we really like people more powerful than ourselves, but we do not cleave to those in power for the good we would do them, but rather for the benefits we would receive from them. We may think the gratitude and loyalty of inferiors springs from friendship, but such gratitude only hides a secret longing for greater benefits to come. Only in the open, free, and equal bonds of noble friendship is there hope for overcoming the degradation of the "vile pantomime" at court, or the insatiable raging demands of self-love,[11] and thus purifying the courtly principle of hierarchy.

Notes

[1] In the sense Max Weber created his typology of authority.

[2] Burke, *A Rhetoric of Motives*, pp. 134–135. Burke's italics.

[3] *Ibid.*, p. 136.

[4] *Ibid.*, p. 137. Or, as even our sociological mechanists are beginning to say, he must "internalize" his culture.

[5] *Ibid.*, pp. 141–142. That is, the scapegoat's punishment and death is a cleansing of one's own evil at the hands of a stranger whom we can confront in ways impossible among members of our own society.

[6] These quotations are taken from *Diderot, Interpreter of Nature* . . . selected writings translated by Jean Stewart and Jonathan Kemp, edited and with an introduction by Jonathan Kemp (London: Lawrence and Wishart, 1937), p. 324. (Pages 235–328 contain a text of *Rameau's Nephew.*)

[7] *Ibid.*, pp. 324–325. The histrionic quality of sex relationships is treated as a comedy until the end of the Enlightenment, when the comedy changes to the tragedy and melodrama of the romantic love story.

[8] *Ibid.*, pp. 332–338. In the last pages of *Rameau's Nephew* Diderot sums up the need for hierarchal pantomime to sustain social order.

[9] Quotations from La Rochefoucauld are taken from "The Maxims and Reflections of the Duc de la Rochefoucauld . . . with an Introduction and Analysis" by Hugh Dalziel Duncan, to be published by The Bedminster Press.

[10] La Rochefoucauld thought that the army, not the court, was the training ground for gentility. "A bourgeois air sometimes wears off in camp, but never in court life." He also equated taste and elegance with merit, in mind as in character. Thus he speaks of "courtesy of the mind," and "gallantry of the mind." There is a "courtly" kind of thought.

[11] La Rochefoucauld placed love between men and women below friendship. "If we judge of love by the majority of its results it rather resembles hatred than friendship." (Maxim 72) "The more we love a woman the more prone we are to hate her." (Maxim 111) "The reason why lovers and their mistresses never weary of each other's company is that they always talk about themselves." (Maxim 312) "It is more difficult to be faithful to a mistress who makes us happy than one who mistreats us." (Maxim 331) "All passions make us commit some faults; love alone makes us ridiculous." (Maxim 474) "There are few women whose merit survives their beauty." (Maxim 474) In sum: "It is difficult to define love: What can be said is that in the soul it is a passion to dominate another, in the mind it is mutual understanding, whilst in the body it is simply a delicately veiled desire to possess the beloved after many rites and mysteries." (Maxim 68)

16

The Rhetoric of Ruling:
Communication and Authority

THE POLITICAL PUBLIC AS AN AUDIENCE:
MACHIAVELLI'S "THE PRINCE"

B U R K E selects *The Prince* as an example of what he calls "Administrative Rhetoric." Machiavelli's *The Prince* can be treated as rhetoric in so far as it deals with the *producing of effects upon an audience*. Sometimes the prince's subjects are his audience, sometimes the ruler or inhabitants of foreign states, sometimes particular factions within the state. If you have a political public in mind, Machiavelli says in effect, here is the sort of thing you must do. The Prince's dealings with his people, short of force,[1] is a communication whose forms must be determined by what purpose the communicative means selected are supposed to serve. Political rhetoric is grounded in exhorting men to ways of acting together for a desired end in the State. It must reduce utopias to practice and show how the bestial—as well as the godly—characteristics of men can be used to motivate men to purposes held desirable by the ruler.

Thus whether it is Machiavelli telling his young prince how to rule, Ovid telling his young (perhaps even his old) Roman how to win and keep a mistress, or Gracian telling his Jesuits how to act in the world beyond the monastery, the problem is not so much one of ends as it is of means and their relationship to ends. When ends as such are not open to inquiry, as in all "how to win friends and influence people" books, we seem to be dealing with magic, or the crude beginnings of "science." Some also think of *The Prince* and *The Art of Worldly Wisdom,* as masterpieces of irony. Thus Machiavelli has been regarded as a wicked cynic, who taught tyrants all the black arts of ruling.[2] He is also the patron saint of "political science," because, so the argument runs, he uses a naturalistic vocabulary, in contrast to supernatural or idealistic terminologies.[3] Still others remind us that *The Prince* was written not by a political scientist but by a great comic dramatist.

After taking all points of view into consideration and turning to Machiavelli's own characterization of himself as "historian, comedian, and tragedian" (who took money from princes to write his *History of Florence*, in which as Machiavelli tells us, "I relieve myself by accusing the princes, who have, all of them, done everything to get us where we are."), it seems better to conclude, with Allan H. Gilbert, that Machiavelli was a great comic artist as well as a great political scientist. If, as Professor Gilbert tells us, Machiavelli's comedy, *Mandragola,* is the greatest of Italian comedies, we must assume that such a genius "does not lay aside his nature when he turns to another type of art or half art, for at first appearance *The Prince* is a political rather than a primarily artistic work. A Machiavelli carries the comic spirit wherever he goes." [4]

There is no question that there is a high vein of political comedy in *The Prince*. But here, as in so many general disquisitions on how to produce an effect upon an audience or in specific discussions on the communication of authority, *comedy becomes a method of inquiry*. Thus, when Machiavelli discusses what kind of allied armies will help to *lose* a war and considers the *dangers* of allies as friends, he *separates* ideas which we are accustomed to think of as belonging together. When he describes ecclesiastical principalities as beyond reason because "they are protected by higher causes, to which the human mind does not reach," he is protesting in a kind of coy, perhaps even pious irony, against the supernatural. When he says "I will omit speaking of ecclesiastical principalities because, since they are set up and maintained by God, it would be part of a presumptuous and conceited man to treat them" he uses comedy to *expose* hidden mysteries because comedy sets the mind to work on what is supposed to be closed to it.

The vocabulary of comedy differs greatly from the "neutral" or "naturalistic" vocabulary of science. A modern political treatise is considered "scientific" if it teaches us to think objectively about various kinds of political systems, not to act as partisans in any one system. *The Prince* makes no such claims. Machiavelli thought the Prince ought to rule for the common good, because he thought such rule to be the best rule. In both *The Prince* and the *Discourses on Livy* he argues that the people will be more just than an upper class because they do not wish to be oppressed and therefore have no wish to oppress anyone else. Machiavelli says "one cannot satisfy the upper class with honor and without injury to others, but it is possible to satisfy the people in that way, because the purpose of the people is more just than that of the upper class, since the latter wish to oppress and the former not to be oppressed." And even on a practical level, "when the people are unfriendly the prince can never make himself secure, for he has too many against him; but he can secure himself against the upper class, because they are few."[5]

Thus we see that comic understanding is possible only when there is deep-seated belief in some end, or in some relationship between means and ends. For if we do not believe in an end we cannot discuss the means which are supposed to produce such an end, and, similarly, when we do not think that a certain means is proper to a given end, we cannot discuss the end which depends on such means. That is, we cannot discuss them as *acts* which arise in, and continue to exist through, the communication of significant symbols in rhetoric. It does not follow that because we choose a rhetorical frame of reference (rather than some kind of "scientific" quantitative approach which, by definition, cannot deal with significant symbols) we have abandoned "objectivity." No social *act* is "objective," for to act at all we must abandon thinking about ends, and their means, to act in terms of an end. The virtue of comedy *as a method of inquiry* is the manner in which it brings to light difficulties, ambiguities, and even the *tragedy* of the experience of those involved in the action.

We are objective in our analysis of means–ends relationships when we show what kind of an action will result from what kind of means. "Means" in conduct must be used to indicate *how* an action is done, *where* it is done, *by what kind of person,* and in *what kind of act.* This Machiavelli does, and although his "case" is limited to showing how Italians, under the leadership of a good Prince, could gain and preserve their liberty and freedom, his analysis of political conduct as a communication, or a staging of authority, is of great help to those seeking to understand how social relations are affected by communication. Machiavelli's conception of politics is a dramatic conception. The community is a great stage upon which heroes and villains struggle for the soul of Florence. In terms of Burke's dramatistic analysis of action, Florence and Italy is the Scene; political integration, the Act; the Prince, the aristocrats, and the people (and their enemies), the Actors; communication of authority in a republic, the Agency (or Means); and the common good of the people, the Purpose.

Like a ruler creating a great community, Machiavelli discusses the political conditions necessary to republic government in dramatic terms,[6] what kind of action ruling such a community involves, how the actors must play their parts, what means of communication are suited to what effects, and, finally, the resolution in the common good of the struggle between the heroes and villains of the community. The voice within *The Prince* is like that of a director mounting a great community drama. He coaches an assembled cast of scene and costume designers, actors who will take part in the play, the audience (or its representatives), himself as author by invoking authorities of the past who have written about the ruling, and community guardians who uphold the principles of the good ruler.

The early chapters of *The Prince* are about principalities; then follows (after an abrupt shift in Chapter 3) direct address of the Prince where Machiavelli discusses the act of ruling (with negative examples from the career of Louis XII). In Chapter 6 he passes from the nature of principalities to the conduct of a prince. Chapter 8, "On Those Who Attain Princely Power Through Evil Deeds," begins discussion on how a prince should rule. In Chapter 21, "What Is Necessary to a Prince That He May Be Considered Excellent," the "great undertakings" of a prince and how he must become a "lover of excellence" are described. And finally in Chapter 26, *The Prince* closes with an exhortation to an ideal prince to "Take Hold of Italy and Restore Her to Liberty from the Barbarians." Thus the structure of *The Prince* is a dramatic structure expressed often in comic, as well as tragic, forms,[7] with the emphasis shifting from the scene to the action, then to the actor (his character), the means he must use to carry on his struggle against the villain (who represents the bad principle of ruling), and ends in evocation to a purified republic in Italy which represents the *principle* of all ideal republics.

What are the principles of political persuasion? Following Burke's analysis of Machiavelli, we note that Machiavelli places stress on the administrator's ability to choose the act best suited to the *situation*, rather than choose the act best suited to the expression of his own nature or character.[8] Defend "weak neighbors and weaken the strong; where you foresee trouble, provoke war; don't make others powerful; . . . do necessary evils at one stroke, pay out benefits little by little, . . . be a combination of strength and stealth (lion and fox); *appear* merciful, dependable, humane, devout, upright, but be the opposite in actuality whenever the circumstances require it . . . be the patron of all talent, proclaim festivals, give spectacles, show deference to local organizations; but always retain the distance of your rank [the mystery of rule] . . .

have a few intimates who are encouraged to be completely frank, and who are well plied with rewards." [9] These, and many other such statements in *The Prince,* are like an actor's prompt book. They tell us how to play the role of ruler before a new kind of audience, the people of a modern city.

Machiavelli is concerned with how the ruler can address the people to make them want to do what they ought to do in a republic here on earth, not in heaven. In a perfect world, he tells us, there would be no need to exhort people to do good. But communities and states are cursed with parties thinking only of their personal good. And even if Italy could be a perfect community, it would still have crafty and powerful enemies seeking to devour it. The ruler who would protect his people must admit the need of adapting himself to things as they are. There have been great and noble men—Romulus, Solon, St. Francis, some of the Medicis—just as there is goodness, wisdom, unselfishness in the Roman people. But it is well to assume that men are capable of the worst evil, and even to realize that virtue, as well as vice, can destroy the state. The practical lawgiver will do well to assume that all men are often bad and "will always employ the malice of their spirits whenever they have a good chance to do so."

The problem of authority is one of using public and private vices, as well as the virtues, to a good end. This cannot always be done by open and rational appeals. The people, in their new roles as citizens of a republic, must be *conspired against* for their own good, just as enemies in turn must be conspired against to bring them to defeat. The enemies of the people are everywhere—within the state as without. Politics thus becomes the organization of conspiracy which often ends in war ("A prince . . . must have no other object and no other thought than war and its methods and conduct. . . . The first cause that makes [the Prince] lose [his] position is neglect of the art of war; and the cause that makes [him] acquire it is skill in that art." [10] Even Fortune or Fate must be assaulted: "Fortune is a woman and, if you wish to keep her down, you must beat and pound her. It is evident that she allows herself to be overcome by men who treat her in that way rather than by those who proceed coldly. For that reason, like a woman, she is always the friend of young men, because they are less cautious, and more courageous, and command her with more boldness." [11]

The common good Machiavelli describes is the national good of Italy, which at the time he wrote was oppressed, enslaved, and divided. Machiavelli's rhetoric shifts to invocation. The comic mask drops for a moment, as he ends in prayer for the deliverance of Italy from barbarism. The suffering of the Italians, like the sufferings of Christ, can become a source of unity and brotherhood in Italy. And, thus, as Burke points out, "by such identification of ruler and ruled, Machiavelli offers the ruler precisely the rhetorical opportunity to present privately acquisitive motives publicly in sacrificial terms." And whether or not we agree with Machiavelli, we know that struggles for advantage always have a rhetorical aspect. Machiavelli attempts to transcend the disorder of his age, not by turning to some Utopia, or by simply exposing the corruption and evil of men and the state, but by trying to scrutinize them as accurately and as calmly as he could. In doing so he gives us many clues for a New Rhetoric which will teach us how to resolve conflict by *confronting*, not denying, the evils of men.

THE RHETORIC OF DOMINATION OF THE SECULAR WORLD BY THE DEVOUT CHRISTIAN. GRACIAN'S "THE ART OF WORLDLY WISDOM"

Bathasar Gracian, Rector of the Jesuit College at Tarragona, Spain, during the second quarter of the sixteenth century, believed, along with his fellow Jesuits, that monastic opposition to the world must be broken down. The way to bridge the gap between the monastery and the world was to make the world Christian by teaching Christians to become worldly. To this end Jesuits must be taught how to gain power, not by going forth as beggars among the humble, but by going among men of the great world and high society.[12] He addresses his Jesuits as men of position, and teaches them how to increase their power because Christian power can be only good power. "The sole advantage of power is that you can do more good." Secular power will not corrupt the Christian because he is "above" worldly vanities. Thus, Gracian, like Machiavelli, is not approving of the world but telling his good Christian, who is about to leave the monastery, how to get along in a world far different from the monastery.

His rhetoric is not directed toward the Christian as a monk but as a Christian who must learn to manipulate men to Christian ends. Thus he speaks as a Christian and as a shrewd courtier. Gracian despises fools, and he sees no quarrel between shrewdness and goodness. He is, as his translator [13] tells us, both "wisely worldly and worldly wise." He speaks in a high tone of Christian authority to a Jesuit seeking to make his way in the world, where men are weak and beset by passions which must be understood if they are to be conquered. His rhetoric of the world is dry and ironic; although not cold, it is marked by a kind of austere irony, as befits a Christian who must reconcile holiness with cunning.

The world of the sixteenth century, Gracian warns his audience of monks, is a complex place. "There is more required nowadays to make a single wise man than formerly to make Seven Sages, and more is needed nowadays to deal with a single person than was required with a whole people in former times." [14] But even in this complex world it is only fools who fail to obtain "the position, the employment, the neighborhood, and the circle of friends that suit him." In the world, men communicate with each other, not with God. The first thing to learn is how to gain admiration. To do this "Keep Matters for a Time in Suspense." Do not declare yourself openly or immediately, for it "is both useless and insipid to play with the cards on the table." Arouse expectation, especially "when the importance of your position makes you the object of general attention." [15]

The best way to attract and hold attention is to create an air of mystery. "Mix a little mystery with everything," for mystery "arouses veneration." When you explain something, don't be too explicit. Be silent, for "Cautious silence is the holy of holies of worldly wisdom." Guesses and doubts about the extent of your talents arouse more veneration than accurate knowledge of them, be they ever so great. Be careful in speaking. Talk as if you were making your will. Do not explain too much, for most "men do not esteem what they understand, [but] venerate what they do not see." Many men praise without being able to tell why. This is because they venerate the unknown as a mystery, and praise it because they hear it praised.

Above all, learn how to display yourself, for such display illuminates your talents. Some men know how to make a great show with small means, and a whole exhibition with great means. If your skill in the arts of display is matched by versatile gifts, you will be regarded as a kind of miracle. There are whole nations given to display, as Spaniards know, for the Spanish take the highest rank in all the arts of display. In this they follow the Creation of God. "Light was the first thing to cause Creation to shine forth." Display fills up much, supplies much, and gives a second existence to things, especially when combined with real excellence. For: "Heaven that grants perfection, provides also the means of display; for one without the other were abortive."

But much skill is needed for effective display. Timing is everything, for even the highest excellence depends on circumstances and is not always opportune. Thus: "Ostentation is out of place when it is out of time. More than any other quality it should be free of any affectation," for affectation is offensive when it borders on vanity, and harmful because it risks contempt. Good display and good address of all kinds consist often in a kind of mute eloquence, a casual display of excellence, for a wise concealment is often the most effective boast. Withdrawal from view piques curiosity. " 'Tis a fine subtlety, too, not to display one's excellence all at one time, but to grant stolen glances at it, more and more as time goes on." [16]

God himself teaches us much about mystification. "[Y]ou imitate the Divine way when you cause men to wonder and watch." All profound secrecy has some of the lustre of the divine. Men venerate what they do not see, or what is far above them. That is why a hero among men should be great and majestic.[17] "In God all is eternal and infinite, in a hero everything should be great and majestic, so that all his deeds, nay, all his words, will be pervaded by a transcendent majesty." To uphold majesty we must avoid familiarity. "The stars keep their brilliance by not making themselves common." "Even God demands decorum." "Familiarity breeds contempt." "In human affairs, the more a man shows, the less he has, for in open communication you communicate the failings that reserve might keep under cover. Familiarity is never desirable; with superiors because it is dangerous, with inferiors because it is unbecoming, least of all with the common herd, who become insolent from sheer folly; they mistake favour shown them for need felt of them. Familiarity trenches on vulgarity." [18]

It is not he that adorns, but he that adores, who makes a divinity. Thus, a wise man would rather see man needing him than thanking him. Create a feeling of dependence; more is won from dependence than from courtesy. When dependence disappears, good behavior goes with it. Keep hope alive without entirely satisfying it, by preserving it, to make oneself always needed, even by a patron on the throne. On the other hand, avoid victories over superiors, for all victories breed hate, and victory over your superior is foolish, if not fatal. Superiority is always detested, and superiors are always very proud. Princes of the world may grant you precedence in good luck or good temper, but none in good sense, for good sense is a royal prerogative; a courtier's claim to that is a case of *lèse majesté*. Princes will allow a man to help them but not to surpass them. Advice given them must be made to appear like a recollection of something they have forgotten, rather than as a guide to something they cannot find.

Cultivate those who can teach you. Let friendly intercourse be a school of knowledge, for culture must be learned through conversation. And since one converses only with friends or equals, and not superiors or inferiors, make your friends your teachers and mingle the pleasures of conversation with the advantages of instruction. In good conversation we reap applause for what we say and gain instruction from what we hear. That is why wise men frequent the houses of great noblemen. Such houses are not to be thought of by the Christian as temples of vanity, but as theaters of good breeding. The great men of the social world are not only oracles of nobleness in themselves, but they surround themselves with a well-bred academy of worldly wisdom of the best and noblest kind. For man is born a barbarian and only raises himself above the beast by culture. Ignorance is very raw, but even knowledge is coarse if without elegance. Not only our intelligence must be elegant, but also our desires, and above all our conversation.

Be expressive, for if we need resolution for the will, we also need expression for thought. This depends not only on clearness but also on vivacity. No act in life requires more attention than conversation, even though it is the commonest thing in life. As the sage said, "Speak, that I may know thee." To be appropriate, talk should adapt itself to the mind and tone of the interlocutor. Talk with friends is not the same as with persons of station. To show respect, talk should be more dignified to answer to the dignity of the person addressed. Do not be a critic of words, or you will be taken for a pedant, nor a collector, a "taxgatherer of ideas," or men will avoid you. Discretion is more important than eloquence in conversation. Never talk of yourself, for if you do you must either praise yourself, or blame yourself, which is little-minded. In ordinary conversation, in discussing official matters, and, above all, in public speaking do not praise or blame yourself. And above all, do not be a bore by becoming a man of one business or one topic. Avoid boring the great, for it is far worse to disturb superiors than inferiors or equals.

Acquire a reputation for courtesy, for it will make you liked. Politeness is the main ingredient of culture, "a kind of witchery," which casts a spell. Better, then, too much courtesy than too little, provided you do not make courtesy the same for everyone. This kind of politeness easily degenerates into injustice. Be courteous to opponents, for this is a sign of courage. Everyone is honored who gives honor. Courtesy helps to fend off hate and dislike. And you will be hated and disliked, for these emotions are a characteristic of the world, so do what you can to lessen the deadly effects of hate.

How things are done, the styles of gesture, bearing, voice, an air of elegance and dignity, play a great part in the world of men. A bad manner spoils everything. Good manners bring joy because they bring beauty into social life. Even a refusal can be softened by good manners. To know how to refuse is therefore as important as to know how to consent. A great man is never little in his behavior. That is why he does not pry too minutely into things, especially in unpleasant matters. Learning what not to see and how to overlook things forms a large part of ruling. You must learn to live with your own failings. Seal up your defects, conceal them from yourself, if you can. To act well, we must learn how to forget, as well as remember. Most things among relatives and friends are better left unnoticed. Even among enemies it is wise to overlook much. Life in the world is made up of contraries, and thus to succeed the courtier must be a philosopher, the Christian holy, sagacious, and worldly wise, and the ruler must learn to live without illusions. For the discovery of deceit is the true delight of a virtuous soul.

Good manners are not the same for those in high positions as they are for common folk. In all things cultivate a tone of authority, but do not parade your position, for the more you seek esteem, the less you obtain it. You cannot take esteem and honor, but must earn and receive them from others. Great positions must have a tone of authority, and those filling them must do so with dignity, for without these no office can be conducted efficiently. Never try to force respect. To insist on the dignity of your office is to show that you have not deserved it, and that it is too much for you to carry well. If you wish to be valued by others be valued for your talents, not for something adventitious. For even kings prefer to be honored for their personal qualifications rather than for their office. Dignity with grace wins all. Without graciousness beauty is lifeless; valor, discretion, prudence, even majesty itself, unattractive.

The secret of majesty and dignity is control of expression. There is art in all kinds of presentations of the self. There is even an art of getting into a passion. This is achieved by considering the effect of your passion on others. The first step toward getting into a passion is to announce that you are in a passion. By doing so you begin the quarrel with command over your temper, for one has to regulate passion to the exact point that is necessary, and no further. Getting into and out of a rage is the art of arts. To keep control of passion one must be attentive to its effects. Keep a store of sarcasms, and know how to use them. Such sarcasms can be thrown out to test a man's mood; often they evoke responses which prove that they are the most subtle and penetrating touchstone of the heart. Allow yourself some venial fault. Let Homer nod now and then, and affect some flaws in your courage or in your intelligence. This will disarm malevolence, or at least prevent it from bursting with its own spleen. "You thus leave your cloak on the horns of Envy in order to save your immortal parts."

But above all, in dealing with the world one must be shrewd enough to use people and events to serve one's own purposes. Select the lucky and avoid the unlucky, for ill-luck is generally the penalty of folly, and there is no disease so contagious to those who share it. Always weigh your luck before you act. Be all things to all men. Notice men's moods. Make use of your enemies, for a wise man gets more use from his enemies than a fool from his friends. Flattery is more dangerous than hatred, because it covers the stains which the other causes to be wiped out. The wise turn ill-will into a mirror. Seek out others, for it is better to be mad with the rest of the world than wise alone. "Do not show your wounded Finger"; everything will knock up against it, for malice always aims where weakness exists.

On the other hand, "Find out each Man's Thumbscrew." Learn how to get at people. All men are idolaters, some of fame, others of self-interest, most of pleasure. In knowing a man's mainspring, you have the key to his will. Guess a man's ruling passion, appeal to it by a word, set it in motion by temptation, and you will check his freedom of will. In sum, "Use human Means as if there were no divine ones, and divine as if there were no human ones." This is the essence of wisdom for the Christian who will preserve his spirit in the world of flesh.[19]

Notes

[1] Even force is analyzed as a *communication* of authority: a continuation of politics by force, to affect the will of the combatants. The *rhetoric* of war (now called psychological warfare) has received far less attention than logistics, or what is called the "science" of warfare.

[2] There is a discussion of Machiavelli's reputation in *Machiavelli: The Prince . . . and other works including Reform in Florence, Castruccio Castracani, On Fortune, Letters, and Ten Discourses on Livy,* new translations, introductions, and notes by Allan H. Gilbert (New York: Hendricks House; Farrar, Straus, 1946). Professor Gilbert's introduction is of great value to sociologists.

[3] Pareto's lions and foxes are discussed in Chapter 18 of *The Prince.*

[4] Gilbert, *op. cit.,* p. 45. Veblen, too, is now being discovered as a "comic artist."

[5] *Ibid.,* p. 123. See also *ibid., Ten Discourses on Livy,* I, 16, pars. 5 and 6.

[6] That is, Machiavelli discusses "environment," "conditions," etc., in terms of their *symbolic* qualities, and shows how these qualities infuse action with meaning.

[7] This does not mean *The Prince* is not serious, any more than *Measure for Measure* is not serious because it is a comedy of community life. Comedy, like tragedy, is very serious, but it is a different kind of seriousness, which resolves struggle through appeals to reason in society, not through belief in some kind of supernatural fate. (This will be discussed in later chapters on comedy.) Even in the moving peroration, when Machiavelli seeks to move his Italians to their great destiny, he ends by saying: "This barbarian rule stinks in every nostril." This is hardly the language of tragedy, and it certainly is not the language of political "science."

[8] This is what is meant by "wise" ruling and also what is meant by a "naturalistic" approach to the study of ruling.

[9] Kenneth Burke, *A Rhetoric of Motives* (New York: Prentice-Hall, Inc., 1950), p. 158.

[10] Gilbert, *op. cit.,* p. 139.

[11] *Ibid.,* p. 176.

[12] *The Spectator* (No. 379, 1712) reported that high-born Spaniards were angry with the famous Gracian for publishing his maxims because he had laid open those maxims to common readers which ought only to be reserved for the knowledge of the great.

[13] *The Art of Worldly Wisdom* by Balthasar Gracian, translated from the Spanish by Joseph Jacobs (New York: The Macmillan Company, 1950). Jacobs' translation was first published in 1892.

[14] *Ibid.,* Maxim i, p. 1.

[15] *Ibid.,* Maxim iii, pp. 1–2.

[16] On the cultivation of mystery, veneration, and awe to produce majesty in the staging of the self before the world, see maxims iii, xiv, lxxvi, lxxxi, ciii, ccli, and cclxxvii, as given in Jacobs' translation.

[17] Gracian describes the proud and spotless Spanish hidalgo in his *El Heroe* (1630) and contrasts him with the prudent courtier as described in *El Discreto* (1647). *Don Quixote,* in which the Don represents the ideal knight and Sancho Panza represents the "real" world of common people, began to appear in 1605. Nothing illustrates better the difference between great art and rhetoric. Cervantes *opens* the mystifica-

tion of *both* knighthood *and* prudence to the light of reason through comedy, while. Gracian shows us how to preserve the majesty of the hidalgo and the greatness of the prudent man.

[18] Maxim clxxvii, Jacobs, *op. cit.*, p. 105.

[19] Maxim ccvxi ("Noble Qualities"). See Jacobs, *ibid.*, pp. 174–175. Thus Gracian ends, as he begins in Maxim iii, by stressing that in seeking to arouse veneration and awe we must "imitate the Divine way" which causes "men to wonder and watch."

17

Rhetoric as an Instrument of Domination Through Unreason: Hitler's "Mein Kampf"

HITLER'S THEORY OF RHETORIC AS A MEANS
TOWARD SOCIAL IDENTIFICATION

OUR FAILURE to study social relations as symbolic acts now bears terrible witness in the rise to power in our time of the greatest rhetorician of evil known to history. Adolph Hitler's *Mein Kampf* (My Battle) invokes hatred and death as guardians of social order. Indeed, it may be called, justly, a book of death. Yet to dismiss this gruesome book as the ravings of a madman or to disregard it is sheer folly, for whenever tyranny raises its hand in the present (and the future) it will owe much to this terrible manual of death and enslavement. Hitler wrote it to teach his followers how to become a "superior" race of killers. He tells us in his Foreword,[1] which he signs in "Landsberg on the Lech, Fortress Prison," that he is not addressing his work to strangers, but to adherents of the movement who belong to it with their whole hearts and who now seek more intimate enlightenment of the purpose of the Nazi party.

Nearly six million Jews and other "inferior races" were to be murdered in Hitler's death camps, before Hitler's voice was stilled. Millions more were to die on battlefields, and other millions to hobble through the streets of Europe and Asia for the remainder of their days, because of the terrible skill of Hitler, the orator, in persuading his Germans that their call to pillage and murder was a divine call. The death camps—Auschwitz, Belsen, Ravensbrück and Dachau—were born in the rhetoric of Hitler. As we stand in sheer horror before the image of these camps, where enslavement, torture, and murder were not only permitted but organized on a mass scale, we ask: "How did these terrible things come to pass?" What was the secret of Hitler's strange hypnotic power over his Germans? How could he convince a people to torture and murder millions of their fellows, not in the wild rage and cold fear of battle, but in the grim efficiency of camps organized for killing "scientifically?" The answer, strangely enough, lies close at hand. Hitler himself tells us how he reduced the German people to monsters. For *Mein Kampf* is truly a manual of how to turn people into self-righteous killers.

The purpose of rhetoric and of all political symbolic action, Hitler repeats many times, is to give people a deep sense of community. The conditions for doing this, the stage on which the political drama must be mounted, is the public mass meeting. The most important political actor, the shaper of men's souls, is the orator.[2] The means by which the orator moves his mass audience is the spoken word. The word, in turn, is an incitement to battle, based on unreason ("will"). It is not the function of the orators to discuss or to argue but to tell people what they ought to do, and then inspire them to do it *by any conceivable means*. Speech is a kind of weapon, and like any weapon it must be used ruthlessly against enemies within, as well as without, the community. All life, nature teaches us, is a battle, and the greatest end of man, the end which purifies his soul and proves his honor, is battle.

Man must live in a state of war because his *"blood sin and desecration of the race are the original sin in this world, and the end of a humanity which surrenders to it."*[3] Pure blood is Aryan blood, and the purest form of Aryan blood is German blood. The Aryan proves that nature's "instinct for race purity" and "will to breed life upwards" is manifest in struggle. All "natural" forms of struggle, such as the struggle for food and mates, improve the health and stamina of the species, "and thus [is] a cause of its evolution." Nature also eliminates the weak by subjecting them to such hard living conditions that only the strongest survive. And as little as nature wishes a mating of weaker with stronger individuals, still less does she want the fusion of a higher with a lower race, since otherwise the whole labor of selective evolution, perhaps through thousands of years, would be "ruined" with a blow.[4] Thus, as history teaches us, by "countless examples" and "with alarming plainness," every mingling of Aryan blood with inferior races results in "the end of the cultured people."[5]

To induce race mixture is, therefore, to sin against the will of the Eternal Creator, as well as to rebel against the "iron logic of Nature." That is why alien blood must be eliminated from German blood—for the fate of Germany is really the fate of the world. "If, with the help of his Marxist creed, the Jew is victorious over the other peoples of the world, his crown will be the funeral wreath of humanity, and this planet will, as it did thousands of years ago, move through the ether devoid of men." [6] Thus, in "dealing with," "settling," the Jewish question "once and for all" and "resisting the Jew," the German simply carries out the Divine Will and obeys the laws of nature. "Thus I believe I am acting in accordance with the will of the Almighty Creator: *by defending myself against the Jew I am fighting for the work of the Lord.*" [7]

The tireless, loyal, honorable, "soldierly," idealistic, brotherly, spiritual German must kill Jews and conquer such "decadent" nations as France, because this alone will save civilization. Only Aryans and the greatest Aryan nation, Germany, can do this. For the German knows how to sacrifice his blood and, if need be, his life for his ideals. Prussia was created by "radiant heroism," and the German empire itself was the reward of a leadership based on power politics and of a "soldierly courage to dare death." The greatness of Germany was born in sacrifice and will continue in sacrifice of blood and, if need be, of life itself on the field of battle. But the German never fights in arrogance, but in humility. When he kills, he does not do so for any personal motive, or even from hate. Like an avenging angel, he is simply carrying out the Divine Will. Extermination of enemies of Germany, hard and dangerous though it may be, is nothing but the extermination of enemies of the Lord.

The purpose of rhetoric, Hitler tells us, is to satisfy the longing of people for communion with each other. Symbols are powerful to the degree that they make it possible for people using them to identify with each other. Communion, the sense of community, is hard to achieve because men are separate and divided among themselves. This came about because men refused to keep their blood pure. Originally the Aryans, the true founders of humanity, were of pure stock, "the Prometheus of mankind from whose bright forehead the divine spark of genius has sprung at all times, forever kindling anew that fire of knowledge which illumined the night of silent mysteries and thus caused man to climb the path to mastery over the other beings of this earth." [8] The Fall of Man in his pure Aryan paradise was not a sexual but a social Fall. Aryan man was expelled from Paradise and thus lost the right to the Paradise which he had made for himself, because he mingled socially, and eventually sexually, with his inferiors to produce a race of "cross-breeds."

Why is Aryan man so miserable when separated from his fellow beings? It is because, of all men, he must live most closely in community with his fellows. The will to sacrifice, to devote personal labor, and, if necessary, life itself to others is most highly developed in the Aryan.

True, the Aryan may not possess the greatest mental qualities, as such, but in the extent of his readiness to devote all his abilities to the service of the community he is unique. "In him the instinct of self-preservation has reached its noblest form, since he willingly subordinates his own ego to the life of the community, and, if the hour demands, even sacrifices it." [9] This is clearly indicated by the German language, which has a word that describes the quality that makes the Aryan capable of surrendering his life for the existence of the community. *Pflichterfellung* (performance of duty) means not satisfaction of the self, but service to the community. This is really what is meant by German idealism and the German character ("Germanity"). True idealism (that is, German idealism) is nothing but the subordination of the individual's interest and life to the community.

This devotion to the community is the first law of the German spirit and the first essential for the formation of any sort of organization in German society. Once let egoism become the ruler of the people, and the bonds of order are loosened; in chasing their own happiness people fall from Heaven straight to Hell. That is why mass meetings of the people are necessary. In them the individual who feels isolated "and easily succumbs to the fear of being alone, for the first time gets the picture of a large community, which in most people has a strengthening, encouraging effect." [10] That is why Marxism has succeeded. It is

the gigantic mass demonstrations, these parades of hundreds of thousands of men, which burned into the small, wretched individual the proud conviction that, paltry worm as he was, he was nevertheless a part of a great dragon, beneath whose burning breath the hated bourgeois world would some day go up in fire and flame and the proletarian dictatorship would celebrate its ultimate final victory.[11]

The community character of a big demonstration not only strengthens the individual, but unites and helps to produce *esprit de corps*.

When from his workshop or big factory, in which he feels very small, he steps for the first time into a mass meeting and has thousands and thousands of people of the same opinion around him, when, as a seeker, he is swept away by three or four thousand others into the mighty effect of suggestive intoxication and enthusiasm, when the visible success and agreement of thousands confirm to him the rightness of the new doctrine and for the first time arouse doubt in the truth of his previous conviction—then he himself has succumbed to the magic influence of what we designate as "mass suggestion." The will, the longing, and also the power of thousands are accumulated in every individual. The man who enters such a meeting doubting and wavering leaves it inwardly reinforced; he has become a link in the community.[12]

A mass meeting, to be effective with the masses, must be staged carefully as a drama of struggle between good and evil. A speech to the masses must be an enactment, not a "report," or simply a gathering. It must be formed carefully to *involve* the mass audience, not to keep them at arm's length. The "so-called bourgeois meetings" failed because they were not staged as dramas but as "discussions."[13] At these meetings they

spoke, or rather, as a rule, they read speeches in the style of a witty newspaper article or of a scientific treatise, avoided all strong words, and here and there threw in some feeble professorial joke, at which the honorable committee dutifully began to laugh, though not loudly, provocatively, but in a dignified, subdued, reserved fashion. . . . [At one such meeting] the speech was delivered or read by a dignified old gentleman, a professor at some university. On the platform sat the committee. To the left a monocle, to the right a monocle, and in between one without a monocle. All three in frock coats, so that you got the impression either of a court of justice planning an execution or of a solemn baptism, in any case more of a religious solemnity. The so-called speech, which might have cut a perfectly good figure in print, was simply terrible in its effect. After only three quarters of an hour the whole meeting was dozing. . . . Three workers, who, either from curiosity or because they had been commissioned to attend, were present at the meeting, and behind whom I posted myself, looked at each other from time to time with ill-concealed grins, and finally nudged one another, whereupon they very quietly left the hall.[14]

Bourgeois leaders do not understand that the broad masses of the people must be won. No social sacrifice is too great to win the masses for the national rehabilitation. Nor do they understand "that the broad masses of a people consist neither of professors nor of diplomats." The masses have small capacity for thought. The slight abstract knowledge they possess directs their perceptions into the world of emotion. Here their positive and negative attitudes are formed. The emotions of the masses are stirred only by a vigorous expression of extremes, never by something floating halfway between the two.[15] But the emotions of the people must not be thought of as passions, but as faith. The speaker stirs up feelings and passions, but only to shape them into faith, for emotion turned into faith brings with it extraordinary stability. This is because faith is harder to shake than knowledge, love less changeable than respect, and hatred more durable than aversion. The driving force in the great upheavals of this earth has been less an intellectual rule of the masses than a fanaticism animating them, and often, indeed, a hysteria hurling them onward.

The great masses are only a "bit of Nature"; they cannot understand a handshake between men who claim to dislike opposite things. They want the victory of the stronger and the annihilation of the weaker, or his unconditional subjection. Thus, he who would win the masses must know that the key which opens their hearts is not objectivity, which, after all, "is weakness," but will and vigor. The soul of the people is won in battle, and the rhetoric of the people's orator must be the rhetoric of battle. Destruction must not be taken as a mere figure of speech, but as a literal description of what is in store for enemies of the people. "The nationalization of our masses will succeed only when, aside from all the positive struggle for the soul of our people, their international poisoners are exterminated." [16] The masses must be taught that Jews and Communists are their enemies. True, many Germans are Communists, but this is only because they have been seduced by Jews, and thus Marxism is really Jewish Marxism. The extermination of Jews is therefore a sacred duty of every good German, for without a clear recognition of the race problem, and thus of the Jewish question, no new rise of the German nation can take place. And if Germans do not arise and exterminate the Jews, they will fail to solve the problem of cultural degeneration and thus fail in their guardianship of human civilization. [17]

The "middle way," the bourgeois way, the "so-called objective standpoint," can never be used to nationalize the broad masses of the people. No people can be made nationalist in the sense of our modern bourgeoisie, i.e., with so-and-so many limitations, but only nationalistic with the whole vehemence inherent in extremes. The people must be given *both* a God and a Devil; the Jew, the Jewish Marxist, and the International Jew (who really controls England and America) must be fought ruthlessly. This cannot be done, and has never been done, by appealing to every faction in the community. A movement's propaganda, to be effective, must aim in one direction only. It is futile to try to appeal to both the masses and the bourgeoisie, for, owing to the difference in the previous intellectual preparation of the two, it would either not be understood by one side or be refused as obvious and hence uninteresting by the other. If mass propaganda sacrifices primitive pungency of expression, it will not find its way "to the feelings of the broad masses."

But if in word and gesture it has the downrightedness of the masses' feelings and their manifestations, it will be objected to by the so-called intelligents as "coarse and vulgar." [18]

Leaders of a new Germany must face the fact that among a hundred so-called speakers there are hardly ten who can speak one day with equal effect before an audience of street-cleaners, mechanics, sewer-workers, etc., and the next day give a lecture with the same intellectual substance before an auditorium of college professors and students. Among a thousand speakers there is perhaps but one who can address mechanics and college professors at the same time in a style that not only suits the capacities of both, but has equal influence on both, "or even carries them away in a roaring storm of applause." And we must keep in mind that even the finest idea for a noble theory must always be promulgated through the smallest of minds. The point of all propaganda is rhetorical, and the way it must be thought about is in terms of rhetoric. What is important is not what the inspired creator of an idea has in mind but what the heralds of this idea transmit to the masses, in what form, and with what success. It is here, says Hitler, that Nazis can learn from Communists. The attraction of the Marxist movement "depended largely upon the homogeneity and, hence, the one-sidedness of the public it addressed. The more seemingly limited, indeed, the narrower its ideas were, the more easily it was taken up and assimilated by a mass whose intellectual level corresponded to the material offered." [19]

These Nazi "heralds of the idea" must learn to stir up the passions of their mass audiences, but they must learn too that the Nazi orator never becomes a tool of public opinion. He is not the masses' menial, but their lord. He must learn to stand against public opinion, "without regard for popularity, hatred, or battle." In the early stages of a movement, he must understand that he cannot court the masses, but must win them away from other faiths and learn how to compete with other speakers. Hitler did not court the favor of the masses (during the early years of the Nazi movement) but "opposed the madness of the people, everywhere." [20] The speaker must be prepared to shatter the convictions held by his audience. For the masses are never neutral, nor do they attend meetings to hear both sides of a case in order to make up their minds.

In the early years of the movement, Hitler tells us, he often appeared before people who believed the opposite of what he meant to say. Then "it was the work of two hours to lift two or three thousand people out of a previous conviction, blow by blow to shatter the foundations of their previous opinions, and finally to lead them across to our convictions and our philosophy of life." This was done by knocking the "weapon of reply out of the enemy's hand myself." This was possible because Nazi adversaries had a definite repertoire, in which constantly recurring objections were made to Nazi assertions. The speaker must realize in advance the probable form and substance of the objections to be expected in the discussion, and then pull these entirely to pieces beforehand in one's own speech. It is expedient to cite the possible objections oneself, and to prove their "inapplicability." Thus the listener, "even if he had come stuffed full of the objections he had been taught, but otherwise with an honest heart, was more easily won over when we disposed of the doubts that had been imprinted on his memory. The stuff that had been drummed into him was automatically refuted and his attention drawn more and more to the speech." [21]

As he progresses, the speaker watches intently the faces of his audience. For the speaker receives constant guidance from the crowd, inasmuch as he can judge from the faces of his audience the impression of his words, in contrast to the writer who does not know his readers at all. If the speaker makes even a small mistake he can correct it. He can read from the expressions of his listeners whether they understand what he is saying, whether they can follow it, and how completely they are convinced of the soundness of what they hear. When the speaker sees that he is not understood, he must make his explanation so primitive and plain that the dullest can grasp it; if he feels they cannot follow him, he must build up his ideas so cautiously and slowly that even the feeblest is not left behind; and if he suspects that they do not seem convinced of the truth of what he says, he must repeat it again and again with new illustrations, putting forward the unspoken objections he can sense, "and go on confuting them and exploding them until at length even the last group of an opposition by its very bearing and facial expression enables him to recognize its capitulation to his arguments." [22]

The political orator of the masses is not appealing to reason but to feeling—for all human beings have prejudices which are not founded on reason. Such prejudices are supported only by feeling, and often people are unconscious of these feelings. False ideas and incorrect knowledge can be corrected by instruction; emotional resistance, never. Only an appeal to these mysterious forces can take effect; and that can be done hardly ever by the writer, but almost solely by the speaker. And even in writing, the more the style approaches the political rhetoric of the speaker the more effective it will be. We see this in the Marxist press. *"The Marxist Press is written by agitators, and the bourgeois press would like to carry on agitation by means of writers."* [23] The speaker may treat the same theme as a book, and he may follow ideas created by party intellectuals, but, unlike the book, the speech must never take on a fixed form. A great and inspired popular speaker will seldom repeat the same subject in the same form. He will always let himself be carried along by the broad masses in such fashion that his feeling will give him precisely the words he needs to move his audience of the moment.

Such speeches ought to be given near the end of the day, because appeals to emotion and feeling are far more effective at night than during the day. The same speech, the same speaker, or the same subject have entirely different results at ten in the morning, at three in the afternoon, and in the evening. In the morning, and even during the day, people's will-power seems to resist the imposition of an outside will and an outside opinion. In the evening, on the other hand, it more easily succumbs to the dominating force of a stronger will. "For, in truth, every such meeting represents a wrestling bout between two opposing forces. The superior oratorical art of a dominating preacher will succeed more easily in winning to the new will people who have themselves experienced a weakening of their force of resistance in the most natural way than those who are still in full possession of their mental tension and will." There is nothing novel about this, for we see the same purpose served "by the artificially made and yet mysterious twilight in Catholic churches, the burning lamps, incense, censers, etc." [24]

A political meeting is an incitement to action, not reflection. But it must be an incitement to controlled action, not mob violence. Mass audiences must see that their speaker and his party are determined to fight to the end, but they must also see that this fighting spirit is under control. There must be displays of heroism, and if necessary these displays must be deliberately staged for the benefit of the audience. *"Any meeting which is protected exclusively by the police discredits its organizers in the eyes of the broad masses."* [25] Because of this an organized group of "regulators" (as Hitler calls them, or bouncers, as we call them in America) must be ready to deal with hecklers and those who try to break up a meeting. These regulators must be "saturated" with the doctrine that if reason is silent, violence must have the last word, and the best defensive is attack. Regulator troops should be preceded by the reputation of being not a debating club but a combat group determined to go to any length. For this reason, the regulators should be composed solely of young lads who can be indoctrinated so deeply with the ideals of the party that they are willing to fight to the last drop of their blood against any odds.

The presence of regulators, ready at a moment's notice to swoop down with flying fists on anyone trying to break up the meeting, must be matched by an air of authority.

No one begged the audience graciously to permit our speech, nor was everyone guaranteed unlimited time for discussion; it was simply stated that we were the masters of the meeting, that in consequence we had the privilege of the house, and that anyone who dared to utter so much as a single cry of interruption would be mercilessly thrown out where he came from. That, furthermore, we must reject any responsibility for such a fellow; if there was time left and it suited us, we would permit a discussion to take place, if not, there would be none, and the speaker, Party Comrade So-and-So, had the floor.[26]

Authority must be *communicated* clearly and simply, by party symbols of all kinds, as well as by words and gestures. The psychological importance of symbols can scarcely be overestimated.[27] Marxist mass meetings where the audience becomes a veritable "sea of red flags, red armbands and red flowers" casts a hypnotic spell, the spell of a grandiose spectacle, over the workers. Bourgeois mass meetings lacked this magic because there were no flags or banners. The problem in selecting symbols is to avoid simply recalling a cherished but dead past, without, at the same time, promising a more radiant future. This can be done if symbols of the greatness of the past and the radiance of the future can be combined. The black, white, and red flag of the old German empire, sacred as it was, could not be a "symbol for a battle of the future." But the colors—the sacred colors which moved the hearts of German soldiers —could take the minds of the people into the future. The new flag was "a Symbol of our own battle" and at the same time it had "a striking poster-like effect," and the poster form of art is the best form for political purposes.

The staging of the popularity of the party leaders and readiness to use force to back him up must always be joined to a great tradition. Popularity alone is not enough. The popular leader must see to it that he generates power out of his popularity. But power, while it seems more stable and reliable than popularity, is not always stronger than popularity. But if *"popularity and force are combined, and if in common they are able to survive for a certain time, an authority on an even firmer basis can arise, the authority of tradition. If, finally, popularity, force, and tradition combine, an authority may be regarded as unshakable."* [28] Failure to link these three elements cost the German Revolution of 1919 dear. The revolutionaries, with their "soldier self-government," exploited only one power, popularity, to build up their authority. This turned out to be a very unreliable basis for authority.

The authority of tradition rests, of course, on the past. But a new party must do more than promise a return to the past; it must offer a future, although this future must always be based on a past and must be explained in terms of history. The Marxists created a "Marxist Heaven," but this "Heaven" is too "economic," and the German, unlike the "Marxist rabble" has too great a tradition to be satisfied only with economic solutions. The problem now is to purify this great tradition, to bring it to life again so that what seems new will really be a return to the old tried and true ways of German life. For the Germans, unlike other peoples, have a great tradition, an Aryan tradition, as every soldier who fought for the Fatherland knows. The popular leader must then use force, not to destroy tradition, as the revolutionaries and the rootless Marxists do, but to purify it so that Germany can return once again to its splendor as the leading nation of Europe, and the standard-bearer of Aryan purity, who will save Europe and the world from degeneration and decay.

Such, then, is the rhetoric of hell. Hitler's appeal to unreason was successful because he understood that symbols, the forms in which we express ourselves, are goads to action, not merely signs or referents to some reality beyond words. Symbols give experience a form and order, which makes action possible. And this form, as Hitler taught his party leaders, is a dramatic form. People must act to live in community with each other, and they must play parts in dramas of community life. For it is only by acting together under great community symbols that men identify and thus rid themselves of loneliness and despair. Hitler knew that men need each other in hate as well as love. He knew also that men do not want to communicate *about* love and hate, but to *express* them in community with other men. He understood the importance of art as a community rhetoric because he believed that motives are the effect, not the cause, of symbols The terrible irony of our time in the use of symbols is that only the tyrants among our political leaders take art seriously into account as a form of political communication. Hitler really believed that art determined life. In Martin Bormann's records of Hitler's conversations [29] we find music and architecture discussed as the disciplines that record "the path of humanity's ascent." In Wagner's music Hitler heard the "rhythms of a bygone world" created by myth and art. Someday, Hitler tells us, "science will discover, in the waves set in motion by the *Rheingold,* secret mutual relations connected with the order of the world." German intellectuals laughed at Hitler's "ravings," but their laughter died swiftly as they saw the German people turn away from them to a leader who taught men to hate and kill by mounting great community dramas in which Germans were exhorted to hate and kill those who disagreed with them at home, as well as those who stood against them in other countries. Intellectual leaders in Germany had taught the people how to think about society; Hitler taught them how to act. He returned words and symbols to life. The tragedy of our time is that tyrants have divined the power of art and have learned how to use the arts for the communication of evil. Democratic leaders too can learn to use the arts for benign purposes, but will they? Perhaps, when all is said and done, it is upon this fateful question that our future hangs.

Notes

[1] All references and quotations from *Mein Kampf* will be taken from the Ralph Manheim translation (Boston: Houghton Mifflin Company, 1943).

[2] In his "Foreword," Hitler is almost apologetic about giving his Nazi elite a *written* manual. He tells us that he knows that men are moved by the spoken, not the written, word and that every great movement owes its growth to great orators, not great writers. He feels justified in writing *Mein Kampf* because the principles of a uniform and unified doctrine must be laid down "for all time."

[3] Hitler, *op. cit.,* p. 249. Hitler's italics.

[4] *Ibid.*, p. 286.

[5] *Ibid.*

[6] *Ibid.*, p. 65.

[7] *Ibid.* Hitler's italics. This is the last sentence of the second chapter, "Years of Study and Suffering in Vienna."

[8] *Ibid.*, p. 290.

[9] *Ibid.*, p. 297.

[10] *Ibid.*, p. 478.

[11] *Ibid.*, p. 473. For Hitler the appeal of Marxism is its promise of vengeance.

[12] *Ibid.*, pp. 478–479.

[13] Hitler seldom curses the good burghers, as he does the Jews and the Marxists. He treats them with irony. Their childishness, dullness, and stupidity are the target of the only consistent vein of humor in *Mein Kampf*. This humor is based on the reduction of political activity to a kind of irrelevant pantomime or meaningless ritual. Business, even "good" German business, is described as a kind of mutual swindle. "Bad" business—that practiced by the Jew—is not funny, but evil, because the Jewish use of money is materialistic, and thus degrades the German spirit of honor and dignity.

[14] Hitler, *op. cit.*, p. 481.

[15] In his discussion of the early days of the Nazi party, Hitler tells us that the party realized as early as 1919 that the new movement must carry through as its highest aim the nationalization of the masses.

[16] Hitler, *op. cit.*, p. 338.

[17] *Ibid.*, pp. 336–339. These are among the fourteen points which were used as a basis for the tactics of the conduct of early and later meetings of the Nazi party.

[18] *Ibid.*, p. 342.

[19] *Ibid.*, Hitler always paid high tribute to the "Marxists agitators" who went into the streets to "stir up" the people. He felt that in Germany the intellectual classes were so isolated and fossilized that they had no living connection with those beneath them. Will, according to Hitler, is always weaker in caste-bound intellectual circles than in the primitive mass of the people.

[20] *Ibid.*, p. 465. That is, Hitler did not gloss over the sufferings and mistakes of the German people. But he *assigned* them not to the "Germanity" of the Germans but to the Jews.

[21] *Ibid.*, p. 467.

[22] *Ibid.*, p. 471.

[23] *Ibid.*, p. 472. Hitler's italics.

[24] *Ibid.*, p. 475. Many local Nazi meetings were held late at night in beer cellars. By ten or eleven o'clock these rooms were filled with men who smoked and drank beer as they awaited the arrival of the speaker.

[25] *Ibid.*, p. 490. Hitler's italics.

[26] *Ibid.*

[27] In the chapter "The Struggle with the Red Front," Hitler discusses the importance of symbols to the masses: symbols are effective because they are the means by which we identify with one another.

[28] *Ibid.*, p. 518. These remarks are made at the beginning of Chapter Nine, "Basic Thoughts on the Meaning and Organization of the Storm Troops." Hitler's italics.

[29] See *Hitler's Secret Conversations: 1941–1944* (New York: Signet Books, The New American Library of World Literature, Inc., 1961), trans. by Norman Cameron and R. H. Stevens, with an introductory essay on "The Mind of Adolf Hitler," by H. R. Trevor-Roper.

18

Social Order Based on Unreason:
The Perversion of Religion by the State

P R A C T I C A L L Y every key concept in Hitler's *Mein Kampf* is a perversion, or a caricature, of a religious concept. It is a perversion of religion because the Nazi world view is one of hate, not love. The Nazi "grace" is found in conflict, battle, and killing, which is done in the name of various supernatural ultimates such as reason, nature, the divine will, fate, and destiny. Yet whatever we say about this terrible book, it is potent medicine for people suffering from guilt and alienation. Hitler's skill in creating symbols which Germans could use to identify with one another is uncanny. We have said, following Burke,[1] that social order is based on a *drama* of guilt, redemption, hierarchy, and victimage. The Nazi ideal and practice of authority certainly upholds this view.

Hitler told his Germans they lost the war because they had sinned by polluting their blood with non-Aryan blood. They must redeem themselves through sacrifice of the Jew and offer themselves as Aryan martyrs who must suffer and die to cleanse the world of sin. Germans, and indeed Aryans everywhere, could atone through "leaders" who would be "responsible" to "Fate" or the "Divine Will" for whatever the Nazis did. The Nazis thus created a hierarchy whose principle of Aryan purity could be upheld only by the strictest observance of the "leadership principle."[2] As Hitler himself tells us: *"The folkish philosophy is basically distinguished from the Marxist philosophy by the fact that it not only recognizes the value of race, but with it the importance of the personality, which it therefore makes one of the pillars of its entire edifice."*[3]

The "personality principle" must be embodied in a strict hierarchy of superiors and inferiors. "The principle which made the Prussian army in its time into the most wonderful instrument of the German people must some day, in a transferred sense, become the principle of the construction of our whole state conception: *authority of every leader downward and responsibility upward."*[4] Parliaments, cabinets, and councilors who act together in democracy as equals who reach decision through discussion and debate, will become advisory bodies. They will also become a training ground for inequality: "Parliaments as such are necessary because in them, above all, personalities to which special responsible tasks can later be entrusted have an opportunity gradually to rise up." [5] No vote will ever be taken, for the Nazi parliaments are to be "working institutions, not voting machines." For, Hitler asks, if we do not vote for our business, cultural, and religious leaders, why should we vote for our political leaders?

Hitler's image of authority is a priesthood that rules the world under a Divine mandate. Carrying out this mandate is difficult because man has corrupted himself through pollution of his Aryan blood (the "inner" curse) and also because powerful devils, Jews and Marxists (the "outer" curse), seek to overthrow the German god. The religious tone (perverted and bastardized as it is) of *Mein Kampf* is struck on the very first page where Hitler dedicates his "Nazi Bible" to the Nazi "martyrs" who died in defense of their "belief in the resurrection of their people." Thus it is the "fighting priest" who is invoked. The Nazis are to be soldiers of the swastika, just as the Teuton knights of old were soldiers of the cross. They are superior to Catholics and Protestants because they "do," instead of "discuss," the will of God.

The significance of this for the future of the earth does not lie in whether the Protestants defeat the Catholics or the Catholics the Protestants, but in whether the Aryan man is preserved for the earth or dies out. Nevertheless, the two denominations do not fight today against the destroyer of this man, but strive mutually to annihilate one another. The folkish-minded man, in particular, has the sacred duty, each in his own denomination, of making *people stop just talking superficially of God's will, and actually fulfill God's will, and not let God's word be desecrated.*[6]

While social and party relationships among the Nazis are "personal," and the leader is given absolute power over his inferiors, all rights to power are derived from Nazi principles of Aryan brotherhood. In his official relations, the inferior is very "unequal," but he becomes equal as he shares with his superiors the principle of Aryan purity (the earthly manifestation of the Divine Will) which is the glory of the Nazis. And if the inferior must subject himself completely to his superiors, he gains, at the same time, the right to make his superiors "responsible" for his acts. Thus the leader, like the priest, can be used for vicarious atonement. The leader "suffers" for his inferiors, just as in battle every volunteer hero climbs the steps to Valhalla by the holy death of sacrifice. The death of the leader in battle is a crucifixion, just as the killing of Jews, Slavs, Communists, and clergymen in the death camps is not murder, but a *ritual* killing which *cleanses* the polluted blood of Aryans.[7]

The Nazi drama of redemption, terrible as it is, returns man to the center of the stage. He is no longer a plaything of social forces. Hitler even denies the power of economic forces. There are no economic cures for the ills of society. It is only by moral and racial regeneration that society is strengthened. It is only by upholding German codes of honor and sustaining Aryan dignity that a community prospers. The community has nothing whatever to do with any particular economic concept or development. It is not a union of economic contracting parties within a definite limited area to perform economic tasks, but the organization of a community of physically and spiritually similar living beings.

The following theorem may be established as an eternally valid truth: . . . . Never yet has a state been founded by peaceful economic means, but always and exclusively by the instincts of preservation of the species regardless whether these are found in the province of heroic virtue or of cunning craftiness; the one results in Aryan states based on work and culture, the other in Jewish colonies of parasites. As soon as economics as such begins to choke out those instincts in a people or in a state, it becomes the seductive cause of subjugation and oppression.[8]

Hitler's personification of evil in the Jew, and materialization of sin in blood-pollution, is very similar to religious use of the Devil. The Jew, like the Devil, is an international figure. Thus, in conquering him, Germany purifies not only her own land, but the world. But the Devil is also a local figure, and his crimes are seen everywhere. He is pure spirit, a principle of evil who is everywhere and nowhere, by turns. Sometimes he is the grasping financier, at other times the "black-haired Jewish youth [who] lurks in wait for the unsuspecting girl whom he defiles with his blood, thus stealing her from her people."[9] In their "folkish" wisdom the people have divined the true nature of the Jew. They know he hesitates at nothing, and his viciousness becomes enormous; "we need not be surprised that among our people the personification of the Devil as the symbol of all evil assumes the living shape of the Jew."[10] And when the Devil is mentioned, he must be cursed if his power is to be exorcised.

Hitler makes his devil an easily understood and completely materialized being, by associative connections of ideas which are treated as images. That is, the *idea* of the Jew, and the *nature* of "Jewishness," is *dramatized,* and dramatized in images which the masses could understand. Hitler thus describes his first meeting with the Nazi devil. "That they were no water-lovers one could tell from their mere exterior—often, I am sorry to say, even with eyes closed. Later I often grew sick to my stomach from the smell of these caftan-wearers. Added to this was their unclean dress and their generally unheroic appearance." Then Hitler links *physical* and *moral* uncleanliness. "All this could scarcely be called very attractive, but it became positively repulsive when, in addition to their physical uncleanliness, you discovered the moral stains on 'this chosen people'!" The images of filth mount. "Was there any form of filth or profligacy, particularly in cultural life, without at least one Jew involved in it? . . . If you cut even cautiously into such an abscess, you found, like a maggot in a rotting body, often dazzled by the sudden light—a kike!" [11] And thus in this kind of sudden light, the "light of reason" for Hitler, a great burden of guilt fell upon Jewry.

But these images and further variations of them ("these slimy creatures in the pelt of humanity"), while they dehumanize the Jew, do not yet prepare him for his final role as the great evil adversary of the Nazi. The Jew must no longer be ridiculed, for ridicule of an enemy is a poor way to prepare for battle.[12] The next step then, was to make the Jew into a great and powerful Satan who would be a fit adversary for the Aryan God. He must become not only a "caftan-wearer" but a strong, cunning adversary. For without such a foe there would be no battle; without battle, there would be no victory and glory for the Nazis. And thus in Chapter Eleven, "People and Race," which follows the chapter dealing with the causes of the collapse of the German empire, we are shown all the steps whereby the Jew who is first introduced in *Mein Kampf* as unclean, shy, and cowardly gains control of the world. We can see this, Hitler tells us, in Russia "where he killed or starved about thirty million people with positively fanatical savagery, in part amid inhuman tortures, in order to give a gang of Jewish journalists and stock exchange bandits domination over a great people." [13]

HITLER'S RHETORIC AS ALLEGORY

Mein Kampf is a political allegory. What Hitler is saying is not "this is how I suffered," but "this is how I, as a symbol of Germany, suffered."

What Germany suffered, all Aryans suffer, and finally, if the world is to be saved in accordance with the Divine Will, what is done in Germany must be done everywhere. Despite his constant use of "I," Hitler is always speaking of himself as identified with Fate, God, Destiny, or Tradition. Whatever he calls these ultimates, and he has many names for them, they are all summed up in the Divine Will of the Creator, and Hitler is the messenger of God.

Thus, in the very first sentence of *Mein Kampf* we read: "It seems to me providential that Fate should have chosen Braunau on the Inn as my birthplace." He then passes, in the next sentence, to a statement of his mission here on earth. "For this little town lies on the boundary between two German states which we of the younger generation at least have made it our life work to reunite by every means at our disposal." This mission is sacred; "German Austria must return to the great German mother country, and not because of any economic considerations. No, and again, no; even if such a union were unimportant from an economic point of view. Yes, even if it were harmful, it must nevertheless take place." This is because: "One blood demands one Reich." But bringing together all Germans in a common realm will not be easy. "The sword will become our plow, and from the tears of war the daily bread of future generations will grow." [14]

Hitler was not simply born to parents, on a certain date (he does not even mention the date), into a family of brothers and sisters (we learn very little about them). His birth is a portent marked by a star. He has been chosen by Fate to be born in a "frontier city" which is "the symbol of a great task." And then begins a series of identifications which *mount* always from simple topical identification with those struggling with the problems of the day, to identification with angels locked in ethereal battle before the ramparts of heaven. Hitler achieves such mounting from the local to the universal, or from the specific to the general, by relating ideas the way a dramatist relates images. Thus, we hear that the

sins of the so-called "German Reichstag" would alone suffice to cover [the Reichstag] for all times with the curse of the German nation. For the most miserable reasons, these parliamentary rabble stole and struck from the hand of the nation its weapon of self-preservation, the only defense of our people's freedom and independence. If today the graves of Flanders were to open, from them would arise the bloody accusers, hundreds of thousands of the best young Germans who, due to the unscrupulousness of these parliamentarian criminals, were driven, poorly trained and half-trained, into the arms of death; the fatherland lost them and millions of crippled and dead, solely and alone so that a few hundred misleaders of the people could perpetuate their political swindles and blackmail, or merely rattle off their doctrinaire theories.[15]

Chapters, paragraphs, sometimes even sentences flash and ring with struggle. This struggle is told in language familiar to the common people. As Ernest Hanfstaengl tells us:

Hitler had caught the casual camaraderie of the trenches, and without stooping to slang, except for special effects, managed to talk like a member of his audience. In describing the difficulties of the housewife without money to buy the food her family needed . . . he would produce just the phrases she would have used herself to describe her difficulties, if she had been able to formulate them. Where other national orators gave the painful impression of talking down to their audiences, he had this priceless gift of expressing exactly their own thoughts.[16]

But the grandiose structure of Hitler's speech contrasts strangely with the common level of his vocabulary. It is the structure, not simply of a dream, but of melodrama. Heroes and villains, gods and devils, the brave and the cowardly, the strong and the weak, struggle ruthlessly. At the end of these struggles "to the last drop of blood" only the victor survives. No one can be neutral. "He who is not for me is against me." Any middle position is unthinkable. Discussion is not a way to arrive at truth, but a "Jewish trick" to wear down the strength of the hero. Reflection and weighing of ends and means are weaknesses. Like the most popular of all dramatic forms on television, Westerns, politics is a struggle of the "bad guys" against the "good guys." These completely opposite characters are clearly indicated at the very beginning of the drama. As the action develops it becomes a chase, a hunt, which ends in a moment of terrible violence as the hero triumphs.

If the events of the day did not provide an adversary who could be symbolized into a villain, Hitler invented one. He would impersonate an imaginary opponent, often interrupt his own argument with the supposed counter-arguments of his imaginary opponent. And then after completely crushing his supposed adversary he would return to his own line of thought. But this struggle was never local. He told Hanfstaengl: "When I talk to people, especially those who are not yet party members, or who are about to break away for some reason or other, I always talk as if the fate of the nation were bound up in their decision, as if they are in a position to give an example for many to follow."[17]

He begins *Mein Kampf* with images of discord. Parliamentary discussion is not a search for common ground for action by simply trading and haggling for jobs. The clashes of national groups within Austria were "the blood turmoil of individual nationalities." The Austrian parliament was a "wild gesticulating mass screaming all at once in every different key, presided over by a good-natured old uncle who was striving in the sweat of his brow to revive the dignity of the House by violently ringing his bell and alternating gentle reproofs with grave admonitions." [18] Journalists are "intellectual robber barons" who live by "attacking the rest of the world in the most scoundrelly way." The Pan-German movement "sold its soul to Parliament" and "instead of fighting, it learned how to 'speak' and 'negotiate.' " The great masses of the people were not led by "discussion" but only by the "force of speech." All great movements are "volcanic eruptions of human passions, and emotional sentiments, stirred either by the cruel Goddess of Distress or by the firebrand of the word hurled among the masses; they are not the lemonade-like outpourings of literary aesthetes and drawing-room heroes." [19]

The stage of these struggles must always be highly public, and every public drama must be a historical drama. The speech must center on troubles of the moment, but these troubles must be given a historical context, and they must be resolved by invocation of some great transcendent future. The orator who will rule the masses must search in the faces of his audience for some indication of what is bothering them. Once this is discovered the orator must give a historical summary of past events which led up to this problem, dwell on the struggle between heroes and villains in the present, and then paint glowing visions of a future in a land of radiant heroes. The speech must end in passion and glory, and as the band crashes into "Deutschland über alles," the orator must stalk out into the night. He must never linger after his speech, for "argument and discussion can completely undo hours of oratorical labor."

Thus did Hitler make his own life a symbolic life. In a day of science, technology, and materialism, he understood that men live by symbols and relate to each other through kinds of identification which must give them a deep sense of community, based on hatred of a common enemy and love of their comrades. By 1923, five short years after the defeat of Germany, Hitler summed up his rhetoric:

Every individual, whether rich or poor, has in his inner being a feeling of unfulfill-
ment. Life is full of depressing disappointments, which people cannot master. Slum-

bering somewhere is the readiness to risk some final sacrifice, some adventure, in order to give a new shape to their lives. They will spend their last money on a lottery ticket. It is my business to canalize that urge for political purposes. In essence, every political movement is based on the desire of its supporters, men or women, to better things not only for themselves but for their children and others. It is not only a question of money. Of course every workingman wants to raise his standard of living, and the Marxists have cashed in on this, without being able to proceed beyond a given point. In addition, the Germans have a feeling for history. Millions of their countrymen died in the war, and when I appeal for an equal sense of sacrifice, the first spark is struck. The more humble people are, the greater the craving to identify themselves with a cause bigger than themselves, and if I can persuade them that the fate of the German nation is at stake, then they will become part of an irresistible movement, embracing all classes. Give them a national and social idea, and their daily worries will to a large extent disappear. It was Count Moltke who said that one must demand the impossible in order to achieve the possible. Any ideal must appear to a certain extent unrealizable, if it is not to be profaned by the trivia of reality.[20]

Such then was the rhetoric of Hitler, "the rhetoric of hell," as it has been so aptly called. Through his power as orator to the masses he unified the German people, led his armies to the gates of Moscow and Cairo, and finally plunged the world into a long and terrible war. But there was one flaw in his oratorical dramaturgy. *He could not talk to equals.* After 1932, when he began the use of microphones, he heard a new voice booming over audiences now increased by many thousands in great halls. He ended by hypnotizing himself. Serious talk with staffs, searching discussion, careful weighing of issues, the ability to listen carefully to devoted followers who disagreed—all this became impossible. Soon he began to address every audience as a mass audience. The Nazi movement soon became a movement of orators. Only those who could move a mass audience to roars of applause were valued. The whole world was a stage only slightly larger than the Hofbrauhaus or the Sportpalast. At the end, when suffering and death was the lot of Hitler's Germans, he was still making speeches to masses who now existed only in his own fevered imagination. In his last weeks his only audience was himself and a few followers.

POLITICAL ACTION AS TRAGIC RITUAL DRAMA

We have argued, following the tradition of Malinowski, James, Dewey, Mead, and Burke, that expressive forms determine action in society. In the case of Hitler we had a terrible example of this. We think of modern tyranny in terms of force, and we are asked to believe that bigger rockets alone will guarantee our security. But Hitler and Stalin, while they did not neglect arms, realized that the *will to use force* must come first. The first stage of a war was, then, a war of words. Churchill, in turn, realized that the *will to resist* force is born in symbols. On June 18, 1940, he spoke to his people, warning them that they had suffered a terrible defeat at Dunkirk, and now stood alone and unarmed before a mighty enemy. Nothing stood between them and the Nazi hordes but their willingness to stand and die as free men. The far greater armies of France had fallen before Hitler's inspired legions. Churchill spoke to his people, telling them they must be prepared to suffer and die in the cause of freedom, even if their allies, the French, had not. What made the British prepare to stand and die, and what made the few squadrons of the Royal Air Force hurl themselves hour after hour against a far more powerful enemy? *Symbols,* the great moving sentences of Churchill, which moved the will of men to dare and to die, in causes that flamed into reality because they were given *form,* and in this form were *communicated.*

The potency of Hitler's witchcraft was derived from his understanding that social relations are *dramatic* relations. His recipe for his black magic is simple enough. In their differences, estrangements, and enmities, men seek unity, brotherhood, and love. This is not achieved in social "process," or in a "return to equilibrium," but through community dramas of guilt, redemption, victimage, and hierarchy. In such dramas, we do not hide or deny guilt but *confront* it (as the penitent does in confessional, or the patient does in psychoanalysis). Germany *lost* a war, Germans *are* sinning by polluting their blood. They can redeem their defeat by sacrifice of themselves on the battlefield with enemies abroad, or of the scapegoat in "rituals of riddance" at home in the death camps. The French, the Slavs, and all the "inferior" races must be subjugated. Jews, Communists, priests, Socialists, and Liberals must be exterminated at home. And all this can be done only through creating a hierarchy in which every leader, on local as well as national and international levels, represents the will of "Der Führer," who is really the incarnation of the "Divine Will," whom we obey, as we obey all gods, to create and sustain social order.

What were the methods and techniques Hitler used to mount the Nazi drama of community life? *How* was it created? The first step, Hitler tells us, is to create a *physical* center, a place, a stage, a shrine, which as the original place of foundation "[with] its school," will serve as a materialized symbol of unity. "Only the presence of such a place, exerting the

magic spell of a Mecca or a Rome, can in the long run give a movement
a force which is based on inner unity and the recognition of a summit
representing this unity." [21] In forming the first nuclei of the organization,
therefore, care must always be taken not only to preserve the importance
of the idea's place of origin, but to increase it until it is paramount.

The representative act which must be developed into a myth of origin
is the cleansing of German blood through sacrifice. The leaders of the
movement must so train its members that they regard battle not as something casually taught them, but "as the thing that they themselves are
striving for." Displays of violence are necessary because in ruthless attack
upon an adversary the people always see the truth of its own just causes;
and they feel that abstention from destroying the other must mean uncertainty of one's own cause—if not a sign that the cause is unjust. In the
eyes of the people, he who exterminates the enemy of the people is not a
murderer but an avenging angel. "The future of a movement is conditioned by the fanaticism, yes, the intolerance, with which its adherents
uphold it as the sole correct movement, and push it past other formations
of a similar sort." [22]

The means by which people are to be won to battle and sacrifice is the
creation of enemies at home and abroad. Give the people a devil whose
evil can be *materialized,* and thus be understood in reference to the problems of the people. Thus, the Jew and the Communist must become the
embodiment of Germany's ills. All social problems must be *personified,*
just as good leadership must be *personal.* Social systems do not have
"equilibrium" or "disequilibrium," they have heroes and villains who lock
in battles which, like the battles of the gods, decide the fate of the world.
For this reason every attempt must be made to *communicate* the purpose
of the Nazi movement to the largest number of people. The people must
know who their leaders are, and they must know what the leaders intend
to do.

Party rallies must be staged with all the care given to a great pilgrimage,
or to the production of a great movie "spectacular." At all such meetings
the audience must be coached not only in mass songs, marching, display
of flags and banners and dress, but in cheering and yelling, after the
fashion of American college football games.[23] For the people must be
allowed, indeed, *exhorted to participate* through response of every kind.
At the party rallies they must sing, dance, march, and cheer, for political
emotions are essentially primitive emotions and must be formed to satisfy

needs for open and public expression. The party must not assemble in secret, "but march in the open air [with] sounding music and with waving banners."

And, finally, a party must have a principle, a purpose, a world-view. This must never be confused with "a mere perception of what is necessary to a state," or of how a state should look in some kind of planned, scientific utopia. The function of a world-view is to move people to *create* a community, to act, not to prepare for action. Political parties are inclined to compromise and discuss with their adversaries. But a world-view must transcend the idea of party. The Nazi party must not remain a German party among other German parties, but must become a world party through its acceptance of the world-concept of Aryan principles. There can only be one world-concept. And here, the Nazis can "learn by the example of the Catholic Church." For although

its doctrinal edifice, and in part quite superfluously, comes into collision with exact science and research, it is nonetheless unwilling to sacrifice so much as one little syllable of its dogmas. It has recognized quite correctly that its power of resistance does not lie in its lesser or greater adaptation to the scientific findings of the moment, which in reality are always fluctuating, but rather in rigidly holding to dogmas once established, for it is only such dogmas which lend to the whole body the character of a faith. And so today it stands more firmly than ever. It can be prophesied that in exactly the same measure in which appearances evade us, it will gain more and more blind support as a static pole amid the flight of appearances.[24]

Notes

[1] Burke's essay, "The Rhetoric of Hitler's Battle" (reprinted in the Vintage Book edition of *The Philosophy of Literary Form*, 1957), contains many observations of the stylistic aspects of Hitler's rhetoric.

[2] Chapter Four of *The National Socialist Movement*, Vol. II of *Mein Kampf*, is entitled "Personality and the Conception of the Folkish State."

[3] Adolf Hitler, *Mein Kampf*, translated by Ralph Manheim (Boston: Houghton Mifflin Company, 1943), p. 448. Hitler's italics.

[4] *Ibid.*, pp. 449–450.

[5] *Ibid.*, p. 450.

[6] *Ibid.*, p. 562. Hitler's italics.

[7] Himmler spoke of killing Jews as a "delousing" operation.

[8] Hitler, *op. cit.*, p. 153.

[9] *Ibid.*, p. 325.

[10] *Ibid.*, p. 324. The "original" sexual act between Aryans and non-Aryans was the beginning of sin. Now the original tempter, Satan, has taken the form of the Jew who "poisons" German blood through organizing prostitution, seducing "hundreds of thousands" of pure German girls, and spreading syphilis.

[11] *Ibid.*, p. 57. In later passages the Jew is linked to every threat to Nazi Germany—threats such as capitalism, democracy, pacifism, modern art, birth control, journalism, syphilis, poor housing, urbanization, loss of religion, the weakness of the old empire, the democratic habit of doing everything by "half measures," and the defeat of Germany in 1918.

[12] Hitler tells us that he learned this during the First World War, when German troops were greatly disgusted to find their newspapers treating the British and French scornfully as "shop-keepers" who did not know how to uphold a soldier's honor. Britain, Hitler pointed out, made no such mistake. Their treating the Germans as "Huns," who raped, tortured, and murdered at will, was, in Hitler's eyes, a master stroke of propaganda. He points out that men do not fight very hard against enemies they scorn. Troops must go into battle in deep hate, but they must also respect their enemy.

[13] *Ibid.*, p. 326. This is an example of Hitler's "Big Lie" technique.

[14] *Ibid.*, p. 3. The first 17 lines of *Mein Kampf* set the tone for the following 600 pages.

[15] *Ibid.*, p. 272.

[16] Ernest Hanfstaengl, *Unheard Witness* (Philadelphia and New York: J. B. Lippincott Company, 1957), pp. 70–71. Hanfstaengl was one of the few literate members of Hitler's inner circle, in the early days of Hitler's rise to power. Before his break with Hitler and his escape to Switzerland, he spent much time in Hitler's company. His observations on Hitler's oratory are very revealing.

[17] *Ibid.*, p. 283.

[18] Hitler, *op. cit.*, p. 77.

[19] *Ibid.*, p. 107.

[20] Hanfstaengl, *op. cit.*, pp. 283–284.

[21] Hitler, *op. cit.*, p. 347. This is discussed in the pages dealing with the "inner structure" of the Nazi movement, which are included in the chapter, "The First Period of Development of the National Socialist German Workers' Party." This is *not* a history of the early days of the Nazi movement, but a description of *how to found a party*.

[22] *Ibid.*, pp. 349–350.

[23] Hanfstaengl tells us: "It was on another occasion, at the house of Heinrich Hoffman, his photographer friend, that I started playing some of the football marches I had picked up at Harvard. I explained to Hitler all the business about the cheer leaders and college songs and the deliberate whipping up of hysterical enthusiasm. I told him about the thousands of spectators being made to roar, 'Harvard, Harvard, Harvard, rah, rah, rah!' in unison and of the hypnotic effect of this sort of thing. I played him some of the Sousa marches and then my own 'Falarah,' to show how it could be done by adapting German tunes, and gave them all that buoyant beat so characteristic of American brass-band music. I had Hitler fairly shouting with enthusiasm. 'That is it, Hanfstaengl, that is what we need for the movement, marvelous,' and he pranced up and down the room like a drum majorette. After that he had the S.A. band practising the same thing. I even wrote a dozen marches or so myself over the course of the years, including the one that was played by the brownshirt columns as they marched through the Brandenburger Tor on the day Hitler took over power. 'Rah, rah, rah!' became 'Sieg Heil, Sieg Heil!'—that is the origin of it and I suppose I must take my share of the blame." (*Unheard Witness*, pp. 52–53.)

[24] Hitler, *op. cit.*, p. 459.

PART SIX

A Sociological Model of Social Order as Determined by the Communication of Hierarchy

19

Social Order as a Form of Hierarchy

THE STRUCTURE OF SOCIAL HIERARCHY CONSIDERED IN TERMS OF THE
COMMUNICATION OF SUPERIORITY, INFERIORITY, AND EQUALITY

WE HAVE SAID, following Mead and Burke, that society emerges
and continues to exist through the communication of significant symbols.
Through the use of such symbols we identify with each other. We do this
through persuasion of the kind we have discussed in our chapters on
rhetoric—a "New Rhetoric," which has been described as a way of using
symbols to create *identifications*. The *function* of symbols in the creation
of social order has been described in terms of guilt, redemption, victimage,
and hierarchy, while the *structure* of these symbolic acts has been described in terms of Burke's dramatistic pentad of scene, act, agent,
agency, and purpose. The next step in our search for a sociological model
of human relationships based on the function of expressive symbols will
be a discussion of hierarchy. We ask: How do we use symbols to create
and sustain hierarchies which are believed necessary to social order?

We begin by pointing out that a group must have superiors, inferiors,
and equals if it is to function at all. New members must be recruited,
authority distributed, proper ways determined of moving from one status
position to another, old or inadequate members eliminated, and means
provided for equals to resolve their differences. Our feudal heritage and
our modern tyrants have taught us much about the authority of superiors.
The literature on the "leadership principle" is written in confidence possible only to those who can draw from a vast number of illustrations (some
very melancholy indeed) of how superiors rule their inferiors. Our modern
psychologies have much to say about dominance. Zoologists who study
the "social" life of animals tell us that organization into some kind of
stable "pecking order" determines the efficiency of the group, and thus of
the individual. Organized flocks of hens, in which each bird "knows his
place" and is fairly well "resigned" to a particular social status, thrive
better and produce more eggs than those flocks where status is uncertain
and the group in constant turmoil over rank.

Religion stresses a somewhat contrary lesson on hierarchy. We are told that the meek shall inherit the earth. In discussions on monastic life and the way to God, much is said about how humility fosters understanding of God. The fourteenth-century English mystic, Walter Hilton, in his guide to holiness, *The Ladder of Perfection,* teaches that humility is the first step to perfection. "One who cannot utterly despise himself never yet found the humble wisdom of our Lord Jesus." We hear too from military leaders that until we learn to obey we cannot command. Such humility is not a permanent condition of the individual, but a role in which he prepares himself for a higher state. For the promise of humility, as St. Luke states, is a promise of power ("He that humbleth himself shall be exalted.") as well as a reminder to the mighty that their days are numbered ("For whosoever exalteth himself shall be abased. . . ."). These preachments warn us that we *must* learn to be inferior, as well as superior, so that when we rise to power we will know how to rule inferiors of the kind we once were.

And if we follow our previous statements about identification and persuasion, we note that superiors gain and retain their power by *persuading* inferiors that they have a right to rule them. Inferiors in turn, soon learn that there is an art to being an inferior, an art of being ruled, as well as of ruling. Not the least of these arts is that of playing our role as inferiors so well that our superior will play his well. For social order depends on *both* being played well. No general, however grand he may be, can win a battle all by himself. But neither can soldiers, however loyal and brave, win battles without generals. Veteran troops *want,* indeed, *yearn* to be led. Inferiors concerned with their survival are very sensitive about how superiors uphold their dignity, because the office, as well as the man, must be protected. As we were taught in the army: "You salute the uniform, not the man."

Hierarchal relations are sustained through persuasion because superiors, inferiors, and equals *must court* each other. Sometimes they do so in love, often (alas!) in hate, and frequently in irony. For if there is any basic fact about courtship, it is that *the responses of the other necessary to hierarchal satisfaction are never taken, but given.* As Mead tells us in his discussion of the genesis of the self, it is the response of the other which defines my response to myself. In "social climbing" the parvenu must wait until he is admitted; he cannot decide by himself that he is one of the Four Hundred. We are all social climbers wherever there is ambition to achieve a higher rank. We parade and strut before our powerful and mysterious superiors who have power to raise us to their level, in hope that their eye will fall upon us and we will be "tapped" for entry into their exalted ranks.

And even with ambition as a goad, hierarchy arises out of the mere process of growth. We are young and old, male and female, stronger and weaker, pupils and masters, new and old employees. And while it is true that I do not have to wait for my elders to accept me before I grow older, it is also true that all such "natural" stages are translated into social classifications. Human beings are not just simply old in the biological sense. They have "rights" of age, as of property, rank, or sex, and they communicate these rights in ways considered proper to their age. Thus we are constantly being admonished to put away childish things if we are to become men, just as we are reminded that there is no fool like an old fool. Every hierarchy is a development of one stage out of another, and a development which at any given time is both up and down. There is no one form of hierarchy which is inevitable, for the crumbling of hierarchies is as true a fact about their development as is their formation and upward progression.

Hierarchy is always based on some notion of exclusiveness, and as we enact our hierarchal positions in society, we depend greatly on hierarchal mystifications to impress those beneath us with our exalted glory. But the *principle* of hierarchy, the beliefs on which glory is based, is not the exclusive property of any rank. An admiral of the Fleet may move in social circles far above those of the midshipman (as Gilbert and Sullivan remind us in *H.M.S. Pinafore*), yet the *glory* of the admiral as an admiral does not come from his role in high society, but from sharing danger and leading brave men into action against an enemy at sea. A rich businessman may head the trustees of a university (and in America businessmen head a good many), but his fame rests on his ability to boss corporations where money is made, not given away, as at a University where all budgets are studies in what business men call "deficit financing." In American lore, "any damn fool can give money away, but it takes a man to earn it."

The entelechial tendency in hierarchy, whereby the culminating stage supplies the image that represents best the whole "idea" of the hierarchy, comes to light whenever questions are raised over the right of an elite to rule. In every generation discussion arises over why certain families are not included in the Social Register. What exactly, it is asked, do we mean by a social elite? How do they justify their exclusiveness? The Four Hundred, and especially its older members, defend themselves in terms of manners, "good breeding," "taste"—with an occasional reference, as befits a Puritanical society, to good works. Why are their manners any better than other manners? It soon becomes obvious that those on top simply "know" that *they* represent the virtue of the hierarchy and have rights to property, privilege, and rank because *they uphold the principle* of hierarchy on which social order rests. It is impossible to submit such belief to rational inquiry because the "ultimates" by which *any* elite lives are beyond the kind of reason we use ordinarily to explore space, time, and motion.[1]

Those on top tend to deny or cloak division, difference, and disorganization. This is clearly indicated in humor which depends for its point on differences between classes and conditions of men and women. The Negro, so many white people tell us, is different from the white, for he is lazy, shiftless, uninhibited, childish, and improvident. Relations with these "children" must be, after all, relations of clientage. And so we hear in the standard jokes about Negroes by whites,[2] the Negro "confessing" his faults and being "forgiven" in the confession by a master who, after all, does love the Negro and has a "personal" relation to him. Such humor disappears whenever the principle of hierarchy, which must be shared by all to be a binding principle, is so rigidly controlled by superiors that inferiors cannot satisfy their needs and expectations, and equals find the means for staging equality constantly narrowed.[3]

Knowing how to play superior and inferior roles is not enough, as we learn when we make our first attempts to play with children of our own age. To cherish one another in the deeply intimate experience of friendship, or to act together under rules in any kind of peer group, we must learn to be equals as well as superiors and inferiors. In relationships with equals we discover the authority or rules that represent the will of equals. Rules cannot be broken unless we are prepared to destroy the group. For it is only *through* them that equals are bound to each other and *in* them that the group of equals has any existence. The parent I disobey is not destroyed by my disobedience; the family will suffer, but will not be destroyed as a social unit if I violate its rules. But, when I violate rules agreed to by equals, action stops, because the relationships, which existed only in the rules and made the group possible, no longer exist.

When courtship turns to irony and finally to hate, identifications which before had been eagerly sought are now denied, and ways are sought to exorcise the elements of life shared with other classes. What we formerly loved, but now hate, is loaded on the back of some hapless stranger within the community, or an alien race, class, or nation outside the community, and the preparation of the scapegoat is under way.

SOCIAL PASSAGE

How we pass from one social position to another is as important to the preservation of social order as what we do when we get there. Every social institution must provide for transfer among equals, as well as promotion and demotion among superiors and inferiors. Successful change in status position safeguards the individual, as it does the group, by providing safe and proper ways to change status. All changes in status are moments of danger, to both the individual and his society. If an adolescent cannot pass from childhood to youth because his parents will not let him, or he is kept apart from older children, and thus cannot learn what it means to grow up, he cannot mature. If a nation cannot abandon civilian for military life, it cannot win wars.

There are many kinds of social passage. Business brokers create "deals" between buyer and seller. Marriage brokers, ambassadors between states, labor arbitrators, social secretaries who arrange coming-out parties for debutantes and entertainments for parvenus—all derive power from communicating between groups where social distance makes such communication difficult and risky. In American politics, crossing from one political party to another often occurs. Practical politics in America cannot be shackled by what Senator Henry F. Ashurst called the "vice of consistency," for "Whoever in his public service is handcuffed and shackled by the vice of consistency will be a man not free to act as various questions come before him from time to time: he will be a statesman locked in a prison house the keys to which are in the keeping of days and events that are dead."

Humor itself is a kind of bridge, a passage by incongruity from one view to another which society provides as an escape from the crushing weight of traditions or the painful anxiety developed by conflicting loyalties. In humor we travel incognito, so to speak. The serious, pious, majestic self can become merry, impious, and wise. Such transfigurations of role within the self, as well as between the self and others, are changes of identity. We must believe deeply in what mystics call the "transcendent fact" of our social principles, but we must keep ways for passage open for times when traditional principles become useless or destructive. The forms of passage offered in humor, the many ways we reverse rank, the inner Saturnalia and the Feast of the Fools which humor brings to the soul are not simply ways of "relieving tension" but of keeping social bridges in good repair. Without such bridges we become islands, and the self is powerless until new ways of reaching real others are established.

Passage from one social position to another may be very slow, as in reincarnation, or very swift, as in plutocratic "climbing." But the difference between the Hindu and American social ladder is one of degree. Both believe social movement from a lower to a higher, a higher to a lower, and among equal positions takes place in some kind of hierarchal progression. American symbols of social position are no more "materialistic" than those of the Hindu. For the Hindu, matter negates spirit, and since money is matter, money negates spirit. For the American, money does not negate, but embodies the spirit. The Hindu may point out the apparent nonsense (to him) of belief in an ever-increasing standard of living where satisfaction is measured only by having more of what we had, yet which could not have been very satisfactory or we would not want to change it. But the American points out, too, how nonsensical it is to teach toleration of suffering, starvation, and death as moments in a progression toward a future life whose benefits can never be tested, yet whose present miseries are obvious to all.

In social passage, the past and the future are not "time" any more than places are "environments." They are images and ideas which determine the form and the content of social relations in a present. The living room is for adults, not children. To enter this room one must be clean, quiet, and polite. Here in this great room, the abode of the family gods, I must be wary. For here I learn what it means to be an adult. I must learn this to become one myself in that mysterious far-off time when I too will be grown up. My parents control this future and discipline me in terms of it. Even when tradition is invoked to legitimize discipline, it is followed because it leads to a desired future. The future, like the past in Edenic myths of original sin, or evolutionary theories of genesis, is socially effective only to the degree it infuses the present with the reality of things to come.

We create myths, traditions, and histories to help us act with more confidence in the present. The past must be ordered. Family traditions must be kept in good repair. Grandparents must behave properly and be respected deeply, for they are guardians of a past which inspires confidence and pride. American traditions contain no struggle between gods, demons, or spirits. Our society originates in the debates of the founding fathers and was reborn in Lincoln-Douglas debates.[4] Our social paradise (as well as our courts and legislature) is well stocked with lawyers. Our struggle between good and evil is a forensic drama; justice, we believe, is reached through open and free debate before impartial juries and devoted citizens. Social order is not "discovered" but created, and will be created again, in such debate. Our political god speaks, not simply through the voice of the people, but through the voice of partisans searching for agreement through reasoned discourse.

As described in Arnold Van Gennep's classic study, rites of passage first cut off the person from earlier social attachments, then pass him through a period of isolation, and finally introduce him into a new social world or reintegrate him into the old one. These rites are always solemn, and sometimes great pain is inflicted to test the courage and endurance of the candidate. The anticipation of pain, of having to endure fearsome meetings with ghosts or spirits, makes all who must undergo such ceremonies take them very seriously. The boy must realize how necessary warriors are to his society; the girl, how important marriage is for orderly familial relations in her society. And since we all must die, we must prepare for death in such a way that our loved ones and the whole community can overcome their sense of loss at our departure.

Anthropologists tell us much about initiatory rites and ceremonies which accompany passage from childhood to manhood, from virginity to marriage, and from life to death. The purpose of all such rites is to prepare the individual for his new role and to change his name, so that the members of his society will know that they must act toward him in a new way. Van Gennep [5] distinguishes three phases in all rites of passage: separation, transition, and incorporation. Rites of separation are prominent in funeral ceremonies, rites of incorporation at marriages, while rites of transition are used at birth. Often, of course, all three are used in the same ceremony. Thus the new-born baby is *separated* from its mother, *incorporated* into the family and the tribe, and is *transmitted* through baptism, or some such ceremony, from a biological to a social identity.

In so far as we experience time in passing from one position to another, it is related to acting in a present. The past we recall and the future we envision are necessary to what we are trying to do in the present. That is, I do not recall a past, or call up a future, to judge their truth or falsity, but to inspire me with confidence in my ability to do what I want to do and to endure the hardships of what must be done. In this sense "pasts" and "futures" are not so much true or false, as relevant or irrelevant to what we are trying to do. On the purely symbolic level, we search the past and the future for help in *naming* things and events, because until we do so we do not know how to act toward them and thus have no control over them. Changing names is always a risk, and such moments of passage from one name to another must be handled with great care.

For, say what we will, we are all haunted by fears of passage from virginity to marriage, from boyhood to manhood, and from life to death. Hierarchal passage may not be as intense as the passage from life to death (although we do hear of shame over social failure causing death), but it is intense enough. All can recall moments of deep apprehension over ability to behave properly with our superiors, inferiors, and equals.[6] We know too that our secret longings to be admitted to certain kinds of relationships can be very intense. And while hierarchal passage may not be as intense as other forms of passage, it is much more frequent. We are born once, we marry but a few times at most, and our death is final, but we move from positions of superiority, inferiority, and equality many times during our lives. In complex societies where we play many roles, we often pass from one position to another several times a day.

Passage is never easy; indeed, for some individuals it is so fearful that it is avoided at all costs. Thus we read in Stekel's *Patterns of Psychosexual Infantilism* of individuals who take to their beds and demand to be treated like infants. Stekel explains such regression in terms of sex, but the phenomena of regression indicate (whether or not we accept Stekel's explanation) that something went wrong in the *social passage of the individual*. He did not want to grow up because there was no means provided for him to do so. The mother who keeps her son in bed with her for many years may be seducing him, but she is also refusing him the *social* experience necessary to passage from boyhood to manhood. For passage, like any aspect of hierarchy, cannot be undertaken by the individual alone. He must pass from one position to another in ceremonies where status change is dramatized. The individual must abandon his old role and be renamed, so that his society will know how to act toward him in his new role. The individual, in turn, must feel that he has a right to his new role.

We move from one position to another through *dramas* of passage. As we move, we change *scenes*. Up to a certain age children live at home in intimate and daily contact with their parents, then they are separated and given their own quarters. As puberty nears, boys are separated from the girls. But in these same years they have also been learning to play with other children in the neighborhood. Such play involves leaving one scene, the home, to enter another, the play place. There are also other stages outside the home. These are the school and the place of work. Thus each passage is a passage from one stage to another. These stages must be carefully prepared, and the individual must be given proper cues for his entrances and exits.

But no matter how well we play our parts in all the great traditional dramas of social life, we know that soon we must prepare to pass into some new and strange stage of life. For the group, as for the individual, life means death, just as death means life. We separate and we are united, we change roles, we die and we are reborn. Nature, too, changes and passes. Summer passes into autumn, autumn into winter, winter into spring, and the spring burgeons once again into summer. As individuals we pass from the day into the night—sometimes a fearful passage, haunted by monsters so terrible that we awaken in anguish and agony. Sleep has been called a kind of death, but it is also a moment of profound passage in which we struggle to attain a new day, so we can banish the fantasies of the night and relate to our fellow beings in society.

All moments of passage are difficult. For in the drama of passage we must kill off the old, prepare to enter the new, and finally begin our new life. All that we have known and cherished must pass away. As the time of death draws near, we know that our domination of those younger, less favored by fortune, subordinate because of sex, race, or education will not last. Soon I will grow old and feeble. I will be killed off (socially if not physically) by delegates of the community who regard my enfeeblement as a threat to their survival. As I pass into old age I must come to terms with my waning powers. My sons will supplant me as family leaders, women will turn to younger men, the young scholars I loved so deeply with all the passion of my mind will turn to others. Soon I will be retired from my office, and my role taken away from me, in ceremonies where those younger and stronger increase the poignancy of my replacement since they exalt the majesty of my role at the same time they banish me from it forever.

THE PRESENTATION OF SOCIAL ROLES AND
SOCIAL ROLES AS A FORM OF HIERARCHY

Institutions, like individuals, must parade and display their glamor, if they are to keep their glory alive. Communities do this in ceremonies, feasts, parades, and exhibitions of all kinds. Superiors, inferiors, and equals use these ceremonies as social stages to display themselves before audiences whose approval sustains their position in the local hierarchy. Thus all such days are a dramatization, and hence a communication, of authority. The content of such ceremonies may be quite various, as when we pass from honoring the dead on Memorial Day to the honoring of military valor on Veterans' Day. Yet in all such ceremonial days, superiors, inferiors, and equals are assigned their positions in terms of some scale of honor, and each displays himself in the community drama according to his right in the hierarchy.

As W. Lloyd Warner points out in his study of the ritualization of the past, anniversary celebrations in a community are a dramatization by the citizens of what they believe themselves to be. In describing Yankee City rites, he tells us: "Five days were devoted to historical processions and parades, to games, religious ceremonies and speeches by the great and near great. At the grand climax a huge audience assembled to watch the townsmen march together 'as one people' in a grand historical procession. This secular rite, through the presentation of concrete historical incidents, stated symbolically what the collectivity believed and wanted itself to be."[7] As the great Tercentenary Procession passed before the reviewing stand, Yankee City was enacting the meaning of its community life to the general public gathered along the street and the city's official representatives on the reviewing stand. At this moment "the collectivity officially accepted the significance of the signs that it had fashioned and now offered publicly to its ceremonial leaders: the sign-maker accepted his own signs in self-communion."[8]

In such community dramas every institution links itself to the sacred values which are believed to uphold social order in the community. This is done by staging—on floats, in pageants and masques, or in large auditoriums—how the community met various crises and the role played by various institutions in this. A certain kind of act is depicted as the mystical moment of institutional or community origin. Thus in such pageantries we see brave soldiers holding the fort against the Indians, honest traders sheltering wagon trains pushing westward, or stern Pilgrims on their knees before God asking for his blessings on their new commonwealth.

Such community presentations serve to *enact* the charter of the society. Like savages dancing the story of their tribe, the inhabitants of Yankee City acted out in expressive forms the *meaning* of their community. But it is *dramatic,* not historical, economic, or political meaning. We find the 42 floats arranged in a *developmental, not simply a sequential order.* The first four floats depict the time of creation, "Before Man Came." The next two floats in Period II depict "The Beginnings of Life on the New Earth." "The Early Fathers" are shown in the next eight floats of Period III. The struggle for independence is shown in the eight floats of Period IV, "The New Nation." In Period V the drama of the procession reaches its climax —as the title of the next eight floats, "Climax: The Power and the Glory," indicates. In the next nine floats, dramatic action falls from the moment of glory to "The Aftermath to Greatness" (Period VI). The two floats of the finale, Period VII, are entitled simply "We Endure." [9]

Warner argues that the historical accuracy of these floats has little to do with their meaning to the citizens of Yankee City.[10] For the meaning of life in Yankee City is dramatic meaning, which can be understood only by how the people enact their roles in the various kinds of social staging which is put on during the "sacred festivals" of the year. The *form* of such dramas, the ways in which the story of Yankee City is communicated, the characters selected as villains and heroes, the kind of acts they perform to bring Yankee City into being, the means they used to achieve a sense of community, and finally the values and ends which Yankee City upholds—these *are* the meaning of Yankee City. Warner's argument that people experience their community life through expressive symbols reduces economic, political, and historical events to communicative events which must be studied in terms of their *communicative* function and structure.[11]

The reenactment of these moments of community origin on holidays and days of celebration is also a kind of social catharsis. As we play our parts we are purged of fear and anxiety over waning community strength. When every dramatic element (scene, act, actors, agency, and purpose) is presented well, a deep feeling of social euphoria is created, as we see in the suffering, death, and resurrection of Christ. In this drama the human community dies and is reborn, the power of Christianity and its church becomes the power of community among men, for now all men are brothers in Christ. There are epics of creation in the words of the Bible, the painting of Michelangelo, the music of Bach and Haydn. Great Christian stages for the enactment of faith have been created in St. Paul's cathedral, Chartres, and Notre Dame. Christian saints and sinners (but Christian still, even in sin) compose the greatest pantheon of heroes we possess. Christians are offered ways to holiness through liturgy and prayer, they are inspired and coached in acts of compassion and atonement, and in the final mystery of the Beatitudes made aware of the great mercies of Christian life.

Ceremonial enactments of community or institutional moments of origin tell us much about power. Whoever controls such ceremonies controls the community. Religious, political, commercial, and cultural institutions seek control through identifying their power with community survival. Thus we hear of community origins in struggle between gods, battles between heroic warriors, political debates on the rights of man, or critical discussions on the wisdom of life. But whatever the myth, those who control its *enactment* have great power over us, because they control the staging, and thus the communication, of authority. If a holy day is turned over to businessmen who create a community drama of purchased gift exchange, it matters little what we tell children in our schools about the Pilgrims, the founding fathers, or the cavalier. The trader controls our community because he controls communication. The community drama he mounts is a drama of buying and selling, and soon we are spending our way to heaven.

The pageantry of social life, wherein we present ourselves to each other in our social roles, is enacted to create confidence in the efficacy of hierarchy to uphold social order. In parades, ceremonies, holidays, festivals, parties, indeed, in every social act, authority is *dramatized* because this is the way authority is glamorized. In Britain alone, more than 60 important public ceremonials are performed throughout the year. At the state opening of Parliament, the Queen proceeds from Buckingham Palace to the Palace of Westminster to deliver a speech from the throne to the House of Lords. Ancient sounds and heraldic colors mark the approach of the royal procession. Hoofbeats ring on the pavement, swords slap on leather as the Life Guards, brilliant in white breeches and plumed hats, provide an escort. In this drama of hierarchy few see the Queen but all see symbols of her sovereignty. Those who hear her speak want no rational disquisition on the relationships between crown and state. Her "loyal subjects" yearn for the *enactment* of kingship, for in such celebration common bonds are created and sustained.

In America there are daily and hourly enactments of earning and spending money. In print, film, radio, and television, thousands of actors spend vicariously for millions who yearn to spend properly and thus become successful Americans. The great fair, once annual or seasonal, is now a daily and hourly "sale." We are cajoled, exhorted, even frightened into buying. Sexual and financial success (so deeply linked in America) will be ours only if we buy the right clothes, the right car, the right house. In the greatest holiday of the American year, Christmas, the reaffirmation of community bonds is acted out in commercial pageants known as "Christmas shopping." The enactment of American brotherhood is turned over to businessmen who create plutocratic dramas of buying and selling which rise to frenzy as millions of shoppers jam through stores and streets to "last-minute gift counters."

We use such symbolic expressions not to "define" or to "celebrate" already existing social bonds, but to *create* them. As people dance and parade together a deep sense of community is born. Shiva as Nataraja, Lord of Dancers, or King of Actors, does not dance to give pleasure but to maintain the life of the cosmos, and to create or enliven the community bonds of his followers. Without the arts of social presentation there would be no community because the sentiments, attitudes, and values necessary to consensus could not be created without them. "Economic laws" do not "determine" Christmas spending. On the contrary, Christmas spending determines economic laws. As we spend we create attitudes toward money which make it possible for us to discipline our lives in terms of money. As we exchange purchased gifts we define degrees of intimacy and social responsibility. As we give to charities we purge the symbol of money. Cleansed and purified through its use for the common good, money can be used again with an easy conscience. As the New Year wanes we return wholeheartedly to the "money game" with little individual concern over the social meaning of the game, because the symbols with which the game is played have been purified of individual greed and have been identified with community good.

MANNERS AND SOCIAL ORDER

The community stages itself in great ceremonies, feasts, parades, on days
set aside for the pomp and circumstance of community life. The individual stages himself through manners. Through dress, gesture, speech,
bearing, he indicates to others, and thus to himself, where he belongs or
wants to belong in his society. He creates stages for himself in his home
and selects those which will set him off to advantage in his public appearance. Thus we can say that all manners are a dramatization of the self,
a way of telling others how we want to be regarded, and in turn how we
regard them. For in manners we live through the responses of others.
These others may be real or they may be imaginary, but they must be
addressed, and we must develop skill in such address if we are to succeed
in the enactment of our social roles.

Manners are the daily language of hierarchy. Manners keep inferiors
"in their place," uphold the majesty of superiors and sustain familiarity
and ease among equals. They are a performance, and like all performances
judged well or ill in terms of style. Everyone bows to a lady, but our
degree of gentility is judged by how well we bow. Every politician assures
us that he is one of the people, but we believe him only if his style of
identification with the people is convincing.

Manners reach purely *formal* moments of social expression in greeting,
addressing, and leave-taking, the rhythmic pantomime of purely *social*
moments in our relationships. Superiors, familiars, and inferiors alike
must use these forms properly. For in the presentation of the self to others
our skill (as well as our "right") in purely social forms of expression give
us rank.

Manners, decorum, and taste are very different from ritual. They are
an *individual* expression of group forms of expression. No one is honored
for his taste because it is the same as everybody's taste, yet, at the same
time, no one is honored if his taste goes so far beyond the expression of
the group that he makes group norms of expression meaningless or ridiculous. Even Beau Brummell, who could tell a prince how to dress, could
vary but not destroy existing fashion. Individuals establish few social
forms. At best they refine and polish gestures which have long been current. Even an absolute monarch must return greetings properly and in
good style. Like all of us he strives to make his greeting a communica-

tion of what he thinks our place to be, and in turn, of how he wants us to regard him. Thus Saint-Simon tells us of Louis XIV:

Never was man so naturally polite or of a politeness so measured, so graduated, so adapted to person, time, and place. Toward women his politeness was without parallel. Never did he pass the humblest petticoat without raising his hat; even to chambermaids, that he knew to be such, as often happened at Marly. For ladies he took his hat off completely, but to a greater or less extent; for titled people, half off, holding it in his hand or against his ear some instants, more or less marked. For the nobility he contented himself by putting his hand to his hat. He took it off for the Princes of blood, as for the ladies. . . . His reverences, more or less marked, but always light, were incomparable for their grace and manner, even his mode of half raising himself at supper for each lady who arrived at table.

Every group—polished aristocrats and street gangs of toughs alike—has standards of "good form." Rules of politeness, being a "regular fellow," the pomp and ceremony of courts, euphemisms in speech, elegant ways of greeting—these seem to lack the great weight of law, tradition, and prophecy in the organization of social life. The mutability of fashion (in all kinds of expression, not only clothes) makes it seem less important than tradition. But, as La Rochefoucauld reminds us, decorum is the least, yet the most obeyed, of all law. A style of dress or a taste in furnishings so affect people that we use the word "rage," in the sense of mania, to define their sudden and overwhelming power. We laugh at fashions of another time, but we do not ridicule rules and fashions of our time so long as we use them to indicate differences in rank and social position we think necessary to social order.

Anger over the ill manners of others arises out of belief that not following our manners is a way of telling us that we are not really important in the eyes of the transgressor. We excuse a *faux pas* made out of ignorance (and soon corrected) because we still feel the importance of our manners as a social bond. We laugh at comic depictions of vulgarity so long as the majesty of what we hold important is not threatened. But we do not laugh at savage ridicule or continued vulgarity, because they endanger the social principle upon which our manners are based.

When we know the limits of gentility, manners excite us, for, like all limits, they are a warning of where to expect novelty, risk, and danger. We address a certain woman as a lady, but a sudden rush of lustful fantasy, or of humor over incongruities of love among animals who would be gods, excites us to say things some ladies might not approve. We smile politely at those who greet and talk with us, but we watch for violations of good taste. We hear ourselves about to say exactly the opposite of what we intend to say, or saying in fun what we mean seriously. We fix limits of decorum but it is the approach to, not the avoidance of, these limits that excites us, just as it is the resolution, not the avoidance, of social tension that brings a sudden rush of pleasure. When we must act in certain ways, as at a party where one prescribed act follows another, or when we must address a superior only as superior, we are soon bored.

Through manners and fashion we keep our social world open to change. Perhaps this is why the individual is permitted to vary forms of expression which the group has approved. In the realm of the sacred there can be little variation. Ritual, not manners, determines sacred hierarchal address. In sacred moments we address the office, not the individual. We want no change, for such change may offend the gods. Thus when we address a bishop, a general, or a college president we are careful to inquire how he should be addressed and to repeat carefully what we have been told. Where there is great social distance between superiors and inferiors such address becomes a kind of incantation or prayer. But the superiors too must be equally careful in such sacred moments. Any change in dress, gesture, speech, or scene, destroys confidence in the power of the sacred leader.

But social supremacy is not won alone by weight of rank, tradition, office, and the right to invoke the supernatural. At Versailles, the king and his courtiers could add majesty and glory to manners, but they could not add wit, gaiety, and fun. Improvisation in dress, in speech, any free and open expression of the self was impossible. For who could argue with a Sun King? The glory of Versailles was in submission to the principle of kingship. Courtship was a way to the king, who in turn was a way to God. Manners could not remain manners but became ritual; they were an expression of devotion to a supernatural power. Such address becomes a form of beseechment, not a free and open expression of the self.

There are gods of manners, just as there are gods of religion and the state. Such gods, called "dandies" in English, dignify and eventually deify manners. But they do this not by conforming to group norms of taste, but by creating norms of their own which the group adopts. For in manners, as in all else, the individual and not the group creates. The dandy, as Baudelaire (himself a dandy in his younger days) tells us, forms "a sort of cult of oneself" even though he is bound by the group he must address if he is to enjoy his cult of self.[12] That is, while he refuses to conform to group norms of expression, and indeed finds them "vulgar," he needs the group as an audience to his elegance and inventiveness. And the group, in turn, needs him, because he keeps fashion and all the arts of social expression open to change, and the group, like the individual, must be prepared to change. Because of this we honor those skilled at meeting new needs, as well as those skilled in upholding tradition and the sacred.

It is often said that dandies are "useless." But if the cultivation of manners is useless, then all social life becomes nonsense. For what the dandy and the fashion leader glorify, and indeed deify, is elegance—the elegance of social expression which lifts the purely social moments of life into high art. We know that we are men of society, as well as politics, business, religion, education. We know that even in politics, business, sex, and religion we will relate to each other through forms considered proper to the occasion. As the businessman who scorns the arts of dress will tell, in every "big deal" and in "contacting" the rich and powerful, manners can "make or break" the deal. Thus in even our most practical moments we depend on those highly skilled in manners to refine and polish the forms we use to address each other in our social roles.

But, however "efficient" (in a purely hierarchal sense) manners may be, there is a final mystification in them which transcends their social reference. We know we must learn to be easy with our familiars, majestic to our inferiors, and modest with our superiors. But in the great art of manners there is a kind of playfulness which indicates that the final power of manners is their ability to create a kind of social euphoria which binds us together simply because we *are* together. Manners are not alone in this, of course. But enough has been said about religion, economics, and politics as sources of our social bonds. In manners, in fashion, in all the arts of personal addresses we act out *as individuals* what we want to be in terms of the *purely social content of experience*.

Notes

[1] Such ultimates are *not* beyond dramatic reason, as we hope to show in later discussion.

[2] We do not yet have many openly told Negro jokes about whites. When we do, we will learn much about what it means to be a Negro in America.

[3] When meetings for discussion are suspect, private clubs infested with spies, and protocol for social events determined by political, evangelical, or any other powers not willing to submit to purely social norms, humor becomes sardonic and bitter, and passes into caricature and the grotesque.

[4] The reenactment of these as sacred community dramas is just beginning in Illinois.

[5] Arnold Van Gennep, *The Rites of Passage*, translated from the French by Monika B. Vizedom and Gabrielle L. Caffee, with an introduction by Solon T. Kimball (London: Routledge & Kegan Paul, 1960). This was first published in 1909.

[6] What we call "stage fright" is an example of this. In society, where ambition is normal, there is great concern with how to get along with superiors, but we must learn, too, how to get along with equals and inferiors.

[7] This is from Part II of *The Living and the Dead: A Study of the Symbolic Life of Americans*, by W. Lloyd Warner (New Haven: Yale Univ. Press, 1959), p. 107.

[8] *Ibid.*, p. 108.

[9] The title of each float and their groupings into various periods are given in "Table I, The Procession" on p. 131 of *The Living and the Dead*.

[10] The various interpretations of the charter of Yankee City tell us much about shifts and changes in authority.

[11] A comparison between Warner's book and the Middletown studies of Robert S. Lynd and Helen Merrell Lynd will indicate the great difference between Warner's approach and the conventional interpretation of community life in terms of economic and political factors.

[12] In his discussion of the dandy in "The Painter of Modern Life," Baudelaire says: "Dandyism arises especially in periods of transition, when democracy is not yet all-powerful and aristocracy is only partially tottering or brought low. In the disturbance of such periods a certain number of men, detached from their own class, disappointed and disoriented, but still rich in native energy, may form a project of founding a new sort of aristocracy, which will be all the more difficult to break because it will be based on the most precious and indestructible of human powers—on those celestial gifts that neither toil nor money can bestow." See *The Essence of Laughter and Other Essays, Journals, and Letters*, by Charles Baudelaire, edited, selected, and introduced by Peter Quennell (New York: Meridian Books, 1956), pp. 48–49.

20

The Communication of Hierarchy

MODES OF COURTSHIP: ACCEPTANCE, REJECTION, AND DOUBT

N o o n e is always superior, equal, or inferior. An absolute dictator, whose word determines life or death, may be scolded by his mistress, snubbed by his consort, disobeyed by his children, or humbled by his priests. Differential status positions are common to all societies, not to democracy alone. Fixed positions of superiority, inferiority, or equality are impossible when social relations are intimate and personal, because in such relationships we play many roles, and we must shift quickly from one to another. Even our experience of hierarchy in highly "official" moments is governed far less by fixed status positions than their expression indicates.

Dislike and hatred of authority rise within us even as we express devout loyalty. Enemies evoke deep compassion—as we are about to destroy them. We struggle to suppress bursts of merriment in the midst of solemn ceremony. A chaotic whirl of images and ideas swarms through us, moods shift and change swiftly and intensely. The order and precision of military drill suddenly become a grotesque pantomime whose rigidity oppresses us as we long for the freedom of walking and talking together. Only in the abrupt shifts of imagery and mood in dance and music, where rage and serenity follow in swift yet harmonic progression, do we find anything similar to the fleeting intensity of the conscious and unconscious states we experience in our relations as superiors, inferiors, and equals.

Anxiety over the responses of others, necessary to us for understanding ourselves, haunts us throughout life. As children we do not want our parents to give us things, but to *communicate* with us. We do not know what we are, just as later in adulthood we cannot be sure of what we are, until others significant to us tell us. We prefer punishment to indifference, as later in life we prefer hate to neglect, because even in the pain of punishment or hate we feel that we really exist. The intellectual condemned to die for treasonable utterances against the state faces death with pride and honor. Like Socrates, he believes that his death will affect the future acts of his countrymen. But the intellectual who is not taken seriously enough to be asked how to think about schools, governments, or armies, cannot even be sure of the reality of thought. If he is not asked to think, and yet must think to live, the incongruities between his individual needs and his role soon become unbearable.

We resent deeply those who will not give us the responses we need to play our hierarchal roles. We are like actors who exist only in the responses of audiences, which allow them to play many and varied roles. We enjoy domination, but we need, too, the experience of submission and equality. I want to be master, but I also want to follow great leaders, to cherish a wise father, to devote myself to great principles, and finally to submit to some power which makes death meaningful. I want equals, for only with equals can I play and joke, and discuss openly problems which I cannot discuss with superiors or inferiors. However noble my superiors and however dutiful my inferiors, I still need to commit myself to a friend. For only among friends can we express openly what we are as individuals, as well as members of a group. Indeed, in friendship we demand individuality, for friendship, like all relationships, is born and sustained in communication. In private, intimate talk, we respond to the private and individual self of a friend, as he does to ours, and thus a self we cannot express to distant superiors or inferiors is born.

I seldom am sure of how others "really" regard me. I witness within myself sudden and violent changes in how I regard others. Even within groups of long standing some members are strange to each other. And since social position is given, it can be taken away. Because of this we struggle to keep our forms of social appeal within the group in good order. We censure bad manners when we believe they threaten our group roles. The neighbor who sends his maid to say he is too ill to see me, the guest who begs off from our dinner because of the sudden arrival of relatives, the hundred and one white lies we all use, are approved because their use preserves the group. An insult, unlike the white lie, requires one individual to take a stand against another. Either he goes or I do. The common front of the group is endangered.

We need an audience to enjoy our hate, as well as our love of each other. We do not simply reject others, and then walk away in indifference. Indeed, in small intimate groups, such as the family, we cannot escape those we hate. Nor perhaps, do we really want to. For there is great pleasure in using those who hate us as an audience to our grandeur. Perhaps this is why there is an air of complicity about two people, or groups, who hate each other. Each tries to lure the other into being his audience, for until he has a real audience he cannot act out his hate, but must submerge it within the self. This is painful, sometimes indeed, unendurable. As we lie in bed alone at night, seething with rage, we rehearse in fantasy what we yearn to do in reality. And if such hate is not to destroy us, it must be expressed in some way before those who cause it.

We all become connoisseurs of manners significant to our group because through their use we obtain our rank within the group. Thus all manners are a kind of plea. We judge according to the style of appeal being made, the conditions under which it is made, and the audience for which it is intended; in short, in terms of how it is *staged*. We communicate differently to those within and without the group, just as we communicate differently to superiors, inferiors, and equals. Yet, whatever the audience, we struggle to perfect our *forms* of hierarchal address, for such forms are an identification, an indication to others and to ourselves of where we want to belong in our group.

HIERARCHAL IDENTIFICATION

The individual must conform to group styles, for such conformity is an indication to superiors of his desire to be accepted by them. But simple conformity is no longer enough when he is accepted by his superiors as one of them. Now he is among equals (as well as superiors and inferiors), and to be equal he must do more than simply play his "official" role as a member of the group. He must become an individual, because only individuals can be equal, as we see in the dialogue of conversation where the "I" responds to a "Thou."

Individuality also flourishes in the spontaneity and mutability of fashion and style. The playfulness of fashion, unlike the solemnity of ritual or the rigidity of public and official roles, lightens the weight of tradition and the staleness of custom and restores individuality to our relationships. As Castiglione tells us, the courtier must be just, noble, and kind, but he must also possess a "grace" which springs out of spontaneity (*sprezzatura*) by which a gentleman "can conceal all artificiality and appear to do everything without design, and as it were, absentmindedly." The courtier must not be content to imitate others, even those of greater charm and address than himself.

The individual must treat style as a variation, not as a theme. To vary a hat style is one thing, to wear a hat so absurd that all hats become ridiculous, or to ban hat-wearing as a sign of the Devil, is another. We may even do without hats, for to do *exactly* the opposite is a kind of inverse imitation. The arbiter on manners, whatever he is called—"gentleman," "master of protocol," or "fashion leader"—refines and polishes gestures of deference, superiority, and equality, but always within clearly understood limits, for no matter how elegant we long to be, our elegance must be understood if we are to enjoy it.

However great the wealth, holiness, beauty, or wisdom of individuals in their official roles, they must subordinate themselves to the purely social demands of hierarchal pantomime when they meet with each other as individuals. As they bow to others, chat together, and take their leave, individuals become aware of a new quality in their relationships. In such moments, social forms free themselves from any meaning beyond their purely social meaning. Even in the solemn moment of death, a funeral becomes a drama of mourning where styles of behavior are approved or disapproved because they indicate degrees of "refinement," not of bereavement. The widow who breaks down in tears and hurls herself onto the grave leaves little doubt of her sorrow, but a great deal about her sense of propriety. The pomp of funerals has more regard to the vanity of the living than the honor of the dead.

We are accustomed to hierarchal pantomime in art and play, where differences in social station are used to charge characters and situations with glamor and mystery. As we watch children play "grownup" we delight in their unconscious parody of what we are. All this, we say, is but fantasy and play. But in the mysterious moments of association when style of dress, speech, greeting, and bearing suddenly affect us deeply and give relationships a deeply social tone, we are very close to the artist who relates forms as forms, with little concern for their immediate content. In every profession we pose and act in what we think others will accept as the "social side" of our "professional role." A surgeon operates but a fraction of the time he spends in his role as surgeon. Few really can judge his competence as surgeon (and even these cannot communicate their judgment beyond the small circle of hospital authorities), but nurses, fellow physicians, hospital administrators, students, and even patients judge him by how well or poorly he plays his role as surgeon.

Style is a social *identification,* and we are dependent on skilled creators of forms for our symbols of identification. In every group certain individuals try to polish and refine social forms of expression. The clever adolescent, the ironic criminal, and the foul-mouthed soldier are no different from the gentleman or lady in their search for better ways to express forms of identification with each other. All such forms are justified so long as their use identifies individuals under some principle of hierarchy. Differences of rank are not thought of as individual and subjective expressions of power, but as roles necessary to identification within the group. All Christians, bishops and vestrymen alike, are equal in the eyes of other Christians because they are all equal before God. Presidential candidates and new citizens are equal before the ballot box. On election day the voice of the people becomes the voice of God. Judge, jury, lawyers—the condemned man himself—are humbled alike before the majesty of the laws. Insignia of office have weight in and of themselves. "The office makes the man"; "When God gives a man an office, he gives him brains enough to fill it"; "A dog's obeyed in office"—are proverbial recognitions of this. We do not question a policeman's knowledge of law, we obey his uniform.

The group functions on a much lower level than the individual, and only those aspects of personality which are common to all can be communicated. It is the simple and not the complex and profound aspects of hierarchal communication which predominate. American business proverbs sum this up by saying: "No one ever lost a buck by underestimating public taste." The devout are not moved by the meaning of religious rites, but by the manipulation of commonly understood holy symbols. The young student cannot prove to himself—or others—the validity of his science, but he feels highly scientific as he manipulates mathematical formulas, punches buttons on calculators, or checks computations with his slide rule. The teachings of a great master *must* be reduced to slogans and clichés (which often parody his teachings) if they are to be made communicable to all.

No system stresses the importance of office, and the hierarchal trappings of office, more than democracy. The equal right of all to occupy almost any office and the assumption that no man is indispensable derive from belief that more people are qualified for superior positions than there are positions, or that the office is so carefully organized that anyone can be taught to fill it. We must believe that many citizens have qualifications required for filling higher positions, even though at any given moment they are doing nothing important. Since military, political, and educational institutions must compete for men with business, where rewards in money and honor (in America, at least) are much greater, the caliber of political, military, and educational office holders is often very low. When such officials are in low esteem as individuals, how is it possible for the institution in which they enact their roles to survive? The institution survives, and indeed even increases in prestige, so long as the hierarchal glamor of the office itself is not tarnished. The office makes the man only if its glory is kept alive through proper use of majestic and sublime symbols which, however awesome and great, must yet be communicable to the meanest citizen.

American leaders in government, business, and education choose opulent and grandiose symbols of power. Vast road nets, huge dams, towering skyscrapers, gothic "halls of learning," bridges thrusting across wide canyons, great amphitheaters, enormous homes—even the huge congested mass of men and machines struggling through the canyons of our cities—are but the pomp and majesty of a technological democracy. Traffic congestion wastes untold amounts of time and money. Technological goods and services are used to increase, not decrease, congestion. As more people pour into our cities, planners bewail the strangulation of urban life and propose "logical" traffic plans. But the congestion of cities creates great audiences, and thus offers unlimited opportunities to see and be seen by others.

We rush to spend money in scenes of great plutocratic splendor, to be served by clerks who simulate elegance and share with us the thrill of fingering and looking at objects far beyond our means. We are seduced, coached, exhorted to buy. We press into crowded streets with our cars and elbow our way through crowds, because in such moments we feel the frenzied responses of others to money. We do not want technology to be efficient, but glamorous. We want the streets to throb with sounds, sights, colors, and rhythms of power and majesty. The streets are not "arteries" where traffic "circulates" or passageways between private islands in great houses where the pomp and ceremony of social position can be enacted among select audiences drawn from the family, church, court, or civic elites. The streets are rather public stages where we enact the drama of plutocracy.

Like the aristocrats of ancient Rome, or the mandarins of old China, who clogged the streets with their awesome retinues and stopped traffic to create a fearful yet envious audience to their power, we seek majesty in public display. But, unlike them, we seek it hourly and daily in the full glare of a public life which is reducing to a memory the private magnificence of "Newport cottages" of a hundred rooms and classical "town houses" costing millions. We spend billions on roads and cars as our homes become smaller and smaller, for the glamor and mystery of American plutocracy is staged in travel. Nineteenth-century streets were designed as stages for the sedate luxury of the carriage. Roads for mechanized carriages enhanced opportunities for public display of all kinds. Soon even the most private acts of family life, weddings and burials, moved from homes into hotels and funeral parlors. Even the home itself opened wide to the street; "picture windows" of glass replaced walls of stone, brick, or wood. The private life of the home, like the curtained carriage, was opened to public view.

The higher *public* standard of living made possible by the expense account and the lavish stage for public life provided by the business community cause severe dislocations in family life. Businessmen "on the road" live far better than they do at home. The secretary accompanying businessmen to their conventions eats, drinks, and sleeps in far greater luxury than the wives at home. The American office building is no longer designed simply as a place to work, but to socialize. Women find husbands where they work, not where they live. The "other woman" in American popular drama is not a siren from the demi-monde, but a colleague in work. She, we are told, "understands" and is "interested" in the husband's work, and she does so in far greater elegance and luxury than the wife.

In America, cars, clothes, and houses are highly communicable symbols of power because they are designed, advertised, and distributed as *mass* symbols. The American plutocrat has several stock cars, many articles of clothing, hundreds of household gadgets. A small, finely designed car, a house designed by Wright or Gropius, is not so easily understood as the "elegant" mass-produced Cadillac, or the ranch house similar to every other ranch house, yet different because it is a hundred feet longer. Perhaps all societies must determine rank on the basis of official insignia, not the achievements of the individual filling the rank. In state ceremony a brilliant staff officer may be far subordinate to field officers. In solemn academic processions, the most gifted scholar will trail far behind administrative officers. In court ceremony, a younger son of a British earl may precede Winston Churchill as a Knight of the Garter, but in doing so he upholds the principle of aristocracy.

In the great acts of social life—birth, marriage, and death—there is intense rivalry for the use and control of highly communicable social symbols. Who should control the burial of the dead? The church wants death rituals kept sacred and performed in church. But those who wish to honor their dead in societies where social position depends on proper communication of wealth cannot be satisfied with a simple church funeral, however holy. A church wedding or a simple civil ceremony in the registry office will satisfy the romantic needs but not the status needs of the bride and groom (and certainly not of their parents). So, too, in birth ceremonies where the contesting claims of the state, church, family, and hospital must be resolved. Even in caste societies where individuals are subject to rigid control, profoundly different social claims struggle for domination within the heart of noble and commoner alike.

Such conflict is not resolved through differential status alone, for we cannot tolerate great differences in status unless we are sure of underlying agreement. Such agreement is possible only when there is belief in some great transcendent principle whose immanence or incarnation infuses the present with the future. The ascetic pariah will occupy a higher rank in heaven than a worldly prince of the church. The worker will cast aside his chains and seize power. The virtues of the poor will humble the majesty of the rich and the great. Humility may become a sign of strength greater than pride, the innocence of a child more to be prized than the learning of the schools, the wisdom of the people more to be trusted than the councils of the great. But whether a social order functions well, as when our leader's commands become our sacred duty, or badly, as when we revolt openly, the same characteristics of status communication obtain. We see to it that "divinity doth hedge a king"—and if he must punish us for disrespect, we must punish him if he degrades the office of kingship.

Manners within the group are directed against the outsider, but they are also used to discipline those within the group to behave correctly. Inner grace, whether religious, military, academic, or aesthetic, cannot be learned save through long apprenticeship to those who possess it. In this lies the power of those who control the social ladder. The aspirant knows where the Grail lies, he finds the path, but he cannot share its radiance until those in power give him entry and approve his state of grace. Social grace is given; it cannot be taken. The inferior, like his superior, must learn to use majestic symbols. And if the paradox of superiority is the need for convincing inferiors to follow us, and yet to keep their distance, the paradox of inferiors is their need for leaders who will attend them, and yet keep distant enough to retain majestic sublimity. It is not the difference in rank between superior and inferior which disturbs a social system, but the inability (for whatever reason) to communicate in terms of a common transcendent principle of social order.

When we want responses and cannot get them from others, we create fantasies of social gratification within ourselves. The rebuffed lover, the child yearning for his parent, the lonely grandparent longing for company, the exile wandering in foreign lands, the prisoner in solitary confinement withdraw within themselves, not to forget, but to keep alive in fantasy what they cannot have in reality. Perhaps in his self-abasement the masochist is only trying to communicate with others significant yet "beyond" communication. The poignancy of all such loneliness and abasement is that only the indifferent, hostile, or departed other, can give us back the self we have lost. When the pain of estrangement of death becomes too great, we turn inward to communicate in fantasy with him whose loss we cannot endure in reality.

Despite the shock of indifference or the deep anger growing out of hostility we cannot express, it is very difficult to do anything that threatens the social principles by which we live. We uphold such principles if only to make sense out of our world. Many actors have been swept off the stage in great revolutions, but revolt is usually directed against the actors, not the play. Few condemn romantic love, although it may lead to suffering and death and, indeed, must lead to suffering and death to be "true" love. Instead we try to "purify" love by placing it in a hierarchal progression toward a higher love, the love of God, as in Dante, or the love of suffering as a way to understanding and compassion, as in Dostoevski.

Generations who witnessed the rise of Stalin and Hitler know that new tyrants often increase the tyranny which they are supposed to change. People who have lost a sense of community will pay any price to regain it. Hitler stated clearly that the German people needed more discipline, not less. German principles of hierarchy (the dynastic state, militarism, etc.) were pure and holy. Authority and discipline, Germanic order, must be purified from the corruptions of plutocracy, Communism, and democracy.

German evil was not really German. Once the Jew was killed, German society would be purified. German social values needed no change; only the world outside Germany must change. Soon, feudal hierarchy, against which men had struggled for centuries, was in power—as it will be again unless we learn to think better about the communication of hierarchy.

All appeals for attention are risks. The loved one we rush to meet may love us no more, the child we cherish may turn against us. In each greeting we seek reassurance from the other that our relationship still obtains. But the danger of rejection never vanishes. This is the secret power of those we love. Like Lear, we know what terrible risks love brings. We must love to exist just as the child must be loved to mature. But sometimes we must hate, too, if only to protect the self and satisfy the dark lusts within us—lusts which among men can be satisfied only in the sufferings of our fellows. We need each other in hate as well as in love. We crave authority to create not justice, but solidarity.

HOW ORDER AND DISORDER DEFINE EACH OTHER

Only in the dream and fantasy can men be satisfied with being audiences to themselves. We learn very soon in life that a social position is given to us by others—significant others, whose responses we must have to gain the place we want in our society. Even in early childhood we soon discover that mother's care is not automatic. Our cry or smile is not a "signal," but a hopeful plea. Mother's response, like the response of all authority for the remainder of our lives, will be "yes," "maybe," or "no." We are never quite sure which it will be, and thus we soon learn that every request involves risk. Most terrible of all are the moments when we get no response, as in the nightmare when we seek to communicate with those who can save us but who will not, or cannot, respond. Placating superiors, bossing inferiors, and persuading equals who hate us, love us, and are indifferent to us, in various forms of address is a hierarchal rhetoric we must all learn.

Our first experience of authority takes place at the breast, in bed, at the table, and on the stool. We soon discover that some ways of sleeping, eating, urinating, and defecating are pleasing and unpleasing to our superiors, inferiors, and equals. We must wait for father to begin before we can eat, we must help a smaller brother or sister (or a pet), and we must share food by passing it to others. As we do these things properly we are praised and fed. We learn too that we can annoy parents, or older brothers and sisters, by eating and defecating improperly. As superiors we learn that withholding food from inferiors fixes their attention on us, and they make greater efforts to do what we ask of them. Equals, we find, must be persuaded, not ordered, to share with us. We *take* food from inferiors, but we *share* with equals through creating rules binding to all those involved in sharing. With equals we discuss who has what right to what part of the food, how it must be eaten, and the order of passing the food from one to another. Once rules are established for passing an ice cream cone, each child becomes a jealous guardian of the rules.

Children must risk angering their parents if they are attended to only in anger. If they cannot overcome the indifference of the parent they must turn somewhere for attention. If the parent seldom says "no" and will not let the child say "no," the child must express his difference, the part of his individuality which is not like other individuals, in ways hidden or secret from the parent. Pent-up needs for the expression of difference may burst out in rage and destructiveness against loved and cherished others who will not let the child express (and thus learn) what it means to be a self different from other selves.

A social order *defines* itself through disorder as well as order. Improprieties set limits; they begin the moment of negation where the positive content of a role ends. Without such limits a role cannot take form. In medieval life the existence of the Devil, as of God, was an article of faith. Satan, the "Grand Negation," had his priests and priestesses—the sorcerers and witches. There was a Satanic Church, in which Satan had his ceremonies and his mass. Such negation is never merely an absence of order, but a carefully formed order, just as the villain of a play is a carefully drawn opposite of the hero. To reduce Satan to a gross and silly figure reduces the meaning of Christianity, for if Satan is trivial what then becomes of the power of the Christian who overcomes him?

Behind every "thou shall" lurks "thou shalt not"; doubt and anxiety beset us at every turn as we try to make sense out of the many social incongruities we must resolve in action. Priests admonish us not to kill; generals reward us for killing. Destruction, torture, murder—almost every crime is permitted so long as it is done in the name of some great social principle. It is not the destructiveness of the mob we condemn, but "wanton" and "undisciplined" destruction. The *name* of the act and those who control the name determine reward and punishment. But we still know killing a civilian is murder, even as we kill in war, and that poverty is a denial of brotherhood, even as we increase money rewards for those who make the rich richer. We doubt and reject our leaders; indeed, in democratic society (as Jefferson warned us) we *must* doubt our leaders, for only then do we learn to reason about, as well as believe in, our leader's commands.

We cannot control hate unless forms are provided for its social expression. Soldiers who hate their officers, children who hate their parents, all who live in deep and constant hate of another soon find their lives organized about those they hate (as well as those they love). If they cannot express such hate to others but must turn it inward, hate soon masters their lives. Perhaps all mental maladies and certain types of insanity derive from inability to *communicate* hate to real others outside the self. When we cannot express hostility directly, we resort to slips, mistakes, oversights, or humor (which is a kind of permitted hate). But when we cannot or do not know how to express hate, and such repression continues over a long period of time, we are like the mute schizophrene who when asked to write "A" wrote "B" and in one work period alone devised 30 incorrect ways of doing the work assigned to his group.

We must be able to communicate freely about social incongruities and disrelationships, for as we communicate we confront disorder within ourselves as well as in society. The patient on the couch, the penitent in his confessional box, the joker telling tales on himself are not "blowing off steam" or getting pleasure out of "a sudden economy in psychic expenditure." They are expressing to a significant other what they cannot express anywhere else without great suffering or degradation. The dreamer who flees madly or rushes savagely at the foe, the daydreamer who becomes a conquering hero, the child who struts about in adult clothes create fantastic others, but others nonetheless. When the paranoid describes his fictive persecutors he struggles to deal with his burden, not to escape or evade it, because only as he *expresses* his anxiety to a significant audience can he discover what it means.

ART CONSIDERED AS THE GUARDIAN OF SOCIAL ORDER

Thus, if the dream is the guardian of sleep, art is the guardian of social order. When society supplies us with no or few benign ways to express our frustrations, we turn to crime, violence, rage or hysteria. In these forms of communication we try to say to others something they cannot, or will not, let us say in other ways. The analyst permits, indeed, *coaches,* us to every kind of hostile expression, for he knows that only when hate is expressed can it be understood. He styles himself as an audience of a certain kind, and we play out our hate before him. As the hidden and secret hate of the patient gushes forth, the physician opens wide the gates. He helps to shape the torrent of words and images into communicable forms. The patient can now *confront* his hate, for it has been made into an object. Now it can be discussed with another who, in his role as physician, priest, or counselor, speaks with the authority of the group which the patient accepts as significant to him.

Confrontation and projection are much the same. The paranoid hearing voices of persecutors and the raging child screaming at his mother are trying to *confront* their agony, as well as blame it on someone else. In tragedy and comedy, villains and fools are reviled, pursued, tortured, and killed. In violence, crime, and war we load our enemy with our burdens to rid ourselves of them in his destruction. We create objects we can *act* toward. In projection we ascribe to others faults we cannot express or can face only with great difficulty in ourselves. The projection is made to create a staged character, a projected self, that we can criticize, revile, praise, blame, or curse.

In private fantasy we communicate with another but submerge him in our self. The social content of the dream is written, staged, directed, criticized, and watched by the dreamer alone. The images used by the autoerotic to stimulate himself are played before a secret audience of the self. In memory and the daydream, the self alone enacts the roles of author, critic, and public. The language of rational discourse, words forged in common action through communication, is subordinated in dream and fantasy to imagery subject to a self beyond communication with real others.

Imagination in art and in the dream are not the same. We create heavens, hells, utopias, ideas, and images as forms which we share in public communication. Milton's *Paradise Lost,* Plato's *Republic,* the *Book of Revelation* are public objects, books that all may share and that mean what they do only because they have been, and will be, shared. We are anxious to communicate well with real audiences because their responses become our responses to ourselves. We become audiences to ourselves through others. The shadowy audience of the dream, the strange and fearful other, is beyond communication. As monsters pursue and reach out we scream in agony, not because we are pursued, but because the other who sits in the next room and who might save us does not see our mad flight and does not hear our screams. In these moments of terror the anguish of communication is born. So long as we communicate with others significant to us, we are like soldiers in the field who can face the agony of death and the pain of wounds because they face them together. In such moments, terror vanishes (even though fear remains), and we are able to act because we are able to communicate.

We do not obliterate fear but we *transcend* fear in conscious communication. In parliamentary democracies we do not fear an opposition so long as we believe such opposition is loyal to the principles of democracy. In Socratic discourse we honor opponents so long as they discourse in ways proper to seeking truth. In sports and games we respect an opponent who plays hard so long as he upholds the rules of the game. As we struggle with the others who share common goals with us, we realize ourselves more fully because our struggle is but a way toward a higher level of action—the maintenance of some principle we hold sacred because we believe it determines social order.

Every institution must define what it considers to be sins against its laws. The most liberal parliaments in the world spend just as much time as, and possibly more than, the worst tyrant in deciding what is order and what is disorder in the community. When we make constitutions, laws, or rules, which tell men how to obey, we then define carefully in various kinds of punishments what will happen to those who disobey. As Hobbes argued, all social organization is really a covenant in which the inferior surrenders his will to the superior because he believes that the superior can guarantee social order. From the view of the ruler, crimes, whether they are called crimes against nature, God, man, or the state, are not simply disobedience, but a breaking of the covenant that is the sole guarantee of order in society.

In the ideal community (from the ruler's point of view), men will obey because they will accept the ruler's commands as their duty. That is, an angel does not obey out of fear, but out of devotion and love. But rulers (or, at least, wise rulers) know that men are not angels. Even God was disobeyed by Adam. We learn from the depiction of Adam's fall that social order cannot depend on perfect obedience, *but on the way such obedience is handled by the community*. The purpose of all punishment and victimage is not to destroy the disobedient individual, but to "rehabilitate" or "reeducate" him so that the will of the leader becomes his will. Thus, if rulers define sin and cause us to be guilty when we transgress their laws, they must at the same time provide us with means for the expiation of the guilt they have caused.

The paradox of all authority is that all-powerful rulers must explain how it is that they are not wise enough, in all their power and glory, to prevent disobedience. Answers to this—the "problem of evil," as it is called in theology—have engrossed many minds for many generations. Here (fortunately) we need not settle this problem on a theological or philosophical level, but turn with better profit (to sociologists, at least) to a consideration of how views on evil affect social organization. The first thing we note is that whatever the intellectual justification of the religious use of sin, there is no question about its efficacy as a means of social control. For if religion gives men comfort, confidence, and security, it also gives men fears and anxieties. Evil spirits, vengeful gods, cunning and cruel devils, and hells of suffering and torture are as much a part of religious experience as loving gods and heavens of joy and song.

And, as those raised on "hell-fire" sermons will attest, the description of the sinner's lot in these kingdoms of evil is very graphic. Indeed, the depiction of evil and the sufferings of the damned compose some of our greatest art. A great amount of social energy goes into exorcising guilt even in our "secular" society.[1] Evil and sin must be put in forms, as it was in the work of Dante or Bosch, before it can be communicated. And unless it is communicated, the "fear of God" cannot be put into us. Thus, before we talk of rituals of avoidance, "mechanisms of expiation," or whatever we term the ways we get rid of guilt, we ought to pay some attention to the ways in which guilt is aroused within us.

We have already said that the final power of all authority lies in the ability of our rulers to mystify us through appeals to some great transcendent principle of social order. They teach us that disobedience threatens, not so much the person or the office of the ruler, but the whole principle on which social order rests. Fathers teach us that if we disobey them the family will suffer, not simply that father will be "unhappy." School principals convince us (more or less) that our disobedience hinders group activities and that we spoil the fun of being together. Christian priests teach that a sin against the Church is a sin against God, and since God upholds order (in nature as well as society), sin threatens the very foundation of the world. And as we have seen, secular leaders in Russia have been able to convince erring Communists that "deviation" was a sin against the people, which could be atoned for only by public confession, as well as imprisonment or death.

It seems then that whatever the form of heirarchy, disobedience and guilt are assumed to be as much a part of hierarchal experience as obedience and innocence. The counterpart to this in theology is the conception of "original sin." While the context of "sinning against the community" and "sinning against God" is often described as a "rational" versus a "supernatural" conception, guilt, sin, and crime are used in much the same way by sacred and secular authorities. And if the *principle* of a hierarchy is just and powerful enough, then all men, regardless of their position, share in it. There is no need for ambition to better one's position, because this has nothing to do with the quality of the experience or the glory of the principle. The monk wandering the roads of Italy with only a few crusts of bread is as holy as the greatest prince of the Church in his cathedral.

But when, as in our hierarchy based on money, we are asked, and indeed, goaded into being dissatisfied with our position in the hierarchy and exhorted daily (even hourly) to want more than we have, we are really being taught that disobedience, as well as obedience, is the way to virtue. And when we are taught that we must be ambitious about our spending but *not* about our earning, economic adjustment becomes very difficult. For how can it be sinful to demand higher wages when it is only through higher wages that we can spend more and thus share in the American glory of an "ever-increasing standard of life"? Such contradiction as this makes clear that *guilt can be intrinsic to social order.*

Thus, both explicitly, by conscious definition, and implicitly, by implicit "inner contradiction," all hierarchies produce guilt. From a purely logical view, or at least in the "neutral" vocabulary of positivism, social disorganization cannot be discussed as guilt, for all mechanical models of sociation assume that "frictionless functioning" is the ideal mechanical function. And from the view of the theologian, or at least the Christian theologian, man sins but God does not. This seems to preserve the principle of Christian hierarchy, although even in Christianity it was necessary for God to give up his only son to suffering and death to save mankind from sin and the world from disorder.

But the question always returns of why a loving God permits man to suffer, just as the good ruler is constantly haunted by questions over crime and injustice in his community, or the father is confronted by a disobedient child whom he treats justly and kindly. In all such moments we recognize that something has gone wrong with our hierarchy. Like Job we find our God to be unjust; like Socrates we find that Athens no longer cares for good men; like the sobbing child we find our father cruel and hateful. Despite the most carefully planned distribution of authority in our hierarchy, there are many moments of disorganization, and we soon learn we must plan for them as carefully as we plan for the perfect moments when obedience, born of love and devotion, is "normal."

As we have already said, the commonest way for ridding a hierarchy of guilt, and of controlling social disorganization, is through victimage. The "perfect" victim, the "ideal" devil, is some poor hapless scapegoat whose sacrifice will wash away all sin. And, whenever we are tempted to think this way of dealing with disorganization is one of the "illusions" of religion, we should recall Hitler's use of the Jews. Perhaps such victimage is not a religious illusion after all; victimage seems to be natural to man. But if there is the tragic scapegoat of religion, there is also the comic scapegoat of art. And thus, as we shall argue in our chapters on comedy, disorganization can be confronted in benign, as well as malign, ways. But both religion and art teach us the same thing, namely, that we must define and confront evil if we are to control it.

Notes

[1] Perhaps, indeed, we spend *more* time and energy in dealing with guilt than is spent in sacred societies. We have no great ritual community drama which offers us a *total* scapegoat, whose suffering and death rid us of *all* our sin.

21

Hierarchal Address

A p p e a l s to superiors, inferiors, and equals, the rhetoric of hierarchy, are forms of address. And since all forms of address involve an audience, the relationship between speaker and audience has much to do with success or failure in such address. Being a member of an audience is a role, not a condition of life. No one is permanently a member of one public. The worker I direct in the plant tells me what to do in his role as a village official. In simple societies, those who watch tribal dances at one hour take part vigorously at another. In every society we change roles as performer and audience. We even become audiences to ourselves, as when we beseech ourselves to do something we think we ought to do, or when we pause to read what we have just written and criticize ourselves from the view of an assumed audience.

Even in the dream where we see more than we hear, there is still address. A dream is a communication to the self, and like all communications it is a drama. In the dream there is a scene in which actors struggle with each other in a kind of dumb-show. The highly visual nature of the dream does not change its nature as a form of address. Gesture, as Mead reminds us in his long description of the language of gesture, is basic to every form of communication. Mead and Freud argue that visual imagery is more primitive and thus more deeply rooted in man than words. In his famous descriptions of dog fights, Mead argues that animals communicate by gestures. For, when one dog anticipates the gesture of another, he is "internalizing" what the other dog might do, and prepares, through gestures of his own, to counter the gestures he anticipates.

The "I" talking to its "Me" is, Mead holds, an internalization of the "I" talking to its "You," just as in turn the "You" we address is formed in part by the "Me" we assume the "You" to be. And while Mead is more concerned than Freud with conscious address (Mead's predominant image is that of a conversation), both are concerned with address. The dreamer trying to outwit the censor, like the child trying to outwit his father, is *addressing* the censor. The Ego, struggling to reconcile the demands of the Id and the Super Ego, *addresses* them. The subterfuges of the dreamer, the ways in which we argue our own case before the bar of our own conscience, the many ways in which we satisfy secret longings for power, are forms of address, "inner" or "outer" though they may be.

Audiences may be real, as when we present ourselves at court to be judged by our peers, or imagined, as when we look forward to a day of judgment before our superiors. They may also be make-believe, as in the night- or day-dream. Memory, too, involves an audience, as when we recall our emotions before the family in some important celebration. How we use audiences in fantasy and reality tells us much about our self in relation to society. I cajole, coach, exhort, or instruct inferiors. Or negatively, I scold, deride, or threaten. I discuss, argue, and agree with equals, or I tease, turn discussion aside through irony and wit, or disagree sharply. I petition superiors in reverence and awe. But I may show dislike for them by being a bad audience. I avoid their presence, arrive late to affairs which they dominate, turn aside and attend to others when they speak or pass before me, insist on the most punctilious observance of the superior's code of manners at times which inconvenience the superior, and finally withhold the responses I know my superior wants.

The kind of pain and horror we suffer in the nightmare has been explained by Ernest Jones as the result of the suppression of incestuous desire. When we turn to the actual descriptions of nightmares we find inability to communicate to be characteristic of them. Jones argues that one typical feature of the nightmare is "utter powerlessness." This he describes as "a feeling of complete paralysis, which is the only response of the organism to the agonizing effort that it makes to relieve itself of the choking expression."[1] Robert Macnish, as quoted by Jones, goes into greater detail.

In general, during an attack, the person has the consciousness of an utter inability to express his horror by cries. He feels that his voice is half-choked by impending suffocation, and that any exertion of it, farther than a deep sigh or groan, is impossible. Sometimes, however, he conceives that he is bellowing with prodigious energy, and wonders that the household are not alarmed by his noise. But this is an illusion: those outcries which he fancies himself uttering are merely obscure moans, forced with difficulty and pain from the stifled penetralia of his bosom.[2]

It may be that our utter inability to express our horror stems from suppressed incestuous desires, yet on the face of the dream itself we note that it is a failure in expression which causes the pain. But if we assume that the disturbed dreamer, in nightmares, sleep-walking, and all forms of painful dreams, is trying to communicate with someone, and if we know with whom, under what conditions, and when he failed to communicate, we could reduce the high degree of inference necessary to sustain sexual theories of the nightmare. For in the horror of the nightmare we are trying to reach somebody, just as in dreams where we are being pursued, we are trying to find a haven, or to reach someone who can help us, as well as simply running away from our pursuers. In one type of nightmare, pain comes from not being able to gain the attention of those who could help us. This is not because they are far distant, or unseen. On the contrary, they may be sitting in the next room, or even watching as the demons close in on us. But they do not attend to our call for help or are indifferent to sufferings.

Perhaps when we know more about the failure to communicate in dreams, we will discover that socialization *is* communication, and that expressive forms, as used in address by individuals, are a kind of exhortation by the individual to form himself in accordance with the communicative norms that seem to produce the cooperative ways of the group significant to him. In this sense we are always talking to ourselves. Through formative ideas and images we seek to persuade ourselves to be what society wants us to be. But we must complete the process within ourselves. When we cannot act, for whatever reason, to tell ourselves (as audiences to ourselves) what the various kinds of rhetoric in our society have tried to tell us, persuasion is not complete. For it is only when voices from without speak in the language of a voice within that persuasion is complete.

The *structure* of the relation between speaker and audience determines motivation because it determines *how* we address each other and thus how we affect each other. These structures are affected by every element of the act. Where and when we speak, what kind of speech we make, the role we assume as speaker, the means we use to move our audience, and the purpose of the speech are *forms* which can be observed like any form. Thus, there is no need for the sociologist to fall back on such concepts as the "psychology of the masses" or the "working class market" to explain the effects of an address. Such phrases tell us very little about how "the psychology of the masses" is affected by communication, just as Freud tells us very little (at least explicitly) about how communication affects sex.

And when we examine closely just how such psychological concepts are used, we often discover that "working class" characteristics are ascribed to an audience, and then later derived as a "cause" of the response to the speaker.

Nor can we say audiences are conditioned alone by environments and "forces," unless we are willing to show how this conditioning takes place. And even as we ask the question we discover that it takes place through forms of some kind. We address each other in scenes designed for some kind of effect, we play a certain role as a speaker (that is, we act in one way and not another), and we try to achieve certain ends. *How* address is staged determines what can be said. Informal seminars cannot be conducted in vast auditoriums. Thoughtful conversation is impossible in a crowded railway station, a speeding car, or a noisy restaurant. The space formed by the architect creates tones, atmosphere, and moods, just as it determines how an audience enters, waits, moves about, applauds, and leaves. Truly, we shape our buildings and then they shape us.

Hierarchal address tells us much about authority. When artists, actors, and speakers choose to be coy, majestic, arrogant, sly, sincere, or thoughtful, we watch for corresponding appeals in all kinds of social address within the society. The difference between publics in Mark Twain's *Huckleberry Finn* and the audience in Thomas Mann's *Mario and the Magician* contains many clues to the distribution of authority in American and German society. Differences in *style* of address to various symbolic audiences should be matched against address to real audiences.

The actor may address his public as a general public, a public of his peers, or as a self struggling to make order out of conflicting roles. In Greek tragedy there is the chorus, in Renaissance court drama the stage audience of noble connoisseurs. In American vaudeville, the members of the orchestra and the master of ceremonies are often addressed familiarly by performers. The actor addresses "asides" to one faction of his audience which are "overheard" by all. The artist may manipulate his audience with skillful eloquence (like Antony in *Julius Caesar*), or he may "let them in" on the fate of other actors (as in many comedies), he may even beat his audiences (symbolically) into submission as in *Mario and the Magician;* he may dazzle through majestic processional as in the ballet *Graduation Ball* or in the music of Chopin's polonaises.

The censor of the dream, the image of the hated and loved authority watching the masochist beat himself, the brethren of the early Christian community gathered to witness martyrdom are necessary to the motivation of the actor; for their acceptance, rejection, or indifference to his appeals will determine his judgment of himself. Self-address in art differs from address in the night- or day-dream because it is public self-address. In dramatic soliloquy we plead our cause with those whom we have selected to "overhear" us. We address various aspects of the self, not to hide or outwit others significant to us, but to communicate with them. We do this to make them respond to us, so that in their reaction we can understand our own action. "Hear me, O ye gods," and all such invocations are statements of a principle of order which the speaker holds sacred. But invocations of such ideals are evidence of struggle within the self to act under conditions where discrepancies exist between principles and practice in social order.

A TYPOLOGY OF AUDIENCES DETERMINED BY HIERARCHAL ADDRESS

Mead argued that the self originated in dialogue between self and society—that is, a dialogue between, on the one side, the "I" and the "Me" and, on the other, a "generalized other," a "They," or the whole community. Freud proposed a somewhat similar model in his descriptions of the Ego trying to deal with the demands of the Id and the Super Ego. Burke describes the nature of rhetoric as addressed to audiences of the first, second, or third person. When we propose, as we have throughout this section on hierarchy, that we think of the self in terms of address between superiors, inferiors, and equals, what kind of model of address must we create? That is, what will be the structure of the relationship between the actor and his audience?

We can distinguish five types of address in the process of hierarchal appeals. These are determined, as befits a rhetoric based on sociology, by the kinds of audiences we must court. First there is the general public ("They"), second, there are community guardians ("We"), third, others significant to us as friends and confidants with whom we talk intimately ("You" which internalized becomes "Me"), fourth, the self we address inwardly in soliloquy (the "I" talking to its "Me"), and fifth, ideal audiences whom we address as ultimate sources of social order ("It"). Drama, and especially comic drama, supplies us with many examples of how these five types of address are used. So too do the courtroom and the staging of political speeches. An American trial is conducted before a general public (either in the courtroom, in the newspaper, or now, on television). Each speaker addresses a jury who are appealed to as responsible citizens; lawyers argue with each other before a judge who personifies the transcendent principle of justice, and finally, each lawyer weighs his case before the community guardians (the jury), in his summation. The American trial thus becomes a contest in the form of a dramatic struggle.

We see the same types of appeal in stage revues led by a master of ceremonies. As he strides on the stage the "MC" greets the general audience, exhorts them to applause, and keeps up a line of "happy talk" with them. He addresses the musicians on the stage, or in the pit, as guardians of art who can be talked to "knowingly" about performance. He singles out other performers for dialogue. Occasionally he turns aside from all to talk to himself for a moment. Finally, he invokes the spirit of art in the "wonderful show," in this "great town," and may even invoke the flag as he finishes. No one is addressed in quite the same way as another. The members of the orchestra are never addressed in the same manner as the audience beyond the footlights. And as the show goes on, the "MC" comments on one audience to another, even though each can hear what he says about the other.

In political rallies the orator greets the good people of the town who make up his general audience, he turns deferentially to his distinguished guests beside him on the platform, and then addresses his "friends and fellow-citizens." During his speech he breaks off into soliloquy ("When I was a farm boy like your boys here, I said to myself. . . ."). He closes his speech with invocations to the great transcendent principles on which the American way of life rests. The political rally is staged as a great community drama, a struggle between good and evil, for the soul of America. At best, the orator's opponent is misled or simply unable to carry out the great responsibilities of public office. At worst he is in league with evil powers, who are using him for malign purposes of their own or direct him in black conspiracy.

But it is in comedy that we see the clearest expression of our five forms of address. The comic hero addresses the general audience, the chorus, or whoever represents the "responsible men of the community," other actors, himself (as when he soliloquizes), and finally invokes some principle of social order. He begins by exposing the vices of one audience to another. He discusses openly and at length, the voices of every faction in the cast. He may even turn to one audience to make side remarks about what others in the cast are doing or saying. There is always an air of conspiracy, as if the audience addressed by the comic hero were gods far above the strife of the actors, assuring each other (as they assure us) that these mortals here below are like children stumbling about in games they really do not know how to play well but play with great vigor.

At "coming out" parties where young men and women are presented to the community as ready for marriage, the same structure of address may be observed, although here address is not wholly verbal. There is a reception line in which the guardians of the community are welcomed to the ball. The girls present themselves to a "king" and "queen," who personify the elegance and grace of the high society the girls are about to enter. The girls dance and chat with boys selected as escorts. Now a general audience has formed who watch and comment on the beauty, breeding, and personality of the debutantes and their escorts. There may also be "gentlemen and ladies" of the press and television. At some time in the evening there is a great processional which is staged as an invocation to the gods of high society. And while soliloquy is not actually provided for in such parties there are "retiring rooms," where the heroines of the evening may go in solitude with a few others.

Thus, we soon learn that there are different kinds of audiences and that we must learn to address them in different ways if we are to be successful. We cannot address friends as we do community guardians, and certainly we cannot talk to ourselves as we do to general publics. But if we are to learn to address each audience properly, society must provide us with the means for doing so and opportunities for using the skill we have learned. When a hierarchy becomes so rigid that inferiors cannot talk to their superiors, or must talk to them always in a highly ritualistic manner, inferiors will soon turn (as they did in Russia and Germany) to other superiors. For we must communicate to live, since it is only through communication that we know what we are.

THE GENERAL PUBLIC

The unseen audience beyond the stage does not enter into dialogue. It may be addressed, and in turn may respond by applause, jeers, or boos. The actor who lets his response to the general audience pass into dialogue steps out of character, while the audience that permits a member to continue in dialogue usurps the role of the players. The heckler must be silenced by the audience itself if the action is to go on. In political gatherings, speeches from the floor are limited by rule. The audience must be persuaded to accept the action and it must make its acceptance known. It cannot help an action forward, although its applause inspires actors to perform better. It can, however, stop a performance, either by refusing to come or by jeers and noisy disapproval. Thus the power of the general audience is negative and positive; it tells us what not to do, and encourages us to continue the kind of expression it approves. The audience may be coached through claques, but, once the performance begins, the actor must cajole, charm, bully, insult, exhalt, or flatter to gain the attention and response he needs to stimulate himself to communicate well.

Political rallies, sporting events, all civic spectacles are a presentation to general publics—a presentation of the community to itself. Who may come, how they are seated, how they are addressed, by what means, by whom they are controlled, how they dress, how they relate to each other, and how they communicate with the actors are indications of how inferiors and superiors relate in a given society. How the general audience is stratified, and how those in various levels relate to each other, is another. Since architecture creates the spatial environment, the scene for social staging, its forms offer many clues to the hierarchal patterns of the community. The artist's attitude toward the general public may or may not coincide with that of the politician, priest, soldier, or educator, but since the artist creates the forms by which we all express ourselves, his symbolic relationship with audiences is decisive. The rhetoric of appeals to audiences, whether "outer," as when we ask an audience to vote for us, or "inner," as when we daydream of making a speech to great applause, differs only in degree. Appeals to audiences in the dream can be analyzed through comparison with appeals to audiences in the shared experience of real life because they are both expressed in common symbols.

COMMUNITY GUARDIANS: THE AUDIENCE AS THE CONSCIENCE OF THE COMMUNITY

The second type of audience, the chorus, or the cast itself where the chorus is not clearly indicated, is usually the conscience of the group. The chorus is never personal or individual. It responds as a group to the individual appeals of the antagonist and protagonist. In Gilbert and Sullivan we have British sailors, nobles, policemen, school-girls, soldiers, or gentlemen; in Aristophanes knights, elders, husbandmen, old men, or women keeping the Feast of Demeter. When the chorus speaks for factions in the community, not for one great hierarchal principle, there are several choruses. Thus in *Lysistrata* there are old men and women; in *The Mikado,* school-girls, nobles, guards, and coolies.

Unlike the general audience, the chorus is a voice in dialogue with other voices. But it is a group, not an individual voice, and while it comments on the problem of the action, it does so from a group, not an individual, point of view. The chorus is antithetical to soliloquy, where the settled convictions of the chorus and the appeals to basic principles of individual actors are turned over in doubt and question. The chorus expresses group ideals. If a troop of soldiers passes by in *Faust* or *Cosi Fan Tutte,* we hear songs about the bravery, loyalty, and comradeship of a soldier's life. If village maidens come tripping over the green, they are all young, beautiful, eager to love. Celestial choric groups of angels, spirits, or gods are solemn, majestic, sublime. As they address the individuals struggling to make sense out of conflicting loyalties, they speak with deep conviction and power, because they speak for the conscience of the community.

Choric comment on individual action becomes critical when the individual's actions violate the common sense of the group. The Captain of the *Pinafore* may be a model sailor and the paragon of all nautical virtues. The sailors of his crew are willing to submit to the Captain's flattery of their own virtues. But when the Captain is carried so far by his own magnificence that he boasts that he is "never sick at sea!," the good sense of the sailors revolts. They seem to say, "Oh, come now, Captain, we are all sailors and we know better." But the Captain persists: he is *never* sick at sea. This is too much for the chorus, who make it plain that they have had enough of this nonsense. As they challenge the Captain again ("What, *never?*"), he knows the game is up, and replies, "hardly ever!" This submission to good sense is a great relief to the chorus, who now sing joyfully: "He's hardly ever sick at sea! Then give three cheers, and one cheer more, for the hardy Captain of the Pinafore!"

The comic chorus is critical and is careful to remain distinct from the actors, but there is a curious air of complicity in their dealing with the general audience. Pious platitudes, drooling sentiment, threadbare slogans are permitted the actors so long as they are used to manipulate inferiors beyond the stage, but once the actors address these to the chorus (especially the comic chorus) they are told off in mockery, disdain, or downright ridicule. Only when the actor, like the politician, admits that he *has* to say such things for public consumption, is he forgiven. After the tenor has serenaded his lady in saccharine or ethereal tones, the chorus is apt to break in with quite earthy reminders of love's problems. In great comedy, as in *Falstaff* or *Don Giovanni,* the beauty of the serenades is not destroyed by this choric comment, but enhanced through the expression of the contrast between ideal and real love. Both young and old come together as the young lovers share their passion with the chorus or with the member of the cast who speaks for the common sense of the community. The old are disenchanted because they can no longer love, the young filled with the enchantment of passion. Who is right? Both. The old smile tenderly, for they know what is ahead once passion wanes, but they know too that even the illusion of passionate love, ridiculous though it may be, is better than no love at all.

INDIVIDUALS AS AUDIENCE TO EACH OTHER

The most important audience is the audience in dialogue between the self and significant others. The self is born in discourse with others. We exhort, command, or mystify general audiences, in hope that we can dominate them. We plead with the guardians of the community, the men of power and authority, to approve our purposes and give us what we need to achieve them. The others we address in soliloquy are not real but fantastic selves, which we address because we cannot address real others or because we cannot find others who understand our problems. We invoke, beseech, and pray to gods who embody the great principles of social order we believe necessary to survival. But in address to other individuals we enter the most profound experience in communication. This is dialogue, the "I" speaking to a "You," whose response is *necessary* to the "I" because in it the "I" discovers *his* meaning and significance, just as the "You" discovers his.

We are human only because others make us human, as we, in turn, make others human. We become individuals only because we enter into dialogue with others who remain others and make us realize that we must learn how to communicate with this strange and unique other. For no self exists, or knows itself, save in the presence of another. The forms of address which arise in dialogue are the fundamental realities of society, because it is what happens between man and man, his *relatedness through communication,* which constitutes society. We *discover* ourselves, as others, in turn, discover themselves through us. We are not selves before we communicate with others, just as others are not real until they communicate with us. There are no "individuals" and there is no "society," as opposed poles waiting to be sparked into being "forces" which "stream" from one pole to the other and form "patterns," "systems," or "fields." But there is *address,* and when it takes place between individuals significant to each other, such address becomes communion, which, in the deepest sense, is what we mean by community.

Address to a significant other is a moment of commitment, and thus a moment of anxiety, and, if failure occurs, a moment of deep anguish. We cannot become selves until we are understood and until we *know* that we are understood. We search through our lives, as we conjure up in our dreams of the night and the day, "ideal" others, who, like the imaginary playmate of the child, will understand us, so we can understand ourselves. We yearn to enter into dialogue because we know that only in dialogue will the anguish of "nothingness," of being related to no one, disappear. We *must* talk to someone, for only in such talk do we really exist as social beings. We must be able to ask others what they think of us, because they are our *real* community, the community which gives us not only our "official" roles, but our public and conscious individuality.

We do not seek to outwit the other with whom we talk intimately. A friend is not a father, an authority, or a superior. He is an equal. Our "covenant" with a friend is not like that between God and man, or the lord and serf, but a communion, an inclusion of the other. We do not want to dominate a friend, for when we do friendship cannot exist and we can no longer converse and discuss, because only equals can discuss. This "otherness" of the friend, our willingness to allow him to exist in his own terms, is granted because we know that he, in turn, grants it to us. We are bound, not because we are alike, but because we are different, and know that in the resolution of the difference we discover a greater self. For it is in sharing differences that we develop, just as it is in coming together as male *and* female that we transcend the solitariness of being male *or* female.

And this is the burden, and the source of hate as well as love, in friendship. It is not that my friend "knows" me like someone who knows my secrets, but that he defines me to myself. In such definition, born in the discussion and expression of dialogue, individuality is born. Before other audiences I play roles, and these roles must be fixed in tradition or determined by glowing visions of a future which must serve as a guide to the community, if the society is to endure. But action in the present is never simply determined by the past or the future. The present is always a problem, a time of struggle and conflict in which action at best is hypothetical. I can expose few problems before superiors and inferiors. For if my superiors are truly strong and great, how can I have any problems? And if my inferiors must find me strong and great, how can I have any problems?

It is not until we discuss problems and express the conflicts raging within us that we become a self. For to become a self we must express the self, in communication with others, with whom we try to *name or designate* our problems, and then struggle to give them some kind of order. Such discussion is never a dramatic rehearsal within the self, any more than the other is a mirror for the self. We don't resolve problems within the self and *then* communicate with others. Dialogue is never abstract and monologic. It is dramatic dialogue, a thinking *in* relationship, *in* the give and take of address to others. For as we speak in dialogue we must stand our ground and wait to be spoken to. In such difference, the real difference of the other in dialogue, in all the oppositions of the other, lies the meaning of conversation as a social event. As we speak together we enter in a mutual agreement not to silence our differences, but to express them.

All words that become names, by which we designate things and events, arise out of the meeting and response of conversation. And such meetings always involve a form of meeting, a staging of the relationship which exists only because of a mutual pledge of the self and the other to continue in dialogue. Such forms, like the stage of a drama, contain the action of dialogue, because they define the relatedness of the actors to each other, and to the things around them. For things, just as people, are brought into relatedness. That is, they are symbolized. And they are symbolized in address, because even though we symbolize them, they must be addressed to become real. In giving a name to something or someone, we differentiate it from ourselves, for only then can we address it. A thing or a person named exists, then, both for itself and for me. Until I name it and it responds it has no existence, because it cannot be addressed; but neither do I have any existence, because I cannot be addressed.

The meaning of my address is in the response of the other. We are not solitary selves who "decide" what to say, and then find meaning in this decision. Nor are we determined selves wholly shaped and formed by forces in nature and society. The reality in which we live is the reality of the *relations* between the things of the world and man, as well as the relation between man and man. And a relation is a form in which communication between the self and the other takes place. In these forms—friendship, the family, all the deeply intimate relationships—the "I" and the "You" become a "We." For so long as the self and the other are bound to a common action—that is, so long as the "I" and "You" struggle, like the hero and villain of a drama, to reach community through the resolution of difference—they are not only an "I" and a "You," but a relationship of "I" and "You" which makes up a "We." Thus, even in dialogue between a single self and another, there is a third element.

This is the social element which makes all relations possible, because we must create social forms in which the relationship *between* the self and the other can exist. For, no matter how subjective I become or how much I try to use another as a thing, I soon discover that I exist in the *relationship* with the other. It is because of this that indifference to others cannot be endured for long, for in indifference there is no relationship, and, hence, no social being. We fear indifference more than hate, because we cannot address those indifferent to us, and we cannot be sure that if we do address them they will respond. Nor can we endure being treated as things, as objects, because this reduces us to quantities and makes relationship impossible. Objects cannot address each other and, hence, cannot enter into any kind of social relationship. And since objects, or men treated as objects, can be determined only by pasts (that is, can exist only in time that has been), time has no future, and man has no purpose.

Dialogue between the self and the other makes society possible, because in such relationships, expression, communication, naming (as designation), and the struggle for consistency in meaning originate. Meaning is always a social meaning, because men create symbols in dialogue, not to measure or to witness a world, but to act in it. And since all such action is dramatic, the life of dialogue is dramatic life. Like actors on the stage, we address each other to find out what we are. We commit ourselves to each other, and this commitment becomes our social covenant, for, as we address another and he responds to us, we discover that we exist in terms of each other. So long as we are bound, we exist. When the bond is broken, when we no longer look the other in the eye, and yearn to hear his words, when we stop trying to speak carefully so we will be "really" understood, we are no longer individuals, but members of a collectivity. We cannot be individuals because we cannot be understood, just as others cannot become individuals because they cannot understand us. For the meaning of symbols arises in the relatedness of man to man.

Notes

[1] Ernest Jones, *On the Nightmare* (London: The Hogarth Press, 1949), p. 22.
[2] *Ibid.*, p. 23.

22

A Sociological View of "Inner" Audiences

FORMS OF APPEAL TO INNER AUDIENCES

S TATUS AUDIENCES are both private and public. I speak to external audiences only through my capacity to internalize them, just as I learn to address inner selves through learning how to address others. The first problem of inner address is to resolve disagreement among the various individuals and institutions among whom I must play many roles. My parents, my playmates, my smaller brothers and sisters often do not agree. If I please one, I anger the other. Not only must I learn to communicate with each actor in his own terms, but I must resolve within myself the different and contending voices of superiors, inferiors, and equals.

We appeal to inner audiences in various ways. Sometimes we are like actors in a play, at others we are like orators appealing to a jury. When I want a promotion, I rehearse how I will act toward the dean in terms of how I think he will act toward me. I become my own audience through imagining myself as an audience to another. Often there is great difficulty in reconciling the competing claims of superiors, inferiors, and equals. Status enactment always involves choice. As we pass from one position to another, we must leave the old properly, as we press on to the new. In initiation rites, sanctioned ways of killing the past, as well as embracing a future, must be provided.

Private and public audiences are mixtures of superiors, inferiors, and equals, whom we love, hate, fear, or disdain. We play our parts to one, but are conscious of all. We often despise those we must please. There is much contempt in the lordly bow of the clown, the deep prolonged bow of the artist in scant applause, or the exaggerated politeness of the husband to his wife as she appears late before guests he has already admitted. By treating her as an entering queen he sharpens the contrast between her genteel pretensions and her boorish manners. As we accept the nomination of one political party, we reject another, and we do so in the presence of both.

Institutions within the same society compete for our loyalty. Often indeed, the same institution makes contradictory appeals. One bank officer urges us to save, another to spend. Our professors exhort us to study, while our fraternity brothers warn us not to become "grinds." We cannot do both, and as we do one we are never quite sure that we should not have done the other. The individual must often bear incongruities which do not exist for the institution which creates them. The bank makes profit from lending me money, as well as from lending my savings to others.

The turmoil of conflicting social roles is matched, and indeed surpassed, by the conflicts which rage within us. We love our friends, but we hate our enemies. In dreams and wishes we rape, murder, and torture at will, and with deep pleasure. Witnessing the suffering and disgrace of majestic superiors, the ridicule and abasement of loyal but stupid inferiors, or exposure of the pretensions and hypocrisies of peers gives us pleasure. We find it easy enough to forgive our enemies when we are about to hang them.

The inner audience is not only a Freudian censor whom we try to outwit, but a judge before whom we plead our case. Attempts to outwit a literary censor are attempts to get work before an audience. In status fantasies we try to outwit or to destroy those who prevent us from reaching authority necessary to social satisfaction. Freud stresses the father as the "ultimate" audience. Only as we placate the father can we relate to others in peace. But there are many kinds of hierarchal failures. Ingratitude of inferiors, rejection by superiors, betrayal by friends are experienced by all. The sudden clutch of envy, the sharp pangs of jealousy, the icy loneliness of pride are but a few of the many powerful emotions experienced in social disrelationships which arise from hierarchal failures.

Often we are so bewildered by how superiors judge that we reach no conclusion about their attitude toward us. We may even wonder if we have communicated at all. We are often puzzled and shocked by the refusal of superiors to keep their own commandments. We find authority puzzling and capricious, like children who find their parents to be mysterious and remote gods who must be placated. When our masters become completely indifferent to us, our sense of reality vanishes and we are literally nothing. Even punishment is better than this, for, in pain afflicted by another, we are sure at least of a relationship, and thus sure of our social being. Difficulties in hierarchal communication occur also when we feel ourselves to be prejudged. The ironic parent who sneers at the child, the teacher who accompanies his assignments with heavy sarcasm over his pupils' ability, the officer who doubts our ability to carry out orders he is about to issue, punish us even before we commit our crime. For the child who has no other superior than the parent, ridicule and sarcasm evoke deep guilt that the parent alone can resolve.

When a distant and majestic superior communicates only to remind us of our unworthiness, and when there is no other authority, our anxiety deepens. The child struggles to make sense of his social torments in the only way he can. He creates fantastic others with whom he *can* communicate, for he must communicate to rid himself of anxiety. His parents are his first experience with absolute authority. He plays before his parents, brings things to them, entices them to play hide and seek. He is learning to attract and hold the attention of his first significant audience. Until he learns how to enact other status roles, especially roles with equals, he will relate to superiors and inferiors as he learned to relate to his parents.

Audiences may be classified by what kinds of appeals *can* be made to them. We may appeal to audiences only as superiors who must be placated, or inferiors who must be terrorized into obedience. Where communication is monopolized, as in church or state censorship of art, or very difficult because of great differences in understanding, as between generations in immigrant families, or impossible because of lack of common language, we cannot expect discussion to be the same as it would be between equals.

Much of our rage and hysteria derives from poor training in status communication. I may not want to fly into a rage with a colleague who criticizes my work, and after I have done so I may feel deep shame. I may admit that hostile criticism is often sharp and thorough, and helps to develop my thought and expression. But if my social experience precluded open discussion of difference with equals and superiors, I cannot be expected to welcome it. Shame passes easily into guilt for which I must atone in the only way I know—through punishment of myself and others.

To relate to a private or public audience means to *perform* before it as before an audience whose praise or blame will determine our own judgment. How we select our audience, how we communicate, in what kind of symbols, by what means, in what kind of action, and for what purpose define the social meaning of such presentation. The applause of the audience inspires us to new heights of social energy, just as the roar of applause deepens the faith of the politician in his own cause. In purely social moments, laughter and smiles encourage us to new audacities in wit.

We kill in piety and with pleasure, so long as audiences approve. The criminal in our press is prepared for official slaughter by working up audiences to "demand" his death. News stories of crimes are dramatized and played out before the reader in highly stereotyped forms. The "killer" is always loose, ready to "strike again." He has been "seen" in several neighborhoods. The police are ready to close in on his hide-out. He is captured after great risks (actual or potential). He is condemned in public long before his trial in court. The trial is not to determine his guilt or innocence but the degree of punishment; the verdict is usually judged as too lenient. If the "killer" is marched off to die, we are relieved because the community has been purged. But our relief is only momentary, for within a day or so (depending on the exigencies of circulation) another "mad dog killer" haunts our streets again.

Whatever increases hierarchal strangeness and mystery increases glamor, but also adds new burdens to open and free communication. In mockery we attempt to laugh away insupportable barriers between the self and others we need. The child playing "grownup" parodies her elders; the college line of chorus boys dressed as girls, with bulging hips and stuffed bosoms, debunk sexual glamor. The woman whose ethereal, intellectual, or glamorous attributes place her beyond approach threatens the solidarity of men and women. Hostility toward her is social as well as sexual. In the mockery and make-believe of transvestitism in festivals such as Purim, farces like *Charley's Aunt,* or annual college reviews, sexual glamor is debunked. The male Jew who feasts and riots in women's clothes throws off the burden of pious rational masculinity, and at the same time mocks excesses in femininity which make communication between men and women difficult. College students burdened with elaborate rituals of romantic love, and subjected to the mystifications of status glamor, cannot work easily beside girls as equals and colleagues. In poking fun at the mystery of love, men—and women—laugh down barriers which increase strangeness and mystery to a point where communication becomes difficult or impossible.

Where transvestitism or parody of women ends in homosexuality, communication is still sought. The homosexual hates women and competes with women for men. In the homosexual drama the unconscious audience may be the woman. If we believe the psychoanalysts, this woman is the mother. It may be too that homosexuality emerges where social distance between the sexes is too great to be overcome. Feelings of inadequacy over failure to reach desired women are solaced by a kind of sexual irony directed at the "hypocrisy" of women. It is as if the homosexual were saying: "Women pretend to be such pure mothers and such great ladies, but here is what they are really after . . . and I will keep it from them."

Obscenity also is used to rob woman of her social glamor. In the work of Rabelais, obscenity is used to attack pride because such pride keeps men and women apart. Rabelais actually spiritualizes lust into moments of profound social communion. His men and women do not "surrender" to each other, but they *play* together. Love lies in laughter and pleasure, not agony and death. The difference between men and women becomes a principle of joy and life. His courtiers delight in their difference because they look forward to overcoming it.

MORTIFICATION AND GUILT

In hate of the real audience there may be love of an imagined (but very real) audience. The hate of the real audience may increase the love of the ideal. Christian chronicles report how the martyrs provoked their torturers. "The martyr chooses the pleasure which exists in the prospect through the present pain." The utmost agony coincided with the joy of paradise experienced in imagination. As the martyr breathed his last the ecstatic idea of bliss was realized. We read descriptions of how early Christians longed for their tortures, how they joyously sang hymns to their last breath. The tortures had spectators—the hated pagans who were responsible for the martyrs' agony and beloved Christians who witnessed the tortures to gain courage for their own public confession of faith.

The prisoner who recants in public to a great audience functions for the state much as the martyr did for the Church. Modern tyrants are careful to avoid public punishment. The Russians prepare their victims for public witness, not trial. Prisoners who cannot be broken are executed secretly by unseen assassins. Russian "brainwashing," like that of the Inquisition, undertakes to change the heretic's will. The Nazis tortured and killed to get information, not to prepare the victim for public witness or to reform him. Those selected for death were not to serve as public redeemers, but as vessels of terror to frighten enemies within who might rise against the state.

In view of the great capacity of Christian martyrs to endure horrible agony and other kinds of mortification where pain is inflicted on the self, there can be little question about the power of the inner audiences. Such audiences are part of an inner drama of purification. Mortification originates in a dramatic struggle between good and evil within the self, for within the self, as on a stage, hero and villain struggle for victory before inner audiences whose approval brings sorrow or joy.

Tyrants rule us because they know we cannot rid ourselves of guilt. Hitler did not try to explain away German guilt. The Germans *had* sinned, they *should* feel deep guilt, but their evil was not theirs alone but a world evil. German Jews were but part of international Jewry, which had duped the Allies and stabbed the German Army in the back. In war against such evil, Germany (like the Teutonic knights of old) was really saving civilization. Such war, like all holy wars, was not for loot, revenge, customers, or territory, but for purification of a social principle. It was pure because it was directed against heretics whose extermination was necessary to social order.

We long to communicate properly with superiors, inferiors, or equals, but often we do not know how to do so. And where there are great social gaps and deep changes in social position, proper forms of communication may not exist because they have not yet been created. So long as I am indifferent to Negroes, I am not embarrassed in their company. But once I think them entitled to a relationship beyond servility, and yet do not know how to relate to them, I am uneasy in their company. The status incongruities in our relationship with adolescents we think old enough to send off to the army, yet too young to remain on the streets after ten o'clock, are equally embarrassing. Perhaps much sexual tension is but a variant of status embarrassment. I am conscious of how silly it is to continue treating the growing girls in my neighborhood as children, yet I cannot relate to them as adults.

It is reaching the other, being able to communicate by giving form to my shame, and doing so before an audience whose power of forgiveness I accept, that makes shame and guilt endurable. Once I apologize openly I am free from shame, even though I may still feel regret. So long as my father will hear me out, my anguish lessens. But guilt in dreams and fantasy deepens when I cannot reach the other who can absolve me. The shadowy powerful figures of the dream who witness our torture, who tower over us as we suffer, who mutter like monsters in the depth of a cave—what are they perhaps but the images of parents who made us feel unworthy yet gave us no way of communicating about our unworthiness? The deep social tragedy of childhood is to be guilty without knowing why, and, even when knowing why, to be left without means of expiation.

Even the worst sinner has his confessional. We do not ask an adult to repent sins he does not understand. Once he repents, we do not let him wander in search of a confessional. The child, however—shut off from communication, not yet able to charm his gods or to placate them through sacrifice of others or mortification of the self—expresses himself in rage. This rage may be directed against the parent or, if the parent refuses attention, against some symbol of the parent. A doll is torn apart, a book cherished by the family is defaced, good clothing dirtied, symbols of the parents cursed. When such rage cannot be expressed, the child may pass into autism. He may even kill himself, but not before one last terrible attempt to communicate with the mother who will not attend to him. The child suicide who dresses as a woman and paints his cheeks kills in effigy the mother he cannot kill in reality.

Exasperation and rage may be turned against the self. The patient who slashes her wrists in the analyst's office, the husband who takes to bed suffering from overwork, and the child steeped in gloom who "lets" himself be seen by his parents seek to communicate with others who can but will not communicate with them. The masochist who coaches his audience of prostitutes and performs before them in pain and degradation uses his drama of suffering to communicate something he cannot communicate in more benign ways.

When we turn against the self in highly public moments, we are like the martyr who demands witness as he enacts his role as sufferer, or like the actor who allows us to "overhear" his soliloquy. In our most tortured and subjective fantasies there is an audience. This mysterious and dark audience has its counterpart in the audiences we seek in public role enactment. Destruction of the self, others, or things is never meaningless. Perhaps rage itself is but a way of attracting the attention of the other we need, so that new conditions for communication may be established.

Guilt, embarrassment, and isolation arise in status communication when there is no transcendent principle strong enough to overcome disrelationships between different classes of beings. Faulkner's Negroes are the sin of his whites. His Negroes and whites meet in guilt. The Negro's guilt is not individual but tribal. He inherits a status position he can do little to change in a land where status improvement is not only a right, but a duty. Two social orders cannot exist side by side unless there are ways of translating one into the other, or unless one transcends the other. When transvaluation becomes impossible one system must dominate. Wars, terrible as they are, become a means for reestablishing common meanings.

Tribal or categorical guilt is often explained by original sin, a drama of the Fall. A class fallen from power often depicts a fall from grace in its art. Hawthorne's Puritans struggle against their fall from grace. An individual suffering from the weakness of old age and premonitions of death, evokes memories of his proud youth. As the sin and decay of the present increase, the innocence and strength of the past increase too. Soon we have a great past, the past of the Fall, whose brilliance and wonder is lighted by the gloom and fear of the present.

When we learn to repair breakdowns in status communication by expressing hate without physical violence, we may not need to fight. Perhaps we should encourage diplomats to become highly skilled in cursing. The press might be taught not to deplore international cursing, but to regard it as the critic does a play. Diplomats might be trained to dramatize, not to mask differences. As we learn to express hostility short of war, our chances of survival increase.[1] Communal life is made possible by love, but hate also binds us together. As Christians we are enjoined to love one another, but no religion has given its followers so many opportunities to hunt down, torture, and kill its heretics—either outside the self, as among infidels, or within the self, as in mortification of the senses.

Inequalities in themselves do not create social disorder nor do specific conditions of ownership, such as private property. Every institution seeks to maximize its power. Every individual believes, indeed, *must* believe, that his view of life should be powerful. Struggle over possession of symbols of hierarchy, whether of the church, army, state, school, or profession, is a condition of all social experience. When a social order does not provide audiences before whom we can enact our difficulties or play out our differences we create such audiences within ourselves. For all fantasy, certainly the fantasy of the dream, soon passes into drama. Who are the audiences of the dream? Is it the father alone, as Freud suggests? Do we dream as much about inferiors and equals as we do of superiors? How do changes of identity take place in dreams? We do not know. The hierarchal drama in dreams may hide clues to a deeper understanding of the nature of social bonds.

The soliloquy is not simply a dramatic "device" but a characteristic of social life. We talk to ourselves, hear others talk to themselves, and hold inner conversations. These talks, normally unheard by others, rage and storm within us. But inner conversation is never buried very deep. Children talk to themselves, as do old people. Drunkards become audiences to themselves. All of us use animals or things to converse with playfully. In humor and playful banter, we comment on ourselves. The conflict between family, school, state, church, and art does not resolve itself in the individual by some kind of social mechanics. It is a dramatic struggle. We appeal to generalized others and to each other, as individuals to community guardians. When resolution of these voices is difficult and action cannot go forward, we step aside to soliloquize.

In public acts it is impossible to narrow our address to inferiors or equals alone. We appeal to superiors, inferiors, and equals in the presence of each other. Our appeals to one are conditioned by needs for creating harmony in our relations with others. A subject loyal and true to his superiors may be found servile by his equals. A man too successful with his inferiors may seem obsequious to his superiors.

The self does not invent conflicting roles. In *The Magic Mountain*, Naptha and Settembrini struggle for the soul of Hans Castorp; God and the Devil battle for Faust; Nigger Jim, Tom Sawyer, and Widow Douglass seek to win Huck Finn. Parent and community struggle for power over the adolescent. The individual struggles to develop an ego strong enough to survive these conflicts. The ego must become the lord of counter-positions, like Hans Castorp. Soliloquy, while "internal," is really an expression of conflict among "outer" roles. Disrelationships among social roles always exist; indeed, they are assumed in every statement of relationship, as when we state punishments for breaking laws we have just passed. Soliloquy on the stage, like talking to oneself and like night- and day-dreams, is an attempt to express problems, to give them form, so we can communicate about them—to the self as well as to others. As we talk to ourselves we address the self in voices of others significant to us in our society.

Since soliloquy is an individual struggle to resolve contradictions and incongruities, it offers many clues to social problems. In Huck's attempt to balance the conflicting claims of the inferior but loved Negro and the superior yet inhuman aristocrat, the inner conflict of America over racial equality is revealed. In those years race problems could be discussed safely only in fun, and the burdens of traditional racial attitudes exposed only in the guise of soliloquy addressed seemingly to no one, yet "overheard" by all. Only in soliloquy can the self become an audience to the general public, to community guardians in the chorus, to the heroes and villains of the day who pursue us with their importunate demands to choose between them, and to the awesome majesty of the ultimate audience. As the individual states his dilemmas in soliloquy, he forces his audience to face disrelationships as he himself must face them.

Note

[1] Perhaps the international cursing matches held at the United Nations are a step toward social order. As each contestant addresses the other he also addresses the world at large. The military power of the United Nations is very limited, but its symbolic power is very great. Like the unseen but potent audience beyond the footlights, it conditions action. Allies must be convinced of causes before they take up arms, for all modern conflicts soon become "world wars," and every nation now must plead its cause before every other nation. Thus, every national event becomes a world event. National honor is no longer "beyond dispute"—on the contrary, skill in disputation is becoming necessary to prestige.

PART SEVEN

Hierarchal Transcendence and Social Bonds

23

Social Transcendence

THERE IS an audience beyond the general public, beyond the guardians of the community conscience, beyond the significant other whom we address in dialogue and the self we address in soliloquy and inner dialogue. This is the ultimate social principle, the God whom we address in final moments of appeal. Such principles are always symbolized in awesome and sacred forms which we address in "fear and trembling." We can distinguish five basic types of these ultimate appeals. There are ultimates of the person, as when the authority of parents, prophets, or gods is invoked; of rules and codes, as when we say "laws, not men, uphold social order"; of environment or nature, as when we ascribe causes of order to "tendencies," "processes," or "laws" in nature; of means, as when we turn to methods, techniques, instruments, or magic; and finally the perfect end or ideal, whose immanence infuses social order with meaning.

While it is common to think of religious experience alone as supernatural or sacred, deep belief in *any* type of social legitimation functions in society in much the same way as the supernatural in religion. We "legitimize" hierarchies through grounding their "causes" in nature (physical or biological), family (as in Freud's Oedipus complex), society, the supernatural, or language.[1] In our roles as scientists, priests, soldiers, statesmen, artists, or philosophers, moments of belief give us confidence to act, because such moments resolve difference, doubt, and ambiguity. Opposites meet in the dialectic of sacred symbols. "Thou shalt not kill [a neighbor]" and "thou shalt kill heretics" meet in religion as "a penny saved is a penny earned" and "spend your way to prosperity" meet in business.

If we believe in the act of creation as the genesis of order, we resolve our conflicts through appeals to Edenic or Utopian myths of origin. If we believe in place or environment, we talk about a nature that determines action through "immutable" forces or laws of space, time, or motion. If we believe in personal charisma, we turn to divine, semi-divine, or heroic

actors whose personal qualities alone determine social order. If we believe in method—as in magic, where how we do something determines
success—we turn to techniques and operations as the way to order. If we
believe in ends, goals, or purpose we turn to ideals, heavens, and utopias
which are known to all true believers (even though they have not yet been
reached).

Any of these types of transcendent beliefs can become very powerful.
In our time we have shifted from belief in acts of creation by divine gods
or inspired heroes, to social and physical "forces" whose natural "laws"
we "discover" and follow. Yet even in our philosophies of materialism
there are several natures, as once there were many gods. Highest of all is
a moment of "nature's perfection." In neo-behaviorism, nature's mystical
moment is its "tendency to self-maintenance" where "equilibrium" determines order. Thus as Parsons and Shils tell us:

> The social system depends, then, on the extent to which it can keep the equilibrium
> of the personality systems of its members from varying beyond certain limits. The so-
> cial system's own equilibrium is itself made up of many subequilibriums within and
> cutting across one another, with numerous personality systems such as kinship groups,
> social strata, churches, sects, economic enterprises, and governmental bodies. All enter
> into a huge moving equilibrium in which instabilities in one subsystem in the per-
> sonality or social sphere are communicated simultaneously to both levels, either dis-
> equilibrating the larger system, or part of it, until either a reequilibration takes place
> or the total equilibrium changes its form.[2]

Once a social system "maintains itself" by equilibrating processes (latent,
as in "adaptiveness," or actual, as in "integration") such processes become
both cause and effect. Suddenly motion becomes, like the celestial mechanics of the Deistic heaven, a "higher" level of explanation. As we enter
this level of final causes, we are in the realm of transcendence.

As the above quotation indicates, operational terms can easily become
"god-terms" which, like all such terms, are "beyond" time and space,
history, and causality, since they are a final and ultimate ground, a transcendence of time, space, history, and causality. A thing, an object, an
event as found in nature is here or there, small or large, round or square,
hard or soft. But when we begin to talk about "putting," "running,"
"equilibrating," just as when we talk about a "must," a "may," an "ought,"
or a "will," we are talking in universals which cannot be directly observed
but must be essentialized from some incomplete example, as when we
point to the running of a particular animal, the equilibrating of two forces,

or the putting of something in a certain place by some kind of agent. All "essentializations" that are beyond observation are peculiarly subject to mystifications.

Personal charisma, as in the power of the hero, the gnomic wisdom of the prophet, the inspiration of the genius, the intuitive understanding of the mother, the elegance of the woman of fashion, are also powerful social mysteries. Every charismatic authority, whatever his social role, subscribes to the proposition: "It is written . . . but I say unto you." It is not the religious context alone (although this context offers many rich examples) that determines such belief. It is belief in the personal power, the divinity of the individual, and finally, whatever symbolizes this divinity characterizes this kind of power.

Forensic appeals based on the transcendence of law are used everywhere in American life to determine justice and truth. We submit the acts of our executive and legislative branches of the government to the courts. *How* the decision is reached, not *who* reached it, is decisive. Thus we read in the article on international arbitration in the *Encyclopedia of the Social Sciences:* "The method of appointing the arbitrators or judges, whether ad hoc by the parties or by election by some independent body, and whether these judges hold temporary or permanent tenure, is less important than the actual judicial process which determines the issue." Arbitration boards are staffed with lawyers [3] because they are considered expert in the rules of judicial process. We think of the judge as an umpire who decides on rules of procedure, not on the quality of the law itself. Belief in judicial process as a way to truth is so ingrained that we find it difficult to recognize incongruities and mystifications in legal process—as when a jury of laymen decide on evidence submitted by experts whose testimony is far beyond their comprehension.

Public opinion rises to great heat if the judicial process is threatened. Those not committed by partisan belief to the guilt or innocence of the surviving Haymarket anarchists were thoroughly aroused once Governor Altgeld made public his view that: "it was no longer a matter of their guilt or innocence but the fairness of their trial." As long as Senator Joseph McCarthy attacked Communists, universities, the army, or the State Department, the public was content to witness a violent but interesting fight.[4] Where institutions (such as the State Department) could not go to the people or where they have not yet learned how to do so (as the universities) they were vulnerable to attack by Senator McCarthy. So long as the drama remained in the legislature, judgment was assumed to be colored by politics. But when the drama shifted from legislative halls to the court room, and people saw the judicial process itself subject to travesty, opinion rose sharply against Senator McCarthy. Conservatives and liberals rallied with radicals, for now the *principle* of democracy itself, judicial process, was in danger.

Absolutely unmodified utterance of traditional spells determines the efficacy of magic. Magical spells must be handed down, without change. The slightest alteration from the original pattern would be fatal, since the principle of order involved is safeguarded by fixed standardized procedures. Our science, by its claims wholly against mystification, is peculiarly subject to this type of mystification. Few people in our society have as much power as scientists who express themselves in symbols far beyond the comprehension of those whose lives are yet determined by them. Even those of us able to make competent judgments in one field must rely on authority in another. Like the faithful swallowing of the bread and wine consecrated by their priest, we swallow digests, abstracts, and résumés. We believe what we read, not because we really know how to test its validity but because the technique used is "correct," or the expression of results is "scientific."

It is characteristic of *any* symbol specialist to carry his symbols to the point where symbolic manipulation becomes a final value. The artist comes to believe that form is life, and thus the manipulation of such form becomes an end in itself. All goals, ends, purposes, heavens, hells, any ideal future whose immanence invests action to such degree that what is happening *now* can only be understood by what will happen *then,* offer peculiar temptations to mystification. Christian eschatology, Marxian classless heavens, and Wagnerian erotic immolations are but a few of these imaginary, yet powerful, futures. How many men have been maimed, tortured, and killed, how many millions doomed to starvation, slavery, and death by such promises of things to come! Once the promise is symbolized and these symbols become sacred, they are no longer subject to critical discussion. No one has returned from heaven, yet the true believer knows it exists and is often capable of torturing and killing those who do not share his vision.

SOCIAL PROGRESSION

The future created by the artist is not a way of escaping (as in make-believe) or of denying the world (as in ascetic religious life). We use art to prepare ourselves to act in the world. Love stories are read to create attitudes necessary to the experience of love. "Success stories" are searched for practical hints or to experience attitudes presumed to be consequent to success. Loyola taught his young Jesuits to envision the most horrible tortures so that they could be endured in reality. Concentration camp survivors tell us that the determining factor in the prisoner's initial reaction to life in a concentration camp was his conception of what would happen to him. The closer this conception came to reality, the less violent was his reaction. Patients can be better prepared for pain, the shock of battle reduced, and the pangs of birth lessened if dramatic rehearsal in the imagination precedes the act. The savage kills his enemy in the pantomime of the war dance to ready himself for the shock of battle when he must kill or be killed in reality.

We invoke posterity, as we do founding fathers, because our acts are burdened with a deep sense of time. Social time has duration because it has both a future and a past. The social order has not *been* created; it is *being* created. We are affected not only by myths of origin, but by apocalyptic myths of perfect ends, revelations of heavenly states of bliss for ourselves and hellish tortures for our enemies. What we are going *to,* as well as what we come *from,* determines social order. Even statisticians invoke the future to explain their data in time series. To say that in the years ahead conditions like those we now know will prevail is simply a statistical fiction. Yet by what we assume will happen in this future time we organize our data in the present. Who can "know" a future—or a past? Yet projections into futures (as in Marx with his proletarian apocalypse) and pasts (as in Darwin and Freud with their myths of genesis) are no less common among scientists than artists.

When the dramatist invokes judgment on the actions of the hero and villain, he does so through symbols infused with sacred pasts and blessed futures. These are invoked to resolve community crises, moments when action cannot go forward. We must observe what community symbols are invoked to resolve the crises. In the name of what community, institutional, or familial symbol does blocked action go forward? All such resolutions are based on principles of social order which find expression in dramatic form as acts. Names are not fictions, labels, or signs, but evocations of some kind of social order.

Christian cosmology, the great drama of man's fall and redemption, is one such symbol. The church links personal familial charisma (God the Father) with the mystery of creation, and then sends us a divine Son, who founds a school of prophecy and preaching where the drama of Christian heaven and hell is created. The whole range of social symbols, every type of transcendence, are combined in one powerful cosmological drama—the most powerful produced thus far in our society.

Social progression involves steps or stages as well as fixed levels. Action must go forward in proper order. Status procedures are not regular but ordinal, with canons of first, second, third, etc.—canons ranging from absolutes in presidents, kings, popes, or generals down to whatever rank is necessary to carry out action on a local level. Magical rites, the king's processional toward his throne, the army parade—these take form in progress from one stage to another through forms regulated by considerations of proper relationships between each step in a developmental sequence. Certain words must be uttered before others, the university marshal must precede the president, members of the faculty must be placed ahead of students. Orderly development in art thus has its counterpart in society. *How* we go from one position to another is as important as our points of arrival and departure. The king could run to his throne, the magician condense his incantation, but in doing so the king would lose his majesty, the magician weaken faith in his spell.

Dramatic progression, the style of action, becomes a form of grace in religion as well as in social and art expression. Hervey Elkins, a Shaker for fifteen years, tells us:

Not a single action of life, whether spiritual or temporal, from the initiative of confession, or cleansing the habitation of Christ, to that of dressing the right side first, stepping first with the right foot as you ascend a flight of stairs, folding the hands with the right thumb and fingers above those of the left, kneeling and rising again with the right leg first, and harnessing first the right-hand beast, but has a rule for its perfect and strict performance.

In social acts, form *is* content. We abstract form out of its context to study it, or, like the artist, to perfect it. But form is a constituent part of the context in which we act, and thus we cannot discuss content without at the same time discussing form.

As I write this page, I often stop and read what I have written. I do not write "in my head" and then copy down what is inside my head. What I write in the first paragraph will determine what I write in the next, just as what I write now is determined by what I imagine I will write in the conclusion. The type of conclusion I imagine is determined, I soon discover, by the structure of my expression. Form is not imposed *on* the work, it is the work. It is not making sexual needs known, but the style of making them known, that determines our erotic life. The nuances of proper form, the "elegant" way to make desire known, takes up a great share of action in every love story—great and popular alike.

All social acts have a structure laden with expectancies in one stage of what will occur in the next. Presenting the flag, celebrating a birth, burying our dead, the most serious as well as the most playful acts, are acts precisely because they have a formal structure in *time*. Even our experience of nature is determined by such forms. Storms have cycles, crops ripen, seasons are born, wax, wane, and die. Thus when we turn to create or use art, the experience of form is already part of our experience. Contrast, comparison, metaphor, are based in our ways of understanding anything. A form is a way of experiencing, a capacity, an ability to function which implies satisfaction in such function. Formal expectancies inspire us to reach out, to extend ourselves toward a future; they do not lie dormant until "triggered" into response. People who like to dress do not wait until they can exercise their sartorial skill; they seek out and create occasions for such display. We all try to establish conditions where we can exercise capacities we enjoy.

SOCIAL MYSTIFICATION AND THE PERFECTION OF HIERARCHY

Authorities expect artists to dignify and spiritualize their symbols of power with such radiance that institutional and individual glory becomes community glory. Burke has shown how such celestialization may be codified. There are terms assigned to the celestial order alone. There are symbols used only in the depiction of the worldly social order. There are symbols used to bridge sacred and secular realms. There are symbols explicitly social but implicitly celestial. There are symbols speciously celestial but actually social. Shifts from one to another of these conditions offer clues to the meaning of each. Carefully tended military cemeteries where crosses are aligned in rows with rank clearly indicated, show how worldly and celestial social distinction become subtly interwoven. We can imagine the dead rising, not perhaps to do battle (although Milton's Protestant heaven is scarcely a peaceful place), but still, as they arise, standing in proper military order, ready to march off in proper military formation.

In our society, the artist must invest the symbol of money with great resonance. Like the Holy Grail, money must become radiant, mysterious, dangerous, a principle of life which moves us deeply. If we refused to believe that money brings success in courtship, dignity in citizenship, and majesty in social relations its power would vanish. We have few sumptuary laws over the use of money. I may be punished for impersonating an officer, a priest, a policeman, or a female, but I am *encouraged* to impersonate plutocrats. I can rent plutocratic clothes, equipage, cars, even houses in which I entertain with a caterer who supplies food, service, and, if need be, guests. The constant and arduous task of keeping in the public eye is not a concession to public curiosity, but a necessity. The American businessman is no different from British royalty with its coronations, public receptions, courts, and world voyages. All symbols of sovereignty must be communicated to remain powerful.

The mysterious power of celestial symbols does not lie in their remoteness, incomprehensibility, or exclusiveness, but in their promise of some kind of higher life. Money in some amount can be had by all. Yet it is not only equality, but the promise of inequality which stirs us as we use money. At the moment I spend I am as good as the next man, yet at the same time I am better than those who do not spend, and superior to those who do not spend as much. In every stage of spending there is immanence of a higher life—what we call our ever-increasing standard of living. This "upward way" of money does not end in a state of financial bliss where everybody will have "enough" and be content. For in the American capitalistic paradise, discontent is truly divine.

Every social transcendence involves choice, and once choice is made, uneven distribution of social power is inevitable. Nor do we always choose correctly. Even when tribal symbols are invested with absolute power, the priest or magician must still ward off new threats to tribal solidarity. Such threats demand reexamination of traditions and goals. The allocation of symbols of power will favor some individuals at the expense of others. In all societies those in control of symbols of class and rank must uphold and yet transcend those of their own institution. In our society the single function of the tribal priest and magician is allocated to many symbol specialists such as journalists, legislators, educators, advertising men, and artists. The priestly stress upon sacred mysteries, which attains its most powerful expression in visions of a celestial hierarchy, is secularized and specialized in many roles.

Each attempts to maximize the mystery of his symbols. Even the educator, devoted to inquiry and reason and by his vocation specifically against priestly mystification, develops awesome ceremonials. Gothic architecture infuses education with feudal mystery. Majestic ceremonial music, stately processionals, and ancient feudal academic gowns evoke images of a sublime ruling class. The voice of the commencement orator becomes solemn and prophetic. Flanked by the flag and the cross, symbols of country and God, the orator's rising periods evoke the wisdom of academia as savior of the world. As we wend our way to the Gothic throne before which the majestic Chancellor stands to offer us our diploma, ancient processional music fills the nave of the cathedral.

The scholar, too, has his great dramatic Passion, even though it is a Passion of wisdom. The persecution and execution of Socrates, the sufferings of More and Erasmus, the struggle of Faust—these make the heroes (and sacrificial gods) of the humanist. As we identify with them a deep sense of community is born. Deans, chancellors, trustees, professors and students are brothers in a common cause because they are now playing parts in an ultimate mystery drama of wisdom. Even critical intelligence requires symbols of transcendent mystery. We cannot be sure; perhaps, after all is said and done, concern over man is a useless concern. But the human spirit quails before this terrible conclusion. As the humanist stands before the abyss of nothingness, he grasps the hand of the priest whose celestial symbols give him confidence to act. The humanist believes, indeed *must* believe, in critical inquiry as an absolute good. He creates Socratic utopias where philosophers are kings. He fashions symbolic paths to his kingdom of grace. For even as he doubts, he must act; and to act in community with others, he must infuse the present with purpose and meaning. He must make doubt a path to wisdom, not absurdity or negation.

All hierarchy rests on progression from a lower to a higher stage. Thus any improvement of status is a kind of transcendence. For those above who control the "mystery" are very powerful indeed. This power does not, however, reside in power of each rank to overlord an inferior rank, but in the acceptance by each rank of the principle of gradation—which acceptance "universalizes" the principle. This makes the spiritual reversal of the ranks just as meaningful as their actual social arrangement, for when we move into the realm of principle, we are not "of the world" but "of God," as Christians say. In this state, the reversal of social status makes as much sense as its actual worldly order. For, here, all that counts is the principle of hierarchy. Its levels, developments, unfoldings, progression, *as such,* are enough to uphold the mystery, since the principle is not dependent on development at all. It is "prior" to any development in time, for it existed before the hierarchy began, will exist after the world ends, and exists outside of all time.

It is easy enough for us to discover the supernatural mystifications of religion, but as we now begin to live in a world which can end at any minute (not by divine fiat, but by the explosion of a few bombs), the mystifications of method as we know them in science begin to weigh heavily upon us. Operational terms, like all terms, are subject to mystification. When we are asked to subsidize "pure" science, even to the end of our world, or when we are asked to believe that societies move "toward an equilibrium," we are in the realm of mystification. True, it is a new kind of mystification, the mystification of method. But it is mystification, nonetheless. "Pure" scientists have brought us to the brink of disaster, but the remedy, we are told, is not less pure science, but more! Now the scientist joins hands with the jurist who said: "Let justice be done, even though the heavens fall!"

The only way we can protect ourselves—if we can at all—from such mystifications is to become highly suspicious of *all* accepted hierarchies of ideas. When we are told that technology will bring us plenty, and thus rid the world of want, we should immediately assume the opposite. For the power of all great ultimates is in their power to make us believe that facts have a direct connection with ideals. In such thinking the god incarnate lurks in every commonplace. When we begin to discover "immutable laws of nature" and "tendencies toward rationalization" or "social forces tending toward equilibrium," we are linking purely material environmental images with some abstract principle or idea. Incarnation—the visit of the spirit to the earth, whether the spirit is a person like a god, a law of nature, a sacred act of creation, or a scientific method—is a mystification and should be treated as such.[5]

Notes

[1] In this book, for example, we say that society arises in, and exists through, the communication of symbols used to express relations between superiors, inferiors, and equals.

[2] Talcott Parsons and Edward A. Shils, *Toward a General Theory of Action* (Cambridge: Harvard Univ. Press, 1952), pp. 226–227.

[3] Tocqueville believed that the profession of the law is the only aristocracy that can exist in a democracy without doing violence to its own nature.

[4] Senator McCarthy's scurrility, like that of Westbrook Pegler, delighted a people who love disputation and who demand vigorous debate sprinkled with salty language from their politicians ("Give 'em hell, Harry"). Even on higher levels we relish exaggeration, caricature, cursing, and violence. Mencken's prose rings with images of violence and slapstick. Veblen's savage ironic cursing is much enjoyed among intellectuals.

[5] This is not an exhortation to do away with the scientific method, but to regard it as a means that must be tested by the human ends or values it produces.

24

Equality and Social Order

RULES AS A PRINCIPLE OF SOCIAL ORDER

OBEDIENCE to rules is a freely given act of the will among equals. In such cooperation reverence for the group is very deep, perhaps in some ways deeper than feudal or patriarchal types of obedience where the will of the master is the will of God.[1] Among inferiors, the cheater is cunning and, if successful at outwitting authority, a hero (as in Aesop). As equals, we make cheaters into villains and banish them from our company, because the rules they break are *our* rules, the common will of equals. The cheater indicates that group will is not *his* will, and, since among equals rules must be honored deeply if there is to be any group at all, such cheating threatens the group.

To the degree that individuals are "free," their social bonds must be deeply interiorized, just as in independent and widely scattered military operations individual soldiers must be deeply convinced of their cause to fight well. When soldiers are slaves, serfs, or mercenaries, we herd them into battle and deploy them in close groups where close personal control is possible. We *expect* such soldiers to break in panic and prepare officers to deal with initial battle shock. Perhaps this is why "people's armies" are always mass armies which fight as mobs. Soldiers given no moral training cannot be individuals as soldiers. Those who follow authority blindly or through fear cannot fight alone, for they obey voices outside, not within, the self.

Submission to rules is no different, in one respect, from submission to personal authority. In each case we obey because we reverence the principle in which the authority rests. The SS officer tortured and murdered his hapless victims in German concentration camps, not simply because he received orders but because he *believed* that in carrying out such acts he was preserving social order. His human victims were "lice"; the operation of the murder camps, "delousing." The principal of a democratic school asks his students to obey, but to obey rules which have been discussed and agreed upon. In obedience to authoritarian command (as in Hitler's "leadership principle") we *surrender* our will; in obedience to rules we *lend* our will to the occasion. We are bound *only* to the task at hand, just as social bonds of the team last *only* as long as the game.

When rules become law in a democratic society, the right to change or repeal of law through popular discussion and parliamentary debates is still upheld. Change, as well as fixity, is provided for. The test of law, as of rules, is its effects on the general welfare of the community. Law among equals is not intended to keep everyone on the same level, for, even in the simple tasks, individual differences in strength, cunning, skill, and luck will operate. Nor is democratic law obeyed as "fate" or "destiny." It is obeyed because we accept individual responsibility for the working of the law. Such law is not some force outside us but a law created and sustained by us. It is *our* law.

In obedience to rules we reserve the right to question and criticize, but since the will of equals is the basis for the authority of rules, differences must be resolved through arbitration. We expect equals to argue long and powerfully, just as we expect teams to argue over rules being prepared for official rule books of their games. The function of the arbitrator is not to create rules himself, but to lead discussion to common agreement and to prepare such agreement for vote by all those bound by the rules. In such agreement we cooperate to act as individuals. We guard our own uniqueness and are highly conscious of the uniqueness of others. Antagonism and hate exist beside friendship and love. Perhaps, indeed, antagonism among equals is a heavier burden than among superiors and inferiors bound by commandments. Equals must assume individual responsibility for their antagonism and hate. They obey a decision, not a person. Authority is a decision reached through discussion; its fairness rests on *how* it was reached, not *who* reached it, and antagonism to decisions can be remedied by periodical reviews in which all those involved can share.

Rules are possible only among equals. And since equals must reach decisions through agreement, the rhetoric of rules is less subject to mystification than truths based on tradition or custom.[2] These truths, which "originate" in some kind of divinity whose truths are revealed, in natures whose workings are "discovered" and "reported" or societies whose "sacred rituals" alone guarantee order, are peculiarly liable to mystification and magic. Where we cannot question, we cannot reason. The purpose, or value, of rules must be subject to reason as well as faith. Parliamentary procedure makes reason possible because it maximizes conditions for discussion and criticism. When we lose faith in open and free discussion, parliamentary debate becomes a sign of weakness, not strength, and rules give way to the "leadership principle."

We respect rules, but we learn to respect them through reason as well as faith. A code of honor must be open to question and doubt, if we are to keep ends and means in relationship between equals open to reason. Within the class subject to codes of honor there will be equality under the code, just as within a team all players and spectators must subordinate themselves to rules. But the question must always be asked: Who *cannot* be equal? We must learn to watch carefully those who promise equality to all, and then tell us that under such equality "some will be more equal than others." Equality is determined by means, as well as ends, and whoever has access to means will reach ends closed to those without them. Some means cannot be equalized, and thus, as we have said, superiority and inferiority will always exist. But where means to equality are kept open to all, and where means-end relationships in conduct are open to critical discussion, equality reaches its highest social function—the dignification of reason in society.

PLAY AND SOCIATION

The purest form of relationships among equals exists in social play (as at a party). Such play has no objective purpose, no content, no result beyond the gathering itself. Its rules depend for their power on the success of the moment. Hence the conditions and results of the game exist only in the interaction of players who, once play begins, subordinate themselves to the rules of the gathering. For whatever power participants possess in other roles cannot be used in a group submitting itself to the authority of rules.

We do not play with superiors, we obey them. We do not play with inferiors, we command them. I can play the fool to the king, but he cannot play the fool to me unless he can step out of his role as king. Only when we forget ourselves, in relation to the world beyond the moment of social play, can there be play. Great games are serious even though everyone knows they are only games, but we are serious about the game itself, not the power and the glory of the players in their roles outside the game. We reduce the power of rank to enhance the power of rules. Only as we are equal under rules, and are willing to risk our skill in terms of the rules, can the excitement of the game increase.

But, however serious, play is still play. The gravity of Japanese manners, the deep concentration of huntsmen stalking game, and the tense solemnity of gamblers are serious but not "sacred." As in every kind of symbolic manipulation, those who are highly skilled in hierarchal etiquette tend to make it an end in itself. We then hear of manners for manners' sake, as we do art for art's sake. But once manners are used solely for power, as when only the king may speak but must not be spoken to, the play element vanishes. For the essence of the game is self-imposed rules, contest between equals, and "umpirage." Once the rules are sacred, and beyond the power of the players themselves, and the "impartial third" is taken over by a priesthood who are not responsible to the players, we are in the realm of ritual, not play. Jefferson thought so highly of "umpirage" that he made it central to justice:

No man has a natural right to commit aggression on the equal rights of another, and this is all from which the laws ought to restrain him; every man is under the natural duty of contributing to the necessities of society, and this is all the laws should enforce on him; and no man having a natural right to be the judge between himself and another, it is his natural duty to submit to the umpirage of an impartial third.

The social spirit of play comes to full expression in the deep sense of solidarity we experience when we play together. As we greet each other, talk, and sip drinks, social excitement and pleasure increase. We play our roles in a drama of sociation, a drama which has no message, no meaning beyond the meaning of sociation itself. Yet the power of this drama is very great. In mixed gatherings we are assailed by every sensual charm of dress, coiffure, perfume. Music, painting, architecture, and dance create an atmosphere of delight. At no time is a woman's body so carefully powdered and perfumed. Yet nowhere is lust so controlled, for the drama of sociation subordinates sensuality to its own ends. The solidarity we develop in play indicates a deep relationship between biological and social elements. Animals play, and among animals, as among men, the stronger withholds his strength so that the game may go on. The subordination of the individual to the game is characteristic of all play. And play, which to be play must be among equals subordinate to rules, is shared by all creation. There is even a kind of cosmological play, as in the myths in which the play of gods produces new creations. The chess player literally plays a feudal world of kings, queens, knights, bishops, and pawns. The two players sit like brooding gods whose thoughtful moves determine the world.

We respect our superiors, assume responsibility for our inferiors, but the touchstone of our relationship with equals is tact. Tactlessness is hated and feared because so long as we must relate as equals we are dependent on limits which the individual must respect if we are to continue enjoying our group role. The tactless person throws individuals back on themselves because he is insensitive to the group-determined phases of their relatedness. When deep individual differences have been transcended by values created in play, roles assume qualities of their own. Ideas take form, wit sparkles, amiability warms us, for now I share myself with other selves. I forget politics, religion, education, and wealth, not because they no longer exist, but because they are transcended by a bond of another kind, a bond which has no meaning beyond its purely social expression of solidarity.

Joking lifts sociation into the realm of play. As we laugh together we feel a deep sense of identification. This cooperative element complements the equally hostile character of wit. Players in any game contest sharply, but their aggressions are created by the game itself, are subject to conscious public control, and vanish once the game is over. We do not love each other less, but more, once we have expressed hostility in approved ways. It is not being hostile, but being unable to express hostility which makes hate dangerous. When I express hostility before a group significant to me, the burden of my hostility lightens. But the price I pay for this is the subjection of myself to the group. If they agree with me, hostility is no longer a burden but a pleasure. If they disagree, I must stop being hostile or leave the group. When we do not want to be a member of the same group as the person we dislike, or we do not know how to express our hostility in ways the group will sanction, we cannot joke.

In any play-form of sociation there will be differences of skill, energy, effort, and will. Some will play harder than others, some will have positions which the rules themselves make more important than others. But this is not the same as differences in wealth, fame, social position, beauty, or erudition, which have been established by factors extrinsic to the rules and which must be subordinated to the rules if the game is to continue. Whatever remains purely personal, or reflects moods of depression, despondency, or exhilaration, militates against play. Intrusion of purely personal elements is tactless, we feel, not because we are insensitive to the sufferings and joys of the individual, but because in so far as we are playing roles in a group bound by rules, highly subjective personal expression spoils the game. This is one reason we use humor so much in play.

Laughter breaks down the distance subjective concern creates between individuals. Gaiety takes us out of ourselves into the moment of sociation because in gaiety we submit to others.

In erotic play the most outrageous flirting is permitted, so long as it is done in fun. The woman desired as partner in this play is not the most beautiful, or even the one who stirs our lust, but the most skilled player of the erotic game. The laughter and gaiety she arouses eliminate all intimacy from sex. We do not need to consider this woman as an individual who must be courted and won. The mind is free; the mysterious difference of sex is overcome. Now sex is expressed in a form communicable within a group, not limited to a couple. Outside the group, flirting is interpreted as a prelude to the sexual act; within the group, erotic desire is transformed from pursuit, consent, or refusal into play. The instinctual drive of sexual passion no longer determines our sexual roles.

"PLAYING SOCIETY": THE SOCIAL FUNCTION OF THE GENTLEMAN

Expression of taste among gentlemen is never simply an "embellishment." To be in fashion is not only to exercise taste, as a child might select ribbons, but to relate to those in power and, in the case of the heroes and heroines of fashion, to *be* a power. The gentleman ideal reaches concrete embodiment through skill in creating and communicating symbols of hierarchy. Books of etiquette deal with the efficiency of various forms of address between different social classes. There are many subtleties in such address, as we see in the expression of humility. Status modesty, like virginal blushes, indicates our awareness, not our ignorance, of what is going on. As we blush while the great man addresses us, we tell him how deeply we feel his majesty, how we long to communicate with him, but how concerned we are over doing it properly and thus upholding the status system in which he is so important. Deference is complicated, indirect, and yet the most elegant of all compliments. Sexual modesty enhances the charm of women because it stimulates curiosity and the virility of men who desire to be the first to possess what others want but have not yet had. Chesterfield and other aristocratic aphorists stress the hierarchal efficiency of modesty. "Modesty is the only sure bait when you angle for praise." The genteel, modest person makes us long to please him, for as we do so he becomes a responsive audience who longs to be won over to the glory of our majesty.

To "play the social game" in any society indicates possession of the right to enhance one's own personality. When the counters in the social game become money, and the right to money is open to all, the enhancement of the self takes on new dimensions. The "social game" can now be played before many different publics, for so long as money can be earned and spent freely anyone who has money can become a public person. This is the final power of every democratic symbol of hierarchy. Through its use we are able to enter many groups necessary to our personal cultivation. Poise, elegance, the stately grace and gay elegance of the ideal nobleman become possible, as Goethe points out in *Wilhelm Meister,* because the nobleman gains a wider range of response than was possible to the burgher of 1800. "A burgher may acquire merit; by excessive efforts he may even educate his mind; but his personal qualities are lost, or worse than lost, let him struggle as he will." But the nobleman "is hampered by no limits," for "his figure, his person, are a part of his possessions, and it may be the most necessary part—he has reason enough to put some value on them, and to show he puts some." Wilhelm turns to the stage, for "On the boards a polished man appears in his splendor with personal accomplishments, just as he does so in the upper classes of society; body and spirit must advance with equal steps in all his studies; and there I shall have it in my power at once to be and seem, as well as anywhere."

Elegant expression of hierarchal address affects us deeply because the form of address idealizes or spiritualizes action of a kind we value. One style of bowing is more elegant than another. As I bow I indicate to the lady my belief in her elegance at the same time as I express my own. Table manners, like style in clothes as established by the gentleman and the lady, create a drama of hierarchy. Table training for children is not so much training in how to get food in the mouth (the child manages this easily enough), but how to indicate status to others (and thus to himself) as he eats. The gentleman perfects the forms of taste (in whatever context) so we all can use them in hierarchal communicatio.a. He becomes, in short, a stylist of social form. Thus social play is not limited to the affairs of "high society," although among ladies and gentlemen the play of manners developed for purely social expression reaches high levels of elegance and grace. Every institution creates and polishes its own style of social play. In America entertainment is a constituent part of business life. Business itself is discussed as a game in which making, not possessing, money brings honor. Few American businessmen give up business once they have made money. Retired executives continue daily visits to the office. The sons of rich families establish a downtown office. American office design sets a varied and rich stage for the social aspects of money making, since the office is a place to socialize as well as to work.

Matters of taste become binding norms because as we express taste we *address* others and thus indicate our sense of community with them. The child, as delegate to groups beyond the intimate family circle, symbolizes the propriety or impropriety of parents' or grandparents' own manners. The contests between the mother and father, between the father and child, or the mother and child have a hierarchal as well as sexual element. As we dress our child for school, church, family visits, or other public appearances, we invest him with status trappings which indicate actual or desired social position. There are great contradictions between realities, wishes, and skill in the child's status enactment. The child, the prototype of all "little fellows" struggling to communicate with powerful "big fellows," must attempt appeals to baffling authorities of all kinds. His status frustrations are legion. Unlike the adult, he cannot use humor, wit, or irony to overcome them. Sometimes he turns to symbolic killing and other symbolic variants of victimage, not because he is more perverse than the adult, but because he has no other way of expressing deep hierarchal frustrations.

The gentleman may be appointed to public office but the office alone does not give him power. The Confucian gentleman became a mandarin and was appointed to public office, not because of technical skill in administration but because of his skill in the humanities. The Whig aristocrats of 1700–1830 and the dandies of Disraeli's time ruled through their charisma as gentlemen, as well as through their skill as administrators. Their philosopher, Shaftesbury, held that good taste had a positive ethical validity, since taste, and taste alone, implied a harmony between morals and art. Their hero, Charles James Fox, essentialized the mystery and glamor of the gentleman. He was trusted in office because he knew the arts of life. For Fox and his friends comedy, wit, irony, the play of mind and reason were as serious as tragedy and were ethically more desirable because laughter banished mystery. Shaftesbury (like Erasmus) thought belief without "folly" (the comic spirit) opened the soul to fanaticism. He distrusted complete abandonment of religion to the tragic sense of life because too often tragic ritual ended in priestly mystification. God could be civil and gay, as well as vengeful and sad. We could understand and forgive in smiles as well as tears.

The gentleman believes that, like the priest, the soldier, the statesman, or the educator, he too creates and sustains public order. He abstracts sociation out of its specific institutional context in religion, politics, or the family and invests it with social grace. He thus becomes the hero of culture, as the statesman and the priest are heroes of politics and religion. His function is to perfect social intercourse—the ways we meet, talk, greet, take leave—the forms of sociation itself. The gentleman creates an art of life; he spiritualizes talk and socialization until poetry finds a home in social life because socializing itself *is* poetic. Until a society produces its gentlemen we do not know its concrete human meaning. The gentleman embodies the "sociable" character of a group.

High society tries to create a poetry of sociation, an elegant drama where characters have an air of living on ambrosia and having only noble preoccupations. Care, want, passion do not exist. Realism, being brutal, is suppressed. The women of this world are like Olympian goddesses visiting the earth. They have no vital organs, no weight; they retain of their human nature only what is needed for grace and pleasure. Such society endows itself with a flattering illusion, that of being in an ethereal state and breathing the life of mythology. Because of this, any vehemence, any cry of nature, any real suffering, any unreflecting familiarity, any frank sign of passion shocks and reverberates in this delicate atmosphere; any crudity at once destroys the collective work, the palace of clouds, the magic architecture created by common consent. Gatherings of such elites unconsciously try to produce a sort of concert of the eyes and ears, an extempore work of art. Neither wealth, social position, erudition, fame, nor great merit alone is enough to assure playing a part in this drama.

PLAY AND EQUALITY

The sociological function of play is to teach us to be equal by subordinating ourselves to the rules which are self-imposed and adjudicated by agreement.[3] We must learn to rule others, we must learn to obey, but we must also learn to be equal. Until we learn this, friends, companions, comrades, colleagues, peers of any kind are impossible because we do not know how to relate to them. We do not choose to be equal, we must be. The specific form of superiority and inferiority under a tyranny or a democracy does not eliminate the need for equality. Where differential status is limited, where there are few top positions open to inferiors, where hierarchal changes are made slowly, and yet where all are taught to be leaders, disrelationships among peers may threaten social order as much as deep hatred between superiors and inferiors. Louis XIV is reported to have said: "Every time I fill a vacant place I make a hundred malcontents and one ingrate." A clever tyrant stirs up discontent among peers, but he must purge his peerage of dangerous malcontents. Purges please those who fear the ambition of their colleagues. By creating new peers Stalin removed threats to his own power and opened fresh hope to ambitious equals and inferiors. Where "few die and none resign" and there are always more applicants than jobs, purges are always popular.

Pleasure in play arises out of contest. We play to win, but to win honorably. Policemen shooting craps could arrest their fellow gamblers, army colonels gambling with enlisted men could order them detained, plutocrats could give millions to other businessmen, fencing masters could easily wound and kill their opponents, but this would destroy the contest. Players feel themselves to be subordinated not to each other but to the game, whose rules, while binding, are so only by consent and are open to question by any player. Whatever destroys equality before these self-imposed rules stops the game. When equality dies, honor dies, for only equals willing to risk with other equals create honor. Honor originates in loyalty to a code, not to persons. Play rules are designed to make the risk the same for all, not to minimize it. Money play is no longer play once the game is fixed. Play rules cannot be used for mystification since questions about rules are permitted. We do not ask a priest or a prophet whether he has interpreted the rules correctly; we ask him to tell us what to do.

As we move from the simple games of childhood, through popular sports, to the most profound cosmologies, the essence of play remains. Gods and devils alike play. Even in Christianity we sometimes stress the fellowship of piety and laughter. In many cultures play is sacred. The Hindus and Chinese hold that joy born in play re-creates social bonds. The god is not danced *to,* he is *danced*. In the joy of play we inspire each other to heights we could never attain alone. The weight of hierarchal difference lifts, and we know joy in these differences. The final greatness of play is reached when we literally play society as among the Greeks and the English in their great dramas of community life. In America we do this in politics, where the stake in the great game of politics is the well-being of the community itself.

Inferiors, like superiors, destroy social play if we cannot become equal to them, and they will not, or cannot, become equal to us. The student who treats me like Socrates at a social gathering bores me and arouses dislike in others, not because I do not want to be thought of as like Socrates in the classroom, but because in a Socratic role I cannot be equal to others in a social gathering and hence cannot play. To intrude inferiority among peers opens the superior to ridicule; to intrude superiority evokes contempt. But in relations among equals, the play form of sociation *must* dominate. More skilled players win, but at least they began as equals. The loser is not dishonored, so long as he gave his best to the game. The winner is not hated, so long as he won according to the rules.

In play all submit to rules, but these rules, unlike legal codes, court protocol, or sacred traditions, are self-imposed, subject to change, and determined by mutual consent. Thus while an equal has no power over equals, rules have power over all. If the king personifies the majesty of aristocratic law; tribal elders, the power of tradition; the prophet, the power of a new life; then the referee personifies the bonds of agreement among equals. Players may challenge the fairness of a discussion, spectators demand a reconsideration of judgment. Rules are sacred only so long as they express agreement in common action. The umpire as guardian of the rules is but the delegate of contesting parties. His power is legitimized solely through our faith in a way of reaching agreement and through the binding quality of these agreements. We do not expect our umpire to be wise, holy, pious, ingenious, or prophetic. We expect him to be fair—that is, to judge each impartially according to rules made or agreed to by all. His expertness derives from knowledge of the rules, but since we can agree to change the rules, his power comes from his application not creation of rules. He represents the will of equals.

As gamblers, we lead lives detached from the cares of the night or the fear of tomorrow. Once my stake is in the pot and the cards are being turned up, I am beyond daily concern with money. The dollar I count so carefully or talk about so judiciously with my banker, is now tossed onto the table. I strive to attain purely social elements in the use of money. As players our differences in other roles vanish, and we enjoy a new communion with each other. In play we recover much of the humanity we have lost in the market. As we honor the amateur we honor the element of sociability which the game abstracts out of experience. The gentleman cricket player, the college football player, and Olympic contestants place competition and rivalry beyond profit. Competition is purified, not because it is eliminated, but subordinated to a higher principle of sociation.

In social play the other is my equal, and I in turn am his equal, not in the eyes of God, as in religion, or of the people, as in democracy, but in terms of charm, amiability, refinement, gaiety, and interest. In this world there are no commands, no majesty. Social distance narrows as the intimacy born of play of mind and spirit inspires all to warmth and joy. Nothing exists outside of the golden moment of sociation. It is, we say, "purely social." Such play is of decisive importance in human relationships because in such joy social euphoria is born and new energy given to our social bonds.

HIERARCHY AND EQUALITY

We do not discuss with superiors; we follow their commands. We do not converse with inferiors; we tell them what to do. But among equals the response of the other is as important as the address of the speaker. For, as we have pointed out in our discussion on dialogue between individuals, all conversation among equals is based on commitment, a trust in the other, and a belief that his response to my address is motivated by a desire to act together in community. Confidence contributes more than wit to conversation (as La Rochefoucauld reminds us). Plato, Montaigne, La Rochefoucauld, and Hume (among others) tell us that the conversation of a friend is the highest pleasure in life because, in such moments, there is a deep sense of communion with another human being, not with a remote and awesome god. Thus friendship becomes the most profoundly social of all relationships.

A great deal has been said in social theory about superiority and inferiority. We have pointed out, in our discussion of Freud, that psychology no less than sociology often confuses order in social relations with authoritarian order. Freud's father is a despot, sometimes benevolent, but in his primitive Oedipal days at least, lustful and cruel. Students of animal life, even those like W. C. Allee who study the social life of animals, describe despotism as "one of the major biological principles." [4] Political philosophers like Tocqueville argue that only in authority of the kind known in religion is there any guarantee of order, for "men will never establish any equality with which they can be contented." [5] It has often been pointed out, too, that the doctrine of equality seldom embraces those who are worse off than its exponents.

But even the most authoritarian social order must have moments of equality, for it is only among equals that we find conversation and discussion. The essence of conversation is that each *talks back* to the other. In such address we do not *know* what we mean, and then announce it to the other, as superiors do when they issue a proclamation, nor do we petition a favor, as inferiors do when they address a superior. I talk to the other to find out what I mean, as he, in turn, talks to me to discover his meaning through my response to him. Much has been made by Simmel, Malinowski, and Mead of the informality of conversation. And while it is true that there are many informal moments in talk, such talk is possible only because many social forms exist in which talkers can meet as equals. Like any social relationship, relationships among equals in talk are carefully contrived forms of association. This is especially true of the many forms of conversation, ranging from searching philosophical discussion to the idle chatter of a casual meeting. Nothing in democratic society is more "formal" than the codification of rules for public discussion. Even on purely informal levels we hear much about the "art of conversation." And where conversation is considered a method of inquiry (as it is in seminars, and as it was in the salons of Paris) much attention is given to creating proper conditions for talk. Equality, and specifically equality in talk, is basic to all forms of conversation, because it is only when we can talk freely and openly (even though the subject may be limited to set themes) that we really converse and thus create what so many students of society [6] have called the "characteristic" human act.

In games, play, and debate (the game of talk) there is always a contest. The honor of winning depends on how the contestants are matched. Where they are unevenly matched, great care is taken to handicap the stronger so that the contest will be, as we say, "equal." As a social form, equality ranges from the simple games of childhood to the most profound conversations of the wise and sacred guardians of the community. It has been suggested that the true function of equality is to act as a counterweight against the power of authority as expressed in superiority and inferiority, but equality, as a form of sociation, exists in its own right and must not be subordinated to superiority and inferiority.[7]

Certainly there is no other way to explain much of what goes on in society unless we give equality a central place in any scheme of hierarchy. The time and effort put into games, play, and contests of all kinds, and the constant use of conversational techniques in activities ranging from the cure of sick souls to the development of science, indicate the importance of equality. We are accustomed to this in parliamentary procedure where all are subject to rules of order, but we forget that much of our social life is equally dependent on rules. Peer relationships are necessary to the efficient functioning of a society as are relationships determined by superiority and inferiority, for only in such relationships can individuality flourish. The "I" becomes an "I" *through conversation* with a "You" which, internalized, becomes a "Me."

From an authoritarian view, equality is a sign of weakness and often of hypocrisy. Conservatives point out how slogans for equality mask inequality. There is much truth in this, for when we raise one group to equal status, we often lower another to inferior rank. This is particularly true of political equality. Radicals point out that those who have power are sensitive enough about equality within their own class but show little concern for granting equality to outsiders. Conservative and radical alike accuse each other of being concerned only with changing the composition of the elite groups who rule society. Equality is simply a slogan, used to convince people to throw off one yoke so that another can be placed on them.

AUTHORITY AND VICTIMAGE

There are perversions of equality as there are in relations between superiors and inferiors. But this does not mean that there is no need for equality or that authority can function without equality. The child needs his playmates, just as he needs his parents. The college student needs his friends, just as he needs his teachers. The worst despot must have councilors and administrators who can act together, if only to administer the state. And if the dangers of equality in "leveling down" are great, so too are the dangers of superiors confusing their wishes with principles of social order equally great. Enough has been said about mystification as a source of social integration to make this clear. Superiors are jealous guardians of mysteries whose rituals are sacred because they are believed to create and sustain social order. The divinity of the king, the authority of the father, like the greatness of a god, are believed *necessary* to the state, the family, and the universe.[8]

Authoritarian leaders often rule by division. They search for differences, and pit those who differ against each other ("Divide and Rule"). Thus they accentuate difference as a technique in ruling. Egalitarian leaders rule through cooperation. They search for areas of likeness and similarity of interest, and bring together those who have common interests. Equals expect conflict among themselves but, unlike superiors, create social forms in which equals can oppose each other to resolve differences by decision reached through discussion. Superiors resolve conflict through identification of their voice with the voice of God.[9] Thus, as we have said, we seek to convince equals, but we petition superiors.

Arguments that aristocracy but not democracy will guarantee social order, have little to do with the observable facts of social life. It is absurd to argue that a child should be equal to his parents, but it is equally absurd to argue that this is the only kind of relationship the child needs to know. Children, like adults, spend a great amount of time with their peers. And the social psychology of Dewey, Mead, Simmel, and Burke certainly makes it apparent that the kind of relations developed in play (both in games and art) *constitute hierarchy, as much as the kind of relationships developed in superiority and inferiority.* For if we must learn to be "good" sons and daughters so we can in turn become "good" parents, we must also learn to play our roles as "good" companions, friends, colleagues, partners, associates, comrades, and all the other social roles in which we must perform as equals.

Authorities who rule by division, and who believe that conflict alone brings out the energy of men, end by encouraging conflict. So long as conflict can be directed against a common enemy abroad, there will be little conflict at home. But when the enemy abroad is defeated, or peace is reached through agreement, some kind of enemy must be discovered at home, and if he does not exist, he must be created. For only the existence of a cunning and powerful enemy justifies demands for power. And finally, the enemy must embody a principle of evil, so that when we torture and kill him, we destroy a *principle,* not merely a person, for only then can we destroy him as a scapegoat in open and public ceremonial. In such purges, the criminal becomes a sacrificial victim whose confession saves him from eternal damnation and whose death purges our community of evil.

The problem for the ruler (democratic and authoritarian alike) is not one of admitting that he is being disobeyed, for he has already admitted by his criminal statutes and the presence of his army that he expects disobedience, disloyalty, and enmity. Rather, it is a problem of how to deal with disobedience so that the principle of social order on which his rulership rests is upheld. Thus the ideal criminal, from the ruler's view, is one who not only confesses to the crime of disobedience but admits that he was wrong to disobey authority. That is, he must not only confess, but recant, and he must be willing to recant before publics significant to those in power. Punishment of disobedience must be symbolized, styled, and staged, so that the majesty of the principle underlying obedience is glorified.

Sublimity has its uses in social life. It keeps the mystery of our majesty alive, and instills awe into those who seek communication with us. Yet inferiors cannot remain forever distant from powers they think sublime. Even though we are affected deeply by the glory of our masters, we must know whether we have communicated with them. Superiors cannot dazzle us too long, for intense radiance of majesty blinds superior and inferior alike. Passage from sublime to common levels must be open if we are to communicate both as superiors and inferiors. Even on the sexual level, a woman who is dressed "fit to kill" or whose appearance is "stunning," must, if she desires communicating with those she is affecting, create conditions where her sublimity may be reduced. Sublimity is only one phase of hierarchy, and if continued too long it becomes insupportable. Even the gods, or at least the classical gods, came to earth to relieve the strain of living on Olympus.

Nothing indicates the need for tyrants to communicate with their inferiors more than the trials that accompany purges. The climax of such trials is usually a confession in which the "deviant" (formerly called the "heretic") confesses not only to his crime, but to the evil in his crime. This is a highly dramatic moment, and like all powerful drama, it is carefully staged. It is important that the culprit play his role well; every effort must be made not simply to obtain a confession of guilt, but a good rousing confession. The state prosecutor, in turn, must do more than prove the culprit's guilt, for it is obvious in such trials that the culprit has been found guilty. The prosecutor, the hero in the drama of persecution and vengeance, must dramatize the horror of the crime.

The tyrant thinks of a trial as *a communication of power,* not a search for the innocence or guilt of the accused. In authoritarian communities the innocence or guilt of the accused is decided *before* the trial; in democratic communities it is decided *during* the trial. The drama of the democratic trial is the struggle between the prosecution and the defense. The confession as such means nothing, and, if it can be proved that it was obtained by force, it is not even admitted as evidence. The drama of the authoritarian trial is the confession of the accused, not to the fact that he committed a crime, but of how he was seduced by enemies of the state and fell into evil ways. Such a confession, a confession which dramatizes and thus communicates the struggle of the community guardians to guarantee the safety of the community, must be prepared as an address, not only to the court, but to the whole community.

Beaten, drugged, or terrified victims make poor figures in court, as the Nazis discovered when they "tried" the Dutch Communist Van der Lubbe for the Reichstag fire, which was staged by the Nazis as Communist sabotage. The foreign press ridiculed the trial because Van der Lubbe was "obviously incapable" of such a crime. Hitler had not learned what Stalin knew, namely, that the power of the devil *dramatizes* the power of God. A poor, witless, bedraggled devil in a struggle against a powerful majestic god makes the god ridiculous.[10] A strong, cunning, and powerful devil enhances the power of God. Like any villain, he must be almost equal to the hero if the hero is to gain honor in vanquishing him. The villain Hitler used to dramatize his struggle against evil was not the enemy within, but without, Germany.

Hitler was able to transfer the public drama of treason (the enemy within) to the drama of war (the enemy without) because he went to war soon after his rise to power. Russian Communists did not (indeed, could not) go to war against an outside enemy until many years after their rise to power. Social disorganization, such as the failure of crops, breakdowns in transportation, and the lack of consumer goods and services, could therefore be explained only by developing an enemy within. In Russia, purges were used to *create* an enemy within the state and to dramatize his power and cunning. Prisoners were selected for their possibilities as stars in these propaganda trials and were trained as carefully as Hollywood movie stars for their public performances. German purges were not mounted as public dramas. The concentration camp was a private ritual drama of purification for the Nazi party. The blood of Jews washed away Nazi sins because racial impurities were washed away. But no Jew could be used in public trial, for how could a "racial degenerate" be allowed to stand up in court to contest the power of Hitler? Tracking down anti-Communists and "convincing" them to confess was a trial of strength, a victory over a cunning and stubborn enemy. Breaking the will of a Jew or any "animal," as the Nazis in the SS were taught to regard those they exterminated, was not a trial of strength but the sacrifice of a scapegoat. Thus the Jew was never "prepared" for confession or allowed to recant and save himself as he was during the Spanish Inquisition, but was slaughtered like any sacrificial animal.

THE RESOLUTION OF HATE AND LOVE AMONG EQUALS

A great flaw in discussions on equality is the lack of stress on conflict among equals. "Sharing" is too often sharing love, but not hate. It is expected that superiors and inferiors will hate as well as love, and a great deal of ruling class rhetoric is devoted to how to deal with the hatred of superiors by inferiors. In art, and most clearly in dramatic art, this principle is recognized in the personification of love and hate in the hero and the villain. In religious ritual, too, God is love and the Devil is hate. And certainly Freud and La Rochefoucauld have taught us that love and hate determine each other. Thus, to discuss any form of hierarchy without taking both hate and love into account is fallacious.

Hate among equals is expressed in competition and rivalry. A superior cannot compete with a rival; he must destroy him. For if the superior is all-powerful, how can there be any other power? If the inferior feels secure in the absolute power of his superior, as the child does with his father, any threat to the power of the superior is a threat to the security of the inferior.[11] To inferiors agreement between equals is a sign of weakness. In their eyes arbitration is surrender and compromise is treason. Evil cannot be cured through wisdom arrived at in open, free, and informed discussion, but through sacrifice and atonement which will affect the will of the superior. Guilt and sin can only be expiated by the superior, for how can a humble inferior affect the will of the gods?

But equals struggle and compete with each other under rules, and before audiences of men, not gods. These rules are not made to discourage, but to encourage, rivalry and struggle, for rules define *how* we can struggle. They are a social sanction for rivalry. They tell us how we can disagree, for if we are in agreement what need do we have of rules? But rules of play, game, and art are careful to contain violence within certain limits, because when force enters a contest among equals they can no longer be equal as their struggle is no longer determined by their will as equals and their agreement to reach and settle differences under commonly agreed rules. When sharp disagreement occurs or the game becomes too one-sided, the contest must stop and new handicaps must be arranged to equalize the players.

We are permitted, indeed, exhorted, to scorn and hate our rivals. In the heat of the game, curses, imprecations, and all kinds of insults are hurled at our opponents by spectators and players alike. The villain in the play is cursed—indeed, some of our greatest art (both sacred and secular) is but a curse. Just as there is vicarious atonement in religion, there is vicarious cursing in art. In art we throw aside the trammels of civilization and the flimsy veil of love. At games we scream and yell at opponents, as at another time the Roman audience at the circus screamed for the life or the death of those struggling beneath them in the amphitheater. In such moments we become gods—gods not of love, but of vengeance and hate. As a member of an audience or a team, *my* hate now becomes *our* hate, a hate I can express with others and thus enjoy free of inhibition.

But, unlike hate in war, where I hate as a vengeful god who must torture and kill to rid the community of evil, hatred in games, play, and art is *symbolic* hate. A member of the audience who rushes onto the stage to kill the villain is seized and hurried off for "observation." The spectator who rushes to the field to grapple with the umpire or the coach of an opposing team is rushed to jail. But the soldier who rushes at his foe to wound and kill him is not punished, but honored. For the enemy cannot be treated as an equal, but as a disobedient, disloyal, and, therefore, evil inferior. What is his sin? Simply that his will is not my will, and, since there can only be one will, I must punish him for setting his against mine.

As we see in games, play, and art, we do not get rid of hate by denying it, but by *expressing* it. As the curtain goes down on *Hamlet, Romeo and Juliet,* or the television Western, the stage is piled with corpses. We have seen the villain hunted and driven like a beast into a corner where he is beaten and killed. As the helpless body of the boxer is lifted by his seconds who wipe the blood from his mouth and eyes, our roars die away. We have had our blood for the day. Even in religion under the sign of a god of love, we cast our opponents into symbolic hells where their suffering will glorify God and insure the good of all his creatures. And, finally, we visit all kinds of hate upon ourselves. This can be endured only if we can turn to others who will let us express our self-hatred and thus confront it. But how can we tell a majestic superior that we are miserable and long to die, or admit to inferiors whose only wish is to be like us, that we despise and hate the very things we have taught them to want?

Equality, then, is a sharing of hate as well as love. And since the very essence of equality is sharing under rules in play, games, and art, before audiences drawn from the community of which the players are members, symbolic playing at hate affects players and spectators alike. Equality is not sameness; it does not limit, narrow, or deny social difference. On the contrary, it stimulates them, because equals can express differences superiors and inferiors must hide. Equals *use* differences not by turning the opposition into an enemy, but through the acceptance by each side of the other as a "loyal opposition" who agrees to struggle and contest under rules acceptable to both sides. Only under these conditions, the conditions of equality, can the self be born, because only as the other remains really another, apart from and yet equal to the self, can we communicate with a strange and distant other who alone can tell us what we are, because he knows that we, in turn, can tell him what he is.

Notes

[1] When society is sacred (as in Durkheim), the family all-powerful (as in Freud), or intimate face-to-face personalized community relationships (as in Ferdinand Tönnies) determine social bonds, equality becomes subsidiary to relationships based on superiority and inferiority. European social theory (Jean Piaget excepted) often confuses social order with authoritarian order.

[2] But even though less subject to mystification, rules become ritual when those in power refuse to consider changes in them. Dogma over *how* we "must" investigate human conduct is as dangerous as any other kind of dogma. The history of science is strewn with the corpses of methodological "truths."

[3] The seventeenth-century Scottish poet and courtier, Alexander Montgomerie, summed this up in the phrase: "Play with thy peer." This has become proverbial in the courtesy literature of almost every nation.

[4] In his *Social Life of Animals* (Boston: Beacon Press, 1958), W. C. Allee argues against Schjelderup-Ebbe's statement that: "There is nothing that does not have a despot . . . usually a great number of despots. The storm is despot over the water; the lightning over the rock; water over the stone which it dissolves." (p. 136) Allee also disagrees with his approval of the old German proverb that God is despot over the Devil. Allee finds cooperation, as well as despotism, common among animals.

[5] *Why* Tocqueville thought men would be more content with authoritarian bonds is never made clear. And why "contentment" is a "natural" goal is never discussed. The "normal" American motive is ambition, which is expressed in competition and rivalry. Thus, among us *discontent* is normal.

[6] Simmel, Mead, Dilthey, Buber, and Burke are but a few of the many students of society who stress this point.

[7] But neither must superiority and inferiority be subordinated to equality. We are not *either* superior and inferior *or* equal, but *both* superior, inferior, *and* equal.

[8] There is a mystery in rules and laws, too, and belief in rules must be submitted to

the light of reason in society (as in comedy) if we are to escape the tendency of faith to become dogma that cannot be judged by reason because it is "beyond reason." Thus, if absolute power corrupts absolutely, as Lord Acton often pointed out, rules placed beyond revision and change also corrupt. But this is not because of their nature as rules, but because of their corruption through ritual.

[9] The voice of the majority in parliament is also the voice of God, but it is a voice which can be questioned and, indeed, in a democracy *must* be questioned.

[10] Hitler learned this when he used the Germany Army against the unarmed Jews of the Warsaw ghetto.

[11] As we have seen, Hitler understood this well.

25

The Establishment of Money as a
Symbol of Community Life

MANDEVILLE, MARX, AND CARLYLE ON THE
TRANSFORMATION OF MONEY INTO A SOCIAL BOND

I T I S S T R A N G E how little is said in anthropology and sociology about
the role of money in human relations. Veblen has much to say about the
rhetoric of money, but he writes about money not as a modern symbol of
community life, but as a means for emulation and display as found in
primitive and medieval life (where money played a small part in social
life). Simmel and Burke both stress that money should be analyzed as a
means of communication, for the first thing we note about money is that
it must be transformed into something else to attain social meaning. Like
any symbol, money stands for something beyond itself and is capable of all
the metaphorical, reductive, analytic, abstractive, and synthesizing powers
of symbols. In American society we are even taught that money is not
simply a means, but an end in itself. A "free" society is a society in which
the "market works freely," and therefore what cannot be related to the
market cannot be related to freedom.[1]

Not only freedom but equality has been translated into money and is
expressed on monetary terms. If all are to spend equally, all must have
equal rights to earn. It is "unfair," we say, for women to do the same work
for less pay than a man; just as it is unfair to prevent a Negro from spending his money wherever and however he likes. We say, too, that prices
must be clearly marked so that we know they are the same for every customer. Money so pervades our life that almost every battle for justice is a
battle for economic justice. Yet at the same time we admit that the power
of money is not only its promise of equality, but of inequality. We spend,
not to show that we have as much as those equal to us, but more than our
inferiors. And where we cannot spend, we identify vicariously, through
cheap imitations, with superiors who can afford the "real thing."

We even have an institution, the stock market, where money is discussed in transcendental terms. The market goes "up" and "down"; stock
values "shrink" and we read of vast losses and gains. The market is even

personified, as when we are told the trading was "brisk," or that the market was "nervous." Yet what has been lost? Not material wealth, for when the market price of motor shares "drops" there are no fewer cars in stock. Yet such losses are discussed as if they were the actual physical destruction of property. Thus we see material goods less in terms of their actual nature as physical goods than as "spiritual" or "ideal" terms of future and of monetary profit. As we soon learn, whatever cannot be translated into money cannot be communicated or, at least, cannot be communicated easily to very large audiences.

The transformation of money from a symbol of evil to a symbol of good and the creation of money as a symbol of hierarchal wonder and mystery have been noted by many observers. Bernard de Mandeville stated in 1705 that spending, not saving, created the glory of money and hence the prosperity of the community. "It is the sensual courtier that sets no limit to his luxury; the fickle strumpet that invents new fashions every week; the haughty duchess, that in equipage, entertainment, and all her behavior, would imitate a princess" who makes us prosperous. The Protestant ethic has been far less efficacious in promoting prosperity "than the silly and capricious invention of hoop'd petticoats." "Religion is one thing and trade is another. He that gives most trouble to thousands of his neighbors, and invents the most operose manufactures, is, right or wrong, the greatest friend to society." Like Gay in his *Beggar's Opera* of 1728 and La Rochefoucauld in his *Maxims,* Mandeville held that man is sociable only because he needs an audience to satisfy his pride.

He argued that while "every want was [regarded as] an evil; that on the multiplicity of those wants depended all those mutual services which the individual members of a society pay to each other; and that, consequently, the greater variety there was of want, the greater the number of individuals who might find their private interest in labouring for the good of others; and, united together, compose one body." And even catastrophes like great fires and wars, deplorable as they may be, are good for trade, and, hence, for the community. "The fire of London was a great calamity, but if the carpenters, bricklayers, smiths," and others put to work in rebuilding, "were to vote against those who lost by the fire, the rejoicing would equal, if not exceed, the complaints." Thus, as Mandeville sums it up, private vices become public virtues. Love of money is the root of all evil, but it is an evil which brings men together in community and thus makes society possible. Men sin their way through greed and emulation to grace in community.

This ironic twist, whereby the sinful luxury of the cavalier against which the Puritan fathers inveighed so strongly, could become a reward of piety, was well understood by John Wesley. "I fear, wherever riches have increased, the essence of religion has decreased in the same proportion." But if labor is the result of the Fall, and is to be regarded as the penalty and the discipline of sin, with laziness and idleness as the refusal to punish oneself for his sin through work, it will not be long, as Wesley said, until diligence and frugality succeed too well. "For the Methodists in every place grow diligent and frugal; consequently they increase in goods. Hence they proportionately increase in pride, in anger, in the desire of the flesh, the desire of the eyes." How then is this inner contradiction to be met? By a sudden symbolic shift, diligence, frugality, and thrift are invoked as riches, not poverty. "We ought not to prevent people from being diligent and frugal; we must exhort all Christians to gain all they can, and to save all they can; that is, in effect, to grow rich." [2]

The owner of wealth or property is but the "Lord's steward," and administers a divine gift which has been entrusted to him. Money, as Wesley tells his followers, "is not your *own*. It cannot be unless you are lord of heaven and earth." There is only one way then to see that money may not sink us to the "nethermost hell." "If those who *gain* all they can, and *save* all they can, will likewise *give* all they can, then the more they gain, the more they will grow in grace, and the more treasure they will lay up in heaven." By giving, Wesley did not mean spending. "Every man ought to provide the plain necessaries of life for his wife and children, and to put them into a capacity of providing these for themselves when he is gone; I say, *these—the plain necessaries of life,* not delicacies, not superfluities; for it is no man's duty to furnish them with the means either of luxury or idleness. . . . The laying up any more than these ends require is expressly forbidden." As Southey, Wesley's biographer, remarks, "Upon this subject Wesley's opinions were inconsistent with the existing order of society. . . . How injurious, if such opinions were reduced to practice, they would prove to general industry, and how incompatible they were with the general welfare of the world, Wesley seems not to have regarded."

As Southey understood in 1820, consuming only "the plain necessaries of life" was not the way to a business paradise where every man would work and spend in complete devotion to money as a transcendent principle of social order. But in his exhortation to Christians "to gain all they can," Wesley endowed money with supernatural power. The whole range of capitalistic production previously denied to the devout Catholic and the good Lutheran was now open to the Methodist. What the Christian had previously denied himself, as a way of mortification, he could now use freely, *ad majorem Dei gloriam*.

Marx and Carlyle thought the social rhetoric of money important—but for very different reasons. The enigma of commodities, Marx stresses, does not arise out of their use-value. Bourgeois hierarchal values ("social hiero-glyphs") stamp labor products as commodities. It is only the common expression of all commodities in money which led to their being recognized as values in bourgeois hierarchy. "In that world [like 'the nebulous world of religion' as Marx called it], the products of the human mind become independent shapes, endowed with lives of their own. . . . I speak of this as the *fetishistic character* which attaches to the products of labour, so soon as they are produced in the form of commodities. It is inseparable from commodity production." The laws imposed by the nature of commodities require us to compare them with some other commodity as general equivalent. The only way a commodity can become a general equivalent is by a social act. "The social act performed by all other commodities therefore sets apart a particular commodity in which they all express their values. Thus the bodily form of this commodity becomes the form of the socially recognized general equivalent. To be the general equivalent is, thanks to this social process, the specific function of the commodity thus set apart from the rest. In this way it becomes—money." With the triumph of labor money will lose its fetishistic character and become a rational means to a just social order.

Carlyle argues that money and the *spending* of money on clothes are necessary, because clothes symbolize a social order, which in turn symbolizes God, who acts through heroes of various kinds. "Clothes, from the King's mantle downwards, are emblematic of God." For *"Man is a Spirit, and bound by invisible bonds to All Men;* secondly, . . . *he wears Clothes,* which are the visible emblems of that fact."[8] Clothes are part of man's social as well as divine nature. "The first purpose of Clothes . . . were not warmth or decency, but ornament." Man's shame over his Fall was not sexual but hierarchal. "Shame, divine Shame (*Schaam, modesty*), as yet a stranger to the Anthropophagous bosom, arose there mysteriously under Clothes; a mystic grove-encircled shrine for the Holy in man.

Clothes gave us individuality, distinction, social polity; Clothes have made Men of us." All this is possible because of money, for "whoso has sixpence is sovereign (to the length of sixpence) over all men; commands cooks to feed him, philosophers to teach him, kings to mount guard over him— to the length of sixpence." [4] Thus both Marx and Carlyle agree that the mystery of money, its transcendence, as expressed by clothes which indicate class differences and differences of power, upholds social order. Both agree that spending to keep up appearances is necessary, although Marx, unlike Carlyle, finds such necessity highly irrational.

THE FREUDIAN SYMBOL OF MONEY

Freudians consider the drive to amass wealth as biologically determined through anal eroticism. Money assumes the role of parts of the body which one could lose, or which one wishes to regain after the fantasy that they have been lost. The "classical traits" of the person with an anal character is parsimony and avarice. We hear of the banker "who again and again impressed on his children that they should retain the contents of the bowels as long as possible in order to get the benefit of every bit of the expensive food they ate." Constipation, like thrift, becomes a virtue and thus the Puritan ethic, which is celestialized in God, becomes bound to the body itself in Freudian psychology. For as Sandor Ferenczi explicitly states: "The excrementa . . . held back are really the first 'savings' of the growing being, and as such remain in a constant, unconscious inter-relationship with every bodily activity or mental striving that has anything to do with collecting, hoarding, and saving."

But Freudians, like Wesley and his Methodists, realized they must deal with spending as well as hoarding. Karl Abraham stated in 1917 that the attitude of the neurotic to the possession of money had evoked far more attention among psychoanalysts than spending, although neurotic spending was met with often enough in practice. His own patients told him that spending money relieved them of depression or anxiety because such spending increased their self-confidence. Abraham rejects such "rational explanations." Anal eroticism, he argues, takes the place of genital eroticism. Morbid fixation of the patient on his father or mother is carried on through the agency of the anal zone. Thus his patient, who spent extravagantly, warded off deepening anxiety by giving out money instead of libido. Buying "objects which have only a momentary value, and passing quickly from one object to another, are symbolic gratifications of a repressed desire—that of transferring the libido in rapid succession to an unlimited number of objects. The allusion to prostitution is unmistakable in this connection; for there, too, money is the means of obtaining transitory and easily changed relationships." When the parental image imposes abnormally strict prohibitions against expending the libido freely, a compromise between instinct and repression is made by which the patient "in a spirit of defiance, does expend—not his sexual libido but an anal currency." [5]

Fenichel [6] points out that, while we must accept anal character described by Freud, Jones, and Abraham, "introjections of every kind can be projected into money." It can represent relations to objects in general "and everything through which the bodily ego feeling and with it . . . self-regard can be increased or diminished." Odier [7] argues that money represents not only the feces but everything which can be taken or given. The wish to receive represents the first relationship of the infant to the object world. As the reality principle establishes itself alongside the pleasure principle, desire to give develops. We realize that we must relinquish something (first the mother's breast, then the feces). The struggle between our desire to keep and the need for giving governs our psychological attitude toward money. The symbolic significance of money is more important than its real significance, since its symbolic meaning is the cause of the origin of money. The symbol of money means milk, food, mother's breast, intestinal contents, feces, penis, sperm, child, potency, love, protection, care, passivity, obstinacy, vanity, pride, egoism, indifference toward objects, auto-eroticism, gift, offering, renunciation, hate, weapon, humiliation, deprivation of potency, besmirching, degradation, sexual aggression, anal penis. And, Fenichel might have added, in America "money talks."

Odier argues further that children introduce money into conflicts over taking and giving long before they can form judgments over the reality and significance of money. Ferenczi holds in his article, "The Ontogenesis of the Interest in Money" (1914), that while the child is influenced by the high appreciation of money among adults and the discovery that money can get him many things he desires, it is not these purely practical considerations but the pleasure-giving qualities of money as a symbol of pleasure over intestinal contents of the body, which determine our use of money. Roheim stresses that taking cannot be enjoyed unless we give. To receive milk from its mother, the child must give up its excrement. Fenichel argues that as we learn more about the ontogenesis of the ego in its drive for power and prestige as a means of warding off anxiety, we discover that the drive to amass wealth is a special form of the instinct of possession which is made possible by the social function of money in a capitalistic society.

THE SOCIAL RHETORIC OF MONEY: SIMMEL AND VEBLEN

In his *Philosophie des Geldes* (1900) and "Die Grossetadte und das Geistesleben" (1902), Georg Simmel discusses the reciprocity of money and society in terms of money as a symbol, the effect of money on society, and of society on money. While money is no more efficient (as a symbol of social order) than kingship, ancestor worship, religion, or ownership of land or office, it has specific qualities and takes certain forms, which we must understand if we wish to understand modern society. Money changes hands in hidden and unrecognizable ways not possible to land, houses, clothes, offices, and rank. It can create effects at a distance—as we see in the ease with which we invest in remote and distant markets. There is a kind of anonymity or neutrality about money. Feudal sumptuary laws set limits to consumption according to class, sex, office, rank, or religion. Capitalistic "laws" of consumption declare rights to an ever-increasing standard of living to be "natural" rights. Money is a great leveler, for purchase by money implies that two heterogeneous things can be juxtaposed and compared by means of a common monetary value. It is highly compressible: a simple piece of paper, a check for a large sum, makes us rich. And, finally, money is highly abstract.

There is a kind of incompatibility between intimate emotional relations and money ties. "Logical" market operations reduce individuality to general elements. Thus, only the objectively measurable achievement or element is of value to the plutocrat or to the intellectual in his function as technocrat or engineer. Production for a market of unknown buyers contrasts greatly with production for a small intimate group. Cold matter-of-factness characterizes urban market relationships. The intellectually calculating economic egoism of the modern urbanite reduces all quality and individuality to the question: How much? The use of money pervades our daily life with weighing and calculating, with constant numerical determinations, and with the constant reduction of qualitative values to quantitative units.

The relation of this mode of social action to the ideal of natural science, in so far as science seeks to transform the world into an arithmetical problem, is obvious. In daily life, as in our technology and research, we seek to fix every part of the world by mathematical formulas. Calculation and precision become social virtues in themselves, as the universal diffusion of the pocket watch shows. Punctuality, calculability, and exactness lead to impersonality, the triumph of the "objective spirit" over the "subjectives." The individual becomes a mere cog in an enormous organization of things and powers. Lifeless clock-measured time flows along side by side with social time, but aloof from it, utterly regardless of the high and low tides of life where no two moments are alike. Money is futuristic, as the notion of investment implies. The investment of money orients us to the future and we learn to think of risks in terms of future rewards. Thus money makes the present highly abstract, pushes us swiftly into an infinitely receding future (for money must always be kept at work, promising greater returns), and thus destroys the past.

To the explanations of money's symbolic power in terms of human nature (the passions), the body (anal eroticism), the supernatural (The Protestant ethic), and the resources of the symbol itself (the intrinsic value of quantification in modern life), Veblen added an analysis of the use of money for emulation. He argues that we cannot understand the social function of the true, the good, and the beautiful until we understand how they are communicated according to "pecuniary canons of taste." Mandeville argued that every institution is held together by pride and that pride depends for its satisfaction on the responses of others. Man is "trapped" by his need for an audience of inferiors, superiors, and peers, for only as he struts and preens before them can he get the response he needs to satisfy his pride. We cannot live without each other because only through each other can we satisfy our vices (as well as our virtues).[8]

Veblen argues that the "cannons of pecuniary decency" are reducible to the principles of waste, futility, and ferocity. Like Mandeville, he grounds satisfaction in the spending of money and in pride, which finds expression in "conspicuous consumption." Only as we become aware of this "invidious" nature of money, will we be ready to think about the "instinct of workmanship."[9] The ignoble capitalist consumer must be replaced by the noble technological worker. Thus Veblen upholds the Puritan ethic by which work becomes sacred while spending (unless to produce more work) becomes evil. But as a dramatic device for exposing incongruities and absurdities, Veblen's innocent technocrat, who works only for the "community" and who looks over in amazed wonder at the false rhetoric of those under the spell of pecuniary motives, is highly effective. Through irony and satire he reduces the mystery of money from a sacred community bond to a kind of magic used by "predatory" and "cunning" businessmen. Thus, in *The Higher Learning in America: A Memorandum on the Conduct of Universities by Business Men,* universities ostensibly devoted to learning actually destroy learning through emphasis on the dignification of wealth. Academicians really teach the art of "genteel expenditure." For in a world where spending determines reputability, learning to spend well will be prized and rewarded.

Thus, by such devious paths and by such different thinkers, has the wonder and glory of money been created. We spend not only to satisfy "needs," but to glorify certain kinds of social relations. What we cannot spend on, we cannot value. What is not on the market cannot be priced. What cannot be priced cannot engage community effort. Teachers cannot be highly paid because they do not make profit, and whatever invokes "deficit financing" cannot bring pecuniary, and hence, social, glory. Only when poor schools threaten urban and suburban real estate values, turn out students with low spending morale, or subject the symbol of money itself to savage ridicule, can something be done. As we pay our teachers more, we increase respect for them, not because people know much more about the glory of teaching, but because the glory of money has shed its radiance over our schools. They are "expensive," so they must be important.

THE SHIFT FROM THE PURITAN ETHIC OF EARNING TO AN
ETHIC OF SPENDING

Money has reached transcendence in our society through freeing spending, as well as earning, from religious and social inhibitions. Symbols of exchange are now treated as symbols of all human relations. We deduce freedom itself from a free market, because we believe that such a market supplies the conditions in which a free social act could occur. American discussion over freedom soon becomes a discussion of freedom to earn and (more recently) to spend. God's laws as well as nature's laws, formerly considered the grounds for freedom, have been replaced by market laws (the law of supply and demand, the iron law of profit, etc.). Money is no longer thought of as a means, a medium of exchange, but as a means to social integration. We do not use money to produce, distribute, and consume more goods and services, but to "develop the community."

We make more money because we believe that money will produce unlimited good. The promise of American life is not an increased, but an ever increasing, standard of living. What we have now is more than we had in the past and is but a promise of what is to come. The past is killed through style (annual and seasonal models). The present is infused with a future which is at once orgiastic, spiritual, and infinite. No material want need be denied ourselves or others, because such satisfactions are but a way to other satisfactions. It is our "right" to spend as we see fit—so long as we spend on the market. It is "unjust" to prevent the Negro from spending. Adolescents (and even children) have a "right" to spend their own money, and, indeed, are coached in how to do so in advertisements of all kinds. We need not think beyond our individual prosperity, because as we prosper the community prospers. And if the community prospers, it is a sign that God loves us. Thus making and spending money is really an act of service, a community satisfaction.

Our commercial magicians and priests of consumption [10] do not urge us to buy things because they will last. On the contrary, it is being merely a step closer to buying another thing, a promise of an infinitely expanding future of bigger and better things, that moves us to buy. *Hierarchal usefulness,* not function or utility, determines our purchases. Even the foreign car which is "made to last" is soon traded in for a new model. The power of style in America derives from its power to communicate to others, and at the same time to ourselves, that we can spend freely and frequently. We are urged to spend before we earn, not after, by the same bankers who in the days of the Puritan ethic exhorted us to abhor debt. We work to pay off debts for houses, cars, and clothes which we have already used, and to go into debt for more things and services (but much more often for things) we do not have. Pecuniary propriety does not allow us to be satisfied with what we have. Obsolescence becomes a standard of value. We are only worth what we spend, and our discontent with what we have is but a mark of ambition to spend more, for as we spend we enhance our stature in the community. The individual who spends upholds prosperity, just as the industrialist who spends on new machinery, or the politician who builds new roads, develops "community resources."

Notes

[1] Even when we agree that this has been true of American freedom, we are discovering, to our sorrow, that other peoples think of money as a means to enslavement, not freedom.

[2] Robert Southey, *The Life of Wesley* (London: Longman, Hurst, Rees, Orme and Brown, 1820, 2nd ed.), Chapter XXIX.

[3] Thomas Carlyle, *Sartor Resartus—On Heroes and Hero Worship* (New York and London: E. P. Dutton & Co., Inc., Everyman's Library, 1954), p. 45. Carlyle's italics. See also Chapter X, "Adamantism."

[4] *Ibid.*, p. 30. Chapter V, "The World in Clothes." Carlyle's italics.

[5] See "The Spending of Money in Anxiety States" by Karl Abraham in his *Selected Papers* (London: The Hogarth Press, 1949), p. 301.

[6] See "The Drive to Amass Wealth" in *The Collected Papers of Otto Fenichel: Second Series* (New York: W. W. Norton & Co., Inc., 1954).

[7] See C. Odier, "L'Argent et les Nevroses," *Rev. Française Psychanalyse,* Vol. II, 1928, and Vol. III, 1929. Odier attempts in these articles to present what is known about the unconscious symbolism of money. See also C. Odier, *Anxiety and Major Thinking* (New York: International Universities Press, Inc., 1956).

[8] Mandeville does not deny the existence of good but insists that to argue that all men are virtuous (as Shaftesbury does) is a "miserable shift and an unreasonable supposition." For while it is possible that men might, without regard for themselves, "consume as much out of Zeal to serve their Neighbors and promote the Public Good, as they do now out of Self-Love and Emulation . . . I argue that it is as possible that Cats, instead of killing Rats and Mice should feed them, and go about the house to suckle and nurse their young ones . . . but if they should all do so, they would cease to be Cats. . . . It is inconsistent with their Natures, and the Species of creatures which now we mean, when we name Cats . . . would be extinct as soon as that could come to pass." See "Remark (M)" of the *Fables of the Bees, or Private Vices, Public Benefits* by Bernard Mandeville, with a Commentary, Critical, Historical, and Explanatory, 2 vols. (Oxford: Clarendon Press, 1957).

[9] Man's salvation, Veblen holds, depends on his ability to think about the social mystifications of money.

[10] The growing school of Madison Avenue apologists hold that successful advertising adds a new value to a product. A lipstick may be sold at Woolworth's under one name and in a department store under another, nationally advertised name. Almost any teen-age girl will prefer the latter, if she can afford to pay the difference. Wearing the Woolworth brand, she feels her ordinary self; wearing the other, which has been successfully advertised as a magic recipe for glamor, she feels a beauty. The new value added here is expense. What the girl is saying is, "The more *expensive* I look (or smell), the more desirable I become."

26

Money as a Form of Transcendence in American Life

I F A M E R I C A has done much to form symbols of equality into transcendent symbols of social order, and thus added to the hierarchal lore of
modern society, it has also created other characteristic forms in the "spiritualization" of money in both religion and art. We see this most clearly in
the celebration of Christmas. The commercial exploitation of the Nativity
in America began about 1890. By 1920 merchants and advertising agencies
recognized the commercial potentialities of holy days; by 1930 their studied exploitation became part of our business life. In 1950, December sales
ranged from 11 to nearly 23 per cent of the year's sales.[1] Merchants open
the "Christmas shopping season" on the Monday after Thanksgiving (also
celebrated by great spending on food and liquor). Carols, both sacred and
secular, blare through business streets. Everything from garbage cans to
automobiles are advertised under headings describing the "joy of Christmas" as the "spirit of giving." Nativity scenes appear in advertisements for
every kind of commodity, under captions of "peace on earth, good will
to men."

The traditional English "Father Christmas" and the German St. Nicholas and Knect Rupprecht, who symbolized the gaiety and feasting of
Christmas Eve, were transformed into gift bringers. After 1890 gifts which
had been made by hand and selected with great care[2] were supplanted by
purchased gifts, lavishly wrapped and sent by mail. The master of revels,
Santa Claus, became a patron of children and the family. Older folk
customs of setting off firecrackers, shooting guns, convivial drinking, and
gay song died out.[3] Christmas is now a family celebration centering
around a gift-laden tree. Women buy and prepare most of the gifts. Even
in stores where men wrap and prepare merchandise for mailing and de-
livery throughout the year, women are hired as gift wrappers for the
Christmas season. Santa, once a Falstaffian knight or a kindly father, now
takes on a soft androgynous body. He is fat, jolly, old, no longer mascu-

line but maternal. At Christmas time woman herself is transformed. Erotic, romantic, and occupational roles must be replaced by maternal and familial images in December advertising. This strengthens other festive images of the American Christmas Madonna who gives, not her breast, but gifts bought for money.

The older personal and intimate gift of home-baked bread or a knitted scarf had little money value. It was a gift of time, an indication of thought and concern for the other. As we take such a gift we know that the giver thought of us and tried to create something for us, and for us alone. But the purchased gift is a thing, an object whose only radiance comes from its price. As with any priced thing, it cannot have any intrinsic value. It can even be exchanged for something else and, indeed, exchange services are a necessary part of Christmas shopping. Thus the symbol of money has replaced the older folk symbol of fellowship created in preparing gifts, reveling together, and the sacred Christian celebration of the Nativity as a fellowship and brotherhood in Christ.[4]

The older, folk Christmas revels, so repugnant to the Puritans and banished from the home by the ascendency of mother and child, have been revived in business life. Work slackens, time for shopping is allowed, vacations and holidays are given, a Christmas bonus is distributed, and (since the end of the Second World War) office parties are held. These parties revived the older American custom among male workers of drinking and joking together on the job throughout the day before Christmas. The office party temporarily banishes distinctions of rank, furnishes unlimited amounts of alcohol, encourages song, jokes, pranks, and sex play. As the popular press describes it:

On one night or another just before Christmas the lights burn late in many American business houses. The occasion is that great leveler, the office Christmas party, an antidote for formality which ranks between a few discreet cocktails and a free-for-all fight. Then all business barriers collapse; executives unbend; the office clown finds a sympathetic audience. This is the only time the pretty file clerk gets kissed in public and the homely one gets kissed at all.[5]

Individual, institutional, and familial gifts are matched by community-wide collection and distribution of money. Millions of dollars are collected and given to the sick, the unfortunate, and the poor. Local welfare agencies, service clubs, churches, the Red Cross, the Salvation Army, the Tuberculosis Association, the American Legion, and Veterans of Foreign Wars send gifts to prisons, jails, mental institutions, convalescent homes, and orphan homes. Newspapers publish appeals for gifts for bed-ridden children, children whose families are killed, or families whose homes are destroyed by fire. Often these "orgies of Christmas generosity" actually run counter to the planned aid program of social work agencies. Hospital patients must give away many of their gifts because they are useless, duplications of what they already have, or highly perishable. Some social welfare agencies refuse such help on the ground that citizens of a free community should not be given gifts but money or help with their family affairs.

SPENDING AND DEATH

The infusion of money with sacred social values can also be seen in our funeral practices. Few funerals are conducted now in homes, yet as late as 1910, most families insisted on bringing their dead from hospitals, or wherever death occurred, to the house as soon as possible. Funeral parlors were used by those who had no home of their own, or had no friends or relatives willing to offer them their homes. The body was laid out by the bereaved or by friends in the neighborhood experienced in handling the dead. Washed, dressed in the best or favorite suit or dress, the body was moved to the parlor where it was put on view even before the casket arrived. Friends visited the bereaved home as soon as news of the death reached them; members of the family seated themselves in the living room to receive condolences. Each caller tiptoed into the parlor to see the corpse. The kitchen was soon piled high with cakes, pies, and meats brought by friends and neighbors. Services at the home were long, solemn, and sad. The mystery of death was a promise of eternal life. Where it was believed that life was essentially tragic and sinful, death was welcomed as a release from suffering and guilt.

By 1900, funeral homes were already advertising their "homelike rooms" and "elegant parlors." [6] The funeral chapel was mentioned discreetly by only 10 per cent of advertisers in 1925; but in 1950 the funeral chapel had become a standard part of nearly all urban and many town and village funeral homes. Funeral "artists," working from a photograph of the deceased, restored the corpse to an appearance of health and life. Powder, rouge, lipstick, mascara, and other beauty aids are used to fit the body for the elegance of the casket and its floral backdrop. [7] The custom of sitting with the dead and holding night-long wakes is no longer thought proper to the "routine of modern funeral home operations," for now the funeral ceremony is held in the funeral home, as well as in the church.

Funeral homes of the 1960s, unlike those of 1880, do not emphasize the "parlor" and do not stress "hominess." They are built around the chapel, which is modern in design, air-conditioned throughout, equipped with the latest in livery equipment (including limousines), and luxuriously appointed rooms that look out over beautifully landscaped grounds. In these modern funeral homes, we are assured, everything moves smoothly with a "reserved elegance." And as the undertakers' advertisement goes on to say: "All this costs no more than an ordinary funeral." [8] The architecture of funeral homes varies widely, from Early Colonial to "modern." But whatever the style, the building must be imposing, accessible to transportation, highly public, and kept in good order. Funeral homes are community showpieces, a fitting background for the funeral director who tends to think of himself as a person who carries out his vocation in surroundings that are scrupulously neat, sanitary, dignified, and even beautiful.

The "elegant reserve" and "dignity" of the funeral home is not created through ageless and traditional forms. The archaic forms of "conspicuous waste" which Veblen found so characteristic of devout observances in 1890, and which characterized the old family mansion taken over as a funeral home, are now replaced by funeral homes which are "the most modern in all America." The crude coffin of Colonial times and the pine box of pioneer days have been replaced by ornate caskets. Casket styles are changing more rapidly each year. "A funeral director who would buy a hundred caskets in 1910 would hesitate to stock a quarter that many ten years later, and five years later might consider ten caskets a precarious inventory." [9] The undertaker, now a mortician, mortuary consultant, funeral counselor, or more generally, a funeral director, no longer takes the corpse wrapped in a shroud to a graveyard in a hearse. He takes the patient in a funeral-car or casket coach dressed in a slumber-robe, from the reposing-room to a memorial park, a Garden of Memories, or a Forest Lawn. Here there is no ground burial, but mausoleum entombment in pretentious and costly tombs of every conceivable style from Gothic to modern.

Death, like birth, has been made salable and, thus, subject to the mystery of money. We now bury our dead "in style." Obsolescence in products and services necessary to decent burial of the dead is a matter of style, not decay. "Long before rolling stock wears out it becomes obsolete, and long before funeral homes actually begin to look shabby many funeral directors feel the urge to redecorate." [10] We submit to the rising costs of funerals because we believe there is a direct connection between the money spent on the funeral and the respect given to the dead. In this moment of symbolic transformation quantity becomes *quality* as the social mystery of money fastens its spell upon us.

But it is a mistake to think of the pecuniary expression of Christmas and of death simply as "secularization." Death has lost none of its mystery or power. The clerk who spends several hundred dollars (which he must borrow and pay back in small installments) on his father's funeral is not "secularizing" funeral rites. Funerals have shifted from churches and homes to commercial funeral homes because spending money in itself has become a way of showing respect, and now in our time, of showing reverence. The indigent family which sinks further into debt to provide an expensive funeral is practicing mortification. Such spending is a penance, a self-punishment. For, in going into debt the debtor pledges many future hours of work to his creditor. And he does it in such a highly public fashion that his good name will be greatly threatened if he does not pay. [11]

We are accustomed to think of asceticism and rituals of renunciation as sacred. [12] But as theologians themselves tell us, Christ's law of mortification implies something more than mere self-restraint. It implies the use of what Jeremy Taylor calls "rudeness" against oneself. Christian temperance implies the control of appetite at those points where its demands are most importunate and difficult to resist. The aim of the temperate Christian is *positive,* not negative. He aims not merely at the subjugation of greed but at the cultivation of moral and spiritual power. He makes circumstances subservient to his spiritual progress and "passes through them upwards and onwards to God." Possession of money means (to those under the spell of money) that we struggled against temptation to sloth. Going into debt to bury our dead is a pledge to meet and fight such temptation again. For in the supernatural as well as the social realm, risk-taking brings us glory. Willingness to take risks is our grasp of faith, and thus in a system of hierarchy based on money, risk brings glory so long as it is money risk.

THE DEIFICATION OF THE BUSINESSMAN

The religion of money reached its apogee around 1925, when Calvin Coolidge, our president, told us: "The business of America is business." By 1929 big businessmen were leaders of the nation. A religion of money, replete with saints (and sinners), developed. Business hagiography became a popular and profitable literary genre. It was written in the spirit of Babcock who declared that "Business is religion, and religion is business." [13] Both political parties turned to businessmen for leaders. The Democratic National Chairman was also a Chairman of General Motors. The words of a Morgan partner were often given more publicity than those of the President or the Secretary of State. Faith in Wall Street ran deep. Money, the new symbol of life, was beyond danger because it was "self-regulating."

The most widely read nonfiction book of 1925, *The Man Nobody Knows: A Discovery of the Real Jesus* by Bruce Barton, a leading advertising agent, makes literal use of money as a symbol of God, and propounds the gospel of service through earning and spending money. The Bible is translated into business terminology.

> Great progress will be made when we rid ourselves of the idea that there is a difference between *work* and *religious work*. We have been taught that a man's daily business activities are selfish, and that only the time which he devotes to church meetings and social service activities is consecrated. Ask any ten people what Jesus meant by his "Father's business," and nine of them will answer "preaching." To interpret the words in this narrow sense is to lose the real significance of his life. It was not to preach that he came into the world; nor to teach; nor to heal. These are all departments of his Father's business, but the business itself is far larger, more inclusive. . . . The race must be fed and clothed and housed and transported, as well as preached to, and taught and healed. Thus *all* business is his Father's business. All work is worship; all useful service, prayer.[14]

Barton links business with religion, explains religion by business, and then uses business terms as religious terms. In the first chapter Jesus becomes an "executive," in the second he is an "outdoor" man, a "he-man," not the "sallow-faced, thin-lipped, so-called spiritual type," in the third Jesus is discovered to be a "good mixer," "the friendliest man who ever lived, yet one who has been shut off by a black wall of theological tradition." In Chapter Four we find that Jesus was the Great Advertiser. "We speak of the law of 'supply and demand' but the words have got turned around. Elias Howe invented the sewing machine, but it nearly rusted away before American women could be persuaded to use it. With anything which is not a basic necessity the supply always precedes the demand. . . . Assuredly there was no demand for a new religion; the world was already oversupplied." But as we study Jesus' teachings, "worthy of the attentive study of any sales manager," we find him using parables—"the most powerful advertisements of all times." The secret of Jesus' success was his recognition that "all good advertising is news." Jesus would have made many great headlines, as a paraphrase of his actions in modern newspaper copy style shows. "If he were to live again, in these modern days, he would find a way to advertise by his service, not merely by his sermons. One thing is certain: he would not neglect the market-place. Few of his sermons were delivered in synagogues. For the most part he was in the crowded places, the Temple Court, the city squares, the centers where goods were bought and sold." [15]

But the "present day market-place is the newspaper and the magazine. Printed columns are the modern thoroughfares; published advertisements are the cross-roads where the sellers and the buyers meet." If Jesus lived today he "would be a national advertiser . . . as he was the great advertiser of his own day." For when all is said and done, Jesus was "the founder of modern business," for did not Jesus make it plain when he said, "wist ye not that I must be about my father's business?" that he "thought of his life as *business*." For modern business, like Jesus, serves mankind. "We are great because of our service." "Service is what we are here for," manufacturers exclaim. They call it the "spirit of modern business"; they suppose, most of them, that it is something very new. But Jesus preached it more than nineteen hundred years ago, as the words and deeds of modern business saints such as George W. Perkins, Henry Ford, Theodore N. Vail, and the partners of J. P. Morgan and Company prove.[16]

AMERICAN ART AND THE DIGNIFICATION OF SPENDING

The dignification of wealth through spending which would match the sanctification of wealth through earning as a "steward of the Lord," was a central concern of Gilded Age families. The marriages of Consuelo Vanderbilt and the Duke of Marlborough, of Anna Gould to Count Boni de Castellane, of Mary Leiter to the Marquis Curzon of Kedleston, and of Pauline Whitney to Sir Almeric Paget, all in 1895, were climaxed in 1899 by the marriage of Prince Michael Cantacuzene of Russia to Julia Grant, the daughter of the president. By 1893 over 90,000 Americans visited Europe each year; those who could not buy a title bought objects of art, pictures, and things whose radiance created identifications with past aristocracies. From Fifth Avenue to Prairie Avenue and Nob Hill the turrets of French chateaux, the spires and crenelations of Rhenish castles, and the gables of English manor houses, offered new American identifications of money. Those who could not afford a grand marital alliance, the Grand Tour, or the grand house enjoyed a pinchbeck splendor in joining the Colonial Order of the Crown for descendents of Charlemagne or the Order of the Crown of America for those ostensibly related to other royalty.

Art of every kind and of every degree of excellence enhanced the glamour of spending. *Walden* shows Thoreau earning his world.[17] Henry James' characters in *The Sense of the Past* and *The Spoils of Poynton* spend their way to significance. People remind James of art and are described as works of art. And it is a trite and conventionally "beautiful" art, little different from the art Hearst or Morgan bought "wholesale" from Europe to decorate their great mansions. Nan, in *The Sense of the Past,* recalls "some mothering Virgin by Van Eyck or Meling," Mme. de Vionnet's head could be found on "an old precious medal, some silver coin of the Renaissance," while the prince's eyes evoke "the high windows of a Roman palace, of an historic front by one of the great old designers, thrown open on a feast day to the golden air." As in the popular romances of Francis Marion Crawford, such as *A Lady of Rome,* the romance of elegance is a drama of purchase, an identification with an honorific world of "culture" which was bought, not made.[18]

Theodore Dreiser's wonder over rich spending has a far different content, but the mystery of money as an expression of hierarchy is equally great. The things money buys in Dreiser's works are not of the hallowed world of European culture. They are from the windows and counters of department stores in Chicago, the new raw city of America that moved Sister Carrie to love and wonder. Like a thousand other American heroes and heroines, her story is a legend of passing from rags to riches. The wonder and enchantment of Chicago is the wonder and enchantment of things money will buy. Clothes, houses, department stores, furnishings, like the jewels, silks, and perfumes of *The Arabian Nights,* are infused with hierarchal magic and mystery. Hurstwood's superiority over Drouet, Carrie's first lover, is foreshadowed through the hierarchal imagery of clothes.

His clothes were particularly new and rich in appearance. The coat lapels stood out with that medium stiffness which excellent cloth possesses. The vest was of a rich Scotch plaid, set with a double row of round mother-of-pearl buttons. His cravat was a shiny combination of silken threads, not loud, not inconspicuous. What he wore did not strike the eye so forcibly as that which Drouet had on, but Carrie could see the elegance of the material. Hurstwood's shoes were of soft, black calf, polished only to a dull shine. Drouet wore patent leather, but Carrie could not help feeling that there was a distinction in favour of the soft leather, where all else was so rich. She noticed these things almost unconsciously.[19]

As Sister Carrie, like Ailene, the financier's wife, moves up the social ladder the mystery of money deepens. Money becomes a force, like nature. "Finally one is lead to conclude that by and large, the financial type is the coldest, most selfish, and the most useful of all living phenomena. Plainly it is a highly specialized machine for the accomplishment of some end which Nature has in view. Often humorless, shark-like, avid, yet among the greatest constructive forces imaginable; absolutely opposed to democracy in practise, yet as useful an implement for its accomplishment as for autocracy." Yerkes (as Cowperwood), his Chicago financier, becomes demonic: "A rebellious Lucifer this, glorious in his somber conception of the value of power. A night-black pool his world will seem to some, played over by fulgurous gleams of his own individualistic and truly titanic mind . . . a clear suggestion of the inscrutable forces of life, as they shift and play— marring what they do not glorify—pagan, fortuitous, inalienably artistic." [20]

Edith Wharton makes villains out of Dreiser's heroes. They are the "new people" whom "New York was beginning to dread and yet be drawn to. . . ." For New York "as far back as the mind of man could travel, had been divided into two great fundamental groups," those who cared about eating, sex, clothes, and money, and those who were devoted to travel, the creation of beautiful homes and gardens, and culture. In her early novels such as the *House of Mirth,* making money is common and vulgar. "[Mr. Rosedale] had his race's accuracy in the appraisal of values, and to be seen walking down the platform at the crowded afternoon hour in the company of Miss Lily Bart would have been money in his pocket, as he himself might have phrased it." [21] As in Henry James, tasteful spending and well-ordered luxury creates a spiritual aura of her characters. In her final analysis of New York society, irony replaces rejection of businessmen, acceptance of families who upheld tradition and culture. Social power in New York was "simply the power of money. . . . Social credit was based on an impregnable bank account." Not only the Rosedales, but all New York society had surrendered to money.

Fitzgerald's rich are created out of deep wonder at the mystery of great wealth. The rich are mythic figures who motivate action because, like all such figures, they *are* the principle, the ultimate value, which shapes the dramatic struggle. Plutocrats are different in kind, not degree, from the middle and lower class. His rich, like Mann's Mynheer Peeperkorn, embody passion and feeling, expressed through the mystery of money which infuses with its power all their relationships.

The scene in *The Great Gatsby* in which Nick, Daisy, and Gatsby walk through the huge, luxurious mansion is a sacred moment. Overwhelmed by the magnificence of a great pile of handmade English shirts, Daisy bows her head and weeps "stormily." In another scene, Daisy becomes a "golden girl."

"She's got an indiscreet voice," [Nick] remarked. "It's full of ——" I hesitated. "Her voice is full of money," [Gatsby] said suddenly. That was it. I'd never understood before. It was full of money—that was the inexhaustible charm that rose and fell in it, the jingle of it, the cymbals' tone of it. . . . High in a white palace the king's daughter, the golden girl.[22]

Americans of the twenties were deeply moved by such depictions of money and love. For Thomas Mann's young Germans money destroys love, even life itself, as in *Buddenbrooks,* where the businessman is coarse, vulgar, and greedy. For Fitzgerald's young Americans, money creates love, what Fitzgerald himself called an "orgiastic future." Fitzgerald's characters are sexually and spiritually aroused by money; Mann's decay, rot, and die under its spell.

The drama of money is also a drama of passage. Cowperwood's rise to power is dramatized through manipulation of money in its purest symbolic form as stocks and bonds. Unlike the heroes and villains of James and Wharton, who move in atmospheres infused with taste expressed in old masters, great country homes, or urban "Renaissance" palaces, the characters of Norris, Dreiser, Fuller, and Herrick move in scenes of crude, bitter, vulgar struggle for dominance in the "money game." Cowperwood's power originates in his ability to spend in good taste, as well as to earn in struggle and competition with powerful rivals.

Even the radical midwesterners in architecture did not deny the transcendence of money. Root, Sullivan, and Wright sought to dignify *both* earning and spending. The office building, the factory, even the "grocer's warehouse" could be beautiful. But the new beauty of these Chicago radicals was very costly. The "simple" Monadnock building of Burnham and Root, the great Auditorium of Adler and Sullivan, like the simple homes designed by Frank Lloyd Wright, were great capital (as well as aesthetic) ventures. Crenelated towers become clean soaring planes in space filled with interlocking cubes of glass and steel, but these "simple" cubes, where, as Mies van der Rohe tells us, "less is more," replace feudal with technological majesty. And, thus even art proper, like religion, becomes subordinate to money. We spend our way to beauty as we do to God.

Notes

[1] In his study, *The American Christmas* (New York: Macmillan and Company, 1954), James H. Barnett gives the following figures: building materials 7 per cent of year's total; department stores 14.8; drugstores 11; eating and drinking places 8.9; family and other apparel 15; general merchandise 14.5; jewelry 22.7; liquor 15; men's clothing and furnishings 16; women's apparel and accessories 13.1. If sales were constant, each month would account for approximately 8.3 of the annual total.

[2] A "boughten" gift was thought vulgar or common unless given by a bachelor or someone who could not make his own.

[3] These elements were revived in the "office party" in the business community.

[4] Merchants seek to counter the impersonality of the purchased gift by offering a wide range of gifts. Concern for the other is indicated by gifts that are in good style and wrapped with elegance and care. Indications of diligent and careful shopping are supposed to personalize the gift. Shopping aids and guides, elaborate check lists of gifts classified according to age, relationship, or sex are given us. It is even possible to order by phone. The impersonality of this is recognized by merchants who list such services as *"Personalized* Shopping Service" and who refer constantly to "a good old-fashioned Christmas."

[5] *Life,* Dec. 27, 1948. Quoted from Barnett, *op. cit.,* p. 140.

[6] I have followed the descriptions given by Robert W. Habenstein and William M. Lamers in their *History of American Funeral Directing* (Milwaukee, Wis.: Bulfin Printers, 1955).

[7] Evelyn Waugh, in his novel *The Loved One,* satirizes the art of "restoration" in American funerals.

[8] Such advertising is common in classified telephone directories.

[9] Habenstein and Lamers, *op. cit.,* p. 547.

[10] *Ibid.,* p. 583.

[11] Habenstein reports that most funeral directors write off only about two per cent of their income to bad debt losses.

[12] We forget that austerity, like consumption, may become highly conspicuous. Thus we hear from India that outward or conspicuous austerity has become a "political imperative." The glorification of asceticism creates many incongruities in a nation struggling for a place among world powers devoted to production of goods and services.

[13] This identification is still very strong in the accounts of success given to the press by businessmen. Great wealth is a "trust," businessmen are "stewards" of wealth who must lead pious, Christian lives of devotion to the community. Businessmen of all faiths use this Puritan stereotype.

[14] Bruce Barton, *The Man Nobody Knows: A Discovery of the Real Jesus* (Indianapolis: The Bobbs-Merrill Company, 1924), pp. 179–180. Barton's italics. Emerson foresaw this in 1860 when he wrote in *The Conduct of Life* that "the gods of the cannibals will be a cannibal, of the crusaders a crusader; and of the merchants a merchant."

[15] *Ibid.,* p. 138.

[16] The "gospel of service" is discussed in Chapter Six of *The Man Nobody Knows,* where Jesus is described as "The Founder of Modern Business."

[17] In one sense *Walden* is a "success" story comparable to the "rags to riches" stories of the popular press. The first and longest section of *Walden*, "Economy," discusses money in various ways and carefully records expenditures. Thus we find our way to the higher life of contemplation *through* money, not outside of it.

[18] James, Wharton, and others use images of art being consumed, not made, that is, from the view of an audience of consumers, not of artists.

[19] *Sister Carrie* (New York: B. W. Dodge & Co., 1907), pp. 107–108. See also a scene in Dreiser's *A Book about Myself* (New York: Boni and Liveright, 1922) at the end of Chapter VIII, where Dreiser describes his own enchantment over the "new, sunny prosperity" of Chicago of the nineties. Elias, Dreiser's biographer, tells us of his belief that if he could wear a satin-lined overcoat and carry gloves and cane, he would be irresistible to women.

[20] Robert H. Elias, *Theodore Dreiser, Apostle of Nature* (New York: Alfred A. Knopf, 1949), pp. 175–176. This is a quotation from Dreiser.

[21] Edith Wharton, *The House of Mirth* (New York: Charles Scribner's Sons, 1905), p. 23.

[22] F. Scott Fitzgerald, *The Great Gatsby* (New York: Bantam Books, 1945), p. 128.

PART EIGHT

The Social Function of Art in Society

———————◆———————

27

Comedy and Social Integration

MUCH HAS BEEN SAID in anthropology and sociology about social integration and religion. Indeed, it could be argued without too much difficulty that whenever the nature of social bonds is discussed, religious imagery will be used to illustrate the nature of such bonds. Thus we hear a great deal about "sacred" and "ritual" in anthropology. And whenever the image of drama is used, as in the phrase "ritual drama," the drama invoked is usually tragic drama. It is not until we come to the work of Burke that we find drama proper, and not religious ritual, offered as a model for thinking about how communication and society affect each other. As Burke points out, if we say a ritual is a drama then we have admitted that ritual is determined by the structure and function of drama, as well as by its use in religion.

When we say this we are saying that art, as well as religion, determines society (just as society determines religion and art). This has been said before, but in discussions about art and society little has been said about how art, *as art,* determines society. Theologians have raised the same complaint about the sociologist of religion who ascribes religion to society, and then derives religion from society. And even when we do turn to tragic art as our image of art in society, we often confuse religion with art. In such discussions (as exemplified by those of Jane Harrison), art soon gives way to religion, and ritual drama soon becomes religious drama. But there is another kind of art which is equally important to society (if not to religion). This is comedy.

The Christian tradition is essentially a tragic tradition. We are saved only by God's sacrifice of his only son, who suffered and died for us. We are born in sin, live in sin, and will be released from sin only in death. Man's corruption, his original sin, finds expression in human association, religion teaches us—in guilt, redemption, hierarchy, and victimage. But if this is true of religious expression, and specifically of Christian religious expression, how true is it of all social experience? Or, more generally, what do we learn from religion about society? We learn a great deal and will continue to learn a great deal so long as we study how religion is expressed and is communicated. When we do this, we are in the realm of *both* religion and art, for religion is worship, an *act* of worship, as well as a state of belief. And when we are in the realm of symbolic action we are in the realm of art, because it is through the symbols supplied by art that we communicate religious experience—or any kind of experience.

Tragedy and religion are so closely linked in our tradition that it is extremely difficult to keep them apart. It is also difficult to avoid being affected by the hierarchy common to all religious thought about art. In this, the highest truth is the revealed truth of religion, with art serving as a means for communicating the truths about religion. Carried to its logical extreme this is like saying that Bach simply "carried out" in music the ideas given him by Luther, or that Milton simply "expressed" the values of Puritanism. In our own day we still hear clergymen discussing art as a kind of rest cure for the weary moralist. Art, so this argument runs, offers refuge from the real world of real moral struggle, by transforming us from participators to spectators in the drama of life.[1]

All such notions about the "delight" of art, or of the artist as simply a kind of messenger or oracle through whom the higher powers of religion (now it is the state) make their commandments known, reduce art to ventriloquism. Like the ventriloquist's dummy, the artist sits in the lap of the church, or the state, mouthing the messages which come from his master. The paradox in this position is obvious once we ask: How do we *know* the revelations from on high, unless through their communication in art? The devout believer of divine truths, as revealed by God or the state, admits that he gets some kind of communication from his divine source, but, he maintains stoutly, this has nothing to do with art. Belief is given in direct communion with the divine spirit. Once the moment of belief has occurred, *then* it can be communicated, but it is not born *in* communication, and the artist has nothing to do with creating it.

But to the artist (as to the sociologist interested in communication) religion is an act of worship, which, like every act, has *form*. In this view, *how* we worship, the ways in which we express our relation to God, *determines the kind of experience we have of God*. For, to the artist, content cannot exist without form, and indeed, it is not until form is created that we can have any experience of content at all. Even the simplest emotion, to say nothing of great religious emotion, depends on form,[2] because an emotion cannot exist (in consciousness, at least) until it is expressed, and it cannot be expressed, in turn, until it is given some kind of form.

It may be that the greatest forms of art depend on religion for their content and for their capacity to move us so deeply. But it could also be argued that the greatest forms of religious life are equally dependent on art. For, until worship is staged it has no existence. A church, a prayer, a hymn, a dance of worship, a cross—all religious symbolization is glorified by art. It may be that a humble peasant stumbling through his prayers with a contrite heart experiences communion with God as much as a worshipper whose heart almost bursts at the cry of agony over Christ's suffering in Bach's *St. Matthew's Passion*. It may be true also that the moment of silent rapture, the moment when silence becomes the voice of God and art vanishes in the sublime experience of the living God, is the most profound moment in religious experience.

But the artist cannot accept this. To him, Bach creates religious experience. And since creation begins in exploration and search for ways to give form to *new* social experience, the artist believes that his forms *constitute* experience. The point is not that Giotto painted on his knees, or that Bach worshipped through music, but that they give religious experience new forms and new realities which would not have been possible without such forms. The difference between Bach and the peasant is a difference, not of holiness, but of creation. In this sense, then, both the artist and the clergymen are priests, and in times of great integration between religion and art both are recognized as such.

Invoking form (and the search for form) as the characteristic act in art and saying that art is not religion soon lead to the question: "What then is art?" Granted it is form, what is the form about? And how do we study art in its purest form as art? The answer to these questions depends on circumstances. There have been no purer forms of art than the religious art of Bach. But in our time, art is no longer dependent on religion. It exists in its own right, as in comedy. We need not argue here over whether comedy or tragedy is the greatest art of our age, but simply point out that artists of our time, like Shakespeare, Cervantes, Swift, Mozart, Verdi, Mark Twain, and Charlie Chaplin, all created great comedy. Sixteen of Shakespeare's plays are comedies, and like Cervantes, Mozart, and Verdi,[3] Shakespeare wrote his greatest comedies at the end of his life, and thus we must assume that he, along with many other artists who created their comic masterpieces in the fullness of experience and creative power, regarded comedy as a profound expresson of art.

It is necessary to point this out because tragedy has a much higher status than comedy, especially among those who do not create art. Even in our own time, Mark Twain complained bitterly about the low esteem in which he was held as an artist by the community guardians of culture in America.

Privately I am quite well aware that for a generation I have been as widely celebrated a literary person as America has ever produced, and I am also privately aware that in my own particular line [comedy] I have stood at the head of my guild during all that time, with none to dispute the place with me; and so it has been an annual pain to me to see our universities confer an aggregate of two hundred and fifty honorary degrees upon persons of small and temporary consequence—persons of local and evanescent notoriety, persons who drift into obscurity and are forgotten inside of ten years—and never a degree offered to me! [4]

But even if we wave such considerations aside, the sociologist who turns to comedy can at least be sure that what he says about comedy is not something he could just as well say about religion, or magic, or ritual. This is necessary because if we say that art determines society, then we must be sure that what we are saying about art really is about art. And even when we do say that art determines society, and use only tragic art as our example of art, we leave a great amount of art out of our scheme. Art is *both* tragedy *and* comedy, and if tragedy was admitted to the sacred festivals at Athens, so too was comedy. And if the tragic hero becomes a god, the comic hero is not without deep and demonic powers of his own. Who is to say that Hawthorne's tortured Puritans tell us more about America than Mark Twain's Huck, Tom, and Jim?

COMEDY AND SOCIAL CONTROL

"Jokes serve as a resistance against authority and as an escape from its pressure." We owe Freud much for his elaboration of this hypothesis, but it is too limited for a social theory of comedy. Comedy *upholds* as well as resists authority by making ridiculous, absurd, or laughable whatever threatens social order. American laughter at the immigrant (German, Irish, Scotch, Scandinavian, Italian, and Yiddish, in turn), like Molière's laughter over parvenus, is a form of social discipline. It serves to keep them in place until they learn how to behave like established Americans. The German was teased for his "dumb" rural ways, the Irishman for his "blarney," the Scot for his thrift, and, as befits a nation of "go-getters," the lazy and shiftless (of whatever background) were ridiculed as bums.

The American comic bum is seldom ironic, like the seedy aristocrat in European comic art. Nor is he holy, like the Yiddish *schnorrer* who helps to keep Baron Rothschild's piety in good repair. The business community, which pays its clowns such great sums, wants laggard spenders disciplined, just as an earlier generation of plutocrats kept a sharp eye on the "sturdy beggar," who could, but would not work. Our television clowns are now "masters of ceremonies" who dress like plutocrats, surround themselves with glamorous "guest stars," and lead us to "commercials" where we are urged to want everything that money can buy. Bob Hope, Milton Berle, and Steve Allen are "live wires." Even those like Red Skelton, who mock the plutocrat with his seedy elegance (in his role as "Freddie the Freeloader"), cigars picked up from the gutter, and talk about "big deals" and wintering in Florida, introduce their acts in highly fashionable dress. For why should they not? Bing Crosby, Bob Hope, Jack Benny, and Steve Allen are millionaires. Their exquisite grooming and general air of well being assure us that comedy pays. Money not only talks in American television—it laughs out loud.

Who are these millionaire clowns "outwitting"? Certainly not the authority of money. Their shows are "parties" with "guests" who are introduced to us, not in their role as clown, but as "great and wonderful" people who obviously can afford luxurious dress, jewels, and elegant coiffures. The clown, as master of ceremonies, is now a gracious host who "asks" his guests to perform for his guests beyond the camera—but not before an exchange of genteel pleasantries over something which only money can buy (the flight back from Europe "just for this show," etc.) or a "build-up" which shows how well the guest is doing in the American quest for fame and fortune. Humor over money is not from the view of the poor, but of the rich. We hear jokes about how the income tax impoverishes, how hard it is to get Jack Benny to spend, how the government borrows from Bing Crosby, etc. The most sophisticated plutocratic humor, the ironic humor of *The New Yorker,* enhances the glamour of money by making fun of unsophisticated and awkward spenders. Even in sophisticated commercials where the "pitch" is very gay and the announcer full of joy in his message (the "bland" in contrast to the "hard" sell) luxury and "gracious living" abound.

The bland comedy and polite mutual teasing by wealthy clowns over the trials and tribulations of living and spending in a world of the "fast buck" is very different from the comedy of Charlie Chaplin or W. C. Fields, the parody of Sinclair Lewis, the satire of Ring Lardner, Groucho Marx's assaults on the dignity of the female plutocrat, or the savage thrusts of Veblen. W. C. Fields makes plutocrats phonies and confidence men. Sinclair Lewis makes Babbitt adolescent and infantile. Ring Lardner scorns the miserliness, stupidity, and meanness of baseball players, the great popular heroes who were supposed to play for glory and love of the game. These comic artists [5] are attacking money, not upholding it.

Life is a continual party in a luxurious house for the genial plutocratic clowns on television. The orgiastic party of the 1920s has been shifted from alcohol and sex to money. We are urged, cajoled, shamed, teased, even frightened into buying. Freedom of the air, it turns out, is freedom to sell. The clown has become a salesman who vies with professional announcers in glorifying anything that is profitable.[6] Thus, as we see daily and nightly, comedy can be highly conservative, as well as radical. Such use is not peculiar to our time, of course. Wise authorities understand well the conservative function of comedy. Greek and Roman Saturnalias, Medieval Lords and Abbots of Misrule, the real and symbolic killing of mock kings, indicate clearly that comedy has long been used to uphold, as well as reject, authority.[7]

Parvenus whose social ambitions far exceed their social skills have been stock figures in comedy for many centuries. We do not laugh at the parvenu to keep him outside our group, but to discipline him so he will learn to act well enough to become one of us. The parvenu knows he can enter good society, what he does not know is *how* to do it, for prestige, like honor, is given, never taken. The established élite discipline the parvenu because they fear he will confuse techniques of social climbing with the spirit of gentility. The parvenu fears his social gods because he is never quite sure of their regard, and because he cannot be sure he worships correctly until they tell him so. So long as we do not have to admit the parvenu to our ranks, and indeed must keep him from our ranks (as in a caste system), manners become ritual whose transgressions are tragic, not comic. Violations of caste can be atoned only through tragic sacrifice, for only in such sacrifice can evils be purged.

Ritual manners are a kind of hierarchal prayer, led by priests who control the "grace" of hierarchy and the means by which we expiate social sins. These sins are acts which threaten the majesty and glory of symbols and offices upon which social order is believed to rest. In a plutocracy such as ours, money and the offices through which money is expressed are held sacred. We must teach our young pecuniary decency. In our colleges and schools, as in the press and television, we use comedy to shame those who are laggard or inept earners and spenders. Jack Benny is now our national miser. He has replaced the thrifty Scot as a threat to the kind of "heroic" individual spending our business community now requires. For the glory of capitalism is *individual* spending, in contrast to institutional or state spending which are the heroics of socialism.

The comic villain, in American business eyes, is no longer the lazy worker or the tramp, but the lazy spender. In the popular comic art of the new urban civilization of America from 1880 to 1930—movies, cartoon strips, vaudeville, and night clubs—the bum is one who will not work, is always after easy money, and who spends in a vulgar and common way when he does have money. The impecunious aristocrat, or the "innocent" aristocrat who cannot understand money, whom we meet so often in British comedy, has faint echoes in Chaplin's Charlie the Tramp. His elegance, while phony, is still elegance. More characteristic of American urban humor is the lazy bum who wants money but will not work to get it. He rejects the Puritan ethic of earning, but not the plutocratic ethic of spending. Moon Mullins, his brother Kayo, and Uncle Willie, in Frank Willard's comic strip "Moon Mullins" are a trio of lazy bums. Red Skelton's Freddie the Freeloader is another.

George McManus' cartoon strip "Bringing Up Father," in which Maggie scrambles furiously for the top rung of the social ladder, is in direct lineage with Molière's *Bourgeois Gentilhomme* of 1670. Jiggs, Maggie's husband, looks wistfully at the simple joys of Dinty Moore's saloon where he can drink, eat corned beef and cabbage, and spend the night at cards with Casey, Sweeny, and Larry O'Girity. But he returns to Maggie and her "swells" in the great cold marble palace sudden fortune has brought them. Hard-driving, ambitious Maggie represents plutocratic majesty, and while we shudder as her rolling pin finds its unerring way to Jiggs' skull, we admit sadly that she is right. Millionaires must not spend their money on beer and corned beef dinners. We love Jiggs for his refusal to give up his old friends, but we realize as good Americans how he threatens the glory of money. For if riches are not to lead to some kind of orgiastic future, why should we work so hard? The older Puritan could spend only as a steward of a Lord. The new plutocrats, and certainly their wives, found such heavenly stewardship too impersonal. They wanted to spend on themselves. And for the common people, the new immigrants of the cities, an earthly paradise was more attractive and much more comprehensible.

Thus, while Jiggs resists authority, he always returns to Maggie, who upholds it. Like the good folk who rescue Huck Finn from the river and the woods, Maggie represents the conscience of the community. She spends as the wife of a plutocrat should and tries valiantly to find a "swell" husband for her daughter. In her are embodied the principles of family and community life among a rapidly rising plutocracy. Jiggs must be punished if the glory of plutocracy is to survive. And so we forgive Maggie her violence and cruelty. She must be obeyed, for only in such obedience can a social order based on money survive.

As Scots, Irishmen, and Germans, we laugh with Americans at ourselves. We understand very well that group judgment has been passed over us, and if we choose to remain in the group, we must accept this judgment and mend our ways. The canny Scot learns to spend. He must learn to owe as well as own money, for among Americans credit, not cash, and bragging, not modesty or secrecy about wealth, determine social prestige. To be in debt indicates confidence in oneself and the future of American society.[8]

THE SOCIAL FUNCTION OF IRONY

But there is another mode in comedy. This is irony which neither accepts nor rejects, but doubts. Irony helps us to endure what we cannot, or will not, change. Man, La Rochefoucauld tells us, cannot love others because he loves only himself. Even a narcissist needs a mirror to reflect the image of the self he loves so deeply. We disguise our vices as virtues to win audiences who will serve as mirrors for our pride. But the paradox of pride becomes painfully obvious as we strut and preen before audiences whom we really despise and who, we know, despise and hate us. The saving grace in ironic comedy is the use of reason to confront our vices. At least we are not deluded; we have *chosen* to confront our vices, not to avoid or deny them. Thus, if we cannot will our fate, we can decide how we meet it.

Such faith in reason is possible only when doubt is considered a way to truth, as in reasoned discourse among equals. Where doubt is considered weakness or heresy, irony cannot be used. Where there are great gaps between classes or conditions of life, irony fails. And where reason in society is not a value, irony easily offends those in power, as the fate of Socrates, the creator of "Socratic irony," warns us. The only social certainty offered by the ironist is the certainty of open and free discussion as a means to truth. He does not predict, he brings back no knowledge from heavens and utopias he alone has seen, nor does he believe in laws discovered by reason which are beyond reason in some kind of nature whose "laws" can be known but not changed. He believes that we must rely on critical intelligence, intelligence born in open and free discourse among men who believe such discourse creates and sustains social bonds.

Ironical address cannot be made to inferiors or superiors. We communicate with general publics through burlesque and broad humor. Slapstick comedy is simple, repetitive, and violent; gestures are exaggerated and prolonged. Differences between superiors and inferiors are accentuated. Action is depicted from the view of the actor. No one steps out of his role to deliver asides to other members of the cast, or to the audience. No soliloquies are held. Slapstick action is often a chase, a pursuit of the "little fellow" by the "big fellow." The big fellow makes clear by menacing gestures that the little fellow will be beaten, even killed, if caught. As the rhythm of the pursuit accelerates, we share the comic terror of the hunted clown. In such comic action no one is a witness, all, audience and actor alike, are participants. Even the scene *acts* as when telephone poles flatten out, and houses crumple under the wind pressure of the racing cars which careen madly down streets where normal traffic laws, and, indeed, the laws of gravity itself, are suspended.

Irony holds belief, the tragic moment of truth, open to doubt. It exposes motives which the actors do not know or seek to hide. Roles shift and change. The audience is suddenly involved in the action through being addressed directly. The ironic actor withdraws from action to become an audience to other actors, and even to himself. He comments on the action in asides, or in soliloquy which audiences are allowed to overhear. Such soliloquy, while "internal," is really an expression of the problem of internalizing "outer" aspects of roles which are in conflict because the roles themselves are in conflict, and it is difficult or impossible for the individual actor to resolve this conflict. Such disrelationships among social roles always exist; indeed, they are assumed in every statement of relationship. We decree punishments at the same time we pass laws; we describe treason in state constitutions which define our duties to the state; we warn men against a devil who has been created by an all-powerful and loving God.

Ironic soliloquy, like talking to one's self or the staging of dreams of the day and night, is a struggle to express problems so we can communicate about them—to the self as well as to others.[9] As we talk to ourselves we take the role of another toward the self. The self replies in turn. The ironic hero does not reject authority, but opens the majesty of authority to doubt and question. He does this through magnification of the distance between ideal and real audiences and actors.

In Chapter XXI of *Huckleberry Finn,* the king and the duke reject feudal dignity. Kingship is burlesqued [10] by being played by ragged and dirty actors before a runaway slave and a boy, on a raft drifting down an American river. Within a few pages a feudal "duel" begins. Soon the burlesque shifts to irony.[11] It also becomes tragic, as we realize that Colonel Sherburn, the southern aristocrat who lives by the code of honor, is really going to shoot Boggs, a helpless drunk pleading for his life, because in a drunken fit of bragging Boggs has insulted the Colonel by threatening him in public.

The majesty of the Colonel is reduced to absurdity by the disproportion between the majesty of the act and the vulgarity of the audience before whom the act is played. Mark Twain underscores heavily the manners and filth of the town and its common people. "All the streets and lanes was just mud, they warn't nothing else *but* mud—mud as black as tar, and nigh about a foot deep in some places; and two or three inches deep in *all* the places. The hogs loafed and grunted around, everywheres." In passages that rival Swift's terrible pages on the rutting, stinking Yahoos, the beasts who think themselves men, Mark Twain describes the townspeople.

There was empty dry-goods boxes under the awnings, and loafers roosting on them all day long, whittling them with their Barlow knives; and chawing tobacco, and gaping and yawning and stretching—a mighty ornery lot. . . . There was as many as one loafer leaning up against every awning-post, and he most always had his hands in his britches pockets, except when he fetched them out to lend a chaw of tobacco. . . . You'd see a muddy sow and a litter of pigs come lallying down the street and whollop herself right down in the way, where folks had to walk around her, and she'd stretch out, and shut her eyes, and wave her ears, whilst the pigs was milking her, and look as happy as if she was on salary. And pretty soon you'd hear a loafer sing out, "Hi! so boy! sick him, Tige!" and away the sow would go, squealing most horrible, with a dog or two swinging to each ear, and three or four dozen more a-coming; and then you would see all the loafers get up and watch the thing out of sight, and laugh at the fun and look grateful for the noise. Then they'd settle back again till there was a dog-fight—unless it might be putting turpentine on a stray dog and setting fire to him, or tying a tin pan to his tail and see him run himself to death.[12]

This is the field of honor where Colonel Sherburn upholds the dignity of a southern gentleman.

But within a few pages Colonel Sherburn changes from villain to hero.[13] The people's rage mounts into hysteria. They rush to the Colonel's home, "ripping and tearing and smashing" the fence palings. The Colonel "steps out on to the roof of his little front porch, with a double-barrel gun in his hand, and takes his stand, perfectly calm and deliberate, not saying a word. The racket stopped, and the wave sucked back." The Colonel "run his eye slow along the crowd; and whenever it struck, the people tried to outgaze him, but they couldn't; they dropped their eyes and looked sneaky." And then begins one of the most damning attacks in all literature on cowards and murderers who confuse punishment with justice.

"The idea of *you* lynching anybody! It's amusing. The idea of you thinking you had pluck enough to lynch a *man*! . . . Why a *man's* safe in the hands of ten thousand of your kind—as long as it's day time and you're not behind him.

"Do I know you? I know you clear through. I was born and raised in the South, and I've lived in the North; so I know the average all around. The average man's a coward. . . ."[14]

As he finishes his mocking tongue-lashing of the crowd, the Colonel tosses his gun across his left arm and cocks it. The crowd "washed back sudden, and then broke all apart and went tearing off every which way. . . ."

We forgive the murder of the drunken Boggs, for now the Colonel upholds a principle of social order which must be upheld if democracy is to be saved from "mobocracy." The individual must stand up for his rights, and he must be brave enough to fight for them. The principle of order which must be upheld is the principle of law. The breakdown of law in mob rule is the curse of democracy. The Colonel asks: "Why don't your juries hang murderers? Because they're afraid the man's friends will shoot them in the back, in the dark—and it's just what they would do." So, "they always acquit; and then a *man* goes in the night, with a hundred masked cowards at his back, and lynches the rascal."[15]

In the figure of the Colonel and his relation to the people, the problem of democracy is explored through every resource of art. Comedy, irony, tragedy, and the grotesque are invoked to express the problem of democracy. Neither the southern gentleman nor the people can be trusted. What then is the solution for democracy, and how can we build a community of free men? Mark Twain did not know. He loved democracy and longed for its realization. As he grew older, despair often overwhelmed him. America was right to reject the southern aristocrat, but it is wrong to find the voice of God in people who are cowards and fools. The people of Mark Twain's town in the Mississippi Valley, the "Valley of Democracy," are not to be purified in some golden day of plenty. They have already fallen from grace. Huck and Nigger Jim return to this grace when they abandon the town and return to the river and the woods, for here and only here can they live in joy and love. Here they meet Thoreau, as later they pass on their spirit to Frank Lloyd Wright, whose Prairie Houses are rooted in the earth. As our cities break up in "flight" to the country and suburbs, it becomes clear that Huck and Thoreau understood the dilemma of a people who would live on freeholds of their own, yet who must bring these islands into some kind of community. For if individuality brings loneliness and isolation, what is its human value?

There is a kind of double-talk in irony where we say one thing, but really mean another. This is not simply an artistic trick, for when we act we act before several audiences, and sometimes we must act before all of them at the same time. We are like the politician making a speech. He speaks to the general public, but on the platform are honored guests who represent the conscience of the community, and somewhere in the audience are opponents waiting to heckle him when they can. Hovering over all are insignias of the flag, the cross, and the institution sponsoring the speech; these are the symbolization of the great principles upon which social order is presumed to rest. None of these must be neglected, yet none can be singled out too much or for too long. Irony permits us to say things we must say to superiors or inferiors to uphold conventions necessary to social order and yet to express our disquiet over these conventions. In ironic address all become equal, since we "let them in" on what is really the truth about the convention.

The strain (sometimes indeed the impossibility) of pleasing different and often antagonistic factions in "outer" audiences, is experienced by everyone in his appeals to his "inner" audiences. Such appeals are an address. We *talk* to ourselves. The Id, Ego, and Super-Ego must communicate to function. Even if the Freudian "cathects" i.e., concentrates desire upon some object or person, it does so in communication. If the Ego cathects "the presentations of objects with libido—to change narcissistic libido into *object* libido," as Freud tells us,[16] what determines these "presentations"? They cannot, as sensory images, arise from soma alone, for an image is a symbol, not a charge.

As we address the Super-Ego whose "calls of conscience" demand response, we feel, at the same time, the call of the Id. Such quandaries are met in ironic comedy by *exposing,* not by hiding, inner conflicts. The Ego *confronts* the Super-Ego with the Id, as the comic actor confronts one audience with another, to let *them* reconcile demands made upon him. Irony is like arbitration where disputants are treated as equals, locked in a room, and told not to come out until they have settled their dispute among themselves. We are never quite sure just how the dispute will be resolved, but we are determined that it shall be faced. It is as if we say: "Well, I don't know how to solve this problem, but at least I admit my ignorance. Certainly I am not taken in, the way those fools are who refuse to see the problem."

Irony is a kind of complicity among equals. The air of detachment, of playfulness so characteristic of irony disturbs a superior, for he is never sure his majesty is believed. Leaders do not want us detached, but committed. Thus Carlyle, a true believer after his conversion in *Sartor Resartus,* tells us: "An ironic man, with his sly stillness, and ambuscading ways, may be viewed as a pest to society." Inferiors dislike irony because they are never quite sure whether the ironist means to insult or compliment them. When we teach children we soon discover that what we think ironical they often find insulting. But with colleagues, friends, brothers and sisters, fellow workers, or with those with whom we share any kind of common dilemma as equals, irony is often used. Through irony we discuss the shortcomings of superiors and inferiors, even as we admit that their weaknesses must be endured, for without superiors and inferiors social order would be impossible.

But irony does not simply "debunk" principles of social order which make authority possible. The ironist makes reason an ultimate value. He believes that doubt is a principle of social order. Like all comedy, irony keeps society flexible and open to change. It does not favor violent rejection, as in obscene comedy (which really is a kind of curse), nor does it favor devout acceptance, as in scornful comedy (which blesses snobbery). It is "the comedy of reason" because it keeps reason at work in situations where it threatens to become subordinate to unreason.

There is a kind of superiority in irony, but it is the superiority of detachment. Perhaps this is why two old friends or husband and wife so often greet each other ironically in formal and ceremonial occasions where protocol and ritual "company" manners must be followed. We mock slightly the rather grand manners we have been putting on to meet the formal demands of the occasion. It is as if we say: "You and I know what trumpery all this bowing and scraping is, but it's the way you keep things going." There are many expressions which convey this kind of ironic comment. The wink, the shrug, raised eyebrows, eyes opened wide in mock amazement—any gesture which expresses doubt over the seriousness of what we are saying—are ways of telling others that while we must do what we are doing, we realize how silly it is after all.

Ironic address of the self (as well as others) is an attempt to control through increased self-consciousness. We address ourselves to *affect* what we do, not simply to comment on our action. Incongruities between ideals and practices are more apparent to the self than to others. The curse of self-love is that we end by knowing our favorite subject—the self—too well. The neurotic deludes others far more easily than himself. Even in the deepest compulsion, the self stands apart as witness. Who has not vowed never to love or to believe again? Yet who has not watched himself begin again to love or to believe those who have caused so much pain and sorrow. At such times we turn to the self and echo La Rochefoucauld's ironic courtier, who tells us that man is constant only in his inconsistency. Yet even as we watch ourselves plunge into causes where faith stifles reason, we struggle to overcome our madness through irony, as at other times we struggle to subdue the senses through mortification. For so long as we confront our madness there is hope of controlling it. In ironic self-address we hope to expose the mystery of the moment of faith which places action beyond reason.

Irony is the great comic means by which various factions within the self and the community question one another, and thus it uncovers the magic and mystery which lurks in every social bond. As he turns to his audience of equals, the ironic clown transcends superior and inferior alike. He can take the point of view of one toward the other without seeming treacherous to either. The tragic hero, in life as in art, must treat difference as heresy and doubt as weakness. The ironic hero detaches himself from belief in any one course of action, so that he can respect and reflect on others. He does not want to mock or "debunk," but to keep faith open to reason in action. The ironist is not concerned with using reason to perceive the world, but to act in it.

Awe and reverence depend on strangeness and mystery; we use such mystery to enhance the "supernatural" power of social bonds. Our styles of punishment, like Greek ritual drama, are community tragedies. The majesty of the law must be upheld. But laws are often broken, or, when obeyed, they sometimes augment the disorders they are supposed to prevent. Incongruities between the ideals and practices of authority often threaten the majesty of the offices they uphold. Even when authorities recognize disrelationships between social ends and means, *how* to admit these with small risk to their majesty, and the social order upon which their majesty rests, is a problem. Tragic invocation to punishing and vengeful gods preserves the mystery and majesty of the principles of social order by which we live.

Comedy, and especially ironic comedy, *institutionalizes* doubt and question. It is *sanctioned* disrespect. The ironic clown lacks the mystery of community priests, but his social office is no less real. Bob Hope "ribbing" the President at the annual Washington gridiron dinner, is not outwitting a censor but performing as a highly honored public functionary—the people's Fool. His laughter, like the incantations of the priests, is sacred because his jokes create comic forms which we use to ward off threats to social order. The incongruities and follies of the President and his staff are brought to light. The mystifications and grandeur of the President's office is opened for examination. It is returned to reason through laughter where it submits itself to the greatest power of all—reason born in discourse among free men.

COMEDY AND GROUP IDENTIFICATION

The burst of glory in comedy has many roots. One of these is our sudden reassurance that while some aspect of authority is threatened, the *principles* of authority are not. The individual priest may be venal, the soldier cowardly, the scholar pedantic, but the church is still holy, the army still brave, the school a community of scholars searching for wisdom. Indeed, only to the degree that the institution is idealized can there be sufficient incongruity between the ideal and the real to excite laughter. We laugh with Swift at the pedantic scholar because he misuses his mind. We laugh with Rabelais at lustful big-bellied monks who use their office to bully and cheat. But this is possible because kindness, love, and intelligence are monkish virtues too, as the inscription of the Abbey of Theleme reads:

> Here enter you, pure, honest, faithful, true.
> Expounders of the Scriptures old and new.
> Whose glosses do not blind our reason, but
> Make it to see the clearer, and who shut
> Its passages from hatred, avarice,
> Pride, factions, covenants, and all sorts of vice.
> Come, settle here a charitable faith,
> Which neighbourly affection nourisheth.
> And whose light chasteneth all corrupters hence,
> Of the blest word, from the aforesaid sense.
> > The Holy Sacred Word,
> > May it always afford
> > > T'us all in common,
> > > Both man and woman,
> > > A spiritual shield and sword,
> > > The Holy Sacred Word.[17]

Against this benign and sunny vision of "neighbourly affection," villainous hypocrites, wrangling barristers, pinching usurers, and "makers of demurs in love adventures" and "peevish jealous curs" become ridiculous. For they set themselves apart from the brotherhood of joyous, loving Thelemites, who are the true citizens of an ideal commonwealth.

As we submit our problems to group consideration we become more confident of solving them. We cannot laugh at what we secretly or unconsciously fear, and we cannot think well about fears we cannot submit to group discourse. We submit to the discipline of comedy because we believe it is necessary to social solidarity and group survival. Communication is kept open and free through laughter because laughter *clarifies* where tragedy *mystifies*. Tragic art and religious ritual lead to victimage and mystification because the ultimate audience of ritual is supernatural power. When the tragic artist and his audience are in complete accord, the most terrible violence and death may be, indeed, must be, visited upon victims who symbolize threats to social order. But comedy opens to reason the mystifications of social hierarchy, whose pomp and wonder is so often enhanced by secular variations of priestly art. Because we possess forms created in the wonderful art of Aristophanes, Rabelais, Molière, Shakespeare, Swift, Mozart, Verdi, and in our own day Mark Twain and Charlie Chaplin, we can communicate over our many social incongruities.

Comedy is a cry of the heart as much as tragedy. Like Don Quixote we grow old and must find in memory and fancies of another time what we can no longer find in a present. Like Gulliver, we see pride confused with reason. Like Mozart, we see lover's vows vanish in a moment of lust. As we laugh together, loneliness and alienation vanish. Such laughter is a moment of reaffirmation. We re-create our social bonds even as we recognize our differences. When we laugh at the haughty gentleman who slips into the swimming pool as he backs away from the lady to whom he has just bowed, we feel superior because his formal dress becomes ridiculous in a swimming pool, and the elaborate status pantomime of bowing to a lady has ended incongruously. If, in helping the drenched plutocrat out of the pool, we too tumble in, laughter mounts until in a moment of complete disregard for the expense of our plutocratic status trappings, we *all* jump into the pool; we are "in the drink" together and flounder about in a mad but glorious moment of solidarity as we reaffirm once again our common human bonds.

We laugh at immigrants so long as we are secure in the glory of our principles of social order. As we laugh at the thrifty Scot, we feel the glory of our boldness with money, and at the same time make him aware of how he must spend if he is to be one of us. There is hostility in our laughter, but it is not the hostility of derisive laughter which ends in alienation and hate. We are anxious to prepare the Scot for membership in the American community. Such joking is really a form of instruction, a kind of social control, directed at those we intend to accept once they learn to behave properly—that is, like us.

Address in comedy is to the supernatural power of society—but a society purified by love and reason whose glory is joy. The comic actor must keep alive belief in reason. His dilemma is how to explain why men so capable of reason and joy are yet so irrational and sad. He resolves this by showing that men sin because they abandon reason. But ignorance is not lack of knowledge of how to think, but of not testing thought for its social relevance. Great comedy is not born in contempt, but in love of man in society. It is a kind of inverse sublimity, exalting and raising into our affections what is inferior to us. But at the same time great comedy returns our superiors to our affections by showing them struggling to make sense out of their world.

"Debunkers" enlist our sympathy by creating the illusion that we do not share the follies of the world we see, and by giving us vicarious victories over vice. But after they have exposed the evil of the villain and convinced us that virtues are but vices in disguise, we suddenly pause. For if no man trust another, how is society possible? Why should vice bind us any more than virtue? At such questions the comic mask must drop. Now we must know what can be right in a world where so much is wrong, if the world is to be worth while.

Thus, all comedy is highly moral, but it is the morality of reason in society. It seeks to unmask vices by confronting ends or ideals with means or practice. The final transcendence in comedy is society itself, people who in hate and love try to resolve differences. Laughter is the scourge of vice, just as tears are the purge of evil. Vice is ridiculous, for its pleasures turn into pain and suffering. Great comic artists distrust tragedy, not because they do not suffer or take a melancholy view of life, but because they think tragedy alone is not enough to purge men of folly. La Rochefoucauld's dislike of tears ("misfortune breeds a variety of hypocrisies"), pride in suffering,[18] and gravity ("a physical mystification to conceal spiritual defects") is not based in destruction of pleasure, but of reason. Whatever removes the individual from a social context is irrational. For if man is beyond society, how can we think about him? And if we cannot think about man, what is the good of thought? Comedy creates joy, joy creates social euphoria which deepens love and trust [19] in each other. Comedy is ethical because it is rational [20] and rational because it leads to good social relationships.

Hierarchal address in comedy begins by exposing authority, as when La Rochefoucauld tells us that virtues are but vices in disguise. But it must end in some kind of authority. Vices may be disguised, but their disguises can be seen through after all. Whoever sees through them is the "true" authority. Clues to such authority abound in moments of address, or presentation of the self. The authority in the courtly act is the king, whose authority in turn comes from a principle of nobility, which in turn is derived from God. But the principle of courtship addressed by La Rochefoucauld is not the noble as warrior, priest, or statesman, but as grand seigneur, the great gentleman, who rules through manners that are based in the authority of God *in,* not beyond, society.

Notes

[1] This is discussed by Von Ogden Vogt in his *Art and Religion* (Boston: Beacon Press, 1960).

[2] There are no unexpressed emotions, and even the unconscious expression of the dream takes place in forms. There are unexpressed *feelings,* but these are not emotions, for emotions depend on the response, and on the attitude we take toward the response, of real and assumed others.

[3] Verdi wrote *Falstaff,* his masterpiece, after he was eighty.

[4] *The Autobiography of Mark Twain,* edited by Charles Neider (New York: Harper and Brothers, 1959), p. 349. Mark Twain goes on to tell us that Oxford University "healed this old sore" by granting him a Doctor of Letters degree. Even in psychology, despite the great legacy of Freud's book on the function of humor, little has been done with comedy; this work of Freud's is still the most neglected of all his works.

[5] Veblen, like Machiavelli and Mandeville, belongs in this tradition, despite his "official" role as economist.

[6] Through some kind of unconscious irony, nonprofit programs are called "public service" programs.

[7] It is significant that Freud uses Jewish humor for his illustrative matter on the social and psychological aspects of humor. Jewish humor is a folk humor. The Jewish God is a tragic God, who never laughs. Dreams are absurd as well as solemn, and we are embarrassed as well as guilty in dreams. This fact led Freud to his book on jokes, and, since jokes and all comedy in Judaism (as well as Christianity) are "low'" and tragedy "high," the use of humor to outwit the majestic Super-Ego certainly parallels the relation between low comedy and high tragedy in Judaism.

[8] With the Americanization of Europe installment buying, which transforms debt from vice to virtue, has now begun. British banks began to make installment loans in 1959.

[9] In acts which have a long tradition and are fully developed, as in acts of worship, erotic acts, or ceremonial civic acts, every sense is involved. We experience the meaning of home as a child through smell, touch, and taste, as well as through the eye and the ear. What we call the "motor phase" of an act is still symbolic since its meaning as a social act depends on the *form* taken by the motor elements. Dance, as much as speech, is a communication.

[10] "Well, next they [the king and duke] made, out of oak laths, a couple of long swords and began to practice the sword-fight—the duke called himself Richard III; and the way they laid on and pranced about the raft was grand to see. But by-and-by the king tripped and fell overboard. . . ." *The Adventures of Huckleberry Finn* (New York: Harper and Brothers, 1899), p. 183.

[11] It also shifts to the grotesque—which is never comic, but a kind of contrived nightmare. The grotesque evokes horror and terror, not laughter. It is used in both tragedy and comedy, but neither the tragic nor the comic hero can be grotesque, because the grotesque character is not disobeying commandments he understands and can will freely to obey or disobey. He is beyond reason, a creature of demonic powers. He is mad, but not evil or comic. Our fear of madmen stems from being unable to communicate with them. We cannot use madmen for sacrificial victims (we must find

our murderers sane before we kill them) because they cannot know moral suffering and thus cannot atone for their sins, or for ours.

[12] Mark Twain, *op. cit.*, p. 189.

[13] Surely one of the most magical moments in American literature.

[14] Mark Twain, *op. cit.*, p. 196.

[15] *Ibid.*

[16] In Chapter II of *An Outline of Psychoanalysis* (New York: W. W. Norton & Co., 1949).

[17] See Chapter LIV, "The Inscription Set Upon the Great Gate of Theleme," in Book I of Rabelais.

[18] "A man convinced of his own merit will accept misfortune as an honor, for thus he can persuade others, as well as himself, that he is a worthy target for the arrows of fate." (Maxim 50)

[19] "Trust contributes more to conversation than does wit." (Maxim 421) That is, reason depends on friendship, where discussion is possible because only equals can discuss.

[20] Spinoza states the case for joy in his *Ethics*: ". . . men being moved not by fear or aversion, but solely by the affect of joy, may endeavor as much as they can to live under the rule of reason." (Appendix, Part IV, xxv.)

28

The Comic Scapegoat

T H E C H I L D, as in *Alice in Wonderland,* or the boy, as in *Huckleberry Finn,* is used to express quite innocently problems that could not be raised in any other way. Those in power may attend to the child's innocent complaints with no loss of majesty. The ingénue, the country cousin, the farmer's daughter of American burlesque, and the king's Fool are all "innocent." We permit the child to ask questions that would be considered rude, insulting, or heretical if asked by a responsible adult. The wide-eyed wonder of the innocent opens up to full view incongruities which have been hidden and suppressed because their expression might subject those in power to mockery or disdain.

In great comedy, unconscious, hidden, and suppressed conflict is brought to light. And if the dream is the guardian of sleep, comedy is the guardian of reason in society because it makes possible confrontation of social disrelationships. Kings *cannot* question, for majesty must be beyond question. A king or a god may answer but never ask, for who can know more than a god? But in the laughter of Aristophanes over democratic demagoguery, of Rabelais over feudal mystifications, of Molière over aristocratic hypocrisy, of Swift over contradiction between man's pride and his bestiality, of Shaw over the incongruities of sex and class, or of Mark Twain over the irrelevance of the genteel tradition to frontier life in the West, leaders could risk their majesty and followers their loyalty.

By the selection of the boy as his comic hero, Mark Twain rendered his humor sexless. But the use of the boy makes it possible to attack the moral conventions that the artist in Mark Twain hated so deeply. Emmeline Grangerford's lugubrious poems to the dead and her early death as a frustrated poet who could not find a rhyme for Whistler (the name of the dead neighbor); the appearance of Tom, Joe, and Huck at their own funeral just as the congregation has broken down in tears at the minister's pathos over the death of the boys, the phony piety of King, the imposter

—these indicate the power gained by the use of the boy as a comic figure. Only someone so simple as a boy or girl, who could not be taken "seriously," was safe as a critic of religion. Mark Twain's mockery of death, like Don Giovanni's rejection of salvation at the price of submission to supernatural power, is in one of the great traditions of comedy, and one of the most telling examples of how great comic art allows us to examine the most sacred and traditional beliefs.[1]

Such beliefs drove sexual themes underground in Mark Twain's time, as we see in his Rabelaisian tale *1601*. Only boys like Huckleberry Finn or Tom Sawyer could rebel openly against woman. No adult could revolt against the pioneer mother, the sacred figure of the new West, who embodied the glamor of the family and was the bearer of the genteel tradition in the East. Mark Twain's ordeal was not sexual alone, but social. His clandestine Rabelaisian writings attack traditions too sacred for open attack. The Elizabethan lady and gentleman discussing the joys of fornication and passing wind return the Victorian lady to common humanity. The Boston blue-stocking and the New England lady are reduced to absurdity in laughter over the incongruity of our noble ancestors' taking such delight, and even pride, in vulgar acts that contrast so ludicrously with the genteel courtly language in which they are discussed.

Comic and tragic art offers formal dramatic expression of the problem of hierarchy. The superior must be majestic and sublime; his sin is pride. The inferior must be loyal, humble, attentive; his sin is churlishness, a refusal to give full and complete loyalty. Unless the inferior really believes his superior submits to a principle of social order common to superior and inferior alike, he will resent his leader's command. A hierarchal system is powerful (as a system) only when it is believed not to be dependent on the subjective will of leaders. It functions as fate, destiny, historical necessity, or, as we now begin to hear, as social equilibrium.

Yet with the best of intentions and the most carefully forged symbols, there will still be areas where majesty and duty do not agree. Majesty purifies itself through loading a scapegoat with its evil. The death of the tragic scapegoat and the villains' corpses on the stage relieve our society of its evil, and we are ready to follow our leaders once more. But the birth of the fool relieves us too, for now we know that things can at last be said (in laughter) that we ourselves long to say, but dare not, for fear of displeasing those we must love or those whose displeasure may cause us pain.

COMIC VICTIMAGE AND SOCIAL CATHARSIS

Tragedy purges through sacrifice of victims whose suffering and death serves as a vicarious atonement for our guilt. The sacrifice of such victims wards off threats to our group. Comedy purges through victims who assume our degradation and suffering so we can confront it together in rational discourse. Both depict struggle between good and bad social principles. Tragedy begins with a firm statement of belief in some social principle and dooms those who threaten it. Comedy begins with exploration of a social principle and ridicules those who place it beyond reason. Tragic heroes and villains cannot be saved, nor can they save themselves. The villain is beyond hope, he is an enemy who must be destroyed, for if he is not he will destroy us. The comic villain can be saved once he allows laughter to be turned against him. He can be laughed *at* but he is also being laughed *with*. We are laughing at him to purge him—and ourselves—of folly, not to torture and kill him.

Art—comic and tragic alike—*embodies* evil. The sacrifice of a speciously "perfect" victim in the formed material embodiment of an "idealized" enemy redeems our sins. Hitler's promotion of social integration through the choice of the Jew as an "ideal" ritual victim is horrible proof that deep guilt is intrinsic to social order in civilized and primitive communities alike. The counterpart of the community scapegoat within the individual is mortification of the self. Whenever there are social burdens to which we must resign ourselves, or when there are social barriers we do not care to (or cannot) scale, the moralistic inhibitions placed upon ambitious attitudes and occasional "sinful" overt acts of "success" lead to sacrificial attitudes. Ascetics who discipline the flesh and masochists who punish themselves through abject submission create highly stylized forms of mortification which must be expressed correctly. No dramatic director holds his actors to the text of his play more carefully than masochists or sadists who, as they inflict pain on themselves or others, do penance for their sins.

But penance, or abstinence, or the self-punishment of mortification, do not occur merely when we are "frustrated" by some external interference. Frustration must come from within. When we accept commandments of authority as our duty, we kill within us motives we think unruly or impious. In highly stylized acts of mortification we *systemize* ways of saying "no" to disorder as we obediently say "yes" to its opposite, order, and "maybe" to express doubt over either. We seek to overcome the deep pain of inner contention by projecting it upon a scapegoat (tragic or comic as the case may be), who becomes the sacrificial vessel upon which we vent, as if from without, a turmoil that is actually within. When we cannot do this, the body itself may be victimized, as in psychogenic illness: our socially goaded entanglements literally tear us to pieces as we suffer from "stress" diseases.

Community motives may serve as the matrix for a corresponding personal motive. Whenever an individual cannot rid himself of generic or tribal guilt by some kind of expiation, he turns, not to the symbolic scapegoat, but to crime or war. In the crime story, the author provides us with symbolic means for expressing hostilities toward communal bonds which we cannot express in other ways. So long as readers use crime stories for voidance of hostility on a symbolic level, we consider them benign. When the symbolic sin passes into actual sin through violations against property or person, we have problems of another order. Good citizens differ from criminals not because they have no hostility, but because they know how to express their hostility in ways considered benign by their community.

Ruler and ruled alike find it difficult to admit that sacred principles of social order bring sorrow, not joy. Peers do not challenge lightly the honor of other peers. If we disobey commandments, or violate a code of honor whose power is thought to be "beyond" the social bonds created in discourse, deviance must be treated as a sin, and we must be made to feel guilty, not merely mistaken. When we are serious and invoke tragic forms of trials (as in murder trials), the punishment must be horrible. For it is by the *form* of the punishment, not the "nature" of the crime, that we learn of its threat to social order. The Jews in Hitler's Germany were evil because they were being punished in certain ways. The German people did not discuss or debate the alleged crimes of the Jews, any more than we discuss or debate the motives and conditions of murder.

Our criminal is not prepared for sacrifice in a temple by priests, but in the daily news by reporters. Like all sacrificial victims, he is kept under lock and key until the altar is ready. No one can interview the murderer. Discussion of the evidence in the public press is often forbidden on the grounds that "trying the case in the front page" threatens the justice of trying it in court. We do not know why the murderer committed his crime, or really whether he did commit a crime, but we are spectators to an elaborate and awesome trial which is a ritual of sacrifice, not a search for justice. Authorities use such trials to make us believe that social disorder does not lie in faults in our relationships as superiors and inferiors, but in the evil machinations of some dark villain who threatens us all.

Shame and guilt are resolved in comedy, through confession of our sins to the group. Unlike tragic confession, when we appeal to some power beyond the group, we assume in comedy that open and free communication will tell us what our guilt means so that we can expiate it. To be guilty in the eyes of God or any supernatural power is very different from being guilty in the eyes of the group in which we enact our social roles. We do not "discuss" our sins with God, but plead for his mercy. In comic absolution, we are forgiven our sins because they surely will not threaten the group once they become "understandable" through open and free discussion.

Tragic victimage *must* end in terrible punishment to "prove" that great majesty was threatened by great crime. For how could a great power be threatened by anything less than another great power? We increase the power of the tragic villain to increase the power of the hero. We enhance the cunning and evil of a hated neighbor to justify the need for our noble self to contest with such rabble in such ignoble ways. The glory of victory depends on the glory of our enemy, when we link punishment to community survival, we condone cruelty, and indeed, enjoy the villain's sufferings. We *yearn* to see the villain suffer, for in his suffering lies our purification.

Tragic victimage is not the only way open to superiors. Like their inferiors, they too may turn to comedy. Louis XIV could not be criticized, and he in turn could not openly criticize his great nobles. The king's dignity was inviolate, the noble's honor beyond discussion. Yet La Fontaine's *Fables,* La Rochefoucauld's *Maxims,* and Molière's plays are profound witness to the vices of courtly life. Molière and La Rochefoucauld create a social pathology of pride. La Rochefoucauld tells us that the clemency of princes, "which is presented as a virtue, is inspired sometimes by vanity, occasionally by laziness, frequently by fear, and almost always by a combination of the three." There have been few sharper scourges of aristocratic pride than the *Maxims* of La Rochefoucauld, but it is the scourge of comedy, not tragedy.

We load the clown with our vices and then beat him mercilessly. We shift our evil to the villain to achieve vicarious atonement through his suffering and death. Superiors, such as Don Quixote or Don Giovanni, find their servants cannot be noble because they live in their stomachs. Inferiors, such as Aesop and Charlie Chaplin, cannot make sense of superiors who are capricious, cruel and, like the Duchess in *Alice in Wonderland,* prey to sudden and inexplicable rage. Equals cannot remain friends because one shuts his heart and mind to the other. The nobleman pokes fun at the gluttony and cowardliness of his servant, the servant in turn shows up the aristocrat's lack of control, and the friend shows his friend throwing himself away in some vain and ignoble pursuit which withdraws him from the society of his peers.

Comedy estranges the clown, so that we can punish him without remorse. But if laughter is to continue, we must be sure that the beaten clown will mend his ways, or at least try manfully to do so. For, so long as he *tries* to follow commands (however ridiculous) or give commands (however impossible to fulfill), he upholds the spirit, if not the letter, of the principles which sustain order within the group. The comic transgressor accepts his beating as just punishment and longs to be accepted again by those who punish him. Such comedy is not only "permitted," it is *institutionalized,* as much as tragic rituals are institutionalized in our legal trials.

Attacks on the court, the schools, high society, even the church, are not only permitted but sanctioned. Molière's plays were given at Versailles. La Rochefoucauld's aphorisms were created in the salons of Paris and repeated at court. "Serious" criticism of the king and his court would have been impossible, but so too would criticism of inferiors. The failure of inferiors is a failure of their leaders. The "un-American" acts of the immigrant are a sign of American failure, as well as a sign of the immigrant's refusal to give up strange ways. In cartoons, jokes, movies, and all kinds of humor, we admit and communicate widely about faults in the Americanization of the immigrant—and in so doing comment on faults in America itself. We laugh at clowns who portray all the "peculiarities" of the immigrant, but we laugh too with the immigrant over incongruities in our way of life.

Under the guise of play (ranging from highly stylized drama to teasing, "ribbing," or "kidding") our most sacred values are opened to reason. Such comic blasphemy occurs in autocratic and democratic societies alike. Perhaps comedy is *more* highly prized in autocratic institutions because solemn expression of hierarchal disrelationships is an affront to those in power. Soldiers cannot criticize their superiors, but they can joke about them. In the aristocratic *No* plays of Japan, elaborately fashioned farces parodied the tragedies given on the same program. The comedies of Aristophanes and the satyr plays were given at the same festivals as the tragedies. This was not done for "comic relief"; fully developed dramas were given on the same day and with the same community sanction as the tragic religious dramas. The gods who had been such heavy judges of men were themselves judged in laughter.

The tragic villain, the "bad guy," seeks to destroy the group. He must suffer and die, or we suffer and die. He does not, like the clown, live in error, but in sin. If he is killed, the sin is killed. But it is not necessary to kill the clown, for he can mend his ways. He can return to the group, even though he has suffered every kind of indignity. His return may only be a promise, and his acceptance far off in a distant future, but he can return because atonement in comedy is atonement for the group as the final principle of life. Comic atonement knows no principle of purgation beyond the social principles which bind the group together. Such bonds, in comic eyes, are purely social, and the essence of social bonds is joy in each other. For, as Rabelais teaches, the comic spirit is human because it makes men in joy, not sorrow, the measure of life. Good Pantagruelists "live in peace, joy, health, making . . . always merry," and are far more worthy of pardon than "a great rabble of squint-minded fellows, dissembling and counterfeit saints . . . who disguise themselves like maskers to deceive the world." The god of Rabelais, Erasmus, and More laughs at the follies of men and forgives them in smiles, even though tears often blind the smile.

The social distance we create in comedy is not to prepare the victim for sacrifice, but for dialogue. For, while we ridicule the exaggerated mannerisms of the immigrant, he is allowed, and, indeed, encouraged, to talk back. As superiors, we must uphold the majesty of our group. But superiority, as well as inferiority, has its burdens. Superiors must face new situations where the glamor and mystery of their power no longer works. Traditions often become irrelevant to new problems. They become useless as symbols of majesty when they cannot be communicated, as so often happens when inferiors are recruited from people new and strange to their masters.

The majestic superior cannot complain of his burdens to inferiors who believe him to be omnipotent. A god cannot doubt, a king cannot be irresolute, a father must settle family disputes. But gods have problems among themselves, and mothers do not share their children's belief in father's majesty. All majesties need fools and clowns upon whom they can project their burdens, if for no other reason than to endure them. They need them to express playfully what they cannot express seriously without risk to the spell of their majesty. Established Americans of the 1880s welcomed dialect comedians, such as Weber and Fields, as they did later Mr. Dooley, because the German and the Irish "outsider" could say things about established institutions that they could not. Mark Twain could have Huck say things about Negroes that would have been impossible for a respectable citizen.

Slang comedians like Josh Billings, George Ade, and Ring Lardner could do things with English that was impossible to those responsible for upholding proper speech. By 1900 urban Americans were speaking American English but writing British English. Open revolt among the gentry was impossible, for how could one be a gentleman and not be English? But in the Middle West, peopled by many nationalities who arrived at about the same time, gentility was not the property solely of the British. Yet even among these new people, American forms in speech (and in music, e.g., jazz) were introduced playfully. In the writings of Mark Twain, George Ade, and Ring Lardner it was safe to speak American because it was done in fun.

Tragic guilt lies in deep fear of the emergence of impulses to violate the commandments of authority. The tragic victim, like the child who feels himself "bad," demands punishment.[2] The severity of his punishment, mournful and painful as it may be, is welcomed unconsciously because it seems a foretoken of coming release from guilt. The tragic victim cannot pardon himself. There is no way for him to communicate easily or openly with the powers he has offended.

Confession requires an audience and means for communicating. A child who is too afraid of his father cannot communicate with him, and must carry the burden of his guilt alone. A compulsive neurotic confesses in pantomime (such as washing ceremonials) what he cannot confess in words. The dark and powerful gods of the sinner, like the gods of legend, must remain silent and invisible. Their names may not be uttered, their visage never looked upon by simple worshippers. Communication with such gods is possible only through solemn and sacred priests.

The comic victim—the clown who is being beaten—like the tragic victim, suffers indignity, torture, and death. He is beaten, kicked, cuffed, cursed, drenched with garbage or offal. All kinds of cruelties are visited upon him. He dies terrible deaths. His lingering agonies are met with indifference, sometimes even ridicule. Even when dead he is treated with contempt. The dead clown is simply thrown away, like a broken doll. These terrible symbolic sufferings at which we laugh so readily are possible only because we have created great social distance between ourselves and the clown. We create social distance in comedy by making the clown a caricature or a complete negation of our virtues. The swaggering portly knight of Saxon legend now becomes the great-bellied Falstaff; the obedient, clean, and pious child of genteel tradition becomes Huck, who obeys no one, wallows in dirt, chews tobacco, worships dark gods of the woods and the river, is expert in black magic, and makes a Negro slave his best friend. Such characters are, as we say, beyond the pale of good society.

Tragedy banishes its victims and then loads them with our evils. Hitler had to convince his Germans that Jews were not Germans before he could finally victimize them in torture and death. He also had to represent them as strong and cunning enemies with secret and terrible powers, to uphold the majesty of the German army whose valiant warriors were to lead armored charges against the truly helpless Jews of Warsaw. The Jew, like all scapegoats on their sorry journey to the sacrificial altar, first became "different," then "peculiar," and finally, "strange and alien." His accent, his gestures, his food, his dress, his face, everything about him, was exaggerated into caricature.

Europeans and Americans who wanted to keep the Jew in their community laughed, as Jews themselves laughed, at the "peculiarities" of Jewish life. In America we believe that strength lies in the resolution of difference. In debate and argument with those who differ from us, we discover greater meanings than we could reach alone. But in Germany, laughter died. The Jew was no longer German. He was not even a heretic, for he could not recant and become German. He was alien and strange and must remain so. His torture and death alone could purify the German spirit which had been degraded by those non-German powers. Only a pure German race could triumph. Only through human sacrifice could this purification take place.

Fortunately for the human community, tragedy is but one face of art and life, as the classical dramatic masks remind us. This double face of art, the tragic and comic, is unique among human institutions. As against victims who absolve us through suffering and death, great art offers us images of our own vices in buffoons and fools whose antics sometimes shame us into wisdom. Even at its worst, as when savage ridicule inflicts pain and suffering on the clown, comedy stops short of the sacrificial altar.

COMEDY AND THE SELF

The comic scapegoat lies within ourselves. We scourge our own follies, as we see in Aristophanes' *The Frogs*. It is the terrible year of 405 B.C. Athens has but a few more months of freedom before she will be vanquished by Lysander and his Spartans. Guilt lies heavy over the city. Like Job of the Israelites, the Athenians challenged the power and the justice of their gods. But this challenge, a pride and presumption for which the God of Israel punishes Job, is to the Athenians a challenge to search their own hearts and minds to find cause for the fearful calamities about to overwhelm them. The gods themselves are but the fierce longings of men. Heracles is a glutton, Dionysus a wanton, a drunkard, and a coward. Like men of Athens, the gods are often clever but not wise, often indeed plain fools saved from danger by sturdy servants such as Xanthias. The curse of Athens is madness, unreason, not sin. The final chorus in *The Frogs* asks the dieties to "grant . . . wise and healthy thoughts to [Athens]." Such thoughts are born only in the discourse of free men who must learn to distrust all revelations—even that of their gods. Laughter guards reason because it reduces fear and submits priestly mystification to reason.

La Rochefoucauld shows us how the snares we set for others become traps for ourselves. Through comic perspective we view the spectacle of the deceiver deceived and laugh at his punishment because he deserves it. The paradox of self-deception is that in an attempting to deceive others we really deceive ourselves. Self-interest blinds us to the interests of others, and if we are ignorant of others, how can we really protect our own interests? Self-love leads to hatred of others, and as hate deepens those we hate become our masters. Self-love becomes self-hate, because as we become more aware of how we use virtues to mask our vices, we despise our own hyprocisy and corruption. The morality of the comic hero lies in the clarity of reason. Self-love becomes more horrible as it is more clearly seen.

We learn in comedy that the virtues of superiors are not so great after all, the humility and loyalty of inferiors are not without limits, and that friends and peers sometimes deceive us. But guilt lightens in laughter as

I admit that if they are rascals, so too am I. We begin by laughing at others only to end by laughing at ourselves. The strain of rigid conventions, of majestic ideals, of deep loyalties, is lessened, for now they are open to examination. They can be questioned, their absurdities can be made plain. Now that we can openly express our vices, there is hope for correction. At least we now have company in misery; we are no longer alone and can take heart for another try. For when all is said and done, what do we have but each other? So long as we can act together we have all the good there is in life.

Comic art is against art itself, as well as against other social institutions. Aristophanes lampoons Euripides, Molière satirizes the high-flown language of the *precieuses,* Gilbert and Sullivan parody Verdi and the Italian opera. Mozart and Shakespeare poke fun at their own art, as well as the art of others. Thus we use comedy to address inner as well as outer selves. Deep incongruity between what we, as artists, censure in others, and what we ourselves do, suddenly becomes clear. The great lord of the self has been caught breaking his own commandments. Usually, like all tyrants, we blame others for our sins. But sometimes we blame ourselves in laughter that is really a confession—one we make with pleasure instead of pain. Such laughter is the scourge of pride. It reduces the deified self to human scale. As we laugh at our own follies we begin to understand ourselves because we take the attitude of others toward us. The hard pride of the self is broken; we return to others, and thus reaffirm social bonds. Reaffirmation in laughter and mirth creates social euphoria which heightens and energizes the spirit. For mirth, as Spinoza reminds us, "cannot be excessive, but is always good; contrariwise, melancholy is always bad."

The difference between tragedy and comedy is not so much in tragedy's "seriousness" concerning evil, for comedy is equally serious; it is rather in the form of exposure and the principles invoked to resolve incongruities. Address in tragedy is to some supernatural power *beyond* question, and thus beyond reason. The tragic actor must keep alive belief in the mysterious and dread power of the principle he invokes. The paradox he must explain is why an all-powerful being can be threatened at all. He resolves this by letting man sin (as an indication of his dignity and freedom), but at the same time he rescues man from sin by making a scapegoat out of the villain whose punishment and death purge him of sin.[3]

Comedy teaches us that men can endure much if they can endure it in rational discourse with each other. When we cannot communicate in reason we are ready for the tortured image of tragedy. We do not laugh at the fearful monsters of the dream. But we laugh at any danger, even death itself, so long as we laugh together. Soldiers moving into battle, slave laborers working in hunger and cold, and prisoners incarcerated for life joke about their grim masters. We do not laugh in the face of great danger or terrible authority to forget or to reach a golden mean of common sense, but to energize ourselves for further struggles. Promethean laughter purges us of fear and guilt by binding us together in sudden deep ecstasy. Tragedy makes our burdens a cross; comedy, a source of joy. We laugh, with Swift, at ourselves as scientists so deeply engrossed in speculation that we are unfit for the society of our fellow men. Our pretentions to grandeur as thinkers suddenly become foolish, for if science does not help us to relate to one another, what good is it?

Ruler and ruled alike reflect, in moments of high comedy, on how absurd it is to preserve social forms whose rigidity threatens our delight in each other. We laugh in a great burst of joy when in *Iolanthe,* Lord Mounteraat and Lord Tolloller, wracked by Phyllis' inability to choose between them, suddenly drop their awesome symbols of exalted rank and burst into dance and song urging the high Lord Chancellor to make a supreme effort to win Phyllis, since "It's love that makes the world go round!"

Gridiron dinners, the Mardi Gras, Feasts of Fools, and modern television programs of "Truth or Consequences" reduce social differences, not by eliminating or hiding them, but by bringing them to light in laughter which makes open communication possible. Even obscene wit directed against a lady is a kind of plea for her to drop her aloofness so we can communicate with her (and perhaps persuade her to satisfy us). Jokes not only "relieve" status tensions but transcend them in a moment of social euphoria which gives relationships new strength, and thus reinforces our social bonds. In moments of danger we turn to the tragic prophet, who may (or may not) lead us into a better life, but we also turn to comic genius. So long as laughter over social incongruities mounts, the tragic scapegoat must wait his turn.

When laughter passes into derision, mockery, and the grotesque, it is no longer comic. The social essence of comedy is joy in reason—the shared joy of he who is laughed at, as well as he who laughs. Savage ridicule is a weapon. It wounds deeply; often, indeed, it kills. Aristocrats recognize this. A grand monarch cannot mock a loyal subject. He may punish him, and through such punishment allow the offender to buy his way back into the group. Ridicule makes us inferiors. Only equals can laugh and tease together. When the clown becomes a monstrous caricature, a grotesque, he loses his identity. For the grotesque, like the nightmare, is sheer horror because it lies beyond communication. We turn away from the grotesque to regain our senses, just as we struggle to awaken from the nightmare, to rid ourselves of terror. We struggle to reach others, to communicate through shared experiences, for only in such experiences do we find our humanity.

Notes

[1] But it must be very great art indeed. When it is not, censure can be swift and heavy, as when Dalton Trumbo's comedy, *The Biggest Thief in Town,* linking business profits and death, was censured by New York critics in 1949.

[2] "Ah, God, punish, we pray thee, with pestilence and famine, and with what evil and sickness may be else on earth; but be not silent, Lord, towards us!" This attitude, expressed by Martin Luther in his *Table-Talk* (LXXXIII), is common to much devotional literature. See *The Table-Talk of Martin Luther,* translated and edited by William Hazlitt (London: George Bell and Sons, Bohn's Standard Library, 1902), p. 37, for this quotation.

[3] The close relation of tragic ritual and religious descriptions of man's fall from grace (the "fortunate fall" by which he is saved) has been noted by many. But the confusion of tragic ritual with all ritual, and, finally, in social theory, its confusion with the social bond itself (as in Tocqueville and Durkheim) prevents us from realizing that there are comic rituals, and that, since comedy stresses disrelationships, ambiguity, and doubt, we are less likely to confuse social order with authoritarian order if we base social theory on comic, as well as tragic, ritual.

29

Comedy as the Rhetoric of Reason in Society

COMEDY AND REASON

IN GREAT COMEDY we glory in our reason and in our dignity as human beings. Don Giovanni can escape eternal punishment if he will recant. Sword in hand, he readies for battle with the commander's ghost, who comes to offer him salvation for repentance. All but the Don give way before the awful messenger. As the fires of hell envelop him he screams in agony, but he screams as a man. As darkness closes in on Strauss's Don Quixote there is a sudden burst of light in the music. In suffering, poverty, and death there are glowing visions of chivalry—visions still, alas! When the music dies away we smile at Don Quixote and ourselves, mortal animals who would be men and gods. But we *will* be men, not slaves cowering on our knees before gods whose power lies in our submission.

The reason of comedy is *social* reason. Like tragedy, it is based on convictions about what is necessary to social order. But comic reason holds that reason must keep convictions about social means and ends *open* to reason. Tragedy seeks belief, even though such belief may not be subject to reason. Comedy seeks belief, but never at the price of banishing doubt and question. Tragedy treats disrelations and incongruities as heresy and sin, comedy as misunderstanding and ignorance of proper social ends. In Twain, Shaw, Dodgson, Gilbert and Sullivan, and Meredith there is a deep laughter over the absurdity of Victorian social disrelationships (Victorian primness about sex does not extend to differences of class, status, or age). Meredith believed that in laughter over the mystery of social differentiation we expose the worst excesses of hierarchy. Social cohesion is strengthened when laughter reduces blocks in communication between different classes who must overcome their difference to act together.

Shaw's characters play their roles in a highly reasonable frame of mind. As they take up their tasks in life, they seem to say: "Ah well, we are but human after all. We must mate, create, fight, suffer, and die. In doing so there must be social differentiation. So long as we submit our differences to reasonable discussion by honest and intelligent men we have little to fear. At times, indeed, social differences can become highly pleasurable, for they are a constant spring of the greatest social pleasure we know—laughter."

In comedy, appeal to good sense is an appeal to cooperation. Comic incongruities arise as we confront one audience with what is meant for another, or as we let one audience "overhear" what is supposed to be kept secret from it. The enjoyment of such moments derives from sudden clarification of the ambiguities arising out of incongruities between social ends and means. The great comic heroes, Socrates, Panurge, Don Quixote, La Rochefoucauld, Don Giovanni, Huckleberry Finn, give such incongruities a *form* that serves to light up the path all men take as they act together in love and hate.

Comic gods do not ask us to surrender reason to faith. They ask: Why should we trust gods if we cannot trust ourselves? How can we know God if we cannot know ourselves? Do we become *less* absurd because we surrender our will to a God whose power lies only in our submission? Yet tragic and comic heroes alike agree that if we lose our will we lose our humanity. Religion teaches us the dignity of man in his suffering; comic art teaches us that dignity *begins* in suffering, but must end in reason. In laughter reason is refreshed, and courage is born. We take heart again for another try. Great comic artists do not believe that salvation can be achieved by controlling forces outside of man—either in "Society," "Nature," or "God"—but only in the struggle of men to communicate in love and hate. Men must live in reason, for only so long as we *confront* the miseries of life and keep staring them hard in the face is there any hope of controlling them. Only so long as we keep our minds flexible and alive in discussion, talk, and laughter do we survive as human beings.

THE SOCIAL FUNCTION OF COMIC OBSCENITY

Comedy is often savage and obscene. In such moments it is used as a curse to degrade whatever threatens our social bonds. Through obscenity we rob evil and malign powers of their majesty. Comic cursing, as in Rabelais and Swift, becomes an incantation, an evil spell we would cast on others to lighten our own burdens. It is also directed at the self as a kind of toughening process, a violent and forced recognition of the need for tearing away veils of sentiment which weaken our vision of reality. In "gallows humor" and the terrible humor of prisons and concentration camps it is a way of overcoming shock and terror.

Concentration camp survivors bear grim witness to the "efficiency" of humor. B. Kautsky says it was the "most infallible means to keep up morale," as he notes that "incredible as it may seem . . . laughter was often heard in the camps." V. E. Frankl states that such humor was a "weapon of the mind in the struggle for its preservation. . . . Humor is better suited than almost anything else in human life to attain aloofness, to rise superior to the occasion." In summing up the effects of humor in the camps, Elie A. Cohen says: "The prisoners who had not yet adapted themselves and still found themselves in the midst of the struggle for daily existence, had little sense of humor." It was only the "wholly or partly adapted prisoner" who could use humor.[1]

In cursing we rid ourselves of anger which makes common action difficult. A soldier swearing at his officer's commands knows that he must do what he is told. But he also knows he will not do it well until his anger is under control. If he is too angry he cannot act well. If he swears seriously at his officer this must be construed as an insult and the soldier punished, so in his cursing he makes a kind of effigy upon which he voids his anger. Comic obscenity struggles to reduce gaps between what was once normal or ideal and what must be done to survive in a new situation. A soldier in the fields lives like an animal. He returns to earth. He lives with death. When he must hold ground against repeated attack, or when he is cut off by the enemy, he must sleep, eat, and live with his dead. He hears his comrades scream out their lives as they die in agony. He brutalizes himself so he can live in a world where men must become brutes to survive.

There is horrible evidence of the "efficiency" of obscenity in concentration camp literature. Eugen Kogon tells us that regression to a primitive state was the only way to survive in German concentration camps. "A cruel laugh, a brutal jest were often no more than protective devices for minds in danger of becoming hysterical or unhinged. There were many dead martyrs in the camps, but a few living saints—though they should have had a field day! We laughed, wretched souls that we were, lest we should grow petrified and die." Even such minor courtesies like "please," "thank you," "would you like," and "may I"—trifles that make life so much easier even though they have often lost inner significance—were rigidly banned.

For months in 1938 the many Austrians who had entered the camps were bitterly hated for their unswerving use of polite phrases that are second nature to the people of Austria. The invariable answer to a "thank you" from them was "kiss my ass." Every "please" drew a plethora of scorn from the primitives. Kogen explains the ordeal of being stripped and beaten before all the inmates.

On the way back, in filth and tatters, would you have dissolved in shame over the ignominy you had suffered? Or would you have mustered the superhuman strength and pride to ignore even the final kick from an SS boot that hurled you back into the communion of prisoners? In any event, you would have had to regress to a more primitive level if you wanted to survive. Then your comrades would have welcomed you with a coarse joke that concealed compassion, would have secretly nursed you back to health without fuss or feathers.[2]

Comic obscenity is a kind of angry plea to others to "make sense," to conform to the demands of the situation. We curse in jest to relieve ourselves of burdens so we can act together. Derision, scorn, and mockery end in caricature and the grotesque. The grotesque cannot be laughed at (in the comic sense) because it is beyond communication, like the monsters of the nightmare who pay no heed to our cries. Obscene humor makes evil laughable because it brings reason and consciousness to bear on what the grotesque leaves in the unconscious. Bosch, Bruegel, and Goya struggle to give horror form so it can be communicated, and thus become subject to reason, for, as Goya entitled his second book of *Caprichos*, "The Sleep of Reason Brings Forth Monsters." [3]

In Rabelais, Swift, and Mark Twain, as in the filthy curses of soldiers, hated authorities are covered with symbolic filth, reviled, and then buried or washed away. Falstaff is buried beneath stinking sheets in a laundry basket. Panurge's Lady of Paris is drenched with dog urine, Elizabeth's courtiers (in Mark Twain's *1601*) are nearly suffocated by Sir Walter Raleigh's roaring flatus. Hated authority is loaded with filth and stinks that degrade majesty and pride. Rabelais depicts Julius III and his cardinals as "whoophoopers," filthy birds "whose delight is to nestle in men's ordure"—an allusion, according to Rabelais' commentators, to his hatred of sodomy. Swift attacks aristocratic female voluptuaries by loading their bodies with stinks, corruption, and blemishes. In the Court of Brobdingnag, the land of the giants, every small blemish on the bodies of the high-born ladies becomes a corrupt mass.

Swift's grim use of filth is very different from Rabelais' exuberant comedy. Swift is clinical. He describes bodily filth with precision and discourses on the causes of putrefaction in a solemn scientific manner. His hygienic protestations over cleanliness are really ways to daub filth over those he hates. Swift contrasts the vulgar sexual tastes and bodily corruption of the great lady with her pride. Hierarchal trappings of dress, furnishings, coiffure, the elaborate symbolization of the body which raised sexual and social passion to such heights, are degraded by sudden shifts from majesty to obscene hideousness. In the last pages of *Gulliver,* man is depicted as a beast of prey who socializes only to satisfy his savage lusts. Yahoos wallow in all kinds of putrefaction, the sexual desire of the female is but animal rutting. The image of man is now that of a filthy ape who breeds in lust, dwells in squalor, and seeks his fellow creatures only to enjoy his hatred of them. Men prize what they possess only if they steal it from others, or keep it from them. The great problem of living among "Yahoo-kind" is how to endure the pride of stinking apes who think themselves men.

The soldier knows he cannot do without his officers, his sluttish prostitutes, or his profiteering businessmen. They cannot be treated in tragic fashion as villains or scapegoats to be loaded with evils and destroyed. Without leaders the soldier knows he cannot win battles, without sluts there will be no sex, without conniving traders there will be no contraband liquor, food, or tobacco. So he turns to obscenity (as the gentleman turns to irony) to endure what he hates, but cannot change. The medical officer becomes a butcher or a croaker, the cook becomes a gut burglar or belly robber, girls who consort with soldiers become pigs, rations are called crap or garbage, eating becomes putting the nose in the trough. Trying to please superiors is brown-nosing. The strict officer is called iron ass; second lieutenants, missing links; sergeants, Simon Legree; corporals, little wolves. A hospital becomes a butcher shop, a casualty list becomes the butcher's bill. Army food is reduced to every kind of filth. Spaghetti becomes worms; cheese, maggots; flake cereals, scabs; oatmeal, glue; corned beef, dead horse; creamed chipped beef, creamed foreskins or dog vomit; meat loaf, ptomaine steak.[4]

As he curses and laughs the soldier reduces the mystery of rank, as medieval priests reduced the mystery of their bishops and Biblical heroes in farces on the Old Testament and Christ's Passion, or as schoolboys do in their drawings of teachers falling into toilets. Army recruits laugh at breakdowns in civilian manners. Old soldiers laugh, too, but much more grimly. They have seen their world become brutish, savage, and filthy. They have seen life turn into suffering and death.

COMIC UNMASKING

We laugh together so long as we share deep conviction in what our group thinks is right. Comedy exposes transgression of rights, but does not question the rights themselves. We cannot long enjoy unmasking and anticipate further unmasking unless we are convinced that something beyond the mask is better than the mask itself. If virtues are mostly vices in disguise, how do we know of the virtues which lie behind the mask? Are they really superior to vices? Are good social ends not often the result of bad motives? As the comic contest begins, we hope that virtue will triumph, but how? Vice and virtue, as villain and hero, are pitted against each other; they are also defined by each other and, as action deepens, determine each other.

The moment of unmasking is the moment of comic truth. The comic hero must now win our sympathy. Until now we have laughed *at* the foolish mortals so distant and far from ourselves, *with* the clown. But the clown has been careful to keep us at arm's length by his cleverness and his foolish guise, which prevents us from seriously challenging him. As his cleverness mounts we become uneasy; we admire the brilliance of the satiric clown but we do not trust him. His suffering—and therefore his humanity—is still hidden. Until the mask drops, we are not even sure he does suffer. For, like the great criminal who avenges himself against society, the satiric clown is highly expert at making us accomplices to his crimes. We laugh at virtue, and, like Tom Sawyer, engage in merry pranks against the good burghers who assume the responsibility for upholding the virtues (shabby though they may be) which make society possible.

When La Rochefoucauld drops his ironic guise, we witness the despair and suffering of a noble who loved and cherished noble ideals but saw them perverted to insolent pride at court. As soldier, lover, statesman, friend, and artist he looked long and searchingly into the abyss of human evil. But the fearful, anxious, foolish creature, man, who would be king [5] yet cannot rule his own passions, merits more than scorn and laughter.

For if men can be beasts they can be men, and noble men, too. Thus La Rochefoucauld helps us to *believe* in human glory even though he exposes the arrogance and pride of men who cannot love others because they love only themselves, and whose struggle with the passion ends in suffering and death.

Only the great can endure this suffering. Out of their woe may come a better life, a life based on deeper understanding of why man tortures himself as he tortures others. As Freud tells his neurotic (and all of us), "Look into the depths of your own soul and learn first to know yourself, then you will henceforth avoid falling ill." The raging demons dwelling deep within the caverns of the soul are brought to consciousness in great art. For this moment at least their dreadful reign over reason is ended. We look our lusts full in the face. It is a terrible vision from which even the brave recoil. For in those terrible moments of clarity, when the abyss of the self is opened, we discover the horror of our lusts.[6]

In all great comedy, we hear the lonely, sad cry of men who yearn for glory in love and beauty, but must live in hate and ugliness. At such moments the heart opens to the great clown, and respect passes into love. A peculiar love, perhaps, for it is tinged with laughter. We smile gravely at such great ironists as La Rochefoucauld who struggle to convince us that reason is fallible, who bring self-love and all its attendant passions to light so that we can see how self-love destroys the self, and who teach us that every man will be king but cannot enjoy his kingship unless he struts and preens himself before an audience of his fellows (whose sole concern is how to destroy his majesty so that they can be king). As our smiles deepen in sadness we pay final homage to the courage and art of the great comedians who tell us that so long as we live in laughter, there is hope of living some day in reason and dignity. Laughter may not be enough to save us, but unless we live under reason and love, what is the use of living at all?

It is this belief in reason as the ultimate social bond which is the tragedy of irony and of all comedy. Franz Schoenberner, the editor of the German humor magazine *Simplicissimus,* who fought to the end against Hitler, warns us that laughter often wards off necessary fear. "An acute sense of the comical side of life is a good antidote against panic. But it sometimes works like a narcotic, because one usually forgets that a situation can be at the same time highly humorous and terribly dangerous."[7] Faith in reason, like all faiths, becomes dangerous when it becomes a fundamental-ist faith in reason as an invincible social principle. It will be invincible only to those who believe in reason. The haunting question for the great comic hero is not whether reason can be a social bond, or whether man is capable of reason, but whether reason is enough for survival.

Man laughs because he must laugh to live with his fellows. As Lockit reminds us in *The Beggars Opera:* "Lions, Wolves, and Vultures don't live together in Herds, Droves or Flocks.—Of all Animals of Prey, Man is the only sociable one. Every one of us preys upon his Neighbor, and yet we herd together." Hate, love, and doubt rule our emotions, and, as comedy reminds us, we must *enjoy* hate as well as love. The paradox of man in society, the ultimate incongruity at the base of all comedy, is that we can enjoy our hate only so long as our fellows, the objects of our hate, help us to do so.

COMEDY AND THE PURIFICATION OF SOCIAL ORDER

Social tensions become unbearable, not when there are great differences between ranks or conditions of life (as in differences between generations), but when there are no common social symbols through which superior and inferior can communicate. The gap between classes and individuals in *Huckleberry Finn, Pygmalion, Iolanthe, The Castle,* and *The Good Soldier Schweik* is very great. In Shaw, as in Gilbert and Sullivan, there is open and frequent communication between individuals who are different, even mysterious, to each other in ordinary life. Much of the wonderful gaiety and soaring wit of Shaw, Wilde, or Gilbert and Sullivan derives from dramatic comment on class differentiation. There is constant play with mystery of class, sex, age—every kind of social differentiation.

In Shaw, Dodgson, and Gilbert and Sullivan the attempts of very disparate people to communicate often become central to dramatic action. There is a kind of initial shock when Shaw's characters meet and begin to criticize each other. Differences in social condition are brought immediately into the open. But the "debunking" of social mystery is well proportioned. If Higgins is allowed to think that class differences are but differences in style of speech and can palm Liza off as a lady after teaching her upper-class usage, he, in turn, is shown up as a petty patriarch and a heartless intellectual snob by his mother and Liza.

Authorities fear attack on the office, not on the individual. A priest, an army officer, a professor, may be ridiculed for conservatism, drunkenness, or radicalism, but when the church, army, or university is ridiculed the issue then becomes the survival of the institution, not of the individual. When the office and the man are so identified that ridicule of one becomes ridicule of the other (as in lese majesty) humor becomes impossible. But when the ruler places himself beyond humor, he risks revolt. So long as we are able to express differences in humor, adjustment of differences is possible.

We laugh at attempts to communicate with authorities who must be obeyed yet outwitted. But we also smile at the inferior who makes his superior's slightest wish a profound duty. By his very piety he widens the gap between the folly of his superior and his own virtue and loyalty.[8] But if he carries his piety too far he becomes ridiculous, for any virtue carried to excess makes the virtue ridiculous because it threatens the social principle it is supposed to uphold. Prolonged mourning becomes ridiculous when it prevents the mourner from returning to society. It also makes religion ridiculous, for if the deceased has gone to his eternal rest, why are we sad? John Wesley, on meeting a widow in deep mourning two years after her husband's death, said: "What, madam, have you not forgiven God Almighty yet?"

The comic artist depicts the incongruities of hierarchy in forms which we use to purge the individual, and thus his community, of fear. The passages in *Huckleberry Finn* when Huck, the white boy, and Jim, the colored man, discover their comradeship in laughter are among the greatest affirmations of democratic principles in our literature. Tom, Huck, and Jim reduce the world of the Grangerfords and the Shepherdsons, the aristocracy of the south, to archaism. White and colored boys live and love in laughter as they travel down the river on their raft, and camp together in the woods. The young white aristocrats hunt and kill each other in feuds which their pride calls affairs of honor, but which Mark Twain depicts as murder. Through the miracle of comedy we see symbols of love and honor shift to the lowly Negro. Huck's teasing laughter at Jim's simple Negro ways changes into love and admiration. In Jim's cry of the heart against Huck's toying with his love, Huck realizes Jim is his moral superior. As he watches Jim walk off to hide his grief at Huck's insensitivity, Huck says:

"It made me feel so mean I could almost kissed *his* foot to take it back.
"It was fifteen minutes before I could work myself up to go and humble myself to

a nigger—but I done it, and I warn't ever sorry for it afterwards, neither. I didn't do him no more mean tricks, and I wouldn't done that if I'd a knowed it would make him feel that way." [9]

Only in comedy would the American Conscience thus search its greatest social burden. In 1889 the Negro was no longer a slave but he was not yet a man. In the guise of the "boy-clown," Mark Twain could depict the warm humanity of the Negro in contrast to the cold pride of the southern gentleman, and the filth and cowardliness of village mobs of poor whites.

"I went to sleep, and Jim didn't call me when it was my turn. He often done that. When I waked up, just at daybreak, he was sitting there with his head down betwixt his knees, moaning and mourning to himself. I didn't take notice, nor let on. I knowed what it was about. He was thinking about his wife and his children way up yonder, and he was low and homesick; because he hadn't ever been away from home before in his life; and I do believe he cared just as much for his people as white folks does for their'n. It don't seem natural, but I reckon it's so. He was often moaning and mourning that way, nights, when he judged I was asleep, and saying, 'Po' little Johnny! It's mighty hard; I spec' I ain't gwyne to see you no mo', no mo'!' He was a mighty good nigger, Jim was." [10]

When Jim finally unburdens himself of his remorse over striking his child Elizabeth, who did not obey him because she had been deafened by scarlet fever (which Jim did not know), Huck is silent. But as Jim's voice trails off into the night over the river, we begin to think. Guilt fills our hearts and our laughter fills with tears of remorse. The comic muse now begins her task of reaffirming social bonds, which must be strengthened if the community is to survive.

Notes

[1] Elie A. Cohen, *Human Behavior in the Concentration Camp*, translated from the Dutch by M. H. Braaksma (New York: W. W. Norton & Co., Inc., 1953), p. 181. Quotations are taken from the same source.

[2] Eugen Kogon, *The Theory and Practice of Hell: The German Concentration Camps and the System Behind Them* (New York: Berkley Books, n.d.), pp. 277–280.

[3] Monsters born in horror are as much a part of art as they are of the dream. They are created and formed and thus can be communicated. Then, and only then, is some kind of control possible. But it is very different from comic control. The grotesque is *not* comic, but neither is it tragic. It has close affinities to the surrealism of the dream.

[4] Army sexual obscenity, if quoted here, would make publication of this book haz-

ardous. Veterans will recall the vigorous application of sexual terms such as "snafu" to military situations in general.

[5] In his essay "A Difficulty of Psycho-Analysis" Freud uses the same imagery as La Rochefoucauld. "You [the neurotic] conduct yourself like an absolute sovereign who is content with the information supplied him by his highest officials and never goes among the people to hear their voice." Freud, *Collected Papers* (London: The Hogarth Press, 1948, 5 vols.), Vol. IV, p. 355. The comic vein in Freud (very wide and deep) is a rich one. The incongruity of an ego, not master in its own house, attempting to rule the houses of others never fails to evoke Freud's irony. Both Freud and La Rochefoucauld depict the passions struggling to outwit reason. Freud does not subordinate reason to the passions; on the contrary, he struggles to give reason ways of understanding the passions so they can be turned to social ends. Freud's heroes, the artist and the scientist, are not the same as La Rochefoucauld's noble hero, but they both share a profound pessimism about the power of reason over passion. This does not, however, lead to any abandonment of reason and of the search for truth.

[6] Hitler's torture and death camps were humanity's latest view into this abyss. There will be others. The atomic bomb, the hydrogen and neutron bombs, and space missiles offer new and terrible ways for satisfying our needs to visit pain, suffering, and death on others, as well as ourselves. We recoil in horror before the bomb and the rocket because we now know that our hates may soon destroy us.

[7] Franz Schoenberner, *Confessions of a European Intellectual* (New York: The Macmillan Company, 1946), p. 5.

[8] Hasek's good soldier, Schweik, throws his officers into hysteria and the Austrian army into chaos, by carrying out literally orders which make no sense whatever and by interpreting as orders whatever his superiors say. Thus any chance remark, or a remark made in anger, is not simply conversation for Schweik, but a command. Sublime commands must be used for sublime purposes. The orders of majestic officers become ridiculous when used for petty ends. We sum this up when we say: "The mountain labored and brought forth a mouse," or, "He found a molehill and left a mountain."

[9] Mark Twain, *Huckleberry Finn* (New York: Harper and Brothers, 1899), p. 123.
[10] *Ibid.*, p. 207.

30

Tragic and Comic Sexual Themes Compared

SEX AND HIERARCHY IN ART AND SOCIETY

ROMANTIC COURTSHIP is a communion of estranged beings whose very strangeness is a condition of their erotic appeal. The awkwardness, respect, reverence, embarrassment, comedy and irony, even the sadism and masochism we find in depictions of romantic love in Western art, are social as well as sexual. A sociological gloss on masochism could begin with Reik's sentence: "[The masochist] By taking the place of authority and chastising himself . . . suspends [authority]." Freud's "moral" and Reik's "social" masochism may be thought of as status as well as sexual perversion. Where the inferior (as woman) is required to submit her body to the male, she may enhance her pleasure by refinements of submission. Where the superior (the male) is required to be lordly, masterful, or proud, he may increase his pleasure and his sense of majesty by refinements in exercising authority and infliction of pain in whipping, binding, or cutting.

In English literature before Richardson, only aristocrats are capable of grand passion. Eighteenth-century art finds love between masters and servants comic. Servants and social inferiors who attempt a grand passion are ridiculous. Like Molière's bourgeois gentleman they can express the letter, but never the spirit, of love. Aristocrats laughed such upstarts out of court, not because they were in love, but because the expression of love as a grand passion risked vulgarization if "anyone" could love. In Dostoevski love is still a noble emotion, but only the dregs of society (as in the figure of the "sacred" prostitute) can now experience it.

American popular art interweaves symbols of sex and hierarchy in many ways. The "glorification of the American girl" by Ziegfeld and Earl Carroll was a status as well as a sexual glorification. Women paraded about the stage in elaborate gowns, rich furs, and gleaming jewels. Men of the chorus were dressed in swallow-tail coats and silk hats and carried gold-topped walking sticks.

In the great outburst of plutocratic power in Chicago after the Civil War, famous madams, such as the Everleigh sisters, used opulent furnishings, expensive wines and foods, and very large fees (never paid in cash but by check in response to bills mailed to the "client") to incite passion. The Everleigh "girls" were trained to wear expensive gowns, to conduct themselves properly on drives through the parks, and to sit in box seats at the theater and the races. The upper-class prostitute was a parody of the plutocratic lady. The Everleigh Club became an elegant mansion. The girls were given daily instruction in etiquette and told to use the library which was one of the show places of the mansion. Sumptuous formal dinners, with music supplied by a string ensemble, were held. Patrons were entertained in richly furnished parlors styled as Moorish, Japanese, Egyptian, or Chinese. There were Silver and Copper parlors for mining kings. The greatest room of all, the Gold Room, was polished every day and refinished each year in gold leaf. Gambling was encouraged, but Minna Everleigh found it necessary to limit the time, if not the amount, spent at the table. In her later years she said: "Admitting that women are a risk, I still say that men prefer dice, cards, or a wheel of fortune to a frolic with a charmer. I have watched men, embraced in the arms of the most bewitching sirens in our club, dump their feminine flesh from their laps for a roll of the dice."

On a lower class level we see the lineage between status and sex in the "strip-tease." The woman enters in formal dress, struts elegantly about the stage, unbuttons her long gloves, and begins to disrobe. This is done with an air of exaggerated refinement, a stylized presentation of a "classy dame" getting rid of rank so she can enjoy sex. Expensively dressed "hostesses" circulate among the audience. Buying such "classy dames" a drink is a way of relating, if only on a vicarious level, to women more expensive, and thus in a money society, of higher station. It is not only the nudity of the "stripper," but the approach to her nudity through symbols indicating actual or simulated expense which excites an audience already charged by the "mystery" of money.

Reik tells us that social degradation of the woman in fantasy, as in reality, affects sexual potency.

A great number of men can develop their sexual potency only with women they do not respect, yes, those upon whom they look down. . . . I learned from Freud how typical this division of love and sexual behavior is for so many men in our culture who cannot love where they sexually desire, and who do not function well sexually where they respect and idealize women. . . . Later on when I treated neurotic patients, I understood why many men need a kind of degradation in their fantasy or in their action with women they highly appreciate or love. They have to degrade them, in order to bring them down from the elevated level which forbids the intimate physical approach.

But there is also the opposite type, in which the superior, not the inferior, stirs lust. The cold, aloof, rich girl of good family who yields to a man of lower rank, like the heiress who marries a waiter, are popular figures in fiction and news stories. In courtship, too, American adolescents learn to "put on the dog." The boys and girls dress far beyond their actual station. Clothes, cars, jewels, anything indicating expense, are borrowed or rented (and sometimes stolen). It is not the ability to know one's station and keep it, but to impersonate a higher station, that determines success in American courtship.

The American woman's opulence becomes an outward and highly visible sign of her husband's real or imputed wealth. She must lead a highly public life where her capacity for "gracious" spending can be seen and tested. Our commercial art depicts the superior woman as a wife or mother housed and clothed in great opulence. As mother, "girl-friend," or wife she becomes a "spiritualization" of the consumer. Thin, bloodless, almost bodiless (the "heiress look"), she is burdened with hierarchal trappings of all kinds and thus expresses the magic link between sex and money which so characterizes the sexual life of our time. In De Sade, feudal symbols of castles, secret dungeons, and great feasts dominate sexual imagery. Symbols of feudal life are not changed, but shifted to a sexual context. The forms of torture of heretics, traitors, and criminals are applied (symbolically) to the woman. Religious rituals become sexual rituals where sexual objects, or the sex organs themselves, are substituted for sacred vessels. The altar is profaned by performing sexual acts before the Host. The woman is treated as a serf over whom the lord has rights of life and death. She is killed at the height of passion. In contrast to plutocratic sexual dramas, where sex is related to money, the sex act is symbolized as a grotesque *sacrificial* act in which the suffering and death of the woman on feudal altars enhances the glory of rank and the mystery of sex.

In the *opera seria* of Handel and Mozart, as in the plays of Racine, passion and aristocratic honor are opposed. Whatever the type of sexual passion expressed, the awesome majesty of rank infuses the plot with grandeur. It is the risk of losing honor, and therefore rank, that moved the aristocratic audiences of Racine and Handel. Where the struggle over honor is between noble men and women, every resource of art is used to preserve the mystifications of aristocratic hierarchy. Even in comedy there are few scenes where noblemen mock their own institutions before publics not composed of their peers. Mozart and Rossini poke fun at their aristocrats, but only when they change clothes with their servants. Once divested of aristocratic insignia they are free to say what they like, just as the servant can woo aristocratic ladies so long as he wears his master's clothes.

COMIC AND TRAGIC COMMUNICATION OF SEX

In *Cosi Fan Tutte* romantic love is satirized because it prevents men and women from taking a reasonable (i.e., social) view of life. The right to love in Mozart is not gained through mortification. Companionship and joy in one another, not death and sin (as in Wagner), charge love with its mystery. In Mozart's humane world the comic spirit resolves crises through forgiveness in laughter. Each character discovers the faults of the other, but anger dissolves in gaiety as he laughs at the weakness of others, and finally at himself. For a wonderful moment we smile like gods as we witness, in tenderness and compassion, the foibles of others and ourselves. We return to each other in laughter, to love others whose differences are necessary as well as threatening to our happiness. The moment of romantic emotion in Mozart is a comic moment. Despina and Don Alfonso agree that passionate love can only be pleasure, amusement, pastime, diversion, merriment. If it becomes too serious and grave, it is no longer love. As Dorabella threatens to go mad for the rest of her life and teach the Eumenides themselves how to scream, the accompanied recitative parodies the dark solemn music of tragedy. Starting on a high G flat she descends slowly while the fiddles who have been supporting her with energetic agitation stop in mock horror as she wonders if she can "survive the horrible sound of her own sighs."

Mozart counters amorous passion with aristocratic pride. In *Figaro* the Count is the sole activator of the plot. His soliloquy in Act III indicates the importance of hierarchal, not sexual, passion in motivating aristocratic drama.

> Must I forgo my pleasures,
> While serf of mine rejoices?
> Must I renounce my passion,
> He have his heart's desire?
> Must I behold my charmer
> To low-born clown united?
> When I for her am burning,
> Dare she disdain my fire?
> No, no, no, no, no, no, no, no.
> I'll show him I'm his master,
> Nor more shall he defy me;
> Dare he be so presumptuous,
> As venture thus to thwart me?
> Dare he, my servant, laugh at me?
> Yes, laugh at me,
> While I am mortified?
> I will endure it no longer,
> Vengeance alone inspires me,
> 'Tis vengeance, only vengeance,
> Can satisfy my pride!

As the lord of the house, the Count could possess Susanna easily enough. But if he uses the cunning of Figaro, or the meanness of Bartolo, he loses his gentility. And this, as Mozart is careful to make plain in music, is the Count's dignity. He struggles to control himself, to preserve aristocratic dignity against the great temptation of a seductive and beautiful woman. When he resolves his struggle in favor of dignity and honor, the play is over. As the Count begs his wife's forgiveness, all join in praises of the Count and Countess.

> Let this day of storm and tempest,
> Day of trouble, day of madness,
> Now give way to joy and gladness,
> And to love and gay delight.

The day of madness gives way to love—not the love of Isolde or Camille, but to a gentleman and lady who subordinate sexual passion to honor and dignity.

Love contains no great transcendent quality beyond sociation itself. For Mozart, as for Casanova, it is the game of love that is important. And it is a game shared not by two, as in romantic love, but by all those living with the lovers. Whatever withdraws or separates the lovers from society is condemned. Don Alfonso in *Cosi Fan Tutte,* tired of romantic protestations and quarrels says: "Take my advice, join hands. . . . Kiss and be friends. And now laugh, all four of you, as I have laughed and shall laugh." Fiordiligi and Dorabella fall back into more romantic protestations to their lovers. "I will comfort your heart with my love and fidelity. I shall adore you forever." Ferrando and Guglielmo have had enough of romance: "I believe you, my sweet delight, but would rather not put it to the proof." Where love binds people together there is laughter, born sometimes in burlesque and farce, but more often in a wonderful kind of serene joy over the warmth and friendliness between men and women.

Racine and Molière differ profoundly over the social evils of their time, but both, like Mozart, honor the social values of the aristocratic community. Every device of Racine's wonderful art is invoked to stir us with the ultimate mystery of aristocratic and kingly honor. In Racine's own life honor ends, not in the reasoned imagination of ladies and gentlemen (as among the courtiers of Rabelais and Molière) but in the religion of Port Royal. Molière, like Mozart, does not find his moment of social transcendence in religion. The worldly social bond between his ladies and gentlemen is his ultimate value. He scores pretentiousness, hypocrisy, and insincerity, not because they offend God, but because they separate men and women from their fellows, and thus magnify their differences. His moral imagination centers in appeals to "reason," the reason of courtiers, for as Rabelais said of his Thelemites, "men that are free, well born, well-bred, and conversant in honest companies, have naturally an instinct and spur which is called honor that prompteth them in virtuous actions, and withdraws them from vice."

Unlike the romantic lover of a later generation, Casanova turns to comic catharsis for love's frustrations. The drama of sex is genial and social. It is also intellectual. "Love is only a feeling of curiosity . . . grafted upon the inclination placed in us by nature that the species may be preserved." The vice of love is the desire to pursue any woman so long as she is a new partner. "A man who has known many women, and all handsome women, feels at last a curiosity for ugly specimens when he meets with entirely new ones." This curiosity must be satisfied "according to established rules" of seduction. Because of this, lovers soon become victims "to coquetry, the monster which persecutes all those who make a business of love." Casanova is curious about relationships, about what happens to people acting together in love. The sexual act is a dramatic act.[1] Sex parties, exchanging mistresses, exhibiting oneself in the sex act and watching others, all kinds of group sex play are described frequently by Casanova in his *Memoirs*. There is little secrecy, no romantic agony, few lonely lovers, and no dignity whatever in frustration.

In the romantic opera of the nineteenth century, dramatic conflict occurs in struggle between duty to the family and to the self. Honor is now family honor. In *La Traviata,* Germont appeals to Alfredo and Violetta in terms of the principle of family life itself. He must protect his daughter and son. When he judges Violetta or Alfredo it is not his own selfish feelings which speak, but the ultimate principle of society, the family, to which he is bound. Germont's affection for Violetta deepens. He realizes the purity of her love for Alfredo. His anguish mounts at the approaching death of Violetta as he understands the terrible punishment he has visited upon her. In the last scene, as Violetta lies dying, he sings to her in great anguish: "I come [to] take you as daughter to my heart." He turns to his son and cries out: "Remorse devours my soul." But he is able to resolve this terrible anguish through invocation of familial symbols. He has become Violetta's father, she his daughter. Even death can now be endured as Violetta tells the doctor: "I'm grateful, Grenvil, do you see? I'm dying in the arms of those whom I love best in all the world." At the very end in the midst of Germont's tragic cries and Alfredo's despair, Violetta, who has suffered and now must die to uphold family honor, admonishes father and son never to weaken in devotion to the mystical principle of family. Alfredo must marry: "And if a gentle maiden in the flower of her youth should give you her heart, make her your bride, make her your wife, I wish it."

Forty years later the principle of hierarchy invoked to create erotic appeal is not the family, but art. In *La Boheme,* Mimi's mystery is aesthetic. Men and women do not love to marry, or to uphold aristocratic lineage, but to reach art through the purification of suffering. The woman now becomes part of an aesthetic myth which now is infused with erotic, not familial symbols. The principle of family which gives radiance to the wonderful music of *La Traviata* is now openly mocked in the ironic words of Marcello to Benoit. Those who uphold the family are now vulgar burghers. The aristocrat is now a poet who finds his greatness outside of the normal community; in a world ruled by plutocrats he will be poor. As Rodolpho tells Mimi: "Who I am?—I'm a poet. What do I do?—I write. And how do I live?—I live. In poverty I yet indulge myself like a Grand Seigneur in rhymes and hymns to love. For dreams, delusions, and castles in the air I've a millionaire's capacity. . . ." Mimi, too, is beyond the normal community in a world of beauty. "I like those things that possess for me a sweet charm, that speak of love, spring, dreams, illusions, that have the name of poetry. . . ." Aesthetic myth, already foreshadowed in the fusion of art, play, and sex in *La Traviata,* is now identified with the erotic. As in Dante, where love of woman leads to love of God, in aesthetic myth woman is a transcendent vessel of beauty.

Sexual appeals are also related to symbols of the nation, and finally to international ideologies. In Tolstoy, as in American art depicting pioneer days, the woman becomes the mother of a nation. This mother is sacred because she bears sons for her country, which in complementary symbolization becomes the fatherland. Out of this mystical union of the woman, the land, and the state come sons and daughters who fill people's armies, open the wilderness, fight plague and famine, and found communities. In Tolstoy the nation is land and the people. In the *First Epilogue* to *War and Peace,* Countess Mary weeps over Nicholas' beating of the village elder. In beating peasants, Nicholas has been "sinning against himself." For these peasants are Russian, and just as Prince Andrew found peace in fighting in the line beside peasants whose suffering and death were transcended in symbols of Russia, so does Nicholas find peace through identification with peasants on the land because they symbolize the new Russia. In contemporary art we see new identifications of international symbols and sex symbols. Race and ideology, as well as class, are now used as symbols of sovereignty to give majesty to love. Miscegenation is still tragic, but it is dignified as love and not a social aberration. Indeed, only in crossing such gaps does love find its power.

SEXUAL AND SOCIAL GUILT IN COMEDY

For the psychoanalyst, social order is always a residual concept. Sex is "natural," society is derived. J. C. Flügel tells us: "It is absurd that a woman visiting friends for the weekend should feel obliged to include two evening dresses in her outfit; the absurdity arises from the fact that, for all but the really wealthy, the additional expense involved is out of proportion to the additional satisfaction (thereby necessitating the sacrifice of potential satisfaction in other directions)." [2] In his discussion on the future of dress, he says: "Only twenty-five percent of the business transacted in America is done in response to a natural demand, and that it is out of the other seventy-five percent that the great country of salesmanship makes its living." It is very naive to talk about status as absurd or unnatural. Even in a nudist camp the care of the skin, nails, hair, the use of the voice as well as bearing and gesture, are charged with social meaning. Meyer Levin, a Chicago novelist, tells how circumcision evoked anti-Semitism in a nudist camp.

Romantic love and Christianity enhanced the social drama of sex by creating new social types in the romantic heroine and the ascetic. Sexual inhibition—a joke, to Ovid and to Casanova—now becomes a sign of purity. By not having sex we gain social or religious status. The lover "etherealizes" and "spiritualizes" his beloved. The monk gains spiritual honor in his struggle against sex. Kirkegaard must break his engagement to find his way to God. Thus we see the power of negation and denial in hierarchy. A principle of hierarchy has both positive and a negative expression; what we do not do is not simply an avoidance, but a clearly expressed negation of what inferiors, strangers, or hated enemies do.

Sexual fantasies, as recorded by psychoanalysts themselves, show many social traits. Not any shoe, but the "elegant shoes of a lady," or negatively, the worn shoe of a worker; not just any handkerchief, but one of the finest linen, are used by fetishists. The lustful idea of the fetish may become entirely separate from the idea of the woman. Sacher-Masoch states explicitly that fur stirs lust because it is a "symbol of sovereignty." His mistresses were required to wear furs as often as possible, and especially when they were in a cruel mood. He wished to regard his mistress as a sovereign power. She must be able to simulate all the arts of "aristocratic arrogance." The sexual act must be authoritarian and predatory, devoid of tenderness and affection, and carried out on a grand aristocratic scale. "Symbols of sovereignty" affected Sacher-Masoch's mental potency too. He kept furs within reach of his hand when he was writing. Even when the sex drive was satisfied, hierarchal passions still ruled.

Pornographic art satisfies sexual and social needs at the same time. The tramp, the bum, the delinquent, the spinster, the farmer's daughter—all the lonely and despised become heroes and heroines in dramas of lust and hierarchy. Ranks are inverted. The authority of the lady as wife, mother, or virgin is reduced by showing her animal lusts. The power of pornography as a political weapon is derived from its efficacy in social degradation. Streicher's linkage of the Jew to pornography prepared him for the kill. So long as the Jew, like the "good" German, possessed an exemplary family life it was impossible to invest him with the evils of Germany. So long as regular army officers lived up to the highest concepts of German honor they could not be purged. Von Fritsch was charged with being a homosexual. The Blood Purge of June, 1930, against Roehm and other storm troop leaders was accompanied by the same charges.

Much of what the psychoanalysts call "forbidden types of instinctual gratification" in pornographic fantasy is forbidden social gratification. In the Sabbat, the Medicus Mass, and the Satanic Mass the female body was used as an altar before which Mass was said or sung. The lady of high society is constantly defamed in the popular cinema comedy of Chaplin, W. C. Fields, and the Marx brothers. Clinical pictures of nudes in medical books are sexual enough, but they do not arouse our lust to the same degree as images which contain *both* social and sexual appeals. Pornographic art is directed to specific publics. Schoolboys are shown obscene acts between teachers and pupils, office workers lascivious scenes between bosses and private secretaries, soldiers lustful scenes between officer's wives and enlisted men, Negroes are offered obscene pictures of perverse sex acts between whites. Raping wives of conquered enemies while the husband is forced to watch at gun point and forcing the women of a conquered nation to serve as prostitutes are other examples of social aggression in sex. Much of the enjoyment for an audience of recently returned veterans in the sexual scenes in *From Here to Eternity* (James Jones' book, later a moving picture) was derived from the seduction of an officer's wife by an enlisted man. In another scene the same enlisted man refused to go to officer's school, even though this might make marriage to a captain's divorced wife possible.

In Beatrice Lillie's comic sketches, upper-class characters hit back at the lower orders. The long, drawn-out sentimental song of the middle-class gallant who assures Beatrice that love lies in the gloaming, in the song of the birds, in the sighs of the trees, etc., is borne with the patience of a lady. But the lady makes it plain to her audience (if not to her gallant) that she has been ready for a trip to the garden long before the song ended, and indeed, is absolutely astonished at the spectacle of a healthy man uttering such sentimental nonsense and taking such a long time at it.

Where the man must be dominant and yet compete with women (as in America), obscene jokes over how women sell themselves serve to subordinate the woman. In her reduction to a thing bought she is now inferior to the male who never sells his body for money. Once she is bought she is inferior, and male dominance through money is assured. In a Puritanical society where ladies are supposed to be "above" sexual need, social degradation brings her down to a lower level. Stories told by one class against another, as when working men impute superior sexual virility to their class through ridicule of a higher class, are other examples. The seriousness of their elders over sex is often parodied by the young, as when the elegance of ballroom dancing is caricatured. The "jitterbug" dancer parodies sexual passion and its attendant social dignification. As the dancers toss each other about in complete abandon, the refinement and intensity in the "mystery of love" as expressed in the stately waltz become ludicrous.

Comedians like the Marx brothers parody upper-class seduction of the "poor working girl" by making refined seduction of the lady ridiculous. The props required for such seduction (the table, flowers, iced champagne, etc.), the expression of high-flown sentiments, are almost too much for Groucho. Nor is he helped by Harpo's lustful outbursts in open chase of the scantily clad blonde who rushes past the table where Groucho is trying manfully to court Margaret Dumont, the great lady. Mae West satirizes the plutocratic lady by mingling sex and hierarchy, as she toys with her enormous string of pearls and rolls her eyes. Marie Dressler suffered constant outrage from the vulgar manners of Charlie and his low-brow friends. Her simpering genteel manners break down as her party degenerates into a brawl. Bearded guests dressed in formal clothes (as the mark of the "swell") lock in battle. Pies fly through the air. Seltzer siphons become insulting weapons. Soon guests and hostess alike are reduced by exuberant "prat-falls" to wallowing together on the floor in a slime of pies, food, wine, and water. The little fellow is now vindicated. The elegance of the gentry is but a veneer after all. Upper class "swells" are no better (if indeed as good) as the common man, the hero of democracy.

W. C. Fields and comediennes like Fanny Bryce reduce the hallowed American mother and her child to cold, greedy, arrogant "ladies" who mask their self-love with sentimental hypocrisy over "mother-love" and gentility. Fields' wives and mothers stuff themselves continually with food, hurl imprecations at their husbands, or sneer and insult the father as they pet and spoil their children. Even physical violence is not beyond these unmasked members of the "gentle sex." As W. C. Fields leaves the house in the motion picture *The Bank Dick*, he barely escapes the vase tossed at him by his loving daughter. He has already submitted to the scornful insults of his mother and wife, and the whining selfish wails of his lovelorn daughter. Here we see the great American authority, the woman, stripped of her majesty. At last, the woman who bosses us as mother, teacher, beloved, and wife, and who, as the great American customer, determines how men make money (and how they spend it) is under attack. The long-suffering American male has found his champion at last. It is no majestic knight in shining armor, no villain clothed in dark majesty of tragedy but the bewildered, frazzled, clown, W. C. Fields. He expects no quarter from his tyrannical women. Always prepared to ward off imaginary blows from his powerful and pitiless madonnas, shuddering in fear and loathing at the sound of his wife's voice, he hurries (like Jiggs) to the nearest saloon where men gather in escape from the tyranny of the genteel American female.

Notes

1 Talleyrand said: "Sexual intercourse is the theater of the poor."
2 J. C. Flügel, *The Psychology of Clothes* (London: The Hogarth Press, Ltd., 1950), p. 186.

PART NINE

By Way of Conclusion

31

A Sociological Model of Social Interaction as Determined by Communication

THE NATURE OF SYMBOLIC ACTION IN ART AND SOCIETY

W E H A V E argued that social hierarchy infuses all symbolic expression and that the kind of symbols available to us determine social hierarchy. Names, we have argued further, are not signs, but goads to action. The symbolic expression of social sentiments and attitudes keeps them alive in the mind and spirit of the individual actor. The social function of symbolism in great community dramas is to maintain and transmit social bonds from one generation to another, and to create and sustain the emotional dispositions on which society depends for its existence. To be so transmitted, emotions, like ideas, must be given forms, for it is only through form of some kind that transmission of a culture can take place. Such cultural transmission is an enactment, a drama in which the community is born and will be born again.

A group is obviously dependent on physical objects, on inherited systems of signs, and on the biological characteristics of individuals acting within the group, but these do not in themselves constitute the group. Only when signs are invested with meaning and emotion can they be used to develop attitudes. The group as an object of reason, faith, or emotion is created and sustained in the communication of attitudes, but these attitudes must be objectified in concrete symbols before we can act together. We love our country through the flag, our church through the cross, our neighborhood through a landmark.

We use proverbs (as we use all symbolic expression) to sum up situations. The proverb is public; it means what it does, not because an individual artist uses it or because it is indigenous to any individual group, but because it has been accepted by many groups over long periods of time. Unlike the image of the dream or the slogan of an institution, it belongs to no one because it belongs to everyone. When we invoke a proverb we invoke the experience of the group itself. "Everybody's guilt is no one's guilt." The folk do not create proverbs any more than Chicagoans created

George Ade's *Fables in Slang*. But the people use a proverb so generally, and so often, that what once seemed highly artificial becomes common. We make the saying of aphorists into maxims of conduct because the forms they impose on experience enable us to act with greater confidence.

An art work exists in its own right. I do not create *Hamlet* and then use it (like a case history is used) to "prove" the hypotheses which inspired me to gather the material for the case history. The "context of situation" for students who use art works begins with the symbolic context. What Freud or Jones says about Hamlet can be examined in the text of *Hamlet*. There is also a body of rich critical thought (from varying points of view) gathered about *Hamlet*. The text of *Hamlet* is a cultural "fact," produced independently of the observer. It is not created by him, and then used as "proof" of what he set out to investigate. Art works, like all symbolic expressions, are *facts,* not inferences. We infer what the Trobriander "did" in his fishing and gardening by citing "factually" a text that tells us what he did.

We get our view of deeds as facts from our sense of words as facts. Thus, even when we refer to nonsymbolic "contexts of situation," we must turn back to the expression of this context for "proof." This does not mean that no inferences or interpretations are smuggled into the text, but that in so far as there is a record, there is an underlying structure of factuality to which we can repeatedly refer in hopes of hermeneutic improvement. The lack of carefully prepared texts, which many workers can use, is one great flaw in all social study. Students of art are at least talking about an object, the art work, which is open to all for inspection. Very few sociological case histories have been prepared for use by students other than those prepared and distributed among sociologists. Often we are told the content of case histories but are not allowed to judge for ourselves whether or not such statements are true—or even plausible.

Proof [1] in symbolic interpretation will contain two elements. First, while grounding itself in reference to the textual facts, it must seek to make clear all elements of inference or interpretation it adds to these facts; and it must offer a rationale for its selections and interpretations. This is very different from symbolic analysis in terms of analogy. If the word "tree" appears in two contexts, we cannot begin by asking what "symbolic" meanings a tree might have in religion or psychoanalysis. We begin with the literal fact that the term bridges the two contexts. Or, even where we might begin with a pat meaning for "tree" over and above its meaning as a positive concept, the fact would still remain that the term had one particular set of associates in some particular work. It is easy enough for the anthropologists to say, "It's not just a 'tree' but a tribal symbol." But such symbolic or analogical meanings, even when correct, still leave the question of how the term "tree" is related to other terms in the text. It is the interconnectedness of an identical term as it recurs in changing contexts within the art work itself that we must search out. This is very different from confining interpretations to equivalences or analogies already established before one looks at the text.

THE STRUCTURE OF THE SYMBOLIC ACT

We have argued, following Burke, that analysis of structure of social action as a symbolic act involves definition of structure in terms of dramatic action. There are five elements in the structure of a social act. These are the time and place of the act, the types of characters who perform the act, the kind of act it is, the means by which the act is performed, and its purpose. In Burke's terminology these are called: scene, agent, act, agency, and purpose. For the purposes of developing a sociological model of communicative action we have adapted them as follows:

Scene is the *symbolization of time and place,* the setting of the act which creates the conditions for social action. The environment of man is symbolic. Even nature is symbolized in spatial or temporal imagery. Social time is always present time because we select the kind of pasts and futures we need to act in a present. Futures and pasts are symbolized in terms of what we want to do *now,* of solutions to problems which must be solved in order for action to go on. Thus, conservatives invoke past traditions, radicals future utopias, to legitimize their acts. In science we invoke a past to explain a present, as in genetic theory. Or, we invoke a future, "the goal toward which the organism presses." In psychology we say that the "child is the father of the man."

Agent is the name for the kind of actor groups select to carry out specified social functions.[2] Who is chosen, who is barred, and who is not eligible to enact certain roles (for whatever reason) tell us much about a society. Roles and the kind of actors held necessary to community survival are honored in all kinds of community presentations. In such presentations we observe what roles are honored, in what style such roles are played, how individuals are trained for such roles, and who controls them.

Act is best understood (from a social view) by watching for acts depicting moments of community origin. Such moments are the creative moment, the moment of social birth. These are the great transcendent absolutes, the final "mystery" of society which are valued because they sanctify social bonds. These may be military, religious, intellectual, or familial. A society may be born in war, created by religious prophets, formed in thought by rational discussion, or conceived by divine parents. We are taught that America was born in debate, and the principles of American union purified in debate over slavery. Our founding fathers are not priests, warriors, teachers, or artists, but politicians who debated to form a constitution. Our sacred act is a parliamentary act.

Agency denotes means or ways of acting. We legitimize power through appeals to belief in certain *ways* of establishing and sustaining authority. In America the way to freedom is through money. A free market guarantees a free society. Justice in our courts is reached through a *method* of trial. Science reaches truth through *methods* of investigation. Magic is effective only when the spell is expressed in rigidly prescribed forms. Manners determine society, for the *ways* we meet, greet, and talk create and sustain the "social graces."

Purpose is belief in certain values as necessary to community survival. If we educate more people and intensify the education of our elites, America will survive; if we are more religious, brotherhood will increase —such "ifs" assume ends, purposes, or goals. Even critical intelligence itself must rest on belief that wisdom, as open and informed discussion, is good for society. Ends, values, and purposes may be described either as pasts or futures. Man lives under immanent symbols, the symbols of promise of things to come. Even rationalists assume an "ideal" rational act to be an ultimate social good. None of these ideal ends can be proved, but their immanence invests action with meanings because they organize the act in a present. Ideal pasts are invoked, not to return to the past, for this is impossible, but to press on into a future. History (in the sociological view taken here) is a goal. Pasts are recaptured only to help us to act in a present.

Scene, agent, actor, agency, and purpose seldom stand alone in symbolic phases of the act. Relationships between two, or stress on various combinations of two or more elements, are common. Burke distinguishes ten dominant types of such relationships which are of specific interest to students of society. Paraphrased for our purposes here, these are:

1. *Scene–act*—All statements which ground social motives in conditions, backgrounds, environments, natural laws, objective situations, existential conditions, historical necessity, equilibrium, time, the body, etc. Whenever space and time become "trends," species "evolve," empires "take the course of destiny," or certain kinds of human relationships are said "to make virtue inevitable," we ground society in scene. All such explanations of social order are both deterministic *and* hortatory, with exhortation smuggled in under the guise of determinism. Thus, to say that only when Negroes can earn and spend as they desire do we have freedom is to say that we ought to let them do so—if we desire a free society based on money.

2. *Scene–agent*—Social conditions here are said to call for actors in keeping with the scene, and the scene, in turn, is depicted as in keeping with the actor. Thus, we hear of politicians who are "prisoners of the situation," former Nazis who explain their crimes as the result of the "leadership principle," or the motivation to motion in a scene where men do not *act* but are *moved to action*.

3. *Scene–agency*—Whenever *ways* of doing something are considered necessary conditions of social action, as when we tell a child that "our family doesn't do that sort of thing." All appeals to customs, usage, traditions, and means, as the condition of ends, enter here.

4. *Scene–purpose*—When the purpose of action is made part of the conditions under which we act. Money determines the "laws of supply and demand," so it is "natural" for men to work for money. Or, as we say, animals and men alike experience the living God because God is in all nature.

5. *Act–purpose*—When a soldier tells us war is necessary to purify the race, the scientist that science alone can save the community, or we are told any kind of act will, in itself, insure community survival, and will do so "inevitably." Here purpose, or the end of action, and action itself are congruent.

6. *Act–agent*—When we explain an action by the character of the agent, or the glory of the role which the agent enacts. Religious "charisma" (the "gift of grace") of the holy man who rules through purely personal qualifications or the office (such as the priesthood), whose glory and mystery transcends the individual who holds it, are examples.

7. *Act–agency*—When we make means into ends, such as the discovery

of the cause of motivation in the "tendency" of the "organism" toward equilibrium. Here motion itself *creates* motion.

8. *Agent–purpose*—When the act of the leader becomes the purpose of the community. When Christ said "I am the way" and Louis XIV told the Parliament of Paris "I am the state" their individual wills became the will of the group.

9. *Agent–agency*—When the instincts, drives, states of mind, character (individual or national) of the actor are said to motivate relationships.

10. *Agency–purpose*—When instruments or techniques become ends, as when we are told that operations determine concepts, that is, how we record temperature *is* our concept of temperature, or, in social actions, when we say: "Manners make the man."

THE FUNCTION OF THE SYMBOLIC ACT

The function of this structure, the content of the drama of society, we argued, is a drama of hierarchy in which superiors, inferiors, and equals communicate by symbols which they believe will create and sustain social order. Our first illustration for this drama was taken from Burke's "dramatistic" adaptation of religious ritual considered as a drama of redemption which is the enactment of guilt and redemption through victimage. These are the great moments in the linguistic experience of man in society. But they are also great social moments, for they are the stages we pass through to create what we call the "social bond." In our view, this bond, in so far as it is determined by symbols, is reached through identification which occurs in the enactment of guilt redeemed through victimage, in social order expressed through hierarchy.

All hierarchy, we argued, is based on a final moment of "mystery," a sacred moment in which social hierarchy ends—and begins. We discussed three basic attitudes toward these ends, namely, acceptance, doubt, and rejection. We then codified hierarchal ultimates, in terms of a dramatistic view of the act based on the work of Mead and Burke. We argued that we ground social motives in scene when we invoke laws of nature to explain hierarchy; in the act, or the nature of the action itself, when we say that a certain kind of act constitutes the social bond; in the actor when we say that a certain kind of person, or a specific role has the charismatic power to identify people with each other; in the agency, or means, when we say that how we do something will determine the efficacy of what we do in creating and sustaining social bonds; and in purpose when we say that ends or values determine our motives.

While we recognized that communication has many functions, we argued that its specific sociological function is that of hierarchal address. The rhetoric of hierarchy was described as a rhetoric of courtship, and courtship in turn involved appeals to general audiences, community guardians, significant others (as in dialogue when the "I" addresses its "Me"), the self (as in all forms of soliloquy), and to some great transcendent principle which is believed to create and sustain social order and is expressed through the glory and majesty of hierarchy. We illustrated one of these principles, the principle of money, by showing some of the steps by which money became a symbol of community and thus transcended its immediate function in trade or exchange.

We declared in favor of democracy as the best form of hierarchy, because it minimized the power of priestly mystification which so often arises when authority is grounded in some kind of supernatural power. We admitted to a mystification of our own, namely, that of reason in society. This, we argued, can be kept under control only when there is open, free, and informed discussion of action in society. Comedy was selected as a "representative case" of such discussion, for in comedy ambiguity, doubt, difference, and all forms of social disorganization are exposed, not cloaked, as in tragedy. The comic hero, the clown, offers hopes for the development of a scapegoat who need not be tortured and killed in ritual murder like the scapegoat whose actual sacrifice begins in the symbolic sacrifice of tragedy. For, we argued, in comedy we confront openly many things we must hide and repress when we are "serious."

Reason in society depends, we said, on equality, and equality in turn can become a form of authority only when experience in creating and obeying rules is made possible. For rules represent the will of equals, and even though rules can also become ritual, there is far less danger of malign mystification under the authority of rules since such authority does not rest on supernatural powers "beyond reason." We do not believe rules "even though they are absurd," but because they work, and when they do not we are prepared to change them so that they will work. We noted how little is really known of the authority of rules, and how small is our social psychology of equality, compared to the great amount of work done on superiority and inferiority as a form of hierarchy. We argued that art, as well as religion, supplied forms of symbolic action which might serve for models for thinking about social integration. But art, we proposed in conclusion, should be studied in its comic, not tragic, forms, for the tragic is too close to religion. *The sociology of art, and especially a sociology of comic art, is a general, as well as a specialized, study of society, in so far as society is determined by the communication of significant symbols.*

Much uneasiness, even despair, pervades our search for a way of thinking about how society arises in, and continues to exist through, communication. This is caused by the spectacle of Hitler and the wide gap between what we know as social scientists about human motivation and what such monsters as Hitler can put into practice. They seem to grasp intuitively that social relations are determined by identification, which is reached through *staging* human relationships in community dramas modeled after horrible perversions of religious drama. What drama of reason can we create to match these terrible dramas of unreason? Can we develop theory and method in symbolic analysis which will tell us *how* to do what we *ought* to do, as citizens of a free world? And can we do it soon enough? Throughout this book we have argued that until the wide gap between humanistic and scientific understanding is closed, there is small reason for optimism. We must return the study of man in society to a study of communication, for how we communicate determines how we relate as human beings.

Notes

[1] Kenneth Burke's treatment of "fact, inference, and proof in the analysis of literary symbolism," as published in *Symbols and Values: An Initial Study* (Thirteenth Symposium of the Conference on Science, Philosophy and Religion), edited by Lyman Bryson, Louis Finkelstein, R. M. McIver, and Richard McKeon (New York and London: Harper and Brothers, 1954), is followed here. Burke's discussion of method deals with specific literary texts which can be readily consulted.

[2] My interpretation of Burke's "dramatism" is biased in terms of a sociological view of human relationships. There is much more to Burke than this necessarily limited view indicates.

Index

Index

Abbey of Thelema, 130, 388
Abraham, K., 351, 352
Absolute: in Hegel as cause and effect, 50; of sociation in Simmel, 186
Absolute idea, as self-developing, 185
Absolutes: as God, nature, society, sex, and mind, 58; make subject residual to object, 74
Absurdity, 198
Acquiescence, as danger to hierarchy, 132
Act: elements in, 147; as exhortation, 151n; hypotheses on structure and function of, 98; logical, rhetorical and symbolic phases of, 147; need for conception of in human studies, 87; in terms of language, 144
Act-agency, 435
Act-agent, 435
Act-purpose, 435
Action: depends on communication, 284; in image of hunt, 243; as a matter of ends, purposes and goals, 74; as mechanical, Intro. 9; as problem solving, 88
Actor, in magical act, 39
Actors, learn what they mean from responses of others, 79
Adam, 284; and generic human nature, 122
Address, 292; comedy as best example of five basic forms of address, 293; by comic hero to various audiences, 293; in the dream, 288; of equals, 289; as exhortation, 290; five types of, 292; forms of as fundamental realities in society, 297; in hierarchy, 288–301 passim; and identification, 165; as inducement to action, 168; of inferior, 289; as "inner," 302; as "inner" and "outer," 289; ironical address possible only among equals, 381; in lyrical discourse, 171; as moment of commitment, 298, 300; not mechanistic, 100; to nature, 100; in ritual as a form of beseechment, 268; of ruler to people, 216; staging of, 291; of superior, 289; ultimate form of, 102

Ade, G., 400
Ade, G., *Fables in Slang*, 431
Adler, D., 111
Admiration, how to gain it, 218
Adoration, creates divinity, 219
Aesop, 398
Aesthetic attitude: adds poetry to action, 83; derived from inward sympathy, 9; involves least artistically endowed, 84
Aesthetic effect, as values in movies, 87
Aesthetic experience: as appreciation of finalities, 82; as delight in outcome, 84; as enjoyment of consummation, 82; as judgment upon quality of a civilization, 65; makes work meaningful in community, 84
Aesthetic joy, as community joy, 84
Aesthetic myths, 424
Aesthetic personification, 99
Aesthetic sympathy, 99
Aesthetics, and psychoanalysis, 16n
Agency-purpose, 436
Agent-agency, 436
Agent-purpose, 436
Agreement, a sign of weakness to inferiors, 343
Alger, Horatio, Jr., 111
Alice in Wonderland, 393, 398
Alienation, 122; as rejection of symbol of authority, 111
Allee, W. C., 337
Allen, S., 377
Allocation of symbols of power, 322
Allport, G. W., 70n
Altgeld, J. P., 317
Amateur, honors sociability of the game, 336
Ambiguity: in action, 124; arising out of incongruities, 407; must be dealt with in any methodology, 150
Ambition: American discontent over money as divine, 345n; as a goad, 255
American burlesque, 393
American Christmas Madonna, 359

American college football, 247
American freedom, as freedom over money, 355
American Legion, 360
American male, as henpecked, 428
American office, as stage for socializing as well as work, 333
American plutocracy, and glamor in travel, 277
American plutocrat, 277
American politics as a great game, 335
American social science, reliance on technique, 137n
American social scientists: failure to study communication, 119; neglect of study of communication as symbolic action, 148; use of imagery of action derived from imagery of motion in space, 175n
American Sociological Society, 153n
American sociologists: lack of theory of symbolic action, 149; of the second generation, 148
American symbols of social position as spiritual, 258
American symbols of power, opulent and grandiose, 276
American trials, 292; as contests in form of drama, 293
American vaudeville, 291
American woman, her opulence as a communication of husband's real or imputed wealth, 419
Analogies: of man in society, 110; of men to animals and machines, Intro. 1
Analyst, as audience, 283
Anguish: in all communication, 165; of nightmare, 284; over nothingness, 298
Anomie, as alienation in religious sense, Intro. 10
Anthropology, as social control, 103
Anxiety: its meaning discovered only through communication, 282; over response of others, 271
Aphorisms, as maxim of conduct, 431
Apocalyptic myths, type of, 319
Appeal to unreason in Hitler, 235
Appeal to reason, negative aspects of, 180
Appeals, to mixed audiences, 310
Appeals for attention, risks in, 280
Appeals to authority, Bentham's typology of, 179
Acquinas, 109
The Arabian Nights, 365
Arbitration: among equals, 327; as treason, 343

Arbitration boards, 317
Arbitrator, social function of, 327
Architecture: beauty and money in work of Root, Sullivan, and Wright, 367; as expression of hierarchy in space, 295
Aristocratic art: mystifications in, 420; struggle between passion and honor, 420
Aristocratic courtship, as obsequious, 207
Aristocrats, of Rome, 276
Aristophanes, 296, 388, 393, 399, 403
Aristophanes' *The Frogs*, 402
Aristotle, 171; his definition of the act, 172; on fear, 173; and nonrational appeals, 172; small audiences of, 166
Army life, as training in manners, 211n
Art: as aid to conspicuous consumption, 369n; of being inferior, 254; both comic and tragic offer clues to sociation, 438; as both instrumental and consummatory in Dewey, 57; as both tragedy and comedy, 376; brings the unconscious into communication, 412; as clue to pure form of sociation, 22; comic art as resolution of struggle between order and disorder, Intro. 13; comic and tragic as formal expression of problems in hierarchy, 394; as communication in society, Intro., 7; confronts evil, 287; considered as the guardian of social order, 282; creates social objects, 90; creative source of communication, 104; as culminating event in nature, 56; as defined by social experience, 63; delight in art as it arises in shared effort in community, 85; and depiction of evil, 285, 295; does not invoke supernatural in same manner as religion, 73; and empiric study of ends, 57; as empirical fact of consciousness, 63; as expression of completed acts, 57; as expression of doubt and ambiguity, Intro. 10; as expression of emotion, 61; as expression of hate, 344; as form of symbolic action, 143, 437; function of as recovery of sense of final outcome of the act, 82; as highest form of communication, 60; as ideal form of communication, 66; and identification, 85; and images of our own vices, 402; impossibility of social theory without making art as communication a constituent part of theory, 45; and integration with religion, 375; as interpretation of shared experience, 85; of life created by gentleman in "poetry of society," 334; linked with the erotic, 423; Mead's theory of art as a movement into

Art (*Cont'd*)
a future, Intro. 6; as means by which we externalize reverie, 85; means by which we take role of other, 85; as means of keeping alive sense of purpose, 67; as message track for other institutions, 374; and morals in harmony, 333; must be more than substitute for reverie, 84; necessary to religion, 375; neglect of by sociologists of our generation, 71n; and order, 320; orders experience, Intro. 6; as participation in community life, 67; personifies hate and love, 343; as play, 21; poster form of best form for political purposes, 234; in presentation of self, 222; the quality of unity in art experience, 63; of rage, 222; raises hierarchal pantomine to beautiful form, 207; as reason in Goya, 409; and religion, 373, 374; religious idea of art as refuge from moral struggle, 374; and social experience in Dewey, 65; social function as vision of possibilities in experience, 67; as social truth, 73; and sociological categories in communication, 111; sociological study of, 153n; as source of knowledge, 68; as source for model of action, 105; as strategy for selecting enemies and allies, 111; as study of ends of acts, 68; and the study of society, Intro. 7; as sympathetic projection, 67; and transmission of custom, 66; how understanding of helps solve basic problems of knowledge, 62; unique in society because it is both comic and tragic, 401; use of comic art in search for model of communication in society, Intro. 10; various uses of to illustrate "sentiments of attachment," Intro. 7; when too private art disintegrates, 87

"Art of Cheating," 171
Art forms: as equipments for living, 111; relation to typical situations, 111
Art work, as object in society, 431
Art works, as cultural facts, 431
Artist: artistic achievement inaccessible to psychoanalysis, 5; belief that form is life, 318; and distortion of symbolic material, Intro. 4; embodies attitude of perceiver, 65; his creation not like creation of God, 62; ventriloquist's dummy (theory of artist), 374
Arts: of display in Spain, 218; popular arts spread average man's reveries, 86; of social presentation, 265
Aryan: martyrs in Hitler's teachings, 238;

Aryan (*Cont'd*)
must live in close community, 227; will to sacrifice, 227
Aryans, as true founders of humanity, 227
Asceticism, enhances power of sex in society, 425
Ascription and derivation in methodology, 116
Ashurst, Senator Henry F., 257
Asides in address, 291
Athens: comedy in sacred festivals, 376; prayer for her safety in wisdom, 402; small intimate audiences of the orator in, 166
Attitude: consciousness as taking the attitude of others, 79; as incipient act, 88; as reaction to stimulus, 88
Attitudes, 155; of acceptance, doubt, and rejection toward authority, 436; and cathexis, Intro. 2; conditions of harmony through reorganization of stimuli, 89; creation of in communication, 180; derived from hearing ourselves as others hear us, 76; evoked by symbols of completion, 89; as exhortation to self, 112; as strategic naming, 110
Audience: always bound to actor, 79; being a member of as role, 288; child learning to attract audience, 304; as clue to meaning in rhetoric, 171; of courtier, 208; in day-dream, 289; and expression of hostility, 344; in fantasy and reality, 289; and fear, 400; inner audience as censor, 303; inner audience as judge, 303; and inner drama of purification, 306; lack of integration in movie audience, 86; as make-believe, 289; in memory, 289; necessary to enjoyment of hate as well as love, 208, 272; of noble connoisseurs, 291; nonneurotic self as audience to neurotic, 17n; players as audience to each other, 78; as political public, 212; relating to private or public audience is a performance, 304; stress on external audience in traditional rhetoric, 166; ultimate audiences, 315; unconscious audience of homosexual, 305
Audiences, 283, 294; of the dream, 283, 309; five types of ultimate audiences, 315; forms of appeal to inner audiences, 302; as imagined, 289; to our majesty, 207; men as audiences to themselves, 280; mixture of those we love, hate, and despise, 302; appeal to inner audiences, 302; classified according to appeals made to them, 304; created by rhetoric, 171; to ourselves,

Audiences (*Cont'd*)
166, 283, 288, 290, 308; of the political administrator, 212; private and public audiences are mixtures of superiors, inferiors, and equals, 302; range of, 131; as real or imagined, 289; sociological view of "inner" audiences, 302–311 *passim;* as taken for granted, 172; typology of, 292
Auditorium Building of Chicago, 367
Augustine on rhetoric, 170
Authoritarian society, Malinowski's tribal image authoritarian, not democratic, 42
Authoritarian trial, 341
Authority, 110, 291; acceptance, doubt, and rejection in, 124; at mass meetings, 234; in American and German society, 291; antithetical thought about, 124; Burke's study of in *Attitudes Toward History,* 137n; cannot function without equality, 339; as combination of popularity, force, and tradition, 235; and communication of social structure, 112; cultivating tone of, 221; as decision reached through discussion, 327; dislike and hatred mingled with love and devotion, 271; and disorganization, 287; distribution of, 117; early discovery in childhood that disobedience fixes attention upon us, 281; early experiences of, 280; expression of in sex, 417; as father image, 10; as final stage in hierarchy, 204; glamorization of depends on dramatization, 264; how it ought to be communicated, 179; of leader downward and responsibility upward as Nazi ideal, 238; legitimized through reference to social order, Intro. 12; loaded with symbols of filth in obscene comedy, 409; local authority seeks to universalize its symbols, 133; must be communicated clearly and simply, 234; must link past with future, 235; must offer a future, 235; mystery and glamor of, 195; paradox of, 285; parents as first experience with absolute authority, 304; as popularity and force combined, 235; power of mystification, 285; problem of in using vices and virtues of people, 216; purification of majesty through scapegoat, 394; as puzzling and capricious, 303; as resolution of conflict in family, · 10; and rhetoric, 179; of rules, 256, 437; and social mystification, 125; staging of for masses, 234; staging of in ceremony, 262; as supernatural, Intro. 9; use of art to celestialize symbols of power, 321; use of clown to

Authority (*Cont'd*)
express in jest what cannot be risked seriously, 393; and victimage, 339
Authorities: fear of attack on the office, not on the individual, 413; need of fools, 400
Autocrat, and secret audience, 283
Autonomous principles in rhetoric, 161

Babbitt, 378
Bach, 374, 375; his art creates religious experience, 375; music as prayer, 375
Bacon, F., on religion in society, Intro. 8
The Bank Dick, 427
Barnett, J. H., 368n
Barton, B., 111, 363
Baseball players, 378
Battle, leader's death in as a crucifixion, 240
Baudelaire, on dandy as "cult of oneself," 268
Beau Brummel, 266
Beethoven, Ludwig von, 134
The Beggars Opera, 201n, 348, 413
Behaviorism, problem of range in, 109
Behaviorist: cannot deal with purpose, 149; lack of moral concern with conditioning techniques, Intro. 16n; and random action, 149; smuggles in purpose in description of action, 149
Behaviorists, stress on non-verbal aspects of communicative act, 171
Belief: and confidence, 315; in divine acts of creation, 316; in ends, goals, or purpose, 316; in method, 316; in nature, 315; in personnal charisma, 315
Benny, Jack, the American "tightwad," 379
Bentham, J., 116, 117, 174; not simply a "debunker," 179; reliance on reason, 181; search for a neutral rhetoric based on reason, 179
Bentham's Handbook of Political Fallacies, edited by H. A. Larrabee, 188n
Berle, M., 377
Bible, 114; translated into business terminology, 363
Birth ceremony, 278
Blake, W., 130
"Block universe," James' description of as a universe devoid of change and novelty, 75
Blood Purge of June, 1930, 426
Blumer, H., 149, 153n
A Book About Myself, 369n
Book of Revelation, 283
Bormann, M., 236
Bosch, H., 285, 409

Bourgeois meeting, lack of drama in discussion, 229

Broom, L., 153n

Brueghel, P., 409

Buber, M., 106n, 345n

Buddenbrooks, depiction of businessman as weak and vulgar, 367

Buildings as stages, 291

Burckhardt, J., 51

Bureaucracy: angelic, 196; and hierarchy, 124; studies of not functional, 145

Bureaucratic men in Soviet Russia, 188

Bureaucratization of the imaginative, 124

Burke, K., 115, 149, 163n, 345n, 373, 433; *Attitudes Toward History* as study in acceptance and rejection of authority, 112; on conditioning, 115; dramatism as a view of human relations, 143; dramatistic model of society, 109–120 *passim*, 436; *A Grammar of Motives* as study of ambiguity, 150; *A Grammar of Motives* and *A Rhetoric of Motives* as studies in symbolic action, Intro. 13; high regard for work of G. H. Mead, 151n; on hysteria, 167; importance of essay, "On Human Behavior Considered Dramatistically," in revised edition of *Permanence and Change*, 119; influence of anthropology on early work, 167; methodological interest in forms of talk about experience, 143; on poet as audience to himself in revision of his work, 14; proportional quality of thought, 119; range of *A Grammar of Motives*, 150; on reductive use of symbols in human studies, 115; search for method, 143; search for models of sociation in art, Intro. 5; social interaction as a dramatic process, Intro. 5; sociology of language, 154–164 *passim*; the structure of the act as act, scene, agent, agency and purpose, 147; the structure and function of the act in Burke's work, 143–153 *passim*; on symbolic analysis, 438n; trilogy on motives in symbolic action, 150; use of Coleridge's image of stairs, 123

Burnham, D. H., 111

Burnham and Root, of the Chicago School of Architecture, 367

Business: "business is religion, and religion is business," 363; as communicative act, 111; as a game, 332; linkage with politics, 363; as service, 364

Business control, of American community based on communication, 264

Business hagiography, as profitable literary genre, 362

Business relations, as named by artists, 110

Businessman: as buffon in Veblen, 199; deification of, 362; as representative American, 110; as trustee of American universities, 255; as villain in Engels, 199

Businessmen, as national leaders, 362

Camille, 421

Capital, 183

Carleton College, Intro., 14

Carlyle, T., 174, 347, 350; on clothes as a symbol of social order, 190; on ironic man as pest to society, 385

Carroll, E., 417

Casanova, 421, 425; use of comic catharsis for love's frustrations, 422

Case histories, lacking in sociology, 431

The Castle, 413

Catastrophies, as good for trade in Mandeville, 348

Catharsis, as stylistic cleansing of the audience, 138n

Cathexis, Intro. 1; cannot be explained by nonmechanical events, 11

Catholic church, 233, 248

Catholics, 350

Celestialization, Burke's codification of relationships between social and sacred symbols, 321

Celestial symbols, 322

Censor: as addressed, 289; of dreams as image of authority, 291

Ceremonies: poignancy of ceremonies of retirement, 261; of community origin, 264

Ceremony: Gothic forms of in education, 134; Greek drama as civic ceremony, 126

Cervantes, 375

Change, may offend the gods, 268

Charisma, 122; in Weber and Burke, 136n

Charley's Aunt, 305

Charlie Chaplin, 376, 378, 389, 398; as compensation for repressed primitive tendencies, 87

Charlie the Tramp, 427

Charter of society, enactment of in Yankee City, 263

Cheater, a villain among equals, 326

Chess players, 329

Chesterfield, on modesty as a bait for praise, 331

Chicago, 103, 365, 418; its wonder and enchantment, 365

Chicago School of sociology, concern with significant symbols in the days of Redfield, Blumer, Wirth, Dewey, Mead, Park, Burgess and Warner, Intro. 15n, 148

Child: as delegate to group, 333; needs peers, 339, 340; shut off from communication, 308; status trappings of, 333

Chinese, use of play, 335

Chopin, 291

Chorus: antithetical to soliloquy, 296; as community voice in dialogue, 296

Christ, as scapegoat, 129

Christian: authority, 218; as courtier, 217; drama of Christianity as illusion, 128; drama of hierarchy, 204; power as good power, 217

Christian cosmological drama, most powerful yet produced in our society, 320

Christian doctrine of the first shall be last and the last shall be first as a pure statement of hierarchal principle, 203

Christian hierarchy, 286

Christian martyrs, 306

Christian tradition, essentially tragic, 373

Christianity: death and life eternal, 157; dramas of Christian social order, 113; fellowship of piety and laughter in, 335; as "ideal" statement of social order, 204

Christians, 275, 306, 309, 350; and riches, 349

Christmas: control of by businessmen, 134; development of in America, 358; as family celebration, 358; feminization of, 358; not secular, 362; as orgy of generosity, 360

Christmas revels, 359

Christmas shopping, 359

Christmas spending, not determined by economic laws, 265

Churchill, W., 176n, 246, 277; great moving sentences of, 246

Cicero, 170

Civic ceremonies: enactment of redemption, 127; as presentation of community to itself, 295

Cities, as stage for people, 276

Clark, K., *The Nude: A study in Ideal Form*, 120

Class relations, as analogous to sex relations, 195

Class rhetoric: Burke's typology of identifications in, 202; general principles of, 202; as magical, analogizing, and specialized, 202; types of identification in as summarized by Burke in writings of Marx, Carlyle, Empson, and Veblen, 202

Classic thought, objectivity of essences in, 60

Classical rhetoricians, concern with pragmatic study of rhetoric, 172

Clothes: of beggar as negative expression of hierarchy, 192; as bridge to divine, 193; in Dreiser as sign of social position, 365; as emblematic of God, 350; instill reverence for rank and uphold principles of hierarchy, 193; as metaphors of hierarchy, 190; reveal and conceal the Mystery of the Divine spirit in Man, 193; and reverence, 194; as social rhetoric, 190; as source of individuality, 191; as spirit of hierarchy, 190; as symbol of spirit of society, 192

Clown: as salesman on television, 378; as satirist must earn our trust, 411; as scapegoat, 397

Code of honor, as open to doubt, 328

Cohen, E. A., *Human Behavior in the Concentration Camp*, 408, 415n

Coleridge, S. T., quotation from *Anima Poetae* to illustrate dialectical method and nature of hierarchy, 123

Collingwood, R. G., *The Idea of History*, 70n

Comedy, 346n, 373; absurdity as created through magnification of social distance, 382; as address to inner and outer selves, 403; as address to society, 389; the American "bum," 379; American laughter at immigrant, 376; antidote against panic, 412; appeal to good sense, 407; and autocracy, 398; banishes loneliness, 403; being laughed at and being laughed with, 395; and belief in doubt and question, 406; belief in reason as ultimate social bond, 412; belief that salvation comes from man himself, 407; as bland and polite, 378; as bland and polite teasing, 378; born of love of man in society, 389; "Bringing Up Father," 379; British and American contrasts, 379; burst of glory in, 387; business use of clown to ridicule laggard spender, 377; Charlie the Tramp, 379; clown as scapegoat in comic art, 138n; and confrontation, 437; as cry of the heart, 389; as cry of mankind, 412; on death must be very great, 405; and "debunking" not the same, 390; the deceiver deceived, 402; and discourse, 403; and disorganization, 287; efficiency of, 119; essence of as joy in reason, 404; estrangement of clown, 398; and excess of virtue or vice, 402; and

Comedy (*Cont'd*)
exploration of social principles, 395; exposes authority to create a new authority, 390; exposes mystifications of social hierarchy, 388; exposes transgression of rights, 411; as exposure of mystery, 213; as expression of unconscious, 393; final transcendence is society itself, 390; as form of instruction, 389; Freddie the Freeloader, 379; Freud's theory limited, 376; glorifies men who will be men, 406; as glory in dignity of reason in society, 406; great question of whether reason is enough for survival, 413; and group identification, 387; gives guilt form so we can express it, 397; as guardian of reason in society, 393; heresy in tragedy and comedy, 406; as highly conservative, 378; human survival dependent on keeping society flexible and alive through discussion, talk, and laughter, 407; and incongruity, 403; indigenous to art and society, 376; inferiors joing with superiors in laughter at themselves, 380; as institutionalized punishment, 398; institutionalizes doubt and question, 387; in irony conflicts are magnified, 385; jokes as resistance against authority, 376; judgment of gods in, 399; lazy spender as comic villain, 379; as low and tragedy as high in Judaism, 391n; as means of discussing sins, 397; as a method of inquiry, 213, 214; miracle of in *Huckleberry Finn*, 414; "Moon Mullins," 379; morality of reason in society, 390; often savage and obscene, 407; over "bum" who wants money but will not work, 379; over death, 394; over rigidity in social forms, 404; over vulgarity, 267; as profound expression of art, 376; purgation in compared with tragedy, 395; as purgation of fear, 414; and the purification of the social order, 413; and reason, 406; as reason and dignity, 406; reduces social differences, 404; as representative case, 437; resolution of civic tension in Aristophanic comedy, 126; resolution of shame and guilt in, 397; returns us to each other, 403; as the rhetoric of reason in Society, 406–416 *passim;* as sanctioned disrespect, 387; as sanctioned expression of doubt, ambiguity, and disrespect, 393; as scourge of pride, 397; as scourge of vice, 390; and the self, 402; as serious as tragedy, 223n; slapstick, 381; and social control, 376; as social discipline, 388; and

Comedy (*Cont'd*)
social distance, 401; and social euphoria, 390; and social integration, 373–392 *passim;* stresses disrelationships as incongruities, 405n; task of reaffirming social bonds, 415; television clowns as plutocratic clowns, 377; uncovers ambiguities, Intro. 13; upholds as well as rejects authority, 378; upholds as well as resists authority, 376; use of reason in ironic comedy, 380; use of in television to shame inept earners and laggard spenders, 379; vocabulary of, 213; when comic mask drops, 390
Comedy and tragedy, differences between, 403
Comic, in art and social theory, 373
Comic art: attacks false art, 403; teaches that human dignity begins but does not end in suffering, 407
Comic atonement, 399
Comic bum: in America, 377; the Yiddish *schnorrer* as God's fool, 377
Comic chorus, 296; replies to actors, 296
Comic gods, do not require surrender of reason to faith, 407
Comic hero, the boy in Mark Twain, 393
Comic heroes: child as "permitted" to question the sacred in religion, 394; give form to life through personification, 407; the innocent one who asks in wonder, 393
Comic incongruities, 407
Comic mask, 217
Comic obscenity: as plea to make sense, 409; social function of, 407; struggle to reduce gaps in communication, 408
Comic scapegoat, 393–405 *passim;* as used in comic art, 287
Comic spirit: forgiveness in, 420; in Machiavelli, 213
Comic truth, as moment of unmasking, 411
Comic types, the child, the boy, the Fool, 293
Comic understanding, 214
Comic victim, 398, 401
Comic villain: his redemption in laughter, 395; as benign scapegoat, 437
Coming out parties, audiences in, 294
Commandments: both negative and positive, 113; as negative and positive determine each other, 281
Commands, 416n
Commodities, values of as result of social act, 350
Common good, as national good, 216
Common man, the hero of democracy, 427

Communal life, based on hate and love, 309

Communicability, as potential of all things, 60

Communication: as address, 9, 101; all arts involved in, Intro. 14n; and animals, Intro., 10; as art, 57; breakdowns in, 309; central to Mead's theory, 92; constitutes society, 298; as a constitutive category in experience, 76; as conversation, 58; Dewey on our lack of knowledge of, 56; Dewey's theory of communication in art and society, 55; in fantasy as a way to get rid of anxiety, 304; fate of free society hangs on proper sociological study of communication, 438; as field of observation of self and society in action, 76; Freud's great contribution to our understanding of unconscious factors in communications, 13; from divine source, 374; of hierarchy, 271–287 *passim;* inability to communicate arising out of lack of transcendent principle of social order, 279; and language theory, 109; as love and hate, 174n; meaning of symbols as determined by sex and work in Freud, 5; as mediator between physical and ideal worlds in Dewey, 56; of motion, Intro. 8; nature, communication, and meaning in Dewey, 58; over social gaps, 307; in the realm of neuroses and psychoses, 15; as reduced to signalling, 93, 149; as role enactment, Intro. 9; and sex, 290; of significant symbols, Intro. 2; social form of, 78; in society, 59; as sociological category of art, Intro. 10; theory of in sociology, Intro. 1; without verbal symbols as conversation of gestures, 95

Communion, as re-enactment of fellowship, 113

Communists, use of enemy within, 342

Community: of scholars, 135; strong among Aryans according to Hitler, 228

Community drama: as the enaction of transcendent principle of social order, Intro. 4; of redemption, 128; use of to ward off threats, Intro. 11

Community dramas, 235, 431; as perversions of religious rites, 438

Community guardians: the audience as the conscience of the community, 295; as voice of community, 295; as "We" in address, 292

Community origin, as mystical moment, 262

Community symbols, and alienation, 235

Competition: and communication, 160; im-

Competition (*Cont'd*)
possible with superiors, 343; and property, 160; purified by amateur, 336

Concentration camps: as death of our civilization, Intro. 11; humor in, 408; perversion of science in, 162; purification for Nazi party, 342

Condition of the Working Class in England, 199

Conduct, as action, 115

Confession, 341; as expression of struggle between good and evil social principles, 342; as public act, 341; requires audience, 400

Confession in purge trials, not only of crime but of evil in crime, 341

Configuration, 149; mechanical images of, 118

Conflict, 278, 340; among roles, 381; lack of stress on in Malinowski, Dewey, and Mead, 16n; as way to higher unity in Simmel, 186

Conflict and the Web of Group-Affiliations of Simmel, 189n

Conformity: among superiors, 273; by inferior, 273

Confrontation, 134; of disorder, 282; of division, 159; of evil and survival, Intro. 12; of hate, 283; and honor, 197

Conspicuous austerity, 368n

Consummation, 101; as aesthetic moment in communication, 82; as crucial moment in the act in Mead's analysis, Intro. 5; as decisive moment in symbolic action, Intro. 5; as final phase of the act, 82–91 *passim;* and the instrumental, 61

Consummatory moment, arises in symbolic action, 144

Contemporary art, international themes in, 424

Contentment, as natural to man, 345n

Contest: in debate as a game of talk, 338; in play, 330

Context of situation, 431; *mana* in, 38; relevance of Malinowski's concept of to communication in modern society, 40; in tribal language, 34

Conversation, 101, 337; among equals carefully contrived, 338; basis of all knowledge, 220; between "I" and "Thou," 273; as characteristic human act, 338; and culture, 220; as Dewey's dominant image of how thought arises in experience, 72n; essence of in dialogue of equals, 338; as a form of sociability, 27; informality of, 338; as Mead's basic image, 288; as a method of inquiry, 209, 338; as pure form of socia-

Conversation (*Cont'd*)
tion, 25; as social event, 299; in society, 209; as talking back, 338

Conversation of gestures, 76, 94; as communication without symbols, 95; not significant below human level, 95

Cooley, C. H., 149; search for models of sociation in art, Intro. 5

Coolidge, C., "The business of America is business," 362

Cooper, L., 176n

Coquetry, as pure form of sociation, 25

Cosi Fan Tutte, 296, 420–421

Cottrell, L. S. Jr., 153n

Coulanges, Fustel de, on social bond as religious bond in *La Cité antique* (Paris: Hachette, 1864), Intro. 7

Court, courtly pantomime, 204

Court of Brobdingnag, 409

Courtesy, and reputation, 221

Courtier: anguish born of pleasing those he hates, 208; great and small alike must live in constant abasement, 208; must not be content to imitate others, 273; society as his god, 209

Courtly thought, 211n

Courtship: as clue to function of rhetoric, 170; and irony, 256; modes of as acceptance, rejection and debt, 271; not a sexual theme in La Rochefoucauld, 201n; persuasion necessary to both sexual and social, 196; as way to king, 268

Courtship in America, as expressed through money, 419

Covenant: and disobedience, 284; as order, 284

Cowperwood, as Chicago financier in Dreiser's novels, 366

Crawford, F. M., 365

Crime, 131

Crime stories, 366

Criminal: condemned in public, 305; and drama of public confession, 341; and good citizen compared as communicators of hostility, 396; and his public audience, 305; prepared as victim by our press, 396; as sacrificial victim, 340

Criminals, scrupulous criminals in Gide, 165

Critical intelligence, 381; its mysteries, 323

Croce, on all history as contemporary history, 50

Crosby, B., 377

Culture, 220, 365; Malinowski's definitive statement of in his article, "Culture," in the *Encyclopedia of the Social Sciences*,

Culture (*Cont'd*)
46n; as a principle of social order, 203; reification of in anthropological theory, 42

Cultural transmission, as an enactment in dramatic form, 431

Curse: of Athens as unreason, 402; in great art, 344; as inner and outer, 239; in jest, 409; use of comedy to degrade through comic cursing, 407; of soldiers to reduce mystery of rank, 410

Cursing: cursing matches at United Nations, 311n; and diplomats, 309; international, 309; as making an effigy, 408; as riddance of anger, 408; as vicarious through art, 344; the villain as social expression of hostility, 344

Daisy, and the glamor of money in Fitzgerald's novels, 367

Dance, as communication, 391n

Dandies, 333; of England as gods of manners, 268

Dandy: Baudelaire's theory of, 270n; mystic significance of, 192; as poet of cloth, 192

Dante, 174, 204, 279, 285

Darwin, 109, 319; Freud's reference to Darwin's work on the expression of emotions, 3

Day-dreaming, as leap to end not expressed in terms of means, 84

Death: celebration of now saleable, 361; church struggle to control rituals of, 278; and drama of mourning, 273; as purge, 340; and rebirth, 261; social function of preparation for, 259

Death camps: of Hitler, 127; origin of in rhetoric of Hitler, 225

Death rites, and communication of wealth, 278

Debate, as forensic drama, 259

Debunking: dangers in, 135; fallacy of, 148

Decorum: demanded by God, 219; limits of, 268; as most obeyed of all laws, 267

Defense, against Jew as Lord's work in Hitler's *Mein Kampf*, 227

Deference, 331

Dehumanization of Jew by Nazis, 241

Delinquent, source for his description of his career, 152n

Democracy: and art, 384; and disagreement, 110; equated with unreason, 73; as guarantor of order, 340; and hierarchal trappings of public office, 275; minimizes supernatural mystification, 437; and "moboc-

Democracy (*Cont'd*)
racy," 383; must match symbolic skill possessed by enemies, 134

Democratic agreement, born of expression not silence over difference, 299

Democratic leaders, must learn to use art for benign purposes, 236

Democratic National Chairman, 363

Democratic society: achieved through resolution, not obliteration or avoidance, of differences, 110; characterized by doubt and ambiguity, Intro. 10; must doubt leaders, 282

Democratic values, based on seeing ourselves as others see us, 89

Demosthenes, 175n

Denotative vocabularies, 181

De Quincey, T., on rhetoric, 171

De Sade, Marquis, feudal symbolization of sex, 419

Despotism, as law of nature, 345n

Destruction, as communication, 308

Destructiveness, and discipline, 281

Devil: dramatizes power of God, 342; fragmentation of his image, 128; Hitler's personification of in the figure of the Jew, 240; ideal type of in scapegoat, 287; as organizer, 139n; in Puritan community, 139n; as villain, 139n

Dewey, J., *passim* 49–72; 149; "attached" emotions described as mechanical not dramatic, 64; difficulties in using his work to create model of action based on communication, 68; discussion of symbolic action in *Experience and Nature,* 56; failure to create a functional model of art in society, 69; failure to define art as form in *Experience and Nature,* 63; great contribution to theory of communication, 67; his social theory of communication, 63; key terms—communication, art, and society—in his system, 57; reflex arc concept, 87; review of Bosanquet's *History of Aesthetic* in 1893, 55; search for models of sociation in art, Intro. 5; search for theory of knowledge based on emotions as well as thought, 55; view of the social function of art, 66; words and things, 59

Dialectic: and antithesis, 131; as "science," 181

Dialogue: between "Moi" and "Lui" in Diderot's *Neveu de Rameau,* 204; between self and other, 297; as dramatic, 299; as "I" speaking to "You," 297; triadic form of, 300

Diderot, D., 174, 204; *Neveu de Rameau,* 204; on the "vile pantomime" of aristocratic hierarchy, 204

"Die Grossetadte und das Geistesleben" of Simmel, 353

Difference, expression of, 281

Differential status, 334; common to all societies, 271

Dilthey, W., 345n; interpretation of expression in speech and writing as basic methodological problem in the human studies, Intro. 5; on social function of symbols, Intro. 2

Dionysius the Areopagite, 196

Dionysus, 402

Discontent: as divine in America, 322; as a virtue, 286

Discourse, nature of, 180

Discourses on Livy, 213

Discussion: dependent on social norms, 270n; as a means to truth, 381; possible only with equals, 337

Disobedience, 340; as threat to principles of social order, 285

Disorganization: must be anticipated, 287; natural to society, 227; reason and hierarchy in, 202

Display, effect of situation on, 219

Disraeli, B., 201n, 333

Disrelationships, 121; among social roles, 310; in hierarchal embarrassment, 121

Divine way, of arousing veneration and awe, 224n

Divine Will, as resisting the Jew in Hitler's *Mein Kampf,* 227

Divinity of the king, 339

Dodgson, C. L., 406, 413

Don Giovanni, 297, 394, 398, 406, 407

Don Quixote, 198, 223n, 389, 398, 407

Dooley, Mr., 400

Dorfman, J., 201n

Dostoevski, F., 417; on suffering as way to understanding through compassion, 279

Doubt: in hierarchy, 194; as path to wisdom, 323

Drama: as best model for human relations, 112; as condition of soul in Christianity, 114; as developed in novel makes it possible to take the attitude of the other, 80; and five types of address, 292; of hierarchy, 134; importance in human society, 80; as a means by which we become objects to ourselves, 79; Renaissance court drama, 291; of sociation, 329

Drama of purchase and elegance, 365

Drama of reason, 438

Drama of redemption, Nazi form of returned man to center of stage, 240

Drama of sex, a family drama in the romantic opera of the nineteenth century, 423

Drama of society, 436

Dramas of guilt and redemption: effect on social structure, 126; and literary plots, 126; in modern literature, 126

Dramatic enactment, creates social structure, 113

Dramatic progression, 320

Dramatic rehearsal in the imagination, 319

Dramatic struggle, paradigm of social struggle, 126

Dramatism: Burke's system of, 114; Burke's version of as gymnastic and clinic of ideas, 148; as intermediate step between material and spiritual, 133; and Kant's categories, 151n; as a method, 114; model of knowledge of motives based on action not reflection about action, 115; reduces inference necessary in observation of conduct, 146; as theory of action, 148

Dramatization: of Jew as evil by Hitler, 241; of status, 146

Dream: as communication with self, 288; as drama, 9; failure to communicate in, 290; as form of address, 14; social content of, 283

Dreamer, and nightmare, 290

Dream-symbolism, as material for dream work, 8

Dream symbols, Freud's insistence that meaning of must be supported by meanings derived from communication in society, Intro. 4

Dreiser, T., 111, 365

Dressler, M., 427

Duncan, H. D.: on dangers of confusing the social bond with the religious bond as discussed in "The Development of Durkheim's Concept of Ritual and the Problem of Social Disrelationships," as given in *Émile Durkheim: 1858–1917,* edited by Kurt Wolff (Columbus: Ohio State Univ. Press, 1960), pp. 97–117, Intro. 15n; discussion of confusion between images of structure and function in "Simmel's Image of Society," as printed in *Georg Simmel, 1858–1918,* ed. by Kurt H. Wolff (Columbus: Ohio State Univ. Press, 1959), Intro. 14n; *Language and Literature in Society* as study of symbols and authority, Intro. 13;

Duncan, H. D. (*Cont'd*) on La Rochefoucauld, 211n; literature as magical art in *Language and Literature in Society* (Bedminster Press, New York, 1961), 46n

Dunkirk, 246

Durkheim, É., 73, 104, 126, 345n, 405n; "collective representations," 92; on social bond as religious bond in *Les formes élémentaires de la vie religieuse* (Paris: Alcan, 1912), Intro. 7

Economic forces, destroy culture in Hitler's view, 240

Edenic myths, 258, 315

Education, and hierarchal means and ends, 135

Educator, his use of awesome ceremonials, 323

Ego: in address, 289; and cathexis, 385; dealing with Id and Super Ego, 292; like actor in address, 385; as lord of counter-positions, 310

Egoism of urbanite, 353

Einstein, A., 134

Eisenhower, D. W., 188n

Elegance: determined by audience, 273; formal affects of, 332

Elias, R. H., 369n

Elites, tendency to cloak division and disorganization, 256

Elkins, H., 320

Embarrassment, 198

Emerson, R. W., 368n

Emotions, 391n; arise in forms of communication, 431; communication of in dramatic forms of expression, 64; must be studied as communication not motion, 12; in religion dependent on form of expression, 375

Empson, W., 174, 196

Emulation, as vicarious identification, 199

Encyclopedia of the Social Sciences, 317

End: determines beginning, 157; mysterious power of when unknown, 186

Ends, 434; empiric study of in James, Dewey, and Ward, 49; as hypothetical in communication, Intro. 6

Enemy: authoritarian need for, 340; as personification of evil, 340

Environment: both scene and agent in Dewey, 69; in politics as symbolic, 223n; as symbolic, 37

Epics of creation, as community myths, 264

Equality, 345n; basic to all forms of conversation, 338; and birth of self, 345; conflict over as depicted by Mark Twain, 311; dependent on rules, 437; as determined by means, 328; and discussion, 338; and efficiency, 339; as equal rights to earn, 347; exists in own right, 338; as a form of authority, Intro. 13; Freud's lack of interest in communication between equals, 10; and hierarchy, 337; highest function as dignification of reason in society, 328; importance of in society, 338; and inequality, 122; as mask for inequality, 136n, 339; must be learned, 334; necessary to tyrannies and democracies alike, 334; need to know more about it as a socio-psychological experience, 10; not a lie anymore than play, games, or art, 24; not sameness, 345; perversions of, 339; principle of may be used to sustain inequality, 122; as promise of inequality, 322; the purest moment of sociability, 23; range of, 338; as sharing of hate as well as love, 344; as sharing under rules, 344; as slogan, 339; and social order, 326-346 *passim;* social psychology of, 437; stimulates expression of differences, 345; sustains honor, 335; translation into money, 347; under a code, 328; unlike superiority and inferiority demands complete reciprocity, 24
Equalization of player through handicaps, 343
Equals, 256, 398; audience of men not gods, 343; bound by rules, 256; can really converse, 210; Christians equal before God, 275; compete under rules and codes, 343; and competition, 343; and conversation, 337; create rules, 281; and the law, 327; make discussion possible, 272; make play possible, 272; must be convinced not commanded, 340; must be persuaded, 281; must be responsible for their love and hate, 327; obey a decision not a person, 327; other as equal necessary to development of the self, 345; resolution of love and hate among, 343; reverence for group among peers, 326; transfer among, 257; under rules, 328; use of differences and opposition among, 345
Equilibrium, 316; as moment of transcendence, 316
Equilibrium theory: claims for as an escape from subjectivism of individual consciousness, Intro. 8; use of communication in, Intro. 8

Erasmus, D., 323, 399; on folly as necessary to sociaton, 333
Erotic desire, transformation in play, 331
Erotic immolation in Wagner, 318
Erotic play, 331
Essentialzations, peculiarly subject to mystification, 317
Ethic of Spending, the shift in the Puritan ethic from earning to spending, 355
Etiquette, and social efficiency, 331
Euripides, 403
European culture, 365
European social theory, subordination of equality to superiority and inferiority, 345n
"Ever-increasing standard of living," 258, 286, 322, 356
Everleigh Club of Chicago, money and sex, 418
Evil: cure of through sacrifice among inferiors, 343; like good defined by religion, 285; must be personified, 247
Existence, depends on bonds, 300
Expectancies, as part of every social act, 321
Experience, meaning in communication as a blend of old and new experience, 57
Experience and Nature, regarded as definitive statement of how to think about symbols in society by Malinowski and Mead, 71n
Expiation: and guilt, 125; of guilt arising out of failure to uphold principles of hierarchy, Intro. 11; must be provided by those who cause guilt, 285
Expressive forms, 290
Expressive symbolism, as data, 146
Extermination, as Lord's work in *Mein Kampf,* 227
Extermination of Jews: and guardianship of human civilization in *Mein Kampf,* 230; sacred duty of Germans according to Hitler, 230
Extra-symbolic, as "reality," 144

Fable of the Bees, or Private Vices, Public Benefits, 357n
Facts: basis of selection must be made clear, 431; expression in religion as observable facts of religious life, 75; and inference in textual interpretation, 431
Faith: controls feeling and passion, 229; in reason, 381
Fall of man: depiction of as art form, 114; from Aryan paradise, 227; labor result of, 349; as social not sexual, 227
Fallacies, as natural to communication, 180

Fallacies of authority, six types of in Bentham, 179
Falstaff, 297, 391n
Falstaff, 401, 409
Familiarity, and superiority, 219
Family: symbol of mother as mother of a nation, 424; as ultimate principle of social order in art and society, 423
Fanaticism, driving force in social change, 230
Fanny Bryce, 427
Fantasies, of social gratification, 279
Fashion: as a communication, 331; as glorification of elegance, 269; keeps society flexible, 268; playfulness in, 273; as realm of change, 267
Fashions, as creation of social order through change, 267
Faulkner, W., on Negro as sin of his whites, 308
Father, as despot in Freud, 337
Faust, 296
Faust, 323
Fear: must be followed by hope to be endured, 173; transcendence of in conscious communication, 284; use of to move men, 173; as way to deliberation in rhetoric, 173
Feast of Demeter, 296
Feast of the Fools, and reversal of rank, 258, 404
Fenichel, O., 352, 353
Ferenczi, S., 351
Fetish, as status symbol, 425
Feudal hierarchy, 280
Fields, W. C., 378, 426, 427; as champion of henpecked American male, 428
Figaro, plot motivated by theme of pride, 420
Film: as catharsis, 87; explores primitive drives, 86
Fitzgerald, F. S., and mystique of money, 361, 366
Flügel, J. C.: his naive thinking about status, 424; on narcissism, 33n; *The Psychology of Clothes*, 428n
Folly, as purgation, 333
Force: as a communication of authority, 223n; use of to purify German tradition, 235
Ford, H., 364
Forgiveness, through laughter, 420
Form: and content in Dewey, 65; as content in social action, 320; and context, 320; as experience, 374, 375; not imposed, 321;

Form (*Cont'd*)
and relationship in experience, 64; as a way of experiencing, 321; of worship determines religion, 374
Forms of hierarchal address, as identification, 273
Forms of Sociation: as art and play in Simmel, 21; as autonomous in Simmel's theory, 21; considered as representative forms of social interaction, 18; Simmel's definition of as reciprocal relations in social space, 20; Simmel's theory of final development in free play of forms as such, 21; as values in themselves, 21
Forms of symbolic expression, as used to create and sustain social order, Intro. 3
Fortune, likened to a woman by Machiavelli, 216
Four Hundred, 254, 256
Fox, Charles James, as hero of taste and manners, 333
Frankl, V. E., 408
Franklin, B., 111
Freedom: exists in choice, 113; as a free market, 347, 355; freedom of the air as freedom to sell, 378
Freud, S., 134, 150, 290, 292, 319, 337, 343, 345n, 352, 412, 431; abondonment of mechanical model of mentation in treatment of patients, 7; on art and literature as the deepest truth," 4; Kenneth Burke's essay, "Freud and the Analysis of Poetry," 16n; comparison of neurotic with absolute sovereign, 416n; his concern over similarities in his case history of Elisabeth von R between his presentation and short story form in literature, 3; on Earl of Oxford as author of Shakespeare's plays, 16n; his contribution to our understanding of blocked communication, 14; intermingling of social and sexual elements, 15; *Interpretation of Dreams* as an analysis of language, 4; on jokes as form of communication, 10; lack of interest in communication as a psychological category, 11; meaning of dream-symbols must find support in our knowledge of communication in social life, Intro. 4; neglect of book on jokes, 391n; Oedipus legend, Intro. 4; respect for literary mind, 5; symbolic-interaction in Freud's work, 1–17 *passim*; use of literary classics and great artists, 3; use of rhetorical images, 8, 166; value of concrete descriptions of action to social view of communication, 9; value of his

Freud, S. (*Cont'd*)
descriptions of children struggling to communicate with elders, 14; value of his observations on dreams and communication, 13; on visual imagery, 288
Freudian catharsis, as verbal purgation, 9
Freudian censor, no basis for in Freudian theory of cathexis, 11
Freudian Ego: as agent in the mind, 7; confusion between mechanical structure of ego and its dramatic function, 7
Freudian psychology, a family, not an individual, psychology, 14
Friend: as audience, 298; and individuality, 272; lack of domination, 298; Negro as friend in *Huckleberry Finn*, 401; as total cathartic agent, 129
Friends, as teachers, 220
Friendship: and mutual analysis of faults, 210; as noble virtue, 210; possible only among equals, 210; as ultimate relationship of equals, 210
Frugality, as way to wealth, 349
Frustration: must come from within, 395; no "romantic agony" in Casanova, 423
Funerals: no longer conducted in homes, 360; pomp of, 273
Funeral artists, 360
Funeral homes: as community showpieces, 361; and modern design, 361; of 1960s do not stress "hominess," 361; range in style of, 361; transformation into funeral chapel, 360
Future, 319; as created by artist, 319; as determined by past, 50; as image in act, 168; as incentive to action, 70n; and living individual, 88

Gaiety, submission to others in, 331
"Gallows humor," 408
Gambler, playfulness with money, 336
Gamblers, 336
Gambling, and sex, 418
Games: and rules, 95; as sanctioned hostility, 344; seriousness of, 328
Game of love, 421
Game of money, 265
Gay, J. 348
General public, 292, 294; negative and positive power, 295
"Generalized other": and Durkheim's "collective representations," 92; in the game, 96

Gentleman: and art of life, 334; as Confucian mandarin, 333; as a creator of social order, 334; as hero of culture, 334; keeps manners within limits, 273; perfects taste, 332; as personification of sociable character of group, 334; social function of, 334
Gentleman ideal, 331
"Germanity," as subordination of individual to community, 228
Germany, greatness of in her soldiers according to Hitler, 227
The German Ideology, 182, 184; as contribution to analysis of rhetoric, 187; happy worker in, 187
German people, 134
German society, purification of through killing of Jews by the Nazis, 280
Gesture: anticipation of, 288; as form of address, 288
Gide, A., 165
Gift: impersonality of money gift, 368n; of money compared with gift of time, 359; purchased gift as thing, 358, 359
Gilbert, A. H., 213
Gilbert and Sullivan, 255, 295, 406, 413
Giotto, 375
Glamor: glorification of the American girl as status glorification, 417; in hierarchy, 276; use of by businessmen, 117
Glory, of rank, 132
Goals, not subjective because imagined when imagination is expressed in public symbols, Intro. 6
God, 279; anthropomorphic notion of, 133; as civil and gay, 333; as creater and ruler, 113; as despot over the Devil, 345n; as *ens perfectissimum*, 133; fear of, 285; Jewish God tragic, 391n; as supernatural principle of order in society, 109; as ultimate audience, 165; as Ultimate Bureaucrat in Kafka, 196; as ultimate in politics, 140n
Gods: of Athens often clever but not always wise, 402; of comedy who judge in compassion, 420; as depictions in Greece of the fierce longings of men, 402; judgment of in laughter, 399
"God-terms," 316
God and Devil, must be given people in community drama, 230
Goebbels, J., 134, 176n
Göring, H., 134
Goethe, W., 134, 332
Good manners: bring joy because of their

Good manners (*Cont'd*)
  beauty, 221; differ according to rank of audience, 221
The Good Soldier Schweik, 413
"Gospel of service," 368n
Gourmont, Remy de, 174
Goya, 409
Grace, kinds of, 278
Gracian, B., 201n; "The Art of Worldly Wisdom" as the rhetoric of domination of the secular world by the devout Christian, 217–222 *passim;* on the rhetoric of the Jesuits, 212
Graduation Ball, 291
A Grammar of Motives, 172
Gray's *Elegy*, as pastoral in Empson, 196
The Great Gatsby, 366
Greek, use of play, 335
Greek ritual drama, 387
Greek Sophists, 171
Greek tragedy: chorus in, 291; as civic ceremony, 126
Gregory the Great, 196
Gridiron dinners, 404
Gropius, W., 277
Grotesque, 415n; as beyond reason, 391n; like nightmare evokes horror not laughter, 391n, 405; not comic, 391n
Group, exists in communication of attitudes, 431
Guilt: arising out of failure in expiation, 125; in Athens, 402; as based on supernatural, 286; best explored in religion, 138n; child guilty without knowing why, 307; confrontation of by Hitler, 246; exorcising of, 285; expiated only by superiors in authoritarian relationships, 343; great energy spent on in secular society, 287; and hierarchal motives, 134; heightens in laughter, 402; as inherited, 125; intrinsic to social order, 286, 395; and lack of transcendent principle, 308; need for study of ways guilt is aroused within us, 285; and negation of principles of social order, 121; no theory of possible when mechanical models of sociation are used, 286; part of all hierarchal experience, 286; as redeemed through victimage, 126, 436; redemption, hierarchy, and victimage, 373; redemption through ransom, 132; and riddance of strain in hierarchy, 287; as sexual and social in comedy, 424; supernatural and social compared, 397; as tribal and categorical, 309; as tribal in figure of the Negro, 308; tyrants rule us

Guilt (*Cont'd*)
  because they know we cannot rid ourselves of guilt, 307; used in same way by sacred and secular authority, 286
Guilt and shame, alleviated only through communication, 307
Gulliver, L., Swift's hero of *Gulliver's Travels* on man's pride, 389, 410

Habenstein, R. W. and Lamers, W. M., 368n
Hamlet, 344, 431; as cultural fact, 431
Handicaps, and equality, 338
Hanfstaengl, E., 249n
Hans Castorp, 310
Harrison, J., 373
Harvard Laboratory of Social Relations, 105n
Haskins, F., 111
Hate, 132, 272, 298; among equals expressed in competition and rivalry, 343; and confrontation, 283; control of depends on communication, 282; failure to consider in social theory, 137n; as "grace" among Nazis, 238; man as only sociable beast of prey, 413; of real audience and love of imaginary audience, 306; riddance through expression as in art, 344; sanction of by audience, 344; as symbolic, 344
Hatred: expected among superiors and inferiors, 343; of self, 344
Hawthorne, N., 309, 376
Haymarket anarchists, 317
Hazlitt, W., 405n
Hearst, W. R., 365
Hegel: Absolute Idea in, 186; common use of his way of thinking, 186; and Marx on ideas and the possibility of combining their views on images of ideas, 203
Hells, as symbolic, 344
Heracles, 402
Hermit, as "beyond" communication, 165
Hero, rules by divine spirit, 194
Heroes, as gods, prophets, poets, priests, men of letters, and kings in Carlyle, 200n
Heroism, must be displayed, 233
Herrick, R., 111
Hierarchal appeals, 288
Hierarchal euphoria, 122
Hierarchal failures, 303
Hierarchal form, as social ladder, 116
Hierarchal glamor, 136n
Hierarchal identification, 273
Hierarchal imagery, as development from one order to another, 157

Hierarchal motive, not prestige alone, 123
Hierarchal order, as developmental order, 122
Hierarchal pantomime, 273
Hierarchal passage, 157
Hierarchal positions, change in common to all societies, 271
Hierarchal principle, must work downwards as well as upwards, 203
Hierarchal psychosis, 122, 132
Hierarchal relations, as obsequious pantomime, 206
Hierarchal roles, as form of hierarchical address, Intro. 11
Hierarchal ultimates: codification of, 436; types of, 122
Hierarchical rhetoric, as expressed in community drama, Intro. 4
Hierarchies: produce guilt, 286; their rise and fall, 255
Hierarchy: based on money, 286; and bureaucracy, 124; channels in, 132; dangers of rigidity in, 294; as a development, 255; entelechial tendency in, 255; and exclusiveness, 255; as fate, 394; function of as guarantor of social order, 116; grounded in mystery, 436; ideal when superiors commands are inferior's duty, 284; and identification, 121; image of as geometrical staircase as image of hierarchy, 123; and metaphor, 136n; and mystification, 134; perfects itself through progression to a "god-term," 134; power of negation in, 425; principle of not exclusive, 255; principle of shared by all, 286; as a progression, 122; as progression from a lower to a higher stage, 323; stages and plateaus in, 122; strange power of, 134; as superiors, inferiors, and equals, 253; in systematic thought, 136n; and undue acquiescence, 132; in which men will continue to grovel and cringe, 206
High society, and poetry of sociation, 334
Hilton, W., *The Ladder of Perfection*, 254
Himmler, H., 134
Hindu, belief that money negates spirit, 258
Hindus, 335
Historical change, as changes in sociological forms in Simmel's view, 19
Historical time, as dramatic time, 152n
History: German need of, 235; as a goal, 434; as interpretation of the present in Mead, 83
Hitler, A., 134, 176n, 182, 342, 346n, 401, 438; on action, 236; admiration for Marx-

Hitler, A. (*Cont'd*)
ist agitators, 237n; application of religious forms to a political context, 238; "de-Germanizing" the German Jew, 401; denial of economic forces as power in community, 240; disbelief of authority among equals, 10; and dramatic form of man appeal, 235; and German guilt, 307; his human slaughter houses, 126; identification with ultimates, 242; image of authority 239; last audience, 245; as messenger of God, 242; need for war, 342; personification of evil in the Jew, 240; power as orator, 225, 245; techniques used by, 246; torture and death camps, 416n; use of enemy without, 342; use of the Jew as enemy, 401; use of Jew as "ideal" victim, 395; use of Jew as scapegoat, 287; use of speciously perfect victim, 129; use of total scapegoat as community catharsis, 129; witchcraft of, 246
Hobbes, on covenants, 284
Holabird, W., 111
Hollywood, 342
Homer, 222
Honor, 425; community dependence on, 240; as family honor in *La Traviata*, 423; as loyalty to a code, 335
Hope, Bob, 188n; 377
Horror, 289
Hostility, 330; expression of and subjection to audience, 330; in jokes, 427; social as well as sexual in courtship, 305
House of Mirth, 366
Howe, E. W., 111, 363
Howells, W. D., 111
Huckleberry Finn, 195, 291, 382, 383, 393, 394, 401, 407, 413, 414, 416n; and the American conscience, 415; and tribal guilt, 121
Hughes, E. C., 33n
Hull House, 91n
Humanity, depends on responses of other human beings, 297
Humanist: his heroes, 323; and priest, 323
Hume, D., 197, 337; on action, 104; on paradox of neutral vocabulary, 179
Humility: as bid for preferment, 197; as mask of pride, 197; as promise of power, 254; as sign of strength, 278; as way to perfection in authoritarian orders, 254
Humor: and adaptation in concentration camps, 408; based on differences, 256; as a bridge, 257; cannot exist when hierarchy too rigid, 256; child's difficulties in use of,

Humor (*Cont'd*)
333; emergence of Negro jokes about whites, 270n; failure to consider humor in anthropological accounts of tribal life, 32n; as form of passage, 257; keeps passage open in society, 258; Negro as inferior who confesses his faults in jokes, 256; over money from view of the rich in American television, 377; in play, 330; plutocratic humor, 377; as weapon of mind in struggle for preservation, 408
Hurstwood, and Drouet as "gentlemen," 365
Hysteria: in communication, 174n; restores original meaning of words in Freudian theory, 4; as result of poor communication, 304; as a rhetoric, 167

"I," internalization of, 288
Idea, as creative principle, 185
Idealism, as doctrine of ends and spirit, 124
"Ideal" criminal, 340
Ideal others, 298
Ideas: appeal of narrow ideas, 231; as "pure" manifestations, 186
Identification, 99, 161, 169, 438; and consubstantiality, 159; as deep communion, 170; dependent on objectification through communication, 112; extra-symbolic roots of, 160; not same as identical, 158; as obtained through property, 169; as persuasion, 169; in rhetoric, 154, 158; of ruler and ruled, 217; in social drama of guilt, redemption, hierarchy and victimage, 436; as source of cooperation, 164n; in strife, 158; symbols of, 275; through popular art, 86; and unconscious rhetorical motives, 162
Identity: changes in, 309; as mystical moment of belonging, 112
Ideologies: as motivation, 186; and social relations, 184
Ideologist, Burke's use of as methodological fiction, 185
Ideology: Burke's seven variants of, 182; as illusion, 188; as sociology and rhetoric in Marx, 182
Ideology and Utopia, 189n
Idolaters, 222
Ill-luck, as penalty of folly, 222
Imagery: of end and its effect on formation of attitudes, 144; function of in conduct, 87; of future organizes action in the present, 89; refers to past only to take us into future, 89

Images: of art are public, 283; as preliminary test of reorganized ends, 89; as real in communication, 89; of struggle in *Mein Kampf*, 243
Imagination, in art and dream not the same, 283
Imitation, 105n
Immigrant: in comedy, 398; in laughing at him we laugh at ourselves, 398; use in comedy as device to discuss native born American, 398
Impersonation, of plutocrat encouraged, 322
Incarnation, 324
Incongruities: and embarrassment, 307; must be borne by individual, 303
Incongruity, 198
Indifference, fear of, 300
Individual: sacrifice of in "block universe" feared by James, 75; and society contrasted in European and American social thought, 73
Individuality: and fashion, 273; as realm of spontaneity, 273
Individuals, as audience to each other, 297
Inequalities, do not create social disorder, 309
Inequality, mystifications in as described in *Sartor Resartus* and *The German Ideology*, 193
Inference, 145; high degree of in social studies, 144
Inferior: basis of submission, 284; fears threat to superior, 343; his sin as churlishness, 394
Inferiority, among peers, 336
Inferiors: and how superiors uphold dignity, 254; rejection of superiors' privileges, 204; use of irony, 198
Initiatory rites, 259
Inner contradiction, 286
Inner conversations, 310
Institutions, 309; compete for loyalty of individual, 303; a functional typology of, 113; make contradictory appeals to individual, 303; must define sins, 284
Instrumentalism, not a theory based on quantification, Intro., 5
Intellectuals: 272, as bound to ruling class, 183; separation from workers, 182
Interaction: between self and society, 73; dilemmas in use of as a category in social theory in Simmel and Freud, 30; language as data of, 73; Simmel on, 19
Interconnectedness of terms, in context of expression, 433

Interests, as content of interaction in Simmel's theory of forms, 18

Intolerance, as basis for social movement, 247

Introspection, as a genuine observation of genuine events, 75

Invocation, of principles of order, 292

Iolanthe, 404, 413

Ironic actor, as audience to others and to himself, 381

Ironic clown: and audience of equals, 386; his social office, 387

Ironic hero, 387; does not reject authority, 382

Irony: air of detachment in, 385; as comedy of reason, 386; comic means of question, 386; complicity with audience in ironic address, 384; as double-edged, 201n; double-talk in, 384; as doubt, 380; as enduring what we cannot, or will not change, 380; Hitler's use of against burghers, 237n; holds belief open to doubt, 381; as increased self-consciousness, 386; and inferiors and superiors, 385; keeps society open to change through reason, 385; as kind of complicity, 385; like arbitration, 385; not "debunking," 385; as prim, 198; and rhetoric, 194; social function of, 380; superiority of detachment, 386

Isolated man, 85

Isolde, 421

Israelites, 402

James, H., 201n, 365, 366

James, W., 49, 149; on "Chicago School of Thought" in 1903, 91n; final position on mental structure, 54; pragmatic approach to religious expression, 52

Jargon: in science, 174n; in sociology, 174n

Jazz, 400

Jefferson, T., 282; on umpirage as central to justice, 329

Jesus: as an executive, 363; as founder of modern business, 364; as Great Advertiser, 363; as "he-man," 363; as national advertiser, 364; success based on advertising, 364; teachings and sales management, 363; would not neglect marketplace, 364

Jew, as symbol of money and degradation in Wharton's writings, 366

Jewish humor, as folk humor, 391n

Jews, as ritually perfect victim, 125

"Jitterbug" dancing, 427

Job, 287, 402

John of Damascus, 196

Joke, and group sanction, 330

Jokes: form of joke, not its "sexual root," determines success or failure, 11; and social euphoria, 404; use to outwit censor through appeal to audience, 11

Jokes and Their Relation to the Unconscious, 166

Joking: not treated by Malinowski, 42; and sociation in play, 330

Joking relationships, Radcliffe-Brown's treatment of as "permitted disrespect," 46n

Jones, E., 352, 431; on nightmare, 289

Jones, J., *From Here to Eternity*, 426

Josh Billings, 400

Judge: as personification of justice, 293; as umpire, 317

Julius Caesar, 291

Jung, C. G., 50

Jury, as an audience, 293

Kafka, F., 196, 199; hierarchal themes as mystery, 195, satire on Celestial Hierarchy, 196

Kant, 134; and Burke's dramatism, 151n

Kautsky, B., 408

Kennedy, J., 175n

Killing: as Divine Will, 227; images of, 158

Killing Jews, as Divine Will and law of nature in Hitler's *Mein Kampf*, 227

Kings: as philosophers who must act, 323; prefer honor for person not office, 221

Kingship: "divinity doth hedge a king," 278; enactment of, 264; principle of in courtship, 208; principle of at Versailles, 268

Kirkegaard, S., 425

Kluckhohn, C., 148, 175n; on personal documents, 152n

Knight of the Garter, 277

Kogan, E., 408; *The Theory and Practice of Hell: The German Concentration Camps and the System Behind Them*, 415n

La Boheme, and aesthetic mystery, 423

Labor, absence of delight in among modern workers, 84

Lady, of Boston and New England, 394

La Fontaine's *Fables*, 397

Language: as action, 172; as address, 155; as critical moment in action, 147; as de-

Language (*Cont'd*)
terminant of social order in Mead and Burke, 144; functions of, 138n; of gesture, 288; Hitler's use of for evil ends, 189n; of magic, 36; and the magic of gardening and food, 37; magical and ritual uses of, 35; Malinowski's reduction to tribal and collective aspects, 41; Malinowski's sacred-secular dichotomy, 43; as mode of action, 34; not to be considered as a benighted kind of prescientific magic, 168; persuasive aspects of, 155; as poetic, 168; as poetic, scientific, and rhetorical, 168; and real others, 283; referent theory of Malinowski neglects referent of symbolic context, 44; as rhetorical, 168; as sacred communication, 114; of sexual courtship, 195; and social change, 42; as a social fact, 144; as social instrument in Dewey, 56; and social organization, 37; and society as parallel not interactive, 43; and technology, 168; transforms life, 147; as triadic interaction, 59; various referents of, 44; and various systems of social thought, 144

La Rochefoucauld, 174, 199, 204, 337, 343, 348, 380, 386, 390, 397, 402, 407, 412, 416n

La Traviata, 423

Laughter: banishes loneliness and alienation, 389; banishes mystery, 333; clarifies where tragedy mystifies, 388; as a confession, 403; and conviction, 411; to create social energy, 404; at danger, 404; danger of laughter when we should be fearful, 412; as derision, mockery, and the grotesque is not comic laughter, 404; dispels subjective concern, 331; and fear do not mix, 388; fends off tragic victimage, 404; as means to break down barriers, 305; at mystery of love, 305; over parvenus, 377; and purgation, 395; rare in dreams, 404; sacred laughter of the people's fool, 387; as scourge of pride, 403; at virtue, 411

Law: majesty of humbles all, 275; as transcendent in American society, 317

Laws, human interaction as a manifestation of laws, 54

Lawyers, 259

Leader: absolute power over inferiors yet vested in ideal of brotherhood, 239; used for vicarious atonement, 239

Leaders, responsibility to "Divine Will," 238

Leadership, must be personal, 247

Leadership principle, 328; among Nazis, 238

Lear, 280

Legitimation, 315

Levin, M., on anti-Semitism in a nudist camp, 425

Lewis, S., 111, 378

Liberal arts, and stylistic identification, 161

Life, as a battle, 226

Lillie, B., 426

Lily Bart, 366

Lincoln-Douglas debates, 259

Linguistic experience, of man in society, 436

Linkage of physical and moral uncleanliness by Hitler, 241

Linkage of symbols between Christianity and the family, 320

Linton, R.: confused use of Mead's role concept, 106n; on role and status, 96; on functioning of societies, 97; role-concept mechanical, not dramatic, 98

Lipps, T., Mead on *Einfuhlung*, 98

Literary critics, use of anthropological studies of language as magic, 167

Literature: common source of hysteria and linguistic symbols in Freudian theory, 4; as equipment for living, 109; as magical art in *Language and Literature in Society*, 120; as precursor of change in society in Dewey, Intro. 6; as public, 283; as ritual and magic, 156

Loneliness, as unrequited need for response, 279

Lord Acton, 346n

Lorimer, H., 111

Lotze, R. H., on problem of symbolic interaction, Intro. 8

Louis XIV: beyond criticism, 397; on filling an office, 335; as skilled actor of manners, 267

Love, 421; between masters and servants as comic, 417; and communication, 158; democratization as vulgarization in aristocratic view, 417; as friendly and joyous, 422; as inferior to friendship, 211n; as joy, light, laughter, and companionship in Mozart, 420; La Rochefoucauld's *Maxims* on, 209, 211n; and the mind in Casanova, 422; purification of, 279; in rhetorical expression, 158; as satisfaction of curiosity in Casanova, 422; vices of in Casanova, 422

Love and Hate, as expressed in community life, 235

Loyal opposition, in democracy, 139n

Luther, M., 374; *Table-Talk*, 405n

Lutherans, 350

Luxury, 349; as evil, 349
Lysander, 402
Lysistrata, 296

McCarthy, Senator Joseph, 317, 325n
Machiavelli, 174, 204, 212; as comic artist, 213
Machine, Mead's approval of art based on technology, 85
Macnish, R., 289
Madison Avenue apologists, 357n
Madmen, fearful because they are beyond communication, 391n
Mae West, satire on the plutocratic lady, 427
Magic: black as well as white based on yearning for unity, 246; compared with language of childhood, 39; confusion with art, 175n; efficacy of, 318; efficacy in how spells are uttered, 137n; of hierarchy, 122; as imputation to things of cultural forces, 60; as inducement to motion in things compared with language as inducement to action of human beings, 168; organizing function of, 40; and realism, 155; as rhetoric, 167; use of in linkage between sex and status, 419; white as well as black, 134
The Magic Mountain, 310
Magical rites, application, not genesis, concerns pre-literates, 38
Magical spell, as social drama, 38
Magician, relation to audience, 40
Majesty, determined by control of expression, 222
Majority, as voice of God, 346n
Malinowski, B., 338; concept of social charter, 50; lack of inquiry into failure and conflict in tribal society, 70n; neglect of form in theory of language, 44; on religious bond as social bond in *Magic, Science, and Religion*, selected and with an Introduction by Robert Redfield (Glencoe, Ill.: The Free Press, 1951), Intro. 7, Theory of the Social Context of Magical Language, 34–46 *passim*
Man: as related to nature in science, 54; as symbol using animal, 129
Mandarins: public staging of themselves, 276; skill in humanities, 333
Mandeville, Bernard de, 347, 348, 354, 357n; on pride as basis of society, 354
Mandragola, Machiavelli's comedy as great Italian comedy, 213

Manners, 273, 390; anger at bad manners, 267; art of, 269; as cult of oneself, 268; as daily language of hierarchy, 266; deification of by dandies, 268; differences between manners and ritual, 266; as dramatization of self, 266; efficiency of, 269; gentleman as arbiter of, 273; gods of in form of dandy, 268; as "grace" of hierarchy, 379; as indication, 266; like fashion manners keep society open to change, 268; for manners' sake, 329; as a plea, 273; not ritual, 134; as ritual, 132, 268, 378; ritual manners as hierarchal prayer, 378; as social mystification, 269; and social order, 266; and spontaneity, 273; as standards of good form in every group, 267; as used against outsider, 278; as used for power, 329; as weapon in hierarchal struggle, 266
Mannheim, K., 116; *Ideology and Utopia*, 51; on social function of symbols, Intro. 2
The Man Nobody Knows: A Discovery of the Real Jesus, 363
Mardi Gras, 404
Mario and the Magician, 291
Mark Twain, 376, 382, 384, 389, 406, 409; bitterness at lack of recognition by American universities, 376; on irrelevance of the genteel tradition to frontier life, 393; "ordeal" of social as well as sexual, 394
Market, as personified through symbols, 347
Market laws, 355
Market relationships, in city, 353
Martyrdom, 292
Marx and Engels, 182
Marx, Groucho, 378
Marx, K., 109, 134, 174, 347, 350; and social action, 181; use of principle of division, 187
Marxism: as analytic tool, 184; and gigantic mass meetings, 228; rhetoric and dialectic in, 181; as rhetorical critique, 185
Masks, often become real, 208
Masochism: Freud's "moral" and Reik's "social" definitions of, 417; as substitution of self for authority, 417
Masochist: attempts to communicate, 279; and communication, 308
Mass, as holy drama, 146
Mass audience: as characteristic modern audience, 176n; and spoken word, 226
Mass audiences, must believe their speaker and party will fight to the death, 233
Mass communication: not study of symbolic

Mass communication (*Cont'd*)
interaction, 149; study of in American sociology, 149

Mass demonstrations, and group integration, 228

Masses: cannot understand arbitration according to Hitler, 230; must be dominated not courted, according to Hitler, 231; never neutral, and do not understand neutrality, according to Hitler, 231; not objective, 230; small capacity for thought, 229; stirred only by vigorous expression of extremes, 229

Mass meeting: as drama of struggle between good and evil, 229; must be thought of as wrestling bout, 233; as political drama, 226

Mass meetings: breaks down isolation, 228; as hypnotic, 234

Mass oratory, not appeal to reason, 232

Mass propaganda: must aim in one direction only, 230; must be primitive, 230

Mass symbols, easily communicated in American society, 277

Maxims, of La Rochefoucauld, 204

Mead, G. H., 104, 149, 163n, 338, 345n; absolutes in, 102; acknowledgment of his debt to Dewey's *Experience and Nature,* Intro. 15n; on animal communication by gesture, 288; basic image of role not dramatic, 98; benign "generalized other," 102; communication and the emergence of the self in the work of George Herbert Mead, 73–81 *passim;* conversation as basic image of thought, 101; failure to construct model of symbolic interaction, 94, 103; failure to develop image of art, 104; "I" and "Me," 102; illustrates but does not demonstrate, 101; knowledge as a good, 103; lack of tragic sense of life, 91n; neglect of form in symbolic action, 101; neglect of form in treatment of address in communication, 100; *The Philosophy of the Present,* 89; play, games, and drama as forms of the act, Intro. 5; rejection of mechanical models of sociation, 92; search for models of sociation in art, Intro. 5; self originates in nature and art, 104; theory of address as dialogue between the "I," the "Me," and "They," 14; theory of significant symbol and problem of form, 92–106 *passim;* value as consummatory imagery, 93; world of benign others, 102

Meaning: always social, 300; arises in relatedness, 301n; as potentiality in action,

Meaning (*Cont'd*)
60; as public, 59; as response of other, 77, 299; social meaning precedes individual, 77; as universal, 77; of words derived from bodily experience, 38

Meaning of symbols, in Freud and Simmel, 33n

Meanings: as modes of interaction, 60; scientific meanings compared with esthetic and affectional, 60; as symbolic or analogical, 433

Means, in conduct, 214

Mecca, 247

"Mechanising the world," Carlyle's critique of Bentham, 200n

Medieval Lords and Abbots of Misrule, 378

Mein Kampf, 225; as book of death, 225; as caricature of religious communication, 238; as manual for self-righteous killers, 226; as Nazi Bible, 239; as perversion of religious communication, 238; as political allegory, 241

Melodrama, in Hitler's speeches, 243

Memoirs of Casanova, 423

Mencken, H. L., 325n

Mental maladies, source in inability to communicate hate, 282

Meredith, G., belief that laughter exposed worst excesses of hierarchy, 406

Merton, R. K., 153n

Method: address and socialization, 298; as analysis of identification of symbols with judgment of status, 164n; architecture as clue to hierarchy, 295; Aristotle and Burke on the elements of the symbolic act, 176n; in Burke's analysis of language, 143; Burke's technique of "indexing," 163n; common fault of ascription and derivation in sociology, 145; confusion of empiric with mechanical, 149; dramatic structure of relationship between speaker and audience, 304; and education, 135; failure of anthropological concepts to deal with symbolic aspects of communication, 148; false use of "psychology of the audience," 291; hate and love define each other, 343; used for humane purposes in Burke's work, 158; moral ground for dramatistic method, 143; need to define social properties of form, 375; need for synthesis, 120; objective difference in naming, 156; pairing opposing rhetorics, 201n; pairing opposites, 136n; and problem of irrelevancy, 139n; socio-anagogic technique of symbolic analysis, 152n, 159; structure of

Method (*Cont'd*)
relationship between actor and his audience, 292; styles of address as clues to authority, 291; symbols used to resolve community crises, 319; systematic development of, 147; thematic analysis, 156; as a value in *A Grammar of Motives* or *A Rhetoric of Motives*, 135; value of emphasis on autonomous fields, 164n

Methodists, 349, 350

Middle Ages, rhetoricians in, 204

Middle position, lack of in Hitler, 243

Mies van der Rohe, L., 111

Miller, H., 130

Mills, C. W.: on art as inferior sociology, 175n; on the image of man in society, Intro. 3; on knowledge of events in society, Intro. 2; neglect of art and communication in *The Sociological Imagination*, Intro. 14n

Milton, J., 155, 156, 163n, 374

Mind: as explained by mechanical model in Freud, 8; as organ of symbol-using animal, 203; social process theory of mind disregards individual, 31

Mirth, as a good in Spinoza, 403

Miscegenation, 424

Moby Dick, 195

Model of sociation: based on communication as rhetoric, 187; in communication, 92; as forms of thought in communication, Intro. 2; Mead's search for in communication theory, 93; of symbolic interaction, 94

Modesty, as communication, 331

Molière, 376, 393, 397, 398, 403, 417, 422; *Le Bourgeois Gentilhomme*, 379; comic villains those who destroy social bond, 422

Monadnock Building of Chicago, 367

Monastery, and worldly communication, 217

Money, 352, 389, 437; amassing of wealth as biologically determined through anal eroticism, 351; American identifications in, 364; as anal currency, 352; and anonymity, 353; and architecture, 367; attacked by popular comic artists, 378; and belief in unlimited good, 356; can be circulated easily, 353; and combination of heterogeneous things, 353; and commercial magic, 356; and communication of respect for the dead, 362; as counter in social game, 332; creates effects at a distance, 353; as credit in America, 380; as democratic symbol of hierarchy, 332; destroys the past, 354; dignification of, 364; dignification of by gilded age families, 364;

Money (*Cont'd*)
and drama of passage, 367; drive to amass wealth as instinctive, 353; as embodiment of spirit in American life, 258; as end in itself in American society, 347; establishment of as a symbol of community life, 347–357 *passim;* and eternal damnation, 349; expression of value in, 350; its fetishistic character in Marxism, 350; as a Form of Transcendence in American Life, 358–369 *passim;* Freudian symbol of, 351; as futuristic, 354; giving money away as Christian duty, 349; as glorification of God, 350; as goad, 286; as great leveler, 353; as highly abstract, 353; and hunger, 193; incompatible with emotional ties, 353; infuses life with calculation, 353; infusion of with sacred social values, 360; and "instinct of workmanship," 354; investment with glory by artist, 322; lack of glamor in deficit financing, 355; laughs out loud in television, 377; loss of symbolized as property loss, 348; makes present abstract, 354; Marx's attacks on mystifications of, 198; as a means of communication, 347; as means to enslavement, 357n; means nothing in itself, 347; as means of obtaining transitory and easily changed relationships, 352; as means to public staging of self, 332; as means to social integration, 355; "money talks" in America, 352; must "work," 354; mystery of as force in *Sister Carrie*, 366; and natural science, 354; as neutral, 180; as "objective symbol" in Marxism, 184; and orgiastic future, 367; parsimony and avarice as anal characteristics, 351; as "pecuniary canon" of taste, 200; and personal cultivation, 332; and plutocratic splendor, 276; and power to command, 351; power as self-regulating, 363; power as symbol, 180; as purely rhetorical in Marx, 183; purely social use of in gambling, 336; as purely symbolic, 200, 347; purgation of, 265; and quantification in science and life, 354; and reduction of individuality, 353; reduction of its mystery in Veblen's comedy and irony, 355; religion of, 362; as reward for struggle against sloth, 362; rhetorical as well as economic, 201n; risk of brings glory, 362; and schools, 355; and sex in Fitzgerald, 367; as a social hieroglyph in Marx, 350; as social identification, 168; and social offices in plutocracy, 379; and social order, 351; as social power in New

Money (*Cont'd*)

York, 366; social rhetoric of, 350; social rhetoric of in Simmel and Veblen, 353; as social symbol in Marx's critique, 183; specific qualities of, 353; and spiritualization of goods and services, 348; spiritualization of through linkage with Christmas, 358; as stewardship in Wesley's teachings, 349; surrender of New York society to, 366; as symbol of community development, 356; as symbol of equality and inequality, 347; as symbol of the feces, 352; as symbol of God, 363; as symbol of justice, 347; as symbol of pleasure, 352; symbolic meanings of, 352; its symbolic power, 348; symbolic significance of, 352; and symbols, 116; symbols of exchange as symbols for human relationships, 355; as transcendental term, 347; transformation of from symbol of evil to good, 348; transformation of into a social bond, 347; and triumph of labor, 350; value, 353; and vicarious identification, 200; wonder and glory of, 355; at work, 188n

"Money game," 367

Monopoly of communication, 304

Montaigne, 337

Montgomerie, A., 345n

More, Sir Thomas, 323, 365

Morgan, J. P., 364, 365

Morgan partners as public seers, 363

Mortification: 130; concern with form in enactment of, 395; as excess of principle, 130; and freeing spiritual energy, 130; and guilt, 306; many variants of, 130; in religion, 130; as "rudeness" against self, 362; social effects of, 130; as systematized way of denial, 395

Motivation, Burke's grammar of, 150

Motive: as categorical, 131; context of, 156; as personal, 131

Motives: community and personal, 396; effect not cause of symbols, 236; formal ways of talking about, 188; internalization of, 167; proper study of not how we discharge feelings but how we express them, 12; as symbols, 115

Mounting devices in Hitler's *Mein Kampf*, 242

Mozart, W. A., 134, 139n, 376, 389, 403, 420, 421; love themes not charged with mystery of romantic love, 420; pits aristocratic pride against passion as in *Figaro*, 420

Mynheer Peeperkorn, of *The Magic Mountain* as the European plutocrat, 366

Mysteries, of class, 117

Mystery, 387; in academic life, 133; of aristocratic honor in Racine's drama, 422; based on unknown, 218; of bureaucracy in Kafka, 196; of clothes, 193; in communion, 121; cultivation of, 223n; of death, 360; of the fetishistic character of commodities in Marx, 183; function of in society, 116; in hierarchy, 118; how to create an air of, 218; increases glamor of hierarchy but also increases difficulties in communication, 305; maximization of symbols of, 323; of money linked with death, 361; as organizing principle, 323; as political glamor, 119; priestly stress on, 117; as prior to its dramatization, 324; in rules and laws, 345n; of sex, 201n; as social, 117; as social bond, 120; source in difference and strangeness, 117

Mystification: American salvation depends on ability to think about mystifications of money, 357n; in Christian eschatology, 318; and class relationships, 193; of method, 324; in persuasion, 154; of ruling class, 184; in science, 134; as "social hieroglyphs" in Marx, 187; taught by God according to Gracian, 219

Mystifications, 324; of bourgeoise in Marx, 183; in love story, 195; Marx's use of religion for examples, 189n; need for doubt of them, 324; as "social hieroglyphics," 183

Myth of origin, as "representative case" of social order, 50

Myths, 258; aesthetic myths, 80n; apocalyptic myths, 319; Edenic, 114; function in society, 50

Names: as mystical power, 39; changing of always a risk, 260; as designation, 299; as goads to action, 431; not signs but evocations of principle of order, 320; and social control, 299; as symbols, 137n

Naming: as function of language, 163n; necessary to action in the present, 260

Narrative, as social and emotive, 35

Nature: as determined by form, 321; several uses of term, 316

Nature's perfection, in neo-behaviorism, 316

Nazi movement, of orators to mass publics, 245

Negation as order, 281

Negative, power of in communication, 281

Negro, white stereotypes in humor about Negro, 256

Neider, C., 391n

Neutral vocabulary: cannot communicate irrational and nonrational, 180; lack of incentive to act in, 179

Newcomb, T. M., 149; 153n

New Rhetoric, 167; 253; based on social function of language, 174; as combination of traditional rhetoric and anthropological study of communication, 167; emulation in, 199; as extension of traditional rhetoric, 176n; resolution of conflict through confrontation, 217

Newspaper, Chicago newspapers of 1870–1930 as creative force in art, 91n

New York, 366

The New Yorker, 377

Nicomachean Ethics, 175n

Nightmare, 290; inability to communicate in as cause of horror, 289

Nobleman, as public person, 332

No plays of Japan, 399

Oakeshott, W., on history as knowledge of present, 50

Obedience: based on reverence for principle on which authority rests, 326; as lending our will, 327; to rules, 326, 327; as surrender of will, 327

Obscene humor, brings reason to bear on unconscious, 409

Obscene jokes over women and money in America, 426

Obscene laughter, as means of survival, 408

Obscene wit, 404

Obscenity: brutalizes man so he can live among brutes, 408; compassion in use of in concentration camps, 409; in concentration camps, 408; as desanctification of evil, 407; as protective device, 408; as regression to primitive, 408; shifts from majesty to degradation, 410; of soldiers, 409, 410; used to reduce social glamor, 306

Odier, C., 352

Oedipus complex, 315; a dramatic, not mechanical, image, 7

Office: glory of must be kept alive, 276; makes the man, 275

Office party, as great leveler, 359

Official insignia, 277

Official Malefactor's Screen of Bentham, 188n

Ogden, C. K. and Richards, I. A., *The Meaning of Meaning*, 71n

Opera seria of Handel and Mozart, 419

Operational terms as mystifications, 324

Opponent, respect for in games, 284

Opposites, how they meet in sacred symbols, 315

Opposition: as loyal to principles we share in democracy, 284; range of images of from opposition as enemy to friend as in "loyal opposition," 345

Orators: effect on men's soul, 226; and great social movements, 236n; Nazi orators as "heralds of the idea," 231; should not discuss or argue according to Hitler, 226

Oratory: as art of attack, 231; explanations must be primitive for mass audiences, 232; and mass audience, Hitler's theory of, 232; and repetition, 232

Order, among "rights," 116

Order and disorder, how they define each other, 280

Organization of perspectives, 101

Original sin: as blood sin and desecration of the race in *Mein Kampf*, 226; as categorical guilt, 121; and disrelationships of social rank, 122; man's deification of self as cause of sin according to La Rochefoucauld, 209

Orwell, G., 136n

"Other woman," as colleague of husband in popular drama, 277

Ovid, 425; on the rhetoric of courtship, 212; on style and form of courtship in *The Art of Love*, 17n

Ownership, of jobs, offices, and ranks, 187

Pageantry: in academic life, 135; of social life, 264

Pain, social function of in iniatory rites, 259

Pantagruelists, belief in joy as social good, 399

Pantomime, and symbolic killing of enemy, 319

Panurge, 407

Panurge's Lady of Paris, 409

Paradise Lost, 283

Paradox, of evil, 403

Paranoid, 283

Pareto, V., 182, 223n

Paring of antithetical terms as methodological tool, 124

Paris, salon life in, 209, 338, 398

Park, reduction of Simmel's theory to social process without communication as a constituent category of interaction, 31

Park and Burgess: on communication as social process, Intro. 8; lack of theory of symbolic forms in their work, Intro. 15n; theory of communication as social force, Intro. 9

Parliamentary discussion: as discord in *Mein Kampf*, 243; maximizes conditions for criticism, 327

Parliaments, as voteless among Nazis, 239

Parody, as unconscious, 273

Parsons, T., 175n, 316, 325; dilemma in his mechanistic theory of interaction, Intro. 8; expressive symbolism and cathectic interests of the actor, Intro. 5; his discussion of symbolism in relation to action, Intro. 14n; and "Harvard mechanists," 93; lack of clarity in discussion on how symbols impose standards in his *The Social System* (Glencoe, Ill.: The Free Press, 1951), Intro. 15n

Party rallies of Nazis: staged like pilgrimages, 247; use of song, dance, marching, and cheering, 247

Parvenu, and social climbing, 254

Pascal, 174, 204

Passage: forms of in humor, 258; from sublime to common levels, 341; and hierarchy, 260; as reincarnation, and in the American way of life, 258

Passions, struggling to outwit reason in Freud and La Rochefoucauld, 416n

Past: as determinant of present and future, 50; false conception of its objectivity, 139n; must be ordered, 258; as object of consciousness, 255

Past and Present, 201n

Pasts, as goals, 434

Pasts and futures, as relevant or irrelevant to present, 260

Peasants, as symbols of Russia in Tolstoy, 424

Pecking order, 253

"Pecuniary canons of taste," 354

Pecuniary decency, 379

Pecuniary propriety, based on discontent, 356

Pegler, W., 325n

Peirce, C. S., 70n

People, new roles as citizens in *The Prince*, 216

People's Fool, 387

Perception: as an act, 88; and attitude toward stimulation in Mead, 88; problems in use of the eye as image for, 81n; visual, not inward, 86

Perfect act, a fiction, 180

Perfection of hierarchy, and social mystification, 321

Performance as prayer, 320

Perkins, G. W., 364

Personal charisma, types of, 317

Personality, 275

Personality principle, and strict hierarchy of superiors and inferiors, 238

Persuasion, 290; as choice, 170; and communication, 170; as generating principle in conduct, 172; various forms of as communication of social order, Intro. 3

Pfuetze, Paul E., *The Social Self* as critique of Mead, 106n

Philosopher, as "above" vile pantomime of aristocratic hierarchy, 206

Philosophie Des Geldes, 353

Physical object, not a thing, 99

Piaget, J., 345n

H.M.S. Pinafore, 255; choric comment in, 296

Pioneer mother, as sacred figure of the West in America, 394

Planners, who is to plan the planners?, 181

Plato, 337; *The Republic*, 283

Play, 256; among animals, 329; among equals subordinate to rules, 329; among gods and devils, 335; as clue to nature of social bond, 22; and equality, 328; and equals as at a party, 328; as freedom, 22; of the gods and creation of the world, 329; of mind and spirit, 331; not possible with superiors or inferiors, 328; and pleasure in contest, 335; and purely personal motives, 330; as random without rules, 78; recovery of humanity in, 336; re-creates social bonds, 335; refinement of, 332; and role playing in childhood, 95; rules of as self imposed, 336; of sociability, 29; and social euphoria, 337; social spirit of, 329; and sociation, 328; sociological function of, 334; and solidarity, 329; and subordination to the game, 329; symbolic significance of, 21; transcendence of individuality in, 330

Players: organic relatedness on team, 78; subordinate to rules, 335

Play-form, of sociation, 330

Play form of sociation, 336

Playfulness: and doubt and irony, 194; of manners, 269

Playing society: as in the art and play of coquetry, 25; the social function of the gentleman, 331

"Play the social game," 332

"Play with thy peer," 345n
Plutocrat, as "Lord's steward," 349
Plutocratic dramas, of buying and selling, 265
The Polish Peasant, Blumer's critique of, 149
Political action: determined by situation or scene, 215; as tragic ritual drama, 245
Political comedy, in *The Prince,* 213
Political conditions, as discussed in dramatic terms, 214
Political equality, 339
Political meeting, incitement to action not reflection among Nazis, 233
Political party, must have a world-view, 248
Political persuasion, principles of, 215
Political public, as audience, 212
Political rallies, as community drama, 293; various kinds of address in, 293
Politics: as a drama in Machiavelli, 214; as organization of conspiracy, 216
Pornography: directed to certain publics, 426; and forbidden social gratification, 426; as a political weapon, 425; sexual and social elements of, 425; social degradation and lust, 425
Port Royal, 422
Pose: in courtship, 205; in professional role, 273
Positivists, and their dogma, 74
Pragmatists, reconstruction in philosophy, 53
Prairie Houses of Frank Lloyd Wright, 384
Prayer, as rhetoric, 175n
Prejudgment in communication, 303
Present: as hypothetical, 299; as infused with future, 356; investment with consequences of future, 64; as locus of past and future, 88; locus of reality in act, 89; never determined by past or future, 299; in relation of past and future, 260
Presentation of the self to others, 266
Prestige, must be given, 378
Pride: as social motive, 174n; as source of society, 348
The Prince: as administrative rhetoric, 212; as community drama, 215; dramatic structure in, 215; early chapters of, 215; views on, 212
Principle of leadership, 134
Principle of order, as determined by means, 318
Prisoner: as actor in purge trials, 342; in public recantation functions like martyr, 306
Private fantasy, 283
Private life, made public by picture window, 277
"Private vices become public virtues," 348

Problem of evil, 285, 287
Problems, and naming, 299
Professional role, social presentation in, 273
Projection, 283; and confrontation, 283; of staged self, 283
Promethean laughter, 404
Prometheus, 227
Proof: must be grounded in symbolic facts, 145; through symbolic interpretation, 431
Propaganda: Hitler's admiration for British propaganda used in World War I, 249n; as rhetorical, 231
Property: in biological sense, 115; and identification, 160; as symbolic, 116; as symbolic construction, 129
Prosecutor, as hero in public drama of confession, 341
Prostitute: as parody of plutocratic lady, 418; as sacred in Dostoevski, 417
Protestant ethic, failure to promote spending, 348
Proverbs: as categorized lore of human foibles, 147; as categories of social experience, 152n; intended to be used in action, 147; as names for typical and recurrent situations, 110; as public, 431; as strategies for dealing with situations, 110; sum up situations, 431
Psychical processes, as quantitatively determined in Freudian theory, 4; as subject to the laws of motion in Freud, 6
Psychology: James on its failure to produce theory of mental structure, 54; of the masses, 290; and rhetoric, 166
Psychology, of William James, 52
Public relations: as character assassination, 135; hierarchal "build up," 135; only one aspect of rhetoric, 172
Punishment: as a communication, 396; for disobedience, 284; must be symbolized, 341; as re-education, 285
Purgation: of social structure, 126; through killing, 127
Purge: and ambition, 335; of peerage, 335; as sacrifice of ritually perfect victim, 125
Purges, 341; create a permanent enemy within, 342; as dramatization of enemy cunning, 342; in Russia, 138n
Purification of German race, 134
Purim, 305
Puritan ethic, 354; shift from earning to spending, 355
Puritans, 309; only one side of American character, *Huckleberry Finn* the other, 376
Pygmalion, 413

Quantification as intrinsic value in modern life, 354
Quintillian, on rhetoric, 171

Rabelais, 130, 306, 388, 392n, 393, 399, 409
Rabelais and Molière, treatment of honor contrasted with that of Racine, 422
Rabelaisian comedy, Mark Twain's *1601*, 394
Race mixture: as rebellion against nature, 226; as sin, 226
Race problems, as symbolized in *Huckleberry Finn*, 311
Racine, 175n, 419, 422
Radcliffe-Brown, A. R., on social bond as religious bond in *The Andaman Islanders* (Cambridge: The University Press, 1922), Intro. 7
Rage: and audience, 308; as result of poor training in communication, 304; turned against the self, 308
Raleigh, Sir W., 409
Rameau's Nephew, in Kemp's edition, 211n
Ratner, on Dewey's *Art as Experience* as his most profound work, Intro. 5
Reality, originates in relationships, 299
Reason: of comedy is social reason, 406; in salon life as reason in society, 210; as social reason among Rabelais' Thelemites, 422; as study of how men relate, 210; as understanding in society, 209
Reason in society, 437; dependent on equality, 437
Red Cross, 359
Redemption, 125; 127; in community through victimage, 126; Nazi drama of, 240
Redfield, Robert, Intro. 14, 148
Red Skelton, 377
Referee, personifies rules, 336
Reichstag fire, 342
Reik, T., 417, 418
Reincarnation, 258
Relation, in communication, 300
Relationship, between self and other depends on social element, 300
Religion: comforts but also causes fear and anxiety, 285; as prime social bond, 337; as source of fetishistic character of symbols in Marx, 183
Religious bond and social bond, 138n
Religious experience: knowledge dependent on expression according to James, 55; problems in study of religion in society, 76

Religious expression: James' on digestive and respiratory metaphors in, 53; James' rejection of Freud's reduction to sexual imagery, 52; as a model for social expression in social theory, Intro. 7
Religious language, how it clothes itself in language in common use, 53
Religious life, and social life, 126
Religious myths: as community myths, 128; and method, 128; perverse use of, 128
Religious principle, fragmentation of, 192
Religious rites, 275
Religious ritual: personifies hate and love, 343; perverted in expression of sexual passion, 419
Religious symbolization and art, 375
Research, dependent on how things are named, 130
Resentment, 272
Reveries, common type in movies, 86
Rheingold, 236
Rhetoric: of acceptance of social hierarchy, 190; as address, 154; as address to self for moralistic or incantatory purposes, 166; as allegory, 241; of appeals to audiences, 295; and attitudes, 170; between speaker and audience as paradigm for relationship between individual and society, 165; Burke's summary of traditional evidences of rhetorical motive, 173; of Christian in the world, 217; commercial use of, 175n; and conflict, 158; designed for use, 165; as determined by character of audience and purpose of speaker, 171; and dialectic, 181; and force, 170; and goals in action, 169; of Hell in *Mein Kampf*, 235; of hierarchy, 280; Hitler's theory of, 225; and identification, 154, 155, 167, 169; as incomplete persuasion, 167; as inducement to incipient action (attitude) and fully developed act, 170; as inducement to social order, 155; as an Instrument of Domination Through Unreason in Hitler's *Mein Kampf*, 225–237 *passim;* and magic compared, 169; as manipulation of belief, 174n; Marxist, 181; as means to achieve reason through passion, 173; as means to decrease reason in Hitler's *Mein Kampf*, 176n; of money in Veblen, 200; of mystification, 187; no rhetoric beyond rhetoric, 181; and poetry, 170; in politics must be spoken, not written, 233; principles of, 155; priority of in social relations, 202; as privately addressed to self, 166; and proving opposites, 160; purpose of in *Mein Kamp*, 227; purpose of

Rhetoric (*Cont'd*)
in political action, 226; range of, 155; as sacred, 175n; of secular domination by devout Christian in Gracian's "The Art of Worldly Wisdom," 217–222 *passim;* of sexual courtship, 195; and social cohesion, 154; and social control, 171; and social order, 155; of social order, 165–176 *passim;* socio-psychological function of, 154; as summed up by Hitler, 244; three aspects of, 154; and Tower of Babel, 160; use in politics, law and education by classical orators, 171; as weapon of attack and instrument of analysis, 162

Rhetoric of hierarchy as rhetoric of courtship, 437

A Rhetoric of Motives as study of social order, 151

The Rhetoric of Ruling, 212

Rhetorical fallacies, Bentham's analysis of, 179

Rhetorical frame of reference, 214

Richardson, S., 417

Ridicule: makes us inferiors, not equals as in comedy, 405; as a weapon, 404

Rights: and conflict, 160; symbolic nature of, 116

Ring Lardner, 379, 400

Rites, of initiation, 302

Rites of passage, phases in, 259

Ritual, 373, 388; in education, 117; not all tragic, 405n; power of poem, 156

Ritual drama, 373; in feudal enactment of redemption, 126

Rituals of avoidance, 285

Rivalry: for control of highly communicable social symbols, 278; rules as social sanction of, 343

Roads, and public display, 271

Roche, M., 111

Roehm, E., 426

Róheim, G., 352

Role: art of playing inferior, 254; in community ceremony, 90; as dynamic aspect of status, 96; Linton's use of Mead on the game, 97; Mead's ambivalent use of term, 96; and renaming, 260; taken from drama, 96; taking role of other as highest capacity of man, 92; transfigurations in social passage, 257; as used by anthropologists, 96

Role of ruler as played in *The Prince,* 216

Roles: art means whereby we take role of others, 85; changes of, 288; as equals must be learned, 340; frequent changes in complex society, 260; and the "generalized

Roles (*Cont'd*)
other," 78; how to play them with equals must be learned in childhood, 304; as modes of social appeal, 112; official and individual, 298; presentation of as a form of hierarchy, 262; as public, 96; role-taking as determinant of child's development, 79; secularization of priestly role in our society, 322; as social offices, 96

Role-taking, 100, 102; as characteristic human act, 96; and the physical object, 98; problems in use of Mead's concept, 96

Roman people, 216

Roman Saturnalias, 378

Romantic love, Mozart's satire on in *Cosi Fan Tutte,* 420

Romantic love and Christianity, and the creation of new social types, 425

Romantic love, sadism and masochism in, 417

Rome, as mecca, 247

Romeo and Juliet, 344

Romulus, 216

Root, J. W., 111

Rossini, G., comic satire on aristocracy and their art, 420

Rule: by division, 339; through cooperation, 339

Rules, 256, 326, 336, 339, 343, 437; among equals, 327; among Shakers for perfect performance, 320; cannot be used for mystification, 335; children as jealous guardians of, 281; and containment of violence in play, games, and art, 343; corruption through ritual, 346n; as encouragement to rivalry, 343; as fixed and held, 77; of the game, 90; of judicial process and role of lawyer in, 317; as law, 327; less subject to mystification, 327; as principle of social order, 326; represent will of equals, 437; as sacred, 329; self-imposed in games, 329; and winning, 336

The Sabbat, 426

Sacher-Masoch, Leopold von, 425

Sacred, admits of little variation, 268

Sacred address, always to office not individual, 268

Sacred legitimation, as paradigm for all legitimation, 315

Sacred pasts, 319

Sacred symbols, as beyond discussion, 318

Sacrifice: as cleansing, 247; God's sacrifice of his only Son, 373; as holy death, 240; hu-

Sacrifice (*Cont'd*)
man sacrifice as means of social purification, 401
St. Francis, 216
St. Luke, on humility as way to power, 254
St. Matthew Passion, 375
Saint-Simon, 267
Saloon, as man's club, 428
The Salvation Army, 360
Samson Agonistes, 155; rhetorical and aesthetic analysis compared, 163n
Sancho Panzo, 198
Santa Claus: change in role, 358; feminization of, 358
Sapir, E., 148
Sartor Resartus, 193, 385
Satan, the "Grand Negation," 281
Satanic Church, 281
Satanic Mass, 426
Satire, "deadpan satire," 199
Satiric clown, makes us accomplices, 411
Saturnalia, as ritual reversal of rank, 258
Satyr plays, as sacred, 399
Scapegoat, 127, 257, 287, 287n, 340; dangers of disregarding, 127; as enemy, 127; as expression of rejection through exorcism of what we hate, 204; and fool compared, 394; and mortification, 395; need for codification of, 138n; petty types, 128; and principle of victimage, 127; secular use of, 129; stages in creation of, 401; as stranger, 211n; as symbolic victim, 137n
Scene-act, 435
Scene-agency, 435
Scene-agent, 435
Scene-purpose, 435
Scenes, change in during social passage, 261
Schilpp, Paul A., Intro. 5
Schizophrene, and negative communication, 282
Schjelderup-Ebbe, T., 345n
Schoenberner, F., 412; *Confessions of a European Intellectual,* 416n
Scholar, passion and mystery of, 323
Science, 404; false equation with quantification, 93; has no method for using data of art and religion as facts of experience, 74; and methodological truths, 345n; and mystification, 318, 324; need for new science to deal with symbolic data, 74; and scapegoat, 127; and symbols as signals, 155; transforms world into mathematics and the laboratory, 354; as an ultimate, 162; as a way of knowing, 74
Scientific method, 325n

Scientific realism, failure to deal with future, 169
"Scientism," failure to deal with language and art, 148
Scientist, and mystification of pure science, 324
Secretary of State, 363
Secular perversions of religious drama, 139n
Security, threats to, 128
Seduction, parody on by the Marx brothers, 427
Self, 104, 307, 403; born in discourse, 297, 299; born in expression, 299; and conflicting roles, 310; and conversation of gestures, 94; as emergent in communication, 76; four phases in development of in Mead, 94; and future, 104; as an island, 258; as locus of emergent and novel, 101; as object to self, 76; originates in dialogue between self and society, 292; originates in taking role of the other, 92; and other in communication, 78; and resolution of difference, 298; and role, 96; turning against the self, 308
Self-address, differs in art and day and night dreams, 292
Self-consciousness, how we attain it in Mead's theory of role-taking, 95
Self-hatred, cannot be expressed to superiors or inferiors, 344
Self-love, 386; becomes self-hate, 402; and clarity of reason, 402; destroys the self, 412; devotion to superiors as devotion to self, 207; La Rochefoucauld's *Maxims* on, 207; leads to hatred of self as well as of others, 402; much still unknown about it, 208; paradox of address among selves who love only the self, 208; as typified by courtship among aristocrats at court, 207
The Sense of the Past, 365
Sex: comic and tragic communication of, 421–428 *passim;* as dependent on forms of communication, 26; drama of as genial and social in Casanova, 422; as grotesque sacrificial act, 419; and hierarchy, 120; in life and art contrasted, 22; link with status, 118; mystical union of the woman, the land, and the state, 424; nude as symbol, 120; as a pantomime, 206; parodies on in the dance, 427; as plutocratic drama, 419; and social aggression, 426; and status in the "strip-tease," 418; symbolic torture in, 419; symbols of linked with national symbols, 424; versus aristocratic dignity,

Sex (*Cont'd*)
421; the woman as a thing, 426; woman as transcendent vessel of beauty, 424

Sex and hierarchy, 417; in art and society, 417

Sex and play, 306

Sex and status: social degradation and potency, 418; social superiority and potency, 418

Sex play, as group play in Casanova, 422

Sex relations, histrionic quality of in comedy, 211n

Sexual act: as authoritarian and predatory, 425; as a dramatic act in Casanova, 422

Sexual courtship, use of mystery in, 117

Sexual fantasies, social elements in, 425

Sexual inhibition, 425

Sexual modesty, 331

Sexual tension, and status embarrassment, 307

Shaftesbury, A. A. C., 33, 357

Shaker sects, 320

Shakespeare, W., 133, 138n, 175n, 376, 388, 403

Sharing hate and love, 343

Shaw, G. B., 393, 406, 413

Shils, E., 316, 325n

Shiva, as Nataraja, Lord of Dancers, King of Actors—an artist as god, 265

Shrine, as physical center in dramatization of community life, 246

Shylock, 133

Sick humor, 138n

Signal, and communication, 155

Significant form, as selection, 62

Significant others, 280; and authority, 283

Signs, must be invested with emotion to become symbols, 431

Simmel, G., 163n, 186, 353, 345n; search for an autonomous form of sociability, 18–33 *passim;* analogy of forms of sociation derived from art, Intro., 5; contribution to social theory of communication, 28; failure to create congruent relationship between structure and function in his model of sociation, 29; on Germany as home of Absolute Spirit in World War I, 189n; his contributions to a social theory of communication, 29; image of sociation spatial and mechanical, 30; on social function of symbols, Intro. 2; use of absolute, 186

Simplicissimus, 412

Sin, 285; as abandonment of reason in comedy, 389; of deviation among Communists, 286; as disobedience of authority, 113; of greed and emulation as way to

Sin (*Cont'd*)
grace in plutocratic community, 348; man sins but God does not, 286; not discussed with God, 397; original and actual, 131; paradox of, 403; passage of symbolic sin into actual sin, 396

Sinclair, Upton, 103

Sister Carrie, 365

Slaying, as a birth, 157

Sleep: as moment of passage, 261; passage struggle in, 261

Slogans, as means of communication, 275

Smith, W. Robertson, on social bond as religious bond in *Lectures on the Religion of the Semites* (Edinburgh: Black, 1889), Intro. 7

Sociability: based on hate, 208; demands subordination of personality to purely social forms, 23

Social action, action in time-space in Mead, 81n

Social bond: dependent on hate as well as love, 137n; as forged in community dramas, 436; must be described in terms of what goes on between individuals, 73; as ultimate value of love in Molière, 422

Social bonds, must be deeply interiorized among equals, 326

Social catharsis, in ceremonies of community origin, 263

Social classifications, as "natural" to social order, 204

Social climbers, common to all hierarchy, 254

Social cohesion: magic and glamor in, 170; through victimage, 125

Social conduct, as stimulation of self through assumed responses of others, 99

Social control: dependence on communication, 264; dependence on control of names, 281

Social courtship, and sexual courtship, 194

Social differences, spice of comedy, 407

Social differentiation, accentuation of by priesthood, 117

Social disorganization, as inability to communicate, 279

Social disrelationships, in Victorian art, 406

Social distance: in hierarchy, 268; makes role of the go-betweens important, 257

Social distinction, and mystery, 194

Social euphoria: necesssary to strengthen social bonds, 337; as result of community drama, 263

Social grace, 279

Social hierarchy: as communication of su-

Social hierarchy (*Cont'd*)
periority, inferiority, and equality, 253; as infusing all expression, 431
Social hieroglyphics, as mystifications, 183
Social interaction: Parsons and Bales on dimensions of action-space, 12; a sociological model of must be based on the communication of significant symbols, 431–438 *passim*
Socialization, as communication, 290
Social ladder, 278; Hindu and American compared, 258
Social mechanists, narrow range of observation, Intro. 7
Social mystification: Burke's analysis of in Bentham and Marx, 179–189 *passim*; need to understand if we are to survive, Intro. 12; and social integration, 190
Social object, 89
Social office, proverbs on, 105n
Social offices, 122
Social organization, 125
Social order, 135, 284; art as guardian of, 282; based on enrollment in many groups, 111; based on unreason: the perversion of religion by the state, 238–249 *passim*; as communication between superiors, inferiors, and equals and passage from one to the other, Intro. 4; in continual process of creation, 319; created, 259; defines itself through disorder, 281; and dependence of toleration on transcendent principles of order, 278; dependent on differences in rank and position, 267; and disorder, Intro. 13; as drama of guilt, redemption, hierarchy, and victimage, 238; as Drama of Redemption Through Victimage, 121–140 *passim*; as drama of social hierarchy, Intro. 10; as expressed in communication, Intro. 3; as form of hierarchy, 253–270 *passim*; and guilt, 129; as maintenance of principle, 284; ordinal, not cardinal, in progression, 124; as a resolution of struggle between superiors, inferiors, and equals, Intro., 11; the "social" considered as residual to sex, 424; social contexts as "referents," Intro. 3
Social passage, 257; cannot be done alone, 260; careful preparation in stages of, 261; in day and night dreams, 261; as drama, 261; fears of must be created yet assuaged, 260; many kinds of, 257; must be ceremonialized, 260; never easy, 260; and time, 258
Social pathology, of pride, 397

Social principles, purification of, 279
Social problems, must be personified, 247
Social process: as being with, for, and against each other in Simmel's theory, 23; as cause and effect, 102; likened to energy affects of atoms in Simmel, 18, 30
Social progression, 319, 320; ordinal not cardinal, 320
Social psychology, of play in Dewey, Mead, Simmel, and Burke, 340
Social Register, 255
Social role, in communication, Intro. 3
Social sciences, hidden use of humanistic studies, 174n
Social scientists, ignorance of basic tenets of rhetoric, 167
Social structure, and catharsis, 126
Social supremacy, dependent on wit, gaiety, and charm as well as rank, tradition, office, and linkage with supernatural, 268
Social symbols, intense rivalry for control of, 278
Social tension, and gaps in communication, 413
Social time, 354
Social transcendence, 315–325 *passim*; involves choice, 322; in Molière and Mozart, 422; types of, 315
Social utility, Bentham's principle of, 180
Sociation: as communication, Intro. 7; fundamental fact of is how men become objects to themselves, 76
Society: as determined by communication in Dewey's theory of art, 49–72 *passim*; as extempore work of art, 334; as pact between arrogant proud selves, 207; prior to "I," 101; as process, 104; as sacred, 345n; in a state of nakedness, 191
Society role, and other roles, 269
Socio-anagogic, 133
Sociological "facts," in history and politics, Intro. 2
Sociological grammar of the act, ratios among scene, act, agent, agency and purpose, 434
Sociological methodology, proportional propositions in, 118
Sociological theory, of social bond as authoritarian bond, 337
Sociologists, neglect of symbolic data by American sociologists, 93
Sociology: as a grammar of the forms of sociation, 18; as science of the structure and function of social interaction in Simmel, 20

Sociology of art, and general sociology, 438

Sociology of knowledge, 136n

Sociology of religion, 373

Sociology Today, neglect of symbolic experience in official contemporary sociological writing, 153n

Socrates, 272, 287, 323, 381, 407

Socratic discourse, 284

Socratic role, 335

Socratic Utopias, 323

Solidarity, 389; in hate and love, 280

Soliloquies, in *Huckleberry Finn*, 136n

Soliloquy, 310, 311, 381; as address by self in roles of others, 79; as attempt at "inner" resolution of voices from without in society, 310; characteristic of all social life, 310; conversational in form, 385; and disrelationships, 311; the "I" talking to its "Me," 292; as ironic, 382; as social, 58; social function of, 310; as taking roles of others toward the self, 382

Sorel, G., on role of myth in society, 51

Southey, R., 349

Sovereign power, woman as symbol of in sexual drama, 425

Soviet Russian Industry, 188

Spanish Inquisition, 343

The Spartans, 402

The Spectator, 223n

Speech: as social communion, 34; as a weapon, 226

Speeches to masses, best given when people are not too alert according to Hitler, 233

Spencer, H., 74

Spending: academic instruction in the art of genteel expenditure, 355; as act of service, 356; before we earn, 356; "canons of pecuniary decency" as reducible to principles of waste, futility, and ferocity in Veblen, 354; on clothes as necessary to symbolize hierarchy, 350; to communicate superiority, 347; and "conspicuous consumption," 354; creates value, 355; and death, 360; dignification of in American art, 364; as evil in Veblen, 354; expense and glamor in advertising, 357n; as giving out libido in Abraham's analysis, 351; as glory of money, 348; and hierarchal expression, 356; humor over awkward spender in *New Yorker*, 378; as mark of ambition, 356; Negro must be free to spend, 356; our way to beauty and to God, 367; as penance, 362; as prayer, 362; as prayer in the American Christmas, 358; private versus public, 379; as release from

Spending (*Cont'd*)
depression, 351; and reputability, 355; rights of adolescent as rights to spend, 356; and transcendence, 355; as transformation of libido, 351; to uphold prosperity, 356; and vicarious identification, 347

Spinoza, 403; on social function of joy, 392n

Spirit: in humanism, 161; as inhabitant of laboratory, 129; materialistic critique of, 188

The Spoils of Poynton, 365

Spontaneity, in manners, 273

SS officer, 326

Stage fright, and hierarchy, 270n

Stage revues, various kinds of address in by master of ceremonies, 293

Staging, of struggles as historical drama by Hitler, 244

Staging of appeals, to mass audiences, 229

Stalin, use of power of devil to enhance power of Communist gods, 342

Standard of living, public versus private among American businessmen, 277

State Department, 317

Status: as ascribed and achieved, 97; as position in a pattern, 97; relation between individual and status position, 97; and sexual frustration, 15; and transcendence, 323

Status changes, as moments of danger, 257

Status enactment: by child, 333; as a plea, Intro. 11

Status needs, in ceremony, 278

Status trappings, as communication of real and desired social position, 333

Stekel, W. *Patterns of Psychosexual Infantilism*, 260

Stendhal, 165

Stereotypes, 121

Stevenson, A., 175n

Streets, as stages for ceremony, 276

Streicher, J. use of the Jew as subject of pornography, 425

Structure: of act a dramatic structure, 433; of social action as dramatic plot, 146; of speaker-audience relationship, 290

Structure of the act: *Act* as the creative moment of community origin, 434; *Agency* as means, instruments, and ways of attaining ends, 434; *Agent* or actor, 433; *Purpose* as belief in social ends which sustain society, 434; *Scene* as the symbolization of time and place, 433

Veblen, T. (*Cont'd*)
mother of necessity, 32n; and ironic appeal, 198; on monastic real estate of University of Chicago, 140n; pretended objectivity, 199; on results of hierarchal psychosis, 140n; on rhetoric of identification, 161; stylistic devices in, 201n; on waste, 161
Verdi, G., 139n, 376, 389, 403
Versailles, 398; ritual in life of, 268
Vestments: capacity to inspire awe and wonder, 133; must be dramatized in action, 152n
Veterans of Foreign Wars, 360
"Vice of consistency," 257
Vices, satisfaction of as basis for society, 354
Victim: demands his own punishment, 400; fragmentation of, 125, 128; the Jew as "ideal" victim, 395; Jew as sacrificial victim, 342; ritual role of, 125; as ritually perfect, 125; sacrificial victim, like Jew in German, cannot recant but must be destroyed, 401; as total, 129
Victimage, 397; and absolute sacrifice, 125; among children, 333; and cleansing, 125; in comedy, 399; and failure in society, 125; in great community drama of Medieval Europe, 126; how it functions in society, 129; of Jews by Hitler, 127; Jew could not be used as public victim in Germany, 342; as natural means for achieving social cohesion, 127; not a religious illusion, 287; perfecting of, 131; psychogenic illness as form of, 396; in religious ritual, 114; and social catharsis in comedy, 395; the symbolization of the "perfect" victim, 395
Victims, Jews as total victims, 127; in public confession must play part well, 342; on television, 138n
Villain: as devil, 342; Hitler's inventions of, 243; must be powerful and cunning, 342; yearning to see him suffer, 397
Virgil, 175n
Virtue, dangers of excess in attacked in comedy, 414
Visual nature of dream, 288
Vogt, Von Ogden, 391n

Wagner, R.: contrasted with Mozart on treatment of love, 420; Hitler on, 236
Walden, 369n; as story of earning a world, 365
Wall Street, 363

War: as community victimage, 131; and guilt, 390, as inducement to cooperation, 163n; of words, 169, 182, 246
Ward, L., theory of teleological forces in *Dynamic Sociology*, 49
Warfare, as imagery, 131
Warner, W. L., 148, 153n, 175n, 262; comparison between his work and Middletown studies of Lynds, 270n; on Greek tragedy as a form of social logic in his work, *The Living and the Dead, a Study of the Symbolic Life of Americans*, Intro. 6; on social meaning of Yankee City ceremony, 263
Wars, holy wars fought to purify a social principle, 307
Warsaw ghetto, 346n
Washington Gridiron Dinner, as means for opening to reason the mystification of the President's office, 387
Waugh, E., on American funerals, 368n
Wealth, as a "trust," 368n
Weber, Max, 109, 126; on social bond as religious bond, Intro. 7
Weber and Fields, 400
Wesley, J., 349; on prolonged mourning, 414; on riches as destructive to religion, 349
Wharton, E., 201n, 366
Whig aristocrats, 333
Whorf, B. L., 148
Wilde, O., 413
Wilhelm Meister, 332
Winning, among equals, 338
Woman: as boss in America, 427, 428; as mother and wife in commercial art, 419
Words: as acts upon a scene, 109; as bridging two contexts, 432; as constituent part of community life, 41; as cultural facts, 431; sexual origin of in Freud, 6
Work, as punishment for sin, 349
Worship, as staged, 375
Wright, F. L., 111, 277, 367, 384; on art of the machine, 91n

Xanthias, 402

Yahoos, 382; 410
Yankee City, 263; changes in interpretation of charter, 270n; community drama of, 263
"You," in dialogue, 292

Ziegfeld, F., 417

Structure of bureaucracy, dependent on communication, 146
Structure and function, in bureaucratic relationships, 152n
Structures: people, not structures, act, 145
Struggle, and self-realization, 284
Style, 273; of appeal and judgment of right to social position, 273; as communication of ability to spend, 356; as identification; 112; kills past, 356; as social identification, 274; in staging of self as necessary to success, 221; a variation, not a theme, 273
Styles in caskets, 361
Stylistic subterfuges, 166
Sublimity: dangers of in communication, 341; and social distance, 341; strain of, 341
Submission, 272
Subterfuges of the dreamer, 8, 289
Suffering in comedy, 412
Suicide among children who kill the mother in effigy, 308
Sullivan, Louis H., 91n, 102, 106n, 111
Sumner, W. G., 50
Sumptuary laws, 353; absence of in American society, 322
Sunday newspaper, 139n
Superior who doubts in irony, 198
Superiority: the "heiress look," 419; paradox of, 279
Superiority and inferiority, 437
Superiors: cannot ask questions of inferiors, 393; dangers of too great use of sublimity, 341; and mysteries of hierarchy, 339
Superiors and inferiors, 299, 393
Superiors, inferiors, and equals, courtship among, 254
Swift, J., 376, 382, 388, 389, 393, 409, 410; satire on science as unsocial, 404
Symbolic and nonsymbolic in social thought, 145
Symbolic act: function of, 436; structure of, 433
Symbolic action: in art and society, 431; confusion in Mead's use of concept, 94; as dramatic action, 144; man's capacity to become object to himself is his distinctive human capacity, 81n; nature of in society, 114; need for general theory, 109; problem of how to study it, 93; problems in demonstration, 75
Symbolic analysis: and free society, 438; weakness of analogical thinking, 432
Symbolic behavior, and biology, 115

Symbolic boasting, as clue to identification, 112
Symbolic devices to "tell off" superiors, 194
Symbolic expression, creates social bonds, 265
Symbolic interaction: in Freud's work, 3–17 *passim;* as greatest clue to understanding of society, 76; need to show how this occurs in society, Intro. 7
Symbolic manipulation, 329; as value in itself, 318
Symbolic material, in case histories, interviews, and life histories, Intro. 4
Symbolic structures, religion and art, 104
Symbolic texts, need for case histories in sociology, 431
Symbolic veil, as intrinsic to human use of words, 203
Symbols: as clothes, 192; as condensation and displacement in the dream, 13; as directly observable data of sociation, Intro. 2; in drama as form of address, 14; as expression of racial heritage in Freud, 5; as hortatory, 155; laws of as prior to economic and political law, 202; means by which masses identify, 237n; as observable facts of social life, 93, 144; of past and future in recall, 234; problem in selection, 234; as a resolution of negative and positive, 41; as social data in James' work, 73; social function of, 431; tendency of to become refined and perfected, 133
Symbols of authority, 111
Symbols of sovereignty, 322, 424; furs in novels of Sacher-Masoch, 425; and mental power, 425; and sexual potency, 425
Symbols specialists, and ideologies, 182

Tact: and equality, 330; a purely social phenomenon, 23
Tactlessness: hatred of, 330; as intrusion of purely personal, 330
Taine, H., James' rejection of, 80n
Talk, as phatic communion, 35
Talleyrand-Périgord, Charles-Maurice, 428n
Taste: in communication of hierarchy, 331; ethical validity of taste as social expression, 333
Tawney, R. H., on religion in society, Intro., 7
Taylor, J., 362
Technocrat, Veblen's innocent and pure workman, 355

Technology: destroys individuality, 354; and impersonality, 354; makes time lifeless, 354

Television Western, 344

Thelemites, 388

Theory, failure in sociological theory to relate structure and function of act to same kind of experience, 98

Theses on Feuerbach, 189n

Things: as determined by money, 359; as objects, 300; as symbolized, 299

Thinking: dependent on reciprocal responses of self and other through symbols, 77; as form of conversation, 86; occurs in relationship with real or imagined others, 299

Thoreau, H. D., 365, 384

Thought, as inner conversation, 92

Time: in act, 319; and form in the structure of the act, 321; must have future as well as past, 300; as social, 319; of social events and things contrasted, 300; in social passage, 259

de Tocqueville, 73, 126, 325n, 345n, 405n; on religion as prime social bond, 337

Tolstoy, A. K., 424; *War and Peace,* Intro. 4

Tom Sawyer, 394, 411

Tönnies, F., 345n

Tradition: must be purified, 235; as way to future, 258

Tragedy, 401; Christian view of, 114; higher status than comedy, 376; not enough to purge men of folly, 390; of our time as the evil use of art and perverted forms of religious appeal, 236; purges through suffering, 395

Tragic actor, must keep belief in supernatural alive, 403

Tragic hero, 386

Tragic invocation, 387

Tragic scapegoat of religion, 287

Tragic victim, cannot pardon himself, 400

Tragic villain, 399

Transcendencies, in symbolic expression, 157

"Transcendent facts," 258

Transcendent principles, incarnation of in society, 278

Transformation: of money into a social bond, 347; of principles in poetry of Milton, 156

Transvestitism, as sanctioned humor, 305

Treasure, in heaven, 349

Trial: in authoritarian and democratic communities compared, 341; as communication of power, 341; to determine punishment, not guilt, 305; drama of in democracy, 341; as stage for confession, 341

Trobrianders, 431

Troeltsch, E., on religion in society, Intro. 7

Trumbo, D., *The Biggest Thief in Town,* 405n

Truths, types of, 327

Tyrants, 279

Ultimate appeals: to means, instruments, agencies, methods, or magic, 315; to perfected ends, 315; to the person, 315; to rules, codes, and laws, 315

Ultimate audiences ("It"), 292

Ultimates, 185; in beginnings of the act, 157; in fulfillment of act, 157; in social order beyond reason, 256; of various kinds invoked by Hitler, 238

Umpirage, 329; by an impartial third, 329

Umpire: applies but does not create rules, 78; as fair and impartial, 336; as guardian of rules, 336; impersonality of, 336; personifies rules, 78; preserves relationships among players, 78; and will of equals, 336

Understanding, Dilthey on, Intro. 5

Undertaker, names for, 361

United Nations, 196

Universals, as essentialized, 316

University of Chicago, 102

Unmaskers, hierarchies among, 140n

Urbanite, reduces all question to: How much?, 353

Utilitarians, doctrine of greatest happiness to greatest number, 180

Utopian myths, 315

Vaihinger, H., on fictions, 69

Vail, T. N., 364

Values, as hypothetical in democratic society, 89

Van der Rohe, L. Mies, technological majesty of his design, 367

Van Eyck, 365

Van Gennep, A., 259

Vanity of princes, 220

Varieties of Religious Experience, James' use of human documents, 52

Veblen, T., 102, 174, 325n, 347, 354, 378; on academic pageantry, 161; as comic artist, 223n; conspicuous consumption, 199; hatred of businessman, 199; *The higher Learning in America: A Memorandum on the Conduct of Universities by Business Men,* 106n, 140n; on instinct of workmanship, 91n; instinct of workmanship never personified, 199; on invention as